The Old Testament Library

. . . provides fresh and authoritative treatments of important aspects of Old Testament study through commentaries and general surveys. The contributors are scholars of international standing. The editorial advisory board consists of James L. Mays, Union Theological Seminary in Virginia; Carol A. Newsom, Candler School of Theology, Emory University, Atlanta; and David L. Petersen, Iliff School of Theology, Denver. See back of jacket for titles.

OLD TESTAMENT THEOLOGY

THE OLD TESTAMENT LIBRARY

Editorial Advisory Board

Horst Dietrich Preuss

OLD TESTAMENT THEOLOGY

Volume I

Westminster John Knox Press
Louisville, Kentucky

Translated by Leo G. Perdue from *Theologie des Alten Testaments,* Band 1: *JHWHs erwählendes und verpflichtendes Handeln,* published 1991 by W. Kohlhammer, Stuttgart

Book design by Drew Stevens

First published 1995
by Westminster John Knox Press
Louisville, Kentucky

This book is printed on acid-free paper that meets the American National Standards Institute Z39.48 standard. ∞

PRINTED IN THE UNITED STATES OF AMERICA

95 96 97 98 99 00 01 02 03 04 — 10 9 8 7 6 5 4 3 2 1

Library of Congress Cataloging-in-Publication Data

Preuss, Horst Dietrich, 1927–
    [Theologie des Alten Testaments. English]
    Old Testament Theology / Horst Dietrich Preuss.
        p.   cm. — (Old Testament library)
    Includes bibliographical references and indexes.
    ISBN 0-664-21844-X (v. 1 : alk. paper)
    1. Bible. O.T.—Theology.   I. Title.   II. Series.
BS1192.5.P6913 1995
    230—dc20   95-19162

CONTENTS

TRANSLATOR'S PREFACE

When I first agreed to translate the Old Testament theology by Horst Dietrich Preuss, I was looking forward to the opportunity to work with him on this project. I had read many previous works that he had written, and I had long admired the clarity of presentation, extensive research, and careful arguments that characterized his scholarship. I was deeply saddened to receive the news of his death in 1993, just before I began the translation of Volume I.

This two-volume theology by Professor Preuss is a splendid example of classical German Old Testament scholarship and theological reflection that follows in the tradition of Walther Eichrodt and Gerhard von Rad. It has been a pleasure to become intimately acquainted with this last important work of Professor Preuss and to make it more widely available to an English-speaking audience.

In presenting this translation, several remarks may be helpful to the reader. Professor Preuss translated his biblical passages directly from the Hebrew, and the English translation has adhered as closely to the German as possible. He also often left the Hebrew, Greek, and Latin words, phrases, clauses, and sentences untranslated and without transliteration. These have been translated into English, and the Hebrew and Greek have been transliterated.

A list of abbreviations has been added by Westminster John Knox Press, allowing the reader to follow bibliographical references. To assist the reader, the Press has also provided a correlation between the important German bibliographical references cited and quoted by Professor Preuss and the English translations of those works.

I am especially indebted to the following people who have been of great assistance in bringing this translation to its completion. Dr. Jon Berquist, editor at Westminster John Knox Press, has been most helpful throughout the stages of this project. The work of Marian Noecker and Carl Helmich as copyeditors has been invaluable. Jean Burnham, Linda Hillin, and Sharlie Tomlinson, three administrative assistants of the Brite Divinity School staff, and Jennie Huff, a graduate assistant at Brite, have carefully prepared the indexes. I am greatly indebted to these individuals for their assistance, patience, and graciousness in bringing this translation to completion.

PREFACE

Radical change and debate characterize much of the scholarly investigation of the Old Testament at the present time. It is therefore a risky venture to present in the current environment a "Theology of the Old Testament." This risk, however, is outweighed, at least in part, by the fact that descriptions of Old Testament theology have a duty to respond to the questions and problems of their own time. In addition, undertaking this risk is also justified by the contemporary study of theology. It has been over thirty years now since the appearance of the significant theological work of Gerhard von Rad, while Walther Zimmerli, in producing his "Outline" of Old Testament theology, wished eventually to write a more detailed description but did not live to do so. What is needed now is a new, comprehensive overview of the witnesses to Old Testament faith that takes into consideration both the present changes in Old Testament research and the positions of the author in regard to these matters. Therefore, references, citations, and bibliographical information are necessary, even as one would find in an introductory text. To print biblical quotations in full of course would be impossible. They will have to be looked up by the reader. In addition, in this kind of presentation, repetitions not only cannot be avoided, they are even intended.

The present volume is aware of its limitations. This also will be true when the second one, God willing, soon appears. Much of what is currently new in Old Testament study will be mentioned, even if the author does not always agree. Other scholars might well choose to set forth their own modifications, corrections, and different orientations. In addition to the purpose of comprehending as fully as possible the witness of the world of the Old Testament, the present work has two other particular interests. One is the quest to discover the essential structure of the faith of scripture that resides both behind and in the Old Testament. However, Old Testament Israel cannot be properly understood apart from its own historical and social context. Another interest is a brief description of this social and cultural environment that is becoming ever clearer to us. It is hoped, of course, that these side glances at the religious and historical environment of the Bible will not take precedence over the major objective of setting forth its theology. Nevertheless the particularities and unique features of Israel's faith at times may be brought out more clearly by comparison to the other religions of the surrounding cultures.

The manuscript of the present volume was finished in the fall of 1990. Scholarly literature that either was written or came into my possession after that time could not be included. However, one work that supports, modifies, and expands much of what is said here ought to be mentioned: J. Assmann's substantial book, *Ma'at: Gerechtigkeit und Unsterblichkeit im Alten Ägypten* (Munich, 1990).

I wish to thank the Reverend Dr. J. Hausmann and Mr. I. Schurig, a theology student, for their considerable help. Ms. A. Siebert introduced me to the intricacies of the computer and produced the final form of the published work. I also wish to thank the publisher, W. Kohlhammer, and its editor J. Schneider, who encouraged me to pursue this work. I am grateful both for the care they gave to this book and for its publication.

Horst Dietrich Preuss

Neuendettelsau
March 1991

Chapter 1.   Setting the Stage: The History, Methodology, and Structure of a "Theology of the Old Testament"[1]

1.1   The Posing of the Question

A course of lectures, even more a book, on the "theology of the Old Testament,"[2] on the one hand, is the most desirable and important undertaking in the study of the Old Testament. On the other hand, it is also the most difficult. In spite of this, the attempt should be made to offer an overview of the world of faith and witness of the Old Testament. The Old Testament is a collection of writings, a library of various texts that originated over the course of eight hundred to a thousand years. Not only does it contain many layers of materials but it also is a wide-ranging book from a distant time with much that conceptually is rather foreign to us. As a result, who can say: "I know and understand the Old Testament"? In addition, each effort to set forth an overview carries with it some of the personal idiosyncrasies or peculiarities of the author. This means that the present investigation contains my own peculiarities and weaknesses and reflects both the character and the limits of my knowledge.[3]

When Old Testament scholars propose or, for that matter, write a "theology of the Old Testament" they provide an account of their own and others' understanding of "the theological problems posed by the multiplicity of the Old Testament witnesses in their context."[4] At the same time, *the* "Theology of the Old Testament" is understood to be that theology which the Old Testament itself contains and presents, and not a theology that has the Old Testament as a subject of study.[5] This latter understanding belongs more to contemporary hermeneutics or fundamental theology. Finally, an "Old Testament theology" should be distinguished from a "history of ancient Israelite religion." These initial issues, only here lightly touched upon, give rise to important problems that call for a more detailed examination.

1.2   The History of Scholarship

a. From Gabler to de Wette

Whenever an inquiry is made into the origins of the critical discipline of "Old Testament Theology" and to discover the most important works within its history,[6] one points to the inaugural address of the theologian from Altdorf, Johann Philipp Gabler.[7] This is true also for the fields of New Testament Theology and Biblical Theology. This address, delivered on March 30, 1787, has the theme: "Oratio de justo discrimine theologiae biblicae et dogmaticae regundisque recte utriusque finibus" ("On the Proper Distinction between Biblical and Dogmatic Theology and the Specific Objectives of Each").[8] Gabler frees biblical theology from its single purpose of serving as the *dicta probantia* for dogmatic theology. While he does not contest the necessity of dogmatic theology, Gabler argues that the primary purpose of biblical theology is to address historical questions, while dogmatic theology seeks to instruct believers in the faith. The language, understanding, uniqueness, and chronological setting of the biblical text are considerations in order to assemble, arrange, compare, and describe "true biblical theology." In this way, Gabler also made more distinct the difference between religion and theology. Gabler distinguished between "true" and "pure" biblical theology: "true" biblical theology was more concerned with the time-bound statements of the biblical authors, while "pure" biblical theology was more interested in discovering "eternal truths" that are valid for all times. This distinction prepared the way for distinguishing between biblical theology that seeks only to be descriptive and biblical theology that evaluates and renders critical judgments about statements of faith.

While these considerations should be taken seriously, it is also necessary to make a distinction between Old Testament theology and New Testament theology, a distinction that Gabler himself did not make. The first effort in this direction[9] was undertaken by Georg Lorenz Bauer in 1796.[10] He wanted to read the Old Testament and its religious ideas (e.g., those about God, angels, demons, and the relationship of human beings to God) in the spirit of the era of the ancient scriptures. He divided this era into five periods and used this temporal framework for comparing the Old Testament with the religions of Israel's environment. He argued that one should read the Old Testament as preparatory for the New Testament, and not as a Christian text or as a reservoir in which to discover only New Testament ideas. However, neither Gabler nor Bauer was able to provide the first actual explanation of how to go about presenting a completely historical interpretation of the Old Testament. Their suggestions, especially those of Gabler, would come to fruition at a later time.

Two scholars, Gottlieb Philipp Christian Kaiser (1813, 1814, 1821)[11] and in particular Wilhelm Martin Leberecht de Wette (1813; 3d ed., 1831),[12] set forth their views on how a historical interpretation of the Old Testament should be carried out. De Wette's title demonstrates that he not only made a clear and complete separation of the Old and New Testaments but also examined two troubling concerns that had emerged since the time of Gabler: the historical interpretation of biblical results and, at the same time, their presentation in a systematic summary. Stated in another way, the concerns are the presentation of the results, on the one hand, and their evaluation on the other. In connection with this, it is clear, especially for de Wette, that the effort should be made in general to determine the relationship of Old Testament religion to both the history of revelation and the New Testament. This effort is necessary, for example, when one is pursuing such questions as the relationship between preexilic and postexilic religion in Israel (i.e., Hebrew religion and Judaism) and between particularity and universalism.[13] At the same time, the critical response[14] that de Wette provoked shows that even by then it was not an easy matter to keep out of the descriptions of biblical theology the interpreter's own problems, prior decisions, philosophical influences (de Wette was especially influenced by J. F. Fries), and valuations. De Wette also sought to locate a kind of "center" for the Old Testament, since he thought God as "holy will" was its "fundamental idea."

b. From Vatke to König

The influence of philosophy, particularly the work of Hegel, on Wilhelm Vatke is rather clear. Vatke's work, *Die biblische Theologie wissenschaftlich dargestellt*, vol. 1: *Die Religion des Alten Testaments*, appeared in 1835.[15] Following his introduction and basic foundation, which sets forth his philosophical and terminological understandings, Vatke sought to use the three features of the Hegelian dialectic (thesis, antithesis, and synthesis) to describe the stages of religion as stages of the development of human consciousness and to see history as the self-realization of pure "Spirit." Of course, it is not an easy matter to derive from the Old Testament Hegel's dialectic which, additionally, does not really conform to Vatke's own historical findings. Anticipating Julius Wellhausen, Vatke placed the law, including its theocratic institutions, and everything else that belongs to this category, in antithesis to the prophets. What he meant by the law is today referred to as the Priestly document. After wisdom literature, seen by Vatke in a positive light, had vanished into that which was specifically Jewish, Christianity offered the crowning synthesis. Old Testament theology would then be presented predominantly as the historical development of Israelite religion from lower to higher forms. His distinction between "idea" and "form of appearance" in the matter of religion expresses once again the tension between pure description and the evaluation of what is described.

A series of additional, preponderantly posthumous[16] works in Old Testament theology then began to appear. Written under the influence of the critical studies of both Wellhausen and the history of religions school (Gunkel, Gressmann, et al.), these works could scarcely set forth a systematic presentation of Old Testament theology. Rather, they appeared much more as descriptions of Israelite-Jewish religious history. Indeed, the senior R. Smend expressly emphasized that he wished to set forth his description in a historical, and not a systematic, form.[17] In 1903, K. Marti edited the third and fourth editions of A. Kayser's *Theologie des Alten Testaments* (2d ed., 1894) and renamed the work *Geschichte der israelitischen Religion*. A biblical theology of the Old Testament that is organized following a pattern of historical sequence and development is the exhaustive, fundamental, two-volume work of B. Stade (vol. 1)[18] and A. Bertholet (vol. 2), appearing in 1905 and 1911 respectively. Similar is the *Biblische Theologie des Alten Testaments* by E. Kautzsch that appeared posthumously in 1911. Such works, oriented to the history of Israelite-Jewish religion, continue to have their successors and to retain their legitimacy unto the present as *one* form of approaching the world of Old Testament faith.[19]

Of more interest for the history of research than for their significance for contemporary questions concerning a "theology of the Old Testament" are the works of G. F. Oehler (1845, 1873, etc., representing a distinctive salvation history and historical-genetic perspective),[20] E. Riehm (1889), A. Dillman (1895), and even H. Ewald (1871–1876).[21]

Quite different is the assessment of the *Alttestamentliche Theologie* of H. Schultz, appearing first in 1869 and bearing the subtitle *Die Offenbarungsreligion auf ihrer vorchristlichen Entwicklungsstufe*. This book underwent several new editions and frequent revisions by its author (5th ed., 1896) and was a favorite textbook for students of the time. Yet the book also has significance for us. Seeing he was in the position to do so, the author felt compelled to take up in the sequence of his new editions the questions and results that came from the scholarly works of J. Wellhausen and B. Duhm concerning the law and the prophets.[22] It should be noted that in the fourth and especially the fifth edition Schultz presented as the first main section (5th ed., pp. 59–309) a history of the religion of Israel under the title "Die Entwicklung der Religion und Sitte Israels bis zur Aufrichtung des Hasmonäerstaates." This was followed by the second main section that sought to describe in a "purely historical" (5th ed., p. 4) manner the themes of God and world, humanity and sin, and the hope of Israel. He entitled this section "Das Heilsbewusstsein der Gemeine des zweiten (!) Tempels." Just as much as the two divisions, the subthemes of the second part would also have their consequences. In addition to discussions about the Old Testament, the history of religions, and the relationship between the Old Testament and the New Testament, it should be noted that Schultz prefaced his presentation with an important chapter dealing with "literary forms in the writings of the Old Testament." In this chapter, for example, he not only examined myth and legend but even set forth the programmatic statement that Genesis may be a book of sacred legends (p. 22). This is a point that H. Gunkel later modified somewhat. According to Schultz, it was the kingdom of God that gave unity not only to the Old Testament but also to the Old and New Testaments.[23] From the remaining members of the closely knit circle of students and friends gathered around Wellhausen, there appeared, in addition to the historically oriented descriptions of the history of Israelite religion already mentioned, only the *Theologie der Propheten* by Duhm (1875). He also asked historical questions in order to provide the theology of the prophets a "foundation for the inner development of the history of Israelite religion."

The first person after Schultz to undertake the effort to present not only a historical but also a systematic[24] description of the data and ideas that have proven to be vital to Old Testament salvation history was E. König in 1922 (3d and 4th eds., 1923). However, owing to many rather opinionated theses and, particularly in part two, to a strongly dogmatic emphasis in the posing of questions, his work, *Theologie des Alten Testaments kritisch und vergleichend dargestellt,* has not had much influence.

c. The Change since 1920

More important for the further development of Old Testament theology were three brief contributions that once more came from the circle of German Old Testament scholars. The year 1921 witnessed the appearance of R. Kittel's address, "Die Zukunft der alttestamentlichen Wissenschaft."[25] According to Kittel, Old Testament scholarship should be engaged not only in archaeology and, especially up to this point, literary criticism and the history of literature but also in the presentation of the "history of Israel's ideas" and "specifically religious information" such as worship and the ethics that special personalities display. This presentation would describe the heights of Old Testament religion. One can see in Kittel's *Gestalten und Gedanken in Israel* (1925) that he was especially interested in personalities and the history of ideas that were associated with them.

In 1926 Otto Eissfeldt distinguished between two different fields of inquiry.[26] The history of religion is a field that proceeds along the lines of intellectual understanding or knowing. In this field, the effort is made to comprehend as a historical entity the religion of Israel as *one* religion among others. A second field, theology, is concerned with faith. Here the religion of Israel is regarded as the *true* religion that witnesses to God's revelation, and the effort is made to assess its veracity. Accordingly, the first field proceeds in a more historical fashion, while the second sets forth a more systematic presentation. Both have methods of inquiry that stimulate each other as they carry out their respective tasks and objectives. However, these methods of investigation should not be so blended together that the tensions between them are eliminated. Their unity is found in the person of the scholar who works in both fields. Reflecting on the questions that had emerged since Gabler, Eissfeldt's argumentation was stimulated by the emerging dialectical theology.[27] He sought not only to search vigorously for the "Word of God" but also to establish the independence of historical investigation.[28]

By contrast, W. Eichrodt wished to see the two fields mentioned above as a unity.[29] One could certainly press toward the nature of Old Testament religion by proceeding only along the pathway of historical inquiry. This would mean that the questions of truth and value would belong to the field of dogmatics but not to biblical theology. However, scholarship may no longer rest content with only a genetic analysis; rather, it must produce a comprehensive systematic work by laying out a cross section through the material that would point out the religion's inner structure and would establish the relationships between the varieties of its content. This way of proceeding would still represent a historical approach and would not place its results under the scrutiny of normative questions of faith. Nor would this approach function as a testimony to the revelation of God. Eichrodt argued that his approach would free Old Testament theology from the chains of an Old Testament history of religion.

It may only be mentioned at this point that the "battle for the Old Testament" that had intensified toward the end of the nineteenth century with the "Bible-Babel controversy"[30] and the nationalistic and racist ideas of developing anti-Semitism and emerging national socialism also entered in general into this discussion concerning the Old Testament.[31]

d. From Sellin to Vriezen

E. Sellin's two-volume work was one of the first results of this debate. He published in 1933 his *Alttestamentliche Theologie auf religionsgeschichtlicher Grundlage* in two volumes. Volume 1 (1933), *Israelitisch-jüdische Religionsgeschichte,* sought to describe the origins and growth of Israelite-Jewish religion, while volume 2 (1933), *Theologie des Alten Testaments,* set forth systematically the religious teachings and faith that the Jewish community had fashioned on the basis of the writings collected in the Old Testament, but "only so far as they have recognized Jesus Christ and his apostles as the presupposition and foundation of the Gospel and as the revelation of the God who has been proclaimed by them" (p. 1). When one traces the changing path on which scholarship was embarking, it is little wonder that volume 2 went through a second edition in 1936 but not volume 1. This second volume, somewhat less inclined toward hypotheses than volume 1, is divided into three parts: God and His Relationship to the World, Humanity and Sin, and Judgment and Salvation (cf. later L. Köhler). This volume distinguishes between popular religion and high religion and between national cult religion and prophetic, moral, universal, eschatological religion. For Sellin, the idea of a "holy God" carries special weight in the Old Testament. Sellin's principle of selection and evaluation leads to the result that Old Testament wisdom literature plays no role in the second volume of his work. Moreover, while the two volumes stand side by side, the relationship between the history of Israelite religion and Old Testament theology is not given a more ready explanation.

If one looks ahead some years, passing over in the meantime other examples, then one is able to discover in the work of O. Procksch a similar dualistic scheme, which Schultz especially introduced. This scheme allowed Old Testament theologians in many areas of inquiry to move beyond such questions as the historicity of Abraham or Moses.[32] Procksch's *Theologie des Alten Testaments* was published posthumously in 1950. It contains two main parts, namely, "Die Geschichtswelt" and "Die Gedankenwelt" of the Old Testament. The first part, in tracing out the world of history, leads from Abraham to apocalyptic, while the second part, dealing with the thought world of the Old Testament, is divided into three sections: God and the World, God and Nation, and God and Humanity. With all that, the programmatic essay at the beginning of the work, entitled "Alle Theologie ist Christologie," could neither be verified nor carried out.

Later on G. Fohrer produced a work following Sellin's two-volume division, the first dealing with Israelite religion and the second with Old Testament theology. Fohrer's *History of Israelite Religion* (1969; ET 1972), in which he wished to treat the development of Israelite religion as a normal history of a typical religion,[33] was followed by his *Theologische Grundstrukturen des Alten Testaments* (1972, see below) in which he also inserted distinct criteria of evaluation.

If one pauses for a moment, prior to mentioning the great work of Eichrodt, to ask what the main problems of Old Testament theology are that have now been encountered, then one would mention: (1) the relationship of Israelite history of religion to Old Testament theology; and, closely related to this, (2) choosing between a historical and/or a systematic presentation. If one reflects further on the second problem just mentioned, then another question arises: (3) From what source does one draw a system to apply to the Old Testament and how does one determine this system's division and structure? For example, the system of God and World, God and Nation, and God and Humanity not only appears to be imposed on the Old Testament from the outside but also raises the question of both the legitimacy and the sequence of this tripartite division. In addition, the tripartite division of God, Humanity, and Judgment and Salvation derives more from Christian dogmatics than from the Old Testament.

There are other fundamental questions in addition to the three main methodological and content problems just mentioned. Gabler introduced a fourth question that Eissfeldt and Eichrodt considered in their own way: (4) the relationship of a historical, descriptive presentation to a contemporary evaluation to be carried out either at the same time or by dogmatics. This question, so it seems, was forgotten or pushed aside for a time. But its reappearance in the more recent period has led to a new examination.

Eichrodt had been a student of Procksch's in Erlangen. In 1933 (!), Eichrodt published the first volume of his *Theologie des Alten Testaments* which bore the subtitle *Gott und Volk*. Volume 2 (*Gott und Welt*) followed in 1935 and volume 3 (*Gott und Mensch*) in 1939.[34] In contrast to Procksch, Eichrodt rearranged the positions of the three major divisions of material and produced a sequence that is more legitimate from an Old Testament perspective. However, above all, Eichrodt wanted to describe "the religion of which the records are to be found in the Old Testament as a self-contained entity exhibiting, despite ever-changing historical conditions, a constant basic tendency and character."[35] Subsequently, by stressing the systematic character of his work, he wanted not only to break away from "the exclusive domination of historicism" but also "to understand the realm of Old Testament belief in its structural unity and . . . , by examining on the one hand its religious environment and on the other hand its essential coherence with the New Testament, to illuminate its profoundest meaning (*Theology*, 1:31).[36] For Eichrodt, there is no question that the Old Testament stands between the ancient Near East and the New Testament. Thus he often takes a look at the religions of Israel's environment and sets forth the scholarly positions on individual themes.[37] The common message of the kingship of God in this world is the theme that connects the Old Testament with the New. In determining the relationship of the Old Testament to the New, the question then arises as to what significance an Old Testament theology has and can have within a Christian theology. It is unfortunate, in this regard, that Eichrodt's position that covenant thinking dominated the Old Testament often prohibited him from placing more value on its eschatological message. But it is important that Eichrodt wanted to see the characteristic mark of a movement of life, that is, to understand the dominating center of the Old Testament as an actual, characteristic element of Israelite religion. Therefore he resisted seeking only after the appropriate vocabulary without seeing its grounding in actual life.

In spite of this, criticism has been directed primarily and with some legitimacy against Eichrodt for making covenant the center of Old Testament theology and for overemphasizing the importance of covenant thinking.[38] This criticism was made at the time Eichrodt's work began to appear, even though the newer works on *berit* (ברית = *běrît*, "covenant") had not yet been published.[39] Nevertheless, Eichrodt could often describe an Old Testament understanding of a matter without digressing from the topic by endeavoring to say something about covenant thinking and without introducing the topic of covenant thinking in an unexpected and surprising manner. Indeed, it is also remarkable to discover the absence of covenant thinking in places and in situations where it would have been especially helpful to the discussion (e.g., sin, forgiveness). Still, the strong theological engagement of the author, which induces him not infrequently toward overinterpretation, leads to theological excessiveness. However, in spite of all the critical questions raised, Eichrodt's work continues to be regarded as a great accomplishment that appeared at the appropriate time. From 1933 and even after 1945 this theology of the Old Testament provided a very valuable service, and it continues to do so in certain areas today because of its profundity and wealth of materials.

In the foreword to the newly revised fifth edition of the first section of his work (1957), Eichrodt could still enter into a discussion of critical questions and underline his own position that he continued to support. Old Testament theology continued to be for him a historical enterprise that resisted all enticements to move into the sphere of the normative sciences. Further, he held fast to the covenant as the central idea in order "to bring to light the structural unity and persistent fundamental purpose of the message of the Old Testament. It is here that the fundamental conviction of Israel about its special relationship to God is grasped" (p. vi). And finally, Old Testament theology is limited neither to the retelling of Old Testament historical narratives nor to the setting forth of the bare facts of this history, since internal events and external facts cannot be separated.

One simply notes at this point that new, additional questions must be raised that are to be appended to the previously mentioned four fundamental problems of an Old Testament theology.[40] However, before doing that, we need to outline further developments in Old Testament theology.

In 1935 L. Köhler published a concise, yet very precise *Theologie des Alten Testaments*.[41] It is no wonder that the strengths of this volume lay in the investigations of ideas, statistics of words, and concise, pregnant language, seeing that Köhler was to be the author of a dictionary of the Old Testament that was being planned at the time. Köhler had written previously: "If it is already theology, then it must be systematic." He thought he could make historical differentiations within the individual parts. But at the same time he stressed that one could not derive this systematic formulation, including its structure and order, from the theological contents of the Old Testament.[42] As a result, Köhler derived his systematic formulation from outside the Old Testament, meaning that his three divisions (God, Humanity, and Judgment and Salvation)[43] derive from Christian dogmatics. The Old Testament idea of God, God as sovereign Lord, is especially important to Köhler, and the first sentence of his foreword makes it immediately clear how the journey through the Old Testament is to proceed: "A book may legitimately be designated an Old Testament theology when its content brings together in proper relationship those views, thoughts, and ideas of the Old Testament which are or can be theologically important" (p. v). The cult presents difficulties for Köhler, a reformed theologian, when it comes to the matter of the "proper relationship." He can and will not attribute the cult to the acts of God, and he does not think it belongs to the section on "Judgment and Salvation." Subsequently, section 52 at the end of his discussion of anthropology is entitled "The Self-Redemption of Humanity: The Cult." This view of the cult represents a significant misunderstanding of the Old Testament's own view.[44] These matters would not have been so mishandled had Köhler carried out what he had set forth in his foreword.[45]

On the occasion of the Göttingen Old Testament Scholars Day in 1935, A. Weiser sought to speak to the objectives that Old Testament theological work at the time had striven to realize.[46] According to Weiser, exegesis may be pursued along with the question of the self-understanding of the Old Testament. This self-understanding presents us with a dynamic comprehension of reality (truth "takes place" here) in which the theological lines of the understanding of humanity and of things proceed from God and lead to God. Accordingly, this understanding of the dynamic of the reality of God is a matter of our concern. It follows then that Old Testament scholarship cannot be only a historical enterprise, remaining in the sphere of the history of religions, for scholarship may not put aside the question of truth. One ought not to separate scholarly from theological investigations of the Old Testament. The fact that an increasing number of scholars writing a theology of the Old Testament saw themselves compelled to set forth a systematic presentation, in spite of the associated difficulties, demonstrates that they saw this issue very clearly and sought to comply with its requirements. The sharp focus on what was normative indeed was avoided to a large extent, although the strong emphasis on the relationships between Old Testament theology and New Testament theology brought the issue into the discussion (see, e.g., Sellin and Eichrodt). Gabler's distinction between pure and true biblical theology[47] was to a certain extent correct and, as a result, continued to be influential.

In 1955, E. Jacob's *Théologie de l'Ancien Testament* appeared.[48] God's nature, his acts (under this category creation and anthropology were brought together), and his triumph at the end of time (sin, salvation, eschatology) were the most important subdivisions of this work. The vitality of God received the special attention and focus of this author whose theology of the Old Testament regrettably never appeared in a German translation. The structure and categories of this work also reveal a clear proximity to dogmatic theology.[49]

After an interlude necessitated by the conditions of the war and the postwar period, the next Old Testament theology in German appeared in 1956.[50] This was the German translation of Th. C. Vriezen's *Theologie des Alten Testaments in Grundzügen* that had been published in 1949 in the Dutch original.[51] Standing on the whole closer to Eichrodt than to Köhler, Vriezen desired to inquire after the "leading ideas" of the Old Testament, seeking thereby to trace out its message and main features. Closely tied to German and Anglo-Saxon scholarship, Vriezen also kept in view the relationship of the Old Testament to its environment. Especially striking are the one hundred printed pages devoted to a comprehensive "prolegomenon" that sets forth his reflections about such issues as the "Christian Church and the Old Testament" and "The Old Testament as the Word of God." "The Way of Israel's Faith in History" also provides a necessary historical orientation to his systematic presentation. The Christian, theological point of departure, which the resulting evaluation of Old Testament proclamation makes clear, is to distinguish between a theology of the Old Testament and a history of Old Testament religion and to accentuate the line of demarcation between dogmatic and historical theology (pp. 97–101). The second part then introduces the leading ideas that are appropriate for this work, namely, the Old Testament understanding of God ("Understanding as Community") as a communal relationship between the holy God and human beings. Vriezen sees this as the center of Old Testament proclamation, arranging about this center such topics as word, history, covenant, and humanity in the image of God. Following that, he treats first the subject of God, then humanity, then the contact between God and humanity (revelation, salvation and judgment, cult), then ethics (the contact between human beings) and finally, God, humanity, and the world in both the present and the future reign of God. In following the features of these programmatic prolegomena, it is little wonder that Vriezen's description is permeated with evaluations, indeed is even determined by them. The standards for evaluation derive from the New Testament. A. Jepsen is correct when he states: "Behind the question about the theology of the Old Testament is concealed the theological question about the Old Testament itself."[52] The relationship of the two Testaments is not only a historical one; indeed, the relationship cannot simply be a historical one.

In a similar fashion to Vriezen, G. A. F. Knight also brought his work, *A Christian Theology of the Old Testament* (London and Richmond, 1959), within proximity of the New Testament, a point demonstrated by the title. Within the four main sections (God, God and Creation, God and Israel, and the Zeal of the Lord), he desires to bring into view "a gallery of pictures"[53] that demonstrates the connections between the testaments. Examples include "Son of God" as a title of both Israel and Jesus Christ, and birth/marriage/death in the life of the Israelites, the people of Israel (e.g., marriage = the Sinai covenant), and Christians. Knight points to these connections in order to make clear the close relationship between the two Testaments. His book is often compared to W. Vischer's *Christuszeugnis des Alten Testaments,* vol. 1 (1934); vol. 2 (1942).

When surveying the scholars of the twentieth century who have addressed the problem of a theology of the Old Testament (O. Eissfeldt, W. Eichrodt, E. Sellin, W. and H. Möller, O. Procksch, E. Jacob, Th. C. Vriezen, and the person last mentioned, G. A. F. Knight), one ought to mention at this point that these undertakings are clearly conditioned by the posing of Christian questions and are decidedly oriented to and brought into line with the New Testament.

On the basis of such findings, it is clear that these efforts prepared the way for the work of Brevard S. Childs that would follow (see below).

e. G. von Rad

After his several brief, preliminary works[54] that broached the issue of the appropriate methodology for doing Old Testament theology and that would portend clearly what was to follow, G. von Rad published in 1957 the first volume of his *Theologie der geschichtlichen Überlieferungen*. Volume 2 (*Theologie der prophetischen Überlieferungen*) followed in 1960. Volume 1 underwent a new revision in its fifth edition (1966).[55] Von Rad's work found enthusiastic readers, especially among students, and continues to exert even to this day an important influence in many areas.

In volume 1, a brief historical overview precedes the theological analysis: "A History of Jahwism and of the Sacral Institutions in Israel in Outline." This introduction intends to set forth the historical contexts and life situations of those topics addressed by the theological section. Von Rad seeks to make clear the historical location of the text and its tradition. In a certain sense, these two major divisions of von Rad's initial volume have taken up the description of Old Testament theology set forth by Sellin and Procksch, although admittedly significantly modified. Above all, von Rad wishes to comprehend the world of the Old Testament witness and not to offer a systematic, ordered world of faith. Indeed, Israel did not formulate catechetical statements about its God; rather, it primarily told narratives about him. Therefore von Rad considers the Old Testament to be a "history book"[56] and thus contends that the most legitimate form of theological discourse for the historical books of the Old Testament is to retell these stories.[57] It is imperative to grasp the *kerygma* (proclamation) of the individual works, books, and prophets, that is, "what Israel at the time had confessed about God." To accomplish this objective, von Rad argued that it was important to comprehend what Israel itself has said about its own history and not the critically reconstructed history that resided behind these testimonies.[58] At the same time, it is important to understand Israel's own interpretations of its traditions of faith. Thus, von Rad sets forth both the *kerygma* and the historical development of the traditions in which this proclamation was located: the primeval history, the history of the patriarchs, the exodus from Egypt, the revelation of God at Sinai, the wilderness wandering, the interpretations of Moses, and the gift of the land of Canaan. Von Rad thought that cultic institutions and festivals played a very influential role in the formulation and transmission of these traditions of faith.

The first volume contains additionally a section that deals with the "Anointed of Yahweh" (judges, monarchy, royal psalms) that allows von Rad to set forth the theology of the Deuteronomistic History, the Priestly source, and the Chronicler's History in a historical sequence, while taking only a preliminary look at prophecy. This volume concludes with a section entitled "Israel before Jahweh (Israel's Answer)." This section takes into consideration the psalms and wisdom (including Job and Qoheleth). Von Rad's form-critical work plays an especially significant role in his description of the theology of the Pentateuch/Hexateuch. It is important to note that, on the whole, von Rad's own thinking comes very close to that of the Deuteronomic and Deuteronomistic writings. This observation may be demonstrated by reference to von Rad's earlier works on Deuteronomy and by the fact that in a very real sense he considered this book to be the central writing for the entire Old Testament (see below).

Volume 2 deals with the prophets. While the first major section is concerned with preclassical prophecy, it also addresses the overarching questions that include the manner in which the prophetic word was transformed into prophetic books, the reception of revelation, the "Word of God" in the prophets, Israel's conceptions of time and history, and prophetic eschatology. The second major section handles the individual prophets and describes their messages (from Amos to Malachi and Jonah). In the segment on "Daniel and Apocalyptic," von Rad renders the surprising judgment that apocalyptic derived from wisdom, a point he continues to make rather explicitly and with more precision in later editions of this volume and in other publications.[59] A third section follows that deals with both the content and the methodology of the entire work. However, this section actually is neither expected nor necessary, chiefly because it is fundamentally different from all that has preceded. Since the individual writings or prophets had been already attractively and meticulously interpreted, especially by reference to the frequent articulation of "salvation history,"[60] far-reaching questions are now discussed that not only lead in the direction of the New Testament but even incorporate it. Now the issues are the actualization of the Old Testament in the New Testament, Old Testament salvation history in the light of New Testament fulfillment, and the Old Testament understanding of the world, humanity, faith in Christ, and the law. Accordingly, hermeneutical questions are incorporated into Old Testament theology that lead in the direction of further thinking about "biblical theology."[61] This would lead neither to a simple listing side by side of the two *kerygmata* (proclamations) of the Old and the New Testament nor to a pure description of Old Testament materials.

The great strength of this work lies in the individual descriptions of writings and books (cf., e.g., those dealing with Jeremiah and Deutero-Isaiah). It delineates precisely the *kerygma* as proclaimed at that time, and it seeks to grasp the inner theological coherence and relationships of its various elements. What is said about the developments and abiding connections of these elements as well as word and history, tradition and interpretation, history and *kerygma*, and the history of tradition is rich in content and valuable reading.

However, perhaps even von Rad himself discovered that his Old Testament theology, in describing Old Testament materials, still required those kinds of recapitulations and modifications which are offered in the concluding part of the second volume.

In any case, questions remained, and these were rather quickly, often times too precipitously and too harshly expressed.[62] The first question involves the relationship between history and *kerygma*.[63] In this matter, von Rad still held the better cards, for he maintained that an Old Testament theology must concern itself with ancient Israel's own view of history and not with that of modern critical study. Even so, in spite of all of the emphasis on kerygmatic and traditiohistorical concerns in von Rad's Old Testament theology, the relationship between faith and history[64] is never specifically discussed.[65] This is probably why von Rad pays scant attention to the ancient Near Eastern setting of Israel and does not go beyond a retelling of Israel's own tellings of its story to consider the acts of God themselves.[66] With the exception of the third section of the second volume, is the rest of von Rad's theology not, in the final analysis, a theologically enriched "Introduction to the Old Testament"? Any effort to set forth a synopsis of Old Testament faith is notably absent. Is it not the case, then, that von Rad offers only a history of the faith of Israel? Can and should one omit the effort to articulate a synopsis of faith, what W. Zimmerli calls the quest to discover the "Word" in words? In what way does the Old Testament have authority when one simply sets in a row the individual messages of the various writings and books?[67] Closely related to these questions is the problem of a possible "center" of the Old Testament. Von Rad vigorously disputed the idea that the Old Testament has a center;[68] indeed, he even denied the legitimacy of searching for one.[69]

In addition to these more comprehensive questions, many specific ones have been addressed to von Rad. These include such considerations as, for example, the value he places on the law; the possibility or, for that matter, impossibility of setting forth the features of the Deuteronomistic History, the Priestly writing (with its idea of sin), and the Chronicler's History, without a previous look at prophecy; the place of the prophets in general; and the relationship between aesthetic and theological judgments.[70] In the present survey, one may only mention these questions as matters for discussion.

Because his work is comprehensive, stylistically elegant, and theological, von Rad's writing has continued to contribute to the main questions[71] that concern Old Testament theology. These questions include (1) the problem of a history of Israelite religion as opposed to a theology of the Old Testament; (2) a historical versus a systematic description; (3) the possibility of a systematic formulation that derives from within the text as opposed to one that comes from the outside; (4) an objective description over against a description that also involves evaluation (and on what basis); (5) the relationship of history and *kerygma;*[72] (6) the possibility or impossibility of a "center" of the Old Testament; and finally (7), the possibility of an overarching "biblical theology" that would include both Testaments of the Christian Bible. The question of faith and *kerygma* may be examined only when one does not overlook the fact that the Old Testament uses religious language to speak of experiences interpreted by faith. The Old Testament does not speak another language. To seek only the "facts" expressed by religious language and to ignore the complexity of its interpretation misrepresents its essential character. The most that one may do here is simply to refer to the voluminous discussion mainly revolving around the fundamental questions of method and content that von Rad's work has elicited.[73] There have been many scholars who expressed their views about how one goes about writing an Old Testament theology or whether one should or even could write one. There have been relatively few, however, who actually have made the effort.

f. After G. von Rad

In 1972 two additional "theologies of the Old Testament" appeared in the German-speaking world. Georg Fohrer, in inquiring about the fundamental theological structures of the Old Testament (*Theologische Grundstrukturen des Alten Testaments*), found them in the expression of different positions concerning human existence. These included magical, cultic, prophetic, and sapiential understandings. He also sought to address the question of unity in diversity and found his answer in the interaction of divine sovereignty and human community. At the same time, he rendered his own judgments about the theological value and veracity of various views and reached the conclusion that the prophetic stance toward existence, as expressed in the preexilic classical prophets, was the most important and enduring understanding in the Old Testament. In his section on "hermeneutical applications," Fohrer also asked about the direct connections between the Old Testament's ways of speaking about God and our contemporary reality. These connections certainly led to his rather direct although inadequate, hermeneutical reflections (e.g., see the discussion of the state and political activities).

Although appearing for the first time after the work of W. Zimmerli (cf. below), C. Westermann's *Elements of Old Testament Theology* should be mentioned at this point because of its close methodological similarities to Fohrer's work. Part 1 seeks to answer the question, "What does the Old Testament say about God?" because, in Westermann's view, an Old Testament theology must begin with a summary and an overview of the Old Testament's speaking about God. In Parts 2 and 3, Westermann then deals with the two fundamental structures that undergird Old Testament theology: the redeeming God's acts of salvation in history and the blessing God's acts in creation. In contrast to Fohrer whose fundamental structures are conceptual, Westermann's fundamental structures are events. This raises the question of whether Westermann is on target when he draws the fundamental distinction between the redeeming and blessing acts of God. In addition, may one not single out or set forth in a preliminary way some feature or idea[74] of the Old Testament as the "center" of its theology? May one not at least inquire about this "center" before embarking on a description? Certainly, Westermann speaks, for example, of the "oneness of God as that which makes possible the coherence of the Old Testament witnesses" (pp. 25–27)[75] when he takes into consideration Deut. 6:4. However, he does not mean by this that the oneness of God is the "center" of Old Testament faith; rather, he is describing the constant, fundamental structure that makes possible the coherence of history. However, does a "fundamental structure" not have something to do with that which, nevertheless, is typical for the Old Testament and therefore addresses the "center" of its theology? Two additional parts follow: divine judgment and divine compassion; and Israel's response— praise, lament, worship, and conception of history. The concluding part (Part 6) has as its theme the relationship between the Old Testament and Christ (largely viewed as an "analogy of structure"). The sequence of the parts follows approximately the arrangement and the order of the Old Testament canon, although certainly not in its Hebrew form.

W. Zimmerli's *Grundriss der alttestamentlichen Theologie* (1972; 6th ed., 1989; ET, *Old Testament Theology in Outline,* trans. D. E. Green [Atlanta, 1978]) has certainly had greater significance.[76] In contrast to von Rad, Zimmerli takes the risk of summarizing the collective, theological understandings of the Old Testament. In doing so, he finds the center of the Old Testament in the revelation of the divine name YHWH (Yahweh): "I am who I am." This name, in expressing divine self-determination and individuality, indicates that, while incapable of being grasped, God continues to be the one who turns toward Israel. Thus, upon the foundation of this revealed name are placed the confessions of "Yahweh, the God of Israel since Egypt"; Yahweh as the God of the ancestors; Yahweh as creator, king, and God of Sinai; and the election of Israel. Yahweh's gifts (e.g., war, land, charismata), Yahweh's commandments, the life before God (obedience, sacrifice, wisdom), and crisis and hope (judgment and salvation, prophecy, apocalyptic) are the additional main sections of this very compactly written volume. The main question that arises from his text is the one concerning the correct determination of the center of the Old Testament. Around this center all else revolves. The impending discussion will move into this problematic area in a more precise manner.[77]

One may observe that biblical scholarship is attributing increasing significance to the Old Testament as canon. The nature of the Old Testament as canon has led to inquiries concerning Old Testament theology, although matters such as how or when the first Testament developed into a canon have not been addressed. The canon of scripture, which produced distinctive and different histories of influence and interpretation in Judaism and in Christianity, became a normative collection of writings for faith, ethics, and cultic worship. This phenomenon of a collection of normative writings perhaps was unique in the history of the religions of the ancient Near East.[78] In considering the Old Testament as canon,[79] attention also is given to the final form of the text and the place of the Old Testament within the Christian Bible,[80] the relationship of Old Testament theology to the New Testament and its message, integrating the theologies of the two Testaments, and then setting forth the meaning of the Old Testament for Christian theology, Christian faith, and the Christian church. These considerations are important for two more recent works in English. The first is R. E. Clements's *Old Testament Theology: A Fresh Approach* (London, 1978; Atlanta, 1979). His introductory chapter mentions and addresses expressly these questions, while his actual description of Old Testament theology intentionally seeks to provide a comprehensive summary that deals with the God of Israel, the people of God, and law and promise. Two concluding sections discuss important issues. The first issue is the relationship of the Old Testament to the other religions of the ancient Near East. The second issue is the place and impact of the Old Testament on contemporary hermeneutics.

Perhaps even more sensational than his introduction to the Old Testament[81] is the provocative theological work by Brevard S. Childs, *Old Testament Theology in a Canonical Context* (London and Philadelphia, 1985). Indeed, in some twenty chapters appear many of the conventional themes and traditions that are found in an Old Testament theology: for example, How God Is Known, God's Purpose in Revelation, Law, Decalogue, Ritual and Purity Laws, Reception of Divine Revelation (Israel, the Nations), Moses, Judges, Kings, Prophets, Priests, Cult, Anthropology, and Life under Threat and Promise. However, it is not fully clear how the "canonical process" is important for Childs within the loci of these themes or how this process is exactly to be understood.[82] In addition to regarding the "editors" as the last valid interpreters, a point that certainly a more exact historical understanding can reach, the other major thesis is that the "canon" is the common ground for understanding the text and is determinative for Old Testament theology. For Childs, the New Testament fulfillment of these interpretations and traditions always must be taken into consideration. The enterprise of Old Testament theology may be carried out in a Christian context and with a Christian design,[83] something that already is indicated even by the name "Old Testament." Nevertheless, this clearly articulated thesis is, in the final analysis, not quite so new as one might be inclined to think, for earlier scholars also have proceeded from this basis.[84] For Childs, however, this now means that the theology of the Old Testament has both a descriptive and a constructive dimension and that the statements of the Old Testament may be critically assessed in the light of the New Testament.

Description and evaluation go hand in hand and lead to an internal biblical dialogue occurring within the Testaments. The theology of the Old Testament is combined with Old Testament hermeneutics. Whether this is an enhancement for the actual theology of the Old Testament or potentially diminishes the description is a question that remains to be answered. In addition to this, the recurring question now must be addressed to the Old Testament as "canon": "Does this collection of writings have a 'center,' and if so, what or where is it?" Jews find the center in the Torah, which usually means both its narrative history and its teaching. Even so, how may one determine the relationship of these two entities to each other, and what role do the Prophets and the Writings play within the Old Testament as canon? Is there an appropriate hermeneutic inherent to the structure and boundaries of the "Hebrew Bible"?

Although the work of E. A. Martens (*God's Design: A Focus on Old Testament Theology,* Grand Rapids, 1981)[85] appeared before Childs's Old Testament theology, we examined both Childs and Clements together because of their common interest in "canon." Martens's theology offers an independent attempt in that he selects the fourfold promise in Exod. 5:22–6:8 as his beginning point. He thinks this text articulates "God's design" (i.e., his plan, his purpose) (Part 1). This theology then develops along the lines of three lengthy, major sections that are ordered according to the history of Israel: the premonarchial period, the period of the monarchy, and the postmonarchial period (Parts 2–4). Old Testament texts are placed at the beginning of Part 3 (Hos. 2:14–23) and of Part 4 (Ezek. 34:17–31). The typical purposes and objectives of divine actions, appropriate for the period, are then discussed within each of these major sections. Thus, for example, liberation, covenant, knowledge of God, and land are described in the section that deals with the premonarchial era, while kingship, prophets, and life in the land are characterized for the monarchial period. In addition, the theology at the end points to certain fundamental structures and themes of divine acts or of divine purpose that continue through the Old Testament. These include, for example, liberation, covenant community, experience of God, and land.[86] In the conclusion, Martens's theology also looks ahead to the New Testament.

While not an "Old Testament Theology" in the strict sense, J. Goldingay's *Theological Diversity and the Authority of the Old Testament* (Grand Rapids, 1987) still makes an important contribution to the enterprise. This work sets forth the diverse understandings of such topics as speaking about God, the people of God, and the relationship between creation and salvation in the Old Testament. The diversity of these understandings may be explained by realizing they arose in different situations and were addressed to their own contemporary contexts.[87] The different theological statements (e.g., those within the multilayered strata of the Deuteronomic text) are contrasted with each other and then evaluated by reference to other understandings in both the Old Testament and the New Testament. For Goldingay, this evaluation is necessitated by the fact that Christians regard scripture as authoritative. However, an Old Testament theology must engage in the risky venture of proceeding with an overview of these topics that seeks not only to be descriptive and reconstructive but also creative and constructive.[88] This overview, according to Goldingay, should seek to discover the lowest common denominator of these different theological expressions. To render necessary theological judgments, the Christian theologian also brings into consideration the New Testament, thereby making it possible to have a biblical theology inclusive of both Testaments.[89] What the common denominator may look like is, unfortunately, not stated. One must continue to seek and test it out.[90]

What the "theology of the Old Testament" announced by R. Rendtorff will look like is recognizable at this point only by reference to a brief sketch.[91] According to this sketch, the first part will describe both the theology of the individual Old Testament books and groups of books in their canonical order and their relationships. A second part will set forth the historical evolution of certain themes. In addition, Rendtorff desires to engage in a lively dialogue with Jewish scholars. The effort to set forth a proper Old Testament theology is obviously gaining ground.

With this, the glimpse at the previous history of the "theology of the Old Testament" comes to an end. It remains to be asked what results from this overview and what conclusions may be drawn. At the very least, one result is that there have been many models for structuring a theology of the Old Testament. While a new effort will also not produce *the* solution, nevertheless the effort still should be undertaken.

1.3 Setting the Boundaries for Methodology

Seven major problems in setting forth a theology of the Old Testament have been mentioned.[92] On the basis of these problems, it is time to determine and define in a precise manner the position represented by the present description of Old Testament theology.

First, this description seeks to set forth, not a history of Israelite religion, but rather a systematically oriented and structured theology of the Old Testament. This occurs quite naturally, not because theology per se is systematic rather than chronological,[93] but because there are other reasons. One should mention at the beginning that a systematically structured description is more capable of seeing the total picture, not only of Old Testament theology but also of its relationship to that of the New Testament. Since both Old Testament and New Testament theology must provide the basis for Christian theology, a systematic description is more conducive to this larger hermeneutical enterprise. Thus one is more easily able to determine where there are similarities, variations, approximations, and significant differences in the theological understandings between the Old Testament and the New Testament, and between the Old Testament and contemporary theology. If one wishes to discover analogous or different basic structures of the witness and faith, a systematic description that provides a comprehensive overview is more helpful. It is also more possible to move from a systematic description into necessary issues concerning the value and validity of Old Testament understandings within the larger structure of Christian theology. Even so, on the whole, a "theology of the Old Testament" still remains a historically oriented as well as a descriptive undertaking.

Second, in regard to the above, evaluations occur, not within the description of a theology of the Old Testament but within the sphere of hermeneutics and fundamental theology.[94] Furthermore, questions of value belong to the contemporary task of hermeneutical reflection on the exegesis of a particular concrete text. A theology of the Old Testament certainly must assist in answering these questions, should take into consideration the entire spectrum of theology in the formation of its own description, and ought to clarify the place of the Old Testament within a comprehensive theology. To work in the field of Old Testament studies requires one to be responsible to the present by bringing this part of the canon into the contemporary, theological debate.[95] Such matters are also important in making the Old Testament accessible to contemporary proclamation and religious instruction.

Third, a systematic description is set forth, because the Old Testament in the final analysis probably does have a center.[96]

Fourth, on the basis of the above it is evident that this systematic presentation, if at all possible, should approach the description of an Old Testament theology, by moving, not from the outside to the inside, but rather from within the Old Testament to the outside. This means then that an Old Testament theology seeks to describe "what the Old Testament says about God as a coherent whole."[97]

Fifth, the systematic formulation must be suitable for setting forth the material in a comprehensive fashion and must bring the distinctive Word of the Old Testament as far as it is possible to clear expression. Necessary historical particularities should not be dropped; rather, they must be integrated into this systematically oriented presentation. After all, God's manner of being and acting with his people is a historical process, indeed a part of history. The drawing in of history includes necessary or accentuating comparative side-glances at the religious environment of the Old Testament.[98] Gerhard von Rad's *Old Testament Theology* almost completely omitted this consideration. "The critical position taken here leads to the recognition that the Old Testament, in spite of its rootedness in the ancient Near East, still in its essential structure cannot be understood by reference to its environment. Rather, the Old Testament may be compared to an erratically shaped boulder that has all the appearance of lying in a particular landscape and belonging to it, but upon closer examination can still be understood only as out of place."[99] Israel's faith has assimilated much from its environment in a form more or less recast. This faith lives, however, at the same time in a polemical debate with this environment. Thus it is not unimportant to observe that the Old Testament does not contain many kinds of religious literature that were dominant and significant in Israel's environment. The Egyptian literature dealing with the afterlife and the typical omen literature of Mesopotamia are both absent in the Old Testament. Also missing in the Old Testament are royal inscriptions and military reports that mark the self-understanding of monarchy in the ancient Near East. In addition, the Old Testament contains neither myths of gods nor astrological and astronomical texts.

As a consequence it is not possible to set forth the various parts of the entire Old Testament on a continuum. Even when one is speaking of a center of the Old Testament, it is necessary to recognize the consequences that derive from the fact that there are some writings and texts that stand close to this center, while others do not. The particular nuances of faith or even the diverse judgments found in the variety of the Old Testament witnesses are therefore not to be eliminated. Nevertheless, there are still typical representations of the witness of faith that predominate in the "central structure of Old Testament faith."[100] The expression of such a center should not ignore either the historical breadth of the Old Testament or the variety of the literary texts and sociological considerations of different kinds. One should be aware of the danger that a systematic description of Old Testament theology represents. A systematic presentation could well conceal the historical diversity of the Hebrew canon.[101] Still, a systematic formulation seeks to offer both the occasion and the context for inquiring after the "unity of the divine activity behind the mutifaceted character of events and the *one* Word that resides behind many words."[102]

1.4   Concerning the Center of the Old Testament

Accordingly, we now address the problem of whether there is a possible[103] "center of the Old Testament."[104] In earlier research, as R. Smend has shown in an instructive way, this center was referred to as the "fundamental principle," "fundamental thoughts," "fundamental character," "fundamental idea," or "kernel." The center has included the following: salvation, redemption, knowledge of YHWH (H. Ewald); the holiness of God (A. Dillmann; J. Hänel); YHWH as a living, acting God (E. Jacob); YHWH as providential Lord (L. Köhler); theocracy[105] or covenant (W. Eichrodt);[106] community between the holy God and humanity (Th. C. Vriezen); community with God and the sovereignty of God (G. Fohrer); promise (W. C. Kaiser); God's presence and mystery;[107] and God's plan and his purposes (E. A. Martens).

Evoking the name YHWH is accompanied by the inherent problem of setting forth specific language about God. Zimmerli has spoken of the oneness of Yahweh in the multiplicity of traditions, whose revealed name means "I am who I am." Yet, how does one speak of God, and how does Israel come into his presence? Moreover, is there within the Old Testament overall a way of speaking about God that remains constant?[108] For example, is the YHWH of Amos identical with the YHWH of Proverbs 10–29? In contrast to Zimmerli, must not the "YHWH from Egypt" be introduced before one can say anything about this YHWH, since it is there, in the event of the exodus, that Israel had experienced in a fundamental way YHWH as its God? Is it possible for one first to speak of "God in and of himself" before one speaks of "God for humanity"? Moreover, how does one evaluate the continuing efforts by Zimmerli to demonstrate that the content of the divine name is understood as the direct(!) self-revelation of God? How much is Karl Barth responsible for this contention?[109] What is one to think or believe[110] about the "self-disclosure of YHWH" (in history)?[111] In addition, the efforts to set forth "YHWH" or "YHWH's self-revelation" as the center of the Old Testament does not provide much further help (see Reventlow; Hasel), since they are in any case too general. In the Old Testament's speaking of YHWH, how does it come to know something of him? How does the revelation of God take place? Surely this occurs, not within the nature of God's own self, but rather in a personal "You." Revelation is not a purpose deriving from within the divine self; rather, it occurs when the community is addressed by this "You." This "You" in the Old Testament is addressed primarily to Israel and through Israel then to the world, that is, the nations. Are Yahweh's acts on behalf of Israel and the world not more precisely describable when they are brought within the "center of the Old Testament"?[112]

One should not attempt to make an "idea" the center, since abstract thinking is foreign to the Old Testament. Westermann[113] has correctly pointed out that the structure of the Old Testament's God language involves events. In addition, this center should not be "static" in nature,[114] since the Old Testament involves historical progress.

On occasion, scholars have pointed to a particular book as the center of Old Testament theology. S. Herrmann thought with good reason that the Book of Deuteronomy served in this capacity.[115] And von Rad from time to time came rather close to this position. As will become apparent, the design of this present volume also seeks to take a good deal from this approach.

Smend[116] sought to set forth the so-called covenant formula ("YHWH the God of Israel"; "Israel the people of YHWH"),[117] including its prehistory and description of present reality in relationship to its expression of future hope, as the center of the Old Testament. This approach also offers important insights, but the question immediately arises as to how the two partners in the covenant formula came to find each other and "what the relationship of Yahweh and Israel actually includes."[118] This question forms the basis for the work of W. H. Schmidt[119] who looks to the first commandment as both the center of the Old Testament and the introductory guide for its theology. This proposal includes the affirmation of YHWH as a God who acts in history (see the preamble of the first commandment) and a God who requires obedience from his people. Indeed, this proposal comes very close to the one suggested in this volume. However, it appears unlikely that the first commandment, with its demand for the exclusive worship of YHWH, is appropriate for the entire Old Testament.[120] Rather, what is addressed in the preamble is more precisely the presupposition for all that follows.

Two other efforts to define the center of Old Testament theology should be mentioned. W. Dietrich's proposal[121] that "justice" is the "red thread" that is woven through the fabric of the Old Testament is not particularly convincing, since this theme is missing in many corpora of texts, especially narratives, that comprise the Hebrew Bible.[122] J. W. Rogerson[123] understands as central the contributions of the Old Testament to the "contemporary questions about the nature and destiny of the human race."[124] However, this statement requires more precise explication lest it remain too general.

1.5 The Present Inquiry

The present effort to set forth a "theology of the Old Testament" seeks to inquire after several related elements: the appropriate center for the Old Testament, the typical features of YHWH faith, and the decisive and formative components that comprise its fundamental structures. How does the Old Testament speak of God, that is, how is "theo-logy" expressed? How does the Old Testament present God as speaking and being spoken to? What is the basis that makes this type of language possible? We certainly do not have before us in the Old Testament God's revelation as such; rather, we have testimonies to this revelation and the various responses to them. We have "data" only in the form of a *kerygma* coming to expression within the wonderment of believing witnesses, along with texts that give voice to their testimony, texts that say that here or there YHWH, according to the conviction of the faith of these witnesses, may have acted and may have revealed himself. Even so, this testimony is not uniform throughout the history of Old Testament faith. This testimony continues to be altered and to allow for new interpretations grounded in the experiences of later witnesses that evoke once more a response.

The Old Testament witnesses primarily, not to the "nature" of YHWH, but to his divine activity. This means that in seeking the center of the Old Testament one must speak of divine activity and not of fundamental concepts or of one idea as pivotal. Rather, one must speak of a fundamental activity and how this activity is comprehended within the language of its witnesses. One should not separate external from internal history or act from interpretation,[125] for these historical happenings now exist *only* as and in language. Furthermore, the tradition history of these interpretations, which are shaped by doxological, soteriological, and polemical[126] considerations, is a part of both the history of Israel and the history of its faith.[127] Thus, insofar as it is exegetically supportable, one may make the effort to differentiate between an event that yields a testimony and an event that has its testimony deleted.[128]

According to the Old Testament, YHWH's activity has to do with Israel, but his actions are not once and for all. Rather, it is through his historical activity that YHWH elects a group, a people, to enter into community with him.[129] In and through this action, YHWH at the same time requires this people to be responsible. In this manner "community with God and divine sovereignty" (G. Fohrer) receive their expression and consequently find their basis. The "election" of Israel took place originally in the foundational events of the exodus out of Egypt and the deliverance at the sea, but election also came to be experienced and then confessed in terms of other events, for example, the installation of the monarchy or the incorporation of Zion within the world of Israel's faith. Accordingly, "election" is open to additional, new acts of YHWH on behalf of his people, provides the model for interpreting new experiences with this God, is a fundamental structure of the Old Testament witness to YHWH,[130] gives the Old Testament its inner unity (Hasel), designates what is typical for the Old Testament and its God, and thus expresses the "foundational dimension" of Old Testament faith.[131] Therefore the necessary integration of systematics and history or of the synchronic with the diachronic is already demanded by the Old Testament itself. Indeed, this foundational structure of Old Testament faith makes this integration possible.

This "center" must be related to the additional, pivotal, foundational structures of Israelite faith that include, for example, the Old Testament witness of revelation, the cult, history, and the ancestors.[132] This present volume will seek to accomplish this task insofar as it is possible, justified, and correct to do so. While one must seek to position writings and texts in varying degrees of proximity to a designated center, one should still remember that "the center of the Old Testament . . . is not the entire Old Testament."[133] There are various corpora of texts in the Old Testament that in and of themselves attempt to set forth their own "theology."[134] This is the case for Deuteronomy, Deutero-Isaiah, and perhaps also the Priestly document. Subsequently, one should have this in view in attempting to keep one's own effort, as far as possible, in close proximity to these earlier theological formulations in the Old Testament.

Furthermore, one should ask whether this articulation of Old Testament theology, including the arrangement of the fundamental structures of Old Testament faith in relationship to a designated center, may be open to the formulation of a comprehensive biblical theology conducive to a Christian perspective without the suspicion arising that this would lead to a denial of the Old Testament to Jews.[135] It would be rather ill-conceived for Christian readers or even Christian scholars to attempt to read the Old Testament as though they knew nothing at all of the message of the New Testament.[136] It is true that a "theology of the Old Testament" is still neither a "biblical theology" nor even a normative theology for Christians after it has been evaluated in terms of the New Testament witness.[137] Nevertheless, even by means of historical, descriptive questions concerning the fundamental structures of Old Testament faith,[138] an Old Testament theology still ought to prepare the way for a biblical theology. This being said, one may hope that many Jewish readers who are concerned with an overview of the "Tanakh" may still be able to view this presentation of Old Testament theology as an appropriate one.

The following presentation views the center of the Old Testament and thus the fundamental structure of Old Testament faith to be *"YHWH's historical activity of electing Israel for communion with his world"*[139] *and the obedient activity required of this people (and the nations).*[140] This presentation will seek to determine whether this center (or fundamental structure) may organize the other fundamental structures of Old Testament faith attaching to or resulting from it, as, for example, the Old Testament ways of speaking about God or the actions of humanity. Yet, even a modest degree of reflection leads to the critical question of how this center relates either to YHWH's activity in creation or to wisdom literature. This presentation will attempt to answer questions such as these.

The current state of scholarship, with its divergent methods, theses, and results, does not appear particularly supportive of efforts to formulate a comprehensive Old Testament theology,[141] even though a comprehensive approach is imperative. This divergence is especially common in the fields of literary and redaction criticisms that particularly impact research in the Pentateuch and the Prophets. It needs only to be mentioned at this juncture that no one is in a position to know in which direction a possible new consensus may lead. However, since this outlook is not likely to change in the near future, the following discussion will dare to venture an opinion here and there about debated issues (e.g., the existence or dating of the so-called Yahwist). While taking such a position is risky, the attempt will still be made. This effort proceeds with the full recognition of the danger that the presentation in both its entirety and each of its parts cannot be "fully informed by the current (and perhaps a very particular) scholarly stance." However, one cannot simply throw up one's hands in despair at either lagging behind the contemporary scholarly understandings of various issues or, having assimilated them, finding that the discussion has moved forward.

It may still be noted, and this is the expressed judgment of another Old Testament scholar, that the contemporary tendency to reject the authenticity of texts is often grounded in reasons not entirely convincing and oftentimes proceeds from unsubstantiated hypotheses[142] that "are based more on the subjective feelings of the interpreters than on the identifiable data of the text. Subsequently, I would rather trust the tradition's representation of authenticity too much than too little."[143] Many of the contemporary views that argue for the late dating of texts and traditions or that almost completely devalue the historical dimensions of Old Testament texts are viewed either as unsubstantiated or as wrong.[144]

PART ONE. LAYING THE FOUNDATION

Chapter 2. An Overview of the Old Testament's
Statements about Election[1]

2.1 YHWH's Acts of Election

YHWH's (historical) action of election and obligation concerning Israel has
been proposed as the possible center, the typical expression, and the most important fundamental structure of the Old Testament witness of faith.[2] Thus one
should ask: "How is this action described in the places in the Bible where it occurs? To what extent is this witness of faith appropriate for the entire Old Testament?"

To begin with, the approach of the present Old Testament theology does not
proceed by noting the appearance or absence of the word "election" and then
choosing to draw or not draw certain conclusions. Furthermore, this approach
does not proceed by reference to either the specific term of election or the distribution of the root בחר = *bāḥar* ("to elect") throughout the Old Testament.
Rather, this approach, on the one hand, looks to the semantic field witnessing
to YHWH's activity of election in order to provide an overview of words that
appear within the linguistic sphere of this concept. On the other hand, this approach points in particular to the realization that YHWH's activity of choosing comprises the most decisive, fundamental structure of the Old Testament
witness. The conception and faith of election are the basis for both Israel's self-
consciousness and its manner of life.

To illustrate briefly this point, Amos 3:2 and 9:7 state that YHWH knew his
people and has brought them out of the land of Egypt. While the term for "election" is absent, its reality is clearly addressed. The same is true of Gen. 12:1–4
(cf. 28:14), a section within the Abraham narratives. While for all practical
purposes the choosing of Abram is described, the specific Hebrew word for
"election" does not appear.[3] Moreover, every word's history has its concrete
prehistory, and the comprehensive meaning of a term does not stand at the beginning of the development of a faith and its manner of expression.

2.2 The Verb "to Elect"

At this juncture, the various understandings of the occurrences of בחר = *bāḥar*
with YHWH/God may be introduced in order to provide a closer examination of

the evidence that will be set forth. The activity of YHWH's election is expressed in this fashion some ninety-nine times.[4] Thus it becomes immediately clear that this concept is not an unimportant idea within the Old Testament (altogether the term *bhr* occurs 146 times). There are thirteen instances that mention that either something or someone has been "elected" by YHWH: for example, Moses (Ps. 106:23), David (Ps. 89:4), and the servant of God (Isa. 42:1). In looking at the distribution of the specifically theological usage of this word, one notes that it receives particular emphasis in Deuteronomy (twenty-nine times), Deutero-Isaiah (seven times), and the Psalms (nine times). When election is mentioned in these texts, it does not require either an introduction or an explanation. In addition, it should be noted that, in good Old Testament fashion, the term occurs in verbal form ("to elect") but not as an abstract noun (i.e., "election"). This contrasts with German and English which require an idea to be expressed as an abstract noun. Even Akkadian has an abstract noun for election (*itûtu*).[5] In the Old Testament, the actuality of election results from God's decision of free will. God turns to the recipients of election in acts of grace and offers them the opportunity for community with him. No reason is given, for example, as to why Abraham or Zion is chosen, and even when Deuteronomy 7 theologically reflects on the election of Israel, the basis for this activity is found only in YHWH himself. In addition, it is clear that YHWH's electing is not contained in some divine decree that exists beyond time (perhaps not even in the form of predestination) but rather takes shape in the historical activity of divine redemption that is grounded in the history of YHWH with his people (Pss. 106:5ff.; 135:4ff.; Ezek. 20:5ff.).[6] And the Old Testament texts point to the fact that YHWH's activity of electing his people cannot be handled without there having developed first the perspective of a universal history.[7]

2.3 Election of the Individual

Whom or what did YHWH elect? His election of individual people,[8] with the exception of the king (see below), is relatively late and is infrequently mentioned in the Old Testament. Nehemiah 9:7 speaks of Abraham's election (cf. his "call" in Isa. 51:2), while Ps. 106:23 refers to that of Moses (cf. also Ps. 105:26). The prophets did not use *bāḥar* to provide an approximate definition for the meaning of their call. This may have been due to the fact that they stood in critical opposition to believers who were themselves the "chosen."[9] It is only with the Servant of God that election and call are combined (cf. Isa. 42:1 with 49:1).

Yet there are instances where election is conveyed through expressions other than *bāḥar*. Even though the root is not used, one may still regard Jer. 1:5 as indicating that YHWH was believed to be a God who also elected individuals. This conclusion may be derived from the use of the two words "to set apart" and "to appoint," terms that in this context can mean nothing other than election. Noah was also, in the final analysis, a chosen individual whose salvation came about only by means of divine "grace" (Gen. 6:8).[10] The same may be said of YHWH's "knowing" (Gen. 18:19) and "taking" Abraham (Gen. 24:7). Finally, when YHWH calls the "major judges" to deliver Israel (Judges 3–16), he elects them to be the instruments of his military activity. These are those who establish justice for YHWH's people in their dealings with their neighbors. Israel's or Judah's election to enter into history with YHWH and the explanation of how this came about are the subjects of reflection and praise in Psalms 68; 78; 105; and 106. Furthermore, these psalms ponder and even lament the consequences that issued forth from election.

According to two texts from the Priestly source (Num. 16:5ff.; and 17:20), priests were divinely elected to the priestly office. There is evidence from one old source (1 Sam. 2:28) that the house of Eli was elected. In later sources, both Aaron (Ps. 105:26) and the Levites are elected to divine service (Deut. 18:5; 21:5; 1 Chron. 15:2; 2 Chron. 29:11). Consequently, election is linked to a commission.

One of the sons of David wore the name Ibhar (yibḥar; 2 Sam. 5:15), derived from the word for election, בחר = bāḥar. This points in the direction of royal figures being elected by YHWH. Late texts use the language of the divine election of kings (cf. Deut. 17:15, an exilic text; and 2 Chron. 6:5). Even if the king is divinely elected, the people who are entrusted to him as his subjects remain the people of YHWH (2 Chron. 6:5: "over my people Israel"; cf. 2 Sam. 6:21; Pss. 28:8f.; 72:1f.; also 78:67–71).

According to 1 Sam. 10:24, YHWH elects Saul to be king. However, the reader, who already knows of this divine act of election of Israel's first king, is soon confronted by YHWH's rejection of this very same man (1 Sam. 15:23, 26). Regardless of the dating of these texts, they underline the fact that election is obviously not a permanent condition. One may also see this in the rejection of Israel mentioned in other sources (2 Kings 17:20; cf. 2 Kings 23:27; Jer. 14:19, 21; Lam. 2:7; etc.).[11] Several presumably ancient texts from the history of the rise of David and the ark narrative speak of the election of David, and, as is often the case in the Old Testament, do so in terms of the election of those of lowly status (1 Sam. 16:8ff. and 2 Sam. 6:21; cf., in regard to Saul, 1 Sam. 9:21; 10:24).[12] One may compare these to texts from the ancient Near Eastern milieu of Israel that speak of the divine election of kings.[13] Additional statements addressing this theme come from later Old Testament texts: 1 Kings 8:16 (Deuteronomistic); Pss. 78:70; 89:4; 1 Chron. 28:5; 2 Chron. 6:5. In 2 Sam. 16:18 Hushai indicates to Absalom that he will serve the king chosen by YHWH. Later texts mention in this connection Zerubbabel (Hag. 2:23) and Solomon (1 Chron. 28:5f.; 29:1). The exilic text, Psalm 89, wrestles with the problem of the final rejection of the house of David, and even offers up a questioning plea about this predicament (vv. 50f.).[14]

Apart from the description of Saul, David, and Absalom as chosen kings and claimants to the throne and the designation of the house of Eli as a chosen priestly line, the mentioning of YHWH's election of individuals, insofar as the term בחר = *bāḥar* is expressly used, occurs again only in exilic and postexilic texts. Even then the statements about the election of individuals are of secondary importance to the election of the people. One may say then that, while the divine election of the king was an early understanding in ancient Israel, the election of other individuals finds a significant place only in exilic and especially postexilic texts.

2.4 Election of the People

Of decisive importance, then, are the statements about the election of the people.[15] The statements that tell of the election of individuals are connected to those which speak of the election of the nation. Indeed, the tradition of the chosen status of Israel gives life to the later understanding of the election of individuals. There are postexilic texts that, looking backward, describe the election of this nation, and especially this nation, in terms of becoming a worshiping community (Isa. 65:9; cf. vv. 15 + 22; also see Ps. 105:6, 43; 1 Chron. 16:13; Ps. 65:5; Num. 16:7). Then there is the designation of Israel as the servant of YHWH in Deutero-Isaiah (Isa. 41:8–10; 43:10; 44:1f.; and 49:7). Here the election of the nation can be associated even with creation (Isa. 43:10ff.; and 44:2), so that historical destiny and creation are seen as one. Ezekiel says in one of his historical surveys that YHWH has elected his people when he made himself known to them in Egypt (Ezek. 20:5). Then, when Israel was brought up out of Egypt, Judah became YHWH's sanctuary and Israel his sovereign domain (Ps. 114:1ff.). Deuteronomy frequently mentions the election of the nation, although (according to Deut. 9:4ff.) this election was not due to the people's special merit (Deut. 7:6–8; 10:15; 14:2; cf. 1 Kings 3:8b).

According to Amos (3:2; 5:14f.; 6:1; and 9:7), the nation's confidence in its secure relationship with YHWH became an expression of faith. While Amos denounced this self-confidence for having turned into a guarantee, even the prophet's speeches of judgment continued to present Yahweh as calling Israel "my people" (Amos 7:8, 15; 8:2; and 9:10). Similar representations are found in Isa. 40:1; Ps. 81:9; Hos. (4:6, 8, 12; and 11:7, but contrast 1:9); Isaiah (1:3; 3:12, 15; 5:13, 25; and 10:2); and Micah (1:9; 2:4, 8, 9; 3:3; 6:3, 5; and 7:14 [a later addition]).[16]

The stories of the ancestors[17] describe individuals who are associated with groups or large families and stand in a personal relationship with the deity. While these narratives portray the relationship as resulting from the deity's electing a group and calling an individual from its midst, they also speak of the group's and individual's choosing of the deity. In fact, Genesis 12:1–4a already takes up the question of the relationship of Israel to the nations in describing the election of Abraham and his descendants. The narratives of the ancestors tell the story of divine guidance and community with God, although without using the term "to elect" (cf., however, Gen. 18:19; 24:7). This means that whereas we tend to look for definitions, these narratives tell stories of how God has established a personal relationship with a particular tribe.[18] The conceptualization of what is here simply narrated occurs later, as Ps. 105:6 indicates ("you offspring of Abraham, his servant, sons of Jacob, his chosen ones"). And when Israel in the making was increasing in numbers and came under the oppression of the pharaoh, YHWH once more, according to the narratives of the exodus, turned toward this band of Moses and elected them to enter into community with him through historical deeds of salvation, guidance, and responsibility. The narrator allows here for the first time YHWH to say Israel is "my people" (Exod. 3:7, 10; 5:1; 7:16; 8:16ff.; etc.), while the people speak of YHWH as "our God" (Exod. 3:18; 5:3, 8). This prepares the way for the compound "people of YHWH" ("your people": Exod. 5:23), as it occurs in other early texts of the Old Testament (cf. already Judg. 5:11; in addition, see 1 Sam. 2:24; 2 Sam. 1:12; 14:13; etc.; and the contrasting formulation in Exod. 32:7f.). YHWH is the God of Israel (so already in Judg. 5:5),[19] its shepherd (Ps. 80:2), and its king (Exod. 15:18).

2.5   The Semantic Field

The various nuances as well as the consistency of the theme of what YHWH has done for his people can now be described by reference to the larger semantic field that surrounds a historical experience of election.[20]

YHWH calls and appoints (קרא = *qārā'*: Exod. 31:2; 35:30; Hos. 11:1; Isa. 41:9; 43:1; 48:12; 49:1; and 51:2; in 45:3, Cyrus is called to be YHWH's historical instrument of salvation). He separated out (בדל = *bādal*, hiphil: Deut. 10:8; 1 Kings 8:53; and Lev. 20:24, 26; contrast: Isa. 59:2), seized (חזק = *ḥāzaq*: Isa. 41:9, 13; 42:6; 45:1; and Jer. 31:32), desired (אוה = *'āwwâ*: Ps. 132: 13f.), knew (ידע = *yāda'*: Gen. 18:19; and Amos 3:2),[21] redeemed (גאל = *gā'al*: Exod. 6:6; 15:13; Pss. 74:2; 77:16; 106:10; Isa. 44:22f.; 48:20; 51:10; 52:3; and 63:9), freely purchased (פדה = *pādâ*: Deut. 7:8; 9:26; 13:6; 15:15; 21:8; and 24:18; cf. 2 Sam. 7:23; Hos. 7:13; 13:14; Micah 6:4; and Jer. 31:11), acquired through purchase (קנה = *qānâ*: Deut. 32:6; Pss. 74:2; 78:54; Isa. 11:11; cf. Exod. 15:16), took or grasped (לקח = *lāqaḥ*: Gen. 24:7; Exod. 6:7; Deut. 4:20; 30:4; and Josh. 24:3; cf. 1 Sam. 12:22; and Isa. 41:9),[22] and "found" Israel (מצא = *māsâ'*: Hos. 9:10 and Deut. 32:10; cf. Jer. 2:2f.; 31:2; Ezek. 16:1ff.). Consequently, Israel became and continued to be a special people (Num. 23:9; cf. Amos 6:1 and Micah 3:11 ["YHWH in our midst"], indicating self-confidence). YHWH himself says or is made to say that Israel is "my people"

(Isa. 1:3, 7; cf. 5:7; Jer. 9:6; Amos 7:8, 15; Micah 6:3; Exod. 3:7 J; 3:10 E; and 7:4 P; the contrasting statement, "not my people," occurs in Hos. 1:9) and also "my inheritance" (a later and more deliberate expression; Deut. 4:20 and 9:26, 29), for Israel is set apart and made holy by YHWH (Jer. 2:3). According to Ps. 74:2, YHWH has acted to make Israel his people within the context of history. The phrase "the people of YHWH's own possession" is used in order to express in a suitable manner YHWH's historical activity of election that leads to his entering into community with Israel (Deut. 7:6; 14:2; and 26:18; cf. similarly Exod. 19:5; Ps. 135:4; and Mal. 3:17). This language of "the people of YHWH's own possession" at the same time expresses the interrelationship between election and obedience. The expression "YHWH's people" (Judg. 5:11 and 2 Sam. 1:12) indicates that it is not through the people's doing, but rather through YHWH's activity of reaching out and setting Israel apart that makes it a "holy" nation, that is, a people consecrated to YHWH (Exod. 19:6; Deut. 7:6; 14:2, 21; 26:19; and 28:9).[23] The image of marriage is used to approximate the relationship between the two partners (Hosea and Jeremiah; cf. Ezekiel 16; 23). Elsewhere the image of the relationship between father and son occurs, an image interpreted as a historical relationship and not as a natural or physiological one in which YHWH fathers Israel (Exod. 4:22; Isa. 1:2f.; and Hos. 11:1; cf. Isa. 43:6; 63:16; Mal. 2:10; Ps. 103:13; and also Deut. 14:1).[24] In addition to the key texts that provide theological reflection on the theme of "election" (i.e., Deuteronomy 7 and 9:1–6), one also should mention Exod. 19:3b–6.[25] This passage summarizes much of what has been stated in the present context about election. Also significant are the remarks in 2 Sam. 7:23f. that pertain to the relationship of YHWH and Israel.

This wealth of biblical statements concerning YHWH's historical activity that leads to his relationship with Israel, to which many others could be added, indicates that the language of "election" could not simply be invented and then proclaimed.[26]

YHWH also becomes known as the God who acted to choose Jerusalem and Zion to be his city and temple.[27] Later on, this activity of choosing a place for worship and a city for divine habitation is added to the election of the people (cf. Ps. 132:13f.). This combination of the election of city, temple, and people is especially frequent in Deuteronomic and Deuteronomistic texts (e.g., Deut. 12:5ff.; 14:23–25; 1 Kings 8:16, 44, 48; 11:32; 2 Kings 21:7; 23:27; etc.) and in Chronicles (2 Chron. 6:5f., 34, 38; 7:12, 16; 12:13; and 33:7; also see Neh. 1:9 and Pss. 78:68 and 132:13). While the formulation of the Book of Deuteronomy as speeches of Moses does not allow for the mentioning of the name of Jerusalem, Isa. 48:2 and 52:1 refer to the city as the "holy city." It is "chosen" (Zech. 1:17; 2:16; 3:2). That this is not simply the result of later reflection is demonstrated by Jeremiah's opposition (cf. Jeremiah 7 and 26) to the people's confidence in the security of the temple, a confidence possibly derived from Isaiah (28:16; 29:8; 30:18f.; and 31:4f.). Later texts speak of the "holy mountain" (Isa. 56:7; 65:11; 66:20; etc.), representing the climax of what YHWH had initiated in his election of Zion.

Israel became the people of YHWH through his historical activity of election and not through divine procreation where a father gives birth to a son. This election came into being within history and not during primeval times. Similarly, Jerusalem did not become the city and sanctuary of YHWH through some mythical act of creation (cf. Ps. 78:54 where קָנָה = *qānâ* refers to Sinai). When the prophets are silent about the faith of election, it is due to their criticism directed against the perversion of this faith (Amos 3:2; 9:7).[28]

2.6   Historical Emphases

What has been described to this point has been only a cursory and rough overview. Even so, when one considers the historical development of election faith, two biblical emphases are noted from looking at the use of בחר = *bāḥar* in the theological realm. While other terms and ways of expressing election faith are found in J, E, and the preexilic prophets, the theological use of בחר = *bāḥar* is absent. It is Deuteronomy that is the first text to emphasize and present a well-developed theology of election.[29] Even so, as the paraenetic texts are able to demonstrate (Deuteronomy 7; 10), this theology was not newly contrived but rather already had an existing prehistory.[30] Deuteronomy 7:6–8 (in 7:1–11) is the classical passage for the idea of election,[31] though Deut. 9:1–6 might also be held up for consideration. In the context of these statements about election, it is not by accident that other, previously discussed expressions for election appear, including "holy people," YHWH's "own people," and "inherited portion." Even so, any possible significance attributed to the chosen people's responsibility toward the foreign nations is passed by in silence. Israel, first of all, must and ought to discover itself again.[32] The statements about election (cf. also Deut. 4:34, 37; 10:15; and 14:2) may well contain older materials or at least presuppose their existence.[33]

Then there is the expression the "place which YHWH chooses" (Deut. 12:5, 11, 14, 18, 21, 26; 14:23f.; etc.).[34] If the election of the king is mentioned, it is done so by stressing that the king is a "brother" who belongs to the chosen people (17:14f.). "The election faith (in Deuteronomy) is the basis for everything else: theocracy, exclusivity (even to the point of particularity), the concentration of worship in Jerusalem, and the rigorous demand that the entire personal and national life be dedicated to God."[35] This first, clearly articulated emphasis on election theology, occurring in a book that may not incorrectly be regarded as the "center" of the Old Testament, influences the Deuteronomistic History where one finds some twenty examples of the verb "elect" with God as the subject.[36]

After Deuteronomy, the second emphasis on election theology is set forth in Deutero-Isaiah with its promises of salvation (Isa. 41:8f.; 43:20f.; and 44:1f.) that often speak of YHWH's "election" of his people (Isa. 41:8–10; 43:10, 20f.; 44:1f.; 49:7; cf. 65:9, 15, 22). As is the case in Deuteronomy,[37] the word "love" appears several times in close proximity to acts of election (Isa. 41:8 and 43:4), including statements about the ancestors (Isa. 41:8; 44:2; cf. 51:2). YHWH has chosen, not rejected (Isa. 41:9; cf. Jer. 33:24–26). "Election in Deutero-Isaiah is first of all an affirmation about God and then, on the basis of this, an affirmation about Israel."[38] In addition, election appears here in connection with Israel's servanthood (Isa. 43:10), an idea that also comes to expression in speaking of the relationship of the chosen people with the nations (cf. Deuteronomy 7 which draws a critical contrast between Israel and the nations).[39] As Israel is the people who, through YHWH's election, is both the servant of God and witness (Isa. 43:10 and 45:4), so it is with the individual Servant of the Lord in the so-called Songs of the Servant (Isa. 42:1 and 49:6).[40]

These emphases on election in Deuteronomy and Deutero-Isaiah make it clear that there are already recognized understandings of election that these two texts render more precisely. A similar example of a text that expresses in a more pointed fashion an understanding of election is Ps. 78:67 which tells of the end of the Northern Kingdom of Israel. It also should be noted that both of these texts, Deuteronomy and Deutero-Isaiah, stress the theology of election during periods of crisis in religious faith, thus giving the theme greater prominence and densifying its meaning.[41] If the early form of Deuteronomy takes shape during the Assyrian crisis, so the crisis of the Babylonian exile is the time for both the Deuteronomistic School's redaction of Deuteronomy and the appearance of Deutero-Isaiah. These were times when Israel believed it was rejected and not elected, as similar views from Jeremiah[42] (cf. Jer. 33:23–26) and Psalm 78 help to demonstrate. Ezekiel could speak of the election of Israel only in a critical fashion (Ezek. 20:5f.), since, according to him, election was supposed to have led to the eradication of idols.

In their reflections over election, both Deuteronomy and Deutero-Isaiah set forth the notion of YHWH as the one God (Deut. 6:4f.) and the one and only true God (Deutero-Isaiah) within the context of a developing monotheism that was becoming more and more theoretical.[43] The combination of both of these circles of thought is clearly elucidated in Deuteronomy 4.[44]

Over against this theological use of election language about the nation, the Priestly source was content with describing only the election of the priesthood (Num. 16:5 and 17:20). Consequently, theological language about the election of the nation and the king is not important in this source. The election of the nation in P is mentioned only in Gen. 17:6, 16 and 35:11, and there is no reference at all to the divine election of kings.

Zechariah is the first text in the postexilic period to speak once more and in fresh ways of the renewed (עוד = *'ôd:* cf. Zech. 8:4, 20) election of the city of Jerusalem that had been rejected (2 Kings 23:27) by YHWH (Zech. 1:17; 2:16; and 3:2; cf. other probably postexilic texts Isa. 14:1; Jer. 33:23f.; and presumably also Ps. 78:68). Close to this is Trito-Isaiah (Isa. 65:9, 15, 22), who considers those who returned from the exile the "chosen." The new beginning after the exile is interpreted by both Zechariah and Trito-Isaiah as a new election. Alongside these texts may be placed several psalms (Pss. 33:12 and 47:3–5 [probably not preexilic]; 105:5f., 42f.; 106:4f.; 132:13f.; and 135:4) and the Books of Chronicles which take up and further develop the semantic field of election that had been so directly impacted by the crisis of faith during the exile (1 Chron. 28:4f.; 29:1; 2 Chron. 6:5f., 34, 38; 7:12, 16; 12:13; and 33:7; cf. Neh. 1:9).[45] David and Jerusalem are closely bound together in Chronicles, and naturally the Levites had to partake in the honor of a special election (1 Chron. 15:2 and 2 Chron. 29:11).[46]

In the Psalter, hymns at times relate election to creation (Ps. 33:6–15; cf. Pss. 95:4ff., 135:4f., 6f.; cf. Deutero-Isaiah: 43:20f.; 44:1f.) and at other times incorporate the theme within the sequence of historical events (Pss. 78:67–72; 89:3–5; and 132:10–14). In the latter case, election is interpreted as a historical event ("we are his people, and the sheep of his pasture," Ps. 100:3; cf. Ps. 79:13). These hymns praise both the God who elects and his actions on behalf of his people. By contrast, any mention of the election of either an individual or the nation by YHWH is absent in Old Testament wisdom literature.

2.7   Election and History

In its historical development, the theme of election eventually includes not only Israel but also David, Saul, the king in general (Deut. 17:15), Levites and priests, and the city of Jerusalem or Zion (cf. Pss. 132:13 and 78:68; according to 2 Kings 21:17, YHWH will make his name to dwell there "forever"). Each of these is interpreted through the lens of expressions concerning election. With the rise of the monarchy and the establishment of Zion, these two spheres are incorporated into Yahwistic faith. This incorporation occurred during the reigns of David and Solomon in Israel, and not before. In addition, the election of the priesthood is established for the first time with the house of Eli. Subsequently, YHWH faith was in a position to integrate later traditions through the concept of "election."

In looking over the entire Old Testament, what is central to the election of the nation are the exodus from Egypt and the choosing of the early ancestors. These are the two components of election to which later developing understandings return and on which expanding "election traditions" are developed.

The importance of the events of the exodus are set forth in Amos 9:7; Hos. 11:1; 12:10; 13:4; Micah 6:3f.; Jer. 2:2ff.; 16:14; 31:31f.; and Ezek. 20:5f. In addition, see Num. 24:8; 1 Sam. 12:6 (Deuteronomistic); Exod. 20:2; Josh. 24:4f.; and Exod. 15:1f. (an expansion of the older text of Exod. 15:21). All of these texts will be examined in more detail later on.[47]

Whether the expression "the God of the fathers"[48] already points to a deity who has elected a group to lead is a matter for debate. Nevertheless, it is still the case that the narratives of the early ancestors understand that YHWH has elected them and their tribes through various actions. This understanding may be seen in Gen. 12:1–4a as well as in Gen. 18:19; 24:7; 28:10f.; and chaps. 16 and 21. By means of the patriarchal narratives that precede the later national history, the ancestors, on the one hand, are bound to the emerging nation through the themes of the promise of the land and the multiplication of their descendants. On the other hand, the stories of the ancestors also are seen as the precursor to the history of the nation whose origins have already been announced. Subsequently, these ancestors and their groups were absorbed into Israel, and it is no wonder that the preponderate discussion of them occurs primarily in Genesis and then only in later texts (from the time of Deutero-Isaiah). It is also likely that, in reference to the "ancestors," it was especially popular faith that primarily believed in and readily defended this tradition. This may explain why critical prophecy primarily tended to pass over the tradition of the ancestors in silence. This fact, along with the chiding references to this tradition by Hosea 12 (Jacob as a deceiver) and probably also by Amos 5:14f. ("he will be with you, as you have said"; cf. "we have Abraham as our father"; Matt. 3:9 and parallels), suggests that the prophets stood in critical opposition to this tradition of faith.

When the tradition of the ancestors and the exodus tradition were brought together (cf. Exodus 3 and 6), the early ancestors were made precursors to the exodus and groups of the ancestors became the forebears of the nation of Israel. In this fashion, Yahwistic faith not only expanded and then anchored its contents in the past but it also augmented its linear, historical understandings that resided within its expression. Therefore YHWH's future directed acts can now be given a still more comprehensive witness. The exodus tradition was probably older and more genuinely "Israelite" and, moreover, would have been transmitted by the more influential tribes among the peoples who came to comprise Israel. At the same time, these tribes were those who "brought along" YHWH with them.[49] The tradition of the ancestors, by contrast, first emerged in the land among groups of worshipers who later came into relationship with the Israel of the exodus, a point made by Joshua 24. What facilitated the coming together of the exodus group with groups already in the land of Canaan, moreover, was that both had their own separate tradition that spoke of the promise of the land.[50] Other fundamental structures that are similar to one another and that could be brought together at this point will be described later.

2.8   The Theology of Election

"Election" in the Old Testament refers not to some kind of supratemporal or primeval divine decree but rather to a historical action of YHWH.[51] Through means of the exodus out of Egypt, Israel/Judah became YHWH's sanctuary and dominion (see Ps. 114:1f.). YHWH's activity of election leading to his relationship with Israel and its connection to him had both a beginning and an intrinsic grounding. The Old Testament knows of such an activity of YHWH's election in several spheres, namely, the exodus, the ancestors, the king, Zion, and the priesthood, and arranges these acts of election in a series in which the exodus clearly had a position of priority.[52] In matters of faith, Israel was oriented primarily to history. It was in history that Israel experienced its God, and it was in this historical experience of God that Israel came to both the possibility and the imperative to believe in him. Thus, through the storytellers and the prophets it was the meaning and sense of history that was always sought after and demanded. The writing of history proceeds from this awareness, even when in the description of the course of events the name of YHWH does not appear (Esther) or appears very rarely (the Succession Narrative, 2 Samuel 9–1 Kings 2; the Joseph Story, Genesis 37–50). This awareness is there even when the prophet Jeremiah does not mention YHWH when he announces the coming destruction.[53] History writing in this case is different from the writing of annals, and indeed it must be, for election faith hears "the Word of God in history."[54]

Election faith is ancient. Amos 3:2 and 6:1 presuppose it, as do Genesis 16 and 21, even if in a simple, conceptually undeveloped form. The conceptual clarification and persuasiveness of the theme of election continue to develop until it eventually reaches its climax in Deuteronomy and Deutero-Isaiah. The Old Testament speaks about election, before defining it. The belief in the reality of election, the awareness of election, and the origin of community between God and the people within history are fundamental for the faith of the Old Testament, even if the term בחר = bāḥar is later. The more definite the theological pervasiveness and repletion of this faith in election became, the more it was recognized at the same time that election includes promise and points forward toward its complete fulfillment and manifest realization. Election entails a setting apart for the purposes of both community and possession and, thereby, being destined for salvation. Accordingly, election is also the promise that awaits fulfillment and the basis for continuing, new hope.[55]

When seeking the motives of election, one discovers that the Old Testament continues to be remarkably reserved (cf. perhaps only Deuteronomy 7 and 9:1–6). Why YHWH called Abraham is not stated. Israel was not better than other nations, and YHWH apparently chooses differently than human beings do (e.g., Lot: Genesis 13). Because YHWH loved his people and wished to keep the oath he had given to the ancestors, he chose his people (Deut. 7:8). The reasons for this election, however, are found only in YHWH himself.[56] Israel can only testify in thankfulness to its election. YHWH "found" his people like grapes in the wilderness (! Hos. 9:10). The Old Testament cannot and does not desire to say more than this.

2.9   Further Questions

If a group or a people has made historical election the experience of its faith, if Israel has interpreted its experience as divine election,[57] then there are further, more far-reaching questions that present themselves. Election causes one to ask about those on the "outside," that is, what of YHWH's and Israel's relationship to other nations and to their gods? In addition, is one also to speak of an election that entails a relationship or responsibility "to" others? Does Israel have a purpose toward other human beings and nations, perhaps to be a witness of YHWH in and before the world? Is what YHWH does to and with Israel exemplary in character? The emergence and the formulation of such questions are not necessarily bound up with a general or overarching universalism. Rather, such questions are connected to a living experience and to a conception of a God who is in the position to reach out to his own particular group. This is already clear in the Song of Deborah (Judges 5), the Yahwist from the tenth century B.C.E., and Amos in the eighth century B.C.E. The interpreter of the Old Testament, who addresses these problems, finds it necessary to inquire after the character of Israel within its contemporary social milieu by seeking to discover the relationship of Yahwistic faith to the religions of the peoples that either border Israel or are found in its midst (= Canaanites). Here it should be said that the idea of the election of a people by a deity is a unique expression to this point within the religious history of the ancient Near East.[58]

YHWH's relationship with Israel primarily is viewed no differently from the relationships of the other nations with their deities (cf. Judg. 11:24; 1 Sam. 26:19; and Micah 4:5; cf. Deut. 32:8f. [LXX]). However, certain historical experiences were so compelling that they led to the recognition of the special, unique, and unmatched character of YHWH. These experiences of YHWH's uniqueness suggested, then, the distinct concept of election that included, for example, both the consequences of being set apart (cf. among others Deut. 14:1f.) and the expansion of faith into the spheres of nature, creation, fertility, the world of the nations, and others. YHWH elected Israel, even though or because he was also the Lord of heaven and earth (Deut. 10:14f.).

The formation of Old Testament election faith rests on presuppositions that are not foreign to its development but rather foster it. This faith continues to develop in observable ways from the occasions that gave rise to it. Therefore it is correct to say that the specific, fundamental structure of YHWH faith consists of the historical activity of election. This activity in its different expressions and various stages should lead through God's dealings with Israel to the consummation of his lordship over his people and over his world. We shall now turn to the ways in which the Old Testament witness speaks of these matters.

Chapter 3. The Election and Obligation of the People

Israel knew its God YHWH as "YHWH from the land of Egypt" (Hos. 12:10; 13:4). As the important preamble of the Decalogue indicates (Exod. 20:2; Deut. 5:6), this confession about YHWH refers to the exodus from Egypt and the deliverance at the sea as the decisive, divine action leading to the establishment of a community between YHWH and Israel in both its outward beginnings and its inward foundation. In this decisive act, the Old Testament witness to God finds both its origins and its center. This means that the primary definition of the divine name in the expression, "I am YHWH, your God," is captured in the statement that follows: "who has led you out of the land of Egypt, out of the house of slaves." This explanation of the divine name is not "added as a secondary definition,"[1] for the relationship between YHWH and Israel did not originate either in a mythical prehistory or from some natural bond. Rather, Yahweh's entrance into history to act on behalf of his people became for Israel an enduring pristine confession (M. Noth). This deliverance was, at the same time, an election; indeed, in this deliverance Israel saw its "primal election." Now we turn to consider how the Old Testament witness speaks about these experiences.

3.1 The Exodus Event as the Primal Election

"When Israel went forth from Egypt, the house of Jacob from a people with a strange language, Judah became his sanctuary, Israel his dominion" (Ps. 114:1f.). "Has ever a god sought to come to a nation and to take it from the midst of another . . . , as YHWH, your God, has done for you in Egypt. . . . Because he loved your ancestors, he has chosen all of their descendants after them and has led you out of Egypt with his own presence, by his great power" (Deut. 4:34, 37). "YHWH your God has chosen you to be a nation for his own possession out of all the nations" (Deut. 7:6).

The oldest texts that witness to this *exodus event as the primal election*[2] celebrated (Exod. 15:21) and described (the J portion of Exod. 13:17–14:31)[3] it as a military action of Yahweh on behalf of his people. With direct language unencumbered by metaphor or simile, the Song of Miriam[4] extols with thankfulness and praise YHWH as a God who acts: "horse and rider he has thrown into the sea." This song, patterned after a victory song, probably originated within the context of this deliverance. Here Yahweh is spoken about in words of adoration and confession.[5] In the form of thankful praise, the song is a direct response to a divine deed, in this case a historical act of deliverance. The event and the response of praise point to the establishment of trust. Finally, the future under this God is extolled at the same time that the past is remembered.

The narrative of Judges 4 is positioned before the older Song of Deborah (Judges 5) and tells the story of what had already been proclaimed in the song. So it is with the narrative of Exod. 13:17–14:31 and the Song of Miriam (Exod. 15:21).[6] Different literary "sources" are woven together in this section of the narrative in Exodus, as is the case in the flood story (Gen. 6:5–8:22). No date is given for the event described in Exod. 13:17–14:31.[7] Normally one thinks of Merneptah as the "pharaoh of the exodus" (1224–1204 B.C.E.), since it is rather certain that the data in Exod. 1:11 pertains to his period of rule. This would mean that his father, Ramses II, is the "pharaoh of the oppression." If the Priestly description of the deliverance at the sea[8] takes part in what is for it a typical exaggeration of what occurs by stressing the miraculous character of the events, the persecution of Israel by the pharaoh himself, and probably also his drowning (Exod. 14:[6?], 8, 17f., 23, 28), then it must be pointed out that there is no pharaoh who died such a death. Subsequently, these statements in P do not lend themselves to "historical" description. Egyptian sources are silent about what is narrated in Exodus 13–14. The question of the location of the event is also not clear, while the differing data concerning the places mentioned are difficult to harmonize with each other (Exod. 13:17f., 20 and 14:2, 9; cf. 12:40). It is not at all clear where Pi-Hahiroth is to be found, while the "Red Sea" could refer to the Gulf of Suez, to the Bitter Lakes, to the Red Sea, or to the Gulf of Aqaba. Whether or not one is capable of harmonizing the different data throughout the narrative, it is doubtful that what one finds is the combination of various, similar experiences of several, smaller groups. Although the later Priestly source regarded the exodus from Egypt as a kind of primal datum of the history of Israel (Exod. 12:41; 16:1; 19:1; Num. 1:1; etc.), we must resign ourselves to the fact that several of the most important narrators within the Pentateuch/Hexateuch tell about the exodus and the deliverance at the sea in their own particular ways and according to their differing emphases and interests. And these interests are not in accord with those of precise history. This becomes especially significant, because the exodus and deliverance do not have to do with some event within the history of Israel but rather represent a "primal datum" of this people's experience of God. If one extends this point, this also means that the entire nation of Israel was not in Egypt at that time and thus not all participated in the exodus.[9] Because of the mentioning of an "Israel" in Canaan on the contemporaneous Stele of Merneptah,[10] one may think at most of a relatively small group, perhaps the Rachel tribes, the "house of Joseph," or, for reasons that will be discussed later,[11] the so-called "Moses group."[12] This group experienced their deliverance from an Egyptian military unit (a border guard?) as an act of YHWH. Through this act of deliverance, YHWH became the divine leader of the Moses group who in turn became worshipers of YHWH. The people's responsibility toward this God was confirmed and established at his mountain where he appeared to them in a theophany.[13] This group later brought into Israel their faith in the deity YHWH who then became determinative for the faith of the entire nation throughout its history. This alone is decisive for a "theology of the Old Testament."

There exist side by side different statements about the event in Exodus 13–14. Apparently no redactor felt it necessary to harmonize or correlate them but rather probably considered it a good thing to weave them together. In addition to differing data about places, there are contrasting descriptions of how the deliverance took place (Exod. 14:16, 21a + b, 24–25), of the defeat of the Egyptians (Exod. 14:27 + 28), of the pharaoh's decision (Exod. 14:5 + 8), of the reasons given for the route taken by the people (Exod. 13:17, 18a; 14:1–4), of the Egyptians who followed after the Israelites (Exod. 14:6 + 7), and probably also of the reaction of Israel (Exod. 14:31a + b). The attendant phenomena (cloud, darkness, and angel) are combined in Exod. 14:19f., while the purpose of the exodus varies. According to Exod. 14:5, it is to escape from Egypt, while according to Exod. 12:31–33 (etc.) it is to celebrate a sacrificial festival.[14]

The Yahwist narrates that YHWH, who previously had marched out in front of his people, separated the Egyptians from Israel by appearing in a defensive position behind the Israelites (Exod. 14:19b, 20). Then an east wind, having blown throughout the entire night, dried up the "sea" so that the Israelites could cross over. The Egyptians, having panicked because of "divine terror," raced into the returning waters and died (Exod. 14:24, 25b, 27aβb).

In this manner, YHWH had fought for the people and rescued them, showing himself to be powerful in war, powerful in ruling over nature, and powerful in defeating a foreign nation (Exod. 14:30f.). Israel learned that "the Lord will fight for you, and you are to be still" (Exod. 14:14; cf. 15:21), according to the testimony of J, who described the event that was to follow in the style of YHWH war. Yet one may also see something of the miraculous in J, for an east wind normally pushes the waves against the west coast, not away from it.[15] "Thus YHWH fights for his own" is the motto that the Yahwist uses, not in turning backward to the deliverance at the sea, but rather for speaking emphatically about the present, telling how this YHWH in this way is important at the present time (cf. Num. 24:8). This datum is integrated fully into the *kerygma;* the past is described as decisive for the present.

The basic text of the exilic Priestly document, by contrast, accentuates the supernatural character of the event, presenting it as a miracle *in* the sea and making clear that YHWH liberates in a marvelous way. Also here the referring of what is narrated to the present is more important than presenting a report that looks to the past. What is reported in P is more of an event between YHWH and "Egypt" in which YHWH prevails (Exod. 14:4, 8, 17f.). YHWH's act, in addition, has a pedagogical effect for Israel (Exod. 14:15), and, as already seen in P (cf. Genesis 1), the narrative attests to the power of the divine word (Exod. 14:26). And if the entire description of P comes close to the promises of a new, second exodus from Babylonia in Deutero-Isaiah, that would be no accident (cf. Exod. 14:28ff. with Isa. 43:16ff.). P desires to awaken a confidence in an analogous, marvelous liberation of the community in exile,[16] and, like J, is oriented more to the present than to the past. Therefore the lack of concern with data about places and other details is not surprising. P was in agreement with what was really essential, and that was nothing other than what the oldest text, Exod. 15:21, had extolled: YHWH was a deity who acts with power in history, who is able to liberate and deliver, and who has his own way. The redactor who brought together these narratives by different authors also recognized and testified to this fact. In the redactional process, the description by P was given a certain predominance, even though it was often modified by the incorporation of J.[17] YHWH reveals himself in an epiphany as one who works wonders and carries out his judgment against both his and Israel's enemies. Thus he becomes the legitimate, only God of the people of Israel who are now finally constituted as a nation, and Moses is his true, authorized representative. The constituent features of the event of the exodus, namely, oppression, the appeal to YHWH, and deliverance, become intrinsic features of further historical writing and of the confession of Israel (cf. Deut. 26:5–9). That a people, nevertheless, would describe the earliest stage of its history as one of bondage ("strangers in Egypt"[18]) in order to be able to emphasize the redemptive act and salvific nature of its God, who, for example, liberates "out of the house of slavery (Egypt)"[19] or has delivered them from the burdens of the Egyptians (Exod. 6:6f.), deserves to be closely noted.[20]

It is no wonder that the Old Testament often and readily reaches back to the exodus event, especially in important contexts, and thereby develops the "exodus tradition(s)." Already in the two oldest festival calendars,[21] the first festival is the Passover festival. This festival not only is oriented to an agricultural economy but also is associated with remembering the exodus (Exod. 23:15; 34:18; cf. Deut. 16:1 for the Passover). Ancient texts that mention the exodus include the sayings of Balaam (Num. 23:21b–22; 24:8) and Amos 9:7. As for Hosea, we have already mentioned the references to "YHWH from the land of Egypt" (Hos. 12:10; 13:4). In addition, there are the word of YHWH who has called his son Israel out of Egypt (Hos. 11:1) and the remembrance of Israel's "youth" when it was brought out of Egypt (Hos. 2:17). It is debated whether Judg. 6:13 is an ancient text in Gideon's lament, although it does mention the exodus out of Egypt as a reason for his prayer to be answered. This text also looks back at this earlier act of salvation by YHWH in order to make it possible to hope for a new deliverance. Jeremiah 2:6 also reaches back to the exodus in order to explain Israel's foolish apostasy from God. By his action in Egypt, YHWH made himself known (Ezek. 20:5f.); he will act against Assyria even as he has against Egypt (Isa. 10:26). Because YHWH led his people out of Egypt in order to be their God and to dwell in their midst (Exod. 29:45f. = P), Israel must be holy, for YHWH also is holy (Lev. 11:45). And for the Deuteronomistic redaction of the Book of Jeremiah, the reference to the exodus from Egypt sets forth the hope for a gathering and return home from the exile and the diaspora (Jer. 16:14f.). With this we are close to Deutero-Isaiah, who could speak of a new exodus out of Babylonia, an idea anticipated by Hosea (Hos. 2:16ff.; 9:1–4; 11:1ff.; and 12:10). This new exodus should and would surpass the old exodus from Egypt (Isa. 40:3–5; 41:17–20; 43:16–21; 48:20f.; 49:7a, 9–13; 51:9f.; and 52:7–10, 11f.; cf. 58:8).[22] In Isa. 51:9f. (cf. Pss. 74:13; 77:17–21; 136:11; and Isa. 63:13 תהום = těhôm, "depths") the historical act of deliverance in the crossing through the sea (cf. Zech. 10:11) is compared with the primeval act of YHWH at creation and his victory over Rahab.[23] By contrast Ezekiel connected this new exodus to a judgment of rejection (Ezek. 20:32–44). The reference back to the exodus in the unfolding of elements of salvation history in Micah 6:3ff. allows YHWH himself to speak of his saving deeds. The preamble to the Decalogue, already mentioned, goes about its arguments in a similar fashion, placing YHWH's reference to his saving act in the exodus prior to his commandments. Thus, as the Gospel precedes the Law, so election is prior to obligation in both time and substance. One not only experienced in the exodus out of Egypt and the miracle at the sea who and what YHWH *was,* one also understood who YHWH invariably *is.* The God of election is also the God who saves and liberates. If one interprets the liberating exodus out of Egypt in distinct terms, then one would speak often of "wonders" or "signs and wonders" that Israel may have experienced.[24] At the same time, however, the extensive use of this language makes clear that "wonders" during the time of the exodus were not isolated events limited to that time; rather, in the continuing providential history of Israel additional "wonders" continued to occur. Individuals and the nation both would hope and could hope for "wonders" to occur in the future.[25] The exodus event proves itself also here to be both the outer and inner foundation of Old Testament faith and hope. These divine actions during the exodus are "particularly the special manifestations of God's works, which, as such, have a fundamental significance that point beyond themselves."[26]

Among the Old Testament legal texts the Covenant Code mentions the exodus only in connection with the "stranger,"[27] who should not be oppressed, for Israel itself was a stranger in Egypt (Exod. 22:20; 23:9). In Deuteronomy, the exodus event is positioned prominently in the center of the book's theological arguments. The event is mentioned frequently not only in the paraenetic sections of the book but also in the actual legal corpus (cf. Deut. 13:6, 11; 15:15; 16:1; and 24:18, 22). Election and the gifts of both the commandments and the land are related to the exodus out of Egypt.[28] F. Crüsemann[29] has pointed to what important roles the references to the exodus play in the Holiness Code (Leviticus 17–26). Here the exodus is bound up with the categories of holiness and sanctification (Lev. 11:44f.; 18:3; 19:36; 20:24–26; and 22:32f.). Through means of the exodus, Israel becomes YHWH's ("separated from": Lev. 20:24b) people, and he becomes their God. The exodus is understood as an act of sanctification, a term that is interpreted to mean "set apart." YHWH's deed is both the presupposition and the foundation for everything. There were priestly circles in the time of the exile who reserved for all Israelites this separation or sanctification as both gift and commission and who therefore created an important basis for the Israelite law of the postexilic period.

The so-called catechetical texts of the Old Testament[30] invariably reach back to the exodus out of Egypt in order to make their response to the "children's questions."[31] Even when Jeroboam I set up the golden "calves" and commanded Israel to worship them, he had to designate them as "your gods who have led you out of the land of Egypt" (1 Kings 12:28). The connection with Aaron and the apostasy at the mountain of God is clear (Exod. 32:8). In this combination of golden calves and the exodus, there is in both texts a positive reference to the exodus in spite of the polemical condemnation of idolatry.

In addition, there are numerous psalms, mostly prayers, that make reference to the exodus from Egypt and the salvation at the sea. These two themes are clearly connected in the psalms. The inference that these two "traditions" originally were separate[32] is suspect.[33] The prayers of various kinds, including laments (cf. also Judg. 6:13), hymns, community laments (cf. also Isa. 63:12–14),[34] psalms of history, and thanksgiving psalms, frequently allude and reach back to the exodus from Egypt and the deliverance at the sea in order to awaken new confidence and to remember both YHWH and his earlier acts of salvation. The exodus from Egypt also finds an important place in more didactically shaped or liturgically conceived psalms, like Psalms 114 and 136 (Pss. 114:1f. and 136:10–15).[35]

The narratives of the "passage" through the Jordan River were shaped to parallel Exodus 13–14 (Joshua 3–4; cf. Ps. 114:3). It is not as certain as S. I. L. Norin thinks when he argues that there was an "exodus festival" or "exodus cult" in ancient Israel beyond that of Passover/Unleavened Bread and its connection to the exodus event.[36] There is more evidence for the "exodus tradition(s)" in the writings of the Northern Kingdom than in Judah during the preexilic period. For example, one finds the tradition(s) in Hosea and in Amos who prophesied in the north, although not in Isaiah. However, a glance at the

Yahwist and Jer. 2:4–6 does not support the traditiohistorical differentiations that are often made of this evidence.

The Old Testament speaks about the liberating, saving activity of YHWH in Egypt in different ways. At first the language probably only speaks of the "release" of the nation (שלח = *šālaḥ*, piel; Exod. 4:21, 23; 5:1f.; etc.). Then, however, YHWH becomes the subject of the verb עלה = *'ālâ* in the hiphil, meaning "to bring up" out of Egypt. This usage predominates in older texts,[37] although it is still found in postexilic passages (Neh. 9:18).[38] The term has more to do with occupation in the land, since the semantic opposite often is "to descend" (ירד = *yārad*) down into Egypt. In late texts of the exilic and postexilic periods, for example, the legal corpora in Deuteronomy and the Holiness Code, the language of Yahweh[39] "leading out" (יצא = *yāṣā'*, hiphil) of Egypt is more frequent.[40] Often the semantic opposite of "leading out," the expression "being led into" the land (הביא = *hābî'*) suggests that one has in mind a location that is outside the land of Israel. This is certainly no accident, since this kind of argumentation prevails in exilic texts like, for example, the Deuteronomistic literature and the Priestly source. Moreover, the aspect of liberation also resonates even more strongly with this impressive revelation, since the verb is also used to speak of the manumission of slaves. The distinction between the two principally used verbs "wanes" in the postexilic period.[41] More clear is the retention of the expression "I am YHWH, your God; I am the one who led you up/out of" from the earliest texts of the Old Testament (Exod. 15:21; Num. 24:8) to one of the latest texts (Dan. 9:15). Through God's action of election that saved this one group and bound them together in community, Israel's faith received its foundation. The narratives of the guidance in the wilderness that follow Exodus 13–14 made clear that this action of divine election placed Israel on an extended journey with YHWH. That Israel showed and continued to show itself to be an ungrateful people toward YHWH is demonstrated in the fact that these stories of the guidance in the wilderness are compelled to speak about the "murmuring" of the people several times and not simply as a single narrative digression. It was only at YHWH's initiative and only by his free gift of grace, grounded in love, that he elected Israel to be his people. Deuteronomy 7:7–11 brings this conviction later into a conceptually concentrated, thankful, theological reflection.

3.2   Israel as an Exodus Community

Regardless of how much Israel saw itself as a community of the exodus and to what extent its faith was formed by the activity of YHWH in the liberation from Egypt, it should be stressed that one still can visualize the ways in which the correlations of meaning given to the exodus by the Old Testament texts take place.[42] When the Old Testament speaks of "YHWH, who has led out of (the land of) Egypt," then this language, for which verbs are characteristically decisive, appears often in a formal, compressed style.[43] Further, this language often has closely related terminology that refers to the exodus, although not always with exactly identical wording.[44] In addition to the two verbs יצא = *yāṣā'* ("go out") and עלה = *'ālâ* ("go up"), two others, גאל = *gā'āl* ("redeem") and פדה = *pādâ* ("deliver"), are also readily used in the interpretations of the event of the exodus.[45] Exodus 6:6; 15:13; Pss. 77:16; and 106:10 speak of the "ransom" from Egypt and the "release" from slavery. It is not surprising that Deutero-Isaiah readily uses these terms to talk about the deliverance from Babylon when speaking of the second, new exodus (Isa. 43:1; 44:22f.; 48:20; 51:10; and 52:9). Deutero-Isaiah also often refers to YHWH himself as the גאל = *gō'ēl* ("redeemer": Isa. 41:14; 43:14; 44:6, 24; 47:4; 48:17; 49:7, 26; 54:5, 8; cf. 60:16). While גאל = *gā'āl* ("redeem") refers more to familial law concerning responsibility for family members, פדה = *pādâ* ("deliver"; in Deutero-Isaiah only 50:2; 51:11 is disputed) has more to do with a legal process. Therefore in Deutero-Isaiah there especially occurs a "stated motivation behind the concept": "the גאל = *gō'ēl* acts always out of an intimate relationship with the ones to be redeemed."[46] In Deuteronomic and Deuteronomistic texts, פדה = *pādâ* ("deliver") is the preferred term.[47] YHWH has "redeemed" his people, and, as Deuteronomy frequently adds, "with a strong hand (and an outstretched arm)."[48]

The event of the exodus was grounded then in Israel's relationship with God and in its knowledge of God.[49] The consequential and necessary rejection of foreign gods is based as well on this event.[50] YHWH's activity of salvation in the exodus event is also the foundation of his commandments to his people.[51] In the exodus out of Egypt, which certainly aims at the entrance into the land, YHWH's gift of the land to Israel has its grounding.[52] Standing in contrast to the exodus event as a demonstration of divine grace is the evidence of Israel's sin.[53] This sin provides the motivation for YHWH's threatened punishment,[54] and this could take the form of a "reverse exodus," namely, being taken out of the land of Israel, into the wilderness, and back to Egypt.[55] Israel's way of life, including, for example, its orientation to kingship, to luxury and urban existence, to the cult, and to other nations, is grounded in and illuminated by the exodus event.[56] It was naturally on the basis of the exodus event that history as a whole was viewed and interpreted (Amos 9:7; Deuteronomy; Deutero-Isaiah). Often the reference to the exodus has a key place in the context of the passages that have been mentioned. What was to be legitimated or critically evaluated had to be measured by Israel's early period, that is, by the exodus event, the time of Moses, and the journey through the wilderness. This is true of the Sabbath according to the Decalogue in Deuteronomy (Deut. 5:15), of the bull idols of Jeroboam I (1 Kings 12:28), of the prophetic criticism of the sacrificial cult (Amos 5:25; Jer. 7:22f.; cf. the rationale for the cultic ordinances in Josh. 5:1–8; 1 Kings 8; 9:21), of the Passover, which originally had nothing to do with the exodus (Exodus and parallels),[57] and even of the "bronze serpent" (2 Kings 18:4).[58] The Deuteronomic literature especially judged many things by the standard set by the exodus and the period that immediately followed. This standard provided the basis for judgment or for the threat of judgment (Judg. 2:1–5; and 2 Kings 17:7–23, 34b–40),[59] for the critical evaluation of Israel's behavior, both during the time of the exodus and in the present (1 Sam. 8:7–9; 10:17–19; 12:6–11; and 2 Sam. 7:1–7), and for motivating additional saving activity (Judg. 6:7–10, 11–13; 11:12–28; 1 Sam. 15:1–6; and 1 Kings 8:21). No apparent consideration was given to the historical accuracy or even probability of what happened. Theology was more important than history.

Particularly succinct is the characterization of "Israel as an exodus community" in Psalm 114. Here, the exodus and the institution of Israel as the sanctuary and dominion[60] of YHWH (vv. 1–2) and the "Lord" and the "God of Jacob" (v. 7) are closely connected. Verse 8 builds on Deutero-Isaiah (Isa. 41:18; cf. Ps. 107:35). "With a succinctness that is almost unrivalled, the history of salvation is here gathered up in a singular manner," and this indeed occurs through the dimension of temple theology's "negation of time," that is, the cult. "This was nothing other than the psalm theology of the postexilic period finally being successful in its efforts to transform entirely, according to its own theological standards, the history of salvation."[61]

The exodus event also provided significant meaning for expectations concerning the future. The importance of the exodus for the language of Ezekiel (Ezek. 20:33ff.) and Deutero-Isaiah has already been indicated.[62] The Holiness Code,[63] exilic in its core, also anchors its expectation of salvation (Lev. 26:40ff.) in this event, for it commemorates YHWH's action in the exodus ("before the eyes of the nations") and in the establishment of the covenant. One believes and hopes in the God of the exodus that his grace will endure forever (Ps. 136:10–16). He continued to guide his people (Ps. 136:16; cf. Exod. 15ff.), and even after their apostasy he continued to be present by means of his angel, his tent, and his countenance (Exodus 33).[64] It deserves to be noted that any reference to the exodus, covenant, and guidance in the wilderness is completely missing in the wisdom literature (Proverbs; Job; Qoheleth). The people of God and their history play no role in this literature. The books of Jesus the Son of Sirach and the Wisdom of Solomon are the first wisdom texts to take up these themes of salvation history and election, and this was probably due to the recognition of a deficiency in sapiential thinking.

Finally, the so-called credo (Deut. 26:5–9; 6:20–24; and Josh. 24:2b–13) stresses the reference to the exodus event by building it into the structure of its text. The exodus is given a theologically determinative position that marks the turn to salvation. Although they possibly may have been edited pieces, these texts today are certainly no longer viewed as ancient or as the kernel from which the Hexateuch's narratives were developed, as von Rad above all had argued.[65] Numbers 20:14b–16, perhaps an older creedal text, already gives a central place to the exodus.

The attention given to the salvific acts of YHWH is decisive for these creedal texts, in their present form so clearly influenced by the Deuteronomistic School that certainly uses them as a summation of its own theology. Accordingly, there was a way, acknowledged in thanksgiving and prayer, on which YHWH had guided his people, a path from the threat of wandering to the gift of the land, from an ancestor to a people, and from imprisonment, oppression, and wilderness through the deliverance of the exodus to the gift of the land for the liberated. YHWH demonstrated that he hears their cry and turns to them when they are in need[66] and that in the course of history, seen as purposefully directed, he brings promises to fulfillment by means of designed acts of salvation. Here the theological consideration of the exodus event reaches its high point in the Old Testament (alongside Deutero-Isaiah).

The Books of Chronicles, however, offer a contrast. It is true that, in ways analogous to the Psalms, the prayers so important for the late postexilic Books of Chronicles[67] reach back to the exodus event in three instances (1 Chron. 17:21; 2 Chron. 6:5; and 20:10). Beyond this, however, the exodus tradition is mentioned only in three additional places in Chronicles (1 Chron. 17:5; 2 Chron. 5:10; and 7:22). Moreover, a different terminology is used in these texts, since the distinctiveness of different words and expressions had already begun to blur by the postexilic period. Furthermore, 1 Chron. 17:5, 21 and 2 Chron. 6:5 are restrained in their remarks about the exodus due to the fact that they are made in the larger context of the promise to David. This does not allow the exodus theme to carry its own weight. This lack of emphasis on the exodus is also underscored through the Chronicler's alterations of his Deuteronomistic precursor when embedding the references to the exodus event into new contexts. Beyond that, he has expunged any mention of the exodus tradition that existed in his Deuteronomistic precursor.[68] "If one seeks an explanation for this striking diminution of the exodus tradition in the Books of Chronicles, then probably the clearest information is found in 2 Chronicles 6. The election of Jerusalem as the place of the sanctuary and the election of King David as the founder of an eternal dynasty and the one who initiated the building of the temple are the decisive events of the history of Israel, according to the Chronicler. . . . The exodus event indeed was still mentioned in the sense of a received tradition; however, it is divested of its dynamic character and the experience of liberation it contains. The tradition becomes a relic of the past. Its significance is surpassed by the temple and its (fictional) origins."[69] There are additional "traditions of election" and "statements about election" beyond those of David and Jerusalem that were forged and transmitted in the postexilic period.[70]

3.3   Israel as a People and as a Community of Faith

With the exodus event, the experience of the salvation of a *group* became fundamental to the faith of Israel. It is not the case that an individual and then later other persons came together around this event but rather a people saw itself placed in community with this God through a historical act of divine election.[71] This faith is quite unique, historically speaking, something of which the Old Testament itself appears to be aware: "Or has any god ever sought to come and to take a nation (גוֹי = gôy) from the midst of another nation by trials, signs, wonders and war, with a strong hand and an outstretched arm and by great terrors, as the Lord your God has done for you in Egypt, before your eyes. This was shown to you so that you may acknowledge that Yahweh is God, there is no other besides him" (Deut. 4:34f.).[72] This people named itself "Israel," and it became at the same time both "a people and a community of faith."[73] Since YHWH was the one who entered into community with this people within the context of history,[74] he was also the one who could dissolve this relationship. In its own customary fashion, Deuteronomy reflects this historical understanding of divine initiative in forming the relationship with Israel (cf. Deut. 8:19f. and 9:14), as do other Deuteronomistic texts (2 Kings 17:7–23). The prophets also proclaimed this understanding in their judgment oracles directed against Israel and Judah.[75]

a.   עַם = 'am ("people") and גוֹי = gôy ("people")

According to the narratives of the ancestors (Genesis 12–36), the Joseph Story (Genesis 37; 39–48; 50), and, in addition, the first chapter of the Book of Exodus, the people of Israel developed from families and tribes. According to the will of YHWH and his providential guidance, "Israel" became a people who descended from the family of one individual (Abraham) and the extended family of the tribal ancestor Jacob ("Israel"?).[76] In the view of Deut. 7:7–9, the theological bases for YHWH's relationship with Israel as his people are twofold: first, Israel's election to be his special possession is grounded in his divine love; and second, Israel's election and liberation are due to YHWH's faithfulness to his oath to the ancestors. Israel was chosen to be YHWH's people even though it was a small group that experienced the saving act of liberation and the exodus from Egypt. This theological interpretation continued to exert a formative influence on the faith of Israel.[77]

Hebrew has only two lexemes for "people": גוֹי = gôy and עַם = 'am. A גוֹי = gôy exists when "a human group comes together on the basis of lineage, language, land, worship, law, and military affairs, and is separated from entities standing on the outside."[78] External factors in the formation and continuing characterization of a "people" are the primary consideration in their designation as a גוֹי = gôy. By contrast, the word עַם = 'am presents an understanding of a human group in terms that are more internal than external. This word perhaps originally designated the father's brother and then, later, referred to the male relatives and ancestors within the extended family (Gen. 17:14; 25:8f., 17; 35:29; Exod. 30:33, 38; Lev. 17:4; 21:1, 4; 2 Kings 4:13; Ezek. 18:18; etc.). The term then came to refer to a league of men. This included all males who were able to bear arms, the full citizens of the legal and cultic community (2 Kings 11:14f.; etc.), and, although not extensively, the army who were selected from the "people" (cf. Judg. 5:13; perhaps also Judg. 11:23; 20:2; 2 Sam. 1:12; later then Exod. 7:4 P; Num. 20:20; and 21:33). Like קהל = qāhāl, עם = 'am later was expanded to include women and children (Deut. 29:9ff.; 31:10ff.; Ezra 10:1; Neh. 8:2; and 2 Chron. 20:13). The occurrences of עם = 'am with personal names correlate well with these findings.[79]

The combination of עם יהוה = 'am yahweh[80] as the "people of YHWH" refers to both the congregation and the cultic assembly (Num. 11:29 and Judg. 20:2) and occurs in association with the "army of YHWH" and "flock of YHWH" (2 Sam. 5:2; 7:7f.; etc.).[81] The combination עם יהוה = 'am yahweh and its reformulation into "my/your people" appear typically in the contexts of deliverance and intercession (cf. Judg. 5:11, 13; then in J: Exod. 3:7, 10; 5:1, 23; 7:16, 26; 8:16ff.; 9:1ff.; and 10:3f.; in addition, see 1 Sam. 9:16; etc.[82]). The frequent occurrences of these formulae in the Deuteronomistic programmatic text of the prayer of the dedication of the temple (1 Kings 8:23ff.) are therefore not surprising.[83] Their absence in the wisdom literature is rather typical, since the interests of this collection of texts are placed elsewhere. By contrast, the formulae are rather frequent within the prophetic corpus (152 occurrences, including Daniel). In these texts, they occur in the genre of the divine speech ("my people"), including those occasions when the relationship between the people and God is expressly challenged (Hos. 1:9; cf. 2:25).[84]

Within the legal texts, the occurrence of the expression of Israel as the "people" ('am) of God in the Covenant Code is rather isolated (Exod. 22:24), while in Deuteronomy it is found only in 14:2, 21 and in the text of prayers (21:8 and 26:15).[85] It is altogether absent in the Holiness Code (Leviticus 17–26). The expression is not typical in legal language; rather, it occurs only in paraenesis and prayers. The expression עם יהוה = 'am yahweh ("people of YHWH") interestingly often occurs alongside the closely related expression נחלת יהוה = naḥălat yahweh, "inheritance of YHWH" (cf. the combination of 1 Sam. 10:1 and 13:14).[86] The "people of YHWH" is his "clan," "kinfolk," and "family" in whose midst he lives (Lev. 26:12),[87] due to his action in history and not through natural means.

At the same time, the so-called covenant formula[88] sets forth the confession that YHWH is Israel's God, even as Israel is his people. N. Lohfink has correctly noted that there is a large group of texts that intentionally use the covenant formula in the context of the exile and the return home: "In the return home from the exile the reality of the עם יהוה = 'am yahweh is set forth anew."[89] The previously mentioned prayer of the dedication of the temple by Solomon, deriving from the Deuteronomistic School, also might be assigned to this group of texts (1 Kings 8:23ff.).

One might conclude, in view of the above discussion, that the term עַם = 'am is reserved exclusively for Israel, while גּוֹי = gôy or its plural, גּוֹיִם = gôyîm, refers to the other nations. However, this is not the case.[90] While considerably less frequently than עַם = 'am, גּוֹי = gôy may also refer to Israel. Examples include the combination גּוֹי קָדוֹשׁ = gôy qādôš ("holy people") in Exod. 19:6[91], the role of גּוֹי = gôy in promises (e.g., Gen. 12:2; 18:18; etc.), and the occurrence of both עַם = 'am and גּוֹי = gôy as designations for Israel in Deut. 4:6.[92] Conversely, עַם = 'am may refer to foreign nations (e.g., Egypt in Isa. 30:5 and Cush in Isa. 18:2). Nevertheless, as one follows the development of the term (cf. Exod. 33:13b), עַם = 'am primarily continues as a designation for Israel and increasingly connotes the "people of God." By contrast, גּוֹי = gôy, especially in its much more frequent plural form גּוֹיִם = gôyim, primarily refers to the foreign nations. It is not surprising, then, that עַם = 'am very frequently has a suffix, while גּוֹי (gôy; pl. גּוֹיִם, gôyîm) very rarely has one.

If Israel is more precisely characterized as the "people of YHWH," then it is spoken of as a "holy nation," that is, set apart by YHWH through a historical act of election to belong to him (Exod. 19:6; Deut. 7:6; 14:2, 21; 26:19; and 28:9). Deuteronomy also speaks of Israel as a "people of (YHWH's) own possession" (עַם סְגֻלָּה = 'am sĕgullâ; Deut. 7:6; 14:2; 26:18; cf. Exod. 19:5; Mal. 3:17; and Ps. 135:4).[93] Other texts personify a juridical concept of the land in speaking of Israel as YHWH's נַחֲלָה (nahălâ, "possession") in order to express the idea that Israel belongs to YHWH through no merit of its own. However, YHWH still has title to his people.[94] It is not surprising that עַם = 'am ("people") often appears in this connection beside נַחֲלָה = nahălâ ("possession") and points to the exodus out of Egypt as the foundation of the relationship between YHWH and the people designated as his (Deut. 4:20; 9:26, 29; 1 Kings 8:51; cf. Ps. 33:12; and 1 Kings 8:53). "If the knowledge of a relational attachment was at stake, (it was still decisive for Israel that) the oneness of the people in the final analysis was grounded in God's actions of union and reconciliation."[95] In the statements to the nation, the Holiness Code stressed that the Israelites became and then were holy,[96] because YHWH sanctified and set them apart through his liberating action in the exodus (Lev. 11:45; 20:24–26; and 22:32f.).[97]

b. "Israel"

This "people of YHWH" are named *Israel*.[98] The word occurs in the Old Testament 2,514 times, although, with the exception of its association with Jacob, it is not encountered as an authentic personal name. What is surprising is the theophoric element "El" (אֵל = *'ēl,* "god") in the name Israel. One would expect instead the divine name YHWH or its short form YH(W). However, this is possibly explained by the suggestion that there already had settled in Palestine a group named Israel who worshiped the god El.[99] When the Yahweh worshipers came out of Egypt and also settled down, they gradually united with "Israel." In the formation of this community of tribes, this new group of arrivals introduced their evidently compelling deity to the ones who were already dwelling in the land, and together they called themselves "Israel." The ancient kernel of Joshua 24[100] reflects a process of the uniting of different groups under the common acceptance of the worship of the God YHWH. This could have reflected the concluding of a covenant in Shechem. Genesis 33:20 speaks significantly enough of an "El" who was worshiped as the "God of Israel." Judges 9:46 mentions, in addition, an "El-Berit" of Shechem, while Judg. 8:33 and 9:4 refer to a Baal-Berit. "YHWH, the God of Israel," replaced "El, the God of Israel," and the host of worshipers dramatically expanded (the successors of?) the original exodus and Moses group to include inhabitants of the land of Canaan.

The meaning of the name "Israel," which also occurs outside Israel,[101] is unfortunately not completely clear.[102] Grammatically speaking, this name is both a clause and an expression of thanksgiving in which "El" is the subject combined with the verbal predicate, that is, "is X." The most common translations of Israel are "El/God is reliable/upright, trustworthy" (if the verb is יָשַׁר = *yāšar*); "El/God rules" (if the verb is שָׂרַר = *śārar*); or "El/God struggles/fights" (if the verb is שָׂרָה = *śārâ;* cf. Gen. 32:29; Hos. 12:4). The name originally designated a union of tribes or clans,[103] for whom YHWH fights (Josh. 10:14, 42; and Judges 5), and "in the entire period prior to the establishment of the state, that is, from Exodus through Judges, referred in strongly theological terms to the union of all the people."[104] With the emergence of the monarchy, the name became a legal, political term for the kingdom (cf., e.g., 1 Sam. 9:16; and 24:15 in regard to Saul and David), in addition to continuing as a "name that bore a religious dignity."[105] Then, after the so-called division of the kingdom following the death of Solomon (926 B.C.E.), the term, above all in the language of the Books of Kings beginning with 1 Kings 11,[106] became the name of the Northern Kingdom. This could have occurred under the influence or revival of a use of the name that had been imposed at an earlier time (2 Sam. 2:9f.; and 3:17; also 1 Sam. 17:52; and 18:16). After the end of the Northern Kingdom, the term is transferred to the Southern Kingdom of Judah. Isaiah may have even used the term to refer to Judah from 734 B.C.E. on.[107] From the time of the exile, the term especially came to designate the people who survived the exile and formed the nucleus of a new beginning. The title "all Israel" was stressed by both the Deuteronomistic History[108] and Chronicles[109] in speaking of the exiles (e.g., Deut. 1:1; 11:6; Josh. 23:2; 1 Sam. 12:1; 1 Chron. 9:1; and 2 Chron. 18:16). Those of the exilic community who returned home were viewed as the core of this new "Israel," and "Israel" became exclusively now the spiritual, religious name of the people of God (cf., e.g., Isa. 43:1, 15; 44:1, 5, 23; Mal. 1:1, 5; Ezra 2:70; 6:17; 1 Chron. 28:8; etc.). This term had always possessed a theological component,[110] so that Israel was never designated only as a people who possessed a common language, history, and land. Rather, in addition to these features, the concept of Israel was also stamped by the character of Yahwistic faith. One said "one does not do this in Israel" (2 Sam. 13:12; etc.) or "this is a scandal in/to Israel" (Gen. 34:7f.);[111] however, one did not say "a scandal in Judah, Ephraim," or the like. Also, YHWH was the "God of Israel," and never the "God of Judah" and so forth. Thus, Israel was "a community characterized by common customs, views of law, and solidarity through mutual participation."[112] In addition, these customs and understandings of law were determined by faith in YHWH, the deity who was common to this association of tribes.[113] This Israel always stood between nation and community, for while Israel possessed "certain characteristics of both entities, neither was entirely identical with it."[114] The factors that influenced the nation were the Yahwistic faith with its defining features (YHWH as the liberating God of history and of law), the solidarity that undergirded the relationship of the groups,[115] and the common connection to the land that people learned to see as the gift of their God to his people. These factors were brought into relationship and closely linked to one another.

c. קהל = qāhāl ("assembly") and עדה = 'ēdâ ("congregation")

In certain groups of texts, Israel is designated as a קהל = qāhāl ("assembly") and/or an עדה = 'ēdâ ("congregation").[116] Israel is called YHWH's קהל = qāhāl ("assembly") primarily in Deuteronomy (Deut. 5:22; 9:10; 10:4; 23:2–9 [cf. Lam. 1:10]; 31:30; cf. 4:10; 18:16). The term קהל = qāhāl generally means "assembly" or "congregation" (including an assembly for war: Gen. 49:6; the verb occurs in 1 Kings 12:21a). However, in certain Old Testament contexts that have theological relevance, the term primarily designated the "community" of YHWH into which one could or could not "enter."[117] This is true particularly when קהל = qāhāl is in the construct relationship with the word Israel. This was the community that was constituted by means of Sinai, law, and cult on the "day of the assembly" and was therefore designated as the community of YHWH. In addition to Deuteronomy and the Deuteronomistic History, there are texts especially in the various strata of the so-called Priestly source (Exod. 12:6; Lev. 4:13; etc.), the history of the Chronicler (e.g., 1 Chron. 28:8; 29:1, 10, 20; 2 Chron. 30 [9 times]; etc.),[118] and Ezra and Nehemiah (e.g., Neh. 8:2, 17) that speak of Israel as קהל = qāhāl ("assembly"). So do some of the psalms (Pss. 22:23, 26; 35:18; 40:10f.; 89:6; 107:32; and 149:1) and Joel 2:16. Earlier cases probably occur only in Gen. 49:6; Num. 22:4; Prov. 21:16; and 26:26.

Women and children could belong to this קהל = *qāhāl* ("assembly"). In the wisdom literature the term is found only in Prov. 21:16 and 26:26 with the commonly occurring meaning of "assembly," while קהל = *qāhāl* ("assembly") and עדה = *'ēdâ* ("congregation") stand beside each other in Prov. 5:14 with the meaning of either a political, legal assembly (cf. Job 30:28) or a cultic gathering. The mentioning of these terms in the wisdom literature carries no cultic, theological, or ecclesiological weight.

"In the Priestly materials, עדה = *'ēdâ* denotes for Pg an attribute that describes the character of the sons of Israel, while קהל = *qāhāl* continues to keep its technical meaning of a present assembly. . . . Ps, by contrast, does not make as clear a separation."[119] Thus, for example, the first occurrence of עדה = *'ēdâ* ("congregation") in the Priestly source is found (not surprisingly in this context) in Exod. 12:3, 6 (Pg), to refer to the assembly coming together to make preparations for the Passover. In Lev. 4:13 (Ps), both terms are used in parallel fashion to refer to the "institutional cultic gathering"[120] (cf. also Ps. 1:5; Lev. 8:3–5; and Num. 8:9–20). In Deuteronomy, עדה = *'ēdâ* ("congregation") is entirely absent. Numbers 1:2f. (cf. vv. 44–47 = P) shows what an עדה = *'ēdâ* ("congregation") looks like. Only men belong to it, and it is arranged according to tribes and clans. The עדה = *'ēdâ* ("congregation") is settled and organized in the camp around the אהל מעד (*'ōhel mō'ēd*, "tent of meeting"; [121] see Num. 2:1–34; 9:15–23; 10:11–28; and 20:1, 22).[122] There in the midst of the community YHWH reveals himself and makes known his will. The עדה = *'ēdâ* ("congregation") is also responsible for maintaining its own purity and has therefore juridical functions, as, for example, those in Lev. 24:10–16 (the execution of one who blasphemes God) and Num. 15:32–36 (the stoning of one who profanes the Sabbath) demonstrate. The עדה = *'ēdâ* ("congregation") is "holy" due to YHWH (Lev. 19:2; Num. 16:3) and must continue to remain so. The terms קהל = *qāhāl* and עדה = *'ēdâ* point thus to the interaction and association of people and community in the Old Testament's understanding of Israel.

d. Differentiations within Israel

The fact that ancient Israel was both the people and the community of YHWH poses the question about the relationship of these two conceptions. Were people and community always identical? Were all of the people at the moment in question always congruent with the "community of YHWH"?

With the exception of the special materials of Deuteronomy, a differentiation between the people and the community of YHWH is not carried out in Exodus through Judges. However, in Deuteronomy one finds Israel as the entire people who should be or should again become the legitimate people of God. Only the late-exilic Deuteronomic texts of Deut. 4:27 and 28:62 probably see the community of the exile as a delivered remnant, who, at the same time however, should and will again become the nucleus of the new people of God. In the Book of Exodus, it is the Moses group that is called the "people of YHWH" and finally stands for the later nation as a whole (Exod. 3:7, 10; 5:1–23; 7:16; 8:16ff.; 9:1, 13; and 10:3). According to the ancient song of Deborah, the groups of tribes gathered for war are the "people = army of YHWH" (Judg. 5:11; cf. 2 Sam. 1:12). However, in the time of the Judges as well as in the texts that tell of this period, we can see that there is no differentiation between people and community.[123] This is also true for the period of the Yahwist and throughout the time of the Davidic and Solomonic empire. According to the Yahwist, Israel saw itself existing in a "covenant" with YHWH that promised divine support (Exod. 34:10).[124] How much of the ancient core of Joshua 24 with its exhortation to fear God and be faithful to YHWH (vv. 14f.) can be attributed to the Elohist is open to debate. In Num. 23:9 the Elohist offers a glimpse of his witness to Israel's own understanding of piety and faithfulness to God. However, Joshua 24 clearly demonstrates that human beings are called to make a decision for YHWH, the God of Israel, a decision in which the "house" of Joshua joins. It is often the case that the "7,000 who have not bowed their knee to Baal" (1 Kings 19:18) are regarded as a circumscribed group within Israel. What is not so very clear[125] is how the conception of a remnant moved from serving as a general reference to a differentiation within Israel to a conspicuous community of people who are faithful to YHWH or who have been preserved by him.[126] Among preexilic texts, one probably may point only to Amos 5:15 as evidence of the latter. Here the prophet offers to his audience the hopeful "possibility" of divine grace that may preserve a "remnant of Joseph" (cf. Amos 3:12). However, it was especially the Old Testament prophetic message of judgment that inserted this idea of a distinctive remnant into the Israel they addressed, even though, as the prophetic books themselves demonstrate, there were very few people at the time who believed the prophetic message that was proclaimed directly to them (Isa. 7:9; Jer. 5:3). To address this problem of unbelief, Isaiah gathered around himself faithful students from among the people in Judah (Isa. 8:16, 18), and it is certainly the case that other prophets had similar groups of students who transmitted the message of their "master" (cf. the books of Hosea, Jeremiah, Ezekiel, Deutero-Isaiah, etc.).

Hosea hoped for a revival of all Israel (Hos. 2:19–25). This was also the case for the corresponding promises made by Ezekiel (Ezek. 34; 36:16ff.; 37:15ff.; cf. also Jer. 31:31–34 edited by Deuteronomists), although some are in particular addressed to the exilic community (Ezek. 37:1–14). The same is true also for Deutero-Isaiah (Isa. 46:3 and 48:1 address those who are from Judah). The "lowly" in Zeph. 2:3 as well as the "poor" and the "silent ones in the land" in the Psalms[127] are mentioned in exilic texts as those who wait expectantly for divine aid. After the exile had led to the destruction of the nation, Israel was reconstituted as a "community." For Haggai, the true people of God consisted of the exiles (Hag. 1:12; 2:2; Jer. 24 = the "good figs"), while the "night visions" in Zechariah 1–8 provide the future form of the new community.[128] Ezra and in its own way also Nehemiah, as well as the postexilic reworking of the Priestly source, seek to create and to shape the new people of God.[129] For these texts, those who return from exile are in particular the forces who give rise to this new community. The Jew becomes the one who keeps the law, and Malachi recognizes among his contemporaries those who are distinguished from the masses of the nation because they "feared YHWH and remembered his name" (Mal. 3:16–20). However, the idea of a community remains a foreign concept to Old Testament wisdom literature.

These differentiations along with the openness to what is new and what is yet to come were possible because the nation elected and placed under responsibility by YHWH did not have a numerically definitive size.[130] Furthermore, "Israel" could be circumscribed *within* the boundaries of the larger nation. Because of this development and the contrasting representations of nation and community that are prompted by a variety of different occasions and reasons, ancient Israel could indeed continue to exist as a community even when as a nation and as a state it had been destroyed. And this understanding of Israel as a community of faith allowed certain schools of thought to be open to the notion of salvation for the nations.[131] God and people as community belong together in the Old Testament as much as Christ and the church do in the New Testament, and the constitutive image of marriage in Ephesians 5 that portrays the relationship between Christ and the church is not simply by accident taken from the Old Testament (see Hosea and Jeremiah).

e. "Amphictyony"?

In looking at the early history of Israel, one sees some important, although, to this point, not fully answered questions. Whether Israel prior to its entrance into Canaan points to a union of the tribes or even some of them is not entirely evident. What was it that brought these tribes of Israel together, unified them, and continued to hold them together? Not too long ago, scholars tended to follow Martin Noth, who had predecessors on this subject, in his presentation of an *amphictyony*.[132] According to this theory, the twelve tribes comprised a sacred tribal band that had a central sanctuary for the worship of a common deity, YHWH. The cult that centered around this God was the unifying force for originating and sustaining this band. That there is no Hebrew word for "amphictyony"[133] says nothing about whether such an entity may have existed. In addition, bringing into consideration parallel phenomena from Asia Minor, Greece, and Italy[134] as Noth does, does not bring into question his hypothesis.[135] However, the existence of a central sanctuary for Israel prior to state formation cannot be clearly demonstrated. In addition to Shechem, the locations of Bethel, Gilgal, and Shiloh have been considered. And while their coexistence causes a problem, their chronological succession as the central sanctuary is not demonstrable. As to the issue of the ark's location in these sanctuaries,[136] there is no evidence for its presence in Bethel[137] and Shechem. It also cannot be demonstrated that the ark's primary role was its association with "central" cultic sites. In Shiloh, the ark became "a symbol of a short-lived military association of tribes that was formed to respond to the trouble caused by the Philistines."[138] While Samuel offered sacrifices and acted as a "judge" in several sanctuaries (1 Sam. 7:6ff., 16; 9:12; 10:8; and 11:15), the thesis of a uniform cult that served as a unifying bond for tribes in the preceding period of the judges is not free of difficulties. While there was a common sanctuary on Mt. Tabor (Deut. 33:18f.)[139] for the tribes of Zebulon and Issachar, what was much more important in binding the tribes together was the shared experience of military threat. YHWH was understood as leading the tribes into battle against the conquest of their land by enemies from within (Judges 5; Joshua 10/11) and to secure their borders against enemies from without (Judg. 3:27; 6:34f.; 7:23; 8:1–3; 11:29; and 12:1–7). It was in tribal war that YHWH was experienced; it was here that one confronted his saving, military power.[140] Here one experienced the military might of this God and the characteristic power that was at his disposal. In its present form, Judges 19–21 is the only text that mentions an undertaking of all Israel. This takes the form of a punitive expedition of "Israel" against Benjamin. However, as is often true elsewhere in Joshua and Judges, it is likely that the text originally dealt with a dispute between Ephraim and Benjamin[141] that was later on rescripted to be an undertaking of "all Israel" (Judg. 20:3). Thus the system of the twelve tribes with its lists of tribes is not an arrangement for the ongoing maintenance of the central sanctuary with each tribe having the responsibility for one month during the course of a year.[142] Rather, as is the case elsewhere in the Old Testament, in particular the popular genealogies, the interest is both to point out and then to substantiate the kinship relationships in which the unity of the tribes found its grounding. For the Old Testament, the number twelve was "the rounded number of an aggregate"[143] and marked the completeness of an entire people.[144] Since Judah according to Deut. 33:7 did not appear to belong to this community, one shall have to conclude that the system of the twelve tribes as a whole did not originate in the period prior to the formation of the state.

On the other hand, however, the summary grouping together of the (six)[145] Leah tribes appears to reflect a previously existing entity that resided in the land of Canaan prior to the formation of the twelve tribes of Israel. Indeed, the Leah tribes may even have been the original bearers of the name "Israel"[146] even though they must not as yet have worshiped YHWH.[147] The Old Testament frequently attributes the "conquest" of Canaan to various tribes and groups,[148] indicating that the taking of the land took place in several phases after a different type of settlement had already occurred.[149] This evidence indicates that the people of Israel as a whole came together only in the land of Canaan and not before.

The existence of a central sanctuary cannot be demonstrated with complete certainty. This does not exclude, however, the existence of contemporary sanctuaries where people would have worshiped YHWH. If YHWH was experienced as a saving deity who was powerful in war, perhaps by either the Moses group or the Rachel tribes who joined together in their worship of this deity, it would be most improbable that this experience was not made concrete in the form of the cultic worship of this God. Further, it is very probable that Israel, uniting together under YHWH, regarded certain principles of law as binding and must have sought to maintain and defend them. These principles would have come into existence bearing their own distinctive, sociocultural character and perhaps would have already been shaped to a degree by Yahwistic faith. This association of Yahwistic faith, law, and the peculiar sociocultural structure of the groups finding themselves coming together as "Israel" appears to have existed, even if one fully breaks from the hypothesis of an amphictyony and wishes rather to see Israel in the period prior to state formation as a "segmentary society that had no head." This is a recent view that appears on occasion.[150] According to this view, the intention of forming a society, faith in YHWH, the egalitarianism of the tribes of early Israel, the worship of YHWH, and law[151] would be closely bound together and related to each other. Even here, Israel was already a societal entity coming into existence within the framework of history. But it was also a community of faith whose testimony to the liberation from Egypt shaped the character of the association of tribes. Furthermore, this community's resolute ideal of freedom and expressed consciousness of faith clearly separated it from the faith and social structure of the Canaanite city-states.

f. Toward the Self-Understanding of Israel

In an important study, H.-J. Zobel[152] has pointed to several texts that reflect Israel's self-understanding as a people as well as a community constituted and closely bound together by its faith. A discussion of these texts will bring this third section to a close.

According to the first speech of Balaam (probably transmitted by E), Israel is "a people dwelling alone" (Num. 23:9). This expression certainly refers not only to Israel's geographical and spatial situation but also at the same time to the inward, even religious dimensions of its life. This means that Israel does not count itself "among the nations" (Num. 23:9b). The context demonstrates why it is that Israel dwells alone and does not count itself among the nations:

since it is not cursed by its God, it cannot be cursed by Balaam. One may and indeed should extend this to mean that God defends, destines, and blesses Israel.

The second Balaam speech (Num. 23:21–24), also transmitted by E, carries this understanding forward. YHWH is "with" this people of his,[153] and he is "acclaimed as king" among them. This "acclamation of a king" most likely points to YHWH as the king of his people[154] who also here is confessed and praised in hymnic song. He is the one who led his people out of Egypt (Num. 23:22)[155] and did great things on their behalf. Magic and conjuration are not found in Israel as a consequence of its experience of YHWH and its faith in him (Num. 23:23; cf. the demarcation from "Canaan" in Gen. 9:26f. = J). The blessing God is also the saving God,[156] and the people of this God have military power (Num. 23:24; cf. Num. 24:5–9 = J). What is special for "Shem," who in Gen. 9:26f. (J) clearly stands for Israel, is his God whose blessing is active in history and in the gift of the land that is described in such an effusive way (Gen. 12:3 and Num. 24:9). "Israel's journey through time is determined both by the presence of Yahweh, its royal lord, and by the response of its profession of faith."[157] Since YHWH who saved and delivered Israel was incomparable, there was no other nation who was comparable to Israel (Deut. 33:29). "Each generation . . . was faced with the . . . task of understanding itself [anew] as Israel."[158]

3.4   Community and Individual

The exodus from Egypt, election, covenant, and the gift of the land are directed toward Israel as a people. YHWH is the God of Israel. Even where and when YHWH elects an individual,[159] this action serves the people as a whole. The individual Israelite saw him or herself as a member of this whole. Thus the question arises as to how the *community* and the *individual* are related to each other?[160]

One must say at the very outset that there was a very close relationship between the individual and the community. "Jacob" could designate both the tribal ancestor and the people of Israel. The Servant of the Lord[161] is both Israel as a people and an individual, either the prophet himself or an exalted godly person. In Deuteronomy, Israel can be addressed both by "you" (singular) and "you" (plural), and the separate uses of the two forms cannot always consistently be attributed to different literary sources. The so-called "little historical, cultic credo" in Deut. 26:5–9 demonstrates in exemplary fashion how the singular "I" and the plural forms of "we" and "us" are interchangeable. Furthermore, in the use of "today" in Deuteronomy, the generations are bound together through the simultaneity of their experience of salvation in history and through their empowerment by analogous experiences with their God YHWH

(Deut. 5:2f.; 29:9–14). The ancestors of the tribes in the tribal epigrams (Genesis 49; Deuteronomy 33) stand for the tribes as a whole. Likewise Esau stands also for Edom (Genesis 27), Cain also for the Kenites (Genesis 4), and Ishmael also for the Ishmaelites (Genesis 16 + 21).[162] The ancestors as individual persons are understood also as representing their extended families or clans. The sisters Oholah and Oholibah stand for Israel/Samaria and Judah/ Jerusalem respectively (Ezekiel 23), while Israel is represented as a woman in Hosea (Hosea 1 and 3) and in Ezekiel (Ezekiel 16). Jerusalem laments over its fate in a manner analogous to that of an individual worshiper (Lamentations 1 and 3). With "you [singular] shall," the commandments of the Decalogue as indicated by their setting in Exodus 20 and Deuteronomy 5 address the responsibility of both the individual citizen who is capable of following the law and the people as a whole. And if we in the modern period raise the question about the identity of the "I of the Psalms" as an "individual or a community," this would have been far less an alternative in Israel at that time. Individual psalms of lament often give voice to the words of the community. The individual Israelite knew himself as a member of the whole, while the nation saw itself as a single person, as a "larger I." The individual worshiper needed the community and lived in and because of it. Loneliness, by contrast, is regarded in very negative terms (Ps. 25:16f.; 1 Sam. 21:2),[163] and two people have it better in a variety of settings than a single person (Eccl. 4:9ff.). It is not good for a person to be alone (Gen. 2:18), and man and woman together are actually "humanity" (Gen. 1:27). The word אדם = *'ādām* means, therefore, an "individual person," simply a "human being," and "humanity" as a whole. If the effort is made to be more precise, then an individual person is referred to as בן־אדם = *ben-'ādām* ("human being"; cf. Ps. 8:5). Ethics were also determined by reference to the community. One says, "This is not done in Israel" or "This is an abomination in/to Israel."[164] As the Covenant Code makes clear, the individual Israelite, the group, and the people as a whole were responsible for observing the stipulations of the law. The same may be recognized throughout Deuteronomy. Hospitality on the one side and blood vengeance on the other are likewise expressions of this spirit of community which is encountered elsewhere in the ancient Near East as well as in other places. However, the relationship between God and people was especially stressed in Israel. The role played by the community had greater significance in Israel than, for example, in ancient Egypt. In Israel the individual and the community were not only biologically, sociologically, and historically bound together, but also were theologically related to each other. This occurred through God's historical election and providential guidance of the people and the individual who lived in their midst. YHWH was the shepherd of both his people and the individual godfearer (Gen. 48:15; 49:24; Pss. 23:1; 80:2; Isa. 40:11; Jer. 31:10; and Ezek. 34:12). And in their prayers to God, both the individual and Israel as a whole could say, "my God."[165] By contrast, Israel, in a manner rather different from the other nations in its social milieu, could confess its sins in the form of "we" and not only "I."[166] One ought not to speak here of a "collectivism" that stands in opposition to an individualism which would be in some fashion an advance over the former. This kind of idealistic thinking is foreign to the Old Testament.[167] The expressions "solidarity" (J. Scharbert) and "conception of the whole"[168] capture better the Old Testament point of view.[169] At the same time, the Old Testament understanding of community cannot be understood as an adding together of individuals. "Much more, community in its various forms (family, tribe, nation) is the natural sphere of life for each of its members."[170]

Joshua 7:16–18 allows one in good fashion to recognize the way in which an individual Israelite was incorporated into the nation and how this nation was organized. When the lots were cast to identify who had stolen what had been banned, "Israel" was first separated into tribes (שֵׁבֶט = šēbeṭ or מַטֶּה = maṭṭeh), then into clans (מִשְׁפָּחָה = mišpāḥâ), then into families (בַּיִת = bayit or בֵּית אָב = bêt 'āb), and then finally into individuals (cf. 1 Sam. 10:20f.). Wrongs that are committed continued to affect "the third and fourth generations" of descendants (cf. also the narrative about David in 2 Sam. 12:10–12),[171] while the activity of the good affected many thousands (Exod. 20:5f.; Deut. 5:9f.; Exod. 34:7). "Father" (אָב = 'āb) designated not only one's immediate parent but also the grandfather and even ancestors farther back (Gen. 28:13; 1 Kings 15:11; etc.). The "fathers" are mainly the previous generations (Exod. 3:15; 20:5; Isa. 51:2; Ps. 22:5; etc.). The significance of lineage and genealogies thus is explained largely from this understanding of community.[172] Even when one dies, one is gathered to the fathers (Gen. 47:30; Deut. 31:16; Judg. 2:10; 2 Kings 22:20; etc.).[173]

The ancestors tell of what YHWH has done for them (Ps. 44:2), enabling supplicants to offer their prayers with comfort and confidence (Pss. 22:5; 78:3f.). However, there can also be warnings of the sins of the ancestors in whose community and evil tradition the "we" who speak now stand (Ps. 106:6f.; cf. Jer. 3:25; 14:20; Neh. 9:32ff.; and Dan. 9:7ff.). Offenses of the children can also affect the ancestor (1 Sam. 2:12ff.: the sons of Eli).

According to the Deuteronomistic History, the actions of the unjust continue to affect the later generations. This is true of the blessings of the ancestors as well as their curses. This is true also of the misconduct of the king, who often in this tradition is represented as the "father" (1 Kings 15:3; 2 Kings 21:19ff.; etc.). The king's misdeeds negatively affect not only himself but also his people, as the case of David in 2 Samuel 24[174] and that of the "sins of Jeroboam" (1 Kings 12:26ff.) clearly show.

Israel's future hope is directed toward the new creation of the nation as a whole (Ezek. 36:16ff.; 37:1ff.; and Jer. 31:31–34), and the nation received more promises in the history of its faith than did individuals.[175] It is only in very late Old Testament texts that one encounters the hope of "resurrection" for individuals or for certain specified groups (Isa. 26:19; Dan. 12:3).[176] The problem of the suffering of the individual is also first reflected in later texts, as, for example, in the Book of Job.

As urban culture grew stronger and social differentiations developed during the period of the monarchy, Israel's thinking about community was negatively impacted. Moreover, the preaching of the prophets, which not only addressed the nation as a whole but also directly concerned individuals, made distinctions as well. While Deut. 24:16 rejects individuals being held liable for the sins of their relatives, it also shows that this was standard practice, as clear evidence from elsewhere in the Old Testament demonstrates.[177] The fortune as well as the decision-making capacity of the individual became increasingly important. Amaziah put to death the murderers of his father but not their sons (2 Kings 14:5f.). The breakup of clans and families occasioned by the exile and the subsequent questions about guilt and responsibility led to a growing individualization, or, better put, personalization, of relationships with God. Jeremiah's emphasis on the individual belongs more to this setting than to explanations directed toward his personality structure. The nation had in view the breakup of its community, yet there was hope for individuals. Consequently, the teaching that the guilt of the fathers necessarily had its affect on the children became problematic. If the fathers have eaten sour grapes, why then must the teeth of their children become dull (Jer. 31:29 and Ezek. 18:2)? In his response to this accusatory (cf. Lam. 5:7) question, Ezekiel individualizes his answer in the name of YHWH (Ezek. 18:3): YHWH inquires about the individual's disposition and ability to change (Ezek. 18:5ff.; cf. also Ezek. 14:12–20 and the different emphasis in Gen. 18:20ff.). However, how much these two opposing views of collectivism and individualism were in tension may be seen in the paradoxical formulation in Jer. 32:18f. Here YHWH causes the guilt of the fathers to come upon the heads of the children, yet he also gives to each according to his ways and the fruit of his deeds.[178] Of course, conceptions about the people of God were not without significance for Ezekiel (Ezekiel 34–37). This is also true for postexilic texts, as for instance Trito-Isaiah, Zechariah, and Daniel demonstrate. These texts were not limited to speaking only about the pious individual but also asked about the future of the people of God and hoped for their eventual reconstitution. There is also a tendency, for example, in the so-called messianic texts, the royal psalms, the confessions of Jeremiah, and the so-called Songs of the Servant of the Lord to move back and forth between the individual and the collective group.[179] However, as was true of the New Testament, the Old Testament knew of no private relationship of individuals with God that was "unconnected with the community either in its roots, its realization or its goal."[180] It is in Isa. 1:5f., and not later in Ephesians 5 or 1 Corinthians 12, that one encounters for the first time the image of the people of God as a "body" with members. The problem of the detachment of personal belief from the community of faith is clearly evident in Job and Qoheleth. These books demonstrate that the separation of individual piety from the people of God and their traditions ultimately leads to a dead end.

3.5   Sinai Tradition and Sinai Covenant

Beside those texts that narrate the story of the exodus events, closely bound together through the person of Moses and the people of Israel who participated in this drama, stand the texts of the so-called Sinai tradition[181] that include both the various features and the problems of the covenant of Sinai.

a. Sinai Tradition

Roughly seen, the texts that belong to the so-called Sinai tradition (Exodus 19 through Numbers 10) move from a theophany that includes the imparting of the Decalogue, through the consummation of the covenant, to the presentation of quite a large number of legal stipulations and commandments. While continuing to expand the discernible structure of the larger Sinai tradition, the extensive Priestly (P) components consisting of various strata and redactions may be separated out for assessment. In addition to Exod. 19:1–2a and 24:15b–18a, the larger units of the Priestly source include Exodus 25–31 and 35–40,[182] the entire Book of Leviticus, and the first part of Numbers found in 1:1–10:10. In addition, editorial activity is responsible for placing the so-called Covenant Code (Exod. 20:22–23:19), which receives its name from Exod. 24:7, in its present location in Exodus 19–24 . Even the Decalogue (Exod. 20:1–17)[183] does not belong to the original form of the Sinai pericope but rather was reworked and then inserted after Exodus 19 by the Priestly redactor (Rᴾ).

The following texts, earlier than P and including some that are Deuteronomic, remain constitutive for the Sinai pericope although in a more limited sense: Exod. 19:2b–25; 20:18–21; 24:1–11; and 32–34. Following the narration of the exodus from Egypt and the preservation of Israel, the redeeming activity of the people's election is consummated by the setting forth of the obligations required of them by the God of salvation. YHWH who liberated the people is the same God who places upon them certain requirements. The God who has rescued the people now reveals to them his will and brings them into a responsible community.[184] For this reason, several collections of Israel's laws, including the Covenant Code and the Holiness Code (Leviticus 17–26), are situated at Sinai and closely associated with it in order to make clear their theological location.

The binding character of the event of Sinai is seen first in the theophany at Sinai (Exodus 19),[185] then in the so-called "law of YHWH's privilege"[186] that is placed in this location, and finally in the texts in the previously mentioned larger structure of the Sinai pericope that deal with duty, including especially the Decalogue. However, the determination of the various textual strata, even in Exodus 19; 24; and 32–34, is especially difficult and much disputed. This makes it hard to define the proper limits of the text. However, the contours of the text are unmistakable. These extend from the appearance of God (Exodus 19), beyond the encounter with God (Exodus 24), to the sovereignty of God (Exodus 34).[187]

The following fragments belong to the Yahwist: Exod. 19:2b, 18a, 20, 21, 25a,[188] while those of 19:2 ("and there Israel encamped before the mountain"), 3, 10, 11a, 14, 15a, 16, 17, 18b, and 19a are characteristic of the Elohist. To be added to the Yahwistic parts of Exodus 19 are not only Exod. 34:1, 4, 5, 8, and 10 but possibly also Exod. 24:4, 5. The Elohistic fragments resume in Exod. 20:20.

The ensuing context of Exodus 32 contains an underlying predeuterono-mistic layer, while material prior to both the Deuteronomic and Priestly sources is found in Exodus 34 alongside the "law of YHWH's privilege" which perhaps comes from J but in any case is Yahwistic in character. Thus the se-quence of events according to the sources prior to P is the theophany as YHWH's self-disclosure, sacrifice, apostasy, and, along with the proclamation of the law, YHWH's obligating of himself to Israel once more.

In an examination of the Priestly portions of the text, one may recognize, above all, that P is silent about any specific Sinai *covenant*. This has probably to do with the fact that, according to the basic Priestly source in its exilic for-mulation, Israel not only was bound by this covenant but also had broken it.[189] In view of the reality of the exile, P prefers rather to reach back to the covenants with Noah (Genesis 9) and above all Abraham (Genesis 17). These are attested as valid not only for people in their own time but also for their "descendants" who are clearly emphasized by the text. What follows for P, then, is "the great institution of worship by which God makes good his promise of a covenant to Abraham."[190]

The Priestly section in Exod. 24:15b, 16–18a demonstrates how P wished to see the event of Sinai interpreted (without the "covenant"). This involves the formal introduction of the proper worship of God. Following a typical Priestly time frame of seven days (Gen. 1:1–2:4a), it is not YHWH himself who de-scends upon Sinai but rather the "glory of YHWH," his *kābôd*,[191] as a sign of divine presence. The *kābôd* of YHWH was an especially well used theologi-cal expression in the cultic theology of Jerusalem that P now places in the ear-lier time of the "period of the wilderness."[192] There YHWH, far away from Jerusalem and the temple, was present among his people and made possible the construction of the sanctuary (Exodus 25ff.). That everything occurs "before the Israelites" and takes place for their well-being is an additional important feature of the Priestly source. "The Priestly source in comparison with the earlier narratives (e.g., Exod. 24:10f.) places a clear emphasis on 'community.'"[193]

Moreover, the pronouncement of the revelation of the word is important for P (Exod. 24:16f.). In addition, the ensuing evidence in Exod. 29:43; 40:34f.; and Lev. 9:4b, 6b, 23–24 shows the significance of YHWH's *kābôd* for P. With these last-mentioned references, the Sinai complex arrives at its objective in the Priestly source: the first sacrifice can take place. While the Sabbath becomes a "sign of the covenant" in Exod. 31:16f., there is the question of whether this is a later addition in this location.[194] The additional and, in many cases, later segments of the structure of the Priestly narrative found in Leviticus 1–6 + 6–7, and 10ff. underline YHWH's instituting and ordering the cult for Israel at Sinai.[195]

By contrast, the narrative that details the theophany in Exodus 19 stands in the foreground of the J and E sources, although the interweavings of their textual stratigraphies are not particularly easy to unravel.[196] The passage in Exod. 19:3b–8[197] did not originate in either of these older literary sources. While standing very close to late Deuteronomistic theology, this passage is not dependent upon later texts. What one has is the intent to set forth a theological summary that mentions what has happened and anticipates what will happen in the exodus and at Sinai (vv. 4–8). Mentioned are YHWH's action on behalf of Israel in Egypt, his guidance, and as a consequence the obedience, soon to follow, to his "voice" and his "covenant." These actions, according to this summary, led to Israel's special status as the chosen people of YHWH, a kingdom of priests, and a holy nation. Israel is dedicated to YHWH and thus confident in him, even as only priests are able to be. In its definition of גוֹי קָדוֹשׁ (*gôy qādôš* = "holy people"; not עַם = *'am* = "people"), Exod. 19:6 moves beyond the typical Deuteronomistic phraseology (cf. Deut. 4:7f., 34; and 9:14—גוֹי = *gôy* = "people" but without קָדוֹשׁ = *qādôš* = "holy"). Moreover, this passage at least indirectly attests to YHWH as "king" by referring to Israel as a "kingdom of priests." Exodus 19:7f. emphasizes the point that the duty of the nation was set forth at Sinai. The formal character of the entire passage may be recognized as a conditional blessing,[198] meaning that future disclosure is both the center and the intent of the text.

According to the Yahwistic components of Exodus 19, which are more of a theological treatise than a literary narrative, the Israelites are encamped in the wilderness. "Sinai" (so also in P; but Horeb in Deuteronomy and Deuteronomistic texts; for E often merely "the mountain/mountain of God") begins to smoke when YHWH "descends" (ירד = *yārad*) upon the mountain.[199] Verse 18 evokes associations with a volcanic eruption (cf. 20:18). The (Yahwistic) references to the pillars of cloud and fire conform well to this image (Exod. 13:21f. and 14:19b, 24). The people who are struck by the awesomeness of this theophany should acknowledge this God as their own. Already for J the theophany aims at receiving Israel's response, and in the continuation of this narrative (Exod. 24:4f.) the worship of Israel is established by offering a sacrifice to YHWH. The corpora of laws and legislation that are added later to the Sinai pericope "originated not with the appearance of God but rather are attracted by its legitimating power."[200] Moreover, this is not to be seen only as a secondary interpretation, for each theophany has a goal and pursues a purpose.

Moses is then called up to the mountain, according to J (Exod. 34:2), offers there a prayer (Exod. 34:4f.), asks for YHWH to accompany Israel along the way, and receives a "covenantal" pledge, that is, YHWH's promise of self-obligation (Exod. 34:9f.).

According to the Elohistic fragments, Israel encamps "before the mountain" (Exod. 19:2b). Moses ascends to God (Exod. 19:3a) and receives the commission to sanctify the people, which includes, for example, the washing of their garments, and then on the third day[201] to have them take up positions around the mountain. Moses descends from the mountain and has these instructions carried out (Exod. 19:14b, 15a). Then the theophany follows, which, in this case, has more the features of a thunderstorm (Exod. 19:16). Moses leads the people out of the camp (cf. Exod. 3:10f.) to "meet God." In this act, the exodus of the nation from Egypt under the leadership of Moses (so says E) reaches its primary goal. The people tremble, the sound of the trumpet, which gives the scene the nuance of worship, grows louder (Exod. 19:18b, 19a), and Moses then explains to the people (in an interpretation evaluated as an "answer": Exod. 19:19b)[202] that the theophany is a test of their fear of God (Exod. 20:20; cf. Gen. 22:1, 12). Only Moses dares to approach closer to God (Exod. 20:21).[203] E. Zenger finds in these fragments of text the literary genre of the "theological treatise that reflects the mode of a day of festival."[204] However, as is also true of J, probably only the first half of this characterization of the text may be appropriate. The theological treatise of this text deals with the typical elements found in a description of a theophany. These typical elements certainly receive their specific emphases in E as well as in J. While E is more interested in the people and their theological fitness and seeks to shape the theophany in the prophetic style of an extensive divine examination, more important for J is the character of this "YHWH from Sinai."

According to many scholars, the present sequence of the traditions of the exodus and Sinai should not be considered original.[205] For instance, M. Noth thought that both were brought together for the first time in a basic source that resided behind both J and E, while G. von Rad thought the Yahwist was responsible for connecting the two. Different circles of tradition or groups, who would coalesce later on in Israel, would have stood behind the two, originally separate traditions. In addition, these respective traditions would have been actualized in the festivals of different sanctuaries. On occasion it is maintained that either the Sinai tradition is prior to the exodus tradition, or there could have been two Sinai traditions, only one of which was associated with the exodus and with Moses.

That the text of the so-called credo[206] does not mention Sinai (Deut. 6:21ff.;

26:5–9; Josh. 24:2ff.) offers no argument for removing the Sinai tradition from other traditions of faith, for this creedal confession names only YHWH's *acts* of salvation for his people and not the duty of this nation toward him. This compares to the Christian credo that gives thanks and confesses divine acts but says nothing about what the present community is to do.

Furthermore, YHWH is the God "from Sinai" (Judg. 5:4f.; Deut. 33:2; and Ps. 68:9), who, consequently, is not to be separated from this mountain. However, he also is not to be removed from the event of the exodus (Exod. 15:21; Hos. 12:10; and 13:4). These two features of Sinai and exodus also are bound together in the figure of Moses[207] and in the entity of Israel. This means that, while one may propose that the two were originally independent traditions, this has neither historical nor theological relevance for the interpretation of the texts that are now connected.

However, if the whole Sinai pericope in its present form is a late product of Old Testament religious and redaction history, it cannot be interpreted in its entirety as a legend of a covenant (renewal) festival that possibly originated at Shechem.[208] In addition, it remains unclear whether the tradition transmitted at Shechem would have shaped the cult or would have been shaped by it.[209]

The problems facing the thesis of the Sinai tradition as a cult legend are similar to those facing the proposal that the Sinai pericope either developed from or has parallels with ancient Near Eastern treaties, in particular Hittite and Neo-Assyrian examples. The *form of the covenant,* for example, Joshua 24, especially has been understood in relationship to these ancient Near Eastern texts.[210] However, a glance at the Sinai pericope indicates that this thesis suffers from problems relating to both form and content. The thesis requires the relocation of certain passages (e.g., Exod. 24:3–8 immediately after 20:1–17), while leaving the Decalogue in its original place. Other features of ancient Near Eastern treaties are missing. Blessings and cursings are not present in the literary context of the Sinai pericope, although they are constitutive features of the ancient Near Eastern treaties. All this means that recent scholarship has not seen as helpful either the thesis of a covenant renewal festival or the theory of a covenant form dependent on ancient Near Eastern treaties.

Located on the periphery of the actual Sinai pericope are texts that often have been attributed to the so-called Kadesh tradition[211] (Exodus [16?]; 17; also 18?; Numbers 10–14; cf. Numbers 20; Deut. 1:46; and 2:14). It is probable that these reflect events and traditions that originally had nothing to do with the exodus and Moses group but rather were associated with groups that later on were incorporated into the larger "Israel." These later members would not have belonged to that original group for whom the exodus and the experience at Sinai were so determinative.

One can probably come closer to finding the solution to many of these problems associated with the Sinai pericope and the events at Sinai when one asks the question about the location of the "historical" Mt. Sinai.[212]

The tradition that locates "Sinai" (so J and P) in the Sinai Peninsula is evidenced as early as the fourth century C.E., though Mt. Sinai has been identified with different mountains: Jebel Qaterin, Jebel Musa, or even Jebel Serbal.[213] Indeed, this tradition possibly goes back even earlier to older (Nabatean?) sources. Numerous Old Testament texts tell about the/a mountain of God in Midianite territory (Exod. 3:1f.;[214] 4:27; 18:5; and 24:13) that takes in the area extending south from Edom to the southeastern coast of the Sinai Peninsula in the proximity of the Gulf of Aqaba. The itinerary of the stations of Israel's journey through the Sinai wilderness (Num. 33:3–49; cf. Deut. 1:2, 19) leads to this region. This means that the original Mt. Sinai could have been a volcanic mountain in Northwest Arabia (this is still mentioned even as late as Gal. 4:25!). The frequently mentioned association of YHWH with Seir also leads one to look in this region for the location of Mt. Sinai (Judg. 5:4f.; Deut. 33:2; cf. Hab. 3:3). Beyond this, the short form of the name YHWH (yhw3) is attested in Egyptian lists from the fourteenth and thirteenth centuries B.C.E., including the mention of a "land of the Shasu yhw3." These texts also point to the region south of Palestine and in the area of the Midianites. They indicate that the name yhw3 could possibly point to the name of a deity as well as a mountain or region.[215]

Added to this geographical and literary evidence is the Midianite or Kenite hypothesis.[216] According to this hypothesis, Moses came to know YHWH at the "Mountain of God" through the Midianites, who were once worshipers of YHWH. In Exodus 2–4, Moses fled from Egypt to the region of Midian and there married a daughter of a priest who, bearing various names (E = Jethro; Reuel or Hobab = J?),[217] is associated with the Midianites or Kenites. This hypothesis adds weight to the possible location of Mt. Sinai in the region of Midian. While J is the first to name this mountain of God "Sinai," later Israelite theologians consciously avoided using this term (e.g., see the Deuteronomic and Deuteronomistic literature). The reason for this avoidance is that the name Sinai reflects foreign influence, or even origins. They thus preferred to use the name Horeb, conscious of the fact that this term only meant "wasteland, wilderness."[218] They preferred to describe the theophany at Horeb in terms of fire out of which YHWH spoke (cf. Deut. 4:11ff.; 5:4, 22f., 26; 9:10, 15; and 10:4). In contrast to these (Deuteronomic) theologians, the later Priestly source spoke once more of the mountain as "Sinai," and, in addition, used the expression, the "Wilderness (!) of Sinai" (Exod. 19:1, 2a; Num. 1:1; etc.). Since there were many mountains of God, the mountain of Kadesh, where perhaps at one time a group (an Aaron group?) practiced the worship of an image of a calf, could have been included among them.

b. Sinai Covenant

The Sinai pericope mentions several times the Sinai *bĕrît* ("covenant, oblig-ation")[219] that appears as the consequence and theological development of the theophany (Exodus 19). In its present context, Exod. 19:1–6 is a theological summary that, in the final analysis, anticipates all that follows. The late text in 19:5 provides the first explanation and classification of the "covenant" as an obligation that the people are expected to keep and obey (שָׁמֹר בְּרִית = *šĕmōr bĕrît*, "keep the covenant, obligation"). Exodus 34:10 is probably the oldest text that presents the contents of the covenant in the language of promise. Covenantal language continues in 34:27ff. that makes reference to 34:11–26.[220] Occurring even earlier in Exod. 24:3–8 are the expressions "book of the covenant" (Exod. 24:7) and "blood of the covenant" (Exod. 24:8;[221] cf. Zech. 9:11—the blood of circumcision?) which is mentioned in Moses' ex-planation of the blood ritual.[222] However, this text is not a single unit and in its present form closely approximates Deuteronomic thought. Exodus 24:1–2 is predominantly redactional, while 24:9–11 contains older features of a theo-phany and a meal. Whether Exod. 24:11 refers to a covenant meal between partners (cf. Gen. 26:28–30; and 31:52–54) is not as certain as some have of-ten claimed. Nevertheless, the association and the establishment of community (without sin!) between God, whose presence is symbolized by the altar, and the people are clearly described and realized in the blood ritual of Exod. 24:6, 8.[223] The form of this ritual, which includes the "throwing" (זָרַק = *zāraq*) of blood on both partners, is unique in the Old Testament. "The appearance of God in vv. 1–2 and 9–11 is both the high point and the climax of the theophany, while the self-obligation of the people and the ratification of the covenant in vv. 3–8 are both the high point and the climax of the proclamation of the law."[224] While Exod. 24:1–11 may contain some older elements, the section as a whole and its placement in its present context are the result of late redactional activity, especially considering the fact that 24:8 appears to allude to the Deca-logue and the Covenant Code. In recent years, a number of important scholarly contributions to the understanding of the phenomenon and meaning of בְּרִית = *bĕrît* ("covenant, obligation") have appeared.[225] In terms of its etymological derivation, the word בְּרִית = *bĕrît*[226] ("covenant, obligation") points, not so much to Hebrew ברה = *bārâ* ("to eat") or to the Akkadian lexemes *birīt*, "be-tween" (M. Noth), and *birītu* "chain"[227] (thus R. Kraetzschmar in an earlier pe-riod and later O. Loretz and M. Weinfeld) but rather to the rarely occurring He-brew word ברה II = *bārâ*, which means "to choose, agree upon."[228] In regard to this last word, one can point with M. Görg[229] to the foreign word evidenced in Egyptian, *bryt*, which often means a "constrained relationship."

Above all, however, the theological evaluation and content as well as the historical location of the concept of covenant have undergone a transformation in scholarship. J. Wellhausen[230] saw in the covenant of the Mosaic period a relationship between God and people that was seen "originally as natural . . . , not as contractual."[231] Thus, Sinai had nothing to do with the giving of the law. R. Kraetzschmar[232] saw the problem in a similar light, and he thought, therefore, that the ideas of covenant were dependent upon the prophets. For J. Pedersen,[233] the important idea was that the covenant set forth a sphere of life for participating partners so that a mutual relationship of solidarity with all rights and obligations would be significant. Most important, however, was the work of W. Eichrodt who considered the conception of covenant to be determinative for the outline and description of Old Testament theology as a whole.[234] For Eichrodt, the fundamental character of the covenant included the clear expression of the divine will, the context for the emergence of a relationship of trust, and the relationship of sovereignty from which developed the idea of the reign of God. In addition, the covenant may have had an important connection to history and as a consequence would have protected Israelite ideas and beliefs against a naturalistic association (contra Wellhausen), for God can dissolve this relationship. L. Köhler, by contrast, stressed in his *Theologie des Alten Testaments* that the ideas of the covenant focused on a reciprocal arrangement involving rights and obligations for both partners.[235]

An essay by J. Begrich, however, came to have particular importance for clarifying the idea of covenant.[236] He investigated first the pre-theological use of ברית = *bĕrît* ("covenant, obligation") and discovered that it means an early form of a unilateral accord or gift (thus, e.g., Joshua 9; the covenant between David and Jonathan in 1 Samuel 18; and 1 Kings 20:34). This early form of covenant, which Begrich called nomadic, knew no laws and obligations imposed on its recipients. A later, and that means also Canaanite, form of the covenant, by contrast, sees the ברית = *bĕrît* ("covenant, obligation") as a two-sided arrangement, that is, as a contractual covenant that may be seen once again in the relationship between David and Jonathan. The early form may often be revised according to the nature of the later form. In this case, the covenant may be more of a relationship and its contents may be described more in terms of *šālôm* ("peace, well-being"). This relationship is where the giver, at least at first, may be active, while the recipient may be passive. The terminology for the earlier understanding of covenant making includes כרת ברית ל (*kārat bĕrît l* = "to cut a covenant for"), while the later understanding is expressed with the prepositions עם (*'im* = "with"), את (*'ĕt* = "with"), and בין (*bên* = "between"). In looking at the theological dimension of covenant[237] and thus the God-human relationship, Begrich argues that the older understanding comes under consideration, namely, the granting of the covenant as a gift. Here, election is always an expression of the covenant that originates with YHWH, and covenant is likewise an expression of the election that originates with YHWH. This means that obligation is not imposed upon the recipient of the covenant. "In other words, there is no connection between ברית and law."[238] This understanding of covenant as gift may have been, in addition, the genuine Israelite understanding, while the understanding of covenant as contract, by contrast, may give evidence of Canaanite influence, influence that also incorporates juridical ideas. "The statements concerning the giving of the law cannot be explained from the idea of ברית" (= bĕrît, "covenant, obligation").[239] The later understanding of covenant (the Elohist Deuteronomy, and Deuteronomistic thinking) was the first to combine the two, that is, covenant and law giving, while the Priestly source, it seemed, remained close to the older understanding of covenant in its evaluation of the covenant of Noah as well as the covenant of Abraham (Genesis 9; 17). However, P did alter to some extent the terminology of covenant (e.g., the verb הקים = hēqîm, "to establish") and introduced the rainbow in the first instance and circumcision in the second as signs of these two covenants. Nevertheless, P is silent about any covenantal document.

This scholarly view of the Old Testament conception of covenant and its development was dominant for a long time. By way of recapitulation, this scholarly understanding consisted of several related features: first, the law was understood to move eventually within the boundaries of the covenant originally conceived as gift; second, the law came to be encompassed, if not entirely absorbed, by the covenant; and third, the attribution of the law to the covenant was understood to be theologically inappropriate. This scholarly view, however, has had and continues to have rather grave consequences for the theological interpretation of Old Testament law and for its theological location.[240] This is the case, for example, in the evaluation of the law in G. von Rad's *Theology of the Old Testament*. However, before moving into an examination of the law, we shall first consider additional scholarly views of covenant in the Old Testament.

In addition to the two types of covenants that Begrich distinguished, yet a third was uncovered in which YHWH was understood as the mediator of covenant.[241] This is where a covenant is established between two partners and a third serves as a mediator between the two (cf., e.g., 2 Kings 11:17; Hos. 2:20; and Ezek. 34:25). A fourth type was later revealed from comparing ancient Near Eastern treaties with the covenant. The so-called covenant formula is more of a bilateral contract that can be concluded between equals. In this treaty, while "the adversaries' obligations can be materially different, they still possess the same binding power."[242]

Further, it should be asked how the act of concluding the covenant was conducted within the circumstances that have been set forth. Is it not possible that the older texts may mention a bilateral covenant (e.g., Gen. 21:27ff.; 26:28–30; 31:44; 1 Sam. 23:18; 2 Sam. 5:3; and 1 Kings 5:26)? If so, then one would not be able to verify the development that Begrich thought he could see.[243] It could then be underscored that שלום = šālôm ("peace, well-being") may be the content of ברית = *běrît* ("covenant, obligation") and that both partners show חסד = *ḥesed* ("steadfast love") to each other (cf. 1 Kings 5:26 and also Josh. 9:15 for the Gibeonites as the less powerful partner).

Above all, however, the major question concerning YHWH's "covenant" with Israel is whether this covenant ever lacked the requirement of an obligation from the partner. Even in the conclusions of the covenants of God with Noah and Abraham, covenants that have more the character of grace, there are still indications of obligations (Gen. 9:3–6 and 17:1c, 9ff.). And in looking at the Sinai covenant, such an obligation may not rightly be excluded. This covenant concerns promise and command (A. Jepsen), pledge, assurance, and obligation all rolled into one. This is a covenant between YHWH and people, but it certainly is not a covenant of mutual obligation between partners reckoned as equals. If YHWH declares, "I will be your God!" there is also included in the gracious promise the statement: "I alone will be your God!" The direction toward the goal and the instruction for the way are entwined. The history of the people held in common with its God also creates room for obedience. That YHWH is a "jealous God" is not accidently stressed within the Decalogue (Exod. 20:5; Deut. 5:9), for this commandment occurs in its present context at the intersecting of covenant and law.

On the basis of this obligatory character of ברית = *běrît* ("covenant, obligation"), one is able to relate covenant and curse to each other (Deut. 29:11; Ezek. 17:18f.).[244] In addition, the ritual of Gen. 15:9–18 (cf. Jer. 34:15ff.), evidenced in a similar form also in Israel's environment,[245] underscores the obligatory character of the event that imposes responsibilities upon the covenant partners. Further, when the verb נתן = *nātan* ("to give") is used with ברית = *běrît* (this occurs regularly in Deuteronomy but also in Gen. 17:2 P), what is in view is probably the handing over of a document. When the verb הקים = *hēqîm* ("to establish"; readily in P: Gen. 9:9, 11; 17:7) is used with ברית = *běrît,* the image is probably that of the erection of a law stele. When the verb כרת = *kārat* ("cut") is used, the idea may be a kind of self-cursing, with the point that the one who breaks the covenant is threatened with a similar fate of being "cut in half." Beyond this, E. Kutsch has rather conclusively demonstrated that ברית = *běrît* ("covenant, obligation") should not be translated consistently with the word "covenant," since this may lead one too quickly to think of a mutual relationship between two partners judged to be equals, an understanding that certainly would not be true of the covenant of YHWH. Therefore he translates the term with the word "obligation." This may involve obligating oneself (e.g., Yahweh) in a way that is very close to a promise or even an oath (e.g., Ezek. 16:8; Gen. 15:18; Exod. 34:10; Pss. 89:4; and 105:9f.),[246] an obligation to a stranger, and a bilateral obligation (Deut. 26:17f.). Finally, L. Perlitt has sought to show[247] that a comprehensive "covenantal theology" in the Old Testament first originated within the structure of Deuteronomic and Deuteronomistic thought.

According to him, Deuteronomic and Deuteronomistic texts are the ones that predominantly speak of "covenant" (chiefly the covenant at Horeb:[248] Deut. 4:13, 23; 5:2f.; Josh. 7:11, 15; 23:16; etc.). Even in the Sinai pericope itself the decisive texts mentioning the covenant seem to be shaped by Deuteronomic/ Deuteronomistic language or to be dependent upon this way of thinking. It is the same in regard to the unique notion of a "covenant at Moab" (Deut. 28:69; cf. 29:8, 11, 13, 20). The entire Book of Deuteronomy and the obedience to what is contained therein are the foundations of this covenant at Moab which may have been a modification of the covenant at Horeb, or perhaps even a substitute, that Israel had broken.[249]

The texts in the Sinai pericope that deal with the covenant already indicate that it has undergone various theological explanations.[250] Two constant features of the interpretation of covenant may be recognized: the covenant always originates with YHWH; and it always addresses the nation, not individuals. Then there are various nuances. At the beginning of the pericope (Exodus 19) stands the theophany that urges a response. This theophany and its response are given theological content in the form of a ברית = bĕrît ("covenant/obligation") as YHWH's promise and self-obligation (Exod. 34:10 = J). In addition, the solidarity and the community between YHWH and his people (Exod. 24:8) are also expressed within the contours of the covenant. The linking of the covenant and the duty to follow YHWH's will, which is in the offing in Exod. 34:27f. and is already indicated in Exod. 24:7, occurs then in the JE passage in Exod. 34:11ff. and comes fully into view in the Deuteronomistic theology in the Sinai covenant. The Deuteronomistic theology of the covenant that requires the people's obligation to YHWH[251] reaches its culmination through the insertion of the Decalogue and the Book of the Covenant (probably through Rp). Thus "covenant" and "law," ברית = bĕrît and תורה = tôrâ, both of which include the Decalogue, could become closely associated ideas (Deut. 4:13; 17:2; 29:20; 2 Kings 22:13; 23:3, 24; and Hos. 8:1). The Deuteronomic and Deuteronomistic literature's preference for the verb צוה (ṣiwwâ; "command"; cf., e.g., Deut. 4:13; Josh. 7:11; 23:16; Judg. 2:20; and 1 Kings 11:11) in combination with ברית = bĕrît ("covenant, obligation") underscores YHWH's imposition of obligation upon the people and their responsibility to obey his "law."[252] In this type of (Deuteronomistic) thought, the tablets of the Decalogue can be designated as the "covenant" (1 Kings 8:21). The covenant becomes a positive reference point for theological reflection (Pss. 106:45 and 111:5, 9). The Priestly source contributes to this when, while consciously passing over the now broken[253] Sinai covenant, it makes the covenant of Noah into an important covenant of grace that possesses signs of the covenant. And it emphasizes the covenant of Abraham as an eternal (עולם = 'ôlām) covenant for him and his seed, along with the signs of the promise of possession of the land and of circumcision.[254] P is inclined to use new verbs in association with ברית = bĕrît ("covenant, obligation"). In stressing the gracious character of a gift, the term נתן = *nātan* ("to give") is used: Gen. 9:12; 17:2, while הקים (*hēqîm*) is used to speak of the legitimate "erection" of a contract stele: Gen. 6:18; 9:9, 11, 17; 17:7, 19, 21; and Exod. 6:4; cf. Num. 25:12 (נתן = *nātan*); Lev. 26:9 (הקים = *hēqîm*). Other late texts also reach back to the covenant of Noah and the covenant of Abraham (Isa. 24:5; 54:10; 61:8; and Ps. 105:8–10).

Consequently, it is not possible to separate the act of concluding the covenant from the relationship of the partners that the covenant sets forth,[255] since this relationship is determined and continues in effect through this act. A number of texts point out that the people can obligate themselves to YHWH through a *bĕrît* ("covenant, obligation"; Ezra 10:3; 2 Kings 23:3; and 2 Chron. 29:10), while the breaking and abandonment of this obligation toward YHWH is a frequent topic in Deuteronomistic theology.[256] In the "New Covenant" passage in Jer. 31:31–34, which is at least redacted by the Deuteronomic School, this breaking of the covenant by Israel is surpassed by the promise of a "new covenant" with a new pledge of the convenant formula (v. 33) in which YHWH's תורה = *tôrâ* will be written on the heart. The full knowledge of God will be possible, and YHWH will forgive his people.

With all of this, it should be said that there was no "historical" Sinai covenant in which all Israel took part,[257] even as there was never a covenant that constituted the nation of Israel either as a unity or in the form of a twelve tribe league. Therefore the covenant of Sinai was not the basis of an amphictyony that is, in itself, a debated idea.[258]

Outside of the Sinai pericope, the Deuteronomic and Deuteronomistic literature, and the literature influenced by the D School, the theological formulation of ברית (*bĕrît*, "covenant, obligation"), which is never encountered in the plural, rarely occurs in older Old Testament literature but, by contrast, is more frequent in texts that are dependent upon Deuteronomic and Deuteronomistic literature. Among the possibly older texts, one should certainly include Hos. 8:1 (cf. 6:7?), whose authenticity need not be questioned because of the language that very much reflects that of Hosea. It further may be demonstrated that the so-called covenant form (see below) in its various parts has a prehistory that goes back to the early period of Israel.

In addition, Old Testament covenant theology is hardly evidenced in Israel's cultural environment[259] in the form of a "covenant" between a deity and people. This theology grew into its more developed form in much the same way that faith in "election" by YHWH did (cf. above, chapter 2). And like faith in election, covenant theology has made an essential contribution to the expression of Israel's faith in YHWH as it continued to evolve and develop. One should not exclude the possibility that there were Canaanite influences, since in Judg. 8:33; and 9:4, 46, El and Baal Berit are mentioned in connection with Shechem. Certainly it is no accident that the scene of Joshua 24[260] unfolds in Shechem.

The development of the Sinai pericope and the emphasis on covenant theology are predominantly and on the whole a later phenomenon within the history of Old Testament piety[261] and are mainly developed by the Deuteronomic/
Deuteronomistic movement. This makes sense, then, of the "silence about the
covenant" (L. Perlitt)[262] in the prophets of the eighth century B.C.E. Amos, Isaiah, and Micah make no mention of this ברית = běrît ("covenant, obligation"),
leaving Hos. 8:1 as the only older prophetic text to come into consideration.
The texts that mention the covenant in Jeremiah (Jer. 7:22f.; 11:1f.; and
31:31ff.) are all edited by the Deuteronomistic School, and Ps. 44:18 occurs in
a community lament that derives from the period of the exile.[263] In Ezekiel,
"covenant" is used as a sign of a divine marriage[264] between YHWH and
Jerusalem (Ezek. 16:8; cf. 23:4 without "covenant"). According to the continuing, later interpretation in Ezek. 16:59ff.,[265] Jerusalem (Judah), nevertheless,
has broken this covenant (cf. Ezek. 44:7). However, YHWH desires to "remember" in a positive way this covenant that he initiated and does not take for
granted (cf. Gen. 9:15f. P), and he will establish an eternal covenant (vv. 60,
62) through which he will create forgiveness[266] for what Jerusalem/Judah has
done. The expressions "commemoration," "eternal covenant," and "establish"
(הקים = hēqîm; cf. Gen. 6:18; 9:9, 11, 17; 17:7, 19, 21; and Exod. 6:4) reflect
the language of P.[267] Covenant theology was, however, not very influential in
the Book of Ezekiel (cf. still Ezek. 34:25; 37:26). Covenant theology appears
to have been, nevertheless, an important vehicle for the expression of postexilic piety, since this was the time when the books of Genesis and Exodus[268] on
through Deuteronomy and Joshua (chap. 24) are given their structure by "texts
dealing with the covenant."

c. The So-called Covenant Formula

As covenant theology developed and took shape, it came to express itself in
the so-called covenant formula[269] ("I will be your God and you will be my people"). In addition to the formula's frequent use in the expressions of limited or
unlimited promise for the future,[270] it also was used in the fundamental situations of the beginning of YHWH's history with his people.[271] It turns out now
that the individual parts of this covenant formula, as, for example, "my people," or "people of YHWH," or "to be your/their God," or "YHWH, the God
of Israel," occur in earlier Old Testament texts. Formulations of the kinds just
named reach back as far as the Song of Deborah (Judg. 5:3, 5, 13); are found
in the earlier exodus tradition (Exod. 3:7, 10; 5:1, 23; 7:16; 8:16f.; 9:1, 13; and
10:3); occur in Judg. 8:30; 24:23 (cf. Gen. 33:20);[272] Amos 7:8, 15; 8:2; Hos.
1:9; 4:6, 8, 12; 12:10; 13:4, etc.; Isa. 1:3, etc.; and later are present in such texts
as Lev. 11:45; 26:45; etc. If one places 2 Sam. 1:12 beside the evidence from
the Song of Deborah, the supposition presents itself that "the relationship between God and his worshipers who appeared later in Israel found its first and

original expression within the context of war that Yahweh led against Israel's and his enemies. . . . If these conclusions are correct, then several elements contributed to the double formula, 'Yahweh, the God of Israel; Israel, the people of Yahweh.' First, there was the 'Yahweh' who came out of Egypt along with the 'people of Yahweh'; and second, there was the 'God of Israel' and 'Israel' who already had settled in Palestine prior to the arrival of the Egyptian group."[273] Since the warlike group belonged to YHWH[274] and the deliverance from Egypt was presented in military terms,[275] this thesis gains in probability. At the same time, in view of what has been said, it is clear that the developed theology of covenant was probably a late product of Old Testament faith. Clearly analogous to election faith, covenant theology grew richer in its expression during certain epochs of Israelite history, with various points and understandings arising out of concrete occasions and in particular out of periods of crisis. Covenant theology discovered in the earlier and continuing history of Israelite faith a foundation for rendering new possibilities.[276]

d. Exodus 32–34

Exodus 32–34 intersects chaps. 25–31, which provide the instructions for the construction of the sanctuary, and chaps. 35–40,[277] which narrate the actual building of the sanctuary. Through the sequence of chapters and the motif of the two tablets, which are given a different designation and function,[278] the apostasy is now introduced (Exodus 32) that turns what was formerly the ratification of the covenant in Exodus 34[279] into a renewal of the covenant. Taken together, all of this stands under the caption of this guiding principle: the apostasy delayed the construction of the sanctuary and along with it the presence of YHWH among his people (Exod. 29:45f.). By contrast, Exodus 33, while making a similar inquiry after the presence of God among his (sinful) people, answers this query in different ways by enlisting various forms of mediating revelation (angel, countenance).[280] This composition obviously presupposes the experience of the exile and this period's theological efforts to cope with its difficulties.

While it was probably the literary stratum of JE that placed Exodus 32[281] before Exodus 34, it was the underlying, basic stratum of Exodus 32 (vv. 1–6, 15a, 19f., 30–34) that ventured to speak of an apostasy from YHWH, who had delivered his people and committed himself to them, to follow after an image of a bull ("calf")[282] who had to be identified characteristically enough as the god of the exodus (v. 4). The use of the plural that appears in 1 Kings 12:28 ("your gods") naturally reflects the two bull images of Jeroboam I in Dan and Bethel. However, this also means that this precursor to Exodus 32 "provides the answer to the question as to why the Northern Kingdom came to destruction.[283] This answer is not meant to be naively superficial, that is, because the

Northern Kingdom had fallen into the worship of idols. . . . The golden calf of Exodus 32 is the opposite picture of the God of Sinai who was revealed in Exodus 19 as the hidden God of the wilderness and the God of prophetic word who fights against the 'natural' inclination of human beings to worship idols that they can see and touch."[284] The polemic of Hosea against the bull cult allows one to recognize similar thoughts (Hos. 8:5f.; 10:5f.). Whether this polemic is directed against the violation of the prohibition against images (Exod. 20:23; 34:17; then 20:4 and Deut. 5:8f.),[285] against a different form of the worship of YHWH (Exod. 32:5, "festival for YHWH"), or against the resumption or continuation of a (El?) bull cult in Bethel is difficult to decide. What compounds the difficulty is the inability not only to date with precision the fully worked out prohibition against images but also to determine its inner presuppositions and its prehistory. In any case, according to Exodus 32 the image of the bull cannot be a symbol of YHWH (Exod. 32:1) leading the nation. This element of guidance and the possibility or impossibility of divine presence among YHWH's sinful people (Exod. 33:5)[286] are followed up, then, in Exodus 33. The apostasy necessarily results in punishment (Exod. 32:35). The later, sizable, intercessory prayer of Moses, inserted in vv. 7–14, develops out of vv. 30–32.[287] Moses consequently no longer desires to live, if the nation is to be destroyed (Exod. 32:32). Nevertheless, this verse does not present the possible death of Moses as a vicarious death for Israel's sin.

The Sinai tradition primarily deals with the duty of the people who are chosen through the event of the exodus. Common sense tells scholars that all the people of Israel did not participate in the exodus and in the events of Sinai.[288] Rather, as a result of their importance for the groups who participated in them and who became the most influential part of later Israel, these events were extended to include all Israel. Nevertheless, these sacred events still continued to have special connections with particular groups and spheres (cf., e.g., the absence of the exodus tradition in Isaiah). Originally, only smaller groups were affected by these events (a "Moses group"? "house of Joseph"? "Rachel tribes"?). These smaller groups introduced to Israel their faith in YHWH and their possible self-understanding as the people of this God, for YHWH became and then was the God of Israel.

The additional themes of covenant, apostasy, and covenant renewal were then combined with the exodus. This means that Israel's failure in its duty to God and the consequences that resulted are brought within the sphere of theological reflection. The effort to trace out and understand the development of this reflection, however, is hampered by the fact that various texts from different periods are brought together in Exodus 19; 24; and 32–34 to comprise an overarching summary. Thus the message and possible origin of each of the various individual texts, the stages of their compilation, and their final redaction are open to question.

e. The Murmuring People during the Wilderness Wandering

Directly after the narrative description of the salvation of the exodus group
at the sea and their response in the form of a song of praise (Exodus 14–15),
the narratives concerning the murmuring of the people during the time of the
wandering in the wilderness are introduced.[289] While these narratives are positioned on both sides of the Sinai tradition, their major emphasis occurs in
those texts which follow it. These narratives, on the one hand, tell about a murmuring or even "rebelling" (לוּן = *lûn*)[290] of the people against (על = *'al*) YHWH
(Exod. 16:7f.; Num. 14:27ff.; and 17:25) because of poor and insufficient pro-
visions during the journey (Exod. 15:24; 16; 17:3) and about a clamorous look
back at the fleshpots of Egypt (Num. 11:4–6; 14:4; 20:5) and the "land flowing with milk and honey" (Num. 16:13).[291] On the other hand, the tradition also
tells about the guidance and sustenance in the wilderness and divine help in
supplying creaturely needs. These narratives include incidents dealing with
water (Exod. 15:22ff.: the bitter water of Marah; Exod. 17:2f.: Massa and
Meribah; and Num. 20:1–13: water from the rocks), food (manna: Exodus 16),
and meat (quail: Exodus 16; cf. Numbers 11). Then there are incidents of murmuring against those in leadership, including Moses (Exod. 15:24; 17:3; cf.
also Numbers 12) and Moses and Aaron (Exod. 16:2, 7; Num. 14:2; 16; and
17:6, 20: so only in P). To these belong Exod. 32:1, Leviticus 10 (Nadab and
Abihu and their own cultic activity), Numbers 11 (the demand for meat and the
gift of quail), Numbers 14 (murmuring when confronted with the report of the
scouts), Numbers 16 (the rebellion of the mob led by Koran, Dathan, and Abi-
ram),[292] and Num. 21:4ff. (the people's murmuring punished by serpents).[293]
These texts are component parts of the literary contribution of every narrator
and editor met in the Pentateuch, for not one of them either could or wanted to
leave unmentioned this murmuring of Israel.[294] Israel's murmuring was combined with local legends and individual traditions in order to arrive at the intended and theologically informative statements.

It is rather astonishing that Israel would speak about itself in this manner,
that is, as unthankful and disbelieving, and that it would in all these ways characterize itself as sinful.[295] Furthermore, the saving God is described also as the
sustaining and guiding deity. YHWH is able not only to deliver through military action but also to sustain and provide for creaturely needs, even those of
a murmuring, disbelieving, and rebellious people. These narratives, in addition, are situated "between Egypt and the land of promise." They pose the question as to whether the people shall and are able to come into this land or
whether they will instead die on the way or, better still, will turn back to Egypt.
Further, the events at Sinai come to have a profound significance within the
murmuring tradition, since here there is a more thorough discussion of punishments, defeats, the wrath of YHWH, and the intercession of Moses. Israel

has entered into a position of responsibility through the Sinai event and therefore is clearly more responsible for bearing its guilt. In rebelling against the
leaders who call them to faith and to continue their journey, they reject the land
of promise (P in Numbers 13/14). All of these topics indicate that the murmuring stories reflect at the same time the reality of the exile when once more
there is a journey through the wilderness to the land and when there is also
faithless and doubting resistance. The topos, "forty years in the wilderness,"[296]
that is described in all of its ghastliness (Deut. 8:15–18; cf. Jer. 2:6) characteristically is found, not in J and E, but more than likely in the texts of the
Deuteronomistic movement that chronologically are close to the exile and in
the Priestly source and later texts dependent upon it. This indicates that this
topos is a cipher for the period of the exile. Here would fit also the narrative
topos about the generation of the murmurers having first to die off before their
children could enter into the land (Num. 14:30–34; Deut. 1:39; and 2:14). It
can be further demonstrated that the majority of the murmuring stories are
transmitted within the Priestly source, and probably in its sections that are exilic. Psalms 78; 106; 136:10ff.; and especially Ezek. 20:10ff. (cf. also Deut.
8:3; 29:5f.; and Josh. 24:7) show how this period in the wilderness, with its re-
bellions and punishments, its support and undeserved divine accompaniment,
is understood as a paradigmatic case of human history and divine providence.

Consequently, there are different evaluations of the wilderness period
within ancient Israel and its history. While Hosea (Hos. 2:16ff.) and Jeremiah
(Jer. 2:1–3) found here the time of the first love between YHWH and Israel,
others found here a time of apostasy and, especially in the narratives that follow the Sinai pericope, the divine punishment that ensued. The stories of murmuring consequently take up anew and continue what is narrated in Exodus
32–34 about apostasy, punishment, and new beginning.[297] Both ways of understanding the wilderness period are in agreement that it was an important
stage on Israel's journey to the land of promise, for it was a time when Israel
not only learned much about itself but, more important, also learned much
about its God.

3.6 Duty and Law: The Theological Basis
of the Law of God

Israel as both a people and a community was elected by YHWH to enter into
fellowship with him. However, at the same time, Israel also entered into a relationship with YHWH that required obligation. Beside the liberating deliverance from Egypt stood the obligation that came through the theophany and
covenant at Sinai; beside (and not before) the indicative stood the imperative
that was subordinated to the indicative both chronologically and especially materially; and beside the creator stood the Lord who issued commandments and
prohibitions (Gen. 1:26; 2:16). Assigned to the Sinai event therefore were also

important Old Testament legal collections and series of commandments, including the Decalogue, the Book of the Covenant, and the Holiness Code. By being located in these legal codes, the self-evident understanding of the obligatory will of YHWH has become both word and text. The Covenant Code and all the following legal materials that develop from considerations of ethos and cult are subordinated to the Decalogue which is presented as a kind of declaration of principle. As the crowning and comprehensive conclusion of the obligatory will of YHWH, Deuteronomy at the same time traces its steps back to the Decalogue and its understanding. Now we shall inquire about the more precise nature of obligation in its relationship to election and about the theological place of law, commandment, and divine justice.[298]

a. Law and Legal Sentences

According to the Old Testament, all Israelite law is associated with YHWH, Moses, and Sinai. This association at the same time says something important about the theological place of law. Law has to do not only with human norms[299] but also with the recognition and carrying out of divine will. The God standing behind this jurisprudence and law is characterized as the one who not only delivered his people but at the same time imposed upon them responsibility. What "is just" in Israel must be identified with YHWH, must be of service to his people as the people of YHWH, and must contribute to their formation. This formation according to Deuteronomy involves Israel's becoming a "holy people" (Deut. 7:6; etc.), and according to the Holiness Code (Leviticus 17–26) Israel is to become "holy, for I (YHWH) am holy" (Lev. 19:2; etc.). These features hold true for תורה = tôrâ ("law"), משפטים = mišpāṭîm ("statutes"), הקים = huqqîm ("ordinances"), מצות = miṣwôt ("commandments"), דברים = dĕbārîm ("words"), עדות = 'ēdôt ("decrees"), and many other terms, for Israel could use a variety of words to denote YHWH's instructions (cf. the interchange of terms in Deuteronomy and Psalm 119).

To take a closer look, there are incorporated within the extensive Sinai pericope various legal corpora that, in terms of content and style, are separate and distinct from each other. For example, the Decalogue (Exod. 20:1–17; and Deut. 5:6–21)[300] is separate from the contiguous Covenant Code (Exod. 20:22–23:19). This requires a more precise investigation that determines distinctions in style and content and then arranges the texts in a historical sequence. This in turn leads quickly to the issue, which continues today to be discussed, about the earliest laws in Israel. Various suggestions have been made about where these earliest laws reside: the Covenant Code,[301] the Law of YHWH's Privilege (Exod. 34:10–26), and probably also Deut. 27:16–25 as well as the Decalogue, the older components of Deuteronomy, and the Holiness Code (Leviticus 17–26) which was not completed until at least the period of the exile. There is no doubt that ancient elements may be contained in many texts that comprise the postexilic formulation of the special material of the Priestly source (P^s). During the past several decades, numerous legal collections and documents have been discovered from the cultures of the ancient Near East (in addition to the Code of Hammurabi which has been known for a long time).[302] These discoveries have enriched the study of ancient Israelite law in regard to its form, content, and theological setting.[303] Following a preliminary effort by A. Jepsen in 1927,[304] A. Alt's investigation, which appeared in 1934, has continued to be fundamental to the study of ancient Israelite law.[305] He conducted what was, above all, a form-critical analysis of ancient legal corpora, especially the Decalogue and the Covenant Code, and he discovered that there were two different kinds of law, namely, casuistic and apodictic. He designated as casuistic law[306] ordinances consisting of the description of an offense or a legal case (protasis) and the determination of the legal consequences (apodosis). Casuistic law is formulated in the objective "if style,"[307] meaning that the main clause is introduced by כִּי = kî ("if"), while a resumptive אִם = 'im ("if") introduces any subordinate clause. In addition to Exod. 21:2 and 22:15f., Exod. 21:18f. can serve as an especially instructive example for this point. While today the term "conditional" law is preferred over "casuistic" law,[308] there is a question whether a formal designation of this type of law, namely, מִשְׁפָּטִים = mišpāṭîm ("statutes"; cf. Exod. 21:1), already existed in ancient Israel, as A. Jepsen and A. Alt had assumed. This type of law had to do with the laws concerning male and female slaves, blood justice, bodily injuries, damages to livestock and to fields, offenses against property, pledges, and marriage.[309] The life setting of conditional (casuistic) law was the customary, secular system of jurisprudence and the legal community. Those who had legal rights, say in a village or a clan, came to "the gate" (cf. Ruth 4:1ff.) for the administration of justice.[310] Subsequently, this form of law was common to the ancient Near East and not specifically Israelite. In spite of that, it is not surprising to find some specifically Israelite elements in collections of this type of law. In addition to the inferior legal position of the slaves vis-à-vis the male who was a full citizen, one also has the inferior position of the woman[311] and the legal distinction between Israelites, foreigners, and strangers.[312] However, there is no class justice that would divide the nation even further. In spite of its retention of the death penalty which was often introduced as the legal consequence in casuistic and especially in apodictic law, this penalty was imposed less frequently in Israel than in the surrounding cultures of the ancient Near East,[313] save for Hittite law.

According to A. Alt, there was a special "spokesperson" of casuistic law in Israel, found among the so-called minor judges (Judg. 3:31; 10:1–5; and 12:8–14).[314] With the exception of this last thesis, most of what Alt said about casuistic law is still accepted today and continues to be seen as helpful. At the most, one may make further refinements by pointing, for example, to other literary styles (without an exact protasis and apodosis) combined with the "setting forth of certain legal stipulations" (Exod. 21:2–6),[315] or to the combination of "if . . . " with the form of direct address ("if you . . . ")[316] that first occurs, not in the paraenetic sections dispersed throughout Deuteronomy, but rather already in the Covenant Code (e.g., Exod. 21:2; and 22:24). One also detects a mixed style between casuistic and apodictic language (F. Horst) in prohibitions (W. Richter) that are clothed in case law (see, e.g., Exod. 22:24f.). Through the study of ancient Near Eastern legal collections, one has come to recognize, above all, that the core of casuistic law consists of judgments from earlier legal proceedings. These judgments are then recorded, collected for further use as precedents, and arranged according to rather clear, ascertainable points of view.[317] Alt thought the self-awareness of being the Israelite people that is present in the law as a whole does not affect casuistic legal materials.[318] However, on the basis of more recent studies of the Covenant Code this view is no longer so certain.[319]

Often the very differently formed apodictic law occurs together with casuistic law in many places in the Covenant Code (cf., e.g., Exod. 21:23ff.; and 22:17ff.), even though for A. Alt[320] the form, nature, and life setting of this type of law is entirely different from the other. Thus the provision for retaliation in Exod. 21:23–25 indeed has a protasis, but it continues with a direct address, a feature that is atypical for casuistic law. A legal case and legal consequences are held in tension within a single framework. The formula for retaliation intrudes in a disturbing fashion into a legal form which, in Alt's view, is uniquely Israelite. One finds a similar formulation in Exod. 21:13–14, only here YHWH in the first person appears alongside the "you" of the one addressed. Also in the Covenant Code, two fundamentally different laws collide against each other. In Exod. 21:12 the apodictic style is especially very clear, which is due to the presence of only five Hebrew words and the force of expression that results from these few words: "Whoever strikes a person so that he dies shall be put to death." Furthermore, the content of this apodictic law is fundamentally different from casuistic laws, for its unconditionality looks to YHWH as its source and has in mind the community of the people of Israel.

The same kind of apodictic laws is found elsewhere, including, for example, Exod. 21:15–17. The typical series of apodictic law intentionally does not go beyond ten or twelve commandments and/or prohibitions. Alt finds additional apodictic laws, for example, in Exod. 31:14f. and Lev. 20:2, 9–13, 15f.; 24:16; and 27:29. However, in these texts there are additions that may be ascertained, and the apodictic style, along with the force of its expression, no longer is set forth in its pristine purity. Alt points then to the enumeration of offenses that lead to curses in Deut. 27:15–26, then to Lev. 18:7–17, and finally to the Decalogue, which certainly must be freed from the mass of additions that have been attached to it. The original form of commandment in the Decalogue is brief: "You shall not commit adultery"; "You shall not steal"; etc.[321] Each sentence was to be as clear and at the same time as apodictic as it could be. For Alt, apodictic law concerns crimes worthy of curse and death, but it does not make a connection with the concrete, individual situation. This type of law does not consist of the concrete instructions of secular jurisdiction; rather, it has to do with sacral law that probably, as Deut. 27 and 31:10–13 show, was proclaimed in Israel's cultus by a priestly speaker during the Festival of Tabernacles every seven years when the covenant was renewed. This was the context to which the Decalogue pointed and with which it conformed. Apodictic law leads to the original character of Israel in which everything is "connected with both the Israelite people and the deity Yahweh,"[322] to use the often cited, easily remembered formula. Since apodictic law also compelled the demarcation from Canaanite legal culture and Canaanite faith, both legal systems had to come into conflict in Israel.

In opposition, for example, to J. Wellhausen, there have been efforts to furnish proof for the existence of a "law" already in early Israel. Alt found in apodictic law, as J. Begrich later did in an analogous way in the covenant of grace,[323] something that was shaped by Yahwistic faith and made specifically Israelite. G. von Rad combined Alt's thesis with that of Begrich. Contemporary scholarship, however, has placed in question the theses that derive from these three scholars. Alt had inquired about the law in Israel in terms that were more historical and form critical. G. von Rad and M. Noth introduced, in addition, questions concerning the content and theology of law and justice.

b. Law and Covenant

In "The Form-Critical Problem of the Hexateuch," which appeared in 1938, G. von Rad wrote that Israel's jurisprudence would exist in the place where it ratified its covenant, namely, in cultic celebration. In this regard, he thought in particular of a covenant renewal festival. The entire Pentateuch was viewed by him as a narrative elaboration of the "small, historical creed" (Deut. 26:5b-9), an elaboration due especially to the work of the Yahwist. However, the Sinai tradition is not mentioned in this creed. As regards its traditiohistorical development, this tradition went its own way. Nevertheless, the Sinai tradition may have cultic roots and may reflect in its final form the course of a cultic festival. The course of this festival, which may turn up in Psalms 50 and 81, Joshua 24, and the framework of Deuteronomy, may have included the sequence of the issuance of paraenesis (Exod. 19:4–6), the historical description of the course of events at Sinai (Exodus 19f.), the proclamation of the law (Decalogue and Covenant Code), the promise of blessing (Exod. 23:20ff.), and the ratification of the covenant (Exodus 24). Taken together, these elements may have comprised the legend of the covenant festival of Shechem[324] and thus the Festival of Tabernacles of the old YHWH amphictyony. In this setting, the law would have its life and its roots. While it may be connected to the covenant, the law was not simply a general religious body of knowledge. When one views the overarching structure of the Sinai pericope in the Hexateuch, it becomes clear how the life of the law and covenant derives from and is nourished within God's salvation history performed on behalf of his people. The preamble of the Decalogue (Exod. 20:2 par.) may sum up this understanding in a brief and appropriate manner. By contrast, G. von Rad directs the tradition of the conquest to the sanctuary at Gilgal, where it, along with the "little historical creed," served as the cultic legend of the Festival of Weeks.

The Sinai pericope could quite naturally be taken to be an old festival legend only if one regards its present redactional structure, which includes the Decalogue and the Covenant Code, also to be ancient. That there are problems with this has already been mentioned.[325] The situation is similar in Deuteronomy,[326] where, moreover, the sequence of the individual components of this festival legend are not identical to those in the Sinai pericope. The form-critical essay of G. von Rad, along with its cultic and theological consequences and implications, was influenced by A. Alt and in turn influenced J. Begrich (1944). Together with the now to be mentioned work of M. Noth, "Gesetze im Pentateuch" (1940), these studies developed the comprehensive and impressive picture of the early history of Israel and of the value of the law and the covenant that came together in G. von Rad's *Theology of the Old Testament.*

In his investigation of the "Gesetze im Pentateuch" (1940), M. Noth does not ask how these laws or "the" law may have originated. Indeed, the Old Testament does not even speak of "the" law. Here, he presupposes the work of A. Alt. Noth is not concerned with the origin and development of these laws but rather with the questions concerning their nature, the assumptions behind their existence, the foundation of their life, and their postulated order. What is the order that these laws maintain and preserve? What is the order that creates these laws? The answer (1940 in Germany!) reads: they are not laws of the state; rather, they are related to the greater entity of "Israel." This is true also for the Book of Deuteronomy, in spite of its possible association with the cultic reform of King Josiah (2 Kings 22–23). Israel's fellowship with "Yahweh, the God of Israel," which is addressed in Old Testament laws, now took the form of Israel as an assembly, a sacred band of tribes that are constituted within a common cult celebrated in a common sanctuary.[327] This covenant and its festival in autumn are constitutive for and preliminary to the laws. The laws seek to preserve the covenant and to defend the sacral fundamental orders of the greater entity of "Israel."[328] A lengthy citation from Noth can illustrate all of this in an exemplary fashion: "Here, having gone into so many individual points, some examples will once more make clear in conclusive fashion the content of Old Testament laws. They will make clear how little these laws could be understood as state statutes and how inappropriate they would have been for the larger regions that had a uniform 'Canaanite' population with extensive states existing in the territory of the Israelite people. They will make clear how much more these laws push decisively a cultic or 'theological' perspective into the center. And they will demonstrate how the existing institution of the sacral league of the twelve tribes is the assumed order of things and serves as the background for the laws."[329] In any event, this is the way it may have been, according to Noth, in the preexilic period. Because of both the prophetic preaching of judgment and the exile, a crisis developed that led to the end of the sacred tribal league and finally to the reversal of conditions in the postexilic community. In this community, the observance of the commandments was no longer subject to the ancient, extant sacral order. Rather, now the observance of the commandments is directed toward the law as an absolute entity that holds the primary position in life. Standing close to J. Wellhausen, Noth argued that it was here that the "Law" of Judaism originated.[330] This view of the postexilic period that in general values the "Law" is often and correctly disputed in modern scholarship.[331]

A. Alt had brought together law and covenant in his form-critical assessment of apodictic law and his view of its "life setting." G. von Rad had underscored this cultic association and had extended it form-critically, traditiohistorically, and theologically. M. Noth had followed up this cultic formulation by enriching it both sociologically and theologically. What J. Begrich wrote in 1944 melded well with these observations. While often looking at what his predecessors had written about apodictic law, he extended these views in pointing to what was specifically Israelite in both the assignment of law to the cultic phenomenon of Israel and the covenant of grace. The law was enfolded by the covenant, indeed absorbed by it. It ordered the existence of the covenant people and functioned to keep and preserve this order. The law was the expression of the gracious covenant will of YHWH, at least in Israel's earlier and preexilic period. All of these efforts were combined then into an impressive whole in G. von Rad's *Theology of the Old Testament* (vol. 1,1962). It is not unimportant to note that von Rad was often guided, not only by his "Form-Critical Problem of the Pentateuch" but also by several of his individual studies on Deuteronomy in dealing with the problem of the theological evaluation of Old Testament law.[332] Where and how far von Rad was indebted in this area to the aforementioned works of his predecessors is not a question to be pursued here. Nonetheless, there are some striking statements that may be put together to make especially clear von Rad's view of the theological value of Old Testament law.

With the proclamation of the Decalogue to Israel, election is realized. "The proclamation of the divine will for justice is like a net thrown over Israel: it is the completion of her conveyance to Jahweh."[333] Thus Israel understood and celebrated the revelation of the commandments as a salvific event of the first order. "The covenant is made, and with it Israel receives the revelation of the commandments."[334] These commandments were not intended to be normative law; rather, they demanded much more a confession of YHWH in certain defining moments. Thus the Decalogue, to a certain degree, set up on the borders of a wide circle signs for life to which the one "who belongs to Jahweh"[335] gave heed. Through reflecting on the Decalogue, one also considered what it meant to abstain from certain practices that displeased YHWH. Such demands were taken to be "easily fulfilled." "Israel only encountered the law in its function as judge and destroyer at the time of the preaching of the prophets."[336] Otherwise, one should not speak of the "Law" in looking at the Old Testament. Naturally Israel should keep these commandments, as, for example, Deuteronomy 27 makes clear in directing words of curse against the violator.[337] Last of all, the Law in the Old Testament is, according to von Rad, *paraclesis*. The Law does not place in question the message of salvation. "It is a special form of comforting or hortatory address to such as have already received the word of salvation."[338] The Law as the demand of God that brings death to human beings is first articulated in the preaching of the prophets.[339] The prophets operated with this completely new understanding of the Law, where, for example, oppression of the poor results in all Israel's receiving the death sentence. Israel has not been a failure as concerns the Law; rather, it has failed to enact YHWH's will for salvation. According to the eighth-century prophets, this sin is shown to be "immediate sin against God's saving action, and not against a law of judgment which stands over against this saving action."[340] G. von Rad refers expressly to Deuteronomy when he states: "The threat to Israel's state of grace does not come from the law."[341] However, is this accurate even for Deuteronomy?

In Deuteronomy it is clear that the law is absorbed by the "covenant," and that obligation is absorbed by election. The law becomes in actuality the form of the gospel.[342] Here Karl Barth's influence may be obvious, a point that also can be emphasized in the discussions of scholarly works over the years. Jews often emphasize that law and grace are not in opposition. Other scholars also have treated this theme in a similar fashion.[343] The problem today exists in the fact that many of the previously mentioned presuppositions of this view have been placed in question. These debated presuppositions include the evaluation of covenantal theology, the theological place of the law in the Old Testament, apodictic law, Israel as a cultic amphictyony, and the relationship of festival, cult, and law. Also questioned is the combination of conclusions about these matters in works like von Rad's *Old Testament Theology* that have exerted great influence.

c. Differentiations

In starting with the problem of apodictic law,[344] one determines first off that this type of law may no longer be viewed as "confined to the people of Israel and to the deity Yahweh" (A. Alt). Rather, ancient Near Eastern parallels exhibit a similar form. These include Hittite contract texts,[345] Mesopotamian royal decrees, oral proclamations of royal policies, public pronouncements of legal testaments,[346] and Egyptian "proscription texts."[347] As a whole, Israel's law belongs in a significant way to the legal context of the ancient Near East, even when the specificity of Israelite law can be determined by comparison to the legal texts that originate within this larger environment. The uniqueness of Israel includes the fact that the Israelite king, in contrast to monarchs of the ancient Near East, did not function as a lawgiver. Another contrast is that one does not find in Israel the ideology of a "world order" that shaped the character of Israelite law.[348] The authority that is named, and not simply implicitly presupposed, who transmits the law is YHWH. He not only sets forth the law but also demands obedience to it.

It has become clear that the law that Alt designated as apodictic is not uniform but rather comprises a diversity of expressions. One expression is the clear and brief apodictic style of "you shall . . . (not)." However, one cannot easily assign to apodictic law legal cases that, in general terms, speak of certain crimes and their perpetrators in participial or relative clauses: "who does so and so . . . "; or "the one who . . . " Furthermore, the transitions between casuistic and apodictic law are also fluid (cf. Exod. 21:12). This is likewise true of the so-called "law of death,"[349] that is, a "case" that defines a situation and sets forth a declaration of the death penalty (cf., e.g., Exod. 21:15, 17; 22:17–19; 31:14f.; Lev. 20:2–27), and it is the case with Old Testament curses.[350] In addition, the formula of *lex talionis* (Exod. 21:23–25 par.)[351] is no longer assigned to the category of the apodictic legal style,[352] as Alt had done.[353] It is also debated as to whether the actual apodictic legal statements (were they designated in Israel with the term חֻקִּים = *ḥuqqîm*?) really had their origins in the cult, although it is probable that they were recited in the cult. Their origins, that is, their original "life situation," have been sought by G. Fohrer and E. Gerstenberger[354] in (nomadic? cf. Jer. 35:6f.) clan wisdom, meaning that this type of law could not be designated as cultic, sacral law. Rather, the family father or the clan elders were the authority standing behind these legal statements. In his social-historical inquiry, K. Elliger had already assumed such a background for the legal statements, similar to the Decalogue, that concern the extended family in Leviticus 18.[355] Further, the designation "apodictic *law*" is rightly questioned, since one does not have in the apodictic statements concrete law but rather in fact apodictic principles that, as basic norms,[356] precede the law and actuate its development. These fundamental norms are shaped more in the fashion of common rules of morality and be-

havior, something shown by the fact that their predominant form is the prohibition.[357] "Apodictic" and "casuistic" function in relationship to each other primarily as the fundamental principles of law and their application to life. Apodictic prohibitions (אל = lō', "no," with the indicative, but without justification)
are to be differentiated from the vetitives (אל = 'al, "no," with the jussive and
often with an explanation) that are similar to sapiential admonitions.[358] Wisdom and law are created from the same sources, but formally they do not travel
exactly the same path.

More precise form-critical refinements have been made, since Alt's significant study. These refinements indicate that his categories are neither sufficient
nor correct.[359] Apodictic law is now seen to be more the legal *foundation* of
the clan and then of the basic community.[360] Casuistic law, originating probably out of judicial proceedings, concerns the settlement of legal cases and has
in mind everyday life in Israelite society. In this setting, there is still no question of obedience to God. Apodictic law, by contrast, sets forth the basic norms
of the common life. Apodictic law takes these norms initially from the family
and then from the legal community that transcends the family. Apodictic law
establishes "the juridical boundary for the legal administration of death and ensures the fundamental norms of both the common life and the survival of the
family through the death sanction."[361] This type of law seeks to protect society and to enable people to internalize its content. Later on, this law becomes
a part of Yahweh faith and is associated with the will of God and the sphere of
sacral law. The speaker of apodictic law becomes the divine "I."

That sacral law was viewed originally as the "law of Yahweh's privilege"
may be especially ascertained by looking at Exod. 34:10–26 (27).[362] For Israel,
the God who issues demands in this context (see vv. 17, 20c, 21ab, 26b set
forth partially in apodictic language) is a "jealous God" (Exod. 34:14b). The
Covenant Code, by contrast, is not a self-contained entity created by a single
process of formation; rather, it has different strata and groupings of texts that
are to be differentiated. Alongside the more secular, casuistic statements of law
(above all in Exod. 21:1–22:19) are cultic stipulations that are close to the "law
of YHWH's privilege" in Exod. 34:10ff. Accordingly, the Covenant Code already gives evidence of the bringing together of sacral law with "secular" law.
In addition, this legal collection not only is permeated by social and economic
relationships but also reflects a later theological development in Israelite law
that points at least to the beginning of the Israelite monarchy. It is clear that
YHWH as the only God of Israel already stands in the background of this legal code,[363] and at times one notes a theological rationale in the Covenant Code
that continues on in Deuteronomy and the Holiness Code. This theological rationale comes not only from Israel's "salvation history" but also from the character of this people and its God and from the announcements of salvation and
disaster that are connected with and result from keeping or violating the law.[364]

In addition to the above, there are more recent differentiations more oriented to form-critical concerns that also set forth the theological inferences of Israelite law. And there are other observations that are in a position to make more precise the theological portrait of "law" in the Old Testament and to correct the earlier representations.

W. Zimmerli critically engaged G. von Rad's understanding and subsequently raised general and important questions for the understanding of the law in the Old Testament.[365] To begin with, Zimmerli pointed to the problem of the relationship of the "law" to the preaching of the prophets. According to Zimmerli, Moses in von Rad's view becomes an evangelist who proclaims the gospel, but, by contrast, the prophets become the Pauline Moses, that is, a proclaimer of the law.[366] For Zimmerli, however, already within the older collections of law, as well as according to the preaching of the prophets[367] who consequently bring nothing fundamentally new to the understanding (cf. Isa. 1:10, 16f.; Jer. 2:8; 7:9; Hos. 4:1f., 6; Amos 5:14f., 24; and Micah 2:2, 9; 6:8), "law" is a commandment "that has the power to expel individuals or the entire nation of Israel from the covenant."[368] For Zimmerli, Israel's law is always very much bound up with curse (cf. Gal. 3:10, 13). He points expressly and emphatically to this theological connection of law and curse.[369] G. von Rad had also seen "that refusal to accept the commandments brought the curse of Jahweh,"[370] yet he did not fully draw the necessary theological consequences. In this connection, one can and must point once more to the so-called law of death already[371] contained in the Covenant Code.[372] This threatening function of Old Testament law is more than made clear here and elsewhere (cf. also Gen. 9:6). And in Exod. 23:20–33, while not placed within the categories of "blessing and curse," there is the very emphatic call to obedience accompanied by the reference to the care and help of YHWH (cf. Exod. 34:10ff.). Beside these examples stand the often very comprehensive series of curses, including Deut. 27:15–26 and vv. 3–6 and 16–19 in the rather extensive chapter of curses in Deuteronomy 28. In these series, Israel recognized the necessity of considering itself as standing under the divine curse. In Deut. 27:15–26, vv. 15 and 26 have a different syntactic structure than the larger textual section that they encompass. This text forms a Decalogue of curses that intentionally stands at the end of the corpus of the laws of Deuteronomy even as the actual Decalogue stands before this corpus.[373] The object that is designated by such curses stands automatically under the powerful word of curse. This word of curse issues in the performance of some action, is judged as realistic language, and, last of all, has as its subject YHWH himself. Those who are cursed stand under the calamity of their own act.[374] Those cursed stand accordingly within the sphere of evil and are consequently excluded from community with YHWH as well as from their interpersonal groups, including the people of God. Series of curses and of judgments requiring death are very similar not only in terms of form but also in terms of content. In the curse series, there "occurs . . . also a collection of capital offenses for intertribal justice in nomadic law."[375] Both series of laws have to do with exclusion from the community's sphere of salvation. The transgression of only one of these laws signifies abandonment of covenant loyalty, and along with that apostasy, curse, and judgment. The validity of the covenant depends upon the obedience of the human partner of YHWH. The enjoining of God's will is found already in the "law of YHWH's privilege" (Exod. 34:12, 14f.) and in the Covenant Code (Exod. 21:12, 15–17). "A commandment is not only the occasion to confess Yahweh in situations on the boundary (von Rad). A commandment can also unexpectedly lead to the place where the curse emerges within the sphere of the covenant."[376] With this the question arises as to whether transgression or curse can lead to the endangerment and termination of the covenant. The prophets, as well as the Old Testament curses themselves, clearly answer this question in the affirmative.

"Thus, through the pronouncement of the divine commandment that encounters it, Israel comes to stand in a peculiar position. Israel hears in the proclamation of God's law that confronts it the remembrance of God's great act of grace, for God is the one who led Israel out of slavery in Egypt and made it into the people of God. This is the means by which Israel became God's own, a God who is long-suffering, rich in benevolence, and will bless abundantly. Israel is, at the same time, the possession of God, who is jealous in carrying out his will and will not be patient when his people become disobedient and begin to abhor him."[377] Both of these features must be kept together if one wishes to understand correctly the Old Testament witness to the theological significance of the law of YHWH. "The God of Israel, by whose gracious gift Old Testament faith continues to live, also remains at all times the merciless one in his holy will. However, the one affirmation should not be dissipated by the other. Ancient Israel lives within the tension between these two affirmations."[378] Israel should "listen to YHWH's voice," as, above all, the Deuteronomic movement formulates it.[379] The strand of Deuteronomistic literature that is particularly interested in the law presents the role of the law and obedience in these Deuteronomistic contexts and in so doing sets forth its own emphases (as, e.g., in Josh. 1:7f.; 23:6, 13, 15f.; 1 Sam. 12:9–25; 1 Kings 9:1–9; cf. also Amos 2:4f. = Deuteronomistic). However, this strand of Deuteronomistic literature also stresses in its own fashion only what has always been positioned within YHWH faith. The communion given by YHWH seeks acknowledgment by human beings, while divine election seeks human acceptance and the response of obedience. " Torah" is instruction for life in the form of the teaching and will of YHWH expressed in the Covenant Code, the Holiness Code, Deuteronomy, and the Pentateuchal assemblage of legal collections overall. At the same time, however, "Torah" is also a demanding and punishing law.

According to Isa. 2:2–4 (v. 3) and Micah 4:1–4 (v. 2), the "Torah" that goes forth from Zion and is sought there by the nations does not speak of the curse against the law's transgressors. This "Zion Torah" did not possess the important and qualitatively transformative significance in the Old Testament that from time to time the "Torah of Sinai" did.[380] However, one should not ignore the obedience that this latter "Torah" requires.

The close, external as well as internal connection between covenant and law, from the "revelation of Yahweh's nature" and "will"[381] to divine gift and thus consequent obligation, is made clear in the Priestly document[382] through the purposeful combination of historical narrative and legal stipulations (cf. in Gen. 1:1–2:4a, creation and Sabbath; in Exodus 12, exodus and Passover). Covenant is not as significant without law, and law is not as significant without covenant. Election cannot be viewed apart from obligation. Moreover, as is true in the covenant of Noah in Genesis 9 and the covenant of Abraham in Genesis 17, the particular emphasis of a bĕrît ("covenant, obligation") is placed on the related features of grace and law. This dual nature of covenant is stressed through the attribution of its "commandments" to the cult,[383] understood especially as the atoning means of YHWH's salvation. This character of the cult is attributed to the gracious will of YHWH. Exodus 24:15–18 and 25:8, and then 29:42–46 and 40:34f., are the most important texts that frame and structure the priestly giving of the cultic law.

The intrinsic relationship between "covenant" and "law" has been underscored by consideration of the Hittite (fifteenth to thirteenth centuries B.C.E.) and, above all, the Neo-Assyrian (ninth to seventh centuries, B.C.E.) treaties.[384] One has seen in them the so-called "covenant formula" and has drawn upon them to interpret Old Testament texts (Exodus 19; Joshua 24) or corpora of texts (the Sinai tradition; Deuteronomy). Although the Hittite texts, for example, had been known for a long time, it was not until G. Mendenhall (1960) that the connection was made with the study of the covenant. Then, in a more detailed way, K. Baltzer used these treaties in interpreting various Old Testament texts, while W. Beyerlin used these ancient Near Eastern documents to explain the Sinai tradition. Beyerlin presented the close relationship between merciful adjudication and demand, a relationship that in actuality is embodied in the exodus tradition and the giving of the law. Today, this covenant formula of the treaties still has a great significance for N. Lohfink and G. Braulik in their interpretation of Deuteronomy, which they regard as a kind of "counter treaty" against the demands of the Assyrian treaty imposed on Judah: Israel is under obligation to YHWH, not to the Assyrian emperor.

The critics of these views, especially G. Fohrer, F. Nötscher, and D. J. McCarthy, have asked whether the Old Testament texts and groups of texts actually correspond form critically to this "covenant formula." We cannot go any deeper into this scholarly debate, but we can say that what can be generally shown is the fact that in these vassal or suzerainty treaties the supreme emperor, who is presented mostly in a preamble and who mentions the prehistory of the new treaty, granted a "covenant" (treaty) to his lower-placed vassal and promised, for example, to defend him. At the same time, the vassal who received this gift is obligated to be obedient to the principal demands of the individual commandments. Since the "covenant" could be dissolved by the vassal by being disobedient, sanctions were imposed by the emperor. In effect this could mean: "Observe this treaty and do not transgress your covenant, so that you will not lose your life."[385] Gods were called on to serve as witnesses to these treaties. Blessing and curse were respectively desired and threatened. Periodic readings of the treaties were required. One should not overlook the structural relationship between these (especially Neo-Assyrian) treaties and Old Testament covenant and legal thought.[386] It is certainly not fortuitous that through these ancient Near Eastern texts one of the substantial theological breakthroughs in the problem of covenant, election, law, and responsibility in Deuteronomy and the related strata produced by the Deuteronomistic movement has occurred.

J. Begrich's alternative between a covenant of grace that contains no obligation, on the one hand, and a contractual covenant, on the other hand, shows itself once more to be too narrow. There is the covenant that is promised and granted, and yet at the same time it is combined with the announcement of responsibility. So one must hold fast to Zimmerli's statement: "The election of Israel is unthinkable without the validity of its divine law and the concealed, threatening judgment within this law."[387] "In retrospect, however, it may become clear that the radical interpretation of the Old Testament as 'Law,' as people from Marcion down to Hirsch have tried to do, is as little justified an interpretation of the Old Testament as its being a pure word of grace, a dangerous understanding appearing on the periphery of the latest phase of Old Testament research."[388]

According to the various strata of Deuteronomy[389] that have discernible nuances in their assessment of the "law," the greatly paraenetically enriched law is given "for life," "for your good" (Deut. 10:13), and also for a long and good life in the good land (Deut. 5:33; 7:12ff.; 11:8ff.; 30:11ff., 15ff.; 32:47; etc.). At the same time, one finds in the same biblical book discussion of extermination (Deuteronomy 13) and curse (Deuteronomy 27–28). The law becomes also a "witness against you" (Deut. 31:26). Whether the law may be given for "life" or for "death" is one of the tensions that Old Testament Israel experienced. Ezekiel 18:9, 17, 23; and 20:11 stand over against Ezek. 20:25f.,[390] while Ezra 7:27 with its "to praise" contrasts with Neh. 8:9–12 and the lamenting that is mentioned there. According to Josh. 24:19, Israel cannot serve YHWH at all, for he is holy and jealous and shall not forgive. Deuteronomy 9:4–6 stresses expressly the deficient "righteousness" of the Israel who is addressed.[391]

However, according to Jer. 31:31–34, redacted by Deuteronomistic editors, YHWH will write the Torah of his new covenant on the hearts of the people and will forgive them. Their hearts will also be purified of guilt, for they will correspond anew with the will of God. Israel saw itself in terms of both election and obligation and as standing under promise and commandment. Israel's hope was also dependent on the belief that when YHWH would consummate his covenant with them, in the form of the new covenant, they could at the same time fully comply with his demanding will (cf. also Ezek. 36:26f.; 37:24; and Deut. 30:6).

Contemporary readers of the Old Testament perhaps may wonder at the fact that cultic instructions not only stand beside ethical instructions in Old Testament legal collections but also are not distinguished by being given less value or importance. According to the understanding of the Old Testament, there exists no distinction in value between the two. Cultic rituals and sacrificial laws (Leviticus 1–7; Numbers 28–29), stipulations about the construction of a sanctuary (Exodus 25–31) and their execution (Exodus 35–40), and stipulations concerning purity and laws of cereal offerings (Leviticus 11–15; Deuteronomy 14) stand beside ethical instructions. In their present context, these cultic laws are closely connected to the ethical instructions. This is the case in the law of YHWH's privilege (Exod. 34:10–27), the Covenant Code (Exod. 22:19, 28–30 and 23:14ff.), Deuteronomy, and the Holiness Code (Leviticus 18–19 in Leviticus 17–26). In addition, these cultic stipulations seek to shape, preserve, and continue to purify the people of God according to the will of YHWH.[392]

What Deuteronomy (Deut. 23:4–9) and the Holiness Code commanded, namely, that the exilic and postexilic communities of Israel ought to live as a holy people separated from the nations and their customs, was not completely followed. For example, mixed marriages are reported in Ezra (Ezra 9:1–5). The community is, however, ready to dissolve these marriages, is obligated to do so, and complies with this responsibility in spite of minor opposition (Ezra 10:1–6; 7–17). According to Neh. 7:72b–8:8, Ezra read "the book of the law of Moses" during a festival before the assembly of the people, while the Levites instructed the people more precisely in this law. Which book Ezra read on this occasion is not known and therefore is debated. Many scholars argue for the Book of Deuteronomy, while others suggest it was the entire Pentateuch.[393] Thus the written law as a book obtained its generally binding position of honor and probably also its place in worship centered on the Torah and the word. It is stressed repeatedly that this law was a reason for rejoicing (Neh. 8:10ff.). The people's festive commitment to follow this law brings everything to conclusion (Nehemiah 10). The reference to joy, the positive assessment of the "law" in Psalms 1; 19b; and 119,[394] and the relation of the law to laudatory worship in the Books of Chronicles[395] allow one to surmise that the postexilic period was not and could not be strictly a period of rigidity and fossilization.[396] Ezra 7 shows how the "law" of Israel, also called the "wisdom of your (Ezra's) God," becomes recognized by the Persians as a law of the empire (vv. 12–16) and for Israel a law that is binding, threatening (v. 26), and to be taught (v. 25). Now the older, different legal collections are brought together and then bound into a new unity as the Pentateuch, which contains the two main areas of law and history.[397]

The historical work of 1 and 2 Chronicles[398] presupposes an already written Torah of YHWH (or of God, of Moses; 1 Chron. 22:12; 2 Chron. 17:9; 23:18; 25:4; 34:21; Neh. 8:18; etc.) that is of "interest to the Chronicler first as the norm that regulates and supports the cult of Yahweh in Jerusalem"[399] and, then, as "the evidence and sign of the continuing election of Israel" that still maintains "its function of accusation and conviction of guilt."[400] The content deals with the rejection of foreign cults, the exclusive worship of YHWH in Jerusalem, and material as well as technical security and organization (cf. also Ezekiel 40–48 and Mal. 3:6–12). Deuteronomy, the Deuteronomistic History, and Priestly concerns were taken up in the Books of Chronicles and absorbed.

The Old Testament wisdom literature, when confined to Job, Proverbs, and Qoheleth, is silent about the "covenant" as well as the "law of YHWH." The combination of "law" and "wisdom" (see only Deut. 4:[5] 6–8),[401] for which the (sapiential?) tribal ethos perhaps paved the way, was clearly consummated in Deuteronomy both in terms of theme and literary character. This combination is developed in Ezra 7:25, the postexilic Psalms 1; 19 (B); and 119, and Ben Sirah (Sirach 24; etc.). By bringing the Torah of YHWH within its confines, wisdom is enriched and is given a more precise location within the sphere of Yahwistic faith. Now wisdom seeks more clearly after the will of YHWH, while at the same time the Torah through wisdom becomes a cosmic law.

3.7 Moses: His Place and the Problem of the Founding and Revealing of a Religion

All of the sources of the Pentateuch show the person of Moses[402] in the center of the events that are associated with the exodus, Sinai, and wilderness journey (cf. also 1 Sam. 12:6, 8; 1 Kings 8:53 = Deuteronomistic). He experienced his call from YHWH (Exodus 3 + 6), was the intercessor at the deliverance at the sea (Exodus 14) as well as during the theophany on Mt. Sinai (Exodus 19), towered over others with spiritual endowment (Numbers 11), and stood like no other in a direct relationship with YHWH (Exod. 33:11; and Num. 12:8).

In following M. Noth and G. von Rad, one speaks in this regard mostly of four tradition complexes in which Moses appears: the exodus from Egypt, the guidance through the wilderness, the revelation at Sinai, and the entrance into the land of Canaan. M. Noth and G. von Rad,[403] who largely agrees with him, have asked in which of these four traditions may Moses originally have been at home.[404] They argue the following about Moses. That he is encountered in all of these traditions may be the result of harmonization. Since both scholars point to an original separation of these traditions (e.g., the exodus from Sinai), Moses cannot have been firmly anchored for this reason within several of them. In the creedal text of Deut. 26:5ff. his name is missing, while in Josh. 24:5 it may be an addition. Moses appears to be anchored in the Sinai tradition in only the loosest of manners. Here nothing is said about him, beyond what is said about his role as spokesman and leader. Also, he may have had no particular relationship to the exodus, for there the only things that are said about him relate to what he did and said after he once had grown into the role of leader. Moses cannot possibly belong to the Kadesh tradition (Exodus 17–18; Numbers 13–14), since M. Noth even disputed that this was actually a tradition. The theme "guidance in the wilderness" may be then only a composite of individual legends in which Moses once again may have played the typical roles of speaker, intercessor, and leader. Furthermore, he may not have been especially anchored in Exod. 17:8ff. (the battle with the Amalekites). His marriage with a foreign woman (Exod. 2:16ff.; cf. Num. 12:1) certainly may well be a kind of very early element of the tradition. Only this woman was no Midianite. The marriage with a Midianite woman appears to have developed from the later combination with the tradition of the mountain of God (Exodus 18). The most original element may have been only the tradition of the grave of Moses (Deuteronomy 34), for even a tradition of a grave may show most clearly where a figure may have belonged originally. However, Moses may have been inserted secondarily into the tradition complex of the entrance into the land of Canaan that became associated with the tradition of the grave. This tradition of the grave was added, because Moses' grave lay on the journey of the Israelites on their way to conquer Canaan. Therefore, what we actually know about Moses and what exists about him in the relatively complete form available to us had to have spun out of the tradition of his burial.

Criticism of these views has rightly been voiced, and John Bright caustically could remark: "Thus it would seem that all we know surely of the historical Moses is that he died—which, if one may be pardoned a flippancy, would seem to be a reasonable assumption."[405] Still, it should be clear that one must not simply conclude, on the other hand, that Moses was indeed liberator, organizer, lawgiver, founder of a religion, and many other things.

However, one should raise important questions about Noth's and von Rad's critical view of Moses. The absence of the name of Moses in the creed of Deut. 26:5ff. signifies nothing at all, since this text sets forth the confession of the salvific acts of YHWH. Indeed, no human name is mentioned at all (cf. only v. 5). Why must what is said about Moses go beyond the description of his role as speaker and leader? Perhaps this is who Moses actually was. *Why* did Moses grow into a tradition in which he was not indigenous? Furthermore, is the separation of the four mentioned traditions justified, since all of them, without exception, are directed at the entrance into the land of Canaan under the guidance of the God YHWH and speak both of YHWH and of Moses? Was Moses not perhaps exactly what M. Noth denied he was, namely, a so-called menial intercessor, a spokesman of YHWH, his mouthpiece and interpreter? What does one make of the connection of the Egyptian name of Moses with the milieu described in Exodus 1–2 and the exodus out of Egypt? Already in the Yahwist,[406] Moses is present as a kind of "inspired shepherd" (G. von Rad) in all of the traditions and functions above all as an announcer and interpreter of deliverance (Exod. 3:16f.; and 14:13f.), as intercessor (Exod. 8:26; 9:28f.; and Num. 11:11), and as a mediator with functions of a deliverer, while YHWH alone is the leader of the nation and the miracle worker. The Elohist sets forth Moses in the form of a leader (Exod. 3:10, 12), a personality who was himself preeminent among the prophets (Num. 11:25ff.; and 12:7), an intercessor (Exod. 20:19), and also one who provided instruction (Exod. 18:19f.). According to Deuteronomy, Moses is, as a "prophet" (Deut. 18:15; and 34:10), the typical interpreter of the Torah (Deut. 1:5; and 18:18), and once more is the prototype of the true prophets. It is only through him that YHWH speaks to his people (Deut. 5:20–26). However, Moses is also an intercessor for Israel (3:24f.; and 9:25–29; cf. chap. 32 and Jer. 15:1) who is even ready to suffer and die for his people (Deut. 3:23ff.). Similarly, Deuteronomy and Deuteronomic texts place him within the so-called murmuring tradition (Exod. 15:22–26; Num. 11:1–3; 14; 21:4–9; cf. also Exod. 32:11–13),[407] where he is often designated as the "servant of YHWH" (Num. 12:7; cf. Josh. 1:1f., 7). According to the Priestly document,[408] Moses alone is given the role of engaging in conversation with YHWH. He is the only and necessary intercessor between YHWH and the people (Exod. 24:15b–18a and 34:29ff.; then see Exod. 12:28; 29:42; Lev. 8:36; and Deut. 34:9b). He receives, however, Aaron the priest at his side, who, during the plagues, functions as a miracle worker, although the plagues are understood to be the mighty displays of YHWH's power. However, both Moses and Aaron were also designated as sinners who, because of their sins, were not allowed to enter into the promised land (Num. 20:10f.). Moses delivered to his successor Joshua his vital force (Num. 27:20) and imparted wisdom to him (Deut. 34:9).

Therefore Moses evidently was or at least was supposed to have been many things: seer, prophet, intercessor, lawgiver, interpreter of the law, and mediator. Above all, however, he was a charismatic figure, that is, a person overcome and seized by Yahweh,[409] and Yahweh's spokesperson who promised and explained the redemption of the exodus event that the exodus group would experience. His interpretation of what happened brings about the interaction of word and event both here and throughout the remainder of the Old Testament. This interpretation of the exodus event made it the foundational faith of Israel, its primal experience, and its primal election.[410]

Thus it is always right to emphasize that, even when scholars continue to debate the historicity of Moses for whatever reasons, they still must discover, whether they like it or not, another figure to perform his functions. This is not to say, naturally, that the historicity of the entire Moses tradition should be defended, but it is to say that we have here narratives that encompass history (G. Fohrer). It is the case that Moses is firmly anchored in the so-called Midianite stratum (Exod. 2:11–4:25; 18). Belonging to a group in later Israel that for a time resided in Egypt, Moses bore an abbreviated Egyptian name, therefore probably was raised in an Egyptian environment, and then was closely tied to the events of the exodus from Egypt as the one who announced and interpreted them. He came to know YHWH on the Midianite mountain of God[411] (Exodus 3),[412] married a Midianite woman (a narrative feature incomprehensible in a later time), proclaimed this YHWH (who was probably also worshiped by the Midianites) as the God delivering the exodus group, and led this group to this very same mountain of God in order to bring them into a responsible relationship with this very same YHWH. Thus Moses was the mediator between Midian and Israel, between YHWH and the exodus, and between the exodus and Sinai.

This search for Moses has led now to a further implication of meaning and to results that are worthy of discussion. If Moses (in following M. Noth) was not original to the traditions that have been mentioned, if he, moreover, was neither a leader nor a spokesman for YHWH, then he would be eliminated as a possible founder of a religion. In this way, then, he would be "dead." If so, how could the origin and development of the faith of Israel be explained?

K. Koch has taken up this question. If Moses is and continues to be "dead" when it comes to his being a founder of religion[413] and if Abraham cannot be regarded as a founder of religion, then the question arises: "How therefore did the exceptional character of Israel originate, an exceptional character primarily seen in terms of its relationship with God? Evidently, it was through multifaceted processes that reached far back into the past that finally led to the constitution of a twelve tribe league in Shechem and to the obligation of the exclusive worship of Yahweh."[414] Three traditions coalesced that are the main roots of this development: the exodus, the event of Sinai, and the early ancestors. However, these were not all the elements that formed the religion of Israel, for other things were added, including the Hittite covenant formula, the concept of holy war, the ark with its accompanying theology, and other things as well. Eventually these different elements came together in forming Israel's religion.[415] However, the whole is also greater than its parts, for all of these parts continued to be shaped increasingly into an Israelite expression. Continuing to contribute to the development of this religion were outside influences, including, for example, Jebusite cult traditions, Phoenician ideas about the temple, and Egyptian rituals of kingship. *"Without these influences from the outside and the proceedings from within* (which they occasioned), *the faith of Israel would not have grown as it did* (until the days of Jesus)."[416] Israel's exceptional character is not conceivable apart from its historical framework. This revelation of the course of a history with many streams encompasses the breadth of human life and not simply the experiences of a single person, as, for instance, Moses. Revelation takes place as history (cf. W. Pannenberg), and Israel's uniqueness consists of the fact "that the people of *election* alone *understood* the things that only *happen to* other peoples, with the result that in history fate becomes destiny."[417]

F. Baumgärtel has vehemently and probably quite correctly rejected Koch's position. Koch's essay clearly demonstrates the limits of traditiohistorical criticism. The uniqueness of Israel's religion may not have developed over a long period of time. Rather, this uniqueness may have been a characteristic feature of Israelite religion from its very beginning, thus separating it from the other religions of the ancient Near East (cf. God as a jealous God; the first and second commandments; etc.). Influences from the outside are not sufficient to explain these unique features, since external forces are not always appropriated. Indeed, they are either reshaped or at times rejected. Even if one today may see many things differently (e.g., see the first or second commandment), the central question of Baumgärtel still continues to be as legitimate now as it was before: how and in what respect was Israel's understanding of revelation unique?[418]

What is central to the Old Testament understanding of God may not be necessarily explained as the result of evolution. And the course of events within history and as history might not be comprehensible when personal forces and decisions are excluded.[419] Israel's ideas of God do not take shape without the involvement of concrete persons and their decisions of faith. External history and internal history are not separable. To this end, Baumgärtel cites N. Söderblom: "It cannot be stressed strongly enough that Yahweh and Israel's religious history remain a complex enigma to the historian without the figure of Moses. Indeed, Moses would have to be invented, if the tradition did not speak of him. To wish to explain this most original and most distinctive revelatory religion by rejecting the giver of revelation and then developing some other person psychologically speaking is critically shortsighted. This would result only in confusing the account instead of simplifying it. If Yahweh should become the God of the prophets and of world religion, then his revelation must first have encountered the spirit of Moses."[420] In this regard, it is no accident that the Old Testament speaks of Moses as a prophet (Deut. 34:10; cf. 18:15; Hos. 12:14; and Num. 12:2–8).

One can add to this that language about revelation, biblically speaking, always encompasses three factors: an event, an interpretation in which the event becomes word, and the personal wonderment of the witnessing of the word. Language about God is chiefly language originating within and issuing from both personal wonderment and a setting of disclosure. Individual testimony is the inextirpable, personal feature of revelation. In addition, the coalescence of tradition does not take shape and come together without bearers of tradition and interpreters. Whether one is able to speak or not of the founding of a religion at the time of the origin of Israel's faith in Yahweh may remain a secondary question. The figure of Moses, nevertheless, may not be removed from the event decisive for Israel's faith. Rather, this figure finds in this event his historical and theological location that is essential for who and what he is.[421]

Whether one actually can obtain even more information from the witnesses of the Old Testament about the religion of the time of Moses is a questionable matter in contemporary scholarship. For example, it is most improbable that sacrifices would not have been offered in this period in spite of the testimonies of Amos 5:25 and Jer. 7:23f. to the contrary. Indeed, the biblical texts from a later period present a particular view of this earlier epoch within the framework of a certain design for a sacrificial cult (cf. also Exod. 24:5, 11b). Furthermore, it is debated as to how old the two symbols of guidance, the tent and the ark, actually are.[422] That the guiding deity of the Moses group was only *one* deity is more than probable. However, the lack of Old Testament witnesses from the early period itself prohibits our knowing whether there existed at this time the exclusive worship of this God (YHWH) as expressed later in the first commandment and whether this deity was already worshiped in an imageless form.

3.8   Yahweh's Will Requires Responsibility

Now it is time to investigate more precisely the Decalogue as a whole and the significance of both the history of its influence and its history of interpretation. And then we shall ask about the age, meaning, and outlook of the first commandment (the imperative concerning the exclusive worship of YHWH) as well as of the second commandment (prohibition of idols). In addition, the problem of the development, form, and history of Israelite monotheism is linked to all of this.

a. The Decalogue

The Decalogue[423] derives its name from Deut. 4:13 and 10:4 ("the ten words"; cf. also Exod. 34:28).[424] It is found twice in the Old Testament, namely, once in the structure of the Sinai pericope (Exod. 20:2–17) and a second time in Deuteronomy as this document's foundational text (Deut. 5:6–21) which later receives its interpretation in Deuteronomy 12–25. The Decalogue was clearly a "self-contained text" that is placed in different settings and then cited. The textual form of both Decalogues is, on the one hand, quite similar, but, on the other, also different, not only in the contrasting rationales given to the commandment concerning the Sabbath but also altogether at least in some twenty different points. These especially include the relationship and separation of the commandment concerning strange gods with the following commandment concerning images, and the combining of commandments by syndesis (consecution with Hebrew *waw*) in Deuteronomy 5 and its elimination in Exodus 20.[425] A third, harmonizing wording of the text[426] that occupies a middle position between the two Old Testament texts is found in the Papyrus Nash from the first century B.C.E. The Old Testament itself has not attempted to make such a compromise. The Old Testament history of the Decalogue and its later interpretation as well as the different numeration caused by omissions and combinations enable one to recognize that even this central textual unit for many reasons would not be regarded as unalterable. In addition, the Decalogue cries out for interpretation because of its terseness and fundamental character. And while the Old Testament mentions the two "tablets" (e.g., Exod. 31:18; etc.),[427] this still does not allow for the division of the commandments.

The formulation in Deuteronomy 5 exhibits its own structure in which the commandment concerning the Sabbath forms the middle point of the collection, and this is probably due to the concrete contrast of the exile.[428] The works of F.-L. Hossfeld, which have continued to be well founded in spite of his critics, have maintained that the formulation of the Decalogue of Deuteronomy 5 is older than that of Exodus 20. The argument is not only based on Gen. 2:1–3 (P), which is very close to the explanation of the meaning of the Sabbath in Exod. 20:10. More precisely said, this means that the Decalogue as a whole is the work of the Deuteronomistic school or movement. The Decalogue then was inserted into the redactional framework of the Pentateuch (by R^P) by being placed within the context of Exodus 19–24, even as the Covenant Code now has been placed secondarily into the context of the Sinai pericope. Exodus 20:18–21 and 24:1 point clearly to the original context. As a consequence of this assignment to Deuteronomistic thought, scholars today largely refrain from seeking an "original" Decalogue residing behind Exodus 20 and Deuteronomy 5 or from constructing such an "original" document by separating out possible additions and reconstructing a consistent form (say of prohibitions).[429]

"Decalogues," meaning series of ten commandments and prohibitions probably formed for mnemotechnical reasons, are also found in other places in the Old Testament, even though their exact limits and contours may not always be clear: Exod. 23:10–19; 34:14–26; Lev. 19:3–12, 13–18; Deut. 27:16–25; and probably also Leviticus 18. Texts similar to the Decalogue form are found in Pss. 15:3–5 and 24:4f. A careful examination of the formulation of the Decalogue in Deuteronomy 5 indicates that its preliminary stages and tradition history already have taken place. These stages are carried out in the form of a progressive generalization of style and validity.[430] Preliminary stages of the Decalogue are found in brief series of commandments in the Old Testament (cf. Hos. 4:2; Jer. 7:9; see also Ps. 81:10f.).

While the "you" addressed by the commandments and prohibitions is both the individual worshiper standing within the collectivity of the nation and at the same time the collectivity itself, the speaker of the Decalogue, on the one hand, is YHWH himself but, on the other hand, is also a priest or a prophet. The first and second commandments (following the Old Testament numeration) are pronounced as a speech of YHWH who is the divine I or subject, while the following commandments either speak of YHWH in the third person and consequently necessitate a human speaker or indicate that the speaker completely withdraws, as appears to be the case with the commandment concerning the parents. Furthermore, the commandments are of varying lengths. The address is evenly shaped either in an "apodictic" or, better said, categorical form consisting of a short prohibition or imperative (see the commandment concerning the parents) or in a mixed form of positive and negative argumentation (see the commandment concerning the Sabbath). The "law concerning God" and "the law pertaining to human beings," commandments that regulated the behavior of human beings toward YHWH and toward their fellow human beings, stand equally beside each other. In the Decalogue, "the God of the covenant defends his status as a God, the election of his covenant people, Israel, and beyond that the worth of each human being."[431]

If the oldest formulation of the Decalogue in Deuteronomy 5, which in its present form stemmed from the Deuteronomistic movement,[432] indeed has a precursor, this would say something about the Decalogue's age and life situation. One can no longer derive the Decalogue in the entirety of its present form from the time of Moses or from Moses himself.[433] While the Decalogue does not contain anything that would stand in the way of its origination in the time of Moses (e.g., L. Köhler), faced with much of its contents one also is not able to say anything (more). Furthermore, it remains questionable whether one is able at all to derive the Decalogue from the early period of Israel. This says nothing, however, either about the age of individual commandments that are incorporated into the present Decalogue or about their social, historical, and theological background. Individual commandments as well as short series could be attributed to tribal wisdom or to general ethical instruction. However, the influence of a prophetic spirit must not be postulated as an unconditional presupposition for any of the commandments. Still, the formative power of the Yahweh faith brought to Canaan by the Moses group and there transmitted to other groups could not have been simply a weak influence. The old "law of God" is present, for example, in Exod. 20:24–26; 22:17–19 (up to 23:19); and 34:12–26, and the Sabbath is also not a new practice dating from the exilic and postexilic period.[434] Without the strong impulse of Yahwistic faith in the beginning (J. J. Stamm), one is unable to explain much of the early history of Israel.

However, if the Decalogue that exists before us in Deuteronomy 5 stems in all probability from Deuteronomy or the Deuteronomistic movement and originated there through the redaction of an older legal series, one is then not able to regard, as does F. Crüsemann,[435] this law code as the document expressive of an ethic of solidarity for the free landowner in Israel that seeks to preserve freedom after the catastrophes connected with the circumstances developing at the end of the Northern Kingdom in 722 B.C.E. Rather, the Decalogue is a Deuteronomistic program for the form of new obedience that is demanded of "all Israel" during and after the exile and that is given its interpretation and amplification in the Book of Deuteronomy (e.g. the consideration given to "widows and orphans").[436] Accordingly, the Decalogue's first "life situation" is probably also its "literary setting."[437] One should also accept the argument that the Decalogue has received its "life situation" in the cult during the postexilic period. It is improbable that the law code was given this cultic "life situation" prior to the exile.

The preamble (Exod. 20:2; Deut. 5:6) with its "formula of grace"[438] ("I am YHWH, your God") sets forth primarily the liberating action of God that precedes obligation. Obedience to the Decalogue is the expression of the community between the God who now imposes demands and the Israelites who are now his people. This community was freely given through divine election. The emphasis upon the "zeal" of this God who elects and now demands (Exod. 20:5; Deut. 5:9)[439] and the reference to the corporate guilt of the generations[440] underline the seriousness of the obligation. The commandments that follow name then the fundamental norms for Israel and provide reasons for the unfolding law.[441]

YHWH has indeed made known his name, yet he has not simply handed it over to humanity.[442] One should not "misuse" this name in witchcraft, magic, false swearing, and cursing (cf. Lev. 24:10–23). How important the commandment concerning the Sabbath is is made clear not only by the weighty argumentation that accompanies it but also by its fullness of expression and its (at least in Deuteronomy 5) central place within the Decalogue. The older wording of the commandment concerning the Sabbath, present in Deut. 5:12–15, includes a theological rationale (v. 15) that argues on the basis of social concerns and salvation history. The later wording in Exod. 20:9–11 has a rationale that points to creation theology (v. 11). Nonetheless, both rationales still appeal to an act of YHWH that provides the Sabbath its significance and dignity. The gift of the Sabbath, however, consists of human beings' resting from labor, in which also the male servant, the maid, and the domesticated animal are included. The wife, however, is not named! The commandment concerning parents seeks to remind the grown son of his responsibility to care for his father and mother.[443] The commandment concerning homicide is directed against killing as an act of vigilante justice, that is, against murder. Killing in war and the death penalty, both of which are known in the Old Testament and are rather common, are not in mind. The commandment concerning adultery seeks to prevent a husband from entering into a marriage with a foreigner, for the husband, according to Old Testament law, is allowed to "break up" a marriage with his foreign wife who belonged to him.[444] What is said in the Sermon on the Mount (Matt. 5:27–32) about this commandment is an intensification of what is said in the Old Testament. The commandment concerning stealing perhaps was related originally to kidnapping.[445] If so, this would demarcate it more clearly from the commandment concerning "coveting" (tenth commandment or ninth and tenth commandment), since the verb חמד = *ḥāmad* ("to covet") is used here not simply to point to an interior "striving" but also to designate the machinations by which one seeks to acquire the property of others. The commandment against stealing then would have been related to the theft of goods in general. The commandment concerning bearing false witness (not lying in general[446]) has as its intent the prohibition of false accusation and perjury. In the wording of the Decalogue in Deuteronomy 5, the coveting of the wife is separated from the larger commandment concerning "coveting" (Deut. 5:21), while Exod. 20:17f. prohibits the coveting of the neighbor's "house" and its property, including his wife. In Exodus 20 the wife is placed alongside the "manservant, maidservant, and domestic animals" and consequently she is more clearly positioned as a possession than in Deuteronomy 5. This difference is not due only to the fact that to make the commandment concerning images in Exodus 20 an independent commandment two commandments must be united at the conclusion in order to reach again the number ten. Rather, this difference is probably also reflected in the postexilic, priestly, cultic devaluation of the wife, a point that cannot be challenged by reference to Gen. 1:27.[447]

The Decalogue's commandments do not encompass all spheres of life, indeed probably do not intend to do so. This is clear in the omission of cultic regulations and in the fact that questions of behavior toward the king, the state, and those persons who require care (widows, orphans, and aliens) are not addressed.[448] These matters were taken up in the remainder of the Book of Deuteronomy that interpret the meaning of the Decalogue and expand its application. This is especially the case with the first commandment, which concerns the exclusive worship of YHWH in Israel.

b. Yahweh's Demand for Exclusivity (the First Commandment)

The first commandment in the Decalogue (Exod. 20:3; Deut. 5:7; cf. what is probably the oldest wording in Exod. 22:19; then see Exod. 23:13, 24; and

34:14, which has the [original?] singular form, לְאֵל אַחֵר = *lĕ'ēl 'aḥēr;* see further Ps. 81:10)[449] does not require any practical or even theoretical *monotheismus.* Indeed, the commandment, through its demand that insists that there be
no other gods in YHWH's "face," presupposes their "existence." The commandment is more concerned that YHWH, and no other god, should be worshiped in and by Israel. "I am YHWH, your God, from the land of Egypt. You
know no other god besides me, and there is no savior besides me" (so already
Hos. 13:4; cf. 12:10). YHWH desires to be the "only" God of his people Israel,
and Israel should not choose for itself "new gods" (so already Judg. 5:8). Israel's sacred experiences with YHWH were not and should not be exchanged
for others associated with different gods.

In addition, YHWH was known as a "jealous God,"[450] and it was no accident that this title was introduced in association with the theophany of Sinai
(Exod. 20:5). It is already present in the so-called "law of YHWH's privilege"
(Exod. 34:14), while its content is found in the Covenant Code (Exod. 22:19;
cf. 23:13, 24). The prohibition against the worship of foreign gods and their
images is based upon YHWH's jealousy (Josh. 24:19, 23; cf. Deut. 32:16; and
1 Kings 14:22f.). Israel had initiated its history with and under YHWH and his
liberating salvation, election, and obligation. Gods who recently appeared did
not share this history with Israel (Deut. 32:17; cf. Judg. 5:8).[451] In the history
with Israel, however, resides YHWH's very own selfhood, for there he and
only he had liberated his people as the God of Israel (Exod. 5:1), obligated himself to them, guided them providentially, and allowed the land to be appor-
tioned to them. YHWH's uniqueness is substantiated in Exod. 18:8a, 9–11*
and is central to his activity in the exodus out of Egypt. In a similar situation,
the Song of Moses asks: "Who is like you among the gods?" (Exod. 15:11).

That the other nations have their own gods and that a foreign land requires
service to other gods are widely accepted views in the Old Testament (Josh.
24:15; Judg. 6:10; 10:6; 11:24; 1 Sam. 26:19; 1 Kings 11:33; 2 Kings 1:2f., 6,
16; 3:27; 5:17; Jonah 1:5; cf. Deut. 32:8; and also Ruth 1:15f.). Every nation
walks in the name of its god; however, Micah 4:5 says that "we walk in the name
of YHWH, our God, always and forever." According to Deut. 4:19f. (cf. 29:25),
YHWH himself had assigned these gods to the other nations.[452] However, when
a prophet appears in Israel who calls upon people to serve foreign gods, then he
shall be killed (Deut. 13:2–6). In addition, apostasy from YHWH receives the
threat of the death penalty (Deut. 13:7ff.), a penalty that was already associated
with the prohibition against sacrifices to other gods in the Covenant Code
(Exod. 22:19). According to 1 Kings 18:40, Elijah massacred altogether 450
prophets of Baal. This type of behavior along with the commandment concerning the exclusive worship of a deity, the prohibition against idolatry,[453] and the
phenomenon of a deity's punishing "apostasy" are unique in the history of religion and in comparative religions.[454] In Israel's neighboring countries, switch-

ing from one privileged god to another was probably wrong and considered evil. However, the polytheistic environment of Israel could not impose a punishment for apostasy, and certainly not the death penalty, for this environment was religiously tolerant. The Old Testament's Deuteronomistic History (cf. also Deut. 29:24ff.), by contrast, saw the final reason for the punishment of the nation in the exile to be Israel's apostasy to "other gods" that they did not and should not know[455] and the closely connected "sins of Jeroboam" that involved the illicit worship of YHWH in the form of calf images (1 Kings 12:28). The punishment for the nation's sins would be the captivity where the exiles would or even must serve "other gods" (Deut. 28:64; Jer. 5:19; 16:13).

"In any case the first commandment has primarily a practical, not a theoretical purpose."[456] YHWH himself is to make clear that he is God in Israel (1 Kings 18:36). Thus prays Elijah. YHWH, however, "is God as and insofar as he has been experienced by Israel at Sinai, in the exodus, and on other occasions and can be newly experienced in Israel's commemorative cult. Therefore, if Israel is forbidden to worship other gods, then it is forbidden to search out other ways of encountering God. . . . Accordingly, the theory of a special revelation issued only to Israel appears to be the proper translation of the jealousness of Yahweh within the language of monotheistic vocabulary."[457] What stands behind the first commandment are YHWH's electing and obligating acts that the Moses group experienced in both the deliverance from Egypt and the theophany and concluding of the covenant at Sinai. These acts were later related to Israel as a whole.

The effort to determine from which period the present formulation of the first commandment stems can be based on the events of the exodus and the revelation at Sinai.[458] The initial impulse necessary for the exclusive worship of YHWH was determined by what Israel had experienced and learned in Egypt, in the Sinai, and in its history with God that continued when he accompanied his people on their way (Exodus 33). While YHWH is not a stationary deity, he is also not a God who devotes himself entirely to human beings.[459] And the events that follow then can only "be formulated as new experiences of the very same God,"[460] be they the encounter with the groups of the ancestors, the origin of the kingdom in its bipolar character, the incorporation of statements of faith about the city of God and the temple,[461] or even the experience of the destruction of the nation that led to the exile and residence in a foreign country with its strange gods who were impressive but also threatening (Deutero-Isaiah). The power and unique character of Israel's God may be shown by his incorporation of many features of other gods, including, for instance, some of those which belong to El. By contrast, the character of YHWH is also defined by the rejection of many characteristics of Baal. In this way YHWH demonstrated, for example, that he was a "living God," not a dying and rising one, and that he, like El, could come to be confessed as "the creator of heaven and earth."[462] "If Yahweh was to continue to be the only God for Israel, he could not remain the God of the wilderness, or of the early tribes, or of the monarchic period, or of Deuteronomy."[463]

One of the results of this demand for the exclusivity of YHWH was the fact that Israel's faith would necessarily have to associate negative experiences with its only God. Negative experiences could not be attributed to other deities or to demons.[464] This is evidenced in the individual and collective psalms of lament in which the one who is offering the prayer turns to YHWH in illness or in political need. However, there would also be the direct statement: "See, this evil comes from YHWH!" (2 Kings 6:33; cf. Exod. 4:11; 5:22; 1 Sam. 2:6; Amos 3:6; Job 2:10; and Qoh. 7:14).[465] The statement that YHWH creates light and darkness as well as salvation and disaster possibly reaches its climax when turned against Persian dualism (Isa. 45:7). It is YHWH who beguiles and entices people to sin (2 Sam. 24:1;[466] and 1 Kings 2:19ff.). YHWH is also the one who made human beings obstinate (Deut. 2:30; and Josh. 11:20), including especially the pharaoh of the exodus (Exod. 4:21; 7:3; 9:12; 10:1, 20, 27; 11:10; 14:4, 8, 17). God also is the one who made obstinate those who heard the prophets (Isa. 29:10), so that one could even say he may have given to the prophets the commission to work actively to harden their hearers' hearts (Isa. 6:9f.).[467] The oneness of God compelled the formation of a unified worldview.

c. The Prohibition of Idols (the Second Commandment)

Closely connected with the first commandment, which speaks of Israel's exclusive worship of YHWH, and serving, so to speak, as this commandment's flip side is the Old Testament prohibition of images (Exod. 20:4; and Deut. 5:8).[468] This prohibition is found already in the law of YHWH's privilege (Exod. 34:17; cf. Exod. 20:23 and 23:23f.) and then in later texts (Lev. 19:4; 26:1; Deut. 4:16ff., 23, 25; and 27:15). YHWH desires to be worshiped without an image, and whoever worships an idol (either carved and then overlaid with precious metal or cast)[469] automatically worships then a god other than YHWH. Images of strange gods and images of YHWH stand under the same condemnation. Thus the second commandment is a more concrete expression of the first, and the imageless nature of the worship of YHWH found acceptance in connection with the exclusive worship of YHWH. Israel not only has borrowed from the religions of its environment but also has at times rejected, criticized, and even ridiculed them. At times Israel mocked the foreign gods and their idols with such expressions as אֱלִילִים = 'ĕlîlîm ("little gods"), גִּלּוּלִים = gillûlîm ("worthless things"), שִׁקּוּצִים = šiqqûṣîm ("horrible things"), הֶבֶל = hebel ("nothing"), or directly stated לֹא אֱלֹהִים = lō' 'ĕlōhîm ("no-gods"; Jer. 2:11 and 5:7).[470]

If this imageless worship of YHWH within the ancient Near East is as unique as is the exclusive worship of YHWH, then it is impossible to accept the notion of a general spiritual development that led to the concept of rejecting divine images. This prohibition of images does not involve either a spiritual worship of God or the belief that "God is spirit" (John 4:24), thus resulting in the rejection of every "image" that one makes of God. That this spiritual understanding is not possible is indicated in the Old Testament by an unbroken, continuing anthropomorphism and often by daring, literary images (Hosea!) in the speech of God.[471] What is more, it is YHWH who did not wish to be accessible through an image. Subsequently, the Old Testament is opposed to making an image of YHWH for reasons that were central to the nature of its faith in God, not for reasons having to do with philosophical epistemology, enlightened skepticism, or a general, aesthetic criticism. At the heart of the prohibition is the recognition that YHWH's freedom was violated by an image.[472] "The prohibition against an image rejects an illustrative depiction and a fixed stylization of God; a sharp, concrete, static representation of God should not be made."[473]

For the ancient Near East,[474] an image of a god had little to do with being either an actual representation or an exact, graphic depiction of a deity. Much more important was the view that the deity dwelt at the time of manifestation within the idol. It was here that the divine aura took possession of a body. Thus one may say: "The gods moved in bodies made out of every kind of wood, stone, and metal in which they have assumed their form."[475]

The danger that certainly always accompanied idols was that one would bring the deity and its image into too close a relationship; indeed, perhaps one would even identify the god with the idol. This was one of the weak points of fraternizing with idols. This weak point, which obviously continued to have an impact, was the object of the Old Testament polemic against idolatry. This polemic has a clear history that may be traced, and it accompanies in a related manner the development of monotheism in Israel.[476] The incisive points of this polemic are found as early as Hosea,[477] then later in Deutero-Isaiah,[478] certain psalms (Pss. 96; 97; 115; and 135), redactional additions of various kinds (e.g., Micah 5:12f. and Hab. 2:18f.), and finally texts of formative Judaism, including Wisdom 13–15. There are also some later additions present within the references in Hosea and Deutero-Isaiah. It is not possible to regard all of these texts as later insertions, since they are too closely linked with the particular message of these respective prophets. In this polemic against idolatry, reflections of YHWH's power, help, vitality, and answers emerge that Israel came to possess and value. These divine characteristics, imagined in these texts, were contrasted with the powerlessness, lifelessness, silence, and even nonexistence of the gods. The particular character of YHWH and the mockery of idols, together with the first and second commandments, are brought together in these polemics. Idols are human works made out of earthly material.

YHWH, by contrast, is the creator of the world and yet transcendent to it. There is no consubstantiation of God and the world. Humanity created by YHWH is his "image," his "likeness"; however, humanity is also created through YHWH's word (Gen. 1:26ff.) and work (Gen. 2:7).[479] According to Gen. 2:7, humanity was indeed made out of earth, but not out of the blood of a god, as narrated in Mesopotamian mythology.[480] The view of humanity being made in the divine image is never coupled in the Old Testament with the prohibition against idolatry, either in a positive or in a negative way. Israel confronts its God, not in an image, but principally in his Word and in history. The function of the idol in worship in the ancient Near East is replaced by the spoken blessing of YHWH in the Old Testament (Num. 6:24–26). The Old Testament reflects theologically upon and gives theological grounding to the prohibition of images for the first time in a later exilic text. This text points to the "word event" that transpires on Sinai/Horeb where one only hears but does not see YHWH (Deut. 4:9–20). This precedence of the divine word over the divine image makes clear that for Israel a divine image is not "the most important medium of revelation and mighty deeds of the Holy," meaning then that the cult (in the ancient Near Eastern sense of taking care of an idol) would not be given precedence over the community's ethics.[481]

One possible contribution to the imageless worship of God according to W. H. Schmidt is the "(half) nomadic past of certain elements of later Israel,"[482] thereby pointing to a sociocultural basis for the prohibition of images.[483] "The nomadic cult is, because of practical necessity, always imageless in particular settings."[484] This does not explain everything, for there also must have been explicit prohibitions against idols in other geographical regions where there would have been imageless worship. The commandment against making an image must be connected primarily with the character of YHWH. Nevertheless, one can say that "the imageless nature of Yahweh had its origin in the wilderness."[485] Out of this Sinai tradition and, above all, out of the character of YHWH that appears in it, the demand for an imageless religion for all Israel, including later Israel, is shaped. It is possible, although incapable of proof, that the ark[486] served as an imageless symbol of guidance that was associated with a deity who himself was not represented by an image.[487]

According to the older narrative about the "golden calf" (JE?),[488] contained in Exodus 32, there was, soon after the theophany at Sinai and the conclusion of the covenant, a dispute about the imageless worship of YHWH. This text serves as the first type case for either the imageless worship of YHWH or at least a worship that would not shape an idol of YHWH in the form of a calf. Similar to the later problem of the "calves" that Jeroboam I installed in his state sanctuaries in Dan and Bethel that were necessary for his reign, the erection of these "calves" in Exodus 32 was judged to be apostasy from YHWH, even though they were designated as "gods"[489] who had led Israel out of Egypt

(1 Kings 12:28), that is, they were identified as the gods of the exodus at the time of the exodus event (Exodus 32; and 1 Kings 12). Both texts (Exodus 32 and 1 Kings 12) contain condemnations of these idolatrous actions. However, these texts also allow one to recognize, even as the second commandment throughout its existence explains, that imageless worship in Israel was not a foregone conclusion.

When Moses prays (Exod. 33:18) that he be allowed to see YHWH's glory after the "golden calf apostasy" but before Israel had embarked on its further journey, the request is denied. What is more, YHWH's כבוד = *kābôd* ("glory") may not become a likeness that may be seen. Rather, the multi-stratified context (vv. 19–23) seeks to offer evidence of substitutes of various kinds ("goodness," "name," "countenance," and "back"), but not one of them is made into the authentic image of YHWH.[490]

The Old Testament frequently mentions the same idols (e.g., the "household gods" or תרפים = *tĕrāpîm*).[491] Numbers 21:4–9 speaks of an image of a serpent that stemmed from the days of Moses (?), later was set up in Jerusalem, and then was finally destroyed (for the first time?) by Hezekiah (2 Kings 18:4). Furthermore, archaeology has continued to present us rich material in this area.[492] The same images[493] associated with YHWH were also related to characteristics of Baal as well as other Canaanite deities,[494] and these images were not limited only to popular piety. The official YHWH cult did not make use of an idol of a deity, but they did use numerous representational elements, especially in the outfitting of the Jerusalem temple (cherubs, a serpent, images of animals). However, an actual idol of YHWH in the Jerusalem temple probably never existed.[495]

It is not at all clear whether an idol of YHWH existed in the (YHWH?) temple in Arad[496] and whether it would have been removed during one of the cultic reforms. That there existed there at least a מצבה = *maṣṣēbâ*[497] ("cultic stele") that probably served as a representation of a deity shows again that the imageless worship of YHWH was indeed a demand that could not in every place and time be carried through. Even in many texts of the Old Testament, it is presupposed without criticism that מצבות = *maṣṣēbôt* ("stelae") found a legitimate use in the cult (Gen. 28:18, 22; 31:13; and 35:14), while other texts either express their criticism about these stones (e.g., Hos. 3:4; 10:1f.; Deut. 12:3; and 2 Kings 17:10) or reinterpret them (Deut. 27:1–8).

The Old Testament often mentions in association with the מצבה = *maṣṣēbâ* (a stone stele) the אשרה = '*ăšērâ* (a "wooden cultic pole") (1 Kings 14:15, 23) or living tree (Deut. 16:21) as an object worshiped in the cult (Jer. 2:27).[498] Already according to Exod. 34:13 (cf. Judg. 6:25–30; Deut. 7:5; 12:3; Micah 5:13; 2 Chron. 34:4; etc.), one is to destroy the אשרה = '*ăšērâ*, an action that Josiah understood in an exemplary fashion (2 Kings 23:4, 6f., 14). It was hoped that in Israel's future, the Asherim will be eliminated (Isa. 17:8; 27:9). Asherah was a Canaanite-Syrian goddess and consort of the god El, and she is attested frequently in the Ugaritic texts.[499] In the Old Testament as elsewhere, this name designates from time to time the goddess Astarte. 1 Kings 18:19 names four hundred prophets of this goddess in the Israel of King Ahab. Now there has been found, moreover, in Kuntillet 'Ajrud (perhaps 50 km south of Kadesh) an inscription on a jar that dates around 800 B.C.E. The inscription (perhaps?) speaks of "YHWH and his Asherah," by whom someone receives a blessing. In addition, from what is probably the same period there comes an inscription from a grave chamber in Khirbet el-Qom (west of Hebron) that mentions YHWH and "his Asherah" who may have delivered Uriyahu from his enemies.[500] The expression "his Asherah" is hardly intended to designate this goddess as the wife of YHWH,[501] since this would require in this case that the personal name of the goddess would be bound with the personal suffix ("his"), something that would be most unusual. In addition, the inscription on Pithos B from Kuntillet 'Ajrud continues in the masculine singular ("he blesses . . ."). Thus this Asherah may have to do with a cultic pole that represents this goddess, and certainly not the goddess as the spouse of YHWH. Nonetheless, this cultic pole certainly gives evidence of religious syncretism when placed beside YHWH. The first and the second commandment obviously did not easily find in Israel general recognition, acceptance, and obedience when they banned every female deity from religious devotion.[502] With the texts just mentioned that derive from the period between 850 and 750 B.C.E., we are led approximately into the time in which Elijah and, following soon thereafter, Hosea engaged in their religious polemics and criticisms directed against false gods and idols.

d. The Formation of Monotheism

If, as has been set forth, the existence of the gods of the other nations in the surrounding regions and of the Canaanites who were connected with Israel at least since the time of the Davidic monarchy was not placed in question by Israel; if the first commandment expressly prohibited apostasy in following "other gods"; if the images of strange gods were used throughout Israel, although prohibited by the commandments, even if they probably belonged to a so-called popular piety, then there can be no discussion of a practical or even theoretical *monotheism*[503] at least in looking at the early period of Israel. Whether one may even speak of henotheism or monolatry is debated.[504] One may assume that even in the polytheism present in Israel's environment the totality of divine reality, for example through the process of equating different gods,[505] is thought to possess a certain unity. Especially in the area of private devotion, this unity often is assumed to be connected to only one ("personal") god who incorporates[506] for its worshipers divine reality. However much this unity may be assumed, it still cannot be demonstrated. Likewise, the phenomenon of a so-called intermittent monolatry, attested in Israel's social milieu in periods of crisis, cannot be substantiated for the Old Testament.[507]

One shall have to differentiate further between the official state cult in Jerusalem and Israelite popular piety. Archaeology demonstrates that in popular piety small idols, figurines of female deities, amulets, and other such things played a role.[508] The bronze statuette of a steer discovered in a premonarchial, Israelite, agricultural, clan sanctuary in the Samaritan hill country, the first uncovered for some time, and the cache of small metal calves in Ashkelon are mentioned in another context.[509]

Nevertheless, in the Old Testament there are clear and recognizable guideposts[510] on Israel's way to monotheism.[511] While in the patriarchal narratives other gods besides YHWH are mentioned,[512] the ancestors themselves and the groups belonging to them still appear to worship in a monolatrous manner only one god (an old Bedouin El?) as their tribal deity,[513] and this worship's influence on later Israel should not be underestimated.[514] This patriarchal religion provides the impulse for Israel's worship of one God, starting with the Moses group's "YHWH from the land of Egypt" in the exodus and the event at Sinai[515] and continuing through this group to influence Israel during its development.[516] In the exodus and at Sinai, YHWH and only he had shown himself to be the God of Israel. Furthermore, while this YHWH was an heir of the solar faith in the god Aton worshiped by Akhenaton, Israel's God was the God of Sinai, not the deity of a sanctuary or city in Lower or Upper Egypt. YHWH is nowhere mentioned in any extra-Israelite pantheon. It is true that psalms that sing of El or Baal were transferred to YHWH (e.g., Psalms 19A; 29). Divine predicates and characteristics of these gods were transferred to YHWH, insofar as they would "adapt" to him and expand and enrich Israel's faith (e.g., Pss. 29:10 and 68:5, 34).[517] YHWH pronounced judgment on and condemned the other gods (Psalm 82; cf. Exod. 12:12 P). In the Song of Deborah, the "sacred acts of YHWH" are praised (Judg. 5:11; cf. v. 23).[518] Then there is the fact that in early Israelite law, that is, the law of YHWH's privilege (Exod. 34:10ff.) and the Covenant Code (Exod. 20:22–23:19; see there 22:19), which are both important for the formation of the Israelite worship of Yahweh, only YHWH is mentioned, while there is criticism directed against the worship of foreign gods.[519] Early Israel, interested in social egalitarianism and therefore also a strongly anti-Canaanite social group, was bound together through the common devotion and duty to YHWH.[520]

The Yahwist (second half of the tenth century B.C.E.)[521] narrates nothing at all about a mythical theogony or a theomachy before creation (cf. Hab. 1:12; Ps. 90:2) but rather begins with the creation by only one deity. This deity is, of course, YHWH, who is neither introduced nor introduces himself. Furthermore, the linkage of YHWH with his people and the gift of the land to Israel are especially important for J (Gen. 12:7; 28:13; and Exod. 3:7, 9). Here, only YHWH shapes and controls events. He is revealed at Sinai as "the God of your fathers" (Exod. 3:16) to Moses (Exodus 3*) and in the theophany (Exodus 19*) to the people, and he promised his help in the taking of the land (Exod. 34:10). The gods of Egypt do not appear as a theme in J's narratives about the exodus and the deliverance at the Red Sea. However, he does frequently use in these contexts YHWH's statement that Israel is "my people" (Exod. 3:7; 7:16; 8:16f.; etc.), and he describes the saving acts of YHWH in the form of a military intervention on their behalf (Exodus 14*). YHWH has his "dwelling place" quite naturally in heaven, from where he from time to time "descends" (ירד = *yārad*, Gen. 11:5; Exod. 19:20). Thus the Yahwist is a witness to a "persistent, nonpolemical monolatry" together with an equally "persistent theology of Yahweh only"[522] where Israel is obligated exclusively to YHWH. Nowhere is there an indication that the character Moses or later Israel as a whole may have ascribed either their liberation from Egypt, the theophany at Sinai, or the gift of the land to another god besides YHWH. It is only YHWH to whom they have witnessed as active in these events.

Then it was the prophet Elijah[523] who promoted the worship of YHWH in opposition to the Baals. 2 Kings 1:2–17aα is directed against King Ahaziah's inquiry of a strange god. The critical, accusatory question of Elijah (v. 6a: "Is it because there is no God in Israel that you are sending to inquire of Baalzebub, the god of Ekron?"), followed by the related announcement of punishment directed against the king, is important for the present context. However, the statement about the situation in v. 2 specifies a historical context that does not appear authentic to the narrative.[524] Within the "drought narrative" (1 Kings 17:1–18:46), the major question in the "divine judgment at Carmel" (1 Kings 18:21–40) appears to be whether in this sanctuary Baal or YHWH should be worshiped.[525] In the larger narrative, developed through several redactions into its present form, YHWH uses the powers of lightning and rain (cf. Jer. 14:22) belonging to Baal[526] in order to demonstrate that he, not Baal, is the true God.[527] Other texts belonging to the Elijah cycle in 1 Kings 17–19 were reshaped in a continuing redactional process to form a narrative in which YHWH is in conflict with the god Baal. Here, "Israel's consciousness of faith is developed."[528] Hosea's polemics against Baal or against the steer images (Hos. 2:19; 4:12–19; 8:4–6; 9:10; 10:1–6; 11:2; and 13:1f.) and his positive statements concerning YHWH (Hos. 12:10; 13:4) should and must have favorable consequences for the carrying out of the worship of YHWH as the only deity.

When Isaiah[529] names YHWH the "Holy One of Israel," this includes a monolatrous worship that is the precursor of Yahwistic monotheism. According to Isa. 6:3, the entire earth is full of the glory of YHWH, the "Holy One."[530] However, this glory refers not only to YHWH's exaltation over the earth and his separation from the world but also to his being the "Holy One of Israel,"[531] who has predisposed himself to this people and has made himself accessible for community. YHWH is therefore not simply one God among others. The predicates "holy," "majesty," and "king" (Isa. 6:5)[532] are probably earlier predications of El that are transferred to YHWH (cf. Pss. 19:2 and 29:3). YHWH has taken these predicates for himself and thus has incorporated El within himself (Isa. 31:1–3). Israel is to worship only the "Holy One" of Israel, the deity whom Isaiah encountered in the temple. And if Isaiah and other prophets assign in the "oracles concerning the nations" other nations to the sphere of YHWH's power,[533] this serves to expand the claims and the influence of YHWH among those who hear.

The hints in popular religion[534] (cf. Numbers 25; 1 Kings 18; Jeremiah 2; and Ezekiel 8), the general recognition that YHWH was worshiped obviously for a long period although not in a uniform way, and the Old Testament itself indicate there are very different ways of speaking about YHWH. This allows one to assume that YHWH was not a changeless being who was understood everywhere in the same way. The Old Testament itself and the more recent excavations show beyond these general reflections and findings that one indeed very often spoke of YHWH and worshiped him, although in the form of a so-called "poly-Yahwism"[535] corresponding to the division of Baal into individual "Baals" in different sanctuaries. YHWH also was worshiped throughout a long period in many different sanctuaries and this was considered fully legitimate (Exod. 20:24—"in every place where I cause my name to be remembered").[536] In 2 Sam. 15:7 the narrative has Absalom speak of "YHWH of Hebron." In 1 Kings 12:28 there is placed in the mouth of Jeroboam I the mentioning of "your gods" who have led "you" (Israel) out of Egypt. The inscriptions on jugs from the caravan inn at Kuntillet 'Ajrud,[537] already mentioned in other connections, speak of a "YHWH of Samaria" and a "YHWH of Teman" (cf. Hab. 3:3!).

The Deuteronomic movement[538] with its program of "*one* YHWH and only *one* legitimate cultic site for his worship" (Deut. 6:4; chap. 12) is to be seen as an effort to bring about the unification of the worship of YHWH and also the image of YHWH himself. The אֶחָד = *'eḥād* ("one") in Deut. 6:4 is to be translated and understood as "one" in the sense of unity, a meaning supported by Exod. 36:16 (the end of the verse), and not as "alone," which would be expressed in Hebrew with לְבַד = *lĕbad*. Only later was the term understood as the "only (God)" in and for Israel and then as the only God at all.[539] Originally the Deuteronomic movement sought to achieve cultic purity through cultic unity. The idea was that through the requirement of monolatrous worship in only one legitimate cultic site Israel would recognize that it is bound and obligated to YHWH alone. It should no longer be said: "for as many as your cities are your gods, O Judah" (Jer. 2:28). YHWH was "one," and that meant that there was only one "single" YHWH (יהוה אֶחָד = *yahweh 'eḥād;* Deut. 6:4) who historically has "chosen," that is, will choose, only *one* sanctuary. This YHWH again (as in Exod. 34:14) is named a "jealous God" (Deut. 5:9; 6:15; cf. 4:24) and also is praised for his singularity (Deut. 3:24; 7:9f.; and 10:17).

However, critically speaking one should not burden this Deuteronomic "YHWH alone movement" with too much responsibility for the development of Israelite monotheism, nor should one evaluate it as a rather egotistical "party" that created monotheism.[540] As has been demonstrated, they were especially influenced by the ideas and requirements of important predecessors that were decisive for the further development of monotheism.

Moreover, whether one is able to maintain that Israel was oriented to polytheism until the end of the period of the monarchy, meaning that YHWH was regarded and worshiped as a national deity,[541] is improbable according to the recent, important, and interesting study by J. H. Tigay[542] of the personal names occurring in the Hebrew inscriptions that are known to us. According to this study, of the 592 known persons between the eighth and the sixth century B.C.E., 94.1 percent of those whose names bore a theophoric element were Yahwistic, while only 5.9 percent contained a pagan feature. The examination of votive inscriptions, formulae of greetings in letters, and other similar data supports this conclusion. Consequently, YHWH was often embraced by and decisive for the sphere of personal piety.[543] J. C. de Moor's[544] renewed examination of the materials that contain personal names and place-names has not fundamentally altered this picture. The names with the theophoric element of El stand beside those with YHWH in the pre-Davidic period. While the number of those with El are preponderate, the possibility still exists that YHWH and El refer in this setting to the same God. In addition, the number of names that are associated with YHWH are so numerous that the worship of YHWH must have played a great role already in the period prior to David. The preponderance of Canaanite divine names associated with the names of locations during this period is not surprising, since Israel was being formed in a land settled by the Canaanites and shaped by their religion.

What role the cultic reforms of Hezekiah and Josiah played in the YHWH alone movement cannot be determined exactly, since these reforms had a more political background in the dissolution of Assyria. Furthermore, the significance of these reforms that are reported in the Books of Kings (2 Kings 18:4; 22–23) are heavily idealized by the Deuteronomic editors and exaggerated in their importance.[545] Nevertheless, one can still accept the view that in addition to the emergence of the Deuteronomistic movement there was also the appearance of a strong orientation toward the worship of only YHWH in Israel and Judah. The abolishment of the "Asherot"[546] and, along with this, the evanescence, even the negation, of every consort of YHWH certainly led to problems for religious piety, and this would probably have been true not only for the female portion of the population but also for the male.[547]

During the Babylonian exile,[548] a clear and theoretical monotheism develops in the Golah, and that means among the upper class who are capable of such convictions. This monotheism is, above all, set forth in Deutero-Isaiah,[549] who based his views on many witnesses of the history of faith that had preceded him. When he speaks of the incomparable nature of YHWH, this is also a common topos of divine exaltation in the hymns of Israel's neighbors.[550] However, YHWH was "compared" with other deities probably even in the exilic community.[551] Deutero-Isaiah takes up this comparison in his polemics, drawing it into his "monotheistic" statements (cf. Isa. 40:18, 25; 44:6–8; 46:9). In judgment scenes between YHWH and the gods of the nations,[552] the purpose is to console the exilic community and to strengthen their hope by demonstrating not only that these gods are powerless and dumb (cf. Jer. 2:5f., 11) but also that they do not exist at all. For example, they are identical with their ephemeral images created by human beings. YHWH, however, is the first and the last, and outside of him there is no God (Isa. 44:6–8; cf. 43:10–13 and 45:14, 18, 21f.). He alone is powerful in history, and whatever his powerful word says will happen. Also, the nations shall recognize this, for the conviction of YHWH's singular divine status shall transcend even these boundaries (Isa. 45:14; 49:26; 55:5; etc.; cf. 42:6 and 49:6).

In any case, probably in the late exilic period, according to G. Braulik,[553] there is an analogous witness to monotheism in a text (Deut. 4:1–40) that stems from the Deuteronomistic movement (cf. also 2 Sam. 7:22; Deut. 32:39 = Deuteronomic). Yet this text not only exhibits no sign of influence from the monotheism of Deuteronomy but also develops before and apart from Deutero-Isaiah. The only God YHWH, who alone is God in heaven and on the earth (Deut. 4:35, 39), is, however, at the same time, the God who is near to Israel (Deut. 4:7; cf. the "Holy One of Israel" in the Book of Isaiah). This is shown, for example, especially in the social order in Israel set forth by YHWH (Deut. 4:8). In close similarity to Deutero-Isaiah, there is articulated in this context the ridiculousness of making an idol (Deut. 4:25) even as, at the same time, there is a polemic against the Babylonian astral cult that perhaps was seducing Israel to apostasy (Deut. 4:19, 28; cf. Isa. 40:26; and 47:13). "YHWH—he is God and no other" (Deut. 4:35; cf. Deut. 7:9; 10:17; 2 Sam. 7:28; and 1 Kings 18:39).

This monotheism became determinative for the religion of postexilic Israel in Palestine[554] and is no longer debated in the texts and redactions of the Old Testament that exist from this period. It is improbable and unnecessary to accept the view that this development of full monotheism was due, not to an evolution within Israel,[555] but to the influences of religions external to Israel, perhaps Persian religion.[556] The YHWH from the time of Egypt, who also was the one from Sinai, had succeeded in demonstrating that he was the only God (Deut. 32:12). As a militarily powerful deity,[557] YHWH became the unifying bond that brought together early Israel in its formation. But if this people should become, not an amphictyony, but perhaps rather a segmentary society, it must be asked what held them together.[558] Israel's demarcation from the Canaanites was also occasioned by religion. YHWH became the deity of the state of Judah/Israel and continued to pursue this claim against both differently oriented influences and various kinds of popular piety in the following period. Since the exile and the teachings of Deuteronomy and Deutero-Isaiah, Yahweh's position as the only deity for Israel in the official religion was hardly contested. The *one* YHWH had himself elected Israel to be his people and had unified them with a single faith into one people.[559] Deuteronomy had made the relationship between these two entities of God and people into its most important theological message (cf., e.g., Deut. 5:1), and this continued to influence not only this period but also Judaism up to the present time. That this was and is an ideal picture[560] does not alter its validity either for faith or for hope (cf., e.g., Ezek. 37:15–28 and Zech. 14:9). Important sections of the Old Testament have articulated just such a hope in their view that the nations may join in this unification.[561]

3.9 Israel's Land

The exodus from Egypt had the objective of entrance into the promised land (Exod. 3:7f.). In the presentation of the promise of the land as conquest, primarily the traditions of the ancestors and the Moses group are brought together in a later Deuteronomistic summary and given a Deuteronomistic interpretation in which "all Israel" (Josh. 1:2; 3:1, 7; etc.) unites together different groups. In addition, the gift of the land is the stated purpose of the Deuteronomistic "credo" in Deut. 26:5–9. The sources of the Pentateuch-Hexateuch point to the entrance of Israel into the land of Canaan. Numbers 32 and 34 as well as the Book of Joshua narrate this entrance into Canaan. The *land*[562] became the historical gift of the God of election to the chosen people.[563] The land became the goal of the near and distant future both for the groups of election and for those who told the story. YHWH gave this land to Israel after military expulsion/conquest of the earlier inhabitants, even as the god Chemosh gave the land to the Amorites (Judg. 11:24).

The fact that a people living upon the land would say they had not lived there "since primeval times,"[564] but rather that there were previous, foreign inhabitants whose title to the land could not be flatly disputed, conforms to the critical investigation of modern scholarship. A conquest may actually have taken place, although there is very little evidence, save in limited areas.[565] The way in which Israel tells the story makes one skeptical of all-inclusive theories about this manner of narration, since the content of what is narrated runs contrary to all other usual ancient Near Eastern "theologies of the land" and consequently enjoys more confidence than one often gives to the others. One would scarcely have narrated that YHWH had only just brought Israel into the land, if this would not have been correct at least for some later, influential groups. Also, the important role that the promises of the land play in the Hexateuch, promises that certainly also seek to legitimate the claims to the land, speaks on behalf of this view.

a. The Promises of Land

The Old Testament speaks of "land" as אֶרֶץ = *'eres* and אֲדָמָה = *'ădāmâ*.[566] The first, more frequently mentioned term is also the more comprehensive. The land (אֶרֶץ = *'eres*) can designate the entire earth (Gen. 11:1), the earth in contrast to heaven (e.g., Qoh. 5:1), and the known cosmos as over against the heavens (e.g., Isa. 1:2; Gen. 1:1). The term also refers to the land in general (Exod. 8:12f. and Deut. 11:25) and especially to the land as a territory (e.g., 2 Sam. 24:8) and as an area with political boundaries (Deut. 1:5; etc.). By contrast, אֲדָמָה = *'ădāmâ*, is connected to the root אדם (*'dm*) and reflects "a reddish brown" soil from which humanity was taken and to which humanity returns (Gen. 2:7; 3:19; Pss. 90:3; 104:29; and Qoh. 12:7). The many allusions to "red" in the references to Esau/Edom (Gen. 25:30) take their content from אדם (*'dm*). The land is the dwelling place of human beings, a civilized world, and an agricultural soil (Deut. 26:10) that "is a unity stretching over the boundaries of the nations."[567] Through the land promised and given to it,[568] Israel has a part in this civilized world and also a territory. The difference between these two terms is especially very clear in Deut. 26:1–11, although they run together in the postexilic period.

Ancient tribal sayings[569] trace back the tribes' possession of land to the gift and in part the military support of YHWH or see in this possession a blessing that is being realized (Judg. 5:11; Gen. 49:13, 14f.; and Deut. 33:12, 20f., 23, 28). Here, the fertility of the land is already derived from YHWH (Gen. 49:25; and Deut. 33:13–16). However, there is no mentioning in these sayings of the promise of the land, and the statements about the land are still not offered in any clearly expressed conceptual form. Only Gen. 49:15 with its mentioning of "rest" in the land is conspicuous (cf. later Deut. 12:9; 25:19).

According to the narratives about the first conquests in eastern Jordan (Num. 21:21ff.; 26:52ff.; 32; and 34) and the effort at a conquest from the south (Numbers 13/14), the Pentateuchal sources have as their intended goal the conquest of Canaan, narrated in the Book of Joshua (Joshua 2–11).[570] This is true, even if other narratives in Joshua come into the picture and the entire book has undergone a Deuteronomistic redaction. In spite of the hope for a new conquest at the time of the return from the exile, so decisive for the Priestly document,[571] this literary source does not appear consciously to end in Num. 32:2, 5, 6,

20–23, 25–32, 33 with the conquest of the east Transjordan. Rather, even if not true of J and E, P on the contrary is at least represented not only by several texts present in the Book of Joshua (Josh. 4:19*, 10–12; 14:1, 2*; 18:1; and 19:51) but also by the rather large section concerning the division of the land (Joshua 13–21).[572] With the exception of Josh. 1:6; 5:6; and 21:43 (entirely Deuteronomistic), the discussion is not about the promise to the ancestors. These last-mentioned texts do not make it entirely clear who are meant by the ancestors. The full arch of the Pentateuchal tradition extends from the promise of the land, to the ancestors, to the Moses group, to Israel coming into existence, and to the realization that even these promises had found their fulfillment (Josh. 21:43–45; 23:15 — Deuteronomistic) with the reaching and possession of the land. The obtaining of this objective did not hinder later Old Testament theologians from reaching back again to the promise of the land and the conquest as elements of new and expanded hopes.

No texts of the religious environment of ancient Israel know of a promise of the land, although they often speak of a conquest of the land. The taking of the land and the conquest of the land of Israel are inserted into the extended arch of promise and fulfillment. They are the object of a long stretch of history that is then seen and must be seen as formed and governed by YHWH.

The Yahwist, the Priestly document, and the Deuteronomic texts, although not the Elohist, know of such a promise of the land, which first is pronounced to Abraham[573] (Gen. 12:7 J; 13:14; 15:7, 18; a later text[574] with the entwinement of the promise of land and covenant theology as the self-obligation of YHWH; 17:8 P; 24:7). The promise of land to Isaac is mentioned only in Gen. 26:3f. (shaped by Deuteronomistic language), while a similar promise to Jacob is mentioned more often (Gen. 28:13 J; 35:12; and 48:4). Other texts refer to the promise of the land to the (three?) ancestors together (Gen. 50:24; Exod. 6:4ff. P; 13:5; 32:13; 33:1; Num. 10:29 J; 14:23; 32:11; Deut. 34:4; Josh. 1:6; 5:6; 21:43f.; and Judg. 2:1). The Yahwist revealed his interest in the אדמה = *'ădāmâ* already in the primeval history (Gen. 2:7, 19; 3:17, 19, 23; 4:2f., 10f., 14; 6:7; 9:20) and in Gen. 12:3.

In Deuteronomy[575] the promise of the land plays a commanding role in comparison to the promise of the multiplication of people and the promise of blessing. This promise culminates in the "oath" of YHWH (thus Gen. 26:3; Num. 14:23; 32:11) where the land is readily designated as the "good land." Here, Deuteronomic and Deuteronomistic concerns both come into play, meaning that there is interest in the preservation of the land as gift as well as the yearning for the winning back of the good land through renewed obedience (Deut. 1:8, 35; 4:21; 6:10, 18f., 23; 7:8, 12f.; 8:1, 18; 9:5; 10:11; 11:9, 21; 19:8; 26:3, 15; 28:11; 30:20; 31:7, 20f.; 34:4; cf. Josh. 23:13, 15; 1 Kings 14:15; etc.). The validity of this promise is underscored by the reference to the covenant of the ancestors (Deut. 7:9, 12; and 8:18). Descriptions of the land, which consciously reach beyond its empirical character, seek to underscore the beauty and size of the territory given by YHWH to his people.[576]

The promised land is readily characterized as the "land flowing with milk and honey,"[577] not in the references to the promises of the land in the ancestral narratives but rather in the narratives of the Moses group and then in ensuing texts (Exod. 3:8, 17 J; 13:5; 33:2f. [early Deuteronomic]; Lev. 20:24; Num. 13:27 P; 14:8 P; 16:13f. J; Deut. 6:3; 11:9; 26:9, 15; 27:3; 31:20; 34:4; Josh. 5:6; Jer. 11:5; 32:22; and Ezek. 20:6, 15).[578] The lack of this expression in the ancestral stories points to the probable original separation of the tradition of the promise of the land to the ancestors from the tradition of the promise of the land to the Moses group.[579] With the distinguishing feature of "land flowing with milk and honey," the land is not portrayed as a land of the gods or painted with the colors of paradise; rather, it is described as an inhabitable land,[580] and perhaps from the view of wandering nomads as an ideal land,[581] so that in Num. 16:13f. even Egypt can have this description. In Isa. 7:15, by contrast, "milk and honey" appear as (poor?) nourishment from the viewpoint of the farmers who use the land. In addition to the promise of the land to the fathers, there is then the promise of the land to the Moses group that builds a bridge reaching unto the conquest. However, those who were rebellious, doubting, and not fully obedient to YHWH were denied entrance into the land (Num. 13:22–33; 14:30–34; 20:12, 24; 26:64f.; and 32:11).[582] Since these emphases occur especially in Priestly and also in Deuteronomic texts (Deut. 1:35, 39f.; and 2:14), the question arises as to whether this "wilderness" treats a situation analogous to the sojourn in the exile when many could not or would not trust anymore in YHWH's guidance.

b. The Land in Israel's History

Israel arrived in a land that formerly belonged to other peoples, a land to which YHWH had "brought" them (הביא/בוא = bô'/hābi'; Deut. 7:1; 9:1; 11:8ff.; Judg. 2:6ff.; cf. Joshua 2–11). The people were to conquer the land and had the capacity to do so, because YHWH opened the land to their conquest and had conveyed it to them as a gift, inheritance, and possession (נתן, ירש/הוריש = nātan, yāraš/hôrîš, "to give," "to possess/inherit," especially in Deuteronomic and Deuteronomistic literature and Pss. 37:9ff.;[583] 44:3ff.; 105:44; and Amos 2:9). Because he was the one who entered history to give Israel the land, YHWH, not Baal, also was and became the dispenser of fertility (Gen. 27:28; 49:25f.; Deut. 28:3–5; 33:13–16; Jer. 5:24; and Hos. 2:10f.).

Thus Israel found "rest" in the land (Deut. 3:20; 12:9; and 25:19),[584] and the Book of Deuteronomy, which was fashioned in the style of speeches of Moses and which placed Israel again at the threshold of its entrance into Canaan, sought through admonitions and warnings to prevent Israel from forfeiting this land. To hold on to the character of the land as gift, Israel spoke in its preexilic time rather sparingly (only 1 Sam. 13:19) of this land as the "land of Israel."[585] However, emphasis was placed on the "land of YHWH" (since Hosea: 9:3;[586] then also Jer. 2:7; 16:18; cf. Ezek. 38:16; and Lev. 25:23) and since Jeremiah and Ezekiel on the land as the "majesty (צבי = *ṣĕbî*) of YHWH" (Jer. 3:19; Ezek. 20:6, 15; Dan. 8:9; 11:16, 41, 45).[587]

Creedal texts combine the exodus and the conquest and give thanks for the gift of the land to YHWH, who has led the people into the land and continues to make it fertile (Deut. 6:23; 26:9f.; and Josh. 24:13). Baal is not mentioned here, and YHWH does not appear as "creator" even though the discussion of the gift of the land centers on its fertility. Rather, the discussion is about the God who has led Israel in history into the land and now is the one who makes it fertile.

Faced with the guilt of the nation, which, for example, is concretized in the form of sinners confiscating the land and enriching themselves illegally by taking possession of it (Micah 2:1–5; Isa. 3:13–15; and 5:8f.), the preexilic prophets of Israel proclaimed as punishment the loss and the devastation of the land and the scattering of the people among the nations (Amos 3:11; 7:11, 17; Hos. 2:16–25; and 4:1–3: land and people together in a common community of fate; 9:2; 10:6f.; Isa. 6:12; 9:18; Jer. 4:23–28; 9:9f.; 12:4, 7–13; 17:1–4; Micah 7:13; etc.). Texts from the Deuteronomistic School take up and affirm this view present in preexilic prophetic preaching.[588]

Israel had to abandon the ("good") land as a consequence of its disobedience,[589] as the D redactors and the prophets had threatened.[590] Israel should not contaminate the land or pollute it with sin.[591] While in exile, Israel lived in an impure land (Amos 7:17; cf. Ps. 137:4; Ezek. 4:3) and hoped for both a fresh gift of the land of Israel and a new entrance into it. This hope, nevertheless, could still fail (Deut. 1:19ff.). However, in this regard, a new obedience toward the law, to which one knowingly is called, plays a special role.[592]

In these contexts, the designation of the land as a "land where milk and honey flow" could also become a new promise (Lev. 20:24; Deut. 6:3; 11:9; 27:3; 31:20; last of all, 26:15; cf. Jer. 11:5; and 32:22), and this motif became the bearer and expression of future expectation. In addition, the promised "rest" was still seen as pending (Deut. 3:20; 12:9f.; 25:19; 28:65: Deuteronomistic, not Deuteronomic[593]) for Israel consequently was always directed forward in a new way to the future, finding itself divinely called within the course of human history. In the Book of Jeremiah, there are also texts that speak of salvation for the land (Jer. 3:12; 12:14–17; 16:14f.; 23:7f.; 29:10ff.; 30:5–7, 10f., 18–21; and 31:2–6, 15–20, 21f.), including, for instance, the future hope signaled by Jeremiah's role of *gōʾēl* in purchasing his cousin's land (Jeremiah 32; cf. v. 15).[594] Further, Israel was also able to speak once again of a conquest of the land. The ancestors, even as their successors, had obtained the land only as a "land of sojourners" (מגורים ארץ = *'ereṣ mĕgûrîm*).[595] And the burial cave of these ancestors, legally acquired without conflict, was the earnest money for the fulfillment and securement of the land of promise (Genesis 23 P).

Thus one hoped for a new guidance into the land where there would be a new possession and a new gathering of the people (Isa. 11:10–16; 14:1f.; 60:21; 65:9; Jer. 12:15; Ezek. 47:13ff.; Micah 2:12f.; Obadiah 19f.; etc.; cf. already Hos. 2:16f.). One can describe this land in the images of paradisiacal fertility.[596] "Life is to receive a portion in the land. Death is the refusal of this eschatological gift."[597]

While Deutero-Isaiah is silent about a return home to the land (as a consequence of a more apolitical expectation of salvation?), he prefers to speak of YHWH's returning and leading back the exiles to Zion[598] (Isa. 40:9–11; 49:14–17, 19, 21, 22; 51:3–11; 52:1, 2, 7–10, 11f.; and 54:1–3). Ezekiel combines thoughts of judgment with his proclamation of the new exodus out of Babylonia and back to the land. Certain apostates should be separated out (Ezek. 20:33–44), and the claim to the land by those who remained behind is rejected by the prophet (Ezek. 11:14–21; cf. 33:23–26). A new conquest is promised then in Ezek. 36:1–11 in opposition to the foreigner's claim (cf. 11:14–21; 34:11–14; 37:1–14),[599] while Ezek. 47:13–48:29 promises a new division of the land west of Jordan (somewhat similar to Joshua 13–21) by YHWH himself.[600] According to this, even the "stranger" (גר = *gēr*) shall receive a portion of the land (Ezek. 47:21–23) that for Ezekiel is the "majesty" (צבי = *ṣĕbî*) of YHWH (Ezek. 20:6, 15).[601]

Zechariah endures pain because of the land (Zech. 1:12; 7:7; cf. Dan. 9:18), although he also promises the return home and a new community of God in the land (Zech. 8:7f.). This new community for Zechariah and other postexilic texts[602] appears especially as Jerusalem (cf. Zech. 14:6–11; Isa. 25:6–8; 26:1–4; and Joel 2:1, 15ff.; also Pss. 69:36f. and 78:54). Joel has YHWH speak gladly of this "beloved land" (Joel 2:21) or even of "my land" (Joel 1:6f.; 4:2; cf. 2:18). According to Zech. 2:16f., YHWH shall elect (cf. Isa. 14:1) this Jerusalem again (עוד = *'ôd*; due to Zech. 8:4, 20, the word hardly means "furthermore") along with Judah as his inheritance so that one may speak of a "holy land." The land was to be bound anew to YHWH even as a beloved wife (Isa. 62:4); it was to be like a mother who gives birth (Isa. 66:7f.).

For Ezra 9:11f., the land to which the person in exile will return home has become impure because of the worship of idols by its inhabitants during the period between the exile and the return from exile. Nehemiah 9:8, 36f. ("rich land" in v. 25), by contrast, makes a positive reference to the promise of the land to the ancestors, and this promise opens up a new future, while 2 Chron. 36:21–23 takes up the law about the land's Sabbath, that is, lying fallow (Lev. 26:34) during the exile, as the rationale for the captivity in Babylon.

The wisdom literature is silent about the promise of the land, the conquest, the loss of the land, the return home, and the land in its relationship to history. However, the sages do mention the land in terms of living space for human beings (Prov. 2:21f.; 10:30; 15:25; 22:28; and 23:10f.; also Ps. 37:9; and Matt. 5:5). By contrast, the psalms often mention the land as the נחלה = *naḥălâ* of Israel (Pss. 37:18?; 47:5; 105:11; 135:12; and 136:21f.; only in 79:1[603] [cf. 68:10] the "inheritance" of YHWH), while in addition Israel also appears as YHWH's נחלה = *naḥălâ* ("inheritance"; Pss. 28:9; 33:12; 74:2; 78:62; 106:5, 40; 114:1f.). Psalms 25:13 and 37:9, 11 allow one to recognize the significance of the land as the portion of blessing for individual piety (cf. Ps. 16:5: "portion" in regard to YHWH).[604] Many words for the theology of the land emerge, and several set forth a partially spiritualized, new interpretation (ירשׁ = *yāraš*, "to possess," Pss. 25:13; 37:9, 11, 22, 29, 34; 44:4; 69:36; נחל = *nāḥal*, "to inherit," 69:37; נפל = *nāpal*, "to fall in terms of one's 'lot,'" 16:6; חלק = *ḥēleq*, "portion": 16:5; 73:26; and 142:6; cf. Lam. 3:24). It is no wonder that the entrance into the land reminded Israelites of the past and created within them thankfulness and new hope (Pss. 44:3f.; 78:54f.; 80:9f.; 105:43ff.; 111:6b; 135:12; and 136:21f.).

c. Terminology

The last-mentioned texts have already allowed us to recognize that, within the Old Testament, statements about the significance of the land made good use of certain *terms*. A closer examination can deepen our understanding of many of the terms that have already been set forth.[605]

The discussion should first address the land as "the" or "a" נחלה = *naḥălâ*.[606] This term designates a portion of land as an inalienable, continually owned piece of earth that one has acquired through inheritance, allotment, or allocation. The term is already found in J/E as an expression that refers to this type of portion of land belonging to a clan or tribe (Gen. 31:14; Num. 32:18f.; cf. Deut. 14:27, 29; Num. 27:1–11; and 36:1–12). Psalm 105:8–11; Ezek. 47:14; and 1 Chron. 16:15–18 mention in this connection the promise to the fathers, which found its fulfillment here. In and since Deuteronomy, the term is readily used for the land of Israel as a whole (Deut. 4:21, 38; 12:9f.; 15:4; 19:3, 10, 14; 20:16; 21:23; 24:4; 25:19; 26:1; 29:7; Judg. 20:6; 1 Kings 8:36; Jer. 3:18; 12:14; 17:4; cf. Ps. 135:12). This term designates the land as the gift of YHWH that is imparted to Israel as an "inheritance" that comes to it without merit or effort. The word is encountered in this way also in P (Num. 16:14; 18:21ff.; 26:52ff.; 27:7; 34:14; etc.; then also in Joshua 13ff.). The designation of an individual's portion of land is seldom found (Num. 27:7; Deut. 21:16; Josh. 19:49b, 50; 24:30; Judg. 2:9; 21:23f.; Ruth 4:5f., 10; and 1 Kings 21:3f.). The conception that the land may be YHWH's נחלה = *naḥălâ* ("inheritance") is missing in the Hexateuch,[607] but it does occur a number of times elsewhere (1 Sam. 26:19; 2 Sam. 14:16; Jer. 2:7; 16:18; 50:11; Pss. 68:10; 79:1; cf. Lev.

25:23 and the אדמת יהוה = *'admat yahweh,* the "land of YHWH, in Isa. 14:2). The people as the נחלה = *naḥălâ* of YHWH are mentioned in a conscious analogy to land as the נחלה = *naḥălâ* of YHWH in Deuteronomistic texts (Deut. 4:20; 9:26, 29; 1 Kings 8:51, 53; and 2 Kings 21:14). Through this analogy, the association of the land and the people is emphasized on the one hand, and on the other hand is given a personalized character.[608]

Since Deuteronomy is interested in the land of Israel as a whole, and not in the sections of land belonging to the individual tribes (Deuteronomy 33 is an exception), it does not speak of the dividing of the land for these tribes by "lot" (גורל = *gôrāl*).[609] However, this is not the case with the Priestly document.[610] The term "lot" is absent in Genesis, Exodus, Deuteronomy, the books from 1 Samuel to 2 Kings, Amos, and Hosea. Joshua 13–19;[611] Ezek. 45:1–7; and 47:13–48:29 portray the division of the land through lots, and Josh. 18:1–10 indicates how the procedure took place.[612] These texts which deal with the distribution of the land may express exilic and postexilic desires and hopes, while Micah 2:4f. testifies to the fact that such a process was carried out. The distribution of the land in its origins was probably concerned only with fixed pastureland for the community, wells, cisterns, and forest.[613] Such a division of the land was designated by the term "lot" (גורל = *gôrāl,* Josh. 15:1; 16:1; 17:1, 14, 17; Ps. 125:3; Micah 2:5; cf. Ps. 16:5f.).

The division of a section of land through, for example, the casting of lots, whether as the distributed inheritance of an individual or of a tribe,[614] is often expressed by using the word חלק = *ḥālaq* ("to divide"; Josh. 14:4; 15:3; 19:9; 22:25, 27; Num. 18:20; 26:53; Hos. 5:7; Amos 7:4; Ezek. 48:8, 21; etc.).[615] More rarely the portion of the land belonging to a tribe or a group is designated by the term חבל = *ḥebel,* which means a measured and meted-out piece of land (Josh. 17:5, 14; and 19:9; cf. Ps. 105:11).[616] The term ירשה = *yĕruššâ* ("possession/inheritance") occurs in Deuteronomic and Deuteronomistic passages (Deut. 3:20; Josh. 12:6, 7; etc.), while אחזה = *'ăḥuzzâ* ("possession") occurs in the Priestly source, the Holiness Code, and Ezekiel (Gen. 17:8; 23:4, 9, 20; Lev. 25:34; and Ezek. 44:28).

The Syrian Naaman sees a clear relationship between God and the land and wishes therefore to take back home from Israel a load of earth carried by two mules, that is, YHWH's land, so that he can then worship YHWH by offering sacrifice (2 Kings 5:17). A foreign land belongs also to foreign gods (1 Sam. 26:19; 1 Kings 20:23; 2 Kings 5:17f.; 17:26; 18:23ff.; Amos 7:17; and Hos. 9:3f.; cf. Deut. 32:8f.; different is Jer. 29:7–14). Thus Israel quite naturally sought to be sure of the dimensions of the land it was promised and to determine the boundaries that YHWH had established.[617] There are several and partially very different expressions about the boundaries of the land. One of these expressions is "from Dan unto Beersheba" (Judg. 20:1; 1 Sam. 3:20; etc.). Some point to boundaries that extend "from the Nile to the Euphrates" or "from the Brook of Egypt (= Wadi el-Arish) unto Hamath or to the Euphrates" (Gen. 15:18; Deut. 11:24; Josh. 15:4, 47; 1 Kings 5:1; 8:65; cf. 2 Kings 24:7; and Isa. 27:12), and there are others (Exod. 23:31; Num. 34:2–12; Deut. 4:45–49; and Josh. 1:4). The Transjordan, for the most part, is not or is no longer reckoned as belonging to the land of promise.[618] This is grounded in a theological argument in Josh. 22:19 that borrows from the language of P. According to this argument, the Transjordan is "impure," while the western Jordan is the possession of YHWH. The dwelling of YHWH is only in the latter location, and it is here alone that there is a legitimate altar for him.

d. The Israelite Law of Landownership

Because the land was the gift of YHWH to his people, Israel shaped its law of the land upon this article of faith.[619] Thus the land as a whole belonged neither to the king nor to the temple or temples. And on account of the land bearing the character of a gift, a character that continued and was constitutive in the final analysis for the "land of YHWH" (Lev. 25:23),[620] Israel apparently knew of no fundamental power of disposition possessed by human beings over ground and earth. The lease or lease tenure of land, for example, in the Code of Hammurabi, either was unknown in Israel or at least is nowhere directly mentioned. There was private ownership of land at least in terms of vineyards and gardens which required a lengthy cultivation and were productive for the first time only after a long period of preparation. However, farmland was probably communal property. The prohibition against the removal of boundaries is also frequently stressed in the law codes of Israel's neighbors, and this receives particular weight within the Old Testament's value of land (Deut. 19:14; 27:17; cf. Hos. 5:10; Prov. 22:28; 23:10; and Job 24:2).

According to the Covenant Code (Exod. 20:22–23:19), the firstfruits of the land belonged to YHWH (Exod. 23:19), since the land was his and he makes it fertile (cf. Lev. 23:10ff.). Thus every farmer with the offering of these firstfruits gives thanks once again for the gift of the land as a whole (Deut. 26:1ff.).

The fallow year, the שְׁמִטָּה = šĕmiṭṭâ (Exod. 23:10f.), should also probably be understood in this connection. During the fallow year, each farmer was to relinquish for himself the produce of his land, and probably at first this period varied from farm to farm. The social intention of this action (v. 11) came to have significance in Old Testament interpretation (cf. Lev. 19:9f.; and Deut. 24:19–22), but the custom of leaving the land fallow originally must have served entirely different purposes, including, perhaps, the appeasing of demons. The custom of leaving the land fallow was later expanded socially in Deut. 15:1–6, 12–18 (cf. 31:10ff.) to include the freeing of slaves and was also provided a fixed time period. Jeremiah 34:8ff. allows one to recognize that there were also problems with this freeing of slaves.

In Lev. 25:1–7 this development is continued even further, for the "Sabbath year" is addressed. Here the Sabbath year is provided a fixed time period that obtains for the entire land and that interposes Sabbath theology (cf. Lev. 26:34f. and 2 Chron. 36:21ff. for the corresponding view of the exile). What is always of concern here is the expressed acknowledgment of YHWH's right of ownership of the land, and not primarily the increase of the land's produce through intermittent periods of leaving the land fallow. When the requirements for the fallow year were increased by Lev. 25:1–7 and it became a regulation that was too difficult to practice,[621] there originated probably during the exile[622] a program accompanied by hope that at least once every seven times seven years there would be the performance of a jubilee year.[623] Thus one wished to believe henceforth in YHWH's care and to respect his claim as the giver of the law of the jubilee year with its predominantly theocentric understanding,[624] even though the law proved to be utopian in the long run. According to 1 Maccabees 6, this law would have been realized on one occasion.

In 1 Kings 21 the conflict between Ahab and Naboth, in which the king wished to bring to fruition his desire to have the vineyard of his subject, appears to rest on different understandings of the law concerning land.[625] In any case, it is striking that the narrator has King Ahab continuing to speak only of the "vineyard" (כרם = kerem) that he can purchase, while Naboth pointedly speaks of his inheritance (נחלה = naḥălâ; cf. Prov. 19:14) that he neither can nor will sell. And Ahab cannot force his subject to do so. In the Canaanite sphere, the land is understood as a private possession that is for sale.[626] Furthermore, Ugaritic documents concerning the transfer and the giving of land by and before the king and an inventory of the transfer of property provide examples that prove the king had a special place in the legal realm concerning this matter of landownership.[627]

According to statements in the Old Testament, human beings without property are in any case "worthless people," as Judg. 9:4 and 11:3 indicate. This is clarified and underscored by the contrast of Micah 2:2, which speaks of the wicked stealing the real estate of others. Real estate belonged to full citizens and could not be acquired by the "stranger" (גר = gēr) and the "foreigner" (נכרי = nokrî).[628] The significant exception of Ezek. 47:21–23 has already been mentioned.[629]

The statement that the Levites[630] intentionally were given no "portion" (חלק = ḥēleq) of the land is true for texts from both the Deuteronomic/Deuteronomistic (Deut. 10:8f.; and 18:1–8; cf. 33:8–11) and the Priestly spheres (Num. 18:20f., 23f., 26; 26:62; and Josh. 14:3; cf. Num. 35:2, 8; and Josh. 21:8). It is unclear whether this should be seen as a reward for the behavior of the Levites, who, because of their loyalty shown to YHWH (Exod. 32:25–29 and Num. 25:10–15), have YHWH as their "portion," or whether this should be seen as a punishment for the insurrection that is mentioned in Num. 18:23 (cf. 16:14). In any case, YHWH is their נחלה = naḥălâ (Num. 18:20; Deut. 10:9; 18:2; Josh.

13:33; Ezek. 44:28f.; cf. Ps. 16:5f.). There should be Levitical cities (Josh. 14:4; 21:8; and Num. 35:2–8), and the Levites should receive the tithes along with other priestly revenues and portions of sacrifices (Josh. 13:14; 18:7; Num. 18:21ff.; and Deut. 18:1). Post-exilic texts mention also the possession of land by the Levites (Neh. 11:20; cf. the pastureland in Num. 35:2ff.; and Josh. 21:2f.).

e. Land as a Historical Gift

The land was never an adiaphoron for the faith of Israel; rather, it much more was a central commodity of salvation. Long life in the land was a promise that should motivate one to be obedient (Exod. 20:12; and Deut. 5:16). To have a part of the land was to have a part in the blessing of YHWH (Gen. 27:27ff.; Lev. 26:4ff.; and Deut. 28:1–14) and a part also in the fulfillments of his promises. However, this combination of God, people, and land according to the witness of the Old Testament was neither mythical nor placed in primeval times; rather, it was historical. Israel came into the land both when and because YHWH led and brought it there. This consciousness of the land as a historical gift of its God is in actuality the reverse side of the historical faith in election of this people.

In contrast to the surrounding countries where, for instance, even Gad was seen as being in the Land of Atharoth "since eternity,"[631] Israel had no mythical relationship to the primeval period. Rather, Israel lived with the singular awareness in the ancient Near East that it did not dwell in the land from primeval times and that it was not autochthonous.[632]

Since there was no natural connection to the land, the land could also be lost. The prophets had threatened this, and the exile had verified their threats. The exile also demonstrated that as a consequence of this historical connection of Israel to the land, it had to lose its land, but it did not at the same time have to lose its God. The land was and continued to be a gift of grace which also could once again be taken away. The texts, which tell of Israel's conquest in the Book of Joshua, is shaped by the consciousness of YHWH's guidance and the land as the gift of God.

Therefore Israel was conscious of the electing, historical acts of its God in reference to its land, for there was a time when Israel was not yet in this land. Further, there was a time of both the preservation and the endangerment of this gift, including the dominion of foreigners. Then there was the period of the loss of the land followed by the return home. Even when the land was lost during the exile, the theology of the land became the fundamental theological theme.[633] However, even the exile made it clear that the loss of the land was not accompanied by the loss of YHWH and that existence in the diaspora was possible. Israel underwent a variety of experiences in its land and in the land of exile, but the future promise was always to be grasped or risked anew.[634] Prophetic threats concerning the loss of the land continued to place disobedience alongside these promises, and Israel had to experience time and again the fact that the land was a gift. Although there was the occasional reflection on the fact that Israel dwelt here primarily as a guest and a stranger (cf. Eph. 2:19ff. as a resumption), the land was always seen as a sign of divine faithfulness. Israel hoped anew that this land would (continue to be or yet again) be inhabited, something promised by Ps. 37:9, 11 and taken up in Matt. 5:5, if in a modified form.

3.10   Yahweh as Warrior and Yahweh War

The Song of Miriam (Exod. 15:21) gave thanks for and praised the deliverance at the sea as a military act of YHWH during the exodus from Egypt. In the components of the text dedicated to the exodus in Exod. 13:17–14:31, where this deliverance at the sea is actualized through storytelling,[635] the Yahwist has also shaped this event with characteristic features of YHWH war.[636] In this regard it cannot be said that the Moses group itself had already interpreted this event of deliverance as YHWH war, even if there is much that speaks for this view. In any case, someone intended to narrate the story in this form. Thus it is clear that this first and fundamental journey through the Old Testament witness of faith, which occurs in the third chapter, that has taken as its charge the delineation of the understandings of the exodus and deliverance from Egypt, should finish with a look at the texts that discuss YHWH as warrior and YHWH war.[637] One should not forget that YHWH is "*eo ipso* a God of war,"[638] because he originally was a deity of groups, a clan, and/or a tribe. This is underlined by early texts or those which are chronologically close to the narratives about the exodus, as, for example, Exod. 17:15f. (cf. Deut. 25:17–19; Judg. 5:31; Josh. 10:10, 12f., 25; 11:6; and 2 Sam. 5:24).[639] It is no accident that there is a reference to a "Book of the Wars of YHWH" (Num. 21:14), while, according to Amos 2:9 (cf. Exod. 15:15f. and many texts in Joshua), the gift of the land was possible only through the military action(s) of Yahweh. In addition, the Old Testament faith in YHWH as the creator or as the God of heaven is bound up with the "battle" of this God, a theme found in ancient Near Eastern thought. The Old Testament speaks of this theomachy only in the remnants of mythological motifs.[640] There is not in Israel an explanatory narrative in the fashion of, for instance, the Babylonian *Enuma eliš*.[641] The wisdom literature is silent to a large extent about YHWH war and about YHWH as warrior. Only Job laments from time to time that he has to experience YHWH as his military opponent (see below).

a. YHWH as Warrior

The later Song of Moses (Exod. 15:2–18), intentionally assigned to the Song of Miriam and to the Yahwistic texts in Exodus 13 and 14, names YHWH a "man of war" (איש מלחמה = *'îš milḥāmâ;* v. 3), that is, a fighter who has "thrown horse and rider into the sea" (v. 2). Within the secular realm, according to the Old Testament, especially outstanding fighters and soldiers were commonly designated in this way.[642] This designation is used for YHWH elsewhere only in Isa. 43:13 (איש מלחמה = *'îš milḥāmâ*). In addition, Deborah's song of victory praises YHWH, Israel's God (Judg. 5:3).

However, more frequently YHWH is described or, above all, hymnically praised[643] as a fighter against chaos.[644] For instance, the battle with chaos in Isa. 51:9f. brings to mind the deliverance at the sea. Similarly historicized is the motif of the warrior fighting against chaos[645] that appears in prophetic words of judgment where the chaos monster is identified with the present enemy.[646] And the relationship between the battle against chaos and the victory over the nations is an element of faith present elsewhere in Israel's Near Eastern environment, since foreign nations and the powers of chaos were seen in close combination.[647]

The involvement of the deity in military activity and also in the primordial battle with chaos is not at all unique to YHWH, since this involvement also is referred to other gods in the ancient Near East. This is true not only of male deities, especially the god Asshur, for example, but also of female deities, such as Ishtar, who for the Babylonians was not only the goddess of love but also the "mistress of battle and struggle,"[648] and Anat (cf. Judg. 5:6?) at Ugarit.[649] It is in no way the case that in ancient Near Eastern thought the military prowess associated with the male god could be moderated or displaced by the influence of the feminine falsely presumed to be weak and passive. In Judges 4–5 the woman Deborah is the leader in battle, while the woman Jael is the one who slays the enemy commander (Judg. 5:24–27).

YHWH is described in the Book of Job as a warlike opponent of human beings (Job 16:12–14; 30:21), although in the Psalms as the one to whom prayers are offered to bring salvation.[650] The ark sayings[651] call upon YHWH to engage in military action (Num. 10:35f.), and it may be that the divine title יהוה צבאות (*yahweh ṣebā'ôt*) points to him as the leader of the armies of Israel.[652] Also, descriptions of theophany and epiphany are permeated with warlike features (cf., e.g., Pss. 18:8–16; esp. v. 15; 68; 96:13; and Isaiah 19; 30–31), and indeed the semantic field related to war and battle in the Old Testament is a rather extensive one.[653] YHWH, who comes from Edom, has bloody garments, because he has trodden upon the nations as in a winepress and has poured their blood upon the earth (Isa. 63:1–6), a statement that echoes closely the description of the goddess Anat in one of the Ugaritic texts.[654] YHWH also is depicted as a mighty warrior fighting against the nations (Isa. 34:5f.; Jer. 47:6; etc.).

YHWH is often designated a "hero" (גבור = *gibbôr*) (Isa. 9:5; 10:21),[655] a "hero in battle" (Ps. 24:8), a saving "hero in Israel's midst" (Zeph. 3:17), and a hero who leads home his people out of exile (Isa. 42:13; cf. Ps. 78:65). And when this hero does not deliver or does not appear to deliver as the "hope of Israel and deliverer during the time of sorrow," then one may ask why he may be a hero without the power to help (Jer. 14:8f.). For Job, this "hero" is indeed a God who now has become his enemy (Job 6:4; 16:14).

b. YHWH War

Not only in the deliverance at the sea, which is clearly described in the older components of the narrative as a military action (cf. Exod. 14:6f., 13f., 20, 24f.),[656] but also shortly thereafter in the battle against the Amalekites (Exod. 17:8–16 J), YHWH once again is shown to be a God of war. It was YHWH himself who in this text led the war against the Amalekites (v. 16), thus his military engagement did not prove to be a onetime effort. The Old Testament reaches back several times to this war and the victory obtained, making the Amalekites the special enemy of Israel.[657] Here the discussion mentions also the "banner" or "battle standard" (נס = *nēs*) of YHWH that then is associated with YHWH's throne (כס = *kēs;* Exod. 17:15f.). Whether the "banner" is a staff, another kind of military symbol, or even a box similar to the ark (cf. v. 16, the altar) with the possible name נס יה = *nēs yâ,*[658] is uncertain. Israel is armed for battle "before YHWH" (Num. 32:20, 21, 27, 29, 32; Josh. 4:13). The designation "holy war"[659] does not occur in the Old Testament, although there are discussions of this phenomenon (Num. 21:14; 1 Sam. 18:17; 25:28). "The war is YHWH's" occurs in Exod. 17:16 and 1 Sam. 17:47, while the "sanctification" of a war mostly referred to a war directed against other nations (Jer. 6:4; 51:27f.; Joel 4:9f.; Micah 3:5) and means essentially "to prepare for or to start a war." The experience of military deliverance by YHWH at the sea gave rise to similar hopes for deliverance in later engagements (Isa. 11:15f.; 43:16–21; and Zech. 10:11).

According to Judg. 5:20f., even the stars fight as a heavenly army (cf. Gen. 32:2f.; 1 Kings 22:19; Pss. 103:20f.; and 148:2) on the side of YHWH and his people. Joshua 5:13–15 mentions a "man," probably an angel, who was the "leader of the army of YHWH." YHWH is also the one who "leads forth" the heavenly army (Isa. 40:26; cf. 45:12). Also hail (Josh. 10:11; cf. Job 38:22), rain (Isa. 30:30; Ezek. 38:22), the sun (2 Kings 3:22; cf. Josh. 10:12f.), and thunder (1 Sam. 7:10), YHWH introduces as instruments of war.

The books of Joshua and Judges (cf. also Numbers 21; 31; 32) are full of narratives about military confrontations between immigrating and already immigrated Israelites and the previous inhabitants and neighbors. These battles were led under the accompaniment and leadership of YHWH (Josh. 4:13; 6:2f.; 8:1ff., 18; 10:7f., 24f.; 11:19f.; Judg. 3:10; 4; 5; 6:16; 7:2ff.; 8:7; and 20).[660] Accordingly, those who did not come to help YHWH were cursed ("to YHWH's help in the midst of the mighty," Judg. 5:23). YHWH came from the south, from Sinai or out of Seir, to the aid of the warriors (Judg. 5:4f.; Hab. 3:3; and Ps. 68:9). In the tribal lands, he executed his "deeds of salvation" (Judg. 5:11; and Deut. 33:21).[661] "This mountain God, strange to the Canaanites though the covenant partner with the Israelite tribes, put more and more fear into the ancient inhabitants (cf. 1 Kings 20:23—'their God is a mountain deity, therefore they have conquered us')."[662] Still at the time of David, when YHWH war was gradually fading away, one finds a divine answer to King David that YHWH is setting out "before you" in order to attack the army of the Philistines (2 Sam. 5:24). The experience of the outcome nourished the faith in the "presence" of YHWH that points to the reality of his power and the assurance of his help.[663] This is true for Saul and his wars as well as for David and his military undertakings. In spite of YHWH's relationship with his people as a tribal and national God, the prophets were especially concerned in their proclamation to make certain that YHWH would not become a "deity ensuring Israel's victories."[664] Therefore they spoke in their message of a God who was militarily active not only on behalf of his people but also at times against them.

Even the Priestly document, which was normally not involved in military matters,[665] still referred to the Israel of the exodus and of the wilderness wandering as the "military host" (צבאות = $s\check{e}b\bar{a}'\hat{o}t$: Exod. 7:4; 12:17, 41, 51).[666] Also עם (' am) can on occasion mean "army, men of war" (Exod. 7:4; Judg. 5:11; and 20:2).[667] The "going out" (יצא = $y\bar{a}\bar{s}\bar{a}'$) or "leading out" (הוציא = $h\hat{o}\bar{s}\hat{i}'$)[668] may be used to describe people departing to battle (Judg. 9:38f.; 1 Sam. 8:20; 18:16; 2 Sam. 5:2; and 10:16; etc.; cf. Num. 27:17 P)[669] as well as for divine acts (Judg. 4:14; 2 Sam. 5:24; and Ps. 68:8). The terms also resonate with the feature of military liberation (cf. the usage in P and P components in Exod. 13:17–14:31).[670] The affirmation "YHWH, your God, who goes before you, who will fight on your behalf" also builds on Deuteronomistic thinking (Deut. 1:30; cf. 20:4—to accompany and to fight). The event of the deliverance at the sea according to P is, above all, a revelation of the majesty of YHWH before and to the Egyptians (Exod. 14:4, 17f.).[671] In addition to the Priestly understanding, there are also within the postexilic community the viewpoints of the Books of Chronicles, the final redaction of the Pentateuch, and the Deuteronomistic edition of the books of Joshua and Judges. In these texts and redactions, the emphasis placed on military features tends to dominate.

In contrast to the peacefully oriented Priestly document, the late postexilic Books of Chronicles with their reports of war and their interest in the constitution of the army of Judah point once more to an emphatic appearance of the conception of YHWH war.[672] Within the Old Testament descriptions of YHWH war, human participation in contrast to divine activity more and more recedes into the background until the culmination is reached in the Chronicles. In the Chronicles, it is YHWH's participation in YHWH war that is underscored and not human activity. According to the Chronicles, the reigning King of Judah always must be assessed in a positive manner. However, there cannot be enough brave warriors who stand at his disposal (2 Chron. 14:7; 17:14–19; and 26:11–15). Not once are less than 300,000 soldiers counted. And these are not mercenaries but rather the civilian troops who are called to service from Judah and Benjamin. In the final analysis, however, the actual warrior is YHWH, that is, God and his priests (2 Chron. 13:12). God is the one who attacks (2 Chron. 13:15; 14:11; and 20:17, 29). In the chronicles of war, the five wars of Jewish kings that went well are especially significant (2 Chron. 13:13–20; 14:8–14; 20:1–30; 26:6–8; and 27:5f.; cf. also 25:10–13). The numbers of warriors mentioned in these texts exceed a million and the fallen number some 500,000. There are prayers (some that look back to the past and contain motifs of salvation history, 2 Chronicles 20) directed to YHWH who alone can save ("no one may prevail against you"; 2 Chron. 14:10) and programmatic, theologically significant addresses to the army with references to the "kingdom of YHWH in the hand of the sons of David,"[673] to YHWH who is on the side of Judah, and to the war cry and the trumpets that the priests blow.[674] The fear of God falls upon the opponents, and God gives them into the hands of the Judeans. The enemy is "broken before YHWH and his military host" (מחנהו = maḥănēhû; 2 Chron. 14:12). All of these texts do not have precursors in the Books of Kings. This means they are the work of the Chronicler and a reflection of his theology, along with his hopes for a renewal of YHWH war, meaning the military powerfulness and activity of YHWH that will come to the support of the postexilic community living a nonpolitical life but wishing it were otherwise. In the reports, "the military powerlessness of Judah is clearly comprehended as well as the miraculous intervention of Yahweh."[675] It is YHWH himself who fights against the enemies of Israel (2 Chron. 20:29). "The war is not yours, but rather God's. Neither fear nor be without courage. Tomorrow go forth against them, and Yahweh will be with you" (2 Chron. 20:15, 17).[676]

c. The Situation of Scholarship

When one reads these descriptions of YHWH war in the Books of Chronicles, they appear to be more in the mold of either wishful thinking or a grandiose design. Indeed, this is what they were in these texts.[677] But what of the scholarly description of the institution of holy war? It should come as no surprise that G. von Rad at the beginning of his book on the subject sets forth "a rather rigid theory of holy war."[678]

First of all in this construction, there is the summons through the blowing of the trumpet. The army, having assembled in the camp, is then called the "people of YHWH/God," which means the amphictyonic body of men. The men stand then as "consecrated people" (Josh. 3:5; 1 Sam. 21:6) under strong, sacramental orders (cf. Deut. 23:10–15). A ceremony of penance or lamentation may be carried out on a special occasion, but, above all, a sacrifice is offered (Judg. 20:23, 26) and God is beseeched (Judg. 20:23, 27; 1 Sam. 7:9; 14:8ff.; etc.). On the basis of oaths that are made to God, the leader announces to the militia: "YHWH has given the (. . .) into your hand" (Josh. 2:24; 6:2, 16; 8:1, 18; 10:8, 19; Judg. 3:28; 4:7, 14; etc.). When the militia goes forth, YHWH goes out either before them or with them (Judg. 4:14; Deut. 20:4; according to Josh. 3:11 in the form of the ark). These wars are YHWH's wars (1 Sam. 18:17; 25:28), for he alone is the one who is acting (Exod. 14:4, 14, 18; Deut. 1:30; Josh. 10:14; etc.). Therefore Israel should not be afraid but rather should believe (Exod. 14:13; Deut. 20:3; Josh. 8:1; 10:8, 25; 11:6; etc.). The other inevitable consequence, however, is that the enemy's courage fails (Exod. 15:14–16; 23:27f.; Deut. 2:25; 11:25; Josh. 2:9; etc.). The cry of war (Josh. 6:5; Judg. 7:20; and 1 Sam. 17:20, 52) and divine terror (Exod. 23:27; Deut. 7:23; Josh. 10:10f.; 24:7; Judg. 4:15; etc.) belong together, while the ban, representing the conveyance of booty to YHWH (Deut. 2:34ff.; 3:6ff.; 7:1ff.; Josh. 6:18f., 21; 8:26; 10:28; 1 Samuel 15; 30:26; etc.; with distinctions in interpretation and execution), forms both the high point and the conclusion of the war.[679] The end of the process, then, was the cry, "To your tents, O Israel!" (2 Sam. 20:1; cf. 1 Sam. 4:10; 2 Sam. 18:17; and 1 Kings 12:16). Von Rad cites at the end of this sketch of the "theory of holy war" the well-known comment of J. Wellhausen: "The war camp, the cradle of the nation, was also the oldest sanctuary. There was Israel and there was Yahweh."[680]

Von Rad sees in the things just described a cultic celebration of something that is, on the whole, historically authentic and not simply a Deuteronomic and Deuteronomistic invention. However, as he concluded, it is hardly the case that a holy war would have been conducted that met fully all of these schematic details. Which wars in Israel's early period (exodus and conquest) actually took place according to this form may not be precisely ascertained because of the character of the evidence. Even so, von Rad considered the time between the battle of Deborah and the time of Saul as the period for holy war. The wars during the time of the Judges are, as a cultic institution, responses of the amphictyony, even if the majority of the twelve tribes did not participate together in these wars even a single time. He noted that, with the rise of the Israelite monarchy, the institution of holy war began to diminish. This happened because the professional soldiers began to replace the civilian militia and because

"Solomonic humanism" began to dissolve the old sacral bonds of the tribal league. Consequently, the narrators of this period no longer experienced real holy wars. Joshua 6 (the conquest of Jericho), Judges 7 (Gideon's victory over the Midianites), Exodus 14 (the narrative about the deliverance at the sea), and 1 Samuel 17 (David's fight with Goliath) are the same kind of narratives certainly possessing ancient motifs. However, for von Rad all of these narratives are already far removed from the sacral-cultic sphere. "All the more weighty [is] their actual didactic and kerygmatic concern."[681] According to von Rad, the thought of YHWH war continued to live in prophecy, and especially in Isaiah, even though Isaiah and the other, sporadic examples show that these were not references to an actual, contemporary institution. Von Rad also argued that Deuteronomy[682] sought to revitalize the ideology of holy war (including the civilian militia) in connection with its thoughts about the people of God who are separate from the other nations. Deuteronomy and the Deuteronomistic movement influenced the later descriptions that are present now in the books of Joshua and Judges. The Books of Chronicles sought to revive YHWH war once again during the postexilic period.

This impressive as well as consistent description by von Rad received through the work of R. Smend[683] some important modifications. Proceeding from the Song of Deborah (Judges 5) in which not even twelve tribes are mentioned as participants in the battle, Smend demonstrates primarily that YHWH war was not an organization of the cultic tribal league and not even a cultic institution.[684] Only individual groups participated in the YHWH wars during the period of the Judges, and not all Israel. A sacral covenant of tribes and YHWH war do not blend with each other either factually or numerically. "Yahweh war does not derive from a sense of nationalism; however, it does lead to a sense of nationalism."[685] The ark, with which the divine name צבאות יהוה (*yahweh sĕbā'ôt,* "YHWH of hosts") was connected, possessed an importance for YHWH war, although not as an amphictyonic central sanctuary. The Rachel tribes probably represented within the amphictyony the feature of YHWH war, while the Leah tribes represented the feature of the amphictyony. The Rachel tribes also had experienced the exodus out of Egypt as an act of war carried out by the God YHWH. Moses may also belong to these contexts. On the whole, Smend's book represents an important contribution for assessing the many problems of the early history of Israel. His book has provided both historical precision and traditiohistorical clarification.

F. Stolz has also demonstrated that YHWH war was not a cultic institution.[686] In addition, he tries to formulate a more precise inquiry. The Song of Miriam, the battle with the Amalekites, the saying concerning the banner (Exod. 17:16), the Song of Deborah, the narrative about the placing of the cities of the king of Arad under the ban (Num. 21:1–3), and the saying of Joshua at Gibeon (Josh. 10:12f.) are classified as the oldest descriptions of religious military leadership. Common to them is the understanding that YHWH is the Lord of war, and this derives, not from cultic celebrations, but directly from historical experience. Chronologically this understanding belongs to the period between the conquest and the formation of the state. Saul's failures brought about the end of YHWH war. Apart from the thesis of the anchoring of conceptions of YHWH war in almost all regions of the tribes, a thesis that is not really established, the book by Stolz provides important historical insights into the theory and practice of YHWH war. The conceptions of YHWH war are evident for the middle Palestinian Rachel tribes, the house of Joseph, and perhaps also the Moses group.

M. Weippert[687] has intentionally looked beyond the boundaries of the Old Testament and Israel[688] and brought into play especially new Assyrian comparative material for the examination of "holy war." The result was that "holy war" was found to be, not a uniquely Israelite institution, but rather an institution that also existed elsewhere, although naturally it was not conducted under the leadership of YHWH. One finds, as Weippert correctly stresses, a common oriental and ancient practice and ideology, together with features that are reckoned among the normal, technical, and cultic apparatus of all ancient warfare and that belong to its ideological superstructure. For the latter, war and deity are brought together in a way that serves to legitimate the war. The legitimation of the claim to the land, however, is especially involved in YHWH wars.[689]

In making his religiohistorical comparisons, P. D. Miller made significant use of those materials out of Syria/Palestine (Baal; Anat) in which the cosmic war of the deity played an important role.[690] Further, he investigated also separate epic and poetic traditions of YHWH war and spoke of holy war as a "synergism" between God and human beings.[691] For M. C. Lind,[692] who studied first the more "pacifistic" narratives of the patriarchs[693] and then tried to set forth a historical, diachronic section of the discourse of YHWH war,[694] the event of the exodus, the deliverance at the sea, is the fundamental basis and most important paradigm for the conceptualization of faith in YHWH fighting on behalf of his own. Lind certainly sees close relationships also to the Sinai tradition and the conception of YHWH as king, something that he did not account for in detail and that remains problematic. Moving beyond this, Lind at the same time searches more thoroughly for the relationship between divine and human actions.

The religiohistorical, comparative material in the first section of the work by S.-M. Kang is presented in an even more comprehensive manner,[695] for here in addition to Mesopotamia and Syria/Canaan also Anatolia and Egypt come under consideration. In his second part, which treats the Old Testament, Kang often arrives at results different from those of earlier scholarship, since he does not find "YHWH war" in the historical realities behind the descriptions of the exodus, the conquest, and the period of the Judges up to Saul. Rather, he thinks that YHWH war occurs for the first time in the wars of David. The synergism between God and human beings, for Kang, is constitutive for YHWH war, and where this does not occur there is no authentic YHWH war. In addition, there must be a clear differentiation between historical reality and later theological interpretation. J. A. Soggin and S.-M. Kang regard all the references to the YHWH wars in the Old Testament to be artificial constructs, as is true in the Books of Chronicles. However, their view is neither provable nor religiohistorically possible (cf. Moab and Assur).

d. The "Ban"

The ban[696] belongs in association with (YHWH) war,[697] for here the booty of war was dedicated to the God YHWH, was taken from human use, and in the end must be and would be given up to destruction (Micah 4:13; cf. Num. 21:2f.). In connection with the (Deuteronomistic) descriptions of the conquest (Deut. 2:1–3:17 and Joshua 6–11), the ban was augmented to include the required annihilation of the conquered population. Nevertheless, this may not have conveyed at all a historical reality; rather, it may describe a portion of the Deuteronomistic program of thought that provides a theological look back at the past. Since the nations continued to dwell in the land in spite of the promise and the gift of the land by YHWH to Israel, it is the judgment of the Deuteronomists that these pagans led Israel into apostasy. Since this was no small theological problem (cf. Judg. 2:20–3:6), the Deuternomists spoke now of the actuality and necessity of a former "ban" (Deut. 7:2; 20:17; and 1 Kings 9:21 — Deuteronomistic). Thus Israel would have to treat under the stipulations of the ban both the nations and an Israelite population of an entire city (Deut. 13:13–19!)[698] abandoned by YHWH[699] so that the nation might continue to be spared testing and punishment. The (Deuterononomic) portion of Deuteronomy is, among the Old Testament legal corpora, the only one to contain laws and speeches pertaining to war.[700] It need not be emphasized that the problem of the ban and the image of God associated with it is not fully "resolved" by removing it from reality and relocating it within a program of wishful thinking,[701] since a series of late texts mention once again the carrying out of the ban against other nations.[702] Also, the Deuteronomistic movement, as Joshua 6–8; Judg. 1:17; and 1 Samuel 15 (?) demonstrate, must have taken over and transformed older texts that spoke of a ban. However, "as strange as it may sound, we have from Israel no historically reliable information about a military consecration of extermination."[703] The Old Testament knew that the Assyrians also practiced the ban (2 Kings 19:11; Isa. 37:11; 2 Chron. 32:14). Cruel conducting of war at that time was not a rare occurrence,[704] and the Moabite Meša inscription proved that the ban was also a Moabite practice of dedication to the deity.[705] In two prophecies (Zech. 14:11; Mal. 3:24), the ban is spoken of once again, only now it will not be carried out against either Jerusalem or the entire earth.

Originally the ban may have had to do with limited, religious extermination on the one hand (Exod. 22:19) and, on the other, with the dedication of war booty (along with the killing of the people to whom the booty belonged) to the deity. Here the text of 1 Samuel 15, in itself not old,[706] may have retained an accurate reminiscence. Also, there may have been a cultic "dedication" of certain goods. This material of the ban may have become the property of the priests (Lev. 27:21; and Ezek. 44:49; both late texts). With the thoughts and beliefs belonging to the categories of the ban, part of the distance of the Old Testament from modern thinking (at least in parts of our world) is indeed clear.

e. YHWH War against Israel

According to the witness of the prophets, the YHWH who fought and fights for his people can and will turn militarily *against* them.[707] YHWH becomes the military leader also of foreign nations, including the Assyrians against Israel (Isa. 5:26–30; 10:5f.; 22:7f.; 30:17; 31:1–3; 29:1ff.; Micah 3:12; and 2 Chron. 33:11), the "foe from the north" (Jer. 1:15; 4:6f.; 6:1ff.; cf. 5:15f.; 22:7), the Babylonians against Jerusalem and its temple (Jeremiah 27; 51:20– 23; and Ezek. 7:21), and, according to Ezekiel (26:7; 28:7; and 29:18–20), Nebuchadrezzar against Tyre. The summons to flee is issued no longer to Israel's opponent but to Israel itself (e.g., Jer. 4:5f.; and 6:1); on the contrary, now it is Israel's enemies—however, not Israel itself—who are called to battle (e.g., Jer. 5:10; and 6:4–6).[708] YHWH now carries out his military judgment against his own people.[709] The "Day of YHWH"[710] is or already was a war against Israel (Ezek. 7:12; 13:5; 34:12; cf. Deut. 28:25f.; etc.). The man of war, YHWH, therefore can fight also against his own people. In spite of what certain prophets thought (Jer. 28:8), YHWH does not simply lead only on the side of and to the benefit of Israel (cf. Numbers 13/14; 1 Samuel 4). In Lam. 2:2ff. this is brought to stunning and shocking expression. He does not interject anymore his "hand" and his "arm" for the benefit of his people (e.g., Ps. 81:15) but rather lifts his hand and arm against them (Lam. 2:4; 3:3; and Ps. 74:11; cf. Job 30:21). Also, he does not allow the king to be victorious anymore in battle, causing then his enemies to rejoice (Ps. 89:43f.).

f. War and Peace

With its witness to YHWH as warrior, to YHWH war, and to the ban, the Old Testament stands within the context of an understanding of the world at that time while keeping its own distinctive features. There can be no discussion of a complete overcoming of military thinking within the Old Testament or of a development to an ever clearer emphasis upon "peace" (שָׁלוֹם = ṣālôm), or of a journey of Israel away from force, or even of its withdrawing from power.[711] The military annihilation of the nations is found also even in many postexilic texts (Zechariah 14; Joel 4; etc.) on down to the apocalyptic elements in the Book of Daniel.[712] While םוֹלשׁ = *šālôm* is indeed the greatest possible contrast to war,[713] it must in no way always be identified with "nonwar" (Judg. 8:9; 2 Sam. 11:7; 1 Kings 2:5).[714] The word םוֹלשׁ = *šālôm* goes far beyond "nonwar." And if YHWH effectuates "peace," then this extends even over cosmic disasters (Psalm 29). If he wipes out war and war materiel from the world, then he also does this through war (Isa. 9:3f.; Pss. 46:10; 76:4; etc.)[715] and exterminates by means of war the enemy nations.[716] An addition in Hosea (Hos. 1:7) is the first description of the salvation of YHWH in terms that are expressly nonmilitaristic, while Zech. 4:6 stresses that the removal of opposing things should happen not through power or force but through YHWH's spirit. However, faith in this nonmilitaristic activity of YHWH cannot be maintained even to the end of the Book of Zechariah (Zech. 10:3ff.; 14). That YHWH delivers from the power of the sword (Job 5:20) is directly contested by Qoh. 8:8 ("no one is spared in war"). The often-cited reforging of the swords into plowshares (Isa. 2:4; Micah 4:3) is neither the only nor the last word of the Old Testament concerning the theme of war and power, as, for example, the formulations of contrast in Joel 4:9ff. show. It is not so certain whether and, if so, to what extent Old Testament Israel even in this area was actually a "society in opposition to" its cultural environment,[717] even if there was no hero worship in Israel. In addition to the hope in eschatological peace,[718] there remains the so-called eschatological power of God. The New Testament is also aware of this. The hermeneutical question concerning the significance and validity of the texts (Mark 13 par.; Revelation) that speak about this matter is passed on there. One can perhaps[719] say that Israel exposes power, looks at it as *the* central human sin, and helps also to dismantle it. It is not correct to see the last prophets, to which Zechariah 9–14 and the Book of Daniel belong, as viewing God's definitive society as a powerless one.[720] Whether the image of God more and more was stripped of its characteristics of power is doubtful even for N. Lohfink, in spite of the Book of Jonah, the Servant of God, and several other texts faced with holding on to judgment against the nations. He writes: "Thus the Old Testament continues to be ambivalent toward power and powerlessness even in its imaging of God."[721] Both Testaments are evaluated in Lohfink's substantial presentation on the theme of power.[722] The central, theological question is stated: How do God and human beings proceed in their quest against evil? And Christians will add what significance the word and work of Jesus Christ have for this question.

Chapter 4. The God Who Elects: His Names and
Titles. His Acts and His Powers of Activity.
Statements about His "Nature."

4.1. The Names of God

The existence of God is contested only by either the godless or the fool on the basis of practical, but not theoretical, atheism (Pss. 10:4; 14:1 = 53:2; cf. Job 2:10). Also, the much too cocksure person thinks that YHWH does neither good nor evil; thus he does nothing at all (Zeph. 1:12; cf. Jer. 5:12; Prov. 19:3). Consequently, while YHWH's existence is not doubted, it also is not the subject of (theological?) reflection in the Old Testament. YHWH is not thought or believed to have an absolute existence; rather, he was thought or believed to exist in his relationship to Israel and to human beings (Hos. 13:14; cf. 12:10). It is in this way that Israel has learned to know its God, and to confess him as its "Lord."[1]

a. Yahweh

This God of Israel has only one name, and the knowledge of his name is acquired at different times according to various witnesses. The Yahwist uses this revealed name beginning with Gen. 2:4b and notes the early dating of its use by human beings in Gen. 4:26.[2] However, according to the witness of the Elohist and the basic Priestly source, Moses is the first to receive the revealed name in connection with the events of the exodus from Egypt and the deliverance at the sea (Exod. 3:14 E; 6:2–9 P). In both of these narratives, the revelation of the name is woven into their contexts. The God who is here made known is identified as the God of the ancestors (Exod. 3:13, 15; 6:3f.), although he was not this as the otherwise ambiguous question in Exod. 3:13b and the statements in Josh. 24:2 and 14 show.[3] The Priestly document, moreover, placed the making known of the name of God within its literary structure. The story of revelation in P is elucidated by a progressive use of the names of God. The Priestly document begins in Genesis 1 with the name אלהים = 'ĕlōhîm ("God"), and then in Genesis 17 introduces אל שדי = 'ēl šadday ("God of the mountains"?; according to P in connection with the covenant of Abraham). Finally, the name יהוה = yahweh (YHWH) is introduced in Exod. 6:3, first of all to Moses. Twice, there is the promise that looks ahead and the reference to the approaching guidance of

Israel into the land by this God who is here made known and who has turned
to liberate the people who have cried out to him (Exod. 3:7ff.; 6:5ff.).

God has therefore a name, in particular יהוה = *yahweh* (YHWH). He is accessible by means of this name, being no "unknown God" (Acts 17:23). One
can call upon him,[4] but one must not cry into the unknown unto a "god whom
I know/do not know" or a "goddess whom I know/do not know."[5] The God of
Israel also has only *one* name, while by contrast Marduk, for example, has
fifty.[6] Accordingly, YHWH is made accessible as a "person," that is, as an authentic "thou" and a personal "other." He makes himself known by name and
may be called upon by name. And, as with the blessing, for example (Num.
6:27; Deut. 10:8; and 2 Sam. 6:18), through his name he is both one who bestows and yet also one who sets forth his claim. His name should not be "profaned" or used in vain, in an empty way, and in an inappropriate manner (Lev.
18:21; 20:3), as in a curse, perjury, or magic (Exod. 20:7; Deut. 5:11). He is
and will be distinguishable from other gods through this name of his and is to
be distinguished from them (Micah 4:5). He desires community and makes it
possible through revealing his name. "For the sake of his/your name" is uttered
either in a prayer for divine help or when God is confessed as savior (Pss. 23:3;
25:11; 143:11; Jer. 14:7; and Isa. 48:9).

A name, for ancient Near Eastern thought, is, however, never "but sound
and fume, befogging heaven's blaze" (Goethe, *Faust* I), but rather the *nomen
est* (or: *atque*) *omen* (Plautus). This means that a name is the expression of
one's nature, and as persons are called, so they are, thus they behave, and so
their lives go (cf. 1 Sam. 25:25, "Nabal" = "fool").

Thus it is reasonable to ask about the meaning of the Old Testament name
for God, יהוה = *yahweh* (YHWH),[7] even if the Old Testament itself is reticent
to provide an answer to this question. The Old Testament attempts within the
6,828 occurrences of this name to provide an explanation only once, in Exod.
3:13f. Already in the pre-Christian period the Tetragrammaton ceased to be
pronounced in order to avoid any kind of misuse. That this name was originally
pronounced as "יַהְוֶה" = *yahweh* (YHWH) can be derived only from early
Christian witnesses and from the Greek transcription of the Samaritan dialect.[8]
The LXX translated יהוה = *yahweh* (YHWH) with κύριος = *kyrios,* so that one
already read and pronounced the name rather early on as "Lord." Later on, the
vowel points of אֲדֹנָי = *'ădōnāy* ("Lord") are used to point the Tetragrammaton
as the so-called Qere perpetuum. אֲדֹנָי = *'ădōnāy* is a plural of intensification
with the first person singular suffix attached to the plural and this possibly with
a pausal accent. In any case, the significance of the ending, ָי = *āy* is debated.[9]
When one attempts to translate this word, one has "my Lords" or "my Mas-
ters." Behind the pointing of יְהוָה (without the defective holem in the ו) in the
Codex Leningradensis (= *BH3* and *BHS*) stands the Aramaic שְׁמָא = *šěmā'*
("the name"). The false reading "Jehovah," which originated perhaps in the

fourteenth century C.E. from the failure to recognize the combination of יהוה =
yahweh (YHWH) with אֲדֹנָי = 'ădōnāy, has been disappearing[10] from use for a
long time now, as one may see, for example, in the hymnals. The name יהוה =
yahweh (YHWH), the meaning of which was probably not well known anymore, even in the Old Testament, becomes only a title. As a consequence of
the regularity of its use, the name is best rendered simply by the word "the
Lord" (Luther: "The 'Lord' as distinguished from human 'lords' "). YHWH is
characterized (with an early Jewish emphasis?) as Lord and Master.

In the Old Testament, the Tetragrammaton is absent only from the books of
Qoheleth and Esther,[11] probably from Canticles,[12] and from the dialogues of
the Book of Job (Job 3–27).[13] In addition, its short form is contained in numerous personal names (וֹ)יְה = yāh(û) or יְהוֹ = yěhô or יוֹ/יְהוֹ = yô/yěhô (Isaiah,
Jeremiah, Jonathan, Nathaniah, etc.).[14] As noted earlier, the only place in the
Old Testament that seeks to explain or interpret the name YHWH is Exod.
3:13f. (15).[15] In this explanation, the name is seen as a verbal form,[16] indeed
either as an (archaic) imperfect of the qal or as an imperfect of the hiphil and
therefore as a short sentence. Further, the name is associated with the verb הֲוָה
= hăwâ, the Aramaic equivalent to the Hebrew הָיָה = hāyâ ("to be"; cf. also
Exod. 3:12). Thus, perhaps one ought to offer the interpretive translation: "he
causes to be, he calls into existence." The short form יְה/יָה = yâ/yāh or יְהוּ =
yâhû and its compressed form יוֹ = yô existed alongside the long form (cf., e.g.,
Exod. 15:2 or הַלְלוּ יָה = hallû yāh). However, the meaning of the name YHWH
cannot be determined by reference to the short form, since it is a secondarily
constructed abbreviation. While this abbreviated form is indeed ancient, it cannot be regarded as the original form of the name.[17]

The meaning attempted in Exod. 3:13f. contains initially an element of re-
buff ("Why do you ask me my name?" cf. Gen. 32:30). However, this is not all
that is involved. The issue is limited neither to YHWH's unapproachableness
nor to his irritation at the question. Israelites heard in the name יהוה (YHWH)
the approximation of the sound of הוה/היה = hāyâ/hăwâ and through this association of sounds drew their inferences.[18] One such inference could be "the
One who is, the One who (truly) exists," as seen, for example, in the LXX
through its (mistaken) translation Ἐγώ εἰμι ὁ ὤν = egō eimi ho ōn.[19] However, this is impossible for Old Testament thought. God's existence is neither
questioned nor given a philosophical definition. Now the Hebrew היה = hāyâ
does mean "to be active,"[20] present tense. At the same time, however, היה =
hāyâ also points to the future in Exodus 3: "You shall behold what I shall do
and who I am"; "I am what I shall show myself to be." The meaning of the
name YHWH might be understood, perhaps, in this way, so that divine mystery may continue to be maintained. In addition, the one asking for the meaning of the divine name is directed to future experiences with and under this God
(cf. also Exod. 34:6f.). Furthermore, indications from Israel's ancient Near

Eastern neighbors point to the recognition that "God is" could be construed as "he shows himself to be a savior."[21] Accordingly, YHWH in this statement neither refuses to disclose himself nor reveals himself in some way; rather, he maintains his majesty (cf. also Exod. 33:19; Ezek. 12:25).[22] However, God wishes much more, according to the meaning of Exod. 3:14, and what he wants fits well the present context. He desires that people in the future will participate in his experiences. Thus, there is the pointing ahead to the exodus event (Exod. 3:12), to the liberation from slavery (Exod. 3:16f.). This God will be "present" (Exod. 3:12) is a statement that is given the weight of a direct, divine speech and therefore is made in the form of אהיה = 'ehyeh ("I will be"; first person sg.). Along with this, the possible character of this divine name could also be seen in the context of cultic thanksgiving. The Priestly document has very probably understood all of this and has continued precisely in this way with its vocabulary (Exod. 6:6–8).

Thus the "sense" of the name YHWH is fully disclosed from its literary context.[23] This is certainly no accident. YHWH was also "the One from Egypt" (Hos. 12:10; 13:4), and in this event the distinguishing feature and means of knowing the bearer of this name occurred. He pointed, then, in a word of promise to his future acts. What the Elohist offers here as an explanation may not be too far removed from the experiences of Moses as well as the Moses group with YHWH. The contrastive statement in Hos. 1:9 (cf. also Isa. 43:10c?) also substantiates this. Here the statement (ואנכי לא-אהיה לכם = wě'ānōkî lō'-'ehyeh lākem; "and I am not present for you") probably already reflects Exod. 3:14 and ought to and can be understood as "I am not your אהיה = 'ehyeh" in the sense of "I am no longer present for you." "Moses and the people of Israel are, therefore, to depend upon their experiences with God. However, they can do this with confidence, for they are told that God shall prove and confirm himself to be what he affirms that he will be and now is."[24]

Do we know anything else about YHWH? In addition to the Old Testament, writings from ancient Israel that contain the name YHWH in the form of the Tetragrammaton include the ostraca of Lachish and Arad, a seal published in 1984, and the texts previously mentioned from Khirbet el-Qom and Kuntillet 'Ajrud.[25] The Meša inscription (circa 840 B.C.E.)[26] offers an extra-Israelite witness. The name is not to be found, in spite of earlier opinions to the contrary, in the Ugaritic texts.[27] The same is true of the texts from Ebla.[28] Exodus 3 seeks to explain YHWH as a purported Israelite name and proceeds to do so with the long form. The preponderance of contemporary scholarship also does this. In contrast to Exodus 3 (cf. Hos. 12:10; 13:4), where YHWH first made his name known to Moses, the Yahwist says in Gen. 4:26 that "at that time," that is, already among the offspring of Cain, people began to call upon the name of YHWH. If this means that God has been known since the origins of human thought, then undoubtedly some indication of this would have been noted in Genesis 2. The same is true if one wished to express the idea that the time prior to Moses was not godless, even if an Old Testament religious person could have thought such a thought anyway.

Some scholars have expanded this first mention of the worship of YHWH (Gen. 4:26) by associating it with the Kenites and often with other texts that are a part of the so-called Kenite or Midianite hypothesis.[29] That the Cain mentioned in Genesis 4 is supposed to be the forefather of the Kenites is derived from the Cainite tribal genealogy in Gen. 4:17ff. as well as from Num. 24:21f. The Kenites, however, were a component of the Midianites so that, for example, Enoch as well as Cain can be assigned also to Midian (Gen. 4:17; 25:4). According to Judg. 1:16 and 4:11, the family of Hobab, with which Moses is supposed to have been related by marriage, belonged to these Kenites. In Num. 10:29 this Hobab, the brother-in-law of Moses, is linked with Reuel, and both stem from Midian. Hobab also takes over at this point the guidance of Israel through the wilderness, since he is familiar with the territory. According to Exod. 2:11ff., Moses fled to Midian and married there the daughter of a Midianite priest (Exod. 2:16ff.), who bears the name Reuel (Exod. 2:18). As noted above, this Reuel was linked with Hobab, the Kenite and Midianite, in Num. 10:29. According to Exod. 3:1, the father-in-law of Moses was the priest in Midian and was now called Jethro (cf. Exod. 4:18). This Jethro visits later on Moses at the mountain of God, praises YHWH as the God of salvation, and offers him a sacrifice. Not only does he know how to do these things, he also shares with the elders of Israel the meal in the presence of YHWH. According to Exod. 3:1f., Moses himself also has had his encounter with YHWH on the mountain of God that is located in the region of Midian.[30] The Midianites dwell south of Palestine (Isa. 60:6 and 1 Kings 11:18), and it is from the south that YHWH comes in order to help his people in the land (Judg. 5:4f.; Hab. 3:3; and Ps. 68:9). The Kenites enjoyed the special preservation of Yahweh, for they bore his signs of protection; yet they must dwell outside the settled land (Gen. 4:12, 14f.). Thus they were linked with Israel in their faith in God (at least for a time) but were separated in terms of the possession of the land. Also, the Rechabites, who were especially zealous on behalf of YHWH (Jeremiah 35; cf. 2 Kings 10:15f.), were Kenites, according to 1 Chron. 2:55. The linkage of the Kenites to Israel is also shown in the fact that the Kenite woman, Jael, fought on Israel's behalf (Judg. 5:24). And under Saul as well as in the early period of David, this linkage became clear once more (1 Sam. 15:6; 30:29). With regard to the Midianites on the whole, the friendship, however, did not last (Judges 6f.; Isa. 9:3).

Thus a hypothesis can be constructed from geographical contacts, the personal kinship relationships of Moses, and the linkages of the Kenites/Midianites with Israel, a hypothesis that provides the following, approximate picture. When he was among the Midianites and on their God's mountain, Moses came to know YHWH. It was to this same mountain of God that Moses led the liberated slaves from Egypt. The Midianites, of whom the Kenites were a part, already worshiped YHWH for a time prior to the Israelites. It was Moses who brought together YHWH and the Moses group as well as Sinai and the exodus.[31] These Midianites dwelt in the region of the land south of Palestine, for example, in the territory of Seir, mentioned often as the place of YHWH's provenance (Deut. 33:2 and Judg. 5:4). All of these combinations receive extra-Israelite support,[32] because the "Shashu" = Bedouin (also called the "Bedouin of Seir") resided in this geographical territory between the Negeb, the Gulf of Aqaba, and the border of Edom. The fact is these very people are mentioned together with YH3 in Egyptian texts that primarily derive from the Nubian Soleb and originate in the fourteenth century B.C.E. Another text even speaks of YHW3-bedouin. The sequence of these consonants is close to יהו (YHW), and they designate probably a deity as well as a mountain and a region. Along with these, there may have been additional extra-Israelite occurrences of the name YHWH,[33] and these would supplement as well the Old Testament evidence. The chronological, geographical, and sociological background of these extra-Israelite occurrences suggests that Israel could have taken over its God from another people. Even so, there is nothing definitive that has been said about the "origins of the faith in God," since we are not able to penetrate behind what the Old Testament tells us (e.g., in Exodus 3 and 14/15), at least at the present time. Thus the total mystery of the name of YHWH is not unraveled. However, perhaps it will be somewhat clear from the above that faith in God and the revelation of God are in a certain way both historical. It pays to inquire about this faith's origins as well as its development. At the same time, the Old Testament itself points to traces of this historical evolution.[34]

b. Yahweh Sebaoth

The name יהוה = *yahweh* (YHWH) occurs 267 times in the Old Testament in the expanded form יהוה צבאות = *yahweh ṣĕbā'ôt* ("YHWH of hosts"; occasionally also הצבאות = *haṣṣĕbā'ôt* = "the hosts"), 18 additional times as יהוה אלהי (הצבאות) = *yahweh 'ĕlōhēy (haṣ)ṣĕbā'ôt* ("YHWH, God of hosts"; e.g., 2 Sam. 5:10; Amos 3:13; 4:13; 5:27; 6:14; Hos. 12:6; Jer. 5:14; 15:16), a construction that often is held to be more original than יהוה צבאות = *yahweh ṣĕbā'ôt* ("YHWH of hosts"), and still further in other combinations as, for example, in the hymnic expanded form יהוה אלהי (ה)צבאות שמו = *yahweh 'ĕlōhēy (haṣ)ṣĕbā'ôt šĕmô* ("YHWH, the God of [the] hosts is his name").[35] Therefore YHWH Sebaoth, including its various combinations, is "the most frequently occurring epithet of God in the Old Testament."[36] The original and (therefore also?) most frequently occurring combination is the short form יהוה צבאות = *yahweh ṣĕbā'ôt* ("YHWH of hosts"). The root residing at the base of צבא = *ṣb'* has meanings both as a verb and as a noun, that is, "to conduct war" and "army." The (feminine) plural noun צבאות = *ṣĕbā'ôt* is formed as a divine epithet, that is, as an attribute of YHWH.[37]

If one looks at the dissemination of the references to this divine epithet, their complete absence in the Pentateuch, Joshua, Judges, Ezekiel, Ezra, Nehemiah, the material unique to the Chronicles, and Daniel is striking. Within the Book of Isaiah the epithet is absent in Trito-Isaiah.[38] When this is coupled with the absence of the epithet in Ezra, Nehemiah, and 1 and 2 Chronicles, one can conclude that there was a decline in use during the post-exilic period. Over against this, however, a great number of references are present in Haggai, Zechariah, and Malachi. The epithet is found especially frequently in Isaiah 1–39 (56 times) and in the Book of Jeremiah (82 times). The references in the Book of Amos (Amos 3:13; 4:13; 5:27; 6:14; each occurrence with יהוה = אלהי צבאות = *yahweh 'ĕlōhēy ṣĕbā'ôt,* "YHWH God of hosts"; in 4:14 and 5:27 שמו = *šĕmô,* "his name," is added) have a formal character and are therefore component parts of a later redaction of the book. In the Books of Kings, it is striking that the references occurring there are found only in association with prophets (Elijah, Elisha, and Isaiah).[39] With the exception of 1 and 2 Samuel (and their parallels in 1 Chronicles) and Psalms, the focal point of use resides in the prophetic literature.

One can think in various ways about צבאות = *ṣĕbā'ôt* ("hosts").[40] They are, first of all, Israel's *earthly hosts* (1 Sam. 17:45; cf. 1 Sam. 15:2f.; 2 Sam. 5:10). Added to this is the fact that this epithet also emerges in association with references to the ark (1 Sam. 4:4; 2 Sam. 6:2), which was certainly among other things, the palladium of war of early Israel.[41] Joshua 5:14 and 2 Kings 3:14 allow one to think about a connection to (YHWH) war. In actual narratives of YHWH war, the combination of יהוה צבאות = *yahweh ṣĕbā'ôt* ("YHWH of hosts") does not occur, however, and 1 Sam. 17:45 is probably not an ancient text. Also, in the prophetic literature, YHWH is not the leader of the hosts of Israel, although he is probably the leader of foreign armies (Amos 5:27; 6:14; Isa. 22:5; 12:25; cf. Isa. 6:3 and 1 Kings 22:19).

Second, the designation *heavenly hosts* may be another rendering of צבאות = *ṣĕbā'ôt* ("hosts"; Isa. 45:13; Josh. 5:14?; cf. Ps. 89:7 beside 89:9), be they stars, angels, or deities deprived of power. In this connection, it must be conceded that the references for this second meaning are rarely to be derived anymore from the Old Testament. It may be that one includes also the cherubim in the "heavenly army" (see below). However that may be, 1 Kings 22:19 and Pss. 103:21 and 148:2 (also Josh. 5:14?) do not exactly understand the expression in terms of this conception of the heavenly army.

A third possibility of meaning, offered by O. Eissfeldt, explains the epithet as an intensive *abstract plural* in the sense of "powerfulness." This explanation, in addition to the first one mentioned, has much to offer. The LXX has translated יהוה צבאות = *yahweh ṣĕbā'ôt* ("YHWH of hosts") most of the time[42] with κύριος παντοκράτωρ = *kyrios pantokratōr* ("Lord almighty"). Thus one may postulate either two different usages or a development from a rather concrete understanding to an abstract one, that is, from Israel's hosts (= armies) as the sign and means of the powerfulness of YHWH to this powerfulness as a divine characteristic. There exists, however, also another, still more probable possibility that the abstract construct of "powerfulness" was applied to this mighty God by looking at the actualization of his distinctive dominancy in war, and this was facilitated with the help of the ark as a war palladium. The name of YHWH and the epithet צבאׄות *ṣĕbā'ôt* ("hosts") are mentioned together first in connection with Shiloh (1 Sam. 1:3, 11). Further, the epithet appears at Shiloh together with the ark as a war palladium, which is the characteristic symbol of YHWH as the one enthroned upon the cherubim. Indeed, YHWH's enthronement upon the cherubim may be a symbol deriving from Shiloh (1 Sam. 4:4; 2 Sam. 6:2 = 1 Chron. 13:6; cf. Isa. 37:16; Pss. 80:2; 99:1). צבאׄות = *ṣĕbā'ôt* ("hosts") "accordingly is the predicate of the royal power of the ruler."[43] Through the combination with both the ark transported to Jerusalem and the cherubim, יהוה צבאׄות = *yahweh ṣĕbā'ôt* ("YHWH of hosts"; cf. in addition 2 Sam. 6:18) receives a privileged position in the Zion tradition, and there as a cultic predicate of God it is often combined with the predication of YHWH as king[44] (Pss. 24:10; 46:8, 12; 48:9; 84:2, 4, 9, 13; 89:9; Isa. 6:3, 5; 8:18; and 31:4).[45] In regard to Zion and temple, one can say that YHWH Sebaoth is "with us" (Ps. 46:8, 12; cf. 2 Sam. 5:10). Whether "יהוה צבאׄות שׁמׄו = *yahweh ṣĕbā'ôt šĕmô*" ("YHWH of hosts is his name") occurs in the language of hymnic praise or whether it is frequently inserted later as an addition into an older text, the power of the God YHWH is articulated by the mouth of the worshiping, postexilic community.[46]

However, one should note that the designation of YHWH as יהוה צבאׄות = *yahweh ṣĕbā'ôt* ("YHWH of hosts"; Ezekiel; P) is apparently avoided by and perhaps even secondarily expunged from certain writings of the Old Testament. Otherwise, the cases of complete omission in a wide range of textual groups and books hardly can be explained. T. D. Mettinger[47] assumes that the expression יהוה צבאׄות = *yahweh ṣĕbā'ôt* ("YHWH of hosts") was mainly avoided, as is also the notion of YHWH's ישׁב = *yōšēb* ("sitting") in the temple, in many contexts and was replaced by other expressions, as for example, the "name," when the temple, with which YHWH Sebaoth was related by means of the ark and the throne of the cherubim, fell under threat and was destroyed by the Babylonians. In the postexilic period, the epithet immediately reemerged in Haggai (1:14) and Zechariah (1:6, 12, 14f.; 2:13, 15; 4:9; 6:15; 7:3, 12; and 8:3, 9, 21f.) when the return of YHWH to Zion is announced and looked forward to with hope.

4.2   The Appellations of God

Besides the especially significant name of God, יהוה = *yahweh,* and its further development in the divine epithet יהוה צבאׄות = *yahweh ṣĕbā'ôt,* the Old Testament also contains other common appellations of God.

a. אלהים = *'ĕlōhîm* ("God")

Among these appellations, the most frequent one is אלהים = *'ĕlōhîm* ("God"), with just under 2,600 occurrences.[48] This name is probably, with the addition of the ה = h, a plural form of either the singular אל = *'ēl* ("God") or of אלוה = *'ĕlôah* ("God").[49] In addition, these latter two appellations can often be used with the same sense as אלהים = *'ĕlōhîm* ("God").[50] However, since the singular אלוה = *'ĕlôah* ("God") occurs only in postexilic texts, it is often regarded as a secondary singular form developing from the primary plural form, אלהים = *'ĕlōhîm* ("God"). This latter name was used in the Old Testament both in the plural sense ("gods") and also predominantly in the singular sense. The divine name אלהים = *'ĕlōhîm* probably describes a plural of intensity or plural of majesty (simply "God" = an abstract plural).[51] Both plurals of intensity and majesty could and did exist openly next to each other so that the "(other) gods" (plural) are placed beside "YHWH your God" (singular) in the first commandment (Exod. 20:3; Deut. 5:6f.). A special word for "goddess" does not occur in the Old Testament. Rather, in 1 Kings 11:5, 33 the discussion is about "Astarte, *the god* of the Sidonians."

From its initial occurrences (present in Genesis 15?) , the Elohist source continues to use אלהים = *'ĕlōhîm* ("God") down to the call of Moses by YHWH in Exodus 3. The Elohist names this God of whom he now speaks (אלהים = *'ĕlōhîm;* "God") YHWH. Quite naturally, this God is the God of Israel; however, it is Moses to whom the name YHWH is revealed in order to refer to the absolute and real God. Subsequently, then, אלהים = *'ĕlōhîm* ("God") is construed always with the singular verb. Similarly, this is true for the use of אלהים = *'ĕlōhîm* ("God") in P from Genesis 1 to 17, that is, from the creation, which is not carried out by just any God (Gen. 1:1), up to the covenant of Abraham. Therefore the special revelation of the Old Testament is spoken about in connection with the divine name יהוה = *yahweh* ("YHWH"), while אלהים = *'ĕlōhîm* ("God") points to general revelation in the Old Testament.[52] This can be underlined by reference to the prophets, with the exception of the postexilic Book of Jonah. Save for Jonah, the prophets do not use אלהים = *'ĕlōhîm* ("God") without enclosing it as a subject within a sentence, "because this appellation of God is for them probably not concrete enough."[53] The use of the name in the form of a direct address shows (Pss. 5:11; 51:3; etc.) that this appellation of God, however, was also understood as a personal name. And the "living God" (Deut. 5:26; etc.) is naturally the one, true God, although the attributive adjective is construed with a plural (i.e., חיים = *ḥayyîm*, "life"). What was important to Israel about its God can be well recognized in the adjectives and construct relationships combined with אלהים = *'ĕlōhîm* ("God").[54] Moreover, the expressions "your (sg. and pl.)/our God" are significant, for YHWH desires "to be (Israel's) God and they are to be his people," to use the words of the so-called covenant formula (e.g., Exod. 6:7; Lev. 26:12; and often).[55] Thus

148   4. The God Who Elects

YHWH is אלהי ישראל = *'ĕlōhēy yiśrāēl* ("the God of Israel"; Exod. 5:1; and often),[56] and the address "my God" points to the relationship between God and
the supplicant, including when the supplicants believe they are abandoned by
God (Ps. 38:22f.; and often).[57]

That אלהים = *'ĕlōhîm* ("God") may also refer to the deities of the foreign nations is obvious, based on what has already been said (cf., e.g., Exod. 12:12;
Josh. 24:15; Judg. 10:6, 16; 2 Kings 18:35; Zeph 2:11; and often). The expression "other gods" (אלהים אחרים = *'ĕlōhîm 'ăḥērîm*)[58] occurs especially often in texts shaped by the Deuteronomic/Deuteronomistic movement and in
passages dependent upon this movement, as, for example, in the texts in the
Book of Jeremiah edited by the Deuteronomistic School or in the Books of
Chronicles. Chronicles warns against the apostasy of following "other gods"
and makes clear that the consequences of following them provide the grounds
for punishment by YHWH. Israelites are not to serve these "foreign" gods, are
"not to pray to" them, and are "not to follow after" them, since they do not
"know" them, that is, the Israelites have no history in common with them.
YHWH has allotted them not to Israel but to other nations to worship.[59] Even
the spirits of the dead can be named אלהים = *'ĕlōhîm* ("God"; 1 Sam. 28:13;
Isa. 8:19; also Micah 3:7?). The comparison of one god, including Israel's,
with other deities and the larger issue of who is really a deity are ancient Near
Eastern themes, but they receive in the Old Testament and especially in the exilic text of Second Isaiah their particular significance as the prophet attempts
to console an impugned faith.[60]

The use of רוח אלהים = *rûaḥ 'ĕlōhîm* ("spirit of God") in Gen. 1:2, where the
translation should be "mighty wind" and not "spirit of God," points to the superlative function of אלהים = *'ĕlōhîm* ("God"). This construction in Hebrew
helps to accommodate for the lack of a regular grammatical form for intensification. Other superlatives include the "mountain of God" to designate an especially high mountain (Ps. 68:16), a "garden of God" to indicate a particularly
beautiful garden (Ezek. 28:13), the "wisdom of God" to point to exceptional
wisdom (1 Kings 3:28), the "cow of god" that occurs in Ugaritic to note simply a splendid cow,[61] and "a great city to God" to refer to Nineveh (Jonah
3:3).[62]

In connection with the observable and intended reduction in the occurrences
of the name of YHWH in the postexilic period,[63] there is by contrast the increasing use of אלהים = *'ĕlōhîm* ("God"). That the postexilic text Qoheleth does
not speak of YHWH but of "God," or rather "the God," results not only from
the characteristic features of its postexilic time period but even more from the
book's own worldview, which includes a portrayal of a rather distant God.[64]
Moreover, the increased use of אלהים = *'ĕlōhîm* ("God") in the postexilic period can be well recognized in the Books of Chronicles and in the Book of
Jonah. This development is also indicated by the so-called Elohistic Psalter

(Psalms 42–83), in which the name YHWH is suppressed in favor of אלהים = 'ĕlōhîm ("God"), which is used here considerably more than in the rest of the Psalter.[65] The fact that here YHWH may be spoken of as אלהים = 'ĕlōhîm ("God") and thereby as "the absolute God" underlines the monotheistic tendency of the Old Testament.[66]

b.   אל = 'ēl ("God")

Common to Semitic languages, with the exception of Ethiopic, is the divine appellative אל = 'ēl ("God").[67] It designates on the one hand (as a title) "god" in the generic sense but on the other hand the Canaanite-Syrian major deity El, who bears this name as his personal name. We know a great deal about the god El because of the Ugaritic texts.[68] Among other things, he is connected with the conception of a heavenly council. His titles include bull, ancient one (cf. Dan. 7:9), hero, king, and creator. He is called "compassionate" (Exod. 34:6), probably also wears the predicate "holy," and possesses the characteristic of "majesty" (cf. Ps. 29:3).[69] He provides the gift of progeny and dwells "at the source of the river, in the midst of the bed of both streams," although other texts place him also on the mountain of the gods in the north. It is easy to recognize that the god El transfers a great deal from his sphere of divination to YHWH, that YHWH in the land of Canaan took over much from him, and that Israel has expanded its faith in God accordingly. Thus the discussion of the council of El is found in Ps. 82:1, his majesty is mentioned in Ps. 19:2 (cf. Ps. 29:3), his throne is found in Ezek. 28:2, and the "sons of El" are present in Pss. 29:1 and 89:7 (cf. Deut. 32:8, following the versions).[70] The mountain of the gods in the north is mentioned in Ps. 48:3, and the "source of the rivers" is perhaps reflected in the four streams of paradise in Gen. 2:10–14.

Etymologically, אל = 'ēl ("God") is connected mostly with the root אול = 'ûl, which means "to be strong, to be in front," with the result that אל = 'ēl can mean something like "leader" or also "power, might." In the Old Testament, there are 238 occurrences of אל = 'ēl ("God"), and indeed in both early (Balaam sayings: Num. 23:8, 19, 22; and 24:4, 8, 16) and later texts (Job). The word is absent in Samuel and Kings as well as in Jeremiah and Chronicles.[71] The Psalms contain the most occurrences (77 times), followed by the Book of Job (55 times). The plural אלים = 'ēlîm ("gods") seldom occurs in the Old Testament.[72] Like אלהים = 'ĕlōhîm ("God"),[73] אל = 'ēl ("God") is also used in the superlative form ("cedars of God" = especially large and beautiful cedars, Ps. 80:11; cf. Ps. 36:7, "mountains of God" = majestic mountains).

In the Book of Genesis different local appellations of the deity El are mentioned in the patriarchal narratives.[74] There appears first in these narratives (Gen. 14:18ff.) the expression אל עליון = 'ēl 'elyôn ("God Most High")[75] by whose name Melchizedek of Salem (= Jerusalem) blesses Abram. Here God receives the titles of the "highest God" and "creator of heaven and earth" (Gen. 14:19, 22). In Gen. 16:13 (J), an אל ראי = ’ēl ro’î ("God who sees") is mentioned in the region between Kadesh and Bered (v. 14), while an אל עולם = ’ēl ‘ôlām ("everlasting God") is mentioned at Beersheba in Gen. 21:33 (J). In Bethel, אל בת-אל = ’ēl bēt-ēl ("God of the house of El"; Gen. 35:3 E) was worshiped as was אל ברית = ’ēl bĕrît in Shechem (Judg. 9:46). These El deities, whose individual components (as, e.g., אל = ’ēl, "God," mainly and then עולם = ‘ôlām, "everlasting," or עליון = ‘elyôn, "most high") are found in some cases in Israel's cultural environment,[76] have no significance in the rest of the Old Testament. The אלים = ’ēlîm ("gods") are not different individual deities but are various forms of revelation and worship of the one El with different epithets.[77] The deity El is met also in the names of places and persons (Bethel, Penuel, Jezreel, Ishmael, Israel, Elhanan, and others). Of special significance for the history of religions is the report out of Gen. 33:20, according to which El (not therefore YHWH) at least during the period of the ancestors was the "God of Israel" (cf. Gen. 46:3) and was worshiped as such in Shechem.[78] This draws attention to the name of the people of "Israel" which contains El, not YHWH or YH, as the theomorphic element. Still, Israel came to equate its YHWH with the Northwest Semitic El, and El was merged into YHWH. This did not happen for the first time in the monarchy.

The Priestly document introduces in Gen. 17:1 the name אל שדי = ’ēl šadday ("God of the mountains"? cf. Gen. 28:3; 35:11; 48:3) for the period of the ancestors down to the revelation of the name of YHWH to Moses (Exod. 6:3 P), therefore providing an overarching connection. This divine name, about which nothing is certain save for the fact that אל = ’ēl ("God") originally was attached to שדי = šadday ("mountains"?) creating then a double name, has a further concentration of use in the Book of Job (there some 31 occurrences), while appearing only 17 more times in the rest of the Old Testament (e.g., Gen. 49:25; Num. 24:4, 16 only שדי = šadday; cf., however, e.g., Gen. 43:14 P?; Ezek. 10:5). Behind שדי = šadday, the exact meaning of which still is not clear (a connection with šadû = mountain?),[79] probably is concealed a pre-yahwistic deity whose name is used as an "archaizing epithet."[80] For P, שדי = šadday ("mountains"?) is the appellation of a deity for a pre-Yahwistic stage of piety, and for the Book of Job it is also a name of a deity who in the dialogues is consciously not named YHWH. K. Koch[81] sees in šadday "a specific form of appearance or entity of activity . . . which stands out from Yahweh," as, for instance, the "angel of YHWH" in the early period or the archangel in the late period of the Old Testament. Supporting this view is the naming of the Šadayin (plural) in the Ammonite Deir ‘Alla inscriptions,[82] a kind of lower order of gods.[83] At the same time, these texts cast light on the Old Testament references to šadday in the speeches of Balaam in Num. 24:4, 16, of which Num. 24:16 (in vv. 15–17) is a very ancient text.[84] Here, Balaam, who also is mentioned in the Deir ‘Alla texts, calls on שדי = šadday.

El then is entirely absorbed by YHWH, stands for YHWH, and can closely approximate him. This is shown by such appellations as קנא אל = *'ēl qannā'* ("jealous God"; Exod. 20:5; and Deut. 5:9; cf. Exod. 34:14; and often), the "great God," the "holy God," and the "compassionate and merciful God" (Ps. 95:3; Isa. 5:16; and Exod. 34:6), where אל = *'ēl* refers always to "God" and it is obvious that, as is the case in Deutero-Isaiah (Isa. 40:18; 43:12; 45:22), YHWH is meant.[85] אל = *'ēl* is (has become), as is true by analogy with אלהים = *'ĕlōhîm* ("God"), purely and simply the "general expression for God, which YHWH claims for himself alone."[86] When the one praying says "my God" (אלי ='ēlî), he or she means quite naturally YHWH (Ps. 22:2; and often).[87]

c. אלוה = *'ĕlôah* ("God")

The appellation of God, אלוה = *'ĕlôah,* is used in the Old Testament only 57 times, of which 41 occur in the dialogues of the Book of Job (Job 3–27). Job and his three friends with whom he is debating are characterized as non-Israelites. Consequently, they do not speak of YHWH and cannot or should not do this, for the Book of Job has as its theme the common human problem of the suffering of the "just," a problem that is not limited to Israelite or to Yahwistic faith, and the related problem of the relationship between deed and consequence that either may be demonstrable or may not exist at all and thus not be legally actionable with God.[88] Among the remaining occurrences in the Old Testament, particular theological nuances in the appellation of the divine name אלוה = *'ĕlôah* ("God") are not to be recognized. These occurrences are found, however, predominantly in the poetic texts (Deut. 32:15, 17; Hab. 3:3; Pss. 18:32; 50:22; 139:19; and Prov. 30:5).

d. Yahweh's Accessibility through His Names

Decisive for the relation of the religious person to God in the Old Testament was, notwithstanding, his knowledge of YHWH, and it was as YHWH that the people of Israel knew the God who chose them, who laid claim to them, who guided them, and who fought for them. If he helped "for the sake of his name" or is beseeched for his aid (Pss. 23:3; 25:11; 79:9; 143:11; Isa. 48:9; and Jer. 14:7), then this means that he acted or should act for the sake of his nature expressed in his name. Other nations do not call on this name (Ps. 79:6). Thus this name also should be "hallowed," and not profaned (Isa. 29:23; cf. Matt. 6:9). One is blessed with the name of YHWH (Num. 6:24–26), and one should walk by his name (Micah 4:5). When the Deuteronomic/Deuteronomistic movement drew up its theology of only one legitimate cultic place for YHWH for the purpose of ensuring "his unity,"[89] this movement also developed a particular theology of the "name" (YHWH).[90] Accordingly, Yahweh will "cause to dwell" (לשכן = *lĕšakkēn*)[91] or rather will "put" (לשום = *lāśûm*)[92] his name in a place that he would choose.[93] It is there that YHWH is near to those who call on him and who come to him. However, YHWH does not put himself at the mercy of someone in this place. Deuteronomy and the Deuteronomistic History do not overvalue or undervalue his nearness or the worth of this cultic place. These texts no longer speak either of YHWH (Sebaoth) himself dwelling in this place or of his "majesty" as a sign and means of his presence there. For instance, if Deuteronomy and the Deuteronomistic History had not also wanted to diminish his presence in the temple and on Zion through this discussion of the "name,"[94] why then was this particular cultic place chosen but not spoken about in terms of YHWH himself dwelling there (cf. Isa. 8:18)? Moreover, in the "name" of YHWH and in the chosen cultic place, according to Deuteronomy and the Deuteronomistic History, Israel now has its external as well as internal center. For Deuteronomic and Deuteronomistic theology, one cultic location still does not possess in itself an abiding or sustained holiness.

"One of the most important things, however, is that for Israel this name never became a 'mystery,' to which only the initiated could have access. On the contrary, each and every Israelite was at liberty to avail himself of it, and once Israel had become fully aware of the distinctiveness of its worship, it did not hide this name of God from the Gentiles in fear, but rather felt itself duty bound to make it known to them (Is. XII. 4; Ps. CV. 1–3). Indeed in the end Yahweh is to be revealed to the world in such a way that all worship of idols vanishes away, and every knee will bow to his name alone (Zech. XIV. 9; Is. XLV. 23)" (G. von Rad).[95]

According to the witness of the Old Testament, the revelation of the name of YHWH took place within history and established a history. YHWH was proclaimed and believed to be the liberator out of Egypt, and his name even gave promise to future and further acts for those who bore his name. YHWH's self-description and therefore the knowledge of his name and nature are fulfilled in a continuous history directed toward this future. "You will know that I am YHWH"[96] (not accidentally elucidated by P during the revelation of the name of YHWH in Exod. 6:7) is a fundamental structure of Old Testament faith in God. Contained in this structure of faith are the knowledge of God deriving from word and history, the promise and dependency of the future on God, and the consciousness of his loyalty and providence. By means of this knowledge of YHWH, the recognition will also take place.

4.3   Yahweh as King

We have spoken of YHWH, of YHWH Sebaoth, and of YHWH as the "one enthroned over the cherubim."[97] These divine appellations lead to the vicinity of the statements that speak of YHWH *as king* and of his *kingship*.[98]

Some thirteen times the verb מלך (*qal;* = *mālak,* "to reign")[99] occurs where it has the broad meaning of Yahweh's "being, becoming, or reigning as king," while the noun "king" occurs some forty-one times as a divine title (מלך = melek).[100] The wisdom literature is noticeably and fully silent about the royalty of YHWH,[101] but this is also true of the Old Testament legal collections, several prophets, and many sections of the narrative literature. The only prose text that contains a verbal occurrence of מלך = mālak ("to reign") is 1 Sam. 8:7. Concentrations of the verb as well as the noun are present in texts[102] that give room to the Zion tradition and the theology of Zion.[103] Furthermore, the collection of Yahweh enthronement psalms contains numerous occurrences (Psalms 47; 93; 95; 96; 97; 98; and 99).[104] Abstract terms[105] deriving from the root מלך = mlk in combination with YHWH are found only in later texts (Obadiah 21; Pss. 22:29; 103:19; 145:11, 12, 13; 1 Chron. 29:11; Dan. 3:33; 4:31). Probably to be added to these are a few texts that call YHWH "shepherd," a predicate that in the ancient Near East was predominantly assigned to the king (2 Sam. 5:2). The references in the Old Testament discussion of YHWH as shepherd over Israel[106] do not, however, offer a direct bridge to statements about YHWH as king of his people or of his world. It is different with the twenty-two occurrences that speak of YHWH's "throne" (כסא = kissê')[107] and the fifty references to his "being enthroned" (ישׁב = yāšab).[108] The "place of his throne" is the temple according to 1 Kings 8:12f. (cf. 2 Chron. 6:2; then Exod. 15:17; Ps. 68:17;[109] and Ezek. 43:7), Zion according to Ps. 9:12 (cf. Jer. 8:19; and Ps. 132:5, 13f.), and heaven according to Deuteronomistic texts or texts dependent on Deuteronomistic thinking that, while speaking of the presence of the "name" of YHWH, still consciously desire to make YHWH more inaccessible[110] (1 Kings 8:30, 39, 43, 49; 2 Chron. 6: 21, 30, 33, 39; cf. 2 Sam. 7:5f.; and Lam. 5:18f.). Earlier texts already speak even naturally of the heavens as the place where God sits enthroned and dwells (cf. 1 Kings 22:19; and Ps. 2:4) and this so that the proximity of the earthly and the heavenly dwellings,[111] that is, of the temple/Zion and heaven, is clearly set forth (Isa. 6:1; Jer. 3:17; Ezek. 43:7; and Ps. 47:9). Later texts likewise do this, however, without once again rearticulating the clear Deuteronomistic accentuation or without already presupposing it as a background of thought (Pss. 33:14; 103:19; and 123:1).[112] Finally, the YHWH predicate, "the one who is enthroned over the cherubim" (ישׁב [ה]כרובים = yōšēb [hak]kĕrûbîm),[113] also belongs to the semantic field of the kingship of YHWH: according to Ps. 55:20, YHWH is enthroned from prehistoric times or "from of old" (קדם = qedem), according to Isa. 40:22 he is enthroned over the circle of the earth, and according to Ps. 22:4 he is "enthroned over the praises of Israel."

   In view of these occurrences, the primary question that now arises is that of their chronological sequence. From the period prior to the formation of the state, there appears to be no instance of YHWH's kingship.[114] This divine predicate was more than likely consciously avoided at that time, for it is very probable that the experience of the state and more precisely the monarchy (cf. the royal psalms, Psalms 2; 45; 72; 110) are necessary for the development of the concept of the kingship of YHWH. Only with the formation of the monarchy can this discussion "be introduced in both affirmative and legitimating as well as critical and negative terms."[115] Exodus 15:17; Deut. 33:5 (cf. v. 26); and Num. 23:21 certainly are important texts in the early period of the state of Israel/Judah, texts that should not too quickly be shoved to the side. For instance, as the parallelism makes obvious, Num. 23:21 refers to the kingship of YHWH and not an earthly kingship. While silent about the kingship of YHWH, the Yahwist is familiar with YHWH's royal court (cf. Gen. 3:22; 11:7; the plural). Other older texts also include Psalm 24 (vv. 7–10);[116] Ps. 29:10;[117] and probably even Ps. 68:25.

Further, it should be asked whether the title "the one who is enthroned over the cherubim," associated with the ark and Shiloh, does not describe an old divine predicate that was eventually transferred to YHWH. However, it is questionable whether the title was always associated with the ark (as a symbol of the presence of YHWH).[118] The title later migrated to Jerusalem with the ark, where the "throne of YHWH" found its place in the temple of Solomon in association with the cherubim in the Holy of Holies (1 Kings 6:23–28).[119] The significance of this "cherub throne" (cf. Isa. 37:14–16, pars.; Ezek. 10:1) for the formation of the conception of the kingship of YHWH should not be underestimated,[120] even if both titles ("king" and "enthroned over the cherubim") are associated with each other for the first time only in Ps. 99:1.

The thesis that the covenant of Sinai was a "king's covenant" and that YHWH, bearing the title of מלך = *melek* ("king"), was a deity who leads since the time at Sinai (so M. Buber) is today no longer an accepted view, primarily because the translation of מלך = *melek* as "leader" cannot be proven. In addition, Judg. 8:22f., with Gideon's rejection of "lordship" over Israel in view of the "lordship of YHWH," may not have originated in the premonarchial period.[121] What is more, there is no mention in this passage of the "kingship of YHWH." Finally, the few additional references, which contrast earthly and divine kingship, derive from Deuteronomistic thought (1 Sam. 8:7; 12:12).

The evidence that in the early period of the state Israel knew something of the kingship of YHWH is suggested by several personal names[122] that are formed with *mlk* (or something similar). Ahimelek (1 Sam. 21:2ff.; 22:9ff.; cf. 26:6; and 2 Sam. 8:17) was related to the priesthood of Nob, while a son of Saul bore the name Malkishua (1 Sam. 14:49; and 31:2). These suggest that the understanding of the kingship of YHWH did take place in the period of state formation in order to function as a modification of and corrective to earthly kingship. When kingship originated in Israel and, in addition, when the Jerusalem temple was built for YHWH, Israel could not close its eyes anymore to the conception of the kingship of God, although in its development the conception of divine kingship still is handled eclectically and reshaped. Kingship and the temple both experienced, in fact, the influence of Canaanite ideology.

In widening the perimeter, it is apparent that the kingship of YHWH is shaped from the beginning of the formation of the state and at times is combined with Zion theology.[123] In this theology, many ideas are appropriated from the kingship of El and to a lesser extent from that of Baal, both of which are found in the Ugaritic texts.[124] In this connection, the oldest reference that may be dated with certainty and that is both clear and familiar in setting forth the conception of YHWH's kingship is Isa. 6:5, which speaks of Isaiah having seen "King YHWH Sebaoth."[125] The "glory" of this divine king fills his court (Isa. 6:1–5). Psalms 29 and 97 reveal clearly a Canaanite heritage where the sons of the gods or gods are to worship YHWH as king (cf. Ps. 96:7ff.).[126] Furthermore, in Jerusalem the god $Ṣdq$,[127] who was probably worshiped there, was addressed as "King," as the royal name of Melchizedek suggests (Gen. 14:18ff.). As in the case of El, royal sovereignty and divine court are connected with each other (Isa. 6:1ff.). While Baal is normally enthroned on צָפוֹן = $ṣāpôn$, Zion becomes the mountain of God in the "north" and the city of the great king (Ps. 48:3).[128]

On the other hand, YHWH's kingship is addressed rather differently from that of El and especially Baal.[129] YHWH indeed is king over the gods (Pss. 95:3; 96:4; and 97:7–9), over all the earth (Ps. 47:3f., 8), and even over the entire world (Ps. 103:19). Yet in addition, he is king over the nations (Ps. 47:3f., 9; Jer. 10:7; and Zech. 14:13ff.),[130] and he is primarily and pointedly the king over his own people and their individual members. Statements of the latter kind are "elsewhere apparently not documented."[131] His royal sovereignty is for the well-being of Israel (cf. Isa. 33:22: "YHWH, our king, he shall help us"), while the gods are no longer real (Pss. 96:5; and 103:19ff.). YHWH has not acquired his royal sovereignty in primeval times through a battle with chaos; rather, the mastery of chaos (cf. Ps. 77:17–20) occurred as the consummation of his kingship (Pss. 89:10f.; and 93:3f.). If YHWH, like Baal, should keep his kingship "forever" (Exod. 15:18; Pss. 29:10; 146:10; cf. Ps. 145:13; Dan. 3:33; and 4:31), he must not, like Baal, continue periodically to descend again into the kingdom of the dead and acquire anew his kingship through battle. Similarly, as with much that is said in the Old Testament about YHWH's court, Zion, the earthly king, and the like, there exists in the statements about the kingship of YHWH an oriental heritage that is reshaped.[132]

Among the references to kingship one shall still have to make another differentiation, as already intimated. In the Old Testament, YHWH is spoken of, first of all, not only as the king of creation, the cosmos, the gods, and the nations, but also, second, as the king of Israel, his people. Further, individual supplicants pray to YHWH as "my" king (Pss. 5:3; 84:4; 145:1; cf. Pss. 68:25; 44:5; and 74:12). The individual statements in this case clearly are applications of common elements of royalty to YHWH by devout persons. Among the references in the Psalms just mentioned, Ps. 5:3 is the one that most likely comes from the preexilic period. Furthermore, YHWH as the king of his people occurs in two ancient texts (Num. 23:21 and Deut. 33:5) and then in later texts in 1 Sam. 8:7; 12:12; Isa. 33:22; Micah 2:13; Zeph. 3:15 (latter part of the verse); Exod. 15:18; and probably also Ps. 10:16 and Jer. 8:19. Thus, a case has often been made for the development of the kingship of YHWH from the rare, "relatively social" statements of YHWH's kingship over his people (O. Eissfeldt). To this might be added[133] the title "shepherd of Israel" (Gen. 49:24; and Ps. 80:2; shepherd is a royal title in Israel's Near Eastern environment) and the "completely hymnic" statements about YHWH as king of the world (cf. also Jer. 46:18; 48:15; and Mal. 1:14). While there are different uses of the title of YHWH as king, at the same time the oldest texts do not reach back to the period before the formation of the state. Along with this, however, the influence of the kingship of El and of Baal can be presupposed, as, for example, in Psalm 29.[134] Certainly the preexilic references point to the "kingship of YHWH" more in terms of his relationship to his people than to his kingship over creation (cf., however, Ps. 24:1f.).

Texts in Ezekiel (Ezek. 20:33–35) and strangely enough especially in the otherwise universalistic Deutero-Isaiah (Isa. 41:21; 43:15; 44:6; and 52:7; cf. Ps. 96:10) speak of YHWH as the king of Israel.[135] This curtailment perhaps has chronological, historical motives that are associated with the situation of the exile. That YHWH is always the king of his people and is demonstrated to be such in the salvation that is breaking into existence at present through him is essential to the content of the message of Deutero-Isaiah. Deutero-Isaiah is familiar with YHWH's court where the book's "prologue" has its setting and where the servant of God is presented (Isa. 40:1–18; and 42:1–4). In the judgment scenes, YHWH demonstrates his preeminence over the nations and their gods, and as king he is the only true deity. Since there are no strange gods at all, this divine status of YHWH, while unexpressed, would still include kingship over the nations (in consideration of the sovereignty of the Persians?). The component of grace in the covenant of David was transferred to God's people (Isa. 55:3–5), and the Persian king became the "messiah" (Isa. 45:1).[136] Here the exodus tradition[137] and the sovereignty of YHWH (cf. Lam. 5:19–21) were bound together. The nations, however, have not dropped from Deutero-Isaiah's view; rather, through what they see and experience they are brought within the inbreaking salvation of YHWH and as a consequence are subordinated to his dominion.[138] "YHWH is king" appears in place of the Babylonian "Marduk is king,"[139] and this king is Israel's and Zion's God (Isa. 52:7; "your God"). The combination of the exodus tradition and the royal sovereignty of YHWH is also found then in later texts (Micah 2:12f.; and 4:7; cf. also Ps. 99:6f.). "When Israel went out of Egypt, the house of Jacob from a foreign people, Judah became his (= JHWH's) sanctuary, Israel his Kingdom" (Ps. 114:1f.; cf. Exod. 19:5f.; also 15:18).[140] Israel's election in history expands to include the choosing God ruling now over this people. If the three Deuteronomistic passages concerning the lordship and royalty of YHWH over his people (Judg. 8:22f.; 1 Sam. 8:7; and 12:12) are also exilic,[141] they on the one hand would take the position of the older texts and on the other hand would consciously seek to speak anew to the situation of the exile.

As the so-called psalms of YHWH's enthronement[142] show (Psalms 47; 93; and 95–99),[143] the royalty of YHWH is celebrated and praised especially in the cult. The thesis of an "enthronement festival of YHWH" in the form of a cult drama in ancient Israel is, however, both uncertain and disputed. In the postexilic period, the celebration of the "enthronement" of YHWH, of his royal status, and of his becoming king on a continuing basis[144] were probably only an element of the autumn New Year's festival. In this context, worshipers experienced and witnessed that YHWH both "rules as king" (מלך יהוה = yahweh mālak)[145] and "has become king" (מלך יהוה = mālak yahweh).[146]

The first of these two expressions is often understood as the "cry of enthronement" (cf. 2 Sam. 15:10; 1 Kings 1:11; and 2 Kings 9:13).[147] With the subject (yahweh) before the verb (mālak), this statement affirms either the sovereignty of YHWH in distinction to other gods or his eternal kingship.[148] Thus one now speaks rather of a cry of acclamation or proclamation that brings to expression the belief that YHWH is really the one who exercises sovereignty. In the cultic festival, the "ascension" of YHWH took place amidst exultation (Ps. 47:6), for "the enthronement of YHWH means taking possession of Zion by the God King."[149] Psalm 93[150] could derive from the preexilic period.[151] While Psalms 93; 97; and 99 hymnically praise YHWH as king, and with this the support given by the exercise of his sovereignty, Psalms 47; 95; 96; and 98 begin by exhorting the worshipers with imperatives to praise YHWH as king. YHWH's kingship is perceived to have no derivation.[152] One ought not to construe an opposition between the exercise of sovereignty and the ritual of enthronement (cf. Pss. 47:6, 9; and 93:1f.), for the poet of the psalm "thinks that Yahweh is king; however, he now describes how he becomes king."[153] "The cultic community proclaims YHWH's becoming king as either presently taking place or as having already taken place (Ps. 47:6, 9). The cult becomes the location of the inbreaking of the reign of God, the place in which the royal sovereignty of YHWH (cf. Ps. 93:1f.) existing 'from of old/from primordial times' breaks into the present reality and confirms its own reality."[154]

Now one may ask about the content the devout person in the Old Testament associates with the discussion of YHWH's royal sovereignty. What does this royal sovereignty evoke or effectuate in the content of faith? What are the reasons for the celebration and praise of this royal sovereignty in the cult?

YHWH's royalty is displayed not only in the primordial defeat of the powers of chaos or the waters of chaos (Ps. 93:3f.) but also in the present and new victory achieved through his role as creator and ruler of the world, the nations (Pss. 47:9; 99:1f.), and the gods (Pss. 95:3; 96:4f.; 97:7, 9). The royal sovereignty of YHWH, expressed through the connection between the earthly and the heavenly divine throne and the temple (Pss. 29:1; 93:1f., 5; and 104:1–3),[155] strengthens the people as a community through the certainty of a saving, royal, divine presence both in Zion (Ps. 48:3; Isa. 24:23) and especially in the sanctuary.[156] His appearance there, his carrying through of law and justice that creates salvation (Pss. 98:1f.; 99:4), his "judgment" of the nations (Pss. 96:10, 13f.; 98:9), and his granting of "sovereignty"[157] provide a basic meaning and content to both worship and human hope.

YHWH's kingship has both a chronological ("eternal") and a territorial (Israel, the nations, the earth) dimension. Further, it has something to do with the mediation of "salvation,"[158] or with the "relief of crisis" (Ps. 93:3f.).[159] The kingship of YHWH includes the maintenance of the world and an ever new conquest of threat (Ps. 104:9), the relationship and mediation of primeval event with the experience of reality actualized during the praise of God by the cultic community,[160] and a continuing, new establishment and carrying through of divine sovereignty. Yahweh's kingship also includes the securing of faith or rather hope in him as the great God and mighty ruler and as the "rock of our salvation." Israel becomes his community, that is, the people of his pasture (Ps. 95:1, 7) who offer praise to this king.[161] Psalms 96–97 already strike their eschatological colors and speak, as does also Obadiah 19–21,[162] of the "kingship of YHWH" as the completion and purpose of history. "The kingship of YHWH" was also a statement of faith that was especially oriented to the future and that continues to set forth hope.[163] "The kingship of YHWH" does not possess negative associations or connotations for religious people in the Old Testament.[164] Therefore one is being too critical as well as too narrow to think that one must warn about the use of the expressions of "divine sovereignty" and "kingship of God," since here the image of the powerful, enthroned God would come close to a triumphal misunderstanding of his nature and would darken "the benevolent countenance of the biblical God by transforming him into a despotic lawgiver greedy for power."[165] Although they worship and rejoice in YHWH as the royal sovereign in the present, human beings shall never realize or bring into full expression the kingship of God in the future. It is, however, the (especially worshiping) community which celebrates, confesses in anticipation, and desires on behalf of the world YHWH's sovereignty. Here, reality is transcended, and it should be noted that prayer is an especially prime location for discourse about divine sovereignty.

This positive and future-oriented course is then taken up in the texts that derive from the very beginnings of apocalyptic[166] (Zech. 14:9, 16; and Isa.

24:21–23) and from the time this new worldview of divine sovereignty achieved its first formulation (Ps. 22:38–32; Dan. 3:33; and 4:31). In this literature, the royal sovereignty of YHWH as the only Lord (Zech. 14:9) once more is consciously extended over the nations (cf. Isa. 25:6–8).[167] Further, it is important to see that even the Book of Daniel, directed toward the fulfillment of the end time, can speak of the royal sovereignty of YHWH[168] encompassing the entire world, not only as an approaching reality but also as a present one in spite of all the adversities in the contemporary period (Dan. 3:33; 4:31; 6:27). This was also the case in the psalms of YHWH's enthronement, which certainly include within the cultic present the tension between the actualization of the past and eschatological hope. The Books of Chronicles sought then to combine earthly and divine kingship in a way that would allow for hope in the future. These books wished to understand the earthly Davidic king as the one in the place of YHWH, that is, as the one in the final analysis sitting on the throne of YHWH (1 Chron. 17:14; 28:5; 29:23; and 2 Chron. 13:8).[169] Nevertheless, in this connection, the royal predicate for YHWH is avoided. Elsewhere the sovereignty of God may be mentioned, although without YHWH being designated as king at the same time.

In spite of the important themes in the texts and collections of texts that have been set forth, one cannot say that the conception of the kingship of YHWH is very central and really basic for the Old Testament. Added to this is the fact that the references to this conception are limited to only a few groups of texts, even if one covers the breadth of the semantic field.[170] Further, it should be noted that the theological language of the royal sovereignty of YHWH gained in significance in the postexilic period (cf. most of the occurrences in the Psalms; Isaiah 24; Obadiah 19–21; Zechariah; Chronicles; and Daniel), while the content of this language is uncovered primarily through a great deal of analogy.[171]

4.4   Yahweh's Powers of Activity

YHWH's activity of election in history is not only attested as a past event by the Old Testament. YHWH acts, moreover, in the present "as a power . . . , active upon the earth"[172] on behalf of his people in order to enter into community with them. One might well ask how and by what means he does this. By what means does he show himself to be a God active in the present? The Old Testament characteristically enough has numerous possibilities for speaking of this present activity and of the revelation of YHWH that occurs within its framework. The most important possibilities will be dealt with in the following.

a. Yahweh's Spirit[173]

There are altogether perhaps 380 passages that deal with the "spirit" in the Old Testament. The word רוח = *rûaḥ* ("spirit") used in this connection shows, moreover, a similar breadth of meaning as does its Greek equivalent πνεῦμα = *pneuma*,[174] namely, from wind or storm (Gen. 3:8; Isa. 7:2; Jonah 1:4; Ps. 135:17; Job 9:18; 19:17; etc.) to breath of life (Job 33:4), vital energy, mind, and will (Exod. 35:21; Num. 14:24; Isa. 61:3; and Ps. 31:6), to the power and the spirit of artistry (Exod. 35:31), and to the spirit of jealousy for the possession and power of God. What holds all of this together is (e.g., in Ezek. 37:1–14) a breadth of meaning openly appearing in the conception of a "wind moving in space" (D. Lys) along with breathing and the breath of life.

The discussion of "spirit" is related to YHWH or God only 136 times in the Old Testament. Of these, the genitive constructs, "spirit of God" (sixteen times in Hebrew and five times in Aramaic) and the "spirit of YHWH" (twenty-eight times),[175] primarily speak to the subject at hand. The idea that "spirit" describes, so to speak, the intrinsic nature of God, say in the manner of John 4:24, is a rare phenomenon in the Old Testament, and even then this occurs with decidedly different emphases (Jer. 31:3; Ps. 139:7; Isa. 40:13).

If one desires to systematize somewhat the Old Testament statements about the spirit as a power of YHWH's activity, then there arise primarily four thematic, distinctive emphases with boundaries that, nonetheless, are often fluid.

YHWH's/God's spirit, first of all, is occasionally an ad hoc gift that is the means by which God is active in certain persons set apart in history for the benefit of his people. There are, for example, the so-called "major judges" on whom falls the spirit of YHWH that makes them into charismatics who are capable then of performing extraordinary military feats (Judg. 3:10; 6:34; 11:29; 13:25; and 14:6). A similar working of the spirit of YHWH is reported about Saul (1 Sam. 11:6; cf. Isa. 37:7). Salvation is achieved through the working of the spirit in Saul, although eventually the spirit of YHWH departs from him, leaving him open to the possession of an evil spirit (1 Sam. 16:14). This kind of military-heroic charisma ceases, though, with the appearance of the monarchy. Only David is supposed to have continued still to possess this "spirit" (1 Sam. 16:13; cf. 2 Sam. 23:2).

The prophetic-ecstatic charisma of prophetic groups mentioned also in connection with Saul (1 Sam. 10:6, 10; and 19:20–24), in which one "will become another human" (1 Sam. 10:6), is witnessed as an active power in other and later places. This power of the spirit is mentioned as being active within older prophecy (Num. 24:2ff.; 2 Sam. 23:2ff.; 1 Kings 18:12; and 22:24). The transfer of the spirit to the successor is important in 2 Kings 2:9, 15f. within an older narrative about Elijah and Elisha.[176] In Deut. 34:9 (P?), there is narrated in a similar way to Num. 27:18ff. (P) the point that the "spirit of wisdom" passes

from Moses through the laying on of hands to Joshua. The prophets of the
eighth century B.C.E. are characteristically silent, however, about the spirit as
a power of YHWH that works upon and within them, a fact that is probably to
be evaluated as their opposition to the "charismatic prophets."[177] The ironic
criticism in Hos. 9:7 allows one to reach this conclusion. In Ezekiel,[178] moreover, this manner of speaking about the spirit reemerges and then is encountered once more in other exilic and postexilic texts.[179] Numbers 11:4 (14ff.) is
occupied with more than the feeding of the murmuring people with quail. This
narrative is also concerned with Moses being a special charismatic leader on
whom YHWH bestows his spirit (cf. Isa. 63:10–14) and with the elders who
shared in this spirit.[180] Mention is made also of the special endowment of the
servant of God with the spirit. It was, above all, in the early period of Israel
that the spirit of YHWH, active and charismatic, took up residence. Postexilic
texts, however, consciously take up this topic, although they see, nonetheless,
the gift of the spirit as being active in a different way than was the case, for instance, with the judges or with Saul. Also, the apocalyptic seer, Daniel, has the
"spirit of the holy gods" (Dan. 4:5ff.; and 5:11, 14), so that he could explain
dreams and mysterious inscriptions (5:12; and 6:4).

However, YHWH can also send a "wicked spirit" and effectuate evil
through it. Consequently, the function of the "evil spirit" is more crucial than
its possession (Judg. 9:23 = Abimelech; 1 Sam. 16:14ff.; 19:10; 19:9 = Saul;
cf. 1 Kings 22:21f. = a "spirit" in the court of YHWH who brings about evil;
then 2 Kings 19:7 = Sennacherib).[181] It is especially early texts that deal with
the "evil spirit," although the experience of reality here is not yet dualistic.

Second, the "spirit of YHWH" is mentioned as God's ongoing gift, as the
breath of life, without which nothing living may continue to live,[182] and as vital energy and will (Josh. 2:11; and Exod. 35:21). The breath of the Almighty
gives life (Job 33:4; cf. Gen. 2:7; Isa. 42:5; Ps. 33:6; Job 15:13; and often), including life to the animal world (Gen. 6:17; 7:15, 22; and Qoh. 3:19, 21).
Wherever this spirit disappears (Josh. 5:1; Isa. 65:14; and Job 17:1), even due
to astonishment (1 Kings 10:5), then the vital energy and the power of life disappears; wherever this spirit returns (again), life revives (Gen. 45:27; and Judg.
15:19). However, whenever God takes (back to himself) this spirit, then the
person has to die, that is, his or her "breath" expires (Gen. 6:3; Ps. 104:29f.;
Job 34:14f.; and Qoh. 12:7). The entire living world is dependent upon the animating power of God.

Thus it is not surprising if the discussion enters into a third area that indicates that the spirit of YHWH is necessary and how it is necessary for the people of God in order that they may live and shape rightly their earthly existence
as the chosen people. This spirit acts upon Israel in the form of a historical
power (Isa. 63:11, 14), and it is the spirit of YHWH in which God's active
presence becomes real for his people (Isa. 34:16; 59:21; Zech. 4:6; 7:12;

Ps. 106:33; Hag. 2:4f.; Neh. 9:20; 2 Chron. 15:1; 20:14; and 24:20). A brief look at these texts allows one to recognize how this topic is treated, especially those texts that originate in the postexilic period. On the basis of the experience of the punishment of the exile that was recognized and accepted as necessary, the postexilic community came to understand that the spirit of God was necessary for a godlike formation of God's people and for a godlike transformation of this community and its devout members (Pss. 51:12f.; and 143:10). Also, the servant of God and the eschatological king of salvation needed this divine spirit in order to bring to proper fulfillment their commissions (Isa. 11:2; 42:1; and 61:1).

In this context are found the two individual Old Testament references that speak of the "holy spirit" (Ps. 51:13; and Isa. 63:10f.). According to these texts, it is the spirit that goes forth from God and resides within his community who is here called "holy."

A fourth sphere of Old Testament statements about the spirit of God, likewise postexilic, speaks then of this spirit as the (necessary, promised, and expected) eschatological gift for the perfection of the people of God, and indeed human beings overall.[183] After correspondingly negative experiences (cf., e.g., Jer. 10:23f.; 13:23; and 17:9f.), and that means after the experiences with apostasy, punishment, and exile, one now hopes for the spirit of YHWH to enable one to act uprightly according to the will of God (Isa. 28:5f.). One awaits the promise of a transformation of the "heart," that is, of the will (Isa. 32:15ff.; 44:3; Ezek. 11:19; 36:26f.; 37:5; and 39:29). In Ezek. 18:31 this was still required as a human work. Joel 3:1ff. (cf. 2:18ff.) especially expanded these thoughts (see also Hag. 2:5; Isa. 59:21; Zech. 12:10; and 13:1f., 8f.). Although the passage does not expressly speak of the "spirit of YHWH," Jer. 31:31–34 also belongs in this connection. Here a perfecting gift of the spirit by YHWH is expected and promised that counteracts the negative experience of both human beings and the community. According to this text, the operation and experience of the spirit in the future would be rather clear, whereas, up to now, what Israel had come to believe and know about the "spirit of YHWH" was in effect contradictory.

Nonetheless, God's gift of the spirit according to the witness of the Old Testament is ever a free gift. The possession of the spirit can come to an end, and it can "depart" (1 Sam. 16:14, about Saul), although the ("false") prophet Zedekiah claimed for himself just the opposite (1 Kings 22:24).[184] "The person is nothing more than the ephemeral vessel of the spirit of God,"[185] and this also when the activity of the spirit is considerably expanded to include the gifts of the power of political leadership (Deut. 34:9 P; cf. Gen. 41:38) and of poetry and art (Exod. 28:3; 31:3; and 35:31). In contrast to this, the idols are without breath, do not possess the power of life, do not have a will, and consequently are without power and strength (Isa. 41:29; Jer. 10:14; 51:17; Hab. 2:19; and Ps. 135:17).[186]

If one looks back at those texts which discuss the spirit of YHWH, one finds most references in narrative and prophetic texts from the early period, then from the exile (Deuteronomistic History; Ezekiel; also Deutero-Isaiah), and last of all from the exilic period. In exilic, cultic texts (Exod. 28:3; 31:3; and 35:31 have a different background) and in legal and wisdom literatures, the lack of corresponding references is certainly not accidental. Proverbs 1:23 is a later text which ties the gift of the spirit to (personified) wisdom, while in the Book of Job the spirit (of God) is mentioned only in statements about general anthropological phenomena.[187]

Whether or not the "spirit of YHWH" is already encountered as a kind of hypostasis in several places in the Old Testament, as it clearly is in Philo and as it might be understood, for example, in 1 Kings 22:21f., this does not appear to prove true, however, for most of the Old Testament. At least this is not the case, if one understands by the term an entity "that takes part in the nature of a deity who through the hypostasis intervenes and becomes active in the world, without the divine nature being depleted through this work."[188]

This hypostasis also would be in some manner independent and a kind of intermediate authority. The "spirit of YHWH" in the Old Testament is one of the active powers of God, but the Old Testament does not ascribe to this spirit an independent form or function.

b. Yahweh's Countenance

When the reference to YHWH's countenance פנים = *pānîm*,[189] a so-called plural of extension, occurs, then it has to do, not with a hypostasis, but primarily with a graphic manner of expression that is close to the secular use of the word. If one "looks" (ראה = *rā'â*) for or wishes to "seek" (בקש = *bāqaš*) "YHWH's countenance," then one searches for a cultic place and prays to or makes a request of YHWH (2 Sam. 21:1; Hos. 5:15; Pss. 24:6; 27:8; 105:4; 1 Chron. 16:11; and 2 Chron. 7:14). As the original source of this expression, the seeking of YHWH's countenance in the cultic place may resonate perhaps with the thoughts about a divine image existing there. In any case, this view no longer plays a role anymore in Old Testament texts and consequently also provides no help in interpreting the meaning of the expression.[190] Thus the so-called shewbread (לחם [ה]פנים = *lehem [hap]pānîm*, "bread of presence") is present only before YHWH (Exod. 25:30), although one did not believe that he would consume it (Exod. 25:30; 35:13; 39:36; 1 Sam. 21:7; 1 Kings 7:48; and 2 Chron. 4:19; cf. Num. 4:7; then Ps. 50:12ff., which expressly denies that YHWH needs nourishment). Who desires to look at YHWH's countenance visits his sanctuary (Exod. 23:15, 17; 34:23; and Deut. 16:16—thus in the so-called festival calendar;[191] then Isa. 1:12; Ps. 42:3; cf. 1 Sam. 1:22, niphal?; and Job 33:26). This image points to a special intimacy with YHWH (Ps. 25:14f.), a trusting devotion to him (Pss. 123:2f.; 141:8; and 145:15), and the experience of his help (Ps. 17:15; cf. 11:7; Num. 6:25f.; Job 33:25f.; and Isa. 38:11). These positive experiences and connotations (e.g., "to cause the countenance to shine") are also mentioned in Pss. 4:7; 31:17; 67:2; 80:4, 8, 20; 119:135; and Dan. 9:17. The conclusion of the so-called Aaronic blessing (Num. 6:26), even as the passages cited before, makes one recognize that this expression has to do with the gift of divine grace. It is the language of the cult, and especially the language of prayer,[192] that favors, and not without reason, this figure of speech.[193]

Furthermore, one even encounters YHWH's countenance as a subject acting in history (Exod. 33:14; Deut. 4:37; Isa. 63:9; and Lam. 4:16) that expresses, as do the "sovereignty of YHWH"[194] and other figures of speech, the personal presence of God. This divine activity through the countenance of YHWH is always a positive occurrence that leads to the well-being of the one concerned. Whether YHWH's countenance "appears" or one "looks" at it in order then to receive divine judgment or punishment is never actually said within the Old Testament texts. Perhaps it is precisely this positive semantic content that explains why there is relatively seldom a discussion of the "face of YHWH" within the prophetic books (Hos. 5:15; Micah 3:4; Isa. 8:17; 54:8; Jer. 33:5; Ezek. 39:23f., 29; Zech. 7:2; and 8:21f.).

Exodus 23:15ff.; 34:20ff.; Isa. 1:12; Ps. 42:3; and others speak of an appearance (expressed in the passive voice) before[195] the countenance of YHWH. That YHWH speaks or associates with someone "face to face" (Gen. 32:31; Exod. 33:11; Deut. 34:10; Judg. 6:22; Ezek. 20:35; cf. Deut. 5:4) occurs with persons especially chosen and set apart and designates an unusual familiarity.

While the "appearance" or "seeing" of the face of YHWH has no negative effects, YHWH, nonetheless, can "set his face against someone" (שׂים = śîm; Jer. 21:10; 44:11; and Ps. 34:17), providing then an additional dimension (cf. Lev. 17:10; 20:3, 6; 26:17; cf. also 20:5: thus in the Holiness Code; for a related use, see Ezek. 14:8; 15:7). Or, YHWH "hiding" his countenance (סתר = sātar hiphil: thus 25 times)[196] means he does not in principle and always in grace turn to human beings. Indeed, this expression also has negative consequences (according to Ps. 104:29, this is true for the entire creation)[197] that are recognized and lamented.[198] Once again it is the language of the psalms with twelve references, in particular the prayer of the individual and less so the prayer of the people (Pss. 44:25; 89:47; Isa. 64:6), in which questions, as for instance "How long?" (Ps. 13:2), and pleas are more frequent.[199] According to Isa. 8:17, the hiding of the divine countenance has negative historical consequences for the house of Jacob (cf. Deut. 31:16–18); however, in spite of this, the prophet ventures to hope. The experience and tribulation of the hiddenness of YHWH may not continue, for people knew something also of YHWH's turning toward them again. The exilic promises in Ezek. 39:24 or Isa. 54:8, for instance, speak of the opposite, namely, that YHWH does not intend anymore to conceal his face or that he has concealed it only for a period of time. "The God who hides himself is the savior"[200] (Isa. 45:15).

Therefore the "face of God" stands for the gift of his grace. When he conceals his face, he thus withdraws this grace (cf. Exod. 33:14f.).[201] This analogously reflects the secular use of פָּנִים = pānîm ("countenance," Gen. 33:10). And the light of the divine countenance means also his concrete, helping intervention. If YHWH promises his accompanying presence, then he himself goes again with his rebellious people, be it through his angel (Exod. 32:34; 33:32)[202] or through his countenance (פָּנִים = pānîm, "countenance," Exod. 33:14f.), both of which incorporate YHWH's presence and carry out his guidance. Thus, פָּנִים = pānîm ("countenance") stands "for a kind of synecdoche"[203] for his "personal presence, relationship, and encounter (or denial of the same)."[204]

c. The Angel of Yahweh

To the powers through which the Old Testament God is active on the earth and among human beings belongs the "angel of YHWH" (מַלְאַךְ יהוה = malak yahweh),[205] who is to be distinguished from the sons of the gods and the angels who belong to the divine court.[206] "The" angel of YHWH appears as an individual, special, and emphasized being, a kind of vizier of God. While the angels within the Old Testament assume no important position, it is different with the angel of YHWH. Messengers of God can be angels, human beings, priests, and prophets. The angel of YHWH (so 56 times in the Old Testament; 10 times the "angel/messenger of God") is conspicuous among them. This raises the question as to whether the mention of him in many texts is a secondary insertion.

It is especially striking, on the one hand, that this angel of YHWH is not mentioned in the prophetic books. The human interpreter (the "man") in Ezekiel 8 and 40–48 and the angel in Zech. 1:9–6:5, often called the angelic interpreter, have nothing directly to do with the "angel of YHWH."[207] They appear in situations that have to do with the exercise of a different function than that of the angel of the Lord. Also, the angel who gives interpretations in Daniel (at times appearing in the form of the "man Gabriel": Dan. 8:15f.; 9:21) develops from the persons functioning in Ezekiel and Zechariah rather than from any association with the angel of YHWH. What the apocalyptic seer sees is to be more clearly "explained" by this angel who provides the interpretation, first, for the reader to understand, and, second, for emphasizing the uniqueness of this apocalyptic seer (Dan. 4:16ff.; 6:23; 7:16ff.; 8:15ff.; 9:20ff.; 10:5, 9ff.; and 12:5; cf. also the angels of nations mentioned in the Book of Daniel: Daniel 10 and 11; 12:1).[208]

On the other hand, the discussion of the angel of YHWH in the narrative texts of the Old Testament occurs rather frequently. This begins in the stories of the ancestors (Gen. 16:7ff.; 21:17ff.; 22:11ff.; 31:11ff.; cf. 48:16), continues in the narratives about Moses (Exod. 3:2ff) and the stories of the judges (Judg. 2:1–4; 5:23; 6:11ff.; 13:3ff.), then occurs in the form of the punishing angel on the occasion of the national census carried out by David in 2 Sam. 24:16f., and concludes with 1 Kings 13:18; 19:7 and 2 Kings 1:3ff.; 19:35. All of these narratives make a rather original impression. In Priestly texts, one no longer finds any mention of the angel of YHWH. The only later references are Gen. 24:7, 40; Ps. 35:4ff.; and Isa. 63:9.

Accordingly, the angel of YHWH often comes with a divine message and/or a mission for action or intervention. In so doing, he speaks and acts for YHWH. Whether there are pre-Israelite, local traditions reporting the appearance of a numen that stand behind these individual narratives must be examined in each case. In most cases, the angel's action is benevolent.[209] However, according to 2 Sam. 24:16f. (cf. 1 Chron. 21:15; cf., however, also Ps. 35:5f.), he turns *against* Israel, while according to 2 Kings 19:35 he turns against Sennacherib, although for the good of Israel. Also, the angel's goodness or wisdom can be spoken about (1 Sam. 29:9; 2 Sam. 14:17, 20; 19:28; cf. Zech. 12:8).

Often it is not easy to establish a distinction between YHWH himself and his angel, since both are often mentioned in close association (Gen. 48:15f.; Exod. 13:21 beside 14:19), whether acting or speaking, so that the angel becomes a kind of form of appearance of YHWH and his representative (cf. Genesis 16 and 21, Judges 6 and 13, as well as Exodus 3; then 2 Kings 19:35 par.; Num. 22:32; and 1 Kings 19:7). He shows each time not only that YHWH turns toward humanity, appears, and is active but also how he does so.[210] As leader of the people in the journey through the sea and in the wilderness the angel of YHWH (along with the "face" of YHWH,"[211] and the fire and the cloud) is mentioned in Exod. 14:19; 23:20f., 23; 32:34; 33:2; and Num. 20:16. In Exodus 33, in the chapter that comprehensively reflects on the possibility or impossibility of YHWH's dwelling among his sinful people, the angel is distinct from YHWH and probably represents him in a limited form (Exod. 33:2f.).

Naturally all of these texts attempt to preserve the tension between the transcendence and the immanence of God.[212] Within the course of this evidence, the discussion of the "angel of YHWH" with the detailing of its functions was probably an older way of holding on to the notion that YHWH and his angel were both separate entities existing beside each other and yet also blending into each other. Later texts are silent about this angel of YHWH. In Job 33:23ff. the discussion focuses on an angel as a heavenly defender who thus probably was considered to be the opposite of the heavenly prosecutor, Satan, in Job 1 and 2.[213] The angel of death in Prov. 16:14 was only a messenger of death. The different theories of scholarly criticism about the origin of the angel of YHWH[214] have offered nothing that can be helpful beyond what was said here for understanding the Old Testament evidence.

d. The Glory of Yahweh

To the powers of divine activity and presence belongs the "glory" of YHWH, his כבוד = *kābôd*.[215] As the secular use of כבד = *kābad* and כבוד = *kābôd* shows, this word signifies "heavy" (1 Sam. 4:18; Exod. 17:12) and then "renown, dignity, importance, wealth" (e.g., Gen. 31:1; Isa. 5:13; 8:7; 16:14; 17:4; 21:16; 22:24; and 1 Chron. 29:28). When the discussion centered on the divine *kābôd*, what was imagined was a certain "weight" associated with God's appearance, as, for example, Ezekiel 1–3 makes clear. This text presents a fiery, shining, and portentous appearance of the divine light of YHWH, who is described as surrounded by brilliance and majesty in the manner of gods and kings in Israel's environment.[216] Thus this brilliance of light, this glory of YHWH/God was the sign and the means of his active presence, especially in his sanctuary.

Isaiah 6:3 is the first indication that this *kābôd* ("glory") of YHWH was connected to the temple in Jerusalem, or rather was and could be experienced there,[217] in a way that was, so to say, the external side of the "holiness of YHWH."[218] In the earthly temple, the prophet sees and hears, as though he is standing in the heavenly pantheon, the creatures of YHWH's *kābôd* ("glory") who praise him (cf. Ps. 24:10) as king. At the same time, it is stressed that his *kābôd* ("glory") not only is a heavenly entity but also fills the earth (cf. Pss. 57:6, 12; 66:1f.; Isa. 42:12). Thereupon, the *kābôd* ("glory") carries out YHWH's turning toward the earth and makes this turning known. YHWH's abundant glory "presses . . . beyond the sphere of the heavenly-earthly temple and the royal palace into the world."[219]

Along with this (cultically influenced) text from Isaiah belong also passages from the Psalms, of which Pss. 19:2 and 29:9 point to Canaanite (כבוד אל = *kābôd 'ēl*, "glory of El") or more specifically Jebusite material reshaped and/or absorbed by Israelite faith in YHWH.[220] Twenty-four times the discussion of the *kābôd* ("glory") of YHWH occurs in the Psalms (e.g., Pss. 24:7–10; 26:8; 57:6, 12; 63:2ff.; 66:2; 72:19; 96:3; 97:6; 102:16f.; 138:5; and 145:5). These texts demonstrate that this theological language of the *kābôd* ("glory") of YHWH belongs clearly to the worship tradition of the Jerusalem temple, while the themes of "salvation history" are not yet demonstrably taken up. In earthly as well as heavenly worship (Psalm 29), and also in nature (Psalm 19), God's *kābôd* is experienced and then praised. It is no surprise therefore that this glory of YHWH present and active in the cult is not mentioned in books such as Genesis, Amos, Hosea, Micah, and Jeremiah. Also Deuteronomy is silent about the theological language of the "glory of YHWH" that is original to Jerusalem and that is the sign and means of his presence (Deut. 5:24 is secondary), even as the ark[221] in Deuteronomy is no longer the sign of the presence of YHWH but rather becomes the container of the tablets of the law. In addition, the name

YHWH Sebaoth, readily associated with the ark, is not found in Deuteronomy. While both the ark and the glory of YHWH appear in 1 Kings 8:11, within a chapter that in its present form has been shaped by the Deuteronomistic editors, their presence represents an addition that conforms to the priestly spirit.[222]

In addition to the Jerusalem temple theology, the second emphasis in the Old Testament discussion of the *kābôd* ("glory") of YHWH comes from exilic texts. The first from this period to mention the *kābôd* ("glory") is the Priestly document[223] which may speak of the glory of YHWH even when the writers are far away from the temple that has been destroyed. According to P, YHWH's *kābôd* ("glory") had been active in the journey through the sea and in the deliverance of Israel in the presence of the Egyptians and their pharaoh (Exod. 14:4, 17, 18: with the verb *kbd;* cf. Lev. 10:3). Later, the *kābôd* ("glory") descended from heaven and appeared to the community on Sinai (Exod. 24:15–18).[224] Then the *kābôd* ("glory") of YHWH, often with the cloud[225] and in association with the "tent of meeting,"[226] migrated with this people through the "wilderness." Divine accompaniment and presence in a portable sanctuary were made possible through God's actual appearance in his *kābôd* ("glory").[227] Accordingly, the *kābôd* ("glory") of YHWH, which is significant for the entire thinking of P,[228] is also in this respect especially appropriate for the cultic sphere and consequently has an effect on Jerusalem temple theology in a modified, though firm manner (Exod. 24:15–18; 40:34f.; and Lev. 9:23; cf. 10:3). In these priestly texts, the appearance of the *kābôd* ("glory") in the "tent of meeting" is readily followed by an ensuing speech of God that has a forward pointing, promising character (Exod. 16:10f.; 29:43: here as YHWH's self-determination;[229] 40:34; Lev. 9:6, 23; Num. 14:10f.; 16:9f.; 17:7ff.; 20:6f.; and Deut. 34:10). The *kābôd* ("glory") appears during the "wilderness wandering" to give emphasis to the purpose of carrying out the threatening power of YHWH, to his salvific might, and to his new promise of additional guidance of the murmuring people (Exod. 16:10; Num. 14:10; 16:19; 17:7; and 20:6).[230] In this way YHWH is with his people, his community. Thus history, cultus, and community are bound together through this moving, accompanying *kābôd* ("glory") that is the means of YHWH's appearance and travel among his people. Also here, as is the case with Deutero-Isaiah (see below), the altered historical situation appears to contribute to these theological nuances, that is, the situation of the exile shines through these narratives and provides them with a paradigmatic character.

It is no surprise that, after the destruction of the temple and within the exilic community, there was a ready return to the discussion of the *kābôd* ("glory") of YHWH in order to find the ability to speak about the active presence of God. It is astonishing, however, that this kind of language is missing in Haggai, Zechariah, Malachi, Ezra, and Nehemiah. At least in Zechariah (chaps. 1–8; and Hag. 2:3, 7, 9; Zech. 2:9 [12] does not belong to the area under present discussion), the interest in the building of the temple perhaps may have been less than is often assumed. If, by contrast, the Books of Chronicles (cf. only 2 Chron. 7:1–3) demonstrate a familiarity once more with this kind of language, this is one more indication that these books do not have the same author as the books of Ezra and Nehemiah. Nevertheless, it can be also acknowledged that temple theology in the Books of Chronicles has once again become more important.

Ezekiel, in whose book the *kābôd* ("glory") of YHWH is mentioned some sixteen times (cf. Ezek. 8:4; 9:3), is allowed to see the "majesty of YHWH" (Ezek. 1:28; 3:23) during his call when he is far from the temple in Babylonian exile (like the basic stratum of P and Deutero-Isaiah). According to Ezekiel 1–3, this "majesty of YHWH" moves about and, according to the textual additions, is even provided on all sides with rolling wheels. According to Ezek. 11:22ff. (cf. before 10:4, 18f.), this "glory of YHWH" had abandoned the temple and was traveling toward the east (!), because of the nation's religious apostasy. As Ezekiel the visionary sees it, this glory of YHWH will return again from the east and will come into the newly rebuilt temple (Ezek. 43:1ff.; cf. 44:4).[231] The exilic text, Deutero-Isaiah, likewise speaks about YHWH's glory and understands it especially as a power active in history that is seen by all the world (Isa. 40:5). At the same time, he does not will to entrust his *kābôd* to anyone else (Isa. 42:8; cf. 48:11; 58:8; and Jer. 2:11). Psalm 79:9f. requests that YHWH help his people for the sake of the honor or the glory of his name[232] and here, as in Ps. 115:1f., provides a lengthy explanation as to what will happen to the nations who normally ask where Israel's God might be. Both psalms probably presuppose Deutero-Isaiah with this argument.

Within the large section of Exodus 32–34,[233] the multilayered addendum of Exod. 33:18–22 (23)[234] still has significance, for here Moses asks to be allowed to see YHWH's "glory." In the present context (mainly Exodus 33), this request is closely connected with the inquiry about the possibility of the continued presence of YHWH among his (wayward) people. In the more narrow textual context, this request to see the "glory" of YHWH is entwined with Moses' desire to "see the countenance (פנים = *pānîm*) of YHWH."[235] In both cases, Moses, like any other human being, may not see either the glory or the face of YHWH but rather is allowed to see only his "back" (v. 23).

Thus a theologumenon (perhaps even taken from pre-Israelite tradition) of the Jerusalem temple theology is rendered through the passage of time into another form so that when one is distant from the temple or when it is destroyed, one may still attempt to speak of the nearness of this mighty God and of the presence of his glory. God's glory does not depart at the expense of human beings; rather, it appears and works to promote their well-being. What one had experienced in the cult, one dared to believe even when separated from the cult during such occasions as the exile. And one hoped for the new diffusion of this divine glory in captivity (Deutero-Isaiah) as well as for its new cultic presence after the return home (Ezekiel). Through concerted language about the *kābôd* of YHWH, the cult, history, and situation of the exile were bound together (P; cf. also Ezekiel). Beyond that, the discourses about the glory of YHWH found in the postexilic period an expanded place in eschatologically colored texts which, in following Deutero-Isaiah, hoped for the complete diffusion of the glory of YHWH (Isa. 4:5; 24:23; 60:1f.; 62:1f.;[236] 66:18f.; Ezek. 39:21; and Ps. 102:17; in the New Testament, see esp. Luke 2:9; John 1:14; and Rev. 21:23).

e. The "Name" of Yahweh

In an obvious and certain (also critical?) contrast to the theology of the ark and the *kābôd* ("glory")[237] and, above all, in response to an altered historical and therefore different theological situation, the movement standing behind the Deuteronomic and Deuteronomistic literature developed a particular theology of the "name" (שׁם = *šēm*) of YHWH.[238] It was not unknown in Israel's cultural environment for one also to speak of the "names" of a deity as the sign of his or her presence.[239] Exodus 20:24 is an important, older, Israelite reference that shows that the Deuteronomic/Deuteronomistic movement established here no new "theology" but rather had appropriated and further sharpened a preexisting idea (cf. also Isa. 18:7, secondary). The Deuteronomic texts now speak of YHWH choosing a place in which he will "cause his name to dwell" (לשׁכן = *lĕšakkēn;* Deut. 12:11; 14:23; 16:2, 6, 11; and 26:2—here only in paraenetic texts; cf. further Jer. 7:12; Ezra 6:12; and Neh. 1:9; but not in the historical stratum of the Deuteronomistic source). In this Deuteronomic view, there is also a consciously different emphasis in the theological judgment about the temple and the city of God. The presence of YHWH believed to be found in Jerusalem and the temple is no longer to be conceived too directly and too narrowly.[240] The realization that the other important ideas of Jerusalem temple theology, such as YHWH's "glory" or the divine name "YHWH Sebaoth," are not mentioned in Deuteronomy and that the ark is transformed in function to become the container of the tablets of the law only underscores this point. This purposeful diminution becomes still clearer through the further (Deuteronomistic) development of the just-mentioned formula, a development that is difficult to explain. According to this, YHWH does not "cause his name to dwell" in the place he has chosen; rather, he "puts" his name there (לשׁום = *lāśûm:* Deut. 12:21; 14:24; 1 Kings 9:3; 11:36; 14:21; 2 Kings 21:4, 7; cf. 1 Kings 8:29f., 44f.; 2 Kings 23:27; 2 Chron. 6:20; and 33:7; "to cause to dwell" and "to put" come together for the first time in Deut. 12:5). Consequently, the conception of dwelling is fully negated, while the attempt is made "to eliminate the misunderstanding of a too narrow bonding of Yahweh to the sanctuary."[241] And the verb that suggests such a conception ("cause to dwell") completely vanishes. With that, the (Deuteronomistic) references join together in affirming that YHWH finally dwells in heaven (Deut. 4:36; 26:15; 1 Kings 8:30, 39, 43, 49).[242] One could still believe from here on that YHWH not only is near his temple and is even present there but also is omnipresent, an option that was especially important for the community in exile (cf. 1 Kings 3:2; 5:17, 19; 8:16, 17–20, 29; etc.). These are the questions that are opened up by the destruction of the temple and the exile to a distant land that should be supplied with a helpful answer. Now YHWH continues to be one who may especially be called upon in heaven, since he did not take away his "name" from human beings. Thus the temple in the Deuteronomistic formulations of Solomon's dedicatory prayer (1 Kings 8:[14], 22–61) is emphasized, not as a place of sacrifice, but as a location of prayer. And the direct presence of YHWH is diminished, perhaps even eliminated.[243] However, YHWH "dwells" also in the midst of his people (cf. Exod. 29:45 P; 1 Kings 6:11–13; Ezek. 43:7–9). The quest for a theology of the name was to serve the purpose of keeping together God and people in a changed situation, without regarding YHWH once again or even in a different way as placed at Israel's beck and call.

f. Yahweh's Justice

According to the earliest and latest witnesses of the Old Testament, the theme of YHWH working for the good of his own[244] and that of the world through his justice is a fundamental, continuing structure of faith.[245] This does not mean that YHWH's works are placed within a relationship of cause and effect[246] that leads to the questioning of divine justice when crisis is experienced or when the innocent and the just suffer (cf. Job). Rather, even as the first and oldest reference to the "righteousness (acts of righteousness) of YHWH" demonstrates, divine justice involves YHWH's historical acts of salvation, acts that he extends to his people (thus, e.g., in the Psalter), to individual persons, and even to his world.

Already in the ancient Song of Deborah, YHWH's "acts of righteousness" are addressed (Judg. 5:11; in the plural). In Judges 5, as well as in the prose report (Judges 4) parallel to this poetic account, the subject of righteous acts is holy war[247] in connection with the conquest and securing of the land for "Israel." Occurring in the song (vv. 6–30) that is a hymn to YHWH who fights on behalf of his own, Judg. 5:11 is part of the description of the battle. In view of these acts of salvation by YHWH, the congregation is called on to give praise to God. And these "acts of salvation" comprise YHWH's military support (or acts of support) for the good of his farmers, or even the deeds performed for Israel in the conquest of the land that YHWH gave to his people (v. 13). This gift of the land, which still required many battles and victories (plural) in the form of historical acts of salvation, is abbreviated in the expression "acts of YHWH's righteousness." In a larger context, these "righteous acts" are regarded as the fundamental deeds of salvation within the framework of the history of the nation with their God. This understanding of God's righteous acts as acts of salvation on Israel's behalf occurs repeatedly wherever YHWH's "righteousness" ("acts of righteousness") is discussed (cf. Deut. 33:21; Micah 6:5; Ps. 103:6; and Dan. 9:16). However, these acts of YHWH's righteousness involve neither retribution nor a compensatory justice; rather, they form a conceptual abbreviation of the (in Judges 5 military) acts of YHWH's salvation for the good of his own. If this view were well known, then it is striking that this abbreviation was not also used to mark the distinguishing feature of the earlier acts of YHWH's salvation and, above all, the exodus event. Disregarding the exceptional text of Deuteronomy 33, there is no mention of the "righteousness" ("acts of righteousness") of YHWH in the Pentateuch. The first reference to YHWH's "righteousness" ("acts of righteousness") emerges in connection with the conquest or the securing of the land. This will be pursued later.

The second reference to this topic among the oldest texts leads in similar directions. In the saying about Gad in the Blessing of Moses (Deut. 33:21), the righteousness (singular) of YHWH is mentioned in a way that it also has to do with the gift of the land and the expansion of territory as an act of YHWH's historical help for the well-being of his own. Thus this reference is once more an abbreviation for such a historical event. God is praised as the one who "creates territory for Gad." When the defenders of the nation are gathered, Gad executes (עָשָׂה = 'āśâ is the verb) the righteousness of YHWH and his just commands for the good of (or "together with"?) Israel. This expansion of the land probably brought Gad the territory of the firstborn (Reuben?) and the commander's allotment (vv. 20–21).

The considerably later reference in 1 Sam. 12:7 also eventually leads in similar directions. This is a text that in the basic Deuteronomistic source is a typical farewell discourse, in this case, by Samuel. In a review of the past, this speech records that YHWH's purpose in salvation was met with rejection while Israel was incomprehensibly guilty before YHWH's "acts of salvation." Indeed, this (Deuteronomistic) conclusion is drawn in vv. 20ff. Then follows last of all a lawsuit (רִיב = *rîb*, "disputation") with Israel, and the theological motifs of this proceeding are the "acts of YHWH's salvation" (12:7; again plural), once more an abbreviation of YHWH's acts in history on behalf of his nation and in this context particularly the conquest and gift of the land (vv. 8ff.).

Also, the (likewise probably later) reference in Micah 6:5 (cf. 7:9) in the pericope of Micah 6:1–5 (8?) reflects YHWH's historical acts of salvation. In response to the accusations of his people, YHWH defends himself by a reference to his past acts that eventually makes its way to the gift of the land. Israel should have and could have recognized these acts of salvation (again in the plural and an abbreviation) that were YHWH's mighty deeds in the early period of his people.

There is no text that refers to the occurrence of YHWH's "righteousness (acts of righteousness)" prior to the conquest. The idea first emerges, then, in connection with the salvific acts of YHWH primarily in winning and securing the land of Canaan. Is this idea the "weighty inheritance[248] of Canaan left to Israel"? In what way was this inheritance so weighty, why has Israel taken it over exactly in this form, and how has Israel administered this inheritance?

In Hos. 2:21 and 10:12, צדקה = ṣĕdāqâ ("righteousness") and צדק = ṣedeq ("righteousness")[249] in both cases are bound with חסד = ḥesed ("loyalty, steadfast love"), a factor that contributes to their meaning. Here this "righteousness of YHWH" concerns salutary activity.[250] In addition, in Hos. 10:12 the association of the metaphors of sowing and harvest as well as the "causing of the rain" is significant for the understanding of righteousness.

The references in the Book of First Isaiah, the "authenticity" of which is not to be examined here, allow one primarily to recognize a relationship of the "righteousness of YHWH" to Zion, that is, to the city of Jerusalem (Isa. 1:26f.; cf. vv. 8 and 17). In Isa. 5:16 and 10:22, one has often wanted to find a punishing righteousness of YHWH, something that, apart from the references in the Psalms which will be mentioned below, is rare and often secondary. The relationship of YHWH's righteousness to Zion may shine through in Isa. 5:16, although here the discussion is of אל = 'ēl ("God"; cf. also Israel/Judah in 5:7), then even more clearly in 28:17f., and also in 9:6 and 11:4f. In the two last-mentioned references, the discussion concerns YHWH's righteousness as an eschatological gift of salvation, while 9:6 could also reflect the Egyptian idea of ma'at as the base of the throne[251] (cf. Pss. 89:15; 97:2, 6; also 72:2ff.; Prov. 16:12; and 25:5). This clear association of צדקה = ṣĕdāqâ ("righteousness") with Zion/Jerusalem suggests now the assumption already addressed that in this previously and, to be certain, non-Israelite, Jebusite city, which derived its name probably from the god Salem[252] (cf. Ps. 76:3 Salem), the deity Sedeq could be worshiped even still. Psalms 85:10ff.; 89:15; and Joel 2:23 may refer to this worship (cf. also Pss. 48:11f.; 97:2; and Jer. 31:23). If so, the possible place of inspiration for Israel's "Canaanite inheritance" mentioned above would be more precisely grasped. Evidence for this deity Sedeq[253] has now been found in the Phoenician-Syrian region. As early as 1400 B.C.E., this god was listed among the Ugaritic personal names and elsewhere.[254] In addition, while the kings Melchizedek and Adonizedek reigned in Jerusalem (Gen. 14:18ff.; Ps. 110:4; Josh. 10:1ff.; and Judg. 1:6?), there are not a few Old Testament texts in which "righteousness" occurs almost in a personified form (Pss. 48:11f.; 85:11 [Salem and Sedeq kiss each other], 12, 14; 89:15; 97:2;

and 112:3). Jerusalem is addressed as both the city and the dwelling of Sedeq (Isa. 1:21, 26; cf. 9:6; 11:4), something that has a later effect in Jeremiah (23:6; 31:23; cf. 50:7) and even in Deutero- and Trito-Isaiah (Isa. 54:14; 60:17). This deity was a solar god and responsible for the divine, just, world order in an analogous manner perhaps to Utu or Shamash in the region of Mesopotamia. The deity of Zion, Sedeq, was a sun god and as such a god of the cosmic order (cf. also Ps. 57:9–12). His order proceeded throughout the world from its place of origin at the mountain of God. The "sun of righteousness" (Mal. 3:20; cf. Ezek. 8:16) was worshiped in Jerusalem, and his sanctuary was destroyed by Josiah (2 Kings 23:11). "Righteousness" provided the rain (Joel 2:23f.; cf. Hos. 10:12) and was emitted as sunlight from Jerusalem (Isa. 60:1). Thus Sedeq and heaven were often connected (Isa. 45:8; Pss. 50:6; 85:12; 97:6). Sedeq moved before YHWH as Maat moved before Re in his sun barque (Ps. 85:14),[255] and the doors of the temple were the doors of Sedeq (Ps. 118:19f.).[256]

The evidence that has been produced points also to the fact that YHWH has usurped this deity, along with his characteristics and functions. As in Mesopotamia Kittu was the right hand of Shamash, Sedeq became the hand or arm of YHWH (Ps. 48:11; Isa. 41:10; cf. 58:8; and 61:3). It is now YHWH who, like Sedeq, gives the light, the sun, and the rain, and in so doing can be expressly equated with Sedeq. In Ps. 17:1 one can translate: "YHWH, Sedeq, give ear!" According to Jer. 23:6, YHWH is "our Sedeq" (cf. Isa. 45:8; and 51:1). YHWH is thus the provider and supporter of fertility (Ps. 85:12f.; Joel 2:23; Ps. 72:6ff.; Gen. 8:21f.; also see Hosea as well as the ancient text Deut. 28:3–6). Along with the city of Jerusalem, Yahweh also took over the functions of the deities who were previously worshiped there before,[257] something that the so-called YHWH enthronement psalms allow one well to recognize (Pss. 96:13f.; 97:2, 6, 8; 98:1–3, 9; and 99:4).[258] It was, above all, in the cultus (with its cultically occurring theophany?) where one experienced the "righteousness of YHWH."[259]

The Old Testament discussion of the "righteousness of YHWH" (or plural), which has been outlined thus far and will soon be summarized in a concise fashion, allows one to recognize at this point that this "righteousness" was actualized in history. "Righteousness" is a term that helped to express YHWH's historical acts of salvation. For example, it is not the gift of fertility that is important but YHWH's gift of the land to his own people through military action. Further, the observation is not unimportant that the discussion of the "righteousness of YHWH" often occurs in texts that in their more expanded or even in their more restricted context speak of a legal disputation (רִיב = rîb) that YHWH has to conduct. He must maintain and enforce his uniqueness against others. It is through YHWH that the natural order also becomes part of the historical experience of salvation (Ps. 103:6; and Dan. 9:16). The history of the contents of the word שָׁלוֹם = šālôm ("peace, well-being"), which develops in a demonstrably analogous fashion, can be drawn on as a piece of supporting evidence.[260] Israel has for the most part independently employed this Canaanite heritage of "righteousness," as may be seen, for instance, in the blessing of Melchizedek (!; Gen. 14:18ff.), which was especially understood to be a historical blessing that granted power for battle and victory.[261]

The relationship of the righteousness of YHWH to Zion is underscored also by Jer. 31:23 (cf. 48:11) and to the promised king of salvation by Isa. 9:6; 11:4f.; and Jer. 23:5f. (cf. 33:14–16; 22:15). Zephaniah 3:5 is indeed to be assessed as an addition, yet it also sets forth the relationship of the "righteous" YHWH to the (unrighteous: vv. 1–4) city of Jerusalem. The Book of Ezekiel, however, contains no references to the "righteousness of YHWH."

The numerous references in the Psalms[262] allow one yet again to recognize the association of the "righteousness of YHWH" with the temple cult. The temple is the preferred location of this idea; here also righteousness is experienced as an active event primarily in the form of salvation[263] for the individual worshipers as well as for the community. At the same time, the "righteousness of YHWH" is also experienced here as a kind of sphere into which one is taken. That *ṣdq* also often occurs here as almost a personal being[264] points to the continuing influence of the deity Sedeq, who was originally connected with Jerusalem and was associated and then identified with YHWH.

According to the witness of the Psalms, the "righteousness of YHWH" provides to the worshiper both confidence and hope (Ps. 4:2), so that he can call[265] on this righteousness and then expect to receive salvation, help, life, and, according to Ps. 51:16, forgiveness as well. Thus YHWH's righteousness is praised, because one knows and has learned to experience it as a positive force.[266] It is said that YHWH in righteousness "judges" even the expanse of the earth.[267] This judgment, however, is a source of salvation, since his "judgments" include the "securing of justice." YHWH loves righteousness and therefore practices it.[268] The righteousness of YHWH extends throughout the world and relates to the entire creation. Consequently, it is associated with the royal sovereignty of YHWH.[269] One apparently experienced this "righteousness" in the cultus, although it remains unclear whether this took place through the cultic operation as a whole and specifically through a cultic theophany (how would one conceptualize this?), or through a special imparting of the word.

Psalm 103:6 makes it clear, however, that YHWH's "acts of righteousness" are his historical displays of salvation which he has "done" (verb: עשׂה = *'āśâ*). According to Ps. 4:2, a lament of the individual, the "righteousness of YHWH" is the basis for the assurance associated with prayer (cf. Pss. 17:1; 94:15; and 143:2). And if YHWH is called "righteous" (e.g., Ps. 116:5), then this is interpreted further to mean that he is gracious and merciful, as well as one who provides succor. Psalm 72 allows one to recognize the important role of the king in realizing צדקה = *ṣĕdāqâ* (Pss. 72:1, 12ff.; 89:15, 17; 45:5; and Isa. 11:1ff.).

Only Pss. 7:10, 12; and 129:4 speak of the "righteousness of YHWH" as a punitive force, although at the same time this punishing action of YHWH takes place for the good of the worshiper.[270] In analogous ways, the destruction of the enemy (e.g., of Zion) also brings about the salvation of creation, or support for Israel encompasses at the same time YHWH's warfare against other nations.

Far from the cult and Zion, Deutero-Isaiah offers in addition to the Psalms another emphasis to the discussion of YHWH's "righteousness"[271] in some fourteen occurrences of the term. Here as well as elsewhere, righteousness is characterized as an action that creates well-being above all through the parallel terms that are assigned to it. That the construct relationship "righteousness of YHWH" (or the plural) does not actually appear is without significance, since this is due to the fact that most of what is said are the direct words of YHWH. This means that in the articulation of his direct address YHWH speaks of "my righteousness," or something similar.

Within the so-called Servant Songs,[272] Isa. 42:6 and 53:11 say something about YHWH having called the servant "in righteousness," certainly meaning the form and the manner of the call but also quite possibly the sphere of this calling[273] and especially its purpose and means. That Isa. 42:6 hardly belongs to the first Servant Song but rather derives from a redactional supplement is, for our inquiry, unimportant. The servant of God is called to bring about salvation for others, and these others, called the "many" in 53:11, reside beyond the sphere of the nation of Israel. YHWH's working of salvation now includes the heathen through the servant. This means that his "righteousness" first of all extends beyond Israel, the people of God, and then second is bound to one person who is declared to be the one who brings salvation before all and for all. Since YHWH has called the servant in a first person predication ("I am YHWH") to be the basis and content of the promise of salvation (42:6a), this clear statement may shed light on the less clear remark in 42:6b. The servant, analogously to Isa. 53:11, would be addressed then as the salvation of the covenant for the nations. Thus the ברית עם = bĕrît ‘am ("covenant of the people")[274] might not be limited only to the totality of Israel. Beyond that, in 53:11 the speech of God begins again, and it appropriates a forensic character by which even here the old connection between sun, light, order, and justice shows forth again.

In Isa. 45:8, a typical, hymnic piece for Deutero-Isaiah, the discussion concerns righteousness and uses the terms of צדקה = ṣedāqâ as well as צדק = ṣedeq. The natural images of the dripping clouds and heaven, which "cause righteousness to rain down," reflect again the deity Sedeq and his functions. The parallel term "salvation" (ישׁע = yēša‘; cf. 45:21; 46:13) makes the positive understanding certain. The terminology of creation not only underscores the subject that is pursued here but also brings a new contribution to the semantic field of the "righteousness of YHWH." Moreover, if one can classify Isa. 45:8 as an "eschatological song of praise,"[275] then the discussion of the "righteousness of YHWH" would here for the first time be related to eschatology.

For rather obvious reasons, five additional references of Deutero-Isaiah to the "righteousness (of YHWH)" are found in the judgment scenes between YHWH and the nations or their gods. Here the more implicit and inwardly turned legal disputation of the older occurrences is explicitly and outwardly set forth. The divine status of the opponents is contested and their nonexistence as deities is demonstrated. In all occurrences,[276] YHWH's acts of salvation on Israel's behalf are set forth and defended in order to demonstrate his divine status in its typical expression. In the legal disputation, the righteousness of YHWH demonstrates his divine nature. The specific features of the divine nature are power over history, works of salvation, the fulfilling of promises, and proclamation already present in the word that points consequently to faith. Isaiah 45:13 and 51:1 (cf. 51:5f., 8; and 42:21) have their place in the so-called disputations between YHWH and Israel. According to Isa. 45:13, YHWH has awakened Cyrus "in righteousness" (cf. 42:6), and in Isa. 51:1 YHWH and righteousness as salvation are placed in parallelism, for salvation is being sought.

Four additional references are found in Deutero-Isaiah in his promises of salvation to Israel (41:10; 46:[12–] 13; 51:6 + 8). According to these texts, Israel is in the hand of YHWH that will bring forth salvation (41:10). His righteousness, which is more precisely translated as salvation, approaches (46:13) and is to be actualized at Zion. Isa. 51:6 + 8 are not clearly connected to their present context. In any case, the nations are pointed with promise to YHWH's righteousness as salvation and light. Even if one eliminates from consideration at this point 51:6 on account of its already rather strong apocalyptic language, one still may recognize by the fundamental direction of the text the proclamation of the future granting of salvation to the nations.

That Deutero-Isaiah so often speaks of YHWH's righteousness that creates salvation probably has to do with the doubts that have arisen about his divine will and power (51:1!). From the acts of YHWH's salvation (plural) comes at this point simply the act of salvation. Deutero-Isaiah causes the plural "acts of righteousness" to issue forth only from the mouth of the heathen. His reference to the act of righteousness, however, remains a historical event, and the nations are now encompassed within its boundaries. The righteousness of YHWH, which in the servant of God can even be associated with one person, serves to demonstrate the divine nature of God and is connected with the idea of the legal disputation as well as with the terminology of creation. Consequently in Deutero-Isaiah the "righteousness of YHWH" is yet again an abbreviation for classifying each act of history, the will to save, the act of salvation, the state of salvation as the goal toward which history moves: gift, lordship, proclamation,[277] and power. The word that proclaims this righteousness can and should be received in faith (41:10; 45:19, 21, 23; 46:12f.; cf. 63:1). That one does not stand far away from the Pauline witness to the δικαιοσύνη θεοῦ = dikaiosynē theou ("righteousness of God") may only be noted here.

The texts in the so-called Trito-Isaiah[278] indicate that, on the one hand, they either have retained the message of salvation in Deutero-Isaiah or have ventured to articulate it anew, and, on the other hand, they inquire about the reasons behind the failure of this announced salvation fully to appear. These reasons, for example, were discovered in the sinfulness of the people, and therefore, precisely because of the proximity of salvation in the form of divine righteousness, the performance of human righteousness was called forth anew (Isa. 56:1; cf. 58:8).[279] Also YHWH himself shall take a new initiative to realize his righteousness (59:16f.; 60:17; and 63:1), which once more is closely connected with Zion (62:1f.; cf. 60:17; also 54:11, 17). The "righteousness of YHWH as salvation" has clearly become the theme in Trito-Isaiah, while Mal. 3:20 ("sun of righteousness") promises in a new and comforting way that YHWH's righteousness will be a power that will bring salvation.

The Chronicler's work of history is not familiar with the eschatological "righteousness of YHWH." However, several times in a retrospective interpretation of history YHWH is confessed in the language of legal doxology as צדיק = ṣaddîq ("righteous"). This confession is used in reference to YHWH's punitive acts as well as to his acts of "leaving behind a remnant" (Ezra 9:15; Neh. 9:33; 2 Chron. 12:6; cf. Dan. 9:7; and Lam. 1:18).[280]

Joel 2:23f. and Isa. 26:9 lead into the early beginnings of apocalyptic. Here creation and Zion are once more mentioned together, thus revealing the cosmic as well as the cultic aspect of the "righteousness of YHWH" in Jerusalem (cf. Hos. 10:12; Pss. 72:3, 5f.; 85:12–14; and 89:17). YHWH's righteousness operates as both a gift and the power to save. He punishes offenses against the law so that his righteousness can bring comfort in times of affliction (Isa. 26:9ff.). This means there is "unconditional trust in the reaching of YHWH into history to bring about order."[281] And it is finally this confidence in YHWH's "acts of salvation" (again plural) that allows one to ask in Dan. 9:7ff. for YHWH's forgiveness and for his deliverance.

In tracing the entire process of the appropriation, transformation, and particular filling out of the contents of צדק/צדקה = ṣedeq/ṣĕdāqâ ("righteousness") by Yahwistic faith, we have noted the characteristic features of righteousness as they relate to both the individual and to history. The relationships to word and faith necessarily followed, while still keeping the relationships to Zion and to creation. Righteousness is an activity of salvation that is appropriate for YHWH and that proceeds from him. Consequently, much of what is constitutive for the content of the "righteousness of God" in Paul[282] is already found in the Old Testament and not for the first time in early Jewish apocalyptic. The "righteousness of YHWH" is not to be seen in close relationship to "world order," as argued, for example, by P. Stuhlmacher.[283] This divine righteousness distanced itself from the thinking about order when Sedeq was incorporated into YHWH.

g. Yahweh's Blessing[284]

Among the almost 400 occurrences[285] of "blessing" (ברכה = $b\check{e}r\bar{a}k\hat{a}$) and especially "to bless" (ברך = $b\bar{a}rak$) as the activity and effect of blessing[286] that are found in the Old Testament, only 87 directly have God as the subject. Still it must and can be said that wherever in the Old Testament the blessing is carried out by human beings, and this is most of the time, it is always actually God himself who does the blessing (cf. Num. 6:22ff.; Deut. 10:8; Judg. 17:2; 1 Sam. 15:13; 2 Sam. 6:18; 1 Kings 8:14, 55; 1 Chron. 23:13; Ps. 129:8; etc.).[287] In Israel's cultural environment, blessing was also "primarily the imparting of a life-promoting power by the deity,"[288] and thus the Old Testament knows "that in its formulation blessing contains nothing that is specifically Yahwistic."[289] Stemming from animistic and dynamistic thinking,[290] the term on occasion retained something of this within the Old Testament, although for the most part it has been transformed. For example, it is the "name" of the deity, "placed upon Israel" in the act of speaking the blessing (Num. 6:27), that grants power to the blessing. However, it is God himself, his form of being, devotion, and salvific activity that are included in his name. Also, through his spirit, God can bless human beings (Isa. 44:3). And so people request, when seeking a blessing for themselves, a blessing from God (Gen. 32:27; 2 Sam. 7:29; Pss. 3:9; and 28:9; cf. Gen. 28:3; 48:16; etc.).

If one surveys the diffusion of the occurrences of this term,[291] then it is scarcely surprising to find that the discussion of the blessing of YHWH is rare in prophetic texts (only Isa. 19:25; 51:2; 61:9; Hag. 2:19). The term is most emphasized in Genesis, Deuteronomy, and Psalms. In the last-mentioned book, the discussion is often about the blessing of God (objective genitive). However, instead of referring to the deity's unlimited supply of beneficent power, the discussion rather is about the "praise of God" that is close to a doxology. The mention of a good deed of YHWH most of the time precedes this praise.[292] In Deuteronomy long life in the "good" land is the preferred gift of blessing (Deut. 7:13; 14:29; 15:4f., 10, 18; 16:15; etc.; here also is an occurrence of ברך בשם יהוה = $b\bar{a}rak\ b\check{e}\check{s}\bar{e}m\ yahweh$, "bless in the name of YHWH"). In addition, the blessing here is clearly connected to the obedience of the people now to be practiced anew (cf. Deut. 12:7, 18; 15:4, 10; 23:21; 28:8, 12f.; etc.). Blessing brings the increase of life, curse by contrast causes it to diminish (cf. for the latter Gen. 3:14–19). In blessing as a potent word, God's freely bestowing power and force are active. God grants this blessing to human beings, who may give it away in turn. He changes the word of curse into blessing (Numbers 22–24, Balaam; cf. Num. 23:7f., 20). Thus God's blessing was spoken to the first human beings (Gen. 1:28), and the Priestly source in which God is here speaking makes clear in the later texts how this blessing is significant as a continuing power (Gen. 5:2; 9:1; 17:16; and Lev. 9:22f.; cf. also Gen. 28:1, 3f., 6; 49:28; and Exod. 39:43). In these texts, blessing and the promise of the land, blessing and productivity, and also blessing and the worship of God are connected. Blessing increases life and brings rest, success, fortune, fertility (Gen. 24:60; 27:27f.; and 30:27, 29f.), peace, and well-being (שָׁלוֹם = *šālôm*; cf. 2 Sam. 8:10; Ps. 133:3). Consequently, it is not accidental that this word שָׁלוֹם = *šālôm* ("peace, well-being") finds usage as a greeting of blessing (Judg. 19:20; 1 Sam. 1:17; 25:6; cf. Matt. 10:12f.), since this "well-being" not only can pertain to an individual but also takes place within the community. Thus, בָּרַךְ = *bārak* can signify then simply "to greet" (Gen. 47:7; 1 Sam. 13:10; etc.).

"Blessing" or "to bless" is also associated with "life" or "fortune" (חַיִּים = *ḥayyîm*, "life"; Deut. 30:16; Ps. 133:3), with righteousness (צְדָקָה = *ṣĕdāqâ;* Ps. 24:4f.), or with help and deliverance (יֵשַׁע = *yēsa‘;* Ps. 28:9; cf. Ps. 29:11 שָׁלוֹם = *šālôm*, "peace, well-being"). And what secures a blessing can be well recognized from Gen. 27:23ff. (Jacob before Isaac). Isaac sought to fortify himself ahead of time by eating so that he could strengthen his blessing. Blessing itself (vv. 28f.) speaks then of cosmic gifts, military victory, fertility of the fields, and lordship over others. Thus, blessing does not remain only in the sphere of undergirding the cosmos. Those who bless the blessed in like measure receive for themselves new blessings. However, those who curse the blessed may likewise be cursed, for both blessing and curse continue to work their effects. After Isaac has thus blessed Jacob, and Esau comes too late, the power of blessing of the ancient father is abated (cf. the end of v. 36; also cf. v. 38). And what the father then can still bestow on his son Esau can no longer actually be designated a "blessing" (vv. 39ff.).[293] Blessing sayings (cf. Jer. 31:23; Gen. 48:15f.) were often rhythmical, concisely made, and formed to reach a climax.[294] This can be seen in Deut. 28:3–6; Gen. 14:19f.; and 1 Kings 1:48.[295] This formula of blessing[296] is always either a testimony to the close solidarity with the one to whom the blessing is issued or an affirmation of community with the person concerned. "Thus God makes use of it in regard to his people and his worshipers; but Israel especially uses it in regard to its God"[297] (cf. Gen. 24:27; Deut. 28:2–6; 1 Sam. 25:32; 1 Kings 1:47; etc.; cf. Isa. 19:25, where it is even related to other nations). The blessing is not only a declaration but much more an act or a speech event. Thus it is no accident that the verb "to bless" occurs chiefly in the intensive form of the piel.

If God blesses animals, the arable land, and the Sabbath (Gen. 1:22; Deut. 28:4; and Gen. 2:1–3a), he does this for the good of human beings. If God desires to enter into community with human beings, then both their well-being and their salvation are to be occasioned through divine blessing. The gifts of blessing are productive harvests, children (especially sons), rain, increase of the herd, and peace (Pss. 65:10ff.; 67:7; 112:1–4; 128; 144:12–14; cf. also Gen. 8:21f.; Deut. 28:3–6). Long life, a substantial number of descendants, riches, and strength are divine blessings also found in Israel's ancient Near Eastern environment.[298] Once again, Israel's solidarity with its neighbors is shown by what was expected, requested, hoped for, and experienced each time from the god or the gods. The blessing of Isaac in Gen. 27:28f., the (Deuteronomistic) blessing of Solomon in connection with the prayer of the temple dedication (1 Kings 8:56–61), the blessing of Jacob (Genesis 49), the blessing of Moses (Deuteronomy 33), and the blessing sayings of Balaam (Num. 23:7–10, 19–24; and 24:5–9, 17–19) allow one to recognize that, according to the witness of the Old Testament, it is not the case that only the creaturely sphere could be assigned to the activity of divine blessing, while the military sphere belonged to the salvific action of God. Such a dichotomy and separation is rather difficult to substantiate within the Old Testament.[299] For example, if the promise of the presence of YHWH was to be an expression of his blessing,[300] a promise that often takes place in connection with military action (e.g., Josh. 7:12 and Judg. 6:16), then war would have something to do with YHWH's acts of blessing but not with his acts of deliverance. This, of course, is not a view supported by the Old Testament. The Old Testament does not separate things so consistently and cleanly, as similar differentiations will make plain. Cosmos and history also flow together under the category of blessing. The "blessed" are YHWH's chosen who are elected within history. They are his people, his inheritance (Isa. 65:22f.; cf. 19:25!).

God blesses whom and when he will. Blessing is grace; it is an event that belongs also to the activity of YHWH's election (cf. just Gen. 12:1–3). According to Gen. 6:8 and 9:1, election and blessing belong together, if one looks at the fundamental event of divine election instead of searching only for occurrences of the word "to elect." "Biblical salvation history is an ever new consummation of divine election and accordingly an ever new requirement for individual decision by the nation. Subsequently, blessing is the ever newly bestowed gift of God that operates within the framework of election and individual decision...."[301]

Blessing continues to produce its effects (2 Sam. 7:29 and 1 Chron. 17:27).[302] Along with the father, the children were also blessed (Gen. 49:26; and Ps. 115:12f.). So were the matriarch and her children (Gen. 24:60), and with Israel's ancestors so were their descendants (Gen. 12:1–7; 17:1–8; Num. 25:12f.; etc.). Along with the king, the nation was also blessed, and with David the King so also the dynasty that followed him (2 Sam. 7:3–16 and 2 Kings 10:30).³⁰³ Blessing creates a kind of sphere and operates there as an active power. Thus, the so-called tribal sayings in Genesis 49 and Deuteronomy 33³⁰⁴ are easily put into the forms of either blessings or wishes. The verb forms in the so-called Aaronic blessing, precisely structured and artistically composed (Num. 6:24–26;³⁰⁵ cf. Pss. 67:2f. and 134:3), are in the jussive³⁰⁶ and are not to be translated as indicatives, that is, not as "The Lord *blesses* you . . . " Rather, the blessing is to be addressed to its recipient in the form of a wish ("may the Lord bless you") or a promise ("the Lord will bless you"), that is, as a performative speech act of the worshiping community (cf. Lev. 9:22 P). This blessing with the name of YHWH (Num. 6:27), which stemmed from Num. 6:24–26, was the high point of worship in Israel's late period. In the early texts of the Old Testament, blessing and cult are not yet brought together in a direct relationship. In Israel's ancient Near Eastern environment, the unveiling of the particular image of the deity served as this cultic high point. The blessing of the Israelite priests when approaching and departing the sanctuary as well as during worship is mentioned first in 1 Sam. 9:13 (the sacrifice is blessed) and then in the late psalms: Pss. 115:14f.; 118:26; 128:5; 129:8; 134:3; and Gen. 14:19f.

The blessing of God is especially significant during the turning points of life. Thus, a blessing is both required and customary at a birth or in taking one's leave (Gen. 24:60; 32:1; Ruth 4:14f.; 1 Kings 1:31; and Jer. 20:15). And the dying bless those who remain behind (Gen. 48:15f.; 49:26; etc.). The dead, though, are blessed no longer, something that points to the fact that the blessing within the Old Testament has been stripped of many magical ideas. Israel's faith in God has also modified the conception of blessing. An aura of power associated with the blessing is no longer magically conveyed; rather, it derives from an encounter with the God who gives and bestows. One offers a blessing "in the name of YHWH" (בשם יהוה = *bĕšēm yahweh;* 2 Sam. 6:18), although not without reason and not without consequence, even as the Levites and Aaron did, or were to do (Deut. 10:8; 21:5; and 1 Chron. 23:13).

How Israel reshaped ancient Near Eastern conceptions of blessing can be recognized by reference to both the form and the significance of the *promise* of blessing important in the so-called Yahwist and in the Deuteronomic and Deuteronomistic literature.³⁰⁷ In and of itself, blessing is an event that affects or is to affect the one blessed either immediately or in the near future. According to the witness of the Yahwist, this "gaining of blessing" or "self-blessing" (ברך = *bārak,* niphal)³⁰⁸ involving Abraham becomes a promise to the nations, more precisely to the "tribes of the earth" (Gen. 12:3; 28:14; differently in 18:18 and in Gen. 22:18 which is secondary), and at the same time is also strongly related to and historically extended into the future. The blessing becomes a motif of salvation history. Deuteronomy also was aware of blessings of promise or at least blessings that were strongly directed toward a wider future (Deut. 1:11; and 16:13–15) and readily connects these—and here lies an important distinction from Gen. 12:1–3—to (the new) obedience (Deut. 7:12ff.; cf. also 14:29; 15:10, 18; 23:21; and 24:19). At this point it is important to note that a corresponding theologizing of the curse and the curse word, which likewise was a word of power,[309] was not carried out in the Old Testament. Indeed, there were no announcements of unfounded curses. Even with all of the weight placed on the curse that often was coordinated with the blessing (cf. only Leviticus 26 and Deuteronomy 27–29; esp. Deut. 27:15–26; 28:16–19), the blessing still contained promises that, in comparison to the threats of the curse, were more powerful (Deut. 30:1–10). "Israel could indeed reckon with the unfounded blessing, but not, however, with the baseless curse."[310] In the Deuteronomistic literature which was compelled to reflect on the punishment of the exile, the curse can belong to the Deuteronomistic interpretation of history (Deuteronomy 28). This is true also in Israel's religious environment.[311] YHWH's compassion, however, is extended to the many thousands, while his punishment is active (only) to the third or fourth generation (Exod. 20:5f.; Deut. 5:9; cf. Exod. 34:6f.).[312]

C. Westermann has investigated[313] Old Testament wisdom literature and has attempted to assign the acts of God mentioned there (and especially in the Book of Proverbs) to the workings of divine blessing in general. This effort already faces terminological difficulties, since "blessing" and "to bless" are not encountered very frequently in this corpus and not at all in the statements that convey wisdom thought.[314] Above all, however, the thinking about order found in wisdom[315] has nothing to do with YHWH's acts of blessing.[316] Thus, later on[317] Westermann paralleled wisdom more with the thinking of the primeval history, that is, to what is generally human, and to the creation faith that appears worldwide. Whether this is legitimate is to be discussed in another place.[318]

"Blessing" in the Old Testament is strongly connected with history. For example, through its combination with promise, as well as through the difficulty associated with the finality of its present formulation,[319] blessing received an "aspect of finality" that thrust itself toward eschatology. Israel saw itself during its journey as a people blessed by YHWH and awaited both complete redemption and the actualization of this blessing (cf. Hos. 2:23f.; Isa. 44:3–5; etc.). In this way, Israel sought to resolve the tension that empirically continued to appear. This tension concerned "whether the condition of a person . . . (ought) to reveal whether or not God had blessed him."[320] However, this connection between a person's condition and divine blessing could be believed only by ignoring any contradictive experiences. Also, through YHWH's blessing, Israel was supported in the further undertaking of its faith. However, "the activity of divine blessing or of human blessing certainly does not at all signify the center of the Old Testament. This center resides much more in the coming and entrance of God into history in order to save."[321]

h. The Connection between Deed and Consequence[322]

According to the testimony of many Old Testament texts, YHWH is believed to be active in the connection between human deed and consequence. In scholarship this connection between deed and consequence is also called the synthetic interpretation of life,[323] the connection between act and fortune, and the sphere of action that determines destiny.[324] The last-mentioned designation especially allows one to recognize what is intended: the power-laden act of a person creates according to its own quality a good or a bad sphere that comes back to affect the doer. Consequently, an evil act results inevitably in a calamitous condition for the doer (cf. Ps. 7:14–17).[325] One speaks of holistic thought in the Old Testament both in this regard and in the corresponding concept of sin with its unity of guilt and punishment.[326] What is meant here can be well illustrated by the expression "His blood be on him/his head." The grammatical structure of this expression is the possessive suffix, plus דמים = *dāmîm* ("blood," in this situation always in the plural), followed by ב = *b* ("in the") + the pronominal suffix, and from time to time the addition of the word "head." This formula,[327] which also stands behind Gen. 9:6, "serves to establish the guilt of one who is condemned to death and thus the innocence of the one who executes the sentence."[328] Here one debates the question of whether this expression may be translated and interpreted as "his blood *comes* upon his head" (so H. Graf Reventlow) or "his blood *remains* on his head" (so K. Koch).[329] In the first-mentioned interpretation, the emphasis is clearly placed on the belief that there is no execution of punishment that does not stand under the authority of the divine Lord who serves as the judge. Any magical understanding may thus be overcome. The prayer in 1 Kings 2:32 (cf. also 1 Kings 2:44) makes this especially clear. The second-mentioned interpretation stresses that the Old Testament has conceived of the connection between human deed and consequence as a rather close one and that this conception receives expression in the idea of "retribution" (cf., e.g., עון = *'ôn*, which signifies both guilt and punishment for guilt).[330] While YHWH's action in this "sphere" is not debated, it is clear that a human judge's pronouncement of judgment in issuing a death sentence against a wrongdoer (מות יומת = *môt yûmat*, "shall surely die") is not even once executed according to the expression "His blood remains upon his head." The blood of the wrongdoer that is to be poured out is far removed from the executing of the death penalty through the so-called formula of protection. Juridical thinking has nothing to do with this notion. The Old Testament often thinks differently from the contemporary world, and the modern way of conceiving things is not always conducive to ancient Israel's manner of thinking. The effect of an evil deed and the ruin called forth against the wrongdoer through YHWH's activity are often closely connected, as, for example, 2 Sam. 16:7f. demonstrates.[331] However, one may ask whether the execution of the death sentence is not a new deed that sets YHWH's will in motion and then is carried out by human beings? Does this also involve a sphere that continues to have effect?

The theory of the connection between deed and consequence in its application to the individual is encountered above all in the so-called wisdom literature (Proverbs, Qoheleth, and Job). This teaching is broadly represented in the Book of Proverbs,[332] although it becomes a problem in both Qoheleth and Job. The fundamental conviction of this conception of faith, so stamped by the interpretation of the world as order,[333] is especially addressed in a concise fashion in Ps. 37:25 where the pious person in a so-called wisdom psalm can say that he has never seen a righteous person abandoned or his children begging for bread. Rather, according to the connection of deed and consequence, things go well with a righteous person. In this situation, one must not speak of "retribution" through YHWH, that is, through a purposeful, forensic intervention of the deity as a judicial act of legal jurisdiction.

In the Book of Proverbs, the teaching of the connection between deed and consequence is formulated in the following ways: the righteous are granted what they desire (Prov. 10:24) and they never once shall stumble, but the godless do not remain in the land (10:30). Furthermore, righteousness rescues from an untimely death (11:4; cf. 11:6), but a heartless person cuts himself in his own flesh (11:17). Since persons are "recompensed" (12:14) according to the deeds of their hands, the work of evildoers can only produce deceitful gain (11:18). No harm afflicts the righteous, for they experience good things, while sinners are pursued by disaster (12:21; 13:21; cf. 11:23). Qoheleth at a later time shall strongly call this teaching into question, while the Book of Job struggles with contradictory experiences. Even so, these examples of the relationship between deed and consequence from the Book of Proverbs could easily be multiplied.[334] Whoever digs a pit for another will fall into it himself, and whoever rolls a stone finds that it will roll back on him (Prov. 26:27).

All of this is so because in the understanding of the "wise" who stand behind this proverbial wisdom YHWH himself has set up this connection between deed and consequence, or act and result, and he watches over this reality. He "recompenses" (שׁלם = *šillēm*) according to this process and thus people according to their deeds (Prov. 11:31; 13:21; 19:17; 25:21f.), and he brings to completion the act and the consequence that belong to human action.[335] If the wrongdoing of the godless shall "fall" upon them (10:6), then YHWH is the one who stands behind the connection between this act and its consequence. He is the one who returns the consequences of a person's action upon him (השׁיב = *hēšîb*, "returns," 24:12).[336] YHWH has established this order, undergirds and maintains it with divine power, operates in and through it, and is its guarantor (12:2; 16:5; 18:10; 20:22; 24:12). That there also are problems associated with such a worldview, including when and precisely why it continues to be related to the life of the individual, is not expressly stated as a theme in these sayings.[337] YHWH functions as the one who originates this order and as the one who continues to oversee it in the present.[338] It may only be pointed out here that this worldview and view of life are encountered also in other ancient Near Eastern wisdom texts that are close to the sapiential literature of the Old Testament.[339] For the sages of Proverbs, God operates within world harmony and the harmony of life and creates a life that has been and continues to be successful for the one who behaves uprightly.

Nevertheless, there are to be found already in the Book of Proverbs some texts that express their doubt in this teaching, by questioning whether this connection between deed and consequence always operates in such a clear fashion, that it may be recognized and seen by human beings.[340] According to Prov. 16:33, a person indeed casts the lot in or out of the fold of the garment, but the decision of the lots still comes from YHWH. This observation is drawn therefore from human insight and calculation. Since it is YHWH's blessing that makes one rich, human effort can neither accomplish nor contribute anything at all to this result (10:22). A person indeed plans, but what he pronounces is effected and directed by YHWH (16:1). So it is with the way of a person and his steps (16:9; cf. 19:14, 21, 30f.). The final insight into divine works is denied to human beings (21:30). The wise person continues to be humble,[341] since God's honor also consists in his concealment of things (25:2).

With all of this said, however, the connection between deed and consequence is still not placed fundamentally in question in the Book of Proverbs in the manner that it is in Job and Qoheleth. Rather, in Proverbs the issue is principally one of the ultimate incomprehensibility of both the connection between deed and consequence and the divine activity toward human beings. Similar statements over the ultimate hiddenness of the divine world order are found in the wisdom texts from the ancient Near East.[342] Consequently, it is initially the empirical experience that opposes more an unambiguous and clear perception of order than it is the Yahwistic faith that assists in recognizing the incomprehensibility of order or even its inaccessibility.

This way of conceiving and believing in a connection between deed and consequence that was established and maintained by YHWH runs headlong into a crisis that fundamentally challenges its validity.[343] In the Book of Job, which is paralleled in many places by Psalm 73, the friends of Job, whose thinking remains fully within the framework of the connection between deed and result, conclude that on the basis of his suffering Job must be a sinner even if he neither recognizes nor acknowledges this. Guilt and suffering, according to the view of the friends, stand in a clear, causal relationship.[344] By contrast, Job concludes that he is a righteous man, and if in spite of this he must suffer, then this may point only to the injustice of God, an argument that nevertheless still operates within the teaching of the connection between deed and result.[345]

Then when YHWH himself proclaims his word in the God speeches of the Book of Job (Job 38:1–42:6), the friends and Job are both pronounced wrong. On the contrary, it is made clear that, while YHWH neither causes nor seeks to cause himself to be incalculable, he nevertheless stands as the creator of the world at an infinite distance from his creatures. Not once in these divine speeches is there a discussion of human beings, and Job himself is mentioned only implicitly in the rhetorical questions directed to him which he cannot answer. While Job must experience existentially the failure of the teaching of the connection between deed and consequence, the authors of this book nevertheless sought as a result to point the problem toward a concrete solution. Qoheleth approached the same problem in a more intellectual fashion and engaged in a reflective disputation with the wisdom tradition by citing and then critically taking issue with its positions.[346] In this way he contests rather energetically the demonstrability and therefore the existence of a connection between deed and consequence. According to Qoheleth, there are righteous people who are treated as though they had carried out the deeds of evildoers and vice versa (Qoh. 8:14). A sinner can do much evil and still live a long life (Qoh. 8:12). Therefore this is "entirely vain," fully absurd, and does not strengthen faith.[347]

With the critique present in Job and Qoheleth, the essential points have been made concerning the view of divine operation in the observable connections operating between deed and consequence. The Old Testament YHWH is neither accessible to nor always understandable by humanity when it comes to divine deeds. YHWH remains the Lord who is not obligated to guarantee harmony in human existence. Thus the image of God in the Book of Proverbs probably stands in tension in many ways with the rest of the Old Testament and with the empirical experience that the books of Job and Qoheleth bring to expression. That YHWH is "totally other" is made quite clear in the speeches of God in the Book of Job. The God speeches are introduced with features of theophany (or contain elements of a theophanic address) that are unusual for the wisdom literature, although not infrequent in the rest of the Old Testament (Job 38:1). Job's and Qoheleth's critique is a fundamental one that also has significance for contemporary questions concerning the comprehensibility of God.[348]

Moreover, since such an understandable picture of God is always an object of human striving and such a comprehensible God is always the object of human hope, it is no wonder that, after Job and Qoheleth, the early Jewish wisdom that follows them has sought to bring back to the table the teaching of the connection between deed and consequence (cf. Ben Sira). However, it is the Wisdom of Solomon that has wished to attribute the full validity of this teaching to the time of eschatological consummation. The New Testament, by contrast, takes up and continues the teaching of the acceptance even of the sinner by God and the fundamental critique of the relationship between deed and consequence, or sin and punishment (cf. Luke 13:2 and John 9:2).

The Old Testament wisdom literature's application of the teaching about the association between deed and consquence to the individual came very close to becoming a "dogma" with an accompanying critique. However, this teaching in the Old Testament is not limited to wisdom texts. Here, especially the Books of Chronicles are to be mentioned,[349] for they have expanded the retributive actions and reactions of God into their most important theological points of interest. Moving into particular details, including more precisely the condition of individual persons, above all the kings, these books seek to demonstrate what punishment ensued from which wrongdoing and what punishment must or at least can be traced back to which wrongdoing.[350] Therefore, for example, everything negative about David, from his affair with Bathsheba to his wars, must be suppressed. By contrast, the Chronicler enlarges upon what is positive about him, including the intentionally expanded preparations for the building of the temple or the order of worship that he carried out. In the same way, much that is negative about Solomon is omitted, as, for example, from 1 Kings 11, for these two ideal kings may exhibit no negative elements in the Chronicler's portrait of them. Otherwise they would have to have fallen under the punishment of God. By contrast, what happens or must happen to an evil king, for example, Jehoram, is described in 2 Chronicles 21. Another king, Amaziah, was victorious only when he was obedient to YHWH, while he eventually had to suffer the usual downfall because of apostasy (2 Chronicles 25; cf. chap. 27). And because the godless Manasseh was permitted to reign and live so long a time, the Chronicler had to invent this ruler's intermediate conversion (2 Chronicles 33; nothing similar in 2 Kings 21). Numerous additional references allow one to recognize how this faith in retribution is also demonstrated in individual narrative features and particular applications.[351] It should be clear that history can neither function nor be written in this way. However, the interests of the Chronicler reside chiefly in Jerusalem and Zion, in the temple and worship, and in the military sphere of war and fortifications, since he hoped again for a strengthened Israel in the new actualization of earlier texts, among these especially the Books of Kings. YHWH or "God" (אלהים = 'ĕlōhîm), which is here more readily used,[352] should be shown to be a "just" deity through the presentation of the association between deed and consequence (2 Chron. 12:1–6). God is the one who persistently reaches into history and consequently can trust people and be trusted by them (2 Chron. 15:2, 7; and 16:9). The Chronicler does not even consider the possibility that such trust, when it encounters the conflict between historical postulates grounded in divine retribution and experiences to the contrary, must eventually lead the nation into crisis.

Also within the Deuteronomistic History[353] one can find a way of thinking and describing that moves within the principle of the connection between deed and consequence. For example, one should think of the Deuteronomistic scheme in the Book of Judges (cf., e.g., Judg. 2:10–23),[354] where YHWH's punishment of his apostate people takes the form of military invasion by a foreign people. Thereupon the people of Israel cry out to YHWH who provides a "judge" as a charismatic military leader by whom Israel is delivered. Then the scheme, or rather the course, of history begins anew.[355] Or in the Books of Kings, Israel's and Judah's history is described in a way that it leads to the necessary punishment of the exile first of the Northern Kingdom and then of Judah because of their continually recurring apostasy (cf. 2 Kings 17:7ff. as a Deuteronomistic summation).[356]

In the Deuteronomistic History, however, the discussion also can focus on the "return" (probably in a certain stratum of the Deuteronomistic History; Deut. 4:25–31; 30:1–10; and 1 Kings 8:46–53).[357] This becomes (e.g., in Deuteronomy 1–3) rather transparent in the possibility of a new conquest, especially since YHWH had "sworn" that this "good" land belonged to the ancestors and their descendants.[358] And the return becomes a hopeful outlook, made possible through the pardon of King Jehoiachin living in exile (2 Kings 25:27–30), a description of which is pointedly placed at the end of the work.[359] In addition, the Deuteronomistic History is written as Israel's great penitential confession before YHWH, in order to show that it might throw itself into the arms of this God once more, and in order to demonstrate that "crying out" to YHWH held out promise. For example, the Deuteronomistically redacted Book of Judges makes this clear. The Song of Moses (Deuteronomy 32), which provides a synopsis of the history of faithless Israel, can speak of YHWH in this connection as the "God of the faithful" (32:4).

That the "Succession Narrative of David" (2 Samuel 9 to 1 Kings 2) inserted into the Deuteronomistic History may be shaped by sapiential ideas has already often been pointed out.[360] More specifically in this regard, E. Otto[361] has indicated that, in association with the narrative's purpose of demonstrating how YHWH brought Solomon to the throne of David, the narrator uses the sapiential teaching of the "return" (הֵשִׁיב = hēšîb) of an evil deed on the head of the doer (1 Kings 2:44). Consequently, YHWH carries out through Solomon the connection between deed and consequence, something David, as the implicit criticism makes clear, was not in a position to do (cf. 1 Kings 2:8f., 33; 1:52 in comparison with 1:6 and several others). The motif of the carrying out of the association between deed and consequence is integrated into the activity of YHWH's providence,[362] which may have been displayed even in the confusion around the succession to the throne. In this case, even "sin and suffering are here lifted up and receive a place of value and meaning in YHWH's guidance toward a beneficent purpose."[363] This motif leads then to a similar view of the Joseph Story (Genesis 37; 39–50)[364] where wisdom influences also have been detected.[365]

There appears in the Joseph Story a critical analysis of the association between deed and consequence, since this principle is neither always and everywhere present nor even immediately and expressly apparent. As an illustration of this, one needs only to point to Joseph's fate following the episode with Potiphar's wife.[366] Thus the association between deed and consequence may be drawn out over a long period of time (cf. the look at the "end" of the enemies in Ps. 73:16ff.), therefore making this teaching conform somewhat more to everyday experience. YHWH's providence, however, envelops this larger, more extended association between deed and result. In this way providence shows how powerful it is. The thematic suffering of the righteous appears in the fate of Joseph, who, according to the Joseph Story, is "not at all distanced from Yahweh but rather is held and supported by him."[367] Two themes or rather solutions of the problem of the synthetic interpretation of life are offered that lead beyond normal wisdom thought. One solution (e.g., in the speeches of the friends of Job) is met in the rigid application of the teaching of the association between deed and consequence in a dogmatic form. In another solution, Joseph is ultimately preserved to become the deliverer of his brothers, who are also the ancestors of Israel. In the final analysis, Joseph's place and function become a part of salvation history,[368] something that likewise leads beyond pure wisdom thinking. It would still require reflection to determine in the Joseph Story the extent to which are present, not only the association between deed and consequence, but also forgiveness and reconciliation that serve to abrogate this association.

Also in the prophets,[369] statements are found that especially move within the association between deed and consequence. K. Koch has brought together and arranged the most important references.[370] In Hos. 8:4b–7 as well as in 10:12f., sin and punishment are addressed in the image of sowing and harvest. What is said here pertains no longer only to the individual but also to the nation and is analogous to what is said in Hos. 12:3, 15,[371] which uses the term שִׁיב = yēšîb ("repay," cf. 4:9). There are deeds of Israel that "surround" it (7:2). The question immediately arises at this point as to whether these statements are composed entirely or only in part by him. Nevertheless, Hosea speaks clearly (e.g., 2:4ff.) about a punishing, personal, intervening activity of YHWH. But the prophet also depicts YHWH as struggling against this punishment because of his compassion (11:8f.).[372] This is similar to the other writing prophets.[373] They proclaim not only a connection between guilt and punishment but also a God who will, desires to, and must punish his people (Amos. 3:2;[374] cf. Hos. 13:5ff.). Indeed, he comes in cosmic and historical events to punish his people anew (Amos 4:6–12; 5:17b; etc.). Yet, at the same time, he can also be the one who breaks through his will to punish (Amos 5:15; Hos. 11:1f.) in order to promise and then to create salvation.[375]

Also in narrative literature not previously mentioned here, K. Koch wishes to demonstrate[376] the existence of a way of thinking about the association beween deed and consequence. So, for example, he points to Judg. 9:23f., where the verb בּוֹא = bô' ("go, come"), as is the case elsewhere,[377] is used in this connection, and also to 2 Kings 21:31–33, where הֵשִׁיב = hēšîb ("return, re-pay") and שׁוּב = šûb ("return") also are used in this way (cf. further Num. 12:11; 32:23). We shall discuss in another context[378] the fact that certain Hebrew terms for sin can designate not only "sin" but also "punishment" and "guilt" (this is true, above all, for עָוֹן = 'āwōn, while צְדָקָה = ṣĕdāqâ means both com-munity loyalty and the fruit that righteous behavior bears; Prov. 21:21[379]).

H. H. Schmid[380] has sought to demonstrate that the view of a "world order" constitutive for the teaching of the association between deed and consequence was the actual center not just of the Old Testament but of the entire biblical theology. U. Luck[381] has followed him in applying this view to the New Tes-tament. This is not the place to discuss the New Testament and the questions of a "Biblical Theology." But one should introduce the various criticisms raised by the problems of the thesis that either the association between deed and consequence or a world order dominates biblical or at least Old Testament thought. For Old Testament wisdom literature and probably also for some other texts and writings, as has already been demonstrated, the significance of the association between deed and consequence for thinking and believing can hardly be disputed.[382] However, does this topic possibly serve as a common perspective of the entire Old Testament? How does the broad consideration of the association between deed and consequence serve overall to explain Old Testament phenomena?

J. Scharbert has investigated the Old Testament use of the verb פָּקַד = pāqad ("visit, attend to")[383] and correctly discovered that when God is the subject of the verb it does not always involve an "automatic, fateful consequence that en-sues from an evil act,"[384] but rather it also has to do with divine, personal in-tervention (Jer. 6:15; 49:8; 50:31; and Ps. 59:6; cf. hiphil in Ps. 109:6 and also Isa. 24:22; Jer. 6:6; and Hos. 4:9). One can already add at this point that also in Hosea, to whom K. Koch points as a valid example of one way of thinking about the association of the deed and consequence among the prophets,[385] YHWH's punishment is understood as being entirely his personal act (Hos. 4:6; 5:2; 7:12, 13; and 10:10). An accounting was required, an offense was punished (Ps. 89:33; cf. Exod. 32:34; Lev. 18:25; Amos 3:2; Hos. 1:4; also Exod. 20:5; and 34:7). Scharbert concludes that פָּקַד = pāqad ("visit, at-tend to") designates, "insofar as God is the subject . . . in these cases, not only the act of placing the sinner within the power of disaster that his sin occasions or that he inherits as a result of his sin, but also a direct or at least indirect in-tervention of God."[386] It is no world order, but rather the personal God who is active here.

Scharbert has considered in addition the use of the verb שָׁלֵם = šālēm[387] that was especially important for the argumentation of K. Koch who readily translated the word (in its piel form, שִׁלֵּם = *šillēm*) "to make complete." Yet the word can also mean "to give back, to pay, to remunerate, and to substitute (for)" when it occurs, for example, in texts that have to do with legal and economic life.[388] The term also designates human reactions to an action of another (e.g., Gen. 44:4; Jer. 18:20). These very references demonstrate at the same time that the term has nothing to do with "making complete." This is also true in theological language where שִׁלֵּם = *šillēm* refers to YHWH's reactions toward human behavior[389] (Judg. 1:7; 1 Sam. 24:20; Isa. 59:18; Jer. 32:18; Joel 2:25; and Ruth 2:12).[390] Here he invariably appears and functions as one who "is directly affected by and then responds correspondingly to"[391] human deeds. Scharbert refers expressly to this while noting "that the Old Testament also is familiar with thinking about the 'deed that shapes destiny' "[392] and the related notion of "retribution." This was already mentioned in the previous investigation[393] of blessing and curse.[394]

R. L. Hubbard[395] has placed in question this notion of a "sphere" created by human actions in his interpretation of certain texts in the Old Testament that have been used to support this idea. He thinks that the "act-result-connection" may be understood not only in "spherical" but also in "linear terms." In addition, for Hubbard, Ps. 17:7 may speak more about a "boomerang" effect than a "sphere" and presupposes a linear but not a spherical ontology. This is similarly the case in regard to Pss. 54:7 and 59:13b, 14a. Nonetheless, with everything said, Hubbard does more pleading for an "alternative term"[396] than demonstrates critical acumen in the matter under discussion and in his grasping of the issue as a whole.

J. Halbe, however, has presented a fundamental and comprehensive critique in an important article.[397] His investigation looks overall at the notion of world order, for which the association between deed and consequence is constitutive. World order is seen as the self-evident horizon of thought and experience for an Old Testament, or even a biblical, theology.[398] This world order is also regarded as the fundamental matter in the human relationship to the world and to the self and as the primary horizon of all experience of the reality of God and of humanity.[399] First of all, in looking at this thesis, Halbe argues that the idea of the (ancient Near Eastern) *conception* of world order is problematic.[400] The conception of cosmic order gives the impression that human beings always experience reality in terms of patterns and then set forth and relate these experiences to each other within the framework of a certain ancient Near Eastern conception of the world.[401] "Related patterns of the experience of the world immediately become indicators of the correlations of culture, specifically religion, and the history of human thought. On the other hand, the recognition of all of these related patterns depends upon making these correlations."[402] Now such correlations may not be uncovered everywhere, although one cannot dispute their presence in the sphere of wisdom literature and its constitutive manner of thought that involves the association between deed and consequence. Halbe's criticism may, however, be on target when he turns to consider Old Testament jurisprudence[403] and asks about the validity of the conception of world order and its principle of the connection between deed and consequence. Stated in a different way, "On what basis, on the strength of what linkage [namely, in Israel][404] did the *integration* of authoritative traditions that unite groups together succeed?"[405] Answer: "Through the common linkage of groups that bore these traditions *with Yahweh.*"[406] This linkage was accomplished not by means of a central power, as, for example, the monarchy, but rather through a solution that "concretely required the confession of the exclusive position of Yahweh and experienced as formative his identity authentically disclosed in the act of the exodus,"[407] that is, in the "turning of Yahweh in his power to gain the victory over his enemies."[408] Nowhere, however, may one recognize or attribute any importance to the construct of an ancient Near Eastern conception of world order in an Israelite form, and this is true even for the Old Testament legal corpora from the Covenant Code to the Holiness Code.[409] For example, not a single legal corpus is traced back to the Israelite king, a legal institution very important for the conception of world order and its dissemination throughout the ancient Near East. Also, there is missing in this Israelite legal material any argument about an order of creation (as generally set forth and understood). And when Halbe concludes that the conception of world order may be "handled" as an ideology,[410] then at least he affirms in this respect that this conception (along with the connection of deed and consequence that is assigned to it) is not suitable for the Old Testament legal texts or for the entire Old Testament itself.

Thus one is able to see for sure that the association between deed and consequence, in which and through which YHWH operates, is important for many spheres of the Old Testament, as, for instance, wisdom literature in which this theme is either especially influential or a problem with which to grapple critically. However, this viewpoint and the conception of world order that accompanies it cannot serve as a key for understanding either the Old Testament as a whole or an entire biblical theology.[411] In this regard, perhaps it will not be inappropriate[412] to ask how the Old Testament worshiper not only experienced and interpreted divine works in history but also recognized them to be problems. For the entire Old Testament, it may be valid to say, in any case, that the teaching of the association between deed and consequence could not become either a completely dominating question or even a "dogma." This is because YHWH as "the God who comes to act within history honors no elements of harmony that are real only within the arena of wishful thinking; he creates changes and he awakens hopes that lead beyond a continually regenerated order."[413] How such a harmony created by wishful thinking appears in an attempted application to the writing of history and how it also distorts have been illustrated above in the example of the Books of Chronicles. On the other hand, it is of significance that the Old Testament has understood by the expression "righteousness (acts of righteousness) of YHWH," not world order, but rather YHWH's historical acts of salvation.[414]

i. Yahweh's Wisdom

Only in an extremely limited group of texts from the postexilic period is there a discussion of divine (!) wisdom through which God acts to create.[415]

Human "wisdom," for example, artistic skill, is considered quite naturally to be a gift of YHWH (Exod. 36:1; 1 Kings 7:14; and 2 Chron. 2:12f.). Likewise the intelligence of Solomon (1 Kings 3:28 and 5:12f., 21) stems from God. God is the one who possesses wisdom, continues to pass it on, and distributes it. And he does so to the farmer as well as to the king, to the judge or official as well as to the artist.[416]

Something essentially different is meant when divine wisdom belonging to YHWH is constituted by him to be a creative force in order to shape the entire cosmos. In this regard, Ps. 104:24 allows one to recognize well what is meant by this type of wisdom. When YHWH has completed all his works in and by wisdom and the earth is full of his created designs, then all has been constructed into a divinely ordained order with one thing properly arranged with another. This is a view that the whole of Psalm 104 portrays in a beautiful way. Divine wisdom was present therefore in the construction of the world as order. This kind of "theological" construct moves wisdom into direct proximity to YHWH and makes it at the same time into a person who as the first, primordial work of YHWH was already present with him in the creation of the world (Prov. 8:22–31) and played before him as his nursling (v. 31).[417] This personification is chiefly a poetic metaphor prompted probably by Egyptian texts as well as by the opposing of a positive portrait of Woman Wisdom with a negative portrait of a seductive, "strange" woman. This personification plays a role that in Proverbs 1–9 surpasses its appearance in Proverbs 10ff. One should not here speak about a hypostasis[418] but about the effort of the sages to strengthen the authority of wisdom in the postexilic period through its personification. These references have their place not accidentally now in the framework of so-called late wisdom as it is encountered in the Old Testament especially in Proverbs 1–9.

One should not enter here into a prevalent misunderstanding developing from what has been said. One has often concluded that, when this divine wisdom was already present during creation or perhaps was even thought to have participated in this activity, it was already accessible to humanity, that is, from the time of creation it may be and must be recognizable. However, this view is present neither in Prov. 8:22ff. nor in the verses in 3:19ff. (cf. also 1:20–33) which are parallel in content. Also in Job 28, a subsequent addition to the Book of Job and a poem that is a strongly theological reflection on divine wisdom,[419] it is expressly denied that wisdom may be accessible to human beings. Even if

one were to dig very deep, deeper than people at that time could excavate a
mine (this is mentioned only here in the Old Testament, vv. 1–11), even then
one could not reach her. There are evidently two different issues in this poem:
whether YHWH established his order of creation and whether humanity can
recognize this order and even God through it. According to Job 28, human beings cannot discover cosmic Wisdom or through her the order of the world and
the God who resides behind it. God alone knows the way to Wisdom and
knows her place. Consequently, one should not cause the text here to say something that it expressly denies. The distance between creature and creator, a
view that the speeches of God also set forth in the Book of Job (Job 38:1–42:6),
is upheld and continues to be upheld. The possibility of the recognition of God
through the order of creation is presented for the first time under the influence
of Hellenistic popular philosophy in Wisd. 13:1–5.

In the later Old Testament period, this view of Job 28 could no longer be
understood or tolerated. Subsequently, an addition was placed at the end of the
poem (v. 28) that speaks and must speak about the significance of human wisdom. The addition of Prov. 8:32–36 to 8:22–31 probably also represents a similar effort.

This manner of thinking then experienced a renaissance[420] that moved beyond Job 28 in the poem on Woman Wisdom in Sirach 24. Here the depiction
of divine Wisdom that took up its dwelling in Israel, on the one hand, associated wisdom with the law and, on the other hand, borrowed from the conception of שׁכן = šākēn ("to take up residence"; cf. the Shekinah in early Judaism).[421] Wisdom 7:22–8:1 and 9:1–8 allow one to recognize a similar
understanding. It is now said that the reign of this divine Wisdom is not limited to the cosmos (8:1), for she can also enter into human beings (7:27; 9:7).
According to Proverbs 1–9; Job 28; and Ps. 104:24, divine Wisdom was active
only in the sphere of creation. Now, however, Israel's history, a topic about
which earlier wisdom literature was silent, is placed under the power of divine
Wisdom's activity who consciously reevaluates this history and extends it forward (Wisdom 10–12 and 16–19; cf. Sirach 44–49).

j. Yahweh's Word

In terms of meaning, use, and frequency in the Old Testament, the most important and most frequent medium of YHWH's revelation and activity is his
word, his דבר = dābār.[422] Already in the review of the Old Testament understanding of blessing,[423] which certainly is a "word," it became clear that word
has to do not only with a spoken statement but also with an activity, that word
according to the viewpoint of the Old Testament witnesses and to that of Israel's
ancient Near Eastern neighbors has the character of both power and activity. A
more detailed analysis of this understanding of word can now be developed.

The question about etymology does not provide very much additional help.[424] The root דבר = *dābār* should somehow reproduce the activity of speech ("to mumble," "to hum") or even portray the function of speech ("what is behind pushes forward"), showing where and how words follow each other. It helps to recognize that דבר = *dābār* is used both for "word" and also for "thing, act, event" (e.g., Prov. 11:13 and 17:9).[425] This is illustrated in the expression דברי הימים = *dibrê hayyāmîm*, which are chronicles recording current events, annals, or historiography (1 Kings 14:19; etc.; Chronicles). The phrase "these words" can also mean "these events" (Gen. 15:1; 22:1; cf. 1 Sam. 14:19; and 2 Sam. 1:4; etc.). Thus the prophets can say that they "saw words" (Amos 1:1; and Isa. 2:1) that were for them objects or events to address. Since a "word" contained or unleashed an event, it consequently was filled with the power and strength either of this event or of the object it named. The "word" not only expresses but also contains the essence of this object (Josh. 5:4; and 1 Kings 11:27). This may be compared to the personal names in the Old Testament or the giving of names as a component of creation in the Babylonian *Enuma eliš*[426] and in Gen. 2:19. The word is a word of power (Genesis 1; Isa. 40:8; 55:10f.; Jer. 23:29; and Ps. 33:4, 9), has a dynamic character, and is much more bound with the concrete meaning or content of what it names than is the case with our more generalized term "word." A "word" has to do with a word event or a state of affairs.

The noun (דבר = *dābār*) and the verb (especially in the piel דבר = *dibber*) with God as the subject are used almost 400 times in the Old Testament. The absolute use of דבר = *dbr* occurs over 200 times when related to God, and three-fourths of these occurrences appear in the prophetic word of revelation. That דבר = *dbr* is typical for the prophets is confirmed also in Jer. 18:18. The noun דבר = *dābār* ("word, event") as a subject predominates over the occurrence of the verbal form. The construct relationship of דבר יהוה = *dĕbar yahweh* ("word of YHWH") occurs 242 times in the Old Testament; furthermore, 225 instances of this construct relation are a technical expression for the prophetic word of revelation, while only seven occurrences refer to the legal word of YHWH.[427] However, this construct relationship never refers to a mechanical or to a mantic divine oracle. The priestly word of God was designated by the term תורה = *tôrâ* ("law, instruction"),[428] while the prophetic revelation of the word of God in both the preexilic and the postexilic period is given in the fixed, formulated expression of דבר יהוה = *dĕbar yahweh* ("word of YHWH"). The plural דברי יהוה = *dibrê yahweh* ("words of YHWH") is found only seventeen times,[429] and דברי אלהים = *dibrê 'ĕlōhîm* ("words of God") occurs only three times (Jer. 23:36; Ezra 9:4; and 1 Chron. 25:5). This plural form can stand not only for the prophetic revelation of the word[430] but also for the word of God of the Decalogue (as דברים = *dĕbārîm*, "words": Deut. 4:13 and 10:4; cf. Exod. 34:28) or the Covenant Code (Exod. 24:3f.; and Ezra 9:4). In Gen. 15:1 (E?), the formula of the revelation of the word is also used by Abraham; however, this person is also a prophet according to Gen. 20:7 (E). In the wisdom literature, the expression of "word(s) of YHWH or God" does not occur.[431]

YHWH's word is not only a medium and expression of his presence, something that also occurs through his "name" or his "glory,"[432] but also a medium of his activity as promise and threat, demand and exhortation, and creative power. דברי יהוה = *dibrê yahweh* means originally the concrete individual sayings of God from the mouth of the prophet that assume the form of an individual revelation of the word. However, the expression is expanded, generalized, and more broadly related to the prophetic writings as a whole and finally then to the entire Old Testament as Holy Scripture and the "Word of God." Consequently, דברי יהוה = *dibrê yahweh* is related to the individual prophetic saying not with the translation "*a* word of YHWH" but rather with the translation "*the* word of YHWH."[433] This is the word that is issued as the present decision or answer, that, for the moment, neither needs modification nor connecting with other words to become the word of YHWH. This word does not call for abstraction. However, through YHWH, who is and continues to be the Lord of his word, it can be canceled by the issuance of a new divine word (cf. Isa. 16:13f.; Jer. 18:5–10; Jonah). The saying of a messenger, the messenger formula, and the prophetic formation of an oracle show in this regard that this reception of the word has to do, not with mystical identity with the divine or ecstasy, but rather with a conscious process where commissioning to service happens through inspiration and where a situation of disclosure occasions the call.[434] As a result, the "word of YHWH" is the central medium of revelation according to the witness of the prophets. The "word of YHWH" is the word that issued forth from YHWH to the prophets as well as the word that issues through the prophets which human beings should hear.[435] Dreams, which elsewhere in the Old Testament are classified as a medium of revelation,[436] are criticized by the prophets (Jer. 23:25, 28). "Word" corresponds to YHWH's personal character and his divine sovereignty, even as a commandment corresponds to his moral will and as words of consolation correspond to his will for community. When YHWH speaks, one is compelled to become a prophet (Amos 3:8). In the word, YHWH makes known his nature and his action; in the word, he is active. The word is the unity of address and action. The word can "descend" to Israel (Isa. 9:7) and be like fire or a hammer (Jer. 5:14; 23:29). Thus, one can also correctly translate the formula of the event of the word ("it happened according to the word of YHWH") with "it became something real by the act of YHWH."[437] Decisive is the recognition that the word is event, and not (perhaps not even eternal) truth in regard to its content. The word, which carries within itself the unity of incarnative and predicative elements, is address and command as well as dynamic event. The word is "communication" and "actualization" of both the divine will and divine power. The word of God from the mouth of the prophets has also animating power (Ezek. 37:4ff.) and thus can mean: "Listen so that you may live" (Isa. 55:3; cf. Deut. 8:3).[438] It has accordingly the clarity of a speech event, yet demands at the same time faith, since YHWH himself remains hidden. However, when YHWH has not "spoken" for a long time, has not revealed himself for a while, people become hungry for his word (Amos 8:11f.; cf. Hos. 5:6; and Ps. 74:9). Ezekiel can and must eat this word (Ezek. 3:1–3), while YHWH places it in the mouth of Balaam and Jeremiah (Num. 22:38; 23:5, 16; Jer. 1:9; etc.). According to the Deuteronomic and Deuteronomistic draft of Israel's constitution (Deut. 16:18–18:22), YHWH promises also that he will awaken from time to time prophets from among the brethren in Israel and will put his words in their mouths. They will speak what YHWH has bidden them to say (Deut. 18:15, 18).

The דבר = *dābār* ("word") of YHWH is consequently not only the proclamation and explanation of history, as is evident especially in the prophets,[439] but also, as, for example, the Deuteronomistic History makes clear, the driving force of history. YHWH leads his nation by an ever new word, desiring the response both of faith and of obedience. Even so, his word is not always and immediately identifiable as his own.[440] Whether it hits the mark or not, his word refers to history,[441] and this history becomes in the word of the proclaimer a demand to the hearer: "You shall know that I am YHWH!"[442] The history of YHWH with his people continues to live as a narrated history and becomes a fresh example that faith can and should work. What binds together all "words" is YHWH's desire for community with his people, a desire that also is made known in his judicial will and that is differently expressed each time, indeed *must* be differently expressed.[443] The "word of YHWH" is the announcement of YHWH, although it is always an indirect, oblique self-revelation. The specific character of this word resides in its "occurrence in or issuance from" a personal encounter with YHWH.[444] YHWH's word has also an exclusive preference over an idol (cf. Deut. 4:10, 15). "This is the mode of the biblical revelation of God: to hear the words of God and to follow after the God who calls. The biblical God is not to be experienced in the contemplation or in the crafting of a beautiful idol but rather in hearing and actualizing his word that both promises and demands."[445] So it is then for YHWH's word that the worshiper hopes and waits (Pss. 107:19f.; 119:81; and 130:5).[446]

In the Yahwist, the word of YHWH that is proclaimed in important passages belonging to the central movement of this narrative is decisive. This movement extends from the words in paradise before the first couple are driven out of the garden by God in Gen. 2:18; 3:16–19, 22, to the command and promise to Abraham in Gen. 12:1–3, 7,[447] to the words of promise to Moses in Exod. 3:4f., and to the promise of the covenant in Exod. 34:10. It remains a question as to whether in the Yahwist the word precedes the event[448] or an event precedes the word (cf. the burning bush). Furthermore, the chronological sequence of the narrated event (e.g., in the exodus) cannot be inferred from the temporal sequence of the narrator's word.

In addition to the books and sayings of the prophets, the Book of Deuteronomy is significant for the Old Testament understanding of the "word of YHWH." Here YHWH's word, as the announcement of his will (Deut. 5:5), is identical with this book of the law (Deut. 28:14; 29:28; and Josh. 1:8), seeks to provide the interpretation of the "ten words" (Deut. 4:13; 10:4) of the Decalogue (Deut. 1:5; 5:22ff.), and not only is but also brings "life" (Deut. 32:47). However, the "word" or "words" (of YHWH) in Deuteronomy are strengthened by words that govern through his laws and in his laws.[449] Also God encounters people as and in human language, even as he does in text and scripture.

In the Deuteronomistic History that is dependent upon the spirit of Deuteronomy, YHWH's word is especially the announcement through the prophet's mouth of the approaching event and the driving force of history. Here occurs the decisive statement "according to the word that YHWH spoke to the prophets,"[450] and the remark that YHWH "fulfilled" his promising (2 Sam. 7:10, 24) as well as his threatening word (2 Kings 17:13). YHWH allows nothing from this word to fall ineffectually to the ground, as the word is readily and explicitly made certain.[451] The (late) salvation history psalms (Pss. 105:8, 42; and 106:12, 24) also speak of the word of YHWH working in history.

In the exilic texts of the basic Priestly source and Deutero-Isaiah, by contrast, the apparent reason for the discussion of this topic is the needed strengthening of the exilic community by YHWH's mighty word that shapes creation and the world. Through God's powerfully active word the world is created (Genesis 1; expressed, to be sure, in this text through the verb אמר = 'āmar; cf. Ps. 33:9),[452] and so history begins that points toward YHWH's dwelling among his people.[453] The appropriate references in the plague narrative and in the narrative about the exodus, with their particular commands and formulae of execution of the events, are of significance for the evaluation of the divine word within the basic Priestly source (e.g., Exod. 6:6; 7:8, 10, 19a, 20; 8:1a, 12a, 13; 9:8a; 14, 15).[454] In the conflict with the Egyptian magicians, Moses and Aaron appeal to the word of YHWH, and this word proves to be superior to the Egyptian magical arts.

According to Deutero-Isaiah, YHWH's word will be realized in the future (Isa. 40:8), in no case remains inactive, and does not return empty (Isa. 55:10f.). False deities and idols by contrast cannot talk. The gods are silent, although YHWH calls on them to speak (Isa. 41:21ff.; 44:6–8, 18; 45:20–25; and 46:7). By contrast, YHWH presupposes what will happen, and this comes to pass on the basis of his mastery of history through his word (Isa. 40:21; 41:26; 43:9; 44:6–8; 45:21; and 46:10f.).[455] In the postexilic period, probably under the influence of Deuteronomy, the "word of YHWH" is identified ever more strongly with the law (cf. Neh. 8:1–12; Psalm 1; 19B; 119; 147:18–20; in Pss. 17:4 and 50:17 with YHWH's commandments). Whether here or already in earlier Old Testament texts this "word" was understood[456] as a hypostasis is both unclear and debated.[457] In the early Jewish period, YHWH's word is still connected with wisdom that is attested again as being especially and primarily active in creation (Wisd. 9:1ff.; cf. Sir. 39:23 [17]; and 42:15ff.).

4.5 Yahweh Reveals Himself

YHWH's acts of election in history aim at community with his people. This is why he freed and then brought Israel under obligation. The previous discussion of the means and powers that YHWH used in order to establish and maintain this community and to make known or to disclose his presence and activity belongs to the theology of *revelation*.[458] What the Old Testament has to say more precisely concerning this topic is now to be set forth. In this regard, it should not be overlooked that we have in the Old Testament texts only words *about* revelations of God, but not the actual revelations of God themselves, even when the evidence of the Old Testament text treats the self-revelation of God. What we do have are texts that give information about revelation(s) in very different ways, and these texts are still written mostly, not by those who were participants in these "revelations," but by later witnesses.[459] Also, this is not the place to ask whether and to what extent the Old Testament as a whole is to be classified as the revelation of God; rather, it is the place to inquire about the discussion of revelation(s) in and according to the witness of the Old Testament. That no human being can remain alive who has directly seen YHWH (Exod. 33:20, 23; cf. Exod. 19:21; Deut. 4:12, 15; and 18:16) is not a fundamental assertion that is confirmed by the entire Old Testament. Rather, this assertion has its special place in the context of Exodus 32–34 which narrates the apostasy and the acceptance once again of the nation[460] and has its basis, moreover, in the later inhibition at looking at God found in many additional texts. That one perfectly well can "look" at YHWH is stated, for example, in Gen. 16:13 and 32:31 ("and I am still alive!"); 33:10; Exod. 24:9–11; and Isa. 6:1. Also, one hopes to see God in the future time of consummation (Isa. 17:7; and 33:17).

a. Terms

The Old Testament knows of no term for revelation, even less a particular or a set one. YHWH can make known his will through the casting of lots, and he can transmit his power through his spirit and his helping presence through his angel, his name, and his majesty.[461] All of these are, nevertheless, not actual "revelations" of YHWH, that is, of himself. YHWH also can make known his plans through dreams. However, their clarity is contested, and, what is more, their validity is debated (Jer. 23:25, 28).[462]

When the Old Testament speaks expressly about the self-appearances of

YHWH, it characteristically uses only verbs, not substantives, and there are several of these. In addition, all of these verbs were used in the theological sphere, and they also exhibit a (often even a predominant) profane use.[463] According to the Old Testament perspective, "only secular language" can be used to speak "about God's revelation."[464] This has to do with the fact that the Old Testament way of thinking is not able and does not want to distinguish between what is for us secular and "theological."[465] That YHWH may have made himself known to the ancestors as שַׁדַּי אֵל = *'ēl šadday* ("God of the mountains"?) and to Moses and through him to Israel as יהוה = *yahweh* ("YHWH," cf., e.g., Exod. 6:3) and that the fundamental revelation of YHWH occurred in his saving act for Israel in its deliverance from Egypt (cf., e.g., Hos. 13:4; and Ezek. 20:5) are two of the most important statements of the Old Testament on the topic of revelation.

The use of secular language for revelation is shown immediately in the first verb to be mentioned, גלה = *gālâ*[466] ("reveal," LXX: ἀποκαλύπτειν = *apokalyptein*), which occurs infrequently with God as the subject. According to this, "God uncovers someone's ear," that is, he opens his or her ear,[467] so that this person hears instruction from him. Samuel learns in this manner that he is to perform the anointing of Saul (1 Sam. 9:15), and David receives the promise of Nathan in the same way (2 Sam. 7:27 = 1 Chron. 17:25). The word designates prophetic revelation in 1 Sam. 2:27; 3:7, 21 with גלה = *gālâ* ("reveal," only niphal). Similarly this happens in the insertion (corresponding to the Deuteronomistic image of the prophet) in Amos 3:7 (cf. also Dan. 10:1). גלה = *gālâ* ("reveal") is not, however, a signature term for the prophetic revelation of the word. Nevertheless, in the process of the "seeing" of the seer Balaam, the "opening of the eye" is expressed through the word גלה = *gālâ* ("reveal," Num. 22:31; 24:4, 16). By contrast, in the much later Psalm 119, the worshiper (in v. 18) prays for such an opening of the eye by which he could see the wonders of the Torah of YHWH. Naturally, this seeing is no longer considered to be a visionary seeing but rather insight or knowledge. גלה = *gālâ* ("reveal") can stand for both. In the Elihu speeches in the Book of Job three times the "opening of the ear" is mentioned (Job 33:16; 36:10, 15), which (after repeated, though unsuccessful "speeches" of God: Job 33:14) takes place through a dream or vision of the night (Job 33:16), or through a bad misfortune (Job 36:10, 15). גלה = *gālâ* ("reveal") designates here the act of hearing itself as well as the behavior resulting therefrom.[468] Important is the reference in Isa. 22:14 that stands alone in the preexilic prophets: "YHWH Sebaoth has revealed himself in my ear," an expression that replaces the messenger formula. The judgment word that follows indicates the content of what the prophet of YHWH Sebaoth heard and what God will do. "The word of threat that sounds in the ears of the prophet and presses toward the event is here declared to be the place of the making of revelation."[469] YHWH's "opening" concerns consequently both seeing and hearing and is decidedly not "whether and how God is revealed, (in whose 'existence' no one doubts), but rather . . . whether and how God is *visible* or *disclosed* within the circle of the human experience of reality."[470]

גלה = *gālâ* ("reveal") can also designate a theophany, as Gen. 35:7 (here in the niphal) shows, a point that relates back to Gen. 28:10ff. The summarizing statement in Deut. 29:28 that appraises Deuteronomy as a whole says that what is concealed resides with YHWH. Yet in helping to make a correction to this, the verse also points at the same time to what is "revealed" in Deuteronomy and what one as a consequence should and can grasp. Isaiah 40:5 promises finally that YHWH's majesty is revealed and all flesh shall see what it is that YHWH shall do to deliver his people (cf. Ps. 98:1f.). Isaiah 53:1 and 56:1 also refer to YHWH's historical activity (here together with בוא = *bô'* = "come, go"). It is only in Gen. 35:7 that גלה = *gālâ* ("reveal") designates a self-revelation of God, but what occurs takes place within the imagination of the narrator.

The presentation of oneself, the appearance of human beings (Lev. 13:19; and 1 Kings 18:1f.), and then especially the manifestation of the deity are designated by the verb ראה = *rā'â* ("see") in the niphal form. According to R. Rendtorff,[471] the last use reflects the oldest, most original linguistic usage of the term. These appearances of God are originally connected with a certain location, so that the narratives that treat them possess the character of a cult etiology (Gen. 12:6f.; 26:24f.; and Exod. 3:2: J). The appearance of the deity precedes the building of an altar that responds to this theophany. Well after the detachment from the cultic site, the Priestly document preserves this narrative scheme (Gen. 17:1–3 and 35:9ff.) which serves as a ceremonial framework for a speech of God. P uses נראה = *nir'â* ("is seen") only for the period of the ancestors (although in Exod. 6:3[472] נודע = *nôda'*, "is known"; niphal of ידע = *yāda'*) in order to contrast this epoch with the continuing event of revelation when the name of YHWH is made known to Moses. One should also recognize that the appearance of YHWH to issue a speech of promise announcing divine action and thus providing the actual content of the scene of revelation (cf. Gen. 18:1ff.; 26:2f.; and Judg. 6:12ff.) recedes into the background in P. Nevertheless, as R. Knierim has emphatically demonstrated, the theophany continues to be retained by the Priestly editors.[473] According to P, YHWH's כבוד = *kābôd* ("glory") also "appears" (Exod. 16:7, 10; Num. 14:10; 16:19; 17:7; 20:6; cf. Lev. 9:23) "in order to announce God's demonstration of power against the disobedient nation."[474] Psalm 102:17, a late psalm, then speaks of YHWH's appearance in hopeful anticipation, while Zech. 9:14 and Mal. 3:2 view a divine appearance as a threatening intervention. Israel could "see" something when YHWH rescued his people in the exodus out of Egypt (Exod. 14:13).[475]

The qal of ידע = *yāda'* ("know") in 1 Sam. 3:7 is associated with the "word of YHWH." Samuel still did not know (ידע = *yāda'*) YHWH, for the word of YHWH had not yet been revealed to him (יגלה = *yiggāleh*). The niphal of ידע = *yāda'* ("know") also occurs in Pss. 9:17; 48:4; and 76:2. "It is the powerful demonstration of Yahweh as the savior and deliverer of Israel that here is designated as his נודע = *nôda'*, his making himself known."[476] It is similarly true for Isa. 66:14 and Jer. 16:21 where this is said about YHWH's "hand." In his powerful acts of salvation, YHWH is visible (cf. Ps. 98) and makes his name known (Isa. 64:1 and Ps. 76:2). And when these acts are more precisely described, the emphasis is placed on the exodus out of Egypt, the act of the primal election of Israel.[477] (Exod. 9:16; Deut. 3:24; Pss. 77:15f.; 78:11ff.; 106:7ff.; cf. Micah 7:15). When YHWH revealed himself and his name in the exodus, he became known by Israel. From that time on, Israel is "known" by YHWH (Amos 3:2; cf. Deut. 9:24 and Hos. 13:4). Thus history is experienced and interpreted by this God in a declaration that from its own wonderment issues forth in a new address. Only a few texts speak of a "coming" (בוא = *bô'*) of YHWH.[478] In Isa. 56:1 the verb occurs together with גלה = *gālâ,* meaning then that it is to be treated in connection with the verbs for "reveal."[479] YHWH "comes" together with the ark (1 Sam. 4:7; thus say the Philistines), and he also comes in a dream to a person (Gen. 20:3; 31:24 E). He comes through his messengers (Josh. 5:14; Judg. 6:11), and he comes, as he himself says (thus in the Covenant Code: Exod. 20:24b), to every cultic place in which he shall cause his name to be remembered for the purpose of blessing. Also, the event of Sinai is interpreted as a coming of YHWH (Exod. 19:9; 20:20), while the theophanic descriptions[480] speak rather of a "descending" (ירד = *yārad:* Exod. 19:18; 34:5: J; cf. Pss. 18:10; 144:5; Isa. 34:5; 63:19; and Micah 1:3). YHWH can nevertheless come to help his people from Sinai, from Seir, or from the south (Deut. 33:2; Ps. 68:18b; Hab. 3:3; cf. Isa. 63:1; in Judg. 5:4f.: יצא = *yāṣā',* "go out").[481] According to the message of the prophets, YHWH "comes" to pronounce judgment over (the wrongdoer in) Israel as well as over the nations (Isa. 19:1; 59:19f.; 63:1; 66:15f.; Jer. 21:13; 25:32; and Mal. 3:1f.), while exilic and postexilic prophetic texts speak of his coming to bring salvation (Isa. 40:10; 42:13; and Zech. 2:14). YHWH's salvation (cf. Gen. 49:10) comes both in the form of "your king" who comes to the daughter Zion (Zech. 9:9f.) and in the form of the Son of Man (Dan. 7:13).[482] Only Ps. 24:7, 9 (cf. Pss. 96:13; 98:9) and Ps. 50:3 ("our God comes and is not silent") speak of a cultic coming of YHWH. YHWH comes in order to do something. His coming is neither a presentation of himself nor an end in itself; rather, he comes primarily to address "Israel's oppression."[483] In this manner, one recognizes YHWH's continuing presence in this world and among his people. At the same time, one can, will, and must speak of YHWH's separate appearance, of his special coming, since he is not completely disclosed but rather continues to be both present and concealed. And he alone can act effectively so as to prove himself to be God and to reveal himself to a human being as God, as YHWH.

b. "Revelation" in Israel's Cultural Environment

In this connection, it is not uninteresting to look at how the gods of Israel's religious environment were "revealed" according to their various witnesses of faith.[484] This happened primarily through and in the cultus and its ritual, as, for example, through the procession of idols and barques, sacrifices with the examination of the entrails and especially the liver, omens, the course of the stars, the cup of divination, and signs and oracles that in Egypt could be transmitted through special animals. Magical sayings could move the deity to a revelation. Deities were revealed also through dreams, which were interpreted then by the help of dream books. The gods also made use of the king as a mediator of revelation who was continually present and who at the same time was often given a divine nature and called the "son" of god. Thus the king transmits knowledge about the deity and his will, for the deity and he know and recognize each other.

c. The Self-Introduction and Knowledge of Yahweh

In order to comprehend further the Old Testament discussion of YHWH and his revelation, we should consider the so-called formula of self-introduction, "I am YHWH," which was enlarged through the addition of "your God" in a so-called formula of grace that provided the basis for further reflection. Through even further additions, this formula became more typically and precisely explicit. These additions included the statement, for example, "I am the one who led you out of (the land of) Egypt," thus expanding and undergirding the formula with dimensions of salvation history.[485] Consequently, it is no wonder that this divine formula is completely absent in the wisdom literature.

The short form of the formula "I am YHWH" may be described as an independent nominal sentence that was the original form devoid of expansion (cf. also Hos. 12:10 and Isa. 42:8). Its expansion to "I am YHWH, your God" (cf. Exod. 20:2), for example, on account of Ps. 50:7,[486] is not to be translated with "I, YHWH, am your God." In its original use, individuals previously unnamed or unknown step forth from their unfamiliarity (Gen. 45:3: "I am Joseph") to reveal themselves and to be called by their proper name.

W. Zimmerli begins with the Holiness Code in his investigation of this formula, where it appears mostly in its short form as a definitive, concluding statement. The formula is later enlarged by the addition of "your God" and then by a continuing relative clause that refers to the acts of YHWH ("I who . . . "). Zimmerli remarks that "the declaration of the self-introduction of Yahweh moves in the direction of expansion[487] (cf., e.g., Lev. 19:36; 22:32f.; 25:38; Judg. 6:10, where the exodus or conquest is mentioned). "Your God" is thus interpreted by reference to the history of salvation (Exod. 20:2; Deut. 5:6; Hos. 12:10; 13:4; and Ps. 81:11). The predication can then become an independent predicate ("holy am I, YHWH, your God": Lev. 19:2). To these extended formulations belongs also the so-called "declaration of recognition" (see below), as it occurs frequently in the Book of Ezekiel. In Exod. 6:2f. the formula (by P) is incorporated into a historical, theological synopsis (cf. Ezek. 20:5–7).[488] "All that Yahweh has to say and to proclaim to his people appears as an expansion of the fundamental declaration: I am Yahweh."[489] And it is through history that this expansion and this recognition of YHWH takes place.[490] The formula appears in the mouth of YHWH as well as in the mouth of those he has sent, and it is certainly not accidental that it has special significance in circumstances involving Moses (Exod. 7:17; 8:6, 18; 9:29; and 11:7: already in J and E).[491] This formula of self-introduction form-critically may be linked to the pressure exerted by polytheism. As its use in the Covenant Code, P, and Ezekiel would suggest, behind the formula of self-introduction by a deity who appears and must introduce himself by name to those addressed, stands, according to Zimmerli, a liturgical process (cf. Pss. 50:5, 7ff.; 81:4, 9; and Deutero-Isaiah) "in which a speaker legitimated by divine command mediates the word that provides the community with its most important nourishment."[492] While the formula of self-introduction is absent in Amos, Isaiah, and Micah and occurs a few times in Genesis,[493] it is of special significance in Deutero-Isaiah. The language of this book is strongly shaped by liturgical elements. This is true both for its own language (Isa. 45:6, 7, 18) and for the statements of divine recognition that are inserted (Isa. 45:3; 49:23). Additional references are Isa. 41:13; 42:8; 43:3, 15, 23; 44:24; 45:22; 48:17; and 49:26 in which this formula reaches its ultimate conclusion in the expression of monotheism: "I am God, no one else"; and "outside of me there is no God" (Isa. 44:6; 45:22; 46:9). In the judgment scenes, disputations, and oracles of salvation, the divine I underscores the trustworthiness of the argumentations and promises that are presented. This can be augmented by the hymnic self-praise of the deity frequently attested in Israel's Near Eastern environment, but found in the Old Testament only in the Book of Job (Job 38:9–11, 23) and Deutero-Isaiah.[494] "I am YHWH, that is my name, my glory I give to no other, nor my fame to the idols" (Isa. 42:8; cf. 41:4; 44:6; 45:5; etc.). The idol polemic and the word of comfort carry greater weight and have a more certain background through the particular emphasis placed on the "I" of YHWH. The frequency of the references of the formula of self-introduction, "I am YHWH," as well as the formula of the declaration of recognition, "You shall know that I am YHWH," even in exilic texts (Ezekiel; P; Deutero-Isaiah; and the Holiness Code) should show in addition that questions were being raised in the exilic community about this "I" of YHWH and his power that must be answered anew. YHWH can call himself simply "I am he" (Isa. 48:12). YHWH's I, his being, is thus declared also in this case to be a saving presence, a historical activity, and an intimate presence (Isa. 43:5).

If one now looks at the already often mentioned formula of the declaration of recognition ("and you shall know that I am YHWH") that stands in clear association with the formula of the self-introduction of YHWH,[495] then the preceding picture will be well supplemented.[496] This formula occurs eighty-six times in the Old Testament, and, according to Zimmerli, it originally belonged either to the sphere of judicial or prophetic demonstration of proof (cf. Gen. 42:33f.).[497] Of these 86 occurrences, 78 are formally bound, while the Book of Ezekiel accounts for some 54 occurrences[498] that chiefly are the goal and concluding statement of a foregoing linguistic construction. A divine action precedes each time the announcement of recognition. This action is mentioned first, and then the prophetic word refers to this action. This can be the case in terms of words of judgment (e.g., Ezek. 7:2–4), words to foreign nations (e.g., Ezek. 25:3–5), and words of salvation (e.g., Ezek. 20:42; 37:5f.). "The knowledge of Yahweh is (consequently here) an event vis-à-vis an action of Yahweh to which the prophet with his word as proclaimer points."[499] The knowledge of YHWH has to do with the foregoing activity of YHWH, not with his being[500] and not with human reflection or speculation. And this activity of YHWH has as its goal the knowledge of this God. This knowledge is the ultimate meaning of the activity of YHWH.

Several occurrences of the statement of recognition are also found for good reasons in the Moses stories. This is true for the Priestly document where this statement in Exod. 6:7 assumes an important place.[501] This is also true in Exod. 7:5 and above all within the narrative of the deliverance from Egypt in the journey through the sea (Exod. 14:4, 17f.). Even the Egyptians should know (cf. Isa. 19:21) "that I am YHWH, when I gain glory over pharaoh, his chariots, and his riders." This language occurs once again in the exodus tradition in the Priestly manna narrative (Exod. 16:6). This context mentions the approaching care of YHWH for his people by means of manna and quail that forms the basis for the knowledge of God (Exod. 16:12). It is not surprising that once again the declaration of recognition appears in the central text (Exod. 29:43ff.) of the Priestly narrative as well as in the Sabbath commandment (Exod. 31:13 with the continuation "who makes you holy").[502]

The corresponding statements of recognition in the pre-Priestly Moses stories, and there, above all, in the narratives of the plagues, have already been mentioned.[503] Thus, it is true for the usage of the declaration of recognition in the Moses stories that "the occurrence of great signs is to effectuate the knowledge of God in Israel, in pharaoh, and beyond them in all the world. That this knowledge is not simply a by-product of the activity of Yahweh, but rather its authentic purpose that God intended, is made rather clear by the frequent attachment of the particle לְמַעַן (= *lĕma'an*, "in order to") to the declaration of recognition."[504] While the statement of recognition in Deuteronomy and in the Deuteronomistic writings appears only occasionally (Deut. 4:32ff., 39; 7:6–9; 29:4f.; and 1 Kings 8:43, 60), the formula is especially frequent in the exilic prophets Deutero-Isaiah and Ezekiel. In Isa. 41:17–20; 45:2f., 4–6; 49:22–26; and 52:6, answers and promises are increased and made conclusive. In the conflict with the nations and their gods, the goal toward which everything is moving is made clear through the recognition formula (Isa. 41:23, 26; and 43:10–12). The epistemologically well grounded reference to the preceding activity of YHWH is retained. Thus the activity of YHWH continues to live in the heralded account of his people and of his witnesses. The statement of recognition makes it especially clear that the history effectuated by YHWH concerns, addresses, and admonishes people anew as a history with God that takes place within the larger, ongoing world history.[505] As a result of all this, a person who is a Christian theologian,[506] who takes seriously the witness of the Old Testament, can well speak of the final, fully valid, definitive (as well as other descriptive terms) revelation of God in Jesus Christ but cannot speak about God's *sole* revelation as having occurred in Christ. In addition, the attempt to distinguish between the Old Testament "manifestations" of God and his sole "revelation" in Christ[507] is not correct according to the Old Testament witness.

d. Fundamental Structures of the Old Testament Language of Revelation

As the employment of the verbs for "reveal," the self-introduction, and the statement of recognition shows, YHWH, according to the witness of the Old Testament, encounters human beings especially in history and in the word.[508] It is said that he appears and speaks (e.g., Gen. 28:10ff.; Exod. 19:1ff.) and that in these ways he is made known. A clear rendering of this encounter as well as of this God is not given, for example, in dream revelations, in the prophetic word, and in the decision of God through other people (cf. 1 Sam. 28:6). Thus it can also be said: "Your way leads through the sea and your path through mighty water, yet no one saw your traces" (Ps. 77:20). Whether an event prepares the way for salvation or for judgment remains primarily open and gives room to different interpretations.[509] It could be maintained (Jeremiah) or contested (Hananiah) that it was YHWH who came to punish Judah anew in the form of the Babylonians and that Judah would remain under their yoke (Jeremiah 27f.). History continues to be ambiguous, as it is expressly stated in 2 Kings 18:25 ("with or without YHWH?"), and the knowledge of YHWH is possible only by faith.[510] In retrospect, history can be known (Exod. 15:1ff.; Psalms 78; 105; Ezra 9; and Nehemiah 9) and written (Deuteronomistic History) as a unity shaped and guided by YHWH, and it can be spoken of as

YHWH's "plan" (Isaiah and Deutero-Isaiah). It was a common ancient Near Eastern conviction that the gods worked in events. Events that affected Israel were also to be recognized and acknowledged as acts of *YHWH*. This name must be proclaimed anew by this God, must again become known by Israel, must be newly spoken, must be brought into play once more, and must be remembered. History is also the place of human decision.[511] There continues in the human consciousness an indirect, mediated self-revelation of YHWH, and the later reader, including the contemporary reader of the Old Testament, possesses the witness to this revelation only in the form of a text or texts, in human language, in human speech. These texts, which interpret[512] divine revelation as thankful confession or fearful bewilderment, ventured to speak of an act of God that has occurred or is occurring in history or in a word that has been issued or is being issued.[513] Israel was supported during its journey and directed toward the future by the act and speech of YHWH ("you shall know. . . "). Israel had experienced YHWH in the liberating exodus from Egypt (Exod. 14:31 and Ps. 77:15ff.) and in the encounter at Sinai when it became obligated to God and received from him new promises.[514] Even here a direct look at God was not and could not be associated with this revelation (Exod. 19:20f.; cf. Exod. 3:5f.; Deut. 4:12). Here, YHWH's revelation is always self-concealment (Exod. 33:20), a passing by (cf. Exod. 34:6a). Later on the recommendation is made to regard Deuteronomy as scripture, since here YHWH may not always remain hidden (Deut. 29:28). With the exodus and Sinai, however, the possibility and the necessity were given to Israel to know and acknowledge YHWH and to speak of the revelation of YHWH in both history and the word, and this occurs "before the nations" (Ps. 98:2f.). An example of this is the Syrian Naaman who, through what he experienced, "recognized" that there is no God on the face of the entire earth outside of the God in Israel (2 Kings 5:15).

Consequently, revelation according to the Old Testament includes several closely related features, namely, an event, a "word" possessing a clear or even an unfamiliar meaning, an address from or to YHWH, an element of personal mystery, and a disclosive and momentous character attributed to what is deeply felt and experienced, what, for example, Judg. 5:4f. or Hab. 3:3f. makes clear.[515]

e. Yahweh's Acts in History

This investigation of the Old Testament discourse of revelation and of the word of YHWH has introduced repeatedly the phenomenon of history and less so the theme of "creation" (cf. Psalm 19A), which is yet to be investigated.[516] The sphere of Old Testament wisdom literature largely avoids, however, the subject of revelation. That YHWH may "reveal" himself in the experiences of the ordinary world that are encountered and described in the wisdom literature is nowhere stated *expressis verbis*.[517] However, that the sages believed that

YHWH is active in the orders that are experienced or postulated in the every-day world is not contested. In addition, it is also uncontested that already within the Old Testament this belief fell into a fundamental crisis (Job; Qoheleth; Psalm 73) that challenged the faith of the wise teachers in both its legitimacy and its capacity to be sustained. Still one shall have to be skeptical about any efforts to secure[518] the wisdom literature as a witness to Old Testament reve-lation. When Israel spoke of YHWH, it did so largely in terms of his acts in history.[519] Old Testament Israel has primarily heard its God YHWH in, with, and by this form of the experience of reality.

The Old Testament discourse of revelation consequently is closely con-nected with its interpretation of history,[520] even though there is no "term" for history in its literature (it also lacks terms for "marriage," "freedom," "con-science," and so on). At most, one could refer to history with such terms as "words" or "events" (דברים = *děbārîm*, "events," or דברי הימים = *dibrê hayyāmîm*, "daily chronicles of events"),[521] often the "way" (Exod. 32:7f.; Josh. 24:17; and Jer. 5:4f.; cf. Exod. 33:12f.; and Isa. 40:14), "work" (Isa. 5:12, 19; and 28:29), and "time" (Isa. 8:23; Dan. 2:28; 4:13; and 12:7). What and how Israel thought about history we still have (and at the same time only have) in the form of its history writing and the witness of its prophets, as well as in the prayers, confessions, and songs about its history. Its image of history is de-cisive for a theology of the Old Testament.[522] We have and know this history only in the form of texts that are transmitted to us, and this history of tradition is a part of the Old Testament history of faith.[523]

Out of the thirty-nine writings of the Old Testament, fifteen books are com-prised of "history" or to a great extent of history (Genesis; Exodus; Numbers; Deuteronomy; Joshua; Judges; 1 and 2 Samuel; 1 and 2 Kings; Esther; Ezra; Nehemiah; and 1 and 2 Chronicles). Also, the books of Ruth, Jonah, and Daniel involve primarily historical matters. Psalms and Lamentations refer to the his-tory of YHWH with his people, and the message of the prophets is closely en-twined with history.

"Historical themes occupy so broad a space in no other religious litera-ture."[524] The "knowledge of YHWH" derives from the process of experience grounded in history. While Israel longed after YHWH's accompaniment in its continuing history (Exodus 33), YHWH himself designated his dwelling in the midst of Israel as the purpose of history (Exod. 29:45f.: P). Thus, myth receded into the background of the Old Testament to a large extent because of and for the good of history,[525] for YHWH is a God of historical coming and interven-tion, and this leads "to a historicizing of mythical functions, that is, to a trans-ference of these functions to the event of history touched by YHWH"[526] (cf. Judg. 5:20; Ps. 77:17–21; or Isa. 51:9f.).

In *distinction from Israel's ancient Near Eastern environment,*[527] nowhere in the Old Testament's "historiography" that we now have available to us is the king the subject commissioning and regulating the account. Royal annals, royal chronicles, royal inscriptions, lists of kings, and royal letters of gods are not present in the Old Testament. It also contains nothing about either the legitimation or the stabilization of the monarchy or of the ruler. According to the material in the Old Testament, there is no relationship between omens and history, and history is not understood as an alternation between periods of disaster and periods of salvation. There are indeed in the Old Testament annals that have been redacted (cf. 2 Kings 18:13–16), and there are references to the existence of annals that may be consulted elsewhere (1 Kings 14:19; 15:7, 23, 31; 16:5; etc.). Also a report of a war appears to have been edited (2 Sam. 10:6–11:1; 12:26–31). However, the Old Testament does not contain historiography associated with a king and exclusively written to the glory of a ruler.

Likewise, we do not possess from the hand of the kings of Israel and Judah building inscriptions which were popular in Israel's ancient Near Eastern environment and were used for historical purposes.[528] Even the Siloam inscription[529] stems, not from the king who commissioned this structure, but from the workers who were active in the building of Hezekiah's tunnel. The great acts of the kings are less significant than the destiny of the nation, and the guidance by YHWH was more important than the fame of human rulers. The monarchy can become in the Old Testament the object of historiography (the Succession Narrative of David; the Deuteronomistic History; the Chronicler's History), but the monarchy was not the subject that produced historiography. Starting with the present problems (e.g., the period of Solomon, the exile, etc.), Old Testament historiography moves backward into the past in order to enlighten the present and to open anew and then to influence the future. Further, while Israel knew quite well the forms of historiography that were purely enumerations, such as lists or genealogies, it either went far beyond historiography in the form of lists and the compilations of annals that were primarily a series or it placed them in the service of theological statements (1 Chronicles 1–9).[530] At the same time, older and perhaps on occasion even contemporary sources could be or were taken up. Israel's history writing is not primarily a question of recording anew a cosmic order or, as especially in Egypt, serving to render an account of the acts of the king as being in concert with this order (*Ma'at*), with both the commission for his activity and its completion corresponding to those of his predecessor. Historiography in Israel also can report defeats, blame, tribute, and captivity. Yet these terrible things must not be passed over in silence or turned into something positive, since there is no interest in their repetition as periodic, recurring events. Old Testament historiography moves beyond mere itemization to authentic narrative, and it can and will do so because it describes history under overarching points of view, as, for example, promise or threat and fulfillment, apostasy and punishment, guidance and providence, destruction and new beginning, Israel and the nations, and YHWH and the nations, including their gods. Even so, there is no desire to record only the typical and the repetitive in history. Among the nations of the ancient Near East, probably only the Hittites had entered into this domain of historiography in an initial way.[531]

In the Old Testament, history is not only a matter of military triumph but also a field of human activity and a testing ground lying under the claim of YHWH. History is a field of guilt and apostasy (Deuteronomistic History) where kings are judged "theologically" (sins of Jeroboam; attitude toward the "high places").[532] History is also a field of obedience and disobedience as well as the place for the new provision for cultic orders. History also is a field of hopeful description for its continuation (Chronicles). History, which chronologically is placed prior to the exodus and Sinai, is described as leading to these key events; it is also described in a transparent fashion. The Priestly narrative of the rescue at the sea in Exodus 14 should strengthen the hope for a comparable, future demonstration of divine majesty and, in addition, for a similar liberation from Babylon in the form of a new exodus. The Deuteronomic and Deuteronomistic description of the conquest (Deuteronomy 1–3) wishes to encourage Israel to hope for a new "conquest." Concrete personalities of narrators or even groups of narrators appear to stand behind the Old Testament descriptions of history with rather concretely shaped theological concerns and interests. Deuteronomic and Deuteronomistic literature deals with the settlement, the possession of the land, the loss of the land, and the winning back of the land. Israel's own past was spoken of as one of slavery, and its early history as one of murmuring in spite of providential guidance and the liberation by YHWH that had taken place shortly before. The desire of the writers of history in the Old Testament was to describe events in terms of their significance for the present as well as for the future, but not to write history that turned back toward the past. This literature is not interested in what actually has been,[533] does not inquire after historical truth, indeed has no term for this,[534] but seeks rather to explain the significance rather than the factual nature of events. The *bruta facta* are picked up in the *kerygma* and continue to exist there as events and experiences in the way that they have been interpreted. For the sake of this *kerygma*, Israel was placed more concretely and continuously within its own historical context. Especially through the prophets, this *kerygma* looked beyond the limitations of a particular nation, even those of Israel, to YHWH as the God who is active in history. The prophets explore the question of how the impact of the nations on Israel relates to the power and the divine nature of the God of Israel. Amos speaks (Amos 1:3–2:3) about and against neighboring nations whose gods, however, he passes over. Other prophets have followed him in this way.

B. Albrektson[535] has correctly pointed out that in Israel's ancient Near Eastern environment the gods also were believed to be active in history. One sees in the lament over the destruction of Ur, for example, the anger of the gods active in history, even if this did not occur, as, for example, in the Erra Epic, as a response to human sin. In the Tukulti-Ninurta Epic by contrast, the failure of a military standstill resulted in the Babylonian gods abandoning their cities, and even the Hittite prayer concerning pestilence asks for freedom from historical punishment that was the result of sins.[536] These ancient Near Eastern examples have to do, however, more with individual acts and particular events than with overarching historical connections. In addition, what was different in Israel was the significance of the divine word in relationship and accord with this history and therefore in its interpretation as either a unity or at least an aggregate consisting of larger components. Israel came to its view of history as an integral whole[537] apparently through the oneness of YHWH and through the unity of the Old Testament faith in God. History became the place where community with God was experienced and maintained, the locus of the activity of the one true God who certainly had no mythical opposite, the context of divine lordship, and the place of human decision for God. In this way ancient Israel has explained and experienced history. Israel was interested in history, not in and of itself, but because it was in history that God had revealed himself. In the form of YHWH's choosing, in his word that becomes event, in his promises that move toward fulfillment, and in his threats that press toward realization lies the binding and interpretive element of the Israelite view of history. In this view, history is not only a unity directed toward a goal but also a linear, not cyclical, movement that is experienced, described, and believed. And thus the ancestors and the later Priestly genealogies were arranged into a chronological sequence, while a place was found for later events that historically accrued to the faith of Israel, as, for example, the monarchy, the city of Jerusalem with its faith tradition, and the temple.[538] History inquires about the future, while Israel's journey with YHWH inquires about a goal or even the goal. Thus history in Israel, having received a religiously motivated teleology, became "theo-teleological."[539] In Isaiah (Isa. 5:11–17, 18f., etc.), Deutero-Isaiah (Isa. 46:9–11, etc.), and later texts (e.g., Isa. 25:1–5 and 2 Chron. 25:1–8), the discussion to be sure is about a historical "plan" of YHWH that is being realized,[540] and this conception may already exist behind the form of historiography that is met in the Succession Narrative of David (2 Sam. 17:14b).

In the exodus, YHWH has entered into relationship with Israel as the God of liberation. In the analogous situation of the exile among a foreign people and hostile deities, Israel, hoping that God would be the same liberating force, wrote on the strength of this earlier understanding about the history of the nation under this deity continuing into the future. What was past became the basis for the present experience, hope, and guiding example of the knowledge of God. R. Smend[541] has spoken correctly, decisively, and revealingly about etiology[542] ("because—therefore") and paradigm ("as—so"), arguing that they provide the foundational categories for Old Testament historiography. He reasons that an etiology has its source not only in a common delight in stories but also in the effort to explain the present on the basis of the past. In this way, etiology exudes a historical consciousness and interest. One can also elucidate Israelite historiography by reference to its categories of explanation, or "coordinates."[543] These include in the relationships of family and national histories (Genesis 12–Exodus 1; 1 Chronicles 1–9) covenant and the breaking of covenant, sin, guilt, and punishment, narrative and established order (Genesis 9; 17), cult and history,[544] and promise and fulfillment. The experience of history and historiography, which is both connected to and determined by this experience, give rise to eschatology. That is to say, eschatology originates as a function of historical experience (V. Maag).[545] Thus it is not then a list or stereotypical formula but rather narration that is a fundamental speech form of the Bible, when it seeks to say something about God.[546] Narration of the acts of God for the transmission of the essential content of faith had in Israel a highly valued place (cf. Deut. 6:20ff.; Judg. 5:11; Joel 1:2f.; Pss. 44:2; 48:14; and 78:3ff.). And when Old Testament writings tell stories, there occurs in these stories a lively variation in the form of sentences, subordination in points of view, the presentation of dialogue, the distinction between the time of narration and narrated time, and the question concerning motive and purpose.[547] "That which exists, beginning with its inception, is comprehended as a process."[548] Thus the appearance of Noah's ark is not described after it is finished; rather, the text describes how it should be constructed (Gen. 6:14–16). This is exactly the case with the Jerusalem temple (1 Kings 6–7). Narration openly furnishes the elements especially appropriate to the discussion about God.[549] This relates to the fact that Israel had experienced historically its God primarily in the events of the exodus, Sinai, and the gift of the land and after these events continued to encounter God in history. Thus the comment of G. Mensching is quite true, for he has argued that in Israel history was the "actual sphere of the divination"[550] of YHWH. Israel pursued the writing of history not only at the high points of its collective life, during its grand periods. It is true that the first historiography came at the time of the Davidic-Solomonic empire (Succession Narrative; Yahwist). However, directly before, during, and on the basis of the exile, Israel deliberated anew on the foundations of its faith, and it understood this again in a special way through a new writing of its history (Deuteronomistic History; P). This historiography assumed the form of an explanation that moved from an interpretation of the past, to an address of the present, to a hope for the future. Israel's historiographers did not ask only about the "Why," that is, the reason events happened (which is more of a Greek view). They also inquired even more about the "What" and the expected "Whereupon."[551] The future for which Israel hoped does not bring with it only the repetition of typical situations but (cf., e.g., Deutero-Isaiah;

Ezekiel 40–48; Daniel; and also Joshua 13–21) also the consummation and even surpassing of the past and the present. Thus Yahwistic faith that was shaped by history wrote its own history that it had experienced and believed. This faith did not do so free of its own particular slant; indeed, there was no intention to do so. Furthermore, this historiography was to be and seeks to be an address to strengthen and to transmit anew the faith, strives to be a response to the word and event that has happened, and also wishes to be a new word from YHWH that witnesses to him.

That YHWH is active in history is not a matter for debate among the worshipers of the Old Testament and in the Old Testament witness. Word and deed (דבר = *dābār*) are bound together. Thus one shall have to say in an Old Testament manner of speaking that YHWH also speaks *through* history. He is active in history, reveals himself in history, and, even more, expresses his purposes and his saving as well as punishing nature *through* history. According to the Old Testament witness, the revelation of YHWH occurs not only *in* history but (also) *as* and *through* history.[552] One does not ask whether YHWH is active in a historical event, for history is personally addressed: YHWH is active (Exod. 15:21), has looked upon (Gen. 19:21; Exod. 4:31; 2 Kings 13:4; etc.), has extricated (Deut. 28:63; Amos 3:12), and so on. However, it certainly can be asked what he wishes to achieve with his historical acts, and why he may have done this but not that (cf. Judg. 21:2f.).

Consequently, history can be narrated with the conviction that God is active within its boundaries, without the discussion having to focus constantly on YHWH or even on his enduring or redeeming word.[553] To illustrate this, one may legitimately refer to the Succession Narrative of David (2 Samuel 9–20; 1 Kings 1–2).[554] The few theological remarks that are scattered throughout this narrative (2 Sam. 11:27; 12:24; 17:14)[555] are regarded from time to time even as secondary additions.[556] In the Succession Narrative, serious politics and the conducting of war are closely interwoven with the most personal matters, and in regard to the first two representatives of the Davidic kingship this linguistically and stylistically remarkable narrative occupies an extremely critical position. Just as reticent in the expression of theological statements, the Joseph Story (Genesis 37; 39–48; 50)[557] describes what happened to Joseph and his brothers as divine providence (Gen. 45:5; 50:20). Joseph as well as his brothers received a sympathetic description of their character,[558] and their ways and errors were clearly and openly mentioned. However, YHWH is also active here, if concealed, in these events and in the persons who can and must reach their own decisions.[559] He is active in their dreams as well as in the ability to interpret them, as the narrator makes clear by scattered remarks or as the persons who are acting in the narrative are made to comment (Gen. 39:3, 5, 23; 40:8; 41:16, 39, 51f.; 42:18; 43:14, 23; 44:16; 45:5, 7; 46:3; 48:3f., 15f.; and 50:20).

According to P. F. Ellis in *The Bible's First Theologian*,[560] the Yahwist,[561] in seeking to tell about God and his activity on behalf of Israel and the other nations, introduces his narrative by moving directly (Gen. 3:16ff.) to the events and words that are appropriate for his own period. As is the case with the rest of the Old Testament, including P later on, J does not begin his narrative with a mythical, prehistorical time or with a theogony or theomachy. His primeval history, along with the one by P, is at the same time foundational history, and the basic, foundational, earliest period for Israel lies not in the time prior to history but rather in history itself.[562] The image of humanity, to which the Yahwist points in Genesis 3, is met again in his description of Jacob and the sons of Jacob. The special feature about Israel's ancestor, Shem, is his deity (Gen. 9:26) who institutes a blessing that provides a pathway with and through Abraham, both for him and his descendants (Gen. 12:1–4a). The promise of blessing, the promise of land (Gen. 12:7, etc.), and the promise of becoming a great nation are fundamental, constituent features for the historiography of the Yahwist, if one wants to designate already his work in such a way. These promises have been made and will be kept in spite of human history characterized by opposition to God. Beyond the ancestors, the narrative moves on to the oppression in Egypt, to liberation from Egypt, to Sinai, to guidance in the wilderness. The theme and promise of the land are important for the Yahwist,[563] and it appears certain that at one time his source contained narratives of conquest.[564]

Israel's prophets[565] have also made an important contribution to the Old Testament understanding of history.[566] They were situated in a time of great historical currents, which included the punishment of Israel, and they recognized and explained[567] history as an event in which YHWH comes anew to his people (Amos 4:6–12). History is his work (Isa. 5:19; 10:12), and the word of the prophets along with their symbolic actions anticipate what it is that YHWH is about to do.[568] YHWH speaks in and outside history to the prophets, and they speak their Word of the Lord within the concrete situations of history (cf. Isaiah 7). They see in history the conversation of YHWH with Israel and at the sight of YHWH's coming the finality and unity of history. "History is for prophecy the purposive dialogue of the Lord of the future with Israel."[569] When the audience of the prophets think they are able to protect themselves through recourse to history, then this use of history is denied them (cf., e.g., Amos 3:2; 9:7; Hosea 12). Prophets, however, reach back themselves to this history in order to bring it into play as the reflection of YHWH's act of salvation, or as an accusatory event, or as a new hope that contrasts with the differently shaped present (Hos. 2:4ff.; 11:1ff.; Jeremiah 2) or even as an experience soon to be surpassed by the new exodus (Isa. 41:18).[570] There are foreign nations that emerge on the horizon of history that come to be seen as the instrument of YHWH's destruction or salvation for his people (e.g., Assyria in Isaiah; the Babylonians in Jeremiah; Cyrus in Deutero-Isaiah). In this way, the prophetic view is expanded to include the comprehension and penetration of history beyond that of the prophets' own people. Prophecy also prepared the way for the universal, historical view of apocalyptic.[571] In his historical surveys (Ezekiel 16; 20; 23), Ezekiel provides a differently oriented overview of the history of Israel, reflecting the Deuteronomistic History. These overviews could describe the history of Israel/Judah/Jerusalem only as a unique history of apostasy and sin (Ezekiel 23), on the one side, and as one that points to YHWH's legacy on the other (Ezekiel 16). This history, then, is one of the lack of gratitude toward the electing and guiding God YHWH, beginning with the liberation from Egypt (Ezek. 20:5ff.).[572] Positive expectations that grow then out of this negative view of history (Ezek. 20:33–38, 40–44) are grounded only in Yahweh himself, who seeks to do such "for my name's sake," "so that you will know that I am YHWH" (v. 44).

The Old Testament prophets do not write history. However, they do speak about history as those who are affected by it. And they provide the means by which to recognize in what way their own faith as well as the faith of their hearers and readers was determined by history. They also allow people to know what YHWH had done, does, and will do to Israel/Judah/Jerusalem in history, and they have sought to enable others to learn from these observations about history in all of its dimensions. The prophets have interpreted history as the place of divine activity, yet they knew that YHWH continued to be a hidden God (Isa. 45:15) whose action is also strange (Isa. 28:21, 29). "Because of this they are not incorrectly to be regarded as the actual interpreters of historical events in the Old Testament."[573]

The multilayered Deuteronomistic History,[574] which reaches from Deuteronomy 1 to 2 Kings 25, allows one readily to recognize where it places its concerns through the particular shape of its language, its farewell speeches, its prayers by important persons that are scattered throughout the text (Deuteronomy attributed to Moses; Joshua 23; 1 Samuel 12; and 1 Kings 8), and its own reflections (Joshua 1; Judg. 2:1–3:6; and 2 Kings 17:7ff.). The temple in Jerusalem and its destiny are a frequent theme that is differently interpreted (with various emphases concerning the "name [חם = šēm] of YHWH").[575] Israel's history is written as a history of recurring apostasy from YHWH (1 and 2 Kings) who responds to save when the people cry out to him (see Judges). In spite of David, who is positively assessed, and his dynasty (1 Samuel), the monarchy places Israel in danger.[576] This is especially so through the self-perpetuating "sin of Jeroboam" (1 and 2 Kings), which contributed decisively to the loss of the land. Consequently, in the so-called Deuteronomistic program for the new beginning after the exile (Deut. 16:18–18:22), the king must be bound to the nation of "brothers" as a brother and be more obligated to the Torah (Deut. 17:14ff.). The promises to (2 Samuel 7 and 2 Kings 8:19) and the judgments against the kings are both set forth in the Deuteronomistic History, as is already clear in the juxtaposed cases of Saul and David. The assessments of monarchs in the Books of Kings, beginning as early as Solomon (1 Kings 11:1–3), are predominantly negative. There was the refusal to obey YHWH whose word was announced by the prophets and whose warnings were not heard. However, new obedience is called for in certain texts and even the possibility of "conversion" (Deut. 4:25–31; 30:1–10; and 1 Kings 8:46–53), so that one may have again a portion of the "good" land that YHWH has "sworn" to the ancestors and their descendants. Along with this, penance is now to be cast aside so that the future may become accessible through both hope in YHWH's oath and allegiance to his people and the appeal for new obedience to the divine will as it is prescribed in Deuteronomy. Here historiography is dominated by theological concerns.

By means of what it narrates and how it tells the story,[577] the Priestly (basic) document[578] aims squarely at the negative situation that has been given to the exilic community to endure. Already with the initial section in Gen. 1:1–2:4a,[579] Mesopotamian material is appropriated, reshaped, or put aside as a threat to Israelite faith in YHWH. Like Marduk,[580] YHWH creates the stars (associated with the Babylonian deities). However, he is able to create light before the stars were brought into existence, and he gave the stars, which had not existed before primeval origins, only a menial function. YHWH also gives them only generic names, allowing their specific names to remain unstated. A battle of YHWH with Tiamat[581] is no longer in view in P's creation story. Neither is a theogony or a theomachy. The image of God is humanity, not, for instance, only the king, and the purpose of creation is the Sabbath, which is the gift of Israel's God to its world. The blessing pronounced over human beings is repeated after the primeval flood, the details of which are found more in P than in J and point to Mesopotamian influence. And the existence of the world is strongly assured through the covenant with Noah with its sign of the rainbow (Gen. 9:1–17). After the Priestly portion of the Table of Nations (Genesis 10), the next great high point of the continuing history of the covenant of God is Abram, who becomes Abraham, and the promises of the validity of his covenant obtain also for his successors as does circumcision, which serves as its sign (Genesis 17). God's speeches are important in these narratives,[582] and the promises to Abraham become confirmed once again to Jacob (Gen. 35:9–13). P wishes to set forth orders that mediate support and orientation. As the covenant of Abraham is to be "eternal," so is what was promised. For example, in the purchase of the Cave of Machpelah (Genesis 23), the sign of the purchase and the purchase price reach their culmination in the division of the land through lots (Joshua 13–21)[583] and in the new possession of the land for which Israel yearned. The hope for the return home and for the new portion in an "alien land" highly valued by P shapes, for example, the description of the deliverance "in" the sea where YHWH shows how marvelously he is able to liberate, and the event of the old exodus shows a clear and intentional proximity to the hopes for the new exodus out of Babylon (cf. the P portion in Exodus 14; Isa. 43:14ff.). YHWH and his servants are also superior to "Egyptian magicians" (P in Exodus 7–9). History before Moses and the exodus was to reach its culmination at this theologically significant period and was to be determined by it. In addition, P makes clear a perceptible usage of various designations for God through its chronology as well as through the progress of the history of revelation.[584] At Sinai, YHWH establishes the cult that remedies sin. P is consciously silent about the *covenant* of Sinai (certainly broken by the people). The first sacrifice (Leviticus 8f.), the Lord appearing on Sinai (Exod. 24:15b–18a), the nation wandering forty years long through the wilderness accompanied by the glory of YHWH,[585] and the "tent of meeting"[586] show the nearness of YHWH in this period and in this place. Several times the creation and the prevailing power of divine speech and words are also stressed. YHWH, the God who is determined to be closer to his people, is the one who could lead them out of Egypt. He intends to dwell again in the midst of his people and to be their God (Exod. 29:42ff.). The sanctuary is (again) erected (Exodus 25ff.). Thus, here history is written in order to mediate the new perspectives of the exilic community which, for example, in the stories of the spies (P portion in Numbers 13–14), perhaps are directed against P's contemporaries unwilling to return home. If people out of the midst of their oppression will call on YHWH (Exod. 2:23f.), he will hear them and intervene to liberate them (Exod. 6:5f.), for he has the power to perform miracles (Exod. 14:29).

The Chronicler's work of history,[587] which here is understood to include only 1 and 2 Chronicles, presupposes the existence of the Deuteronomistic History along with Deuteronomy and the Priestly document within the Pentateuch and often points out the sources used.[588] This work, like the Deuteronomistic History, does not have a single author, and also undergoes later additions and expansions. Even in its "genealogical vestibule" (1 Chronicles 1–9), it points to some of its essential concerns. While humanity in general is indeed initially introduced, this is followed by Israel and Judah, and Saul and David. Chronicles was primarily intended to be a report about the history of the monarchy, and in particular the monarchy in the Southern Kingdom. This narrative of history also has a clear relationship to the present, for only the successors of the Southern Kingdom and those residing in its former territory in the postexilic period are the "true Israel."[589] Inhabitants of the former territory of the Northern Kingdom can join in the new nation only through a "return" that involves repentance (2 Chron. 30:6). The monarchy of the Southern Kingdom, where the ruler is the one who stands in the place of King YHWH,[590] obtains its significance for the cult and the temple especially by means of the figures of David and Solomon. The purpose of this often paradigmatic historiography is to provide the help necessary for the people in their own present context to organize after the exile. This help is to be found in the cult, the (problematic) Levites,[591] the hope in a just YHWH who already is given the stronger name אלהים = 'ĕlōhîm ("God"), and the new political and military power of "all Israel" existing now only as a cultic community.

Confessions, psalms, and songs that speak of YHWH's works in history very aptly show how history was experienced and understood in Israel.[592] This begins at first with texts that praise and give thanks for only a single historical event understood as YHWH's act of direct intervention into history. This is the case, for example, in the so-called Song of Miriam (Exod. 15:21) and the Song of Deborah (Judges 5). After that, the prayer of Jacob (Gen. 32:10–13) encompasses a section of the life of the one who offers it, and the short credo in Num. 20:15f. encompasses the journey from Egypt to Kadesh. The texts originating from the Deuteronomistic movement (Deut. 26:5–9; Deuteronomy 32) as well as those dependent upon them (Nehemiah 9), the psalms of salvation history (Psalms 78; 105; 106), and the prayer of Daniel (Dan. 9:4–19) seek, by contrast, to write about Israel's history as a whole during their time or about major epochs that belong to this history. They do this under different, often consciously contrasting categories of explanation, including the lament for God's turning toward slaves, deliverance from need, the wandering and guidance into the land (Deuteronomy 26), the loyalty of YHWH in spite of human unworthiness and disloyalty (Deuteronomy 32; Psalm 105), the movement from individuals to a great nation and from oppression to liberation, YHWH's salvific turning toward Israel and the nation's unthankfulness and sin, judgment and grace, the thanks and the praise of YHWH for his deeds in this history, and the new petition for compassion heartened by the look back into history. All decisive "coordinates" (J. Hempel) of the faith connecting itself to history and of the historiography of Israel are here incorporated and clearly recognized. History as tradition is seen as "revelation," and it comes in the form of language, as a thankful or penitential confession in the personal appropriation by the worshiper, and as the penitential unburdening to YHWH that is new in its origin and meaning. "The reality of the language brings forth the event in the word, and now the word as the interpretation of the event transmits salvation for faith."[593] History, word, and language, and this is the religious discourse of mystery, constitute here what we commonly call revelation. Thus God does not "reveal" himself through history, although he does allow people to recognize in history something of his divine nature.[594]

f. "Time" according to the Witness of the Old Testament

Israel's understanding of time is also shaped by its experience of history and its faith oriented especially toward history.[595] As is true with the phenomenon of "history," there is no comprehensive, abstract, or general term for time in the Old Testament (or in its environment).[596] The Hebrew עת = 'ēt[597] designates, above all, the concrete moment (e.g., the evening time: Gen. 8:11; the time of the evening sacrifice: Dan. 9:21), the "right time," as one can readily recognize in Qoh. 3:1–8, and the "time of grace" (Isa. 49:8). The term involves the appointed time (e.g., Gen. 29:7: time of driving home the cattle), and "to its time" likewise points to the right time (Pss. 1:3; 104:27; etc.). One can form a plural for עֵת = 'ēt (cf. "my times stand in your hands": Ps. 31:16; also Ezek. 12:27; Job 24:1). Also מוֹעֵד = mô'ēd stands for the fixed moment (Gen. 17:21: "set date"), especially for the cultic festivals (1 Sam. 9:24; Exod. 13:10; Lev. 23:2ff.; etc.), and יוֹם = yôm for the day filled with a concrete event ("on the day that YHWH made earth and heaven": Gen. 2:4b). This latter understanding can be recognized also in "the day of YHWH," that is, the day determined by and filled with the action of YHWH,[598] in the day of Midian, in the day of Jezreel, and in the day of Jerusalem (Isa. 9:3; Hos. 2:2; and Obad. 11, 14). Israel's history is qualified by the events transpiring on certain days and in earlier times (Deut. 4:32; and 32:7), and one frequently and readily reflects on these days.[599] One also looks with hope to future days of salvation (Hag. 2:15, 18f.; Zech 4:10; 8:9).

YHWH does everything "in accordance with its time" (Jer. 5:24; Ps. 145:15), so that L. Köhler is able to enlist the Old Testament idea of time as the Old Testament's means for describing God as the one who sustains the world.[600] Unique is the Old Testament discussion of the past (קֶדֶם = qedem) and the future (אַחֲרִית = 'aḥărît; cf. Isa. 46:10), since "future" is something that lies "behind" and is not accessible to a person (Jer. 29:11), while the "past," quite to the contrary, is "before" him or her so that one can act in response to it (Ps. 143:5).[601] In this connection, however, what is past (קֶדֶם = qedem) lies not in mythical prehistory but rather in that which YHWH has done on behalf of the ancestors (Pss. 44:2ff.; 74:2; etc.). Joining these terms also is the word עוֹלָם = 'ôlām, which can stand for distant time both in the past (Pss. 90:2; 93:2) and in the future (Isa. 55:3). The term also expresses long duration. However, it is also true that what gives time its meaning and shapes its understanding is the variety of contexts in which it is used. This is true, as we have seen before, of the inquiry concerning Hebrew lexemes that do not set forth fully their own etymology or lexical semantics but rather provide their meaning from their context. As with the case with "history," one should not expect to find in the viewing and evaluation of time that the same understanding and the same experience of time would be present everywhere in the Old Testament, due to the differences between wisdom literature, historical writings, prophecy, and cult.[602] However, since the Hebrew for these different groups of literature is a common language that possesses general structures of understanding and comprehension, it is possible to ask with all caution what the understanding of time in the Old Testament and its language may be. The following statement is a succinct summary that, it is hoped, is not too concise:

"In the language of Biblical Hebrew, one may more precisely describe the nature of time in the grammatical categories of the relationship of tense (aspect: perfect, imperfect), the coefficient of direction (retrospective, prospective), and the course of action (punctual and durative). At the basis of this description lies an understanding of time as a one-dimensional, irreversible 'river' running in one direction." For the representations of the locations of time, there is a register of words (now, then, at that time, here, there, etc.) that establishes the relationship of the speaker or narrator and his or her own situation of communication to other points in time. "This description of the location of time and its function for the understanding of language presupposes a conception of time as a continuing and comprehensive medium of experience."[603] Consequently, the present is bound with the past and opened to the future, something that one may readily recognize in the narrative form and narrative purpose present within the narratives of history.[604]

In spite of the possible differences in the experiences and comprehensions of time for the persons of the Old Testament, the significance of the qualitative understanding of time as a succession of events takes precedence over the quantitative understanding of time as a sequence of temporal units. In this connection, S. de Vries, who uses the conceptual pair of terms, quantitative and qualitative, brings to attention the fact that the prophetic writings speak more frequently of יוֹם = *yôm* ("day"), while wisdom[605] and apocalyptic literatures speak more of עֵת = *'ēt* ("time").[606]

For the Old Testament, time does not begin in the mythical, primeval era;[607] rather, the "beginning" (Gen. 1:1) of the world is the beginning of human time and history (cf. also Gen. 2:4bff.). The commandment to multiply, which contains a blessing (Gen. 1:28 P), is that which also causes the small tribe of Jacob to become a great nation (Exod. 1:7 P). The course of time is structured generally by the alternation of day and night (Jer. 33:20; Ps. 74:16) and the appearance of the various "lamps" in heaven that are connected to this alternation (Gen. 1:4f.; cf. Ps. 136:8f.), but in a more specific way by the Sabbath (Gen. 2:1–3). At the same time, the Sabbath was related to Israel who was alone among the nations in knowing the Sabbath as a commandment.[608] The week as the ever recurring cycle is integrated into the progress of time as a line and a route that has a "beginning," orders the succession of days, and actualizes a time of cessation. The descendants of Adam listed in Genesis 5 mark the continuing history in the form of additional genealogies. These genealogies encompass periods of the course of history and explain at the same time that the decreasing life spans (Genesis 5) are due to the continuing diminishment of the power of life that results from the human distance from God. All of humanity receives in the covenant granted to Noah and his descendants a promise for future progeny (Gen. 9:1–17). Then time is moved forward with history by promises that are often issued repeatedly and with purpose. These promises include descendants, land, blessing, and assistance to the ancestors, the Moses group, the people of Israel as a whole, and then David and his dynasty, for YHWH "is" certainly indeed "the one who shall prove himself" (Exod. 3:14).[609] Prophetic threats and promises follow and hold Israel to the pathway of time and history.

Genesis 8:22 shows that something consequently can be said about time in the Old Testament without having recourse to the actual conception ("In the future, so long as the earth shall stand, sowing and harvest, frost and heat, summer and winter, and day and night are not to cease": J; cf. Ps. 74:17). Here, all that pertains to time appears as a cycle, better said, as a rhythm. However, this rhythm of time is included in the continuing course of history narrated by the Yahwist as a sign of YHWH's enduring patience with human beings following the primeval flood.[610] This enduring patience is expressed "in the incomprehensible duration of the natural orders in spite of continuing human sin."[611] The ancestors' sayings of blessing are formed to survey time and history and to be a plan for realization (in the final analysis Yahweh's plan) that extends from individuals to the tribe and then to the nation (Genesis 27; 48; 49). In Deuteronomistic and Priestly texts, although not in J and E, "forty years in the wilderness,"[612] on the one hand, is a cipher for the period of the exile and, on the other hand, serves as an indication to the following generation of Babylonian captives that they can expect to return from exile, a promise that is expressly made into a theme elsewhere (Num. 14:22f.; Deut. 9:7ff.). As the chronological indications in P and in the Deuteronomistic History suggest, theology also is transmitted and advanced by means of temporal numbers and periods of time.

When Qoheleth, who uses the noun עֵת = 'ēt ("time") forty times, reflects about time in 3:1–8,[613] he does so in order to show that human beings cannot recognize each proper moment of time (Qoh. 3:1: זְמָן = zĕman, "time," and עֵת = 'ēt, "time") to bring to success a particular matter or deed (Qoh. 3:11). This perspective is certainly already present in the wisdom of Proverbs (Prov. 15:23; 25:11; cf. Isa. 28:23–29). Time in Qoheleth is not primarily a fixed time or chance but rather contains an ever new pitfall or risk in the sight of given but not recognizable possibilities (cf. Qoh. 8:6), so that in addition to "time" the "fortuitous event" (פֶּגַע = pega') can and must be mentioned (Qoh. 9:11f.). Time can be seen by the oppressed only as the same, ever occurring experience, when there is nothing new under the sun (Qoh. 1:4, 9, 11).[614] The day of death is better than the day of birth (Qoh. 7:1).[615] In view of the brevity of human life, Qoheleth commends to his audience the delight of joy, when and however this is possible (Qoh. 5:18f., etc.), so long as a person is young (Qoh. 11:9ff.). Qoheleth 3:11 is to be seen, then, within this context. God's giving עוֹלָם = 'ôlām into human hearts means that reflecting on time and the future is a wearisome task (cf. Qoh. 6:10; 7:14).[616] And thus Qoheleth in 6:10

probably turns even against the Book of Job and stresses that one cannot argue with one who is stronger. God, like human existence, remains inaccessible and inscrutable, and thus it is for time as well.

What Qoheleth determined through reflection Job offers in complaint in his first sustained lament (Job 3).[617] Since his lifetime has produced nothing positive, he curses the day of his birth. For Job, the day of birth and the day of death should have coincided. Later on, other speeches of Job address the days of human life, weep over their brevity, and lament the unawareness and suddenness of their end (Job 7 and 14; cf. Wisd. 2:1–5). Or Job contrasts the former days that were good with the tragic present (Job 29). By contrast, Qoheleth placed no stock in such comparisons (Qoh. 7:10). Contacts between the understanding of time in sapiential thought and God's acts on behalf of his people are not discernible.

A *cultic event* is shaped by chronologically determined, repetitive, and regulated festivals that follow a temporal course.[618] The Old Testament festival community achieved unity in its experience of time marked off by the cult. Nevertheless, through the historicizing of these festivals and their relationship to "salvation history," this community was placed not only within a recurring cycle but at the same time found itself confronted continually by history and brought within its boundaries on a repeated basis. To celebrate this kind of festival, to interpret it, and to fill it with this kind of content appears so far to be without analogy in Israel's environment. Such a festival is, then, "the day which YHWH has made" (Ps. 118:24) and is purely and simply a time that is filled with content. One can compare the relationships and references of the Christian church year and its festivals to the New Testament events of salvation. Here the calendar found its special meaning. The authoritative chronology within the Old Testament stems out of priestly circles.[619] Moreover, this chronology is oriented characteristically, not to astral or to other natural phenomena, as, for example, occurred in Egypt,[620] but rather to the exodus out of Egypt (Exod. 12:40f.; 19:1; cf. 1 Kings 6:1). The "calendar," nevertheless, still is determined by astral factors (Gen. 1:14ff.). The concurrence of past and present experienced in the cult, as Psalm 114 well makes clear, also is done directly and intentionally, as, for instance, in the event of the Passover (Exodus 12; cf. 13:8–10),[621] in the "today" (occurring seventy times) in Deuteronomy, and in the simultaneity of generations taking place within the ratification of the covenant also stressed in Deuteronomy (Deut. 5:2f. and 29:9–14). The sequence of different festivals with their individual legends that, as narratives of divine acts of salvation, were constitutive for Old Testament piety influenced on the one hand the development of an understanding of time as bound to a history viewed as a course and span of time and events. On the other hand, this development of the understanding of time was shaped by the cultic remembrance and actualization of the fundamental past of YHWH's salvific events contained in the word of its legends and narratives. By means of the word of these festival legends and cultic narratives, Israel's fundamental past was remembered and reactualized. This development of the understanding of time was also aided by the festival experiences of the acts of YHWH that followed each other in sequence. "It was God who established the continuity between the various separate events and who ordained their direction as they followed one another in time."[622] Thus the question is newly placed from different sides whether it is very meaningful or even correct to speak of "cyclical" and "linear" understandings of time (already perhaps in an opposition that is mutually exclusive), or whether one[623] should not speak rather of the necessary joining together of the "rhythmic" and "continual" division and experience of time. However, it can be asked whether and where one of these two perspectives on time tends to predominate. Nevertheless, for the Old Testament it can thus be said that the rhythm of time is integrated within and subordinated to the course of time and to historical time as both a path and a span.

According to the Book of Daniel[624] with its chronological details (Dan. 7:25; 8:14; 9:2; 11:11f.; and 12:7), its discussions of world periods (Dan. 3:33; 4:31; 7:14, 27; etc.), and its efforts to comprehend time (Daniel 9), the continuation of time must, at the same time, be endured (Dan. 12:11f.), since the "end" that is addressed here ($\gamma\bar{p}$ = $q\bar{e}s$: Dan. 9:26; 12:13) and understood as the end of earthly time, of empires, and of history overall approaches. The sequence of the world empires (Daniel 2 and 7) indeed reveals a trend toward a clearly diminishing and falling value of these governments (Daniel 2). The passing of these empires and the present concrete history now being experienced (Daniel 11) point to this approaching end and to the advent of the kingdom of God through YHWH's action. Yahweh's intervention alone breaks into and ends all time and history.

As in Hebrew, the understanding of time in the languages of the ancient Near Eastern environment of ancient Israel[625] cannot be ascertained only through an analysis of the terms used. Likewise there is nowhere in Israel's Near Eastern environment an understanding of "time" as an abstraction. If one seeks to summarize the conceptions present there and the scholarship that is both disputed and difficult, then the following picture perhaps emerges. The course of the year and the calendar determined by the circuit of the moon, by the stars and the sun, and by the change of the seasons were central in Egypt as well as in Mesopotamia for both the experience and the divisions of time that were comprehended as an automatic "cycle."[626] For the more precise determination of the course of the day, there were sun and water dials. In Egyptian, one word was used for "day" in the sense of a calendrical day, while another word refers to "day" in the image of bright sunlight or a day formed by the sun. Akkadian has expressions for "point in time" and "appointed time" and speaks of "days" and "years" for the past and the future.[627] In Egyptian, the understanding of time has less to do with the course of time, and more to do with repetition (cf. the course of the day or the overflow of the Nile) and recapitulation, for example, in the festival, so that the year is called "that which is rejuvenated" (*rnp.t*). Time in Egyptian has more to do with what abides and continues to be true than with what happens once.[628] The Babylonian king Hammurabi could say of himself that he already "at that time" was given his names before all human history, when the gods transmitted to Marduk the rank of Enlil and also named the city of Babylon with its exalted names.[629] Every Egyptian king brought about anew the unification of both the empire and the entire world order. He performed deeds which belonged to this order, or he at least portrayed it as actualized. Here, time becomes ritual. Further, even in Egypt time was readily determined by its contexts and relationships. Thus there is among the numerous Egyptian words for time a word, *3t (at),* for the point in time, the moment when, for example, Ramses II can say, "I am like Baal in his time."[630] The word *p'w.t* (= *pa.ut*) is an expression for prehistorical time, while *tr (ter)* is a word for the right time. There is also a term for (a measured) "lifetime" (*'ḥ'w* = *aḥau*) that stands in opposition to the unmeasured fullness of time ("eternity" in this sense: *nḥḥ* = *neḥeḥ*). The other term for "eternity" is pronounced *ḏt* (*dyet*), and its difference, much discussed by Egyptologists, from *neḥeḥ* (past/future; resultative/virtual) will not be pursued here.[631] However, both terms are connected together by the fact that while they have almost nothing at all to do with human time, they do have something to do with the time of the cosmos and with cyclical time, especially the course of the sun and thus the sun god Re who determines the courses of the year and of the day. "Existence and history cannot be conceptualized in these categories,"[632] although, practically speaking, a person could not avoid an understanding of linear time. It is the cosmic fullness of time that moves and sustains the Egyptian, and his or her life is embedded within the flow of time that is guided and determined by the gods.

Certainly neither the Old Testament understanding of time nor "the Old Testament understanding of history . . . is purely and simply the key for Old Testament faith in God."[633] One only has to think of the different spheres of law, creation, cult, and wisdom. However, in the law, the cult, and Old Testament statements about creation, the steady development of significantly stronger influences of history on Yahwistic faith can be recognized.[634] This is true of early Jewish wisdom (Wisdom and Sirach) that saw it necessary to appropriate elements of the Old Testament witness to history. Thus, this Old Testament witness to time and history in its complexity, which allows one, nevertheless, to recognize even common basic structures, still remains important for the comprehension of the Old Testament picture of God and the discussion of revelation. YHWH is the one who forms time and fills history. And if one confesses him (Deut. 26:5–9) and desires to thank him, because his goodness endures forever (Psalm 136), then one tells of his historical deeds.

4.6   Yahweh as Creator

According to the witness of the Old Testament, YHWH is not only the Lord of the history of Israel and the nations but also the *creator of the world*. What do the statements about the creator and his creation mean theologically?[635]

a.   Concerning Worldview

The picture of the world expressed in and lying at the basis of the Old Testament statements about creation[636] widely resembles the common ancient Near Eastern view, in spite of many differences in details. The earth was viewed as floating on the water or was seen as a disk that is stationary on the cosmic ocean (Gen. 7:11; 49:25; Exod. 20:4; Pss. 18:16; 104:5; Job 9:6; 26:11; 38:4, 6;[637] and Prov. 8:29), and water is found (Gen. 1:7; Pss. 104:3, 13; 148:4; and Job 26:11) above the heavenly firmament (Gen. 1:6; Job 37:18) in which the stars follow their course (Gen. 1:16–18). The throne of God was located in the region above the heavenly ocean (Isa. 6:1; 66:1; Ezekiel 1; and Ps. 104:3),[638] while the place of the dead was under the earthly ocean (Ps. 88:7 and Job 26:5f.). The Old Testament does not actually have a comprehensive term for "world." The "circle of the earth" is indeed mentioned (תבל = *tēbēl*), but this term certainly designates more the inhabited earth,[639] while הכל = *hakkōl* occurs only in Isa. 44:24 (also 45:7?); Jer. 10:16 [= 51:19]; Qoh. 3:11; Pss. 8:7 and 103:19 with the meaning, "the universe." Otherwise, the Old Testament speaks readily of "heaven and earth" in attempting to designate both the creation in its entirety (e.g., Gen. 1:1–2:14; etc.) and the two basic segments of reality as, for example, in Exod. 20:4; Ps. 135:6; and Job 11:8f.

The world was viewed in the ancient Near East in general as the creation of the gods, often a particular deity who had carried out this creation in the mythical, primeval period frequently in the form of a battle with another god or following a victorious battle with this opponent.[640] The essential differences between the ancient Near Eastern religions reside not simply in the "How?" of their depictions of the world, but more in the "How?" the "From What?" and the "What For?" of creation. Even though Israel's faith describes YHWH's power over the natural forces in the deliverance at the sea during the exodus event, this faith in YHWH as creator is added here for the first time (see below). Thus, while one cannot introduce Old Testament theology with the consideration of the witnesses to creation, one shall certainly have to think clearly what it means for the Old Testament itself to begin with such witnesses.

YHWH is the Lord and creator of the world who then turns to the ancestors of Israel (Genesis 12ff.) and later to the people of Israel (Exodus 1ff.), and he elects Israel as the example and paradigm of humanity to enter into community with him.

The discussion of YHWH as the creator occurs now in various textual contexts and in a variety of ways. In addition to numerous narrative texts, there are hymnic statements, and in addition to references in the promises of salvation as well as laments, there are also contemplations about wisdom and creation. One speaks of the creation of the world and of human beings in general; however, individual worshipers can name YHWH also as their personal creator. Thus the main questions arise as to when and why Israel began to speak of YHWH as the creator. The how of this creation apparently could be stated in different ways, as the location of Genesis 1 beside Genesis 2 already demonstrates. Further, one must ask whether the Old Testament even knows about a "revelation" of YHWH through creation.[641]

b. Hymnic-Sapiential Language about Creation

If one closely inspects its statements about creation, the Old Testament allows one to recognize textual and historical emphases in this discussion. First to be mentioned is the so-called hymnic-sapiential tradition, which consists largely of texts as well as forms of sayings that Israel held in common with or even borrowed from the ancient Near East. In this context, creation is set forth in language that is hymnic, occurs in the present tense, and has to do with first things.

One of the first, older psalms (and originally a hymn to the sun?), which now may exist in a later form, is Psalm 19A.[642] This hymn sings about the Sun, the deity who has made his tent from where he begins his cycle. According to this psalm, the heavens tell of the majesty of El (!), although this telling is without words and consequently cannot be heard by human beings (v. 4).[643] So that this psalm will not conclude with this negative saying, Israel attached a later addition, Psalm 19B. This combination of 19A and 19B provides an Israelite interpretation that, like early Jewish wisdom, combines Torah and creation (cf. Sirach 24 and Wisdom 9).[644] The effect of this addition is to make clear where YHWH is now to be perceived actually and plainly, namely, in the Torah (cf. Deut. 29:28).

Psalm 104[645] is surely no ancient, unredacted psalm. It nevertheless preserves in its blending of tradition, experience, and reflection (and indeed especially in vv. 20–30, more narrowly in vv. 25f.) reminiscences of the great hymn to the sun by Pharaoh Akhenaton.[646] Attached to these verses is an addition, "to sport in it" (v. 26), which underlines YHWH's sovereignty over Leviathan.[647] Further, the psalm praises creation as a well-structured order of its creator who has made all things "in wisdom" (v. 24), including humanity, which, like all other creatures, is dependent upon God's support (Ps. 104:27–30). The creator has assigned all things their place within creation, and humanity is provided a special place in his work (Ps. 104:14f., 23). Creation is here primarily seen as providential maintenance, and through the ordered system of the world something of God's nature becomes known. The frequent personal address with "you" (sg.), as well as the constantly occurring "you have . . . " and "you do . . . ," which culminate in the praise of God (v. 24), demonstrate this. All the more striking is the concluding verse (v. 35), which speaks all of a sudden of sinners who apparently disturb and impair this order and are to vanish. According to this psalm, the theological problem of creation is the human being as sinner, something that is very relevant for today. If this final verse is to be treated as an addition,[648] then the one who was capable of such an addendum is to be congratulated.

Psalm 8 is not a postexilic text dependent upon Genesis 1 (P); rather, both texts together probably go back to the same previous tradition. This psalm is strongly stamped by temple theology and appears to derive from a New Year's night worship service (the sun is not mentioned: v. 4).[649] The psalm presupposing originally a (Canaanite?) king as the one who offers it in praise, was "democratized" by Israel who associated it purely and simply with human beings.[650] In spite of the creation, the psalm nevertheless makes no statement about God but rather speaks about humanity. In the framing refrain (v. 2 + v. 10), the community hymnically announces and praises the majesty of YHWH in every land. All of these "creation psalms" do not appeal to the creation as the initial act that constitutes the world but rather praise the creator God as the Lord of his present creation. He is the one who sustains this life (Ps. 104:27ff.). The praise of the creator thus is even older than the "instruction" by the creator and the "teaching" about the creation, and the praise of God's maintenance of creation is more significant than the reaching back to the initial act of divine creation.[651]

Some texts in the prophets and in the Psalms in addressing the divine "you" refer to the personal, individual creation of the worshiper. This reference to the creation of the individual leads to the consecration of his or her call (Jer. 1:5; Isa. 49:1), or enables him or her to express new hope (Ps. 22:10f.), or even allows him or her to offer the general praise of God (Pss. 119:73; 139:13, 15).

By means of its list-like recording of the reality of creation, Psalm 104 clearly reveals how close it is to the sapiential discussion of creation. In this psalm, the description of YHWH as sustainer of creation's orders is not brought into relationship with the history of Israel. What is said in Psalm 104 about God as sustainer is similar to what is said in the older collections of Proverbs (Proverbs 10–29).[652] In these sapiential collections, YHWH is the creator of the rich as well as the poor, of the righteous as well as the wicked. Consequently, there are, according to God's will, differences in the creation

and in human beings, and these are not easily altered. However, all of this probably indicates that the wise were those who were "rich" in the social order of
that time. It is only in Israel's later, postexilic sapiential tradition that the sages
reflected comprehensively on YHWH's wisdom as the intercessor (Prov.
8:22ff.) between creation and him (Proverbs 1–9).[653]

In the Book of Job,[654] the speeches of God (Job 38:1–42:6) offer, above all,
the most comprehensive witness to the creator and his creation within the Old
Testament. Only they are silent, and with full intention of being so, about humanity and especially about Job. They do speak about YHWH as the creator
(Job 38:4–21) and sustainer (Job 38:22–39:12; cf. 39:13–30) of this world,
make clear his majesty and exaltation over all creation, and also allow YHWH
in the self-praise occurring only here (Job 38:9–11, 23; 39:6) and in Deutero-
Isaiah[655] to address a hymn to himself. "The God who is finally turned now toward the suffering Job shows then who he is in the preeminence of his being
God,"[656] namely, the one who is purely and simply incomparable and superior
to mortals. The Book of Job, along with its statements about creation, stands
in close proximity to doxologies and to the psalms and creation hymns already
mentioned. Also Job 38ff. has nothing to do with making a statement about first
things or YHWH's initial workings of creation but has everything to do with
his present status as the creator and Lord whose power sustains creation. He
seeks to show to human beings, furthermore, that they are not the center of the
world and that they should not and cannot interpret and evaluate every event
as having to do with them. Thus, animals, which are of no use for human beings, are described in the divine speeches. This list of animals, along with similar ones in Genesis 1 and Psalm 104, probably imitates ancient Near Eastern
wisdom's onomastica. There are also texts with a similar view of creation that
have been inserted as additions into the Book of Job that now in fact anticipate
the theme of the speeches of God in Job 38ff.[657] However, these additions lead
naturally toward the divine speeches so that they do not provide answers that
sound contrary to what has preceded (Job 9:5–10; 12:7–11; 26:7–13; and
34:10–15). The real purpose of the other statements about creation in the Book
of Job is to present the distance between humanity as creature and God as the
creator (Job 4:17ff.; 5:8ff.; 7:17ff.; 15:14ff.; 25:1–6; cf. 34:19; and 37:1–24).
Further, Job brings into play his creatureliness in his laments in order to mention not only his dependence on God but also his relationship to him. It is also
typical for the Book of Job that these petitions to God have no effect (Job 10:3,
8–13; 14:13–15; and 31:15) on Job's circumstances. In this connection, even
Psalm 8 and its view of humanity in creation is subverted (cf. Job 7:17–18;
15:14). Human beings are clearly placed *below,* not beside, their creator, and
they cannot recognize the orders dwelling within creation. They are closed to
them and should continue to be so, for creation does not find its exclusive purpose in human beings. This is emphasized by the hymn on divine wisdom (Job

28), which is more inaccessible to human beings than if it were residing within a deep mining shaft.[658] The world that "lifts up its voice" (S. Wagner) to humanity knows its unmistakable challenge.

In Qoheleth,[659] direct statements about God as creator are rare, although they are contained implicitly in several sayings. Thus it is said of God (Qoheleth never speaks of YHWH) that he "gives" (נתן = *nātan*)[660] something. However, in this connection, the point consists mostly of the fact that he does this for humanity unseen. Thus, while he gives the breath of life or the life span (Qoh. 5:17; 8:15; 9:9; and 12:7), he does this in order to take it back again whenever he wills, thus making clear that time is inaccessible to human beings. God "created" also the world (הכל = *hakkōl*: Qoh. 3:11;[661] עשׂה = *'āśâ*; 12:1 ברא = *bārā'* [662]), and indeed even made it "beautiful" (Qoh. 3:11 יפה = *yāpâ*, not טוב = *ṭôb*), although there occurs a "however" followed by the statement that everything is concealed from human beings (Qoh. 3:11; cf. 7:13, 29). God creates the good day as well as the evil day so that humanity cannot know what shall be the future course of things (Qoh. 7:14 and 11:8f.). The work of God remains once and for all concealed to humanity (Qoh. 11:5). Consequently, recourse to creation or to the activity of God as creator secures for Qoheleth no support either in terms of knowledge (Qoh. 6:10 and 8:17) or experience. Creation encounters a person as fate,[663] and for that reason achieves special significance, for the Qoheleth finally cannot speak of God save as creator. That the world, then, is created "beautiful" (Qoh. 3:11) is for Qoheleth the basis of the only positive good that he knows, namely, the enjoyment of life with happiness. Still, even this joy is darkened by the shadow of death,[664] and consequently this at last is also folly (Qoh. 2:1, 11; 6:7; and 7:2, 4).

In the Old Testament discussion of creation, it is in the hymnic, sapiential tradition,[665] within which Qoheleth occupies a special (negative) position as a consequence of his critique of wisdom, that Israel has especially borrowed sayings and views from its ancient Near Eastern environment. Canaan and more specifically Jerusalem had the capacity to be the contact point for this borrowing to have occurred. For example, it was in Jerusalem where "El, the creator of heaven and earth" was worshiped (Gen. 14:18ff.). El as "creator" and Baal as the one who sustained creation are clearly attested in the Ugaritic texts.[666] Here, the world is seen in a predominantly positive way as creation. When YHWH is introduced or praised as its creator, then he is differentiated from Baal and El, including when sayings about them are transferred to him. With this appropriation of understandings of creation from the surrounding cultures, Yahwistic faith undergoes an expansion. Yahwistic faith was also in the position to usurp the foreign sphere of divination, though this proved not to be completely alien to its faith. This adaptation of Yahwistic faith was urged upon Israel by the new situations it came to face that contrasted with its origins in the wilderness and at the mountain of God.[667] Now the majesty of El is no longer praised and the king is no longer the only one receiving God's attention and positive visitation (Psalm 8). Rather, YHWH creates the world in wisdom and order, although he certainly remains widely concealed behind this world and its order.

c. The Yahwist, Priestly Source, Deutero-Isaiah, Postexilic Psalms

Around 950 B.C.E. the Yahwist in the (Davidic) Solomonic empire provides new documentation of YHWH as the creator. The Yahwist does this at a time in which the Canaanite portion of the population along with their religion were incorporated into this Israelite empire. The way was paved, then, for the controversy with Canaanite religion, which was later continued by Elijah and Hosea and which also, for example, found expression in the ongoing historicizing of the agrarian festivals taken over from the Canaanites.[668] Hosea and Deuteronomy argue remarkably differently in this regard, as one would perhaps expect them to do. They do not in this manner emphasize YHWH as the giver of the fertility of the land by appealing to him as the creator; rather, they witness to him as the God who acted in history to lead Israel into the land, and therefore he is the giver of the land's yield (cf., e.g., Hos. 2:7ff.; Deut. 8:7ff.). Also in Deut. 26:5–9 YHWH is thanked for the gifts of the land in connection with his guidance in history.

Similarly, the Yahwist had already spoken of YHWH as the creator and of creation. J does so in the fashion of narrative literary forms that consequently are necessarily different from those present in sapiential and hymnic texts. The dry land that is in need of watering (Gen. 2:5f.) serves as the point of departure for the Yahwist who takes his narrative nevertheless beyond YHWH's initial activity of creation (according to Gen. 2:4b–3:24), which is more centered in humanity than is the case in Genesis 1, to the course of human history and to YHWH's activity on behalf of Israel.[669] This he does for the first time, not in Genesis 12ff., but already in his primeval history by means of both the אדמה = 'ădāmâ ("land") motif that runs from Genesis 2 to 12:3 and the clear demarcation from the Canaanites that occurs as early as 9:25f. The Yahwist says nothing of the origin of the gods or of battles between the gods, and human labor is not, as is true, for example, in the Atra-ḥasis epic, on behalf of the gods but rather for the support of human beings themselves (Gen. 3:19).

In the Yahwist's testimony to creation it is also good to recognize that here as elsewhere in the Old Testament the creation of the world by YHWH and the *maintenance* of his creation[670] are closely related. The rhythm of creation, which sustains and continues to move this world forward (Gen. 8:21f.; cf. Pss. 74:16f.; and 136:8f.), is established by YHWH and is held in course by him, however, not by Baal. YHWH also is the one who distributes the rain and moisture, not Baal (Gen. 2:5f.; cf. 1 Sam. 12:17f.; 1 Kings 18:41ff.; Jer. 10:13; 14:22; Amos 4:7; and Ps. 104:10, 13f.). Also, the world as well as humanity is not created out of divine material. Humanity's initial creation becomes a part of a clear *creatio continua* (Gen. 2:8ff., 18ff.), and through this creation fundamental orders were established for the continual relationship of God with disobedient human beings (Genesis 3) and for the relationship of human beings to each other (Gen. 3:14ff.). To the maintenance of the world by its creator belong also his establishment of boundaries for the flood (Jer. 5:22; Pss. 104:5–9; 148:6; Job 26:10; 38:8–11; and Prov. 8:29), his giving of nourishment (Deut. 87:13; Pss. 104:14f.; and 145:15ff.), his gift of birth and blessing of children (Gen. 21:1f.; 29:31; and Ps. 22:10f.), and his enabling each person to be seen as the creature of God (Ps. 22:10; 139:13–15; Job 10:8–12; Prov. 16:9; and Mal. 2:10).[671]

However, the Yahwist is not in the position to speak only positively about the world, as do for instance Psalm 104 and Psalm 8; rather, he mentions the diminishments of life that burden contemporary existence (Gen. 3:15ff.). Thus creation is oriented to history in the Yahwist, and the statements about YHWH as the creator result in a polemical expansion of the faith in God and in the reformulation of or differentiation from similar statements in Israel's ancient Near Eastern environment.

It was this relationship with the statements in the surrounding cultures that suggested to the Elohist that he should renounce any primeval history. He began his narrative work, which is preserved for us in broken pieces, with Abraham and thereby with Israel's more distinct character. Later on, the Deuteronomistic literature follows this tradition of silence, while the creedal texts likewise say nothing at all about YHWH as creator, choosing instead to begin with YHWH's activity on behalf of the ancestors (Deut. 26:5–9; cf. 6:20ff.; and Josh. 24:2bff.). An Old Testament "confession of faith" that speaks of YHWH as creator first occurs in Jonah 1:9: "I am a Hebrew and fear YHWH, the God of heaven, who has made the sea and the dry land." While the sea is mentioned in this credo, it is probably not accidental that Israel's salvation history is not recited before pagans who would neither understand nor know anything of this particular history.[672]

A greater and especially more important emphasis on the Old Testament discussion of the creator and creation takes place during the period of the exile. To be mentioned first in this regard is the Priestly (basic) document, which with Gen. 1:1–2:4a shaped a text that was moved back not incorrectly to the beginning of the entire Old Testament. In concentrated, well thought through, instructive, and at the same time hymnic language, God is portrayed as the creator working through his powerful speech. This happens with the critical appropriation and reformulation of Mesopotamian concepts and terms such as תֹהוּ/וּתְהוֹם = *tōhû/tĕhôm* ("void?"/"deep"), the storm of God (v. 2), the creation and at the same time the depotentiation of the stars whose names are suppressed and whom God does not need for the previous creation of light, and the utilization of scientific lists. Also important is P's pointing to the history and salvation history of Israel through the prominence given to the Sabbath as the gift of God and as the goal of creation. For the divine act of creating, which is understood also as "to divide" (הבדיל = *hibdîl,* hiphil), the verb ברא = *bārā'* ("create")[673] is prominently used, with only God appearing as the subject and with no indication of any material used to "create" something. In this regard, the compilers of P knew nothing about creation out of nothing, although at the same time one must ask whether they could even think of "nothing." However, ברא = *bārā'* ("create") still touches "in some way"[674] upon this argumentation, which is found clearly for the first time in Wisd. 11:17 and especially 2 Macc. 7:28. Israel's God is the one who has created the world and maintains it through its orders (cf. Gen. 9:1–17 P). Here, no theory about the origins of the world is to be imparted; rather, trust in the power of this God is newly strengthened: "There are pathways, courses, and roads for the clouds, air, and winds which shall also reveal ways where your foot can travel." What God has created is "very good," something that cannot be guaranteed too often (Gen. 1:4, 10, 12, 18, 21, 25, and 31; Qoh. 3:11 uses the term "beautiful"). Human beings are introduced and dignified as the partner of God,[675] and the commission in which they are blessed does not abandon the earth to their arbitrary rule but rather obligates them to be responsible before God (Gen. 1:28f.).[676] The commission has to do with taking possession (cf. Num. 32:21f. [24], 29; Josh. 18:1; and 1 Chron. 22:18f.) and ruling in order to preserve creation (cf. Ezek. 34:4 and Ps. 49:15), and not with dominating or treading underfoot, as the verbs in Gen. 1:28 unfortunately have been misunderstood to mean for a long time. The Sabbath, not humanity, is the crown of creation (Gen. 2:1–3).[677] A commission for lordship within the Old Testament could never include exploitation. This is made clear by the prohibition against the eating of flesh (Gen. 1:29f.), directed to both human beings and animals, who also have received the blessing for multiplication (Gen. 1:22; cf. 8:17).[678] This prohibition is valid until the time following the primeval flood. When the enjoyment of animal flesh was allowed and the commission to multiply the species was repeated once more to human beings in the period after the cosmic flood (Gen. 9:1–6), animal blood was still forbidden for human consumption. Also here the boundaries of human lordship were stressed, at the same time animals were included in the covenant of Noah (Gen. 9:10f.). It may here only be intimated as to how the Priestly discussion of creation continued in a formative way through the narratives about the ancestors (Gen. 17:2, 20f.; 28:3f.; 35:11; 47:27; and 48:3f.: P) and reached into the narratives about the sojourn in Egypt (Exod. 1:7 P; cf. Lev. 26:9) and the Sinai pericope (Exod. 24:15b–18a), including even the portrayal of the construction of the tabernacle[679] as the consummation of the entire creation.[680] The statements about creation clearly have, for the basic Priestly document at any rate, the function of seeking to defend the faith in YHWH's further, salvific works in history.

This is true in a similar and even clearer fashion for Deutero-Isaiah.[681] He can speak hymnically about YHWH's activity of creation and thereby can use many of its typical images.[682] However, the creative working of YHWH is clearly attributed to his historical activity, and this happens in the oracles of salvation (e.g., Isa. 43:1-7), in the words of disputation between YHWH and his people (e.g., Isa. 40:26), and in the judgment scenes between YHWH and the nations or their gods (e.g., Isa. 45:18-25). This attribution of creation to divine action in history happens in the last-mentioned literary form certainly less frequently, since YHWH brings into greater prominence the essential character of his historical activity that he has predicted in his word. Creation can be equated with election (in the "rather limited manner" of using creation terminology[683]) (Isa. 43:1; 44:24ff.; 46:5; and 54:5), and the statements of creation have the task of serving to defend faith in salvation and in history (cf. Isa. 40:12-31; 42:5; 43:1-7; and 44:24b-28).[684] Deutero-Isaiah must evidently go farther back[685] in order to make his message of salvation as certain as possible. When Deutero-Isaiah speaks of the knowledge of YHWH, it is striking that this is conceived of being mediated through creation only in Isa. 40:12-31. By contrast, the knowledge of God is continually associated with the historical acts of YHWH.[686] Mythical activity in the primeval time is related to Israel's exodus out of Egypt (Isa. 51:9f.), for YHWH is the guide of history because he is the creator. Consequently, Israel's history in the exile resides also in the hand of this divine creator, not, however, in the hands of Marduk, the god of Babylon. Statements about YHWH as creator also have here a clear relationship to the present. The creator of the world directs history and summons therefore the Persian king Cyrus to be his instrument of salvation ("Messiah": Isa. 44:24ff.; 45:1f.). This is analogous to YHWH's acting through and with Nebuchadrezzar (Jer. 27:4-6), although the purpose is different: Nebuchadrezzar is called forth to punish Israel. The pointed statement in Isa. 45:7 is that YHWH creates salvation as well as disaster, light as well as darkness. Something that is not directly stated in Gen. 1:2f. has already assumed a critical posture against Persian dualism at the end of the oracle to Cyrus:[687] YHWH has everything in his hand; there is no power either besides or against him. Creation is attested as an activity that is relevant to the present, and assigned to the proclamation of history and salvation. If YHWH is the creator, then Deutero-Isaiah speaks not only about a God who *desires* to create new salvation for his exilic community but also about the mighty Lord who *can* create this salvation. Like P, Deutero-Isaiah therefore emphasizes the active power of the word of YHWH (Isa. 40:6-8; 55:8-11; cf. also Ezek. 37:1ff.).

Similarly, the discussion of YHWH as creator in a series of exilic and post-exilic psalms, like Psalms 74; 89; and 102, has the function of either making possible once more or of supporting election faith.[688] In psalms that express confidence (Psalms 33; 115; and 124) or venture forth a confession (Psalm 135), an analogous argumentation exists.[689] The word is in the hand of YHWH, since it originates with him. The actualization of salvation and the strengthening of its certainty occur as a consequence of the discourse about the creator.

Statements about YHWH as creator are present in those texts which Israel itself had formed primarily by its own faith and which were chiefly used for the defense and undergirding of salvation faith. These texts serve in addition to expand this faith and its horizons beyond its own people and land.

d. Creation, History, and Salvation

As one reviews what has been said about Israel's understanding of creation, it becomes clear that Yahwistic faith, whether active in its own formulation or in its transformation of ancient Near Eastern statements, does not shape an isolated, separate creation theology. Rather, this faith of Israel reasons about works of creation and acts of salvation in the entwinement of creation and history.[690] Creation theology was to defend, enhance, extend, and undergird the structures of life. Creation is presented as the beginning of the salvation history of Israel, indeed is integrated with this history, while the history of the nation is anchored within the primeval history. Later psalms, including Psalms 33; 74; 89; 136; and 148, show this very clearly. Psalm 19A flows then into Psalm 19B and can become rightly understood only in connection with the addition of this counterweight. Psalm 104 receives an addition in v. 35 that asks for an act of salvation. Thus Israel was compelled, through its experiences of history and its faith in YHWH bound up with the historical acts of election, to go beyond the praise of the creator that was the earliest theological understanding of creation. Thus the discussion of creation does not continue to be limited to the praise of God, as takes place, for example, in the Babylonian epic of the *Enuma eliš*.

It was forbidden in the Old Testament, however, to see creation as a primordial event involving more than one deity. When in the Old Testament motifs appear from the mythical sphere, as, for example, the battle with the dragon, the restraining of the primeval floods, or similar themes,[691] they are often stripped of their own particular weight. Instead, one is able to say that the common motifs and mythical reminiscences at that time, such as the battle with the dragon, serve the glorification of God.[692] These reminiscences do not, however, always serve as motifs of creation. For example, the battle with chaos in the the Old Testament does not always evoke images of creation as is the case in the Babylonian epic of creation, the *Enuma eliš* (Tablet IV).[693] Rather, this battle, on the contrary, often exhibits a certain analogy to the battle of Baal with

Mot and/or Yam,[694] which has nothing to do with a creation of the world at its beginning[695] but rather probably has to do with its maintenance. In the Old Testament, then, the battle motif supports the stabilization of reality and the carrying through of divine lordship and power.[696] However, the descent of the deity into the realm of the dead and his resurrection, mentioned in the Ugaritic texts in connection with the battle motif, are expunged from the Old Testament. Further, the mythical is historicized in the use of תהום = tĕhôm (or plural) when biblical texts speak of the guidance through the "floods," that is, of the deliverance at the sea during the exodus out of Egypt (Exod. 15:5, 8; Isa. 51:9f.; 63:13; Pss. 74:13f.; 77:17; 78:15; and 106:9). The battle with the dragon can also be given an eschatological character (Isa. 27:1), while רהב = rahab (Rahab) can also be a designation for Egypt (Isa. 30:7; 51:9; Ps. 87:4; cf. Ezek. 29:3; 32:2). These mythical remnants were used in statements that are related to the primeval events (Pss.74:13f.; 89:11; Job 9:13; 26:12f.; and Prov. 8:24, 29) but also in passages that speak of the support and present preservation of creation (Hab. 3:8–15; Pss. 18:5ff.; 89:10–15; 104:23; Job 3:8; and 40:15 [ff.]; cf. Job 7:12).

Creation consequently becomes a historical act in the Old Testament, and through the possibility of thinking ahead to the "new creation," which resides in the future and not as a golden age in the past, creation additionally becomes (finally) an eschatological idea "in the theology of the Old Testament."[697] The activity of creation flows into the creatio continua (Genesis 2–3), culminating in the Sabbath as a gift of the rest of God (Gen. 2:1–3), a Sabbath that, in contrast to the six preceding days of creation, has no evening, thus allowing it to extend openly into the future. Creation faith leads to hope in a new creation that will bring not the return of paradise but the completion of the history of YHWH's salvation for his people and his world. One can compare to this the combination of creation and nation in Jer. 31:35–37; and 33:19–22, 23–26.[698] Consequently, creation is tied up with the eschatological fulfillment of other traditions of Israel's faith, as the new covenant, new temple, new Jerusalem, new people of God, new David and Davidic ruler, and others.[699] These hopes and with them the theology of creation are thereby included in the historical journey of YHWH with his people leading to the perfection of his lordship and of the world, and not only to the perfection of humanity.

Creation is an act of YHWH. However, this act is not once seen in the Old Testament after Genesis 1–2 as only or even primarily an act he performed in the past. Creation is chiefly related to the present and applies to what already exists.[700] Since in the world of Old Testament faith "creation has no particular weight," it cannot be of special importance within a "Theology of the Old Testament." Old Testament theology cannot be introduced with "creation."

However, one should consider what it means to have the Old Testament in its present form begin with creation. It should be explained accordingly that the world is YHWH's free gift allocated to human beings[701] and that all that follows within the Old Testament not only is a transaction between God and his people but also aims at the world, the other nations, and the cosmos. In opening the Old Testament with creation, it is to be understood that the Lord of this world wills to speak (cf. Jer. 27:5f. and 32:27), and not only a national deity, even though YHWH began his journey with Israel in this way. In addition, there cannot be an independent, isolated theology of primeval history that does not foresee and interlock with Israel's history,[702] particularly since Genesis 1–11 is already shaped by Israelite faith in YHWH. In their present form, these chapters are not materials of faith common to all humanity. Yahwistic faith is primarily election faith on which is based faith in salvation.[703] Israel has experienced and testified to its deity YHWH primarily as a liberating deliverer, whose revelation consisted in redemption and whose redemption was and ever became again the decisive revelation.[704] Through the statements about creation that were allocated and accrued to faith in YHWH, statements that can be very differently articulated,[705] Yahwistic faith experiences both an expansion and an enrichment. Creation is not only the front end but also the extension of salvation history, and the creator deity and redeemer God are (against E. Bloch) not opposites but rather the same. The world is the locus of YHWH's devotion, and if YHWH, for example, maintains his people's creaturely needs during their wandering through the wilderness, then at the same time he supports this people with the promise of salvation in the gift of the land. Creation theology, like the monarchy, the kingdom of God, the temple, and the agrarian festivals, belonged to the elements of the piety of a sedentary civilization which were later assigned to Yahwistic faith. Moreover, whatever is connected with the god El (Gen. 14:18ff.) to a large extent can be integrated into Yahwistic faith. Whatever is connected with Baal, who was believed to be a dying and rising deity and was very active sexually, was taken over from a very restricted selection and then transformed (Psalm 19A). Also, a particular way of thinking about world order, closely linked with the theme of creation, was strongly reshaped by and then incorporated into Yahwistic faith. The historical acts of YHWH's salvation emerged from this cosmic order and its deity (צדק = *ṣedeq*).[706] Consequently, a creation theology closely entwined with ancient Near Eastern thinking about order can receive no central theological significance for the Old Testament in spite of the arguments by H. H. Schmid.[707]

History and nature were closely related to each other through the attribution of Old Testament statements about creation to history and salvation. History and nature were not at all separated from each other.[708] Human beings were bound up with the world[709] and with each contemporary generation with which they shared a common fate. This is shown in the primeval flood and expected in the new creation that is to produce not only a new humanity and a new people of God but also a new world. Creation speaks of what is and is to be, not in the first instance of what was. Statements of creation are confessions of God's rulership over the world and therefore often are connected with statements about the kingship of YHWH.[710] God and the world are, however, never identical and cannot be. The world, however, does not confront human beings in a threatening manner; rather, human beings and their contemporary world are the creation that comprises all things. From the beginning, God has given the world to humanity. The world, and that does not simply mean fellow human beings, is the object of human moral behavior and discourse (cf. Psalm 8), and humanity may and should order the world responsibly before this God and in relationship with him. God is the one who has opened himself up to community, and that means he is one who elects and obligates. The world and humanity are also, as, for example, the Yahwistic primeval history shows, dependent upon God's will to redeem the world, since it is also a world full of evil and guilt. The world is directed toward YHWH's blessing and toward his activity of deliverance (J), and the world is supported by YHWH's orders for life (Gen. 8:21f. J; then P). This understanding, along with the fact that human beings live in this world as sinners (Ps. 104:35) and still are responsible for the world, moves in the direction of a proper theology of creation and the world.

The Old Testament's development of a creation theology not only has historical, religious, and phenomenological significance but also evokes questions concerning its understanding of history, salvation, and eschatology. The relationship of human beings to the world ought not to be an autonomous or direct one, but rather it is the human relationship to God that shapes and reconciles human existence. This relationship with God, however, is not mediated primarily and only through creation and faith in the creator. Rather, the Old Testament also speaks of divine acts of election in history that undergird this community between God and humanity. That the world, then, is the creation of YHWH, the God of Israel, cannot be recognized from the creation itself. Thus, while "creation" continues in the Old Testament statement of faith, the Old Testament knows nothing of a "nature." Faith reveals YHWH's works also in creation, and YHWH has shaped the orders of creation. However, the Old Testament says nothing about YHWH fully "revealing" himself to human beings in creation.[711] Salvation faith says that YHWH wants to create salvation.[712] The electing God places his people within his creation, and he gives them the land that brings together God, people, and creation.

Thus the world and humanity are bound together into a holistic display, held together in a historical movement, and oriented toward a common hope. Creation, salvation, and history in the Old Testament are bound together by the important place of land in Old Testament faith. Along with this, statements of creation possess a certain background of experience which they seek to penetrate more deeply. Acknowledgment of one's own creatureliness means then in Israel both the recognition of one's guilt and ephemerality and the knowledge of God who brings about support for his world and helps set right the sinful creature. For P, creation leads significantly therefore to the erection of the cult that remedies sin. "My help comes from YHWH, who has made heaven and earth" (Ps. 121:2). In this sentence of thankful recognition, the Old Testament's theology of creation may be summarized very well.[713]

4.7   Old Testament Statements about the "Nature" of Yahweh

It is only seldom that one finds in the Old Testament statements about the nature or the characteristics of God,[714] and when such occur, they concern, not the nature of God in and of itself or his absolute being, and so forth (also not in Exod. 3:14),[715] but rather his relationship to human beings.[716] Characteristics of God are mentioned, not because God in and of himself is thus and so, but because he does or did this or that, behaves or behaved in this way or in that manner, and he shows or showed thereby something of his own nature. While there are inferences that may be drawn from the Old Testament's understanding of the nature of God, one should be careful about the use of later philosophical, theological categories of thought to set forth the Old Testament's view of reality (e.g., "aseity").

a.   Yahweh as an Eternal God without Origin

The Old Testament does not tell how YHWH "originated," how he prevailed against other gods (through battle), or so forth. The Old Testament knows of no theogony and no theomachy in contrast to the *Enuma eliš* or to Egyptian mythology.[717] The Old Testament is also silent about many other patterns of divine behavior and activities that Israel's ancient Near Eastern environment narrates about its gods. "Before the mountains were given birth and before the earth and the inhabited world went into labor, you were, O God, from eternity to eternity" (Ps. 90:2; cf. Deut. 32:40; Isa. 43:10; 45:5f.; and Ps. 102:27). YHWH is the "first and the last" (Isa. 40:28; 41:4; and 44:6), he is an *eternal* God. The world created by YHWH has a beginning; he himself, however, has no beginning. He does not grow older (Job 10:5), does not "die" (Hab. 1:12 conjecture?). eats no flesh of bulls and drinks no blood from goats (Ps. 50:13).[718] He has no need of human beings and their gifts (Isa. 40:16 and 43:22f.). He is great and high, exalted over the world and human beings.[719] There is no cultic image of him. Also, at least according to the Old Testament evidence,[720] he has neither a wife nor a family, nor were amorous adventures told about him, as, for instance, they were of Baal.[721] Perhaps this absence can be due to the fact that the Old Testament that we now have is a work of postexilic redaction that may have expunged or obscured many things. According to the witness of the Old Testament, God is encountered as a considerably more "transcendent" deity than the gods of Israel's environment at the time, without, however, endangering or reducing thereby the community with human beings that he strives after and makes possible. YHWH as an eternal God (Gen. 21:33;[722] Pss. 9:8; 10:16; 29:10; 33:11; 92:9; 93:2; 102:13; 145:13; and 146:10) has disclosed himself through his election of human beings to enter into community with him. The God exalted over the world and human beings has lowered himself to them (Isa. 57:15; Pss. 113:5f.; and 138:6).

b. The Holy One and the Holy One of Israel

Thus YHWH is the *holy God*[723] (1 Sam. 6:20; cf. Josh. 24:19), the majestic and set apart (Exod. 15:11) deity, and the one who swears by his own holiness (Amos 4:2). One encounters YHWH in sacred places where he speaks from the "sacred mountain" and from Jerusalem the "sacred city."[724] Those who would encounter him must themselves become holy (Exod. 19:10f.). The praise of the holy God is sung in his heavenly court by the seraphs (Isa. 6:3; cf. Psalm 99).[725] However, YHWH as a holy God is holy not for and by himself, meaning that he is exalted over and separated from the world and humanity; rather, he is "holy in your (= Israel's) midst" (Hos. 11:9), that is, he is the "Holy One of Israel."[726] This is expressed according to Isaiah chiefly in YHWH's acts of judgment against his people and against Assyria (Isa. 10:17) and according to Deutero-Isaiah and Trito-Isaiah in his works of salvation. He indeed is holy, mighty, and to be feared (Ps. 111:9f.), and as such he leads his people (Exod. 15:11, 13). He makes himself known as the Holy One when he demonstrates he is holy by his punishing righteousness (Isa. 5:16) and when he does *not* forgive sins (Josh. 24:19). He comes as the Holy One to his people (Hab. 3:3), and he reveals himself before the eyes of the nations as holy while he rescues Israel (Ezek. 20:41f.), for no one is as holy as he is, no one is like "our God" (1 Sam. 2:2). Because he is holy, his people also should be[727] and can be holy in existing in community with him (Exod. 19:6; 22:30; Lev. 19:2; 20:7, 26; 21:8; Deut. 7:6; 14:2, 21; and 26:19),[728] for he is the one "who sanctifies you" (Lev. 20:8, 24f.). YHWH's name should not be profaned: "I may be sanctified among the Israelites; I am YHWH who sanctifies you, for I brought you out of the land of Egypt in order to be your God. I am YHWH" (Lev. 22:32f.).[729] The holiness of YHWH determines both the existence and continuation of his people[730] and the particular character of his temple. "Holiness possesses a double significance: a real and personal significance on one hand and a cultic-ritual and election conditioned significance on the other."[731] Holiness involves purity and separation. In the temple, the "Holy of Holies" (דביר = *dĕbîr*) is dark and contains no image of God, and in the postexilic period only the high priest may enter this part of the temple once a year on the Day of Atonement (Lev. 16:2). What functions as the altar, what is presented as sacrificial offerings, and who as priest comes into contact with the altar must be "consecrated" (Exod. 28:3; 29:21, 33, 36f.; 30:29; Lev. 6:11, 20; etc.).[732] The high priest wears on his turban a plate with the inscription "holy for YHWH" (Exod. 28:36), while YHWH himself has "consecrated" for human observance the Sabbath as a day of rest and of community with him (Gen. 2:3; Exod. 20:8f.; and Deut. 5:12f.). Apart from places and times, the adjective "holy" is used to designate only persons (Lev. 6:9, 19ff.) and objects. The holy, that is, transcendent God becomes immanent while continuing to be the one who is over against his world.[733]

c. Yahweh's Jealousy

YHWH is a *"jealous"*[734] (קנא = *qn'* in the form of an adjective, verb, and noun) and passionate God who wills to have his way. This description of himself in first person speech occurs in the important locations in the Decalogue (Exod. 20:5; Deut. 5:9) and in the so-called law of YHWH's privilege (Exod. 34:14[2]). In this statement (missing in the Old Testament wisdom literature), first to be found in Exod. 34:14 and then rather commonly throughout the Deuteronomic and Deuteronomistic literature (Deut. 4:24; 6:15; 29:19; 32:16, 21; and Josh. 24:19; cf. 1 Kings 14:22), the issue no longer involves the oath of the gods and battle of the gods but rather YHWH's desire for Israel to share his divine status with no one. On the basis of the special relationship that he has introduced historically to Israel, YHWH's jealousy is directed against his and their enemies (Nahum 1:2) and especially against Israel's apostasy to other gods. This jealousy is put in the form of a prohibition and the response of punishment. This evidence about YHWH's jealousy is closely connected to the understandings of his holiness ("jealous holiness"; cf. Josh. 24:19) and his love (cf. Deuteronomy). The discussion of divine jealousy is a further expression of the trend existing within Yahwistic faith toward the exclusive worship of YHWH from which developed practical as well as theoretical "monotheism" of Israel.[735]

According to the witness of the postexilic period, YHWH's jealousy also is turned against Israel's enemies or the nations (the jealousy of YHWH for the *well-being* of the nations is not in evidence) while serving by contrast to bring about salvation for Israel. However, already before, YHWH's jealousy is directed not only *against* an apostate Israel but also to benefit his nation. Israel's apostasy to foreign gods would have signified a conversion to nothingness, to powerless deities, or to idols.

d. Exodus 34:6f.

A small compendium of statements about YHWH's form and nature, found rather seldom in the Old Testament, comprise the formula (shaped by JE) in Exod. 34:6f.[736] that perhaps should be understood in its context as a self-predication of YHWH:[737] "Yahweh, Yahweh, a compassionate and merciful God, long-suffering and abundant in loyalty and truthfulness, the one who maintains loyalty, forgiving guilt, rebellion, and sin, who however still does not allow to go fully unpunished, visiting the iniquity of the ancestors on the children and on the children's children, to the third and fourth generation."[738] This "formula of grace" (H. Spieckermann) perhaps was first inserted into the context of Exodus 34 in connection with apostasy, the confession of guilt, and later the formation of the commandments. It occurs several times within the Old Testament (in Joel 2:13 and Jonah 4:2 with a somewhat different word order and the addition, "relents from doing evil"; then Pss. 86:15; 103:8ff.; 145:8; and Neh. 9:17; cf. also Exod. 20:5f. = Deut. 5:9f.; and Num. 14:18);[739] reveals strongly, liturgically colored language; finds its place frequently in prayers; and always states something about YHWH's nature, as, for instance, his behavior toward Israel. In Jonah 4:2 the formula speaks about YHWH's behavior toward humanity, and indeed the wicked Ninevites, who on the basis of prophetic preaching have, in general, consummated their conversion. The formula presupposes Jeremiah and Deuteronomy and has a longer prehistory that is disclosed in the appearance of its individual parts, as, for instance, in the different style of Exod. 34:6–7 and in the expression "merciful and compassionate," which can be traced back to the predicates of the Canaanite-Syrian El. Through this double predication placed before YHWH, all that is yet here to be stressed is related to him (Exod. 33:19).

"*Compassionate*" (רחמים = *raḥămîm;* often with חסד = *ḥesed*)[740] designates loving care in terms of a concrete act, but not an attitude. Twenty-six times the term is used to speak of YHWH, although primarily not in preexilic texts (Hos. 1:6; 2:6; and Isa. 9:16; cf., however, Hos. 11:8f.). In exilic and especially post-exilic texts, YHWH's new activity of salvation and the ground of its actualization are often called the compassion of YHWH.[741] YHWH's compassion is expressed, moreover, in the form of the gift of preservation, new beginning, forgiveness, and hearing the cries of the poor. YHWH shall neither abandon nor ruin Israel, and he will not be forever angry so that a turning back is possible.

"*Gracious*" (חנון = *ḥannûn*)[742] designates the grace and favor of a highly placed person, who, for example, like a king, hears a plea and condescends to the lowly. As an adjective, the term is found in the Old Testament only in reference to God,[743] and in addition to the references mentioned within the formula there are also occurrences in Exod. 22:26; Pss. 111:4; 116:5; 2 Chron. 30:9; cf. Jer. 3:12; 9:23; and Neh. 9:31; etc. Merciful turning and compassionate *loyalty* are praised here and elsewhere as the prominent characteristics of YHWH (Deut. 7:9f.; 32:4; Jer. 42:5; Hos. 2:22; Pss. 33:4; 100:5; 115:1; 117:2; and 143:1; cf. Psalm 89; etc.).[744] The following predications construe these adjectives. YHWH is merciful and his goodness endures forever (Pss. 106:1; 136; etc.).[745]

Further, YHWH is *"long-suffering"* (אפים ארך = *'ōrek 'appayim*), that is, he restrains his justified wrath, and in addition he is *"abounding in goodness and loyalty"* (ואמת חסד רב = *rab ḥesed we'ĕmet*). Along with that, he abounds in free will, in opening up to human need, in turning toward people, in goodness and in the fullness of untiring faithfulness to the community.[746]

After these more conceptual descriptions of divine conduct, the polarity of divine reactions to sin and guilt are spoken about (v. 7). YHWH preserves his grace and removes the guilt, sins, and offenses of thousands, but he visits the iniquity (עון פקד = *pāqad 'āwōn*) upon the third and fourth generation. Blessing continues to have its effect for a long period, while curse quickly destroys. The grace of God stands above all else, but there is also the solidarity of guilt, that is, suffering for the guilt of the ancestors. YHWH's forgiveness, nevertheless, is always new (cf. Ps. 103:3).[747] That the formula of grace has found its place chiefly in prayers clearly says something about where one has praised this YHWH above all as a God full of grace and compassion.

e. Yahweh as a Living God

YHWH is also a "living God" (חי אל = *'ēl ḥay*).[748] At first glance, it might be here assumed that this designation is directed toward a conception of God that (cf. the "grove of Adonis": Isa. 17:10f.) speaks about the death[749] (and resurrection) of the deity. This is, however, only rarely found within the Old Testament (Hab. 1:12 [?]; Ps. 102:26ff.). One speaks rather of the living God when one wants to emphasize his power and might (1 Sam. 17:26, 36; and Josh. 3:10) and when one wants to bring oneself into relationship with him (Hos. 2:1). This expression also has to do with YHWH's works, not with his being. This is demonstrated in the same way by the optative names Jehiah and Jehiel (1 Chron. 15:18, 24; etc.; cf. Hiel, 1 Kgs 16:34) and then by the oath formula that appears in the Old Testament fifty-three times "as YHWH truly lives" (חי יהוה = *yahweh ḥay*),[750] in which God at the same time becomes both the witness of the oath and the one who watches over it. Twenty-two times YHWH himself says אני חי = *ḥay 'ănî* (Deut. 32:40 has אנכי חי = *ḥay 'ānōkî*). One swore also by the life of the king (1 Sam. 17:55; cf. Gen. 42:15f.), while in Ugarit the (cultic?) cry *ḥay aliyan ba'al* ("alive is Baal the mighty one") was known, which probably occurs on the basis of a dream in which is seen new rain and the streams that flow once again.[751] One speaks also of El in terms of "eternal life,"[752] and he is the one who bestows life as well upon human beings.[753] Close to the oath formula are hymnic statements (cf. Ps. 18:47). YHWH, however, has demonstrated his living power in the exodus out of Egypt (Jer. 16:14f. and 23:7f.: Deuteronomic) or in causing Solomon to succeed to David's throne (1 Kings 2:24). He redeems out of need (1 Sam. 14:39; 2 Sam. 4:9; and 1 Kings 1:29) or receives the men of God into his service

(2 Kings 3:14 and 5:16). Israel has heard the voice of the living God at Horeb/Sinai from the fire (Deut. 5:26). Thus one praises the living YHWH as a God who historically and also militarily (Josh. 3:10; 1 Sam. 17:26) delivers (Ps. 18:47ff.). And the promise is issued to the Israelites that they shall no longer be named "not-my-people" but rather "sons of the living God" (Hos. 2:1). The kingdom of the living God, of the eternal king (Jer. 10:10), will exist without end (Dan. 6:27f.). Since he is the living God who gives life to human beings (Jer. 38:16), he is also known as the source of life (Jer. 2:13; 17:13; Pss. 36:10; 42:3; and 84:3). Here YHWH is shown to have a closer connection to El than to Baal.

f. Anthropomorphisms and Anthropopathisms

While YHWH is spoken about as a living God, he is not presented as a "principle" in modern, abstract terms. In the Old Testament, this description means rather that he is open to change, can cause himself to be "sorry" about something. This addresses the problem of Old Testament anthropomorphism and anthropopathism.[754] God is also a living God when he wants to have community even with sinful people. In the final analysis, this is also the meaning of Old Testament anthropomorphism.

After Israel's apostasy in worshiping the "golden calf" (Exodus 32), YHWH was capable of being moved to pardon his people (Exodus 34), due to the intercession of Moses and to his own "nature" which finds expression in Exod. 34:6f. (see above). The punishment (Exod. 32:25ff.) does not afflict the entire nation and does not remain the last word. In the primeval history, YHWH "regrets" that he has created human beings and consequently brings the deluge, because "the thoughts and inclinations of the human heart were always evil" (Gen. 6:5f.: J). The same rationale is given at the end of the flood (Gen. 8:21: J). The flood has therefore not altered human nature, although YHWH's grace has now triumphed. These kinds of anthropomorphic statements are due, not to a naive, childlike manner of speaking, but rather to the human perspective in which God is considered to act in a spontaneous manner, since he wishes to turn toward human beings and seeks to enter into community with them.[755] He watches "jealously" over his own people and over his exclusive status as God.[756]

According to Old Testament statements, YHWH has a face, a mouth, eyes, a heart, hands, ears, feet, and a voice. He takes a walk in a suitable, invigorating time, comes, sees, laughs, blows, tires, and smells.[757] He experiences regret, hate, anger, and pain.[758] Too little attention is given to the recognition that YHWH's speech or his "word," his "name," as well as his appellations, are examples of anthropomorphic language which cannot be avoided when human beings speak about God. Also, the same kinds of anthropomorphisms are found not only in the older texts of the Old Testament, so that one might be able to say that these are the undigested remnants from a period that still possessed little theological clarity, but also, as the evidence shows, even from later periods. For example, one finds these anthropomorphic statements even in Deutero-Isaiah, which also presents a "theoretical monotheism." The late postexilic text of 2 Chron. 6:40 mentions the ear of God that is an addition to the older parallel text of 1 Kings 8:52. Israel had (and has) no philosophical conception of God, and the Johannine confession, "God is spirit" (John 4:24), is close to being an "unbiblical" definition, if one understands it as an absolute statement when removed from its context.[759] The Old Testament pictures for God often venture forward to the point of almost being problematic.[760] Thus, one did not and cannot get along without an anthropomorphic way of speaking, if one wishes to speak as a human being about God. Consequently, there cannot be a way of speaking about God in spiritual or even abstract terms,[761] for an abstract speaking about God remains at the same time anthropomorphic. Rather, the issue is to examine the appropriateness of the anthropomorphisms. Particular, specific, personal, and concrete statements, at times embarrassing, are to be preferred over general, abstract, and material statements. Of God's liver, blood, and bones the Old Testament is silent. God exists not in and of himself but as a you (personal). He desires a relationship between himself and us, us and himself. While through his act of election he presents himself in the language that human beings propose,[762] there is still nothing with which one can compare him (Isa. 40:25). Anthropomorphisms underscore the personal character of the Old Testament God, make God accessible to human beings, and intend to do so. The effort to speak appropriately of God must always be ventured anew. This new theological language continues, however, at the same time to remain open to further efforts, which already within the Old Testament seek to fold much into allegory (Isa. 59:17: armor of salvation; helmet of salvation; garments of vengeance; and mantle of anger).

While God is, without doubt, thought of also in human form, more specifically as a man (Isa. 50:1; 54:1–6; 62:5; Jer. 2:2; Ezekiel 23; and Hos. 2:18),[763] there is no further reflection about these representations (cf., e.g., 1 Kings 22:19; Isa. 30:27; and Ezek. 1:26), and in Hos. 11:9b (cf. v. 3) YHWH indeed ensures about himself: "For I am God and not a man (איש = 'îš)." The divine name יהוה = yahweh and the divine appellation אלהים = 'ĕlōhîm were both always bound with masculine predicates. The Hebrew of the Old Testament offers no particular word for "goddess."[764] YHWH's sexuality, in distinction, for instance, from that of Baal in the Ugaritic texts or from that of other deities in Israel's environment, is not an expressed theme in the Old Testament and plays no specific (or even sexist) role. The Old Testament commandment against images[765] and its theological background are well worked out in this regard. In Israel's ancient Near Eastern environment, goddesses can also be spoken about in military terms,[766] while "motherly" ways of conduct and experiences can be used to speak about YHWH. YHWH is a father (Deut. 32:6; Isa. 63:16; 64:7; Mal. 1:6; and 2:10; cf. Exod. 4:22; Hos. 11:1; Ps. 2:7; etc.), although he comforts like a mother (Isa. 49:15 and 66:13) and bears his people like a mother her suckling child (Num. 11:12; cf. Ps. 13:12). In God's role as creator, both names of mother and father were used (Isa. 45:9–11). YHWH turns himself in a loving way toward humanity (Hos. 11:1–9), while at the same time he also like a father takes pity on his children (Ps. 103:13).[767] One should not eliminate features of wife and mother (Isa. 42:14), nor should those of the male and patriarchy be especially featured.

That the Old Testament anthropomorphisms ought not to be taken purely and simply as declarative statements but also already can develop a tendency toward metaphor is shown in the fact that often opposite statements can coexist. Thus, while YHWH is "sorry" in Gen. 6:6, this is contested elsewhere (Num. 23:19; 1 Sam. 15:29; and Jer. 4:28; cf. Mal. 3:6). According to Isa. 31:2, YHWH does not take back his words, but this stands in the final analysis in opposition to what is narrated in the Book of Jonah. YHWH is called upon to awake (Pss. 7:7; 35:23; and 78:65ff.; cf. concerning Baal 1 Kings 18:27), while, at the same time, the Old Testament speaks of him as not being tired and neither sleeping nor slumbering (Isa. 40:28f. and Ps. 121:4). Also, YHWH sees (Ps. 94:7); however, he does not see with human eyes (Job 10:4f.). YHWH's heart recoils within him because of compassion, while at the same time he is God and not a human being (Hos. 11:8f.). YHWH's sorrow[768] can bring about the consequences of his punishing action (Gen. 6:5f. and 1 Sam. 15:11, 35), as well as, on the contrary, can induce him to take back his plan to punish (Exod. 32:14; Amos 7:3; and Hos. 1:8). YHWH is a punishing (Amos) but also a loving God (Hosea and Deuteronomy). He is simply the living God and wants to be taken seriously as such. He wishes to be near human beings, elects them to exist in community with him, comes to the world (E. Jüngel), and therefore assumes already in the Old Testament a human form (Phil. 2:7). Old Testament anthropomorphisms consequently deal with God as a you (personal), as a "person," with God's community with human beings, with God in human language, with an event between God and human beings, and not with divine characteristics in and of themselves. God acts humanly, not in spite of, but rather on the strength of his divine status.[769] He is near and far (Jer. 23:23).

g. Fundamental Structures of the Old Testament Witness to God

The Old Testament witness to God under the name YHWH (W. H. Schmidt),[770] to whom the Old Testament owes its meaning, is therefore many-sided. This has its basis in the fact that the Old Testament develops over a rather long period of time and contains many different kinds of literature. The variety of the Old Testament witness also results from the fact that very many different readers can continue to discover the experiences of God that are brought to language in these texts. If one seeks a summary of what has been reconstructed heretofore about the Old Testament discussion of YHWH/God, then one has the following.

The Old Testament praises, recounts, and testifies that YHWH is the God who has created the world and continues to maintain it. He is also the God who has elected Israel to be his people, an act that also was directed toward the world and the nations. As the God of the ancestors (Genesis 12ff.), he is the promising, accompanying, personal deity of the tribe. This God and the tribe are the components out of which the nation is constructed, and the tribe is the location in which the individual now finds himself situated and where he solemnly remembers. God as YHWH from Egypt on (Hos. 2:10; 13:4; and Exodus 3; 13–15) is the one who has led Israel up from and out of Egypt. YHWH is the saving, militarily active (Exod. 15:3, 21) liberator of the nation to whom he has made himself known as the God associated with the mountain of God/Sinai in the revelation of the name (Exodus 3 and 6) and in theophany (Exodus 19). And he commits himself to those to whom he also gives instructions and for whom he will be their only God (Hos. 13:4; Exod. 22:19; and the first commandment). That he had already been worshiped before by the Midianites is possible, but, for the Old Testament, that is no longer important. God's word is issued as both promise and command, which, made known by the intercessor of the word, points out and announces God's acts, looks back at their significance, gives thanks for them, and on the basis of Israel's experiences provides warnings and makes hearers aware of their guilt. The Old Testament believed that the decisive experiences of the faith of Israel, related to history, were the exodus and Sinai. Existence came to be understood as history under YHWH, as the journey with him, and as providential guidance. YHWH's act of liberation precedes his commandments in terms of both time and substance, and he keeps faith with this nation even during their apostasy and murmuring. He punishes; however, he does not reject. He is a deity who is more bound to a group than to a place. He leads into the land, coming from the south, in order to help militarily his people (Judg. 5:4f.; Deut. 33:2; and Ps. 68:8–11), secures the possession of the land, and provides the fertility of the soil. Agrarian festivals of the Canaanite environment were attributed to him and historicized. Monarchy, Zion, and temple were "elected," adapted, and at the same time interpreted in a way that differed from Israel's pagan neighbors. Other spheres of ancient Near Eastern piety were consciously eliminated (little by little?), as, for example, the cult of the dead, faith in demons, magic, astrology, and myths about the gods. The cult is not a means to influence the deity but rather the gift of YHWH to his people. Sacrifices are the means to achieve the sanctification of the people of God. Elijah and Hosea are the first to resist popular piety that embraced Canaanite religion shaped by the presence of El and Baal and that developed into the form of a poly-Yahwism and a syncretistic mixture of Baal with YHWH. Then came the opposition of the Deuteronomic/Deuteronomistic movement with its programmatic "YHWH is One" (Deut. 6:4) and its demand for cultic purity through cultic unity (Deuteronomy 12). And it is important that Israel never once added to the event fundamental for its faith several deities or another deity outside of YHWH. YHWH was and became the God of Israel as it expanded, and the rejection of an image for the worship of YHWH became increasingly one of its major characteristics. Predicates and characteristics of the Canaanite high god El, however, were transferred to YHWH (holy, majesty, king, royal household, living god, and creator) and to a large extent came first to their full development in the postexilic period. Perhaps still other (father) gods (besides El) were incorporated into him (Sedeq; Salem). YHWH's "character," however, goes far beyond that of a deity who is only a god of a pantheon, a place, a particular region, or the cosmos.

The preexilic prophets, however, had to proclaim YHWH as the God who, because of the social, cultic, and political sins of his people, came now and again to punish them. "Prepare yourself, Israel, to meet your God" (Amos 4:12). YHWH fights now also *against,* not only *for,* his people, and his "day" becomes darkness, not light, as expected and hoped. When Israel experiences the punishment of the exile, it becomes necessary there to develop precisely a new knowledge of YHWH (Ezekiel; P: Deutero-Isaiah) in order to become self-aware and to receive a continuing existence. These things are promised to Israel, however, in a positive manner, and it is freed precisely by its recognition of the powerlessness of the foreign deities. YHWH is not subject to these deities, and it is not Babylon and Marduk who triumph over YHWH and Israel. Rather, YHWH's activity (Lamentations) points to Israel's return and new beginning (Ezekiel; Deuteronomistic History; and Deutero-Isaiah), so that new designs for the form of the postexilic community can be ventured (Ezekiel; P; Deutero-Isaiah; Deuteronomistic History with Deuteronomy; and the night visions of Zechariah). In Deuteronomy, the basic Priestly document, and Deutero-Isaiah, the most detailed "theology" is found, providing the witness that reflects most thoroughly on God in the Old Testament.

All epochs and forms of the Old Testament discourse about God in the final analysis are transmitted and accompanied by the language about him (prayers, psalms), and the hymn is probably the oldest form of theological discourse. One unique form of theology was likely associated with certain social groups that produced the older Old Testament wisdom literature (Prov. 10–29 [31]). This theology featured YHWH as the founder and guarantor of the principle of the connection between deed and consequence. Job and Qoheleth, who, however, precisely because of their special testimony about God make it possible for many to have an entrance into the Old Testament, contested this effort to associate God with world harmony, while the Books of Chronicles undertook once again the hopeless effort to refer to YHWH as the overseer of retribution who requites exactly according to individual acts. YHWH should not and cannot be believed or even postulated to be a God who guarantees an unscathed world.

The Old Testament wisdom literature was strongly influenced by similar texts from Israel's ancient Near Eastern environment as well as by the general human problems that are expressed in this corpus. This Old Testament wisdom literature could speak of YHWH (apart from Job 3–27 and Qoheleth)[771] and only of YHWH as God. This was not solely due to the consequences of the first commandment.[772] The wisdom texts of ancient Israel's religious environment also spoke mostly of *one* deity.[773] This both limiting and generalizing form of speaking about God in this literature was not due to a specifically Israelite understanding but rather was present and operative in these texts as both a normal and an avant-garde theology.

According to the Old Testament, YHWH is both the Holy One and the Holy One of Israel, who is both near and far. He is the one who elects but also rejects, the delivering but also the punishing, the personal You, the deity from whom one cannot escape (Psalm 139; Jonah), the one before whom one cannot exist, and the one who cannot be gazed upon. He is present for human beings only in his freedom and refers them to obedience, faith, and the future. He makes himself known and has his powers of activity, but he remains concealed and enigmatic (Qoheleth; Job; Jeremiah; Genesis 22). One not only can praise him but must and may, however, also offer a lament to him (Psalms; Jeremiah). And if the prophets have to proclaim YHWH's judgment, for which YHWH uses as his instruments also the foreign nations (Isaiah: Assur; Jeremiah: Babylonians), the question arises, and not for the first time in contemporary Old Testament scholarship, whether this may be the end (Amos 8:2) of the way of YHWH with his people, whether this may be a final rejection (Deuteronomistic redaction in Jeremiah) or whether there is the possibility of deliverance and salvation, if also not without judgment. YHWH is a compassionate God who himself laments for his people even as his prophet does (Jeremiah), whose heart recoils within him (Hosea 11). When he promises new knowledge and opens up a new future, then these are possible only because of him. He is their basis. One knows nothing of God's changelessness, for he can allow himself to "regret" something. However, the Old Testament does know something of his loyalty (Exod. 34:6f.; Deut. 7:9; and Ps. 143:1), on which Israel believed they were able to depend even when they were faithless themselves (Deuteronomy 32). The community of God and the transcendence of God, the election that precedes and the obligation that follows, the combination of exodus and covenant, the association of trust and obedience, history, law and ethos, worship, and life are the fundamental structures of Old Testament faith in God.

Chapter 5. The World of God and the
World Distant from God

The areas of Old Testament faith that are to be treated here play a more subordinate role. In the Yahwistic faith to which the Old Testament witnesses, demons, angels, and Satan, for example, do not have a significant place. For example, YHWH does not have a direct antagonist. Further, the wilderness deity YHWH, who was certainly more seminomadic earlier on, originally had no relationship to the sphere of the dead, the cult of the dead, and the kingdom of the dead. Early Judaism and the closely related New Testament place far greater importance on these matters. As a consequence of the strengthening of divine transcendence and the placing of an intermediate being between God and humanity, early Judaism and the New Testament have much in common with respect to the themes to be discussed in the following pages. In addition, some of what here may be called less significant for Yahwistic faith has become more important in the course of the history of theology and religion and therefore for us (e.g., Satan). However, these themes are presented in this chapter, because the topics to be addressed, for instance, the tent, the ark, and the heavenly court, are closely connected with other, more important, coteries of themes, as, for example, the kingship of God or the presence of God with his people. Furthermore, there is much about the topics that follow that will not be treated or addressed here, although they ought not be passed over in silence. One might compare this to Augustine's similar formulation about the three "persons" in the teaching of the Trinity (*De Trinitate* 5.9, 10).

5.1 Yahweh's Places of Dwelling[1]

If YHWH elects for himself a people, opens himself up to enter into community with human beings, and comes to their aid, then one should ask, "Where does he originate these actions?" "Where does YHWH dwell?" If he comes to his own, he comes from the south according to the testimony of several Old Testament texts, therefore probably from Sinai/Horeb/the mountain of God.[2] Also Seir, mentioned in connection with this location, points to the region south of Palestine proper (Judg. 5:4; cf. Deut. 33:2; and Hab. 3:3). And when Elijah traveled to the mountain of God to save his life by finding YHWH, he hurried into and through the wilderness, beyond Beersheba, to the south, to

Horeb (1 Kings 19:3ff.). Certainly, the Old Testament does not report that any kind of "pilgrimage" was taken to this mountain of God, although there was a station marker on the way there (Num. 33:3–49).

Then there is the statement that YHWH dwells in heaven (Pss. 2:4; 123:1; Deut. 4:36; and 26:15), and from there he descends to the Sinai or to another place.[3] From there he looks below (Pss. 33:13f. and 102:20); he also descends from his heavenly dwelling to the temple (cf. the shout in Hab. 3:20; Zeph. 1:7; and Zech. 2:17), where he then takes up his temporary presence. Psalm 104:3; Amos 9:6; and Exod. 24:10 speak of his palace over the heavens, while Ps. 29:10 tells of his throne over the heavenly ocean (?),[4] a view corresponding to the usual ancient Near Eastern worldview. However, מָכוֹן = *mākôn* ("place") can designate the heavenly as well as the earthly dwelling place of YHWH.[5]

According to the ancient temple dedication speech in 1 Kings 8:12f., the temple is now the dwelling of YHWH, and the verbs שָׁכֵן = *šākan* ("dwell") and יָשַׁב = *yāšab* ("inhabit, sit") are used reciprocally to speak about this divine dwelling. The temple and Zion perhaps are seen in the same way (Amos 1:2; Ezek. 37:26f.; and Zech. 2:14; cf. 1:16). However, when Isaiah receives his call in the Jerusalem temple, he does not see YHWH himself there. Rather, YHWH dwells and remains unseen in the heavens, while only the border of his train in the temple can be noticed, symbolizing thus a connection between heaven and the earthly temple (Isa. 6:1ff.). Psalms 9:12; 132:13f.; Isa. 8:18; and Joel 4:17 also speak of Zion as the dwelling place of YHWH, while 2 Sam. 7:4–7 vehemently protests against a "house" for YHWH. If the discussion is of YHWH as the "one who is enthroned over the cherubim" (cf. Ps. 99:1 and 2 Kings 19:15), then it can also be asked whether the thought is of an earthly dwelling place in the temple or a heavenly one that still must stand in some sort of relationship to the temple.[6] The "throne of YHWH that towers up to the heaven" is established in the Jerusalem temple.[7]

According to the Book of Deuteronomy,[8] YHWH will cause his "name" to dwell in the place which he will choose or, as the Deuteronomistic continuation and attenuation of this formula reads,[9] "will place his name."[10] That YHWH himself dwells there is certainly and intentionally not stated here. Elsewhere in Israel's ancient Near Eastern environment, for example, in Ugarit,[11] one sees the "name" of a deity, for instance, the name of Baal, serving as his cultic appearance or presence. This was in a weakened form as compared to his own presence, since the goddesses Astarte and Aṭṭart had to represent him. Thus, YHWH himself did not dwell in this place he had selected, but "only" his name dwelt there. On the one hand, this was more than likely directed in a critical fashion against the theology of divine presence (1 Kings 8:11; cf. Exod. 40:34f.) that was associated with the ark and the conception of the כָּבוֹד = *kābôd* ("glory").[12] The Book of Deuteronomy is meaningfully silent about both the ark and the *kābôd*, along with the divine name "YHWH Sebaoth."[13] On the other hand, the theological significance of the temple was to be secured by other means. There, people were always able to address YHWH, and the operation of the cultus was possible (1 Kings 8:52f., 59f.). Early on, worshipers could appear "before YHWH" in various sanctuaries (Exod. 23:14ff.; 34:20c) and could remember his name in different places (Exod. 20:24). But according to Deuteronomy (Deut. 16:16), this access to Yahweh would be decided differently.

If one attempts to provide an overview of YHWH's dwellings, one cannot construct a line of development that goes directly from Sinai to the sanctuaries of Canaan, to the temple, to heaven.[14] For instance, there are parallel statements about God being in heaven and in his sanctuary (cf. Ps. 68:34–36 with Isa. 60:13, or Ps. 11:4 with 1 Kings 6:13 and Ps. 5:8).[15] The temple, or according to Ps. 132:7f. the ark, is the footstool of his feet (Lam. 2:1; cf. Isa. 6:1ff.).

As, for example, Gen. 28:16ff. and Isaiah 6 (and Ps. 29:10) make clear, the sanctuary was also the place where the boundaries between this life and the future life, and between heaven and earth, are established. Thus, the throne of YHWH is established in the sanctuary but also rises up into the heavens (Isa. 66:1; Ezek. 43:7), a point that is similarly true of the mountain of God (Isa. 14:13f.). "Whoever sets foot into the sanctuary stands before the God who is enthroned in heaven."[16] The sanctuary and heaven are also mentioned together in Pss. 11:4 and 150:1. Thus each time a feature of divine presence is stressed by the description of heaven or the temple as the place of YHWH. These features include, namely, his majestic transcendence and omnipresence, his supportive nearness, his magnificence, and his solidarity. That YHWH was not tied to his sanctuary was demonstrated by the experience and the overcoming of the exile. Heaven was then stressed (in the late Deuteronomistic texts) as the place of YHWH, and his throne was located there (1 Kings 8:30, 39, 43, 49 with the statement "in heaven" clearly recognizable as a correction; cf. 2 Chron. 6:21, 30, 33, 39).[17] Or YHWH's "majesty"[18] abandoned this temple in the direction of the east (Ezekiel 11) in order either to meet the prophet in distant Babylonia (Ezekiel 1–3) or to march with the people "through the wilderness" (thus the Priestly document). Although the temple is destroyed at that time, one can still pray to YHWH (Jer. 29 and 1 Kings 8:23ff.), for he hears in heaven (1 Kings 8:36 and often). Prayers in the temple and God's hearing in the heavens occur together (1 Kings 8:30). YHWH's presence with his people and his succor that he provides them are not affected by the destruction of the temple. YHWH can be a God who is far as well as near (Jer. 23:23; 1 Kings 8:27; cf. Isa. 66:1f.), and he is "near" especially for prayers (1 Kings 8:52f., 59f.) or in the wisdom of his law (Deut. 4:6–8). These last-mentioned texts both probably stem from the period of the destruction of the temple. Thus it was never too difficult evidently for Israel to reorient its view from a conception about YHWH's "dwelling" to another understanding. Since YHWH is not a part of the cosmos, he also is not subjected to its limitations. He is the distant God who becomes present in theophany and in the speech that accompanies most of these appearances, and his revelation is experienced as redemption. YHWH also promises that he desires to dwell among his people Israel (1 Kings 6:13 Deuteronomistic; Exod. 29:45f. P), a point made in texts from the time and experience of the exile where YHWH and Israel appear to be separated (Deut. 31:17f.) and perhaps when YHWH no longer dwelt in Israel's "midst."[19] The YHWH who is both near and far is not unconditionally bound to his temple, yet he desires to bind himself anew to his people Israel whom he himself has chosen as his community.[20] For Qoheleth, however, distance is important: "the God" is in heaven, but humanity upon the earth, so that one should not talk so pretentiously (Qoh. 5:1).

5.2   The Ark[21]

The ark (Hebrew "chest")[22] also is representative of divine presence and a symbol of God who is present with his own people and accompanies and fights for them. Besides the ark sayings in Num. 10:35f. (cf. 10:33 and 14:44 J?), the oldest texts[23] that deal with the ark are the references in the so-called ark narrative (1 Samuel 4–6 and 2 Samuel 6), which are to be compared to ones in Joshua 3; 4; and 6. According to these texts, the ark is less an empty throne of God and more a part of this throne, namely, a throne's footstool (Isa. 6:1; 1 Chron. 28:2 and Ps. 132:7) or at least an "impressive pledge of Yahweh's presence."[24] The term אֲרוֹן = *'ărôn* ("chest") might have been chosen to refer to the ark because of the object's appearance, while כִּסֵּא = *kissē'* ("throne") might have been consciously avoided. At the same time, it is nowhere specifically said that YHWH sits enthroned on the ark. Further, the ark is already present during the period of the wilderness. Though it is seldom mentioned there, this results from the fact that certainly not all groups during this period, which later are incorporated into Israel, made their journey under the symbol of the ark.[25] If the ark was not already created as a typical, portable, migrating shrine and war palladium (1 Sam. 4:4; 2 Sam. 6:2)[26] before the conquest, then why would it be built after the settlement? Since Shiloh (1 Sam. 3:3), it was obviously connected with the title "enthroned upon the cherubim" (cf. again 1 Sam. 4:4 and 2 Sam. 6:2).[27]

In the ark narrative, the ark is the symbol of the presence of YHWH among his own people during their battles. The estimation of the ark by the Philistines (1 Sam. 4:7: God has come into the camp) and the contest between YHWH and the Philistine deity Dagon (1 Samuel 5) clearly point to YHWH's presence with the ark. The ark both blesses (2 Sam. 6:11) and destroys (2 Sam. 6:6f.), and the name of God, "YHWH Sebaoth," which originally may have been related to the earthly military hosts of Israel (1 Sam. 17:45), often was associated with it.[28] According to 1 Sam. 2:22 and 2 Sam. 7:6, a tent also belongs with the ark, leading one to conclude that this combination is not originally due to the work of P.

Deuteronomy and the Deuteronomistic literature subsequent to it make the ark into the (יהוה) אֲרוֹן (ה)בְּרִית = 'ărôn (hab)běrît (yahweh), "ark of the covenant of (YHWH)," cf. 1 Kings 8:21),[29] meaning the container of the tablets of the law (Deut. 10:3, 8 and 31:9, 25f.). At the same time, these texts theologically devalue and carry out an indirect polemic against the old Jerusalem ark theology. According to J and E, the tablets already existed (Exod. 31:18),[30] but they were not in the ark. By contrast, the predeuteronomic texts were familiar with the ark, but not with the tablets of law in it. Thus the question emerges, what was in the ark before? Holy stones from Sinai[31] or nothing at all? Why does 1 Kings 8:9 stress so much that nothing else was present in the ark "save" (רַק = raq) for the tablets? The Priestly document takes over from Deuteronomy the function of the ark as the container of the tablets of the law (Exod. 25:16 and 40:20), puts a jar of manna into the ark (Exod. 16:33f.), gives it a precise description (Exod. 25:10–22 and 37:1–9), places it in the tent of meeting[32] in the midst of the camp of Israel (Exod. 26:33; 40:21),[33] and names it the "ark of witness" (הָעֵדֻת אֲרוֹן = 'ărôn hā'ēdut, Exod. 25:22; 26:33f.; and often).[34] Possibly these texts out of P have replaced an older description of the ark found in JE and an older report of the making of the ark that once stood between Exod. 33:6 and 7.

Following the taking of Jerusalem, David transported the ark there (2 Samuel 6), a fact that speaks rather forcibly against the notion that it originated in Canaan. In Jerusalem the ark stood later in the temple (1 Kings 6:19; and 8:1–11) underneath the wings of the cherubim (1 Kings 8:6).[35] Thus YHWH was transformed from a God who marched with his people to one who "dwelt" in their midst as an enthroned ruler.[36] Apparently destroyed with the temple (Jer. 3:16f.), the ark by then had probably already lost its significance, since it scarcely is mentioned in later texts. YHWH and the ark were once again closely associated in Ps. 132:8, a text that is probably not early, but rather influenced by Deuteronomistic redaction.[37] That the ark was used during cultic processions to the temple is not as certain as has often been assumed. The references that are enlisted for this argument (Psalms 24; 47; and 132) do not provide the clarity one would wish.[38] In 2 Maccabees 2:4f. we learn more about the later fate of the ark.

5.3   The Tent (of Meeting)[39]

The tent, both in connection with as well as separate from the ark, has been called the sign and means of divine presence.[40]

The tent is mentioned 182 times in the Old Testament, and 140 of these references belong to P. The "tent of meeting" (אֹהֶל מוֹעֵד = 'ōhel mô'ēd, derived from the Hebrew verb יָעַד = yā'ad, "to appoint") is mentioned 133 times, of which 120 references occur in texts of the Priestly document and its strata.[41] The references in Josh. 18:1 and 19:51 are similar to the texts of the Priestly document and perhaps are to be assigned to it.

The Priestly "tent of meeting" (Luther: "tabernacle") is apparently for P "the copy, not the prototype, of the temple at Jerusalem,"[42] and is mainly mentioned in Exodus 25 to Numbers 10. With its dimensions shaped according to those of the Solomonic temple, this (exilic) tent at the same time also served as the planned model for the desired temple of the future. Moses had seen on Sinai the "model" (תַּבְנִית = tabnît, Exod. 25:9) and heavenly exemplar of this tent. The tent of meeting was the place of cultic activity (Exod. 25:22; 29:10f.), which may be performed only by ordained persons.[43] Here, YHWH is continually present in the midst of the Israelites (Exod. 25:8).[44] The tent, constructed out of gold-plated boards and carpets and for P the location for the ark,[45] stands in the midst of the camp of Israel (Exod. 25:8; 29:42–46). The כְּבוֹד יהוה = kĕbôd yahweh ("glory of YHWH") descends into the tent (Num. 14:10; 16:19; 17:7; and 20:6). One of the central purpose statements of Priestly theology (Exod. 29:42–46) focuses all of this in a clear, understandable manner,[46] for P's portrayal, already as early as Genesis 1 to Exod. 24:15ff. and beyond, points toward this tent of meeting as the place where divine presence occurs among the nation during its journey through the wilderness.[47] It is disputed as to whether or not there are traditiohistorical connections between this Priestly tent of meeting with its developed, theological elaboration and the tent which is already mentioned by the Yahwist and the Elohist.[48]

Besides the connection with the camp, the ark, and the cult, this "tent of meeting" is significant for P in the so-called murmuring narratives where the appearance of the כָּבוֹד = kābôd occurs each time as a salvific event during a time of murmuring and need and where the leaders of Israel are strengthened and confirmed by this appearance. "The sanctuary so constituted as to provide for both blessing and sin is the purpose of God's way with Israel, yes even with creation itself."[49] The terminology of creation that occurs in Exod. 39:32, 43; and 40:17, 33b, 34 inescapably points to this conclusion.

In the older traditions[50] of J and E, which contrast with P, a tent[51] is mentioned in Exod. 33:7–11; Num. 11:16f., 24–30; and 12:4f., 10. Exodus 33: 7–11[52] is the introduction to Numbers 11 and 12. Deuteronomy 31:14f. cannot be counted here, and Exod. 34:29–35 has been redacted. After a tent is erected outside the camp, Moses goes there to meet with YHWH. And the fact that YHWH "descends" (יָרַד = yārad)[53] each time to the tent in a pillar of cloud demonstrates that he is not always present here. He encounters Moses in the tent, and the important decisions for the people and their journey occur through the oracle he receives (Exod. 33:7–11; and Num. 12:4). Joshua functions as a "servant" to this tent of meeting.[54] Since this tent is still probably considered empty, the exact cultic functions that go beyond what has heretofore been said are unclear. Possibly the tent was to function as a place for the obtaining of an oracle, although a completely empty tent is improbable. If this tent should actually reach back to the time prior to the conquest, "it would not be separated from the person of Moses."[55]

It is improbable that the ark was placed within a tent in the premonarchial period (1 Sam. 2:22; 2 Sam. 7:6).[56] The tent of David (2 Sam. 6:17; cf. 7:6),[57] often mentioned as a third tent, was probably nothing other than a protective tent for the ark (cf. 1 Kings 1:39 and 2:28–30).

Behind the tent and the ark one shall have to suppose the existence of different tradents or immigrating groups of later Israel, especially since both sacred objects in the time of P are clearly separated and differently attested. Moreover, whether one can associate different "theologies"with them, for instance, a theology of presence (ark) and a theology of manifestation (tent), is open to critical debate.[58] They are not mutually exclusive subjects, and the particular nuances of each are complementary.[59] For the Priestly document itself, both sacred objects belong together, whereas before P they were never mentioned together. The tent is more closely oriented to the theme of the "wilderness wandering," while the ark is mentioned in connection with this theme only in Num. 10:35f. (14:14). Later, "the terminology of the tent enters into the language about the temple" (Pss. 27:5 and 61:5; cf. 15:1; 78:60; and Isa. 33:20f.).[60]

5.4   Yahweh's Court: The Cherubim, Seraphim, and Angels[61]

YHWH is indeed an unparalleled or even the only God, but he is not alone.[62] With him in his heavenly world, he has his court (1 Kings 22:19; Isa. 6:1f.; Job 1 + 2; cf. also Gen. 6:1–4; Deut. 32:8f.; Pss. 8:6; 29:1; 82:1; 89:7f.; and Dan. 7:9f.) to which the often used divine plural also refers (Gen. 1:26f.;[63] 3:22; 11:7; and Isa. 6:8; cf. 40:1–8). Thus, even as the god El collected and continued to have around himself his pantheon (see the Ugaritic texts),[64] a retinue over which he presided as the highest deity and king of the gods, so YHWH is surrounded in a similar fashion by his own court. According to Ps. 82:1, this court consists of "gods," although it is clear even here that they are characterized as deprived of divine power. The members of this court have their respective functions and are part of a larger cosmology that assumes political forms of expression (cf. the royal court as an analogy). For example, the court includes cherubim and especially angels who are a medium of the divine, cosmic government and God's providential direction of the world.

The *cherubim*[65] mentioned especially in 1 Kings 6–8 and Ezekiel 10 belong to this court. As many archaeological discoveries, especially Babylonian, demonstrate, these cherubim are to be seen as a kind of hybrid creature probably of mythological origins and represented usually as a winged sphinx. They are closely associated with the throne of YHWH and with his court, and they perform especially the responsibility of guard duty for the heavenly throne and the tree of life (Ezek. 28:13ff.; cf. Gen. 3:24; 1 Kings 6:29, 32, 35; and Ezek. 41:17ff.). As either the bearers or even as a part of this throne, they are the ones who transport the deity. As the ark is in other ways,[66] the cherubim are the symbol of YHWH's presence. They function as his vehicle (Ezekiel 10; Ps. 18:11, par.), for which reason they were also regarded as a personified stormcloud (cf. Isa. 19:1 and Ps. 104:3). They were present in the temple of Jerusalem (1 Kings 6:23–28; cf. 1 Kings 8:6–8), and already had been mentioned in the premonarchial period in connection with the ark,[67] where the title "enthroned above the cherubim" (2 Kings 19:14f. and Ps. 99:1) was connected to YHWH perhaps in Shiloh (1 Sam. 4:4 and 2 Sam. 6:2). To what extent the conception of YHWH as king was associated with the cherubim is not entirely clear,[68] even though the related iconographic[69] and semantic evidence (throne; cf. Ezekiel 10)[70] makes this association probable. The cherubim were employed originally, not so much for the linkage of God and humanity, but to illustrate divine majesty. "They defend the holy precinct, they mark off the boundaries of the presence of the holy, and they are bearers of the holy."[71] The cherubim throne of YHWH links therefore his earthly throne in the temple with his heavenly throne. The cherubim throne both describes and establishes once again, as the temple as a whole does,[72] the combination of the heavenly and earthly dwelling places of YHWH and thereby both the distance and the nearness of God. However, after the destruction of the (first) temple, the idea of the cherubim was consciously retained (Ezekiel) although somewhat reinterpreted (P: Exod. 25:17ff.). They were adapted now to serve the desire to enable YHWH to be present among his people in spite of the loss of the temple (cf. Ezek. 11:22 and the closeness of the four creatures in Ezekiel 1 to the cherubim).

The *seraphim* are mentioned only in Isa. 6:2f., although they are presupposed there as being well known. Perhaps comparable to the Egyptian uraeus, they are probably to be conceived as winged creatures with the body of serpents (cf. Num. 21:6; Isa. 14:29; 30:6; also Deut. 8:15; and 2 Kings 18:4?) and with human hands and feet. The heavenly adoration of the God sitting on his throne is their primary function. Submissive to God, they sing praises to the holy YHWH who thus does not remain dependent only on earthly doxologies. They must cover themselves with their wings before the majesty of YHWH. The root שׂרף = *śārāp* that is used to designate them causes one to think of lightning,[73] which would fit the original association of the cherubim with a personified thundercloud (Pss. 18:12f.; 104:3; and Isa. 19:1).[74]

Whether the *angels* (plural!)[75] were originally members of YHWH's court who served as his messengers is debated.[76] That they could also be named "the strong ones," "the holy ones," and "the sons of the gods" on the one hand suggests such a relationship and on the other hand characterizes them as mascu-line beings.[77] They are probably also to be identified with the "army of heaven" (1 Kings 22:19; Isa. 24:21; 40:26; Jer. 33:22; Pss. 33:6; 148:2; etc.; cf. "army of YHWH" in Josh. 5:14 and also Dan. 7:10), and quite possibly as such they even had some connection with the stars (Judg. 5:20: the stars fight; cf. Job 38:7). Since the stars were also seen as the messengers of God, it might be that they provided a bridge to the angels. A connection to the function of messen-gers is likewise suggested through the Hebrew designation for angels, מלאכים = *mal'ākîm,* which is derived from the verb לאך = *lā'ak,* ("go, send"), a verb that is attested also in Ugaritic. These heavenly beings have no wings (Gen. 28:12) and are, above all, YHWH's "messengers," thereby serving as repre-sentatives of his presence and as functionaries of his will. Human beings and even forces of nature can also be called YHWH's "messengers" (Ps. 104:4). The possible religiohistorical roots and backgrounds for angels are no longer important for the Old Testament. Here the angels do not have an actual inde-pendent signification but rather, as the mediators of protection, revelation, pun-ishment, and divine opposition, are an expression of YHWH's distance and proximity.[78] It is important to note that God is the one who sends forth these angels. However, they do not provide any occasion to speculate about the heav-enly world.[79]

While in Ezekiel a "man" assumes the leading role of describing and inter-preting the new sanctuary (Ezek. 40:3; etc.; cf. also Dan. 8:15 and 9:21), Zechariah is familiar with an angel who offers interpretations (Zech. 1:9ff.; 2:2; etc.) and also makes intercession (Zech. 1:12). From Daniel on, these an-gels are then placed into divisions, receive names, and appear as both guardians and heavenly representatives of the other nations (Gabriel: Dan. 8:16; 9:21; Michael: Dan. 10:13; cf. Raphael in the Book of Tobit). A further development of angelology in the postexilic period and in early Judaism (Qumran![80]) is brought about through both the increasing transcendence of God in this period and the religiohistorical influences from Parsiism.[81]

5.5 Demons[82]

According to the witness of Old Testament faith, Israel felt itself endangered or oppressed by demons far less than did the other cultures of the ancient Near East. In Babylonia the fear of demons was especially great, and the practice of exorcism directed against these sinister powers was of great significance.[83] By contrast, the reason for Israel's modest concern with demons resides clearly in its experience and image of God that include the unique character of YHWH. The discussion of demons, rarely documented for ancient Israel in the Old Tes-tament, is "inherited and then suppressed,"[84] being rather a "jetsam of the pagan milieu's belief in demons."[85] While one can espouse the view that the fear of demons was much more extensive in the popular religion of ancient Israel than is apparent in the Old Testament, one cannot clearly demonstrate this.

According to the Old Testament, magic and divination are forbidden in order to preserve YHWH's majesty (Exod. 22:17; Lev. 19:31; 20:27; Deut. 18:9ff.; 1 Samuel 28; cf. 2 Kings 23:8; and Isa. 2:6). In some passages, however, their practice and the rites closely associated with them are narrated (Gen. 30:14ff.; 37ff.; Num. 5:11ff.; 2 Kings 2:19ff; and 4:33ff.). On account of these relatively meager data, one finds in the Old Testament only very sporadic and mostly minor statements about demons. These include the mentionings of the "animal of the wilderness" (? Isa. 13:21), the "hairy demon" or the "goat spirit" (Isa. 34:14), Lilith as the female night demon (Isa. 34:14),[86] and the wilderness demon Azazel in Lev. 16:10.[87] Also, one should note 2 Chron. 11:15, where even priests for the demons are mentioned, certainly an indication of the terrible sin of Jeroboam. Deuteronomy 32:17 and Ps. 106:37f. (also Lev. 17:7; Isa. 8:19; and 1 Sam. 28:13?) allow one to recognize that these demons were viewed as divine beings, even as in Mesopotamia the names of gods and the names of demons were both given the divine determinative. In many cultic as well as other practices (Lev. 19:9; cf. Job 31:38–40), in food laws and especially in customs concerning the dead, rites of protection against demons that are found also in Israel's religious environment may be hidden (Isa. 22:12; Jer. 16:6; 41:5; Ezek. 7:18; Micah 1:16; etc.: often in prophetic polemic!).[88] Illnesses in the Old Testament, however, were not attributed to demons but to YHWH himself (Lev. 26:16; Num. 12:9–14; Deut. 28:21f.; 2 Samuel 24; and Job 6:4ff.; then see the psalms of individual lament and other examples). In portrayals that reflect the influences of demonic presence, YHWH, who is active in these contexts, is addressed with the personal "you" (Ps. 22:13–17; cf. there v. 16c). The "destroyer" (Exod. 12:23) comes from God, yet he is also Israel's physician (Exod. 15:26).[89] Since there are no other gods but YHWH, there also are no other spirits besides him (Ps. 91:5f.; cf., however, 1 Kings 22:21). This is different from what one will find in the postexilic period, in early Judaism, and then in the New Testament where demons play a somewhat greater role than in the Old Testament. This is also true of statements about angels and Satan.[90] "According to the Old Testament revelation, human beings have to do with God and only with God."[91]

5.6 Satan[92]

Satan, who is late to appear in the Old Testament, likewise plays a rather small role. In the search for his possible origins and derivation,[93] the thought has usually been limited to a literary figure, to a malicious being of folktale and fable.

Satan has also been traced to Babylonia or Persia, seen as a member of the divine police, as the antipole to the personal, guardian deity, and as a personified
function of God. In any case, he may have "originated first after the exile."[94]

The name "Satan" is derived from the Hebrew root שׂטן = śāṭān, which
means "to show hostility toward, to accuse, and to prosecute" (Pss. 38:21;
71:13; 109:4, 20, 29; cf. Ps. 55:4; Job 16:9; Gen. 27:41; 49:23; and 50:15).
Consequently, this means that the word itself designates neither a fixed function, nor a title, nor even a personal name. Such adversaries can primarily be
human beings, thus, for example, David for the Philistines (1 Sam. 29:4), a personal opponent, or an opponent in a litigation (2 Sam. 19:23; Pss. 109:6; and
71:13). The term also refers to opponents in the political arena (1 Kings 5:18
and 11:14, 23, 25) or to the angel of YHWH who confronts Baalam and his
she-ass (Num. 22:22, 32). To be an adversary is therefore not to be a continual
opponent; rather, this opposition is ad hoc and temporary. Thus, standing at the
very beginning of the use of this root is the behavior that occurs between human
beings.

In Zech. 3:1f. and Job 1–2, "the Satan" (with the article) appears in the role
of a heavenly prosecutor[95] within the court of YHWH and under his direction.
He is here in dialogue with YHWH, stands under his power, and acts according to his orders. He is not assigned the same rank as God and, what is more,
can do nothing without his permission (Luther: "God's devil"). The staunch
opponent of Job is God himself, not the Satan. If the Satan should have been
added at a later time to the prologue of the Book of Job,[96] then these references
to him in the narrative frame would join those in Proto-Zechariah in the (early)
postexilic period.

In 1 Chron. 21:1 "Satan" appears in the late postexilic period as a personal
name that lacks the definite article. The content of the older parallel in 2 Sam.
24:1 matches this text in Chronicles. When both texts are compared, it becomes
clear that in 1 Chron. 21:1 Satan is spoken about in a manner in which he carries out the wrath of God. In carrying out the divine commission, Satan is an
opponent of human beings, although he is not the opponent of God, the originator of wickedness, or something similar. Also, "satanology" was developed
in this direction for the first time in the period of early Judaism,[97] and is, as was
demonology, present in the New Testament more significantly than in the Old
Testament. If God in the Old Testament was originally the one who brought
into existence what is negative, tragic, and harmful to human beings,[98] Satan
was later moved into this role. This occurred in order to disassociate God from
evil and from what was negative, due to more astute theological ethics and a
growing sense of divine transcendence. In this sense, one may compare, for instance, Job 2:7 with Exod. 11:5; 12:23; Lev. 26:16; Deut. 28:20ff.; 1 Sam.
16:14; 2 Sam. 24:15f.; and 1 Kings 22:22f. Thus, two conceptions now become
separated from each other, YHWH as the originator of the good, and YHWH

as the one who also brings about the negative. In order to shift evil eventually away from YHWH, the strong Old Testament faith in one God must have been set aside. It is possible that a dualistic influence of Persian religion was increasingly at work. Thus Satan now assumed certain divine actions that were originally ascribed to God, for example, when great suffering was experienced in an incomprehensible way.[99] Whether one had "solved" this problem of inexplicable suffering in an appropriate way or whether the problem is rationally solvable at all remains to be seen. However, the Satan in the Old Testament is still not brought together with the origin of sin, not even in Genesis 3 where the serpent is the tempter. This combination first occurs in Wisd. 2:24.

5.7   The Kingdom of the Dead[100]

In view of the fact that the Old Testament witnesses to YHWH as the only, mighty God, it is striking that he could not or would not extend his powerful influence from the beginning over the kingdom of the dead, that is, upon שְׁאוֹל = šě'ôl.[101] The result was that the realm of the dead in the Old Testament had to be assigned to the world that is far removed from God.[102] The Old Testament is familiar with שְׁאוֹל = šě'ôl only as the place of the dead and knows nothing, however, of a hell as the place of the damned.[103]

When death befalls human beings and they fall victim to the insatiability (Prov. 27:20; 30:15f.) of the realm of the dead, then they are separated there from YHWH (Ps. 88:6). YHWH has no interest in the dead who stand outside his activity in the world. There is no longer any community with God in the underworld (Isa. 38:18; and Ps. 88:6, 11–13). The person who offers prayers on the earth can be a witness of YHWH, but the dead person is excluded from testimony.[104] This is true in spite of the strikingly contrary statements in Deut. 32:39; 1 Sam. 2:6; Amos 9:2; Job 26:6; Pss. 30:4; 49:16; 86:13; 139:8; etc.[105] On the one hand, these texts suggest that a living person cannot escape from YHWH even in Sheol. On the other hand, these texts provide information that YHWH also can extricate people from the power of Sheol. Nonetheless, the power of the kingdom of the dead is seen as afflicting people in this life.[106] Sheol reaches with its power into this existence (Prov. 7:27; Pss. 18:5f.; and 116:3), because an illness already signifies that the person who has been afflicted by it is in the grip of death.[107] Thus, Sheol not only is a place but also encompasses with its arms and snares a region and forms a sphere of death (Ps. 18:5f.). Consequently, there is salvation before death, but not from death (Pss. 9:14; 16:10; 30:4; 56:14; 71:20; and Isa. 38:10). In the valley of darkness, YHWH must guide and protect his worshiper from the danger of death (Ps. 23:4).[108]

How things appear in Sheol according to the imagination of the Old Testament is especially clear in Isa. 14:9–11; 38:10ff.; Psalm 88; and Ezek. 32:17–32.

A dark realm, Sheol lies in the interior of the earth under the primeval ocean, so that conversely God's palace is to be sought above the heavenly ocean.[109] A place into which one descends, Sheol is also called the "pit" and the "deep" and possesses doors and bars.[110] One leads there a shadowy existence[111] and no longer speaks but rather only chirps.[112] The dead person remains forever in this place of silence and in this land from which there is no return.[113] A dead person may be brought up again from there only in violation of all prohibitions against this practice (1 Samuel 28: Samuel). In the realm of the dead, one does not praise YHWH, for one is certainly separated from him (Pss. 6:6; 30:10; 88:11–13; 115:16–18; and Isa. 38:18; cf. Sir. 17:27f.). Thus, in the Old Testament the form of existence of the dead in Sheol (Isa. 26:19) as "shadows"[114] is no longer called life. Sheol is simply known as the "non-world,"[115] and the dying person entering Sheol must in fact take leave of God.[116] And if the person was rich, he or she could not take along any wealth (Ps. 49:17f.; Qoh. 5:14; Isa. 14:11f.). In this connection, the Old Testament conceptions about the realm of the dead are very similar to those of ancient Mesopotamia,[117] which are encountered in exemplary fashion in Tablet XII of the Epic of Gilgamesh.[118]

Thus one finds in Sheol indeed a true, although only shadowy image of earthly life, and if one was not properly buried, was slain by the sword, or was not buried at all, then these conditions would have negative consequences in Sheol. Thus one must be content there with a negatively defined existence (1 Kings 13:22; Isa. 14:3–21; 34:3; Jer. 16:6; 26:23; and Ezek. 32:17ff.).

In addition to Sheol, the grave was also known as the place of the dead (Isa. 22:16), and the fact that both can apparently exist beside each other in an unreconciled manner is probably to be evaluated as a so-called "intellectual archaism"[119] where one consciously is not interested in such a reconciliation.[120] In any case, Sheol is not to be understood as a common grave or as a concentration of graves; rather, the grave and Sheol exist side by side as two different strands of tradition or, better, traditions with different roots.

However, how is it to be explained that the sphere of the dead within ancient Israel, as the Old Testament allows us to understand it, would be regarded for so long a time as not standing under YHWH's activity and influence (Job 14:7ff.; Ps. 115:17)? First of all, there appears to be carried out a conscious rejection and delimitation of various views of Sheol, as is attested, for example, by the rejection of customs of the dead. Customs and beliefs about the dead in Israel's ancient Near Eastern environment were a widespread phenomenon that also was often bound up with other gods. Thus Ugarit knew of the god Mot ("death") and told of him and his opponent Baal in a variety of circumstances. The realm of the dead and dying was linked with these episodes of Mot and Baal.[121] All of these customs and beliefs concerning the dead were rejected and forbidden as "unclean" (e.g., Lev. 19:31; 20:6; 21:1; Deut. 14:1f.; and 18:11).[122] YHWH was a God of the living and wanted it thus, but he was not the God of the dead (cf. Matt. 22:32, par.). Second, it was the case that some ideas about the future life (perhaps beyond the realm of the dead) were borrowed from the cultures of the ancient Near East, since Yahwistic faith showed no particular interest in these questions. If one wishes to consider these in context, one must collect the statements about the topic within the Old Testament. In so doing it is clear that the psalms, prophets, and wisdom literature (Job!) typically provide considerably more information than the narrative literature. A literature about the future life, which, for example, ancient Egypt knew, was not developed in ancient Israel. Third, the anthropology of ancient Israel[123] offered no possibility of any connection that would allow positive views to be expressed about an existence after death. Perhaps Yahwistic faith, with its reticence to express hopes and statements about a future life, continued to preserve a piece of nomadic heritage[124] regarding the questions addressed openly by a sedentary piety that can speak of a "graveyard." And fourth, an ancestor cult cannot be shown to have existed in ancient Israel,[125] even though the graves of the fathers played no small role (Genesis 23) and the dying and burial is often mentioned, usually with the words "to be gathered to the fathers" (or "to lie down," "to enter") (Gen. 47:30; 49:31; 50:25; 2 Sam. 17:23; 19:38; etc.).

Thus, one was able from time to time to hope and to pray that YHWH would not allow his worshiper to see the kingdom of the dead and would heal the person from his or her illness (Pss. 16:10; and 49:16) so that one, having rejoined the living, could once more offer praise to God (Ps. 115:17f.). However, once one had died and was in the realm of the dead, there was no more hope. One could then only ask with resignation where this person may actually be (Job 14:7ff.; esp. v. 10). YHWH has indeed power over the realm of the dead (Amos 9:2 and Ps. 139:8; cf. Hos. 13:14); however, this kingdom and its inhabitants lie outside YHWH's interest, according to the testimony of the Old Testament (Isa. 38:11; and Ps. 88:6, 11). To a large extent, the Old Testament worshipers are resigned to this. Their community with YHWH, limited to this life, within their clan and their people, whom YHWH had established and made possible through his historical action of election, was enough. As were all their ancestors, these worshipers were both guests and strangers (Ps. 39:13).

ABBREVIATIONS

AHw	W. von Soden, *Akkadisches Handwörterbuch* (1965–1981)
AnBib	Analecta Biblica
ANET	J. B. Pritchard, ed., *Ancient Near Eastern Texts Relating to the Old Testament* (3d ed., 1969)
AOAT	Alter Orient und Altes Testament
AOF	Altorientalische Forschungen
AOT	H. Gressmann, ed., *Altorientalische Texte zum Alten Testament*
ARM	*Archives royales de Mari*
ATD	Das Alte Testament Deutsch
AThANT	Abhandlungen zur Theologie des Alten und Neuen Testaments
AuS	G. Dalman, *Arbeit und Sitte in Palästina* (1928–1942)
AUSS	*Andrews University Seminary Studies*
B.C.E.	Before the Common Era
BA	*Biblical Archaeologist*
BBB	Bonner biblische Beiträge
BETL	Bibliotheca Ephemeridum Theologicarum Lovaniensium
BH3	*Biblia Hebraica*, ed. R. Kittel (3d ed.)
BHS	*Biblia Hebraica Stuttgartensia*
BHHW	B. Reicke and L. Rost, eds., *Biblisch-Historisches Handwörterbuch* (1962–1979)
BHTh	Beiträge zur historischen Theologie
Bibl	*Biblica*
BibOr	Biblica et orientalia
BiKi	*Bibel und Kirche*
BiLe	*Bibel und Leben*
BiTod	*Bible Today*
BK	Biblischer Kommentar
BL	Herbert Haag, ed., *Bibel-Lexikon*
BN	*Biblische Notizen*
BRev	*Bible Review*
BRL	K. Galling, ed., *Biblische Reallexikon*, HAT I/1 (2d ed., 1977)
BTB	*Biblical Theology Bulletin*

BThSt	Biblische-Theologische Studien
BThZ	*Berliner Theologische Zeitschrift*
BuL	*Botschaft und Lehre*
BWANT	Beiträge zur Wissenschaft vom Alten und Neuen Testament
BZ	*Biblische Zeitschrift*
BZAW	Beihefte zur Zeitschrift für die alttestamentliche Wissenschaft
C.E.	Common Era
CB OT	Coniectanea Biblica, Old Testament series
CBQ	*Catholic Biblical Quarterly*
CBQMS	Catholic Biblical Quarterly Monograph Series
Conc	*Concilium*
DBAT	Dielheimer Blätter zum Alten Testament
DPfrB	*Deutsches Pfarrerblatt*
E	Elohist
EdF	Erträge der Forschung
EKL	*Evangelisches Kirchenlexikon*
EMM	*Evangelisches Missions-Magazin*
ET	English translation
EThL	*Ephemerides Theologicae Lovanienses*
ETR	*Etudes théologiques et religieuses*
EvErz	*Evangelische Erzieher*
EvTh	*Evangelische Theologie*
FOTL	The Forms of the Old Testament Literature
FRLANT	Forschungen zur Religion und Literatur des Alten und Neuen Testaments
FF	*Forschungen und Fortschritte*
FS	Festschrift
GK	E. Kautzsch, ed., *Gesenius' Hebrew Grammar;* 2d English edition by A. E. Cowley, 1910
GuL	*Geist und Leben*
HAT	Handbuch zum Alten Testament
HdO	Handbuch der Orientalistik
HKAT	Handkommentar zum Alten Testament
HorBibTheol	*Horizons in Biblical Theology*
HSM	Harvard Semitic Monographs
HThR	*Harvard Theological Review*
HUCA	*Hebrew Union College Annual*
HZ	*Historische Zeitschrift*
IKZ	*Internationale kirchliche Zeitschrift*
Interp	*Interpretation*
IrBibStud	*Irish Biblical Studies*
J	Yahwist

JBL	*Journal of Biblical Literature*
JBTh	*Jahrbuch für biblische Theologie*
JETS	*Journal of the Evangelical Theological Society*
JSOT Suppl	Journal for the Study of the Old Testament Supplement Series
JSS	*Journal of Semitic Studies*
JSS Mon	Journal of Semitic Studies Monograph Series
KAI	H. Donner and W. Rollig, *Kanaanäische und Aramäische Inschriften* (2d ed., 1966–1970)
KD	K. Barth, *Kirchliche Dogmatik*
KS	*Kleine Schriften*
KTU	M. Dietrich, O. Loretz, and J. Samartín, *Die Keilalphabetischen Texte aus Ugarit,* I (AOAT 24, 1976)
KuD	*Kerygma und Dogma*
LÄ	W. Helck and W. Westendorf, *Lexikon für Ägyptologie* (1975ff.)
LeDiv	Lectio divina
MIO	*Mitteilungen des Instituts für Orientforschung*
MThZ	*Münchener theologische Zeitschrift*
NBL	*Neues Bibel-Lexikon*
NEB AT	Neue Echter Bibel, Altes Testament
NedThT	*Nederlands theologisch tijdschrift*
NF	Neue Folge = new series
NGTT	*Nederduitse Gereformeerde Teologiese Tydscrif*
NRTh	*Nouvelle revue théologique*
OBO	Orbis Biblicus et Orientalis
ÖBS	Österreichische biblische Studien
Or	*Orientalia*
P	Priestly writing
par.	parallel(s)
Protest.	*Protestantismo*
PTh	*Pastoraltheologie*
Qoh	Qoheleth = Ecclesiastes
RB	*Revue biblique*
RExp	*Review and Expositor*
RGG	*Die Religion in Geschichte und Gegenwart*
RGT	*Religionsgeschichtliche Texte*
RHPhR	*Revue d'histoire et de philosophie religieuses*
RHS	*Religionsunterricht an höheren Schulen*
RivBibl	*Revista biblica*
RLA	E. Ebeling et al., eds., *Reallexikon für Assyriologie und vorderasiatische Archäologie* (1932ff.)
RScRel	*Revue des sciences religieuses*
Saec.	*Saeculum*

SBAB	Stuttgarter biblische Aufsatzbände
SBB	Stuttgarter biblische Beiträge
SBL MS	Society of Biblical Literature Monograph Series
SBL SP	Society of Biblical Literature Seminar Papers
SBS	Stuttgarter Bibelstudien
SBT	Studies in Biblical Theology
Sir.	Sirach = Ecclesiasticus
SJOT	*Scandinavian Journal of the Old Testament*
StANT	Studien zum Alten und Neuen Testament
StGen	*Studium Generale*
Sth St	Sinziger theologische Texte und Studien
STh	*Studia Theologica*
TB	Theologische Bücherei
TGI	K. Galling, ed., *Texte zur Geschichte Israels* (2d ed., 1968)
THAT	E. Jenni and C. Westermann, eds., *Theologisches Handwörterbuch zum Alten Testament* (1971–1976)
ThG	*Theologie und Glaube*
ThLZ	*Theologische Literaturzeitung*
ThPh	*Theologie und Philosophie*
ThQ	*Theologische Quartalschrift*
ThR	*Theologische Rundschau*
ThSt	Theological Studies
ThViat	*Theologia viatorum*
ThWAT	G. J. Botterweck and H. Ringgren et al., eds., *Theologisches Wörterbuch zum Alten Testament* (1970ff.) (ET: *Theological Dictionary of the Old Testament*)
ThZ	*Theologische Zeitschrift*
TRE	*Theologische Realenzyklopädie* (1976ff.)
TThSt	Trierer theologische Studien
TThZ	*Trierer theologische Zeitschrift*
TUAT	O. Kaiser et al., eds., *Texte aus der Umwelt des Alten Testaments* (1982ff.)
UBL	Ugaritisch-Biblische Literatur
UF	*Ugarit-Forschungen*
VT	*Vetus Testamentum*
VT Suppl	Vetus Testamentum Supplements
VuF	*Verkündigung und Forschung*
WdF	Wege der Forschung
WdM	H. W. Haussig, ed., *Wörterbuch der Mythologie* (1965; 2d ed., 1985)
WMANT	Wissenschaftliche Monographien zum Alten und Neuen Testament

WO	Die Welt des Orients
WuD	Wort und Dienst
WZ	Wissenschaftliche Zeitschrift
ZA	Zeitschrift für Assyriologie
ZÄS	Zeitschrift für Ägyptische Sprache und Altertumskunde
ZAW	Zeitschrift für die alttestamentliche Wissenschaft
ZdZ	Zwischen den Zeiten
ZDPV	Zeitschrift des deutschen Palästina-Vereins
ZRGG	Zeitschrift für Religions- und Geistesgeschichte
ZThK	Zeitschrift für Theologie und Kirche

NOTES

Chapter 1. History, Methodology, and Structure

1. The following offer a historical orientation: L. Diestel, *Geschichte des Alten Testaments in der christlichen Kirche* (1869 and its new printing); H. Karpp, *Das Alte Testament in der Geschichte der Kirche* (1939); R. C. Dentan, *Preface to Old Testament Theology* (2d ed.; New York, 1963); E. G. Kraeling, *The Old Testament since the Reformation* (New York, 1969); J. S. Preus, *From Shadow to Promise: Old Testament Interpretation from Augustine to the Young Luther* (Cambridge, Mass., 1969); R. E. Clements, *One Hundred Years of Old Testament Interpretation* (Philadelphia, 1976); H.-J. Kraus, *Geschichte der historisch-kritischen Erforschung des Alten Testaments* (3d ed., 1982); idem, *Die Biblische Theologie: Ihre Geschichte und Problematik* (1970); W. Zimmerli, "Biblische Theologie. I: Altes Testament," *TRE* 6 (1980), 426–455; John H. Hayes and Frederick C. Prussner, *Old Testament Theology: Its History and Development* (Atlanta, 1985); R. Smend, *Deutsche Alttestamentler in drei Jahrhunderten* (1989); W. H. Schmidt, " 'Theologie des Alten Testaments' vor und nach G. von Rad," *VuF* 17, 1972, 1–25; and J. Scharbert, "Die biblische Theologie und der Suche nach ihrem Wesen und ihrer Methode," *MThZ* 40, 1989, 7–26.

2. Authors and abbreviated titles are used for the following standard works that are often cited:
   E. Sellin, *Theologie des Alten Testaments* (2d ed., 1936) (cited: *Theologie*).
   W. Eichrodt, *Theologie des Alten Testaments.* Teil 1: *Gott und Volk* (8th ed., 1968); idem, Teil 2/3: *Gott und Welt/Gott und Mensch* (7th ed., 1974); ET, *Theology of the Old Testament,* trans. J. A. Baker, OTL; vol. 1 (London and Philadelphia, 1961) [= Teil 1: *Gott und Volk,* 6th ed., 1959]; vol. 2 (London and Philadelphia, 1967) [=Teil 2/3: *Gott und Welt/Gott und Mensch,* 5th ed., 1964]. (Cited: *Theology*).
   L. Köhler, *Theologie des Alten Testaments* (4th ed., 1966) (cited: *Theologie*).
   O. Procksch, *Theologie des Alten Testaments* (1950) (cited: *Theologie*).
   E. Jacob, *Théologie de l'Ancien Testament* (2d ed., 1968) (cited: *Théologie*).
   Th. C. Vriezen, *Theologie des Alten Testaments in Grundzügen* (1956) (cited: *Theologie*).
   G. von Rad, *Theologie des Alten Testaments.* Vol. 1: *Die Theologie der geschichtlichen Überlieferungen Israels* (5th ed., 1966); vol. 2: *Die Theologie der prophetischen Überlieferungen* (4th ed., 1965); ET, *Old Testament Theology,* trans. D. M. G. Stalker; vol. 1: *The Theology of Israel's Historical Traditions* (New York, 1962) [=Band 1: *Die Theologie der geschichtlichen Überlieferungen Israels,* 2d ed., 1957]; vol. 2: *The Theology of Israel's Prophetic Traditions* (New York, 1965) [=Band 2: *Die Theologie der prophetischen Überlieferungen Israels,* 1960]. (Cited: *Theology*).
   H. H. Rowley, *The Faith of Israel* (1956; London, 1965) (cited: *Faith*).
   E. Jacob, *Grundfragen alttestamentlicher Theologie* (1970) (cited: *Grundfragen*).
   G. Fohrer, *Theologische Grundstrukturen des Alten Testaments* (1972) (cited: *Grundstrukturen*).
   A. Deissler, *Die Grundbotschaft des Alten Testaments: Ein theologischer Durchblick* (1972) (cited: *Grundbotschaft*).
   C. Westermann, *Elements of Old Testament Theology,* trans. D. W. Stott (Atlanta, 1982) (cited: *Theology*).

R. E. Clements, *Old Testament Theology: A Fresh Approach* (London, 1978; Atlanta, 1979) (cited: *Theology*).

H. Graf Reventlow, ET, *Problems of Old Testament Theology in the Twentieth Century* (Philadelphia, 1985) (cited: *Problems of Old Testament Theology*).

B. S. Childs, *Old Testament Theology in a Canonical Context* (London and Philadelphia, 1985) (cited: *Theology*).

W. H. Schmidt, *Alttestamentlicher Glaube in seiner Geschichte* (6th ed., 1987) (cited: *Alttestamentlicher Glaube*).

W. Zimmerli, *Grundriss der alttestamentlichen Theologie* (6th ed., 1989) (cited: *Theologie*); ET, *Old Testament Theology in Outline*, trans. D. E. Green (Atlanta, 1978) (cited: *Theology*).

3. For the problem of one's own standards and limits, see in addition E. Gerstenberger, "Der Realitätsbezug alttestamentlicher Exegese," VT Suppl 36, 1985, 132–144; and J. W. Rogerson, "What Does It Mean to Be Human?" in David J. A. Clines et al., eds., *The Bible in Three Dimensions* (JSOT Suppl 87; Sheffield, 1990), 285–298.

4. Cf. G. Ebeling, "Was heisst 'Biblisches Theologie'?" in G. Ebeling, *Wort und Glaube*, vol. 1 (3d ed., 1967), 88 (quotation is abbreviated).

5. Cf. Th. C. Vriezen, *Theologie*, 94.

6. Cf. also O. Procksch, *Theologie*, 19–47.

7. For an examination of the previous period, see J. H. Hayes and F. C. Prussner, *Old Testament Theology*, 5ff.

8. The Latin text is found in J. P. Gabler, *Opuscula academica* 2 (Ulm, 1831), 179–194. The German translation is most easily accessible in G. Strecker, ed., *Das Problem der Theologie des Neuen Testaments* (WdF 267; 1975), 32–44. For an English translation, see Ben Ollenburger, Elmer A. Martens, and Gerhard F. Hasel, *The Flowering of Old Testament Theology* (Winona Lake, Ind., 1992), 489–502. See R. Smend, "Universalismus und Partikularismus in der alttestamentlichen Theologie des 19. Jahrhunderts," *EvTh* 22, 1962, 169–179; idem, "Johann Philipp Gablers Begründung der biblischen Theologie," *EvTh* 22, 1962, 345–357; and M. Saebø, "Johann Philipp Gablers Bedeutung für die biblische Theologie," *ZAW* 99, 1987, 1–16.

9. Chr. F. von Ammon (*Entwurf einer reinen biblischen Theologie*, 1792) was actually still a step behind Gabler.

10. G. L. Bauer, *Theologie des Alten Testaments oder Abriss der religiösen Begriffe der alten Hebräer: Von den ältesten Zeiten bis auf den Anfang der christlichen Epoche.* Zum Gebrauch akademischer Vorlesungen, Leipzig, 1796.

11. G. P. Chr. Kaiser, *Die biblische Theologie, oder Judaismus und Christianismus nach der grammatisch-historischen Interpretation und nach einer freymütigen Stellung in die kritisch-vergleichende Universalgeschichte der Religionen, und die universale Religion.* The title of the work indicates not only that the Old and New Testaments may be separated but also that the general approach of the history of religion may be related to each Testament. At the same time, the Old Testament's thoughts and beliefs, so alien to our own, may be set forth.

12. W. L. M. de Wette, *Biblische Dogmatik Alten und Neuen Testaments. Oder kritische Darstellung der Religionslehre des Hebraismus, des Judenthums und des Urchristentums.* For further information for G. P. Chr. Kaiser and W. L. M. de Wette, see W. Zimmerli, *TRE* 6, 429f.; and J. H. Hayes and F. C. Prussner, *Old Testament Theology*, 91f. and 98f. For de Wette, see R. Smend, *W. M. L. de Wettes Arbeit am Alten und am Neuen Testament* (1958).

13. See R. Smend, "Universalismus und Partikularismus in der alttestamentlichen Theologie des 19. Jahrhunderts."

14. See the brief but instructive discussion in W. Zimmerli, *TRE* 6, 430f. Also note in Zimmerli as well as in J. H. Hayes and F. C. Prussner, *Old Testament Theology* (pp. 92f.) brief outlines of two scholars whose works are passed over here: D. G. C. von Cölln (published posthumously in 1836): and C. P. W. Grambert (1829, 1830).

15. See L. Perlitt, *Vatke und Wellhausen* (BZAW 94; 1965).

16. Cf. W. Zimmerli, *TRE* 6, 433 (see the names of the persons and their works). Cf. B. Stade, *Biblische Theologie des Alten Testaments*, vol. 1 (1905), 22: "The biblical theology of the Old Testament is a science of posthumous works." See also once again J. H. Hayes and F. C. Prussner, *Old Testament Theology*, 103f.

17. R. Smend, *Lehrbuch der alttestamentlichen Religionsgeschichte* (1893; 2d ed., 1899).

18. Cf. the first sentence: "By biblical theology of the Old Testament is meant the history of religion under the old covenant" (B. Stade, *Biblische Theologie des Alten Testaments*, 1/1). The expression "biblical" theology is used because of the connection with the New Testament (ibid., 1/2.5.13; etc.). For more about Stade, see R. Smend, *Deutsche Alttestamentler*, 129f.

19. Cf. for instance: E. König, *Geschichte der Alttestamentlichen Religion* (1912; 3d and 4th eds., 1924); R. Kittel, *Die Religion des Volkes Israel* (1920); G. Hölscher, *Geschichte der israelitischen und jüdischen Religion* (1922); G. Fohrer, *Geschichte der israelitischen Religion* (1969); W. Eichrodt, *Religionsgeschichte Israels* (1969); G. W. Anderson, *The History and Religion of Israel* (1966; Oxford, 1971); H. Ringgren, *Israelitische Religion* (1963; 2d ed., 1982); W. Kornfeld, *Religion und Offenbarung in der Geschichte Israels* (1970); W. H. Schmidt, *Alttestamentlicher Glaube in seiner Geschichte* (1968; 6th ed., 1987). In its first edition (1968), Schmidt's work appeared under the title *Alttestamentlicher Glaube in seiner Umwelt*, and it is perhaps worth noting that it certainly has continued to take on more of the character of a "theology of the Old Testament" in later editions.

20. Cf. the much later work of W. and H. Möller, *Biblische Theologie des Alten Testaments in heilsgeschichtlicher Entwicklung* (1938). This work also takes a salvation history approach. It is conservative, follows largely the sequence of Old Testament texts, and relates them in an often typological manner to New Testament materials.

21. See W. Zimmerli, *TRE* 6, 433–436. For the few, usually not very significant works in Old Testament theology that appear outside Germany in the nineteenth and the beginning of the twentieth century, see J. H. Hayes and F. C. Prussner, *Old Testament Theology*, 123f.

22. For H. Schultz, cf. W. Zimmerli, *TRE* 6, 436f.

23. A typical citation that expresses H. Schultz's view reads: "A devout person of the Old Testament does not need a religious conversion to become a Christian. What is required is only the decisive act of faith, demanded by each prophetic proclamation, and the disposition of repentance, also an unwavering demand by all prophets, who announce the coming of the reign of God" (*Alttestamentliche Theologie*, 5th ed., 37f.).

24. Compare to this, however, the "brief reflection" of A. Jepsen ("Theologie des Alten Testaments: Wandlungen der Formen und Ziele," in *Bericht von der Theologie*, Berlin, 1971, 15–32, esp. 15). W. Eichrodt, during the Bonner Orientalistentag, 1928, lifted up the systematically structured theology of the Old Testament by König as particularly praiseworthy. "E. König stood up (in the discussion) and explained that his theology was not a systematic but rather a strongly historical work. Thereupon Paul Volz, who was presiding, noted that it was a remarkable situation that colleague König had received great praise for his systematic work, but he would not accept it." Jepsen remarks: "In fact, both were correct." The essay by Jepsen is, on the whole, valuable reading.

25. R. Kittel, "Die Zukunft der alttestamentlichen Wissenschaft," *ZAW* 39, 1921, 84–99. For the period of scholarship that was beginning here, see also R. E. Clements, *A Century of Old Testament Study* (Guildford and London, 1976) = *One Hundred Years of Old Testament Interpretation* (Philadelphia, 1976), 118f.

26. O. Eissfeldt, "Israelitisch-jüdische Religionsgeschichte und alttestamentliche Theologie," *ZAW* 44, 1926, 1–12 = *KS* 1 (1962), 105f. This study was taken up yet again and developed in Eissfeldt's *Geschichtliches und Übergeschichtliches im Alten Testament* (1947).

27. For a summary of this investigation, see J. H. Hayes and F. C. Prussner, *Old Testament Theology*, 154f.; and H. Graf Reventlow, *Problems of Old Testament Theology*, 19–43. The content of early dialectical theology is characterized in the collections of essays edited by J. Moltmann, *Anfänge der dialektischen Theologie* 1–2 (TB 17; 1962).

28. Cf. also W. Staerk, "Religionsgeschichte und Religionsphilosophie in ihrer Bedeutung für die biblische Theologie des Alten Testaments," *ZThK* NF 4, 1923, 289–300. C. Steuernagel reached conclusions similar to those of Eissfeldt: "Alttestamentliche Theologie und alttestamentliche Religionsgeschichte," in FS K. Marti (BZAW 41; 1925), 266–273.

29. W. Eichrodt, "Hat die alttestamentliche Theologie noch selbständige Bedeutung innerhalb der alttestamentlichen Wissenschaft?" *ZAW* 47, 1929, 83–91.

30. Cf. K. Johanning, *Der Babel-Bibel-Streit* (1988).

31. Cf. R. Abramowski, "Vom Streit um das Alte Testament," *ThR* NF 3, 1937, 65–93; and H. Graf Reventlow, *Problems of Old Testament Theology*, 16–18, 40–42. See further the sections

devoted to the interpretation and influence of the Old Testament by A. H. J. Gunneweg, *Understanding the Old Testament* (OTL; London and Philadelphia, 1978); and H. D. Preuss, *Das Alte Testament in christlicher Predigt* (1984).

32. The discrepancy between the view of history set forth by historical criticism and that of the Old Testament already had been seen by A. Köhler (*Lehrbuch der biblischen Geschichte des Alten Testaments*, 1875–1893). He sought to think through this matter by proceeding in the direction of the question of the relationship of salvation history and revelation. For him, Old Testament salvation history may only be the history of the revelations of God that are reflected in the consciousness of the Old Testament community! Therefore the history of divine revelation takes place neither beside nor outside the secular history of Israel but rather within it. History may be seen not simply as facts but also as interpretation and appropriation. One may read a similar understanding in the work of J. Köberle (1905 and 1906) (cf. H.-J. Kraus, *Geschichte der historisch-kritischen Erforschung*, 3d ed., 380f.). G. von Rad's later, provocative theses could have received some elucidation from these earlier discussions.

33. G. Fohrer, *History of Israelite Religion*, trans. David E. Green (Nashville, 1972), 23.

34. Eichrodt's three volumes later appeared in two volumes. Volumes 2 and 3 of the first edition were published together. A detailed evaluation of this work, along with the work of G. von Rad (see below), is found in D. G. Spriggs, *Two Old Testament Theologies* (SBT 2d series 30; London, 1974).

35. Foreword to the first edition (also printed along with the later editions). See W. Eichrodt, *Theology*, 1:11.

36. W. Eichrodt wrote in 1953 a "Religionsgeschichte Israels." It first appeared within the larger collection, *Historia Mundi* (vol. 2, pp. 377–448). In 1969 Eichrodt's work reappeared separately in an edited form as Dalp-Taschenbuch Nr. 394D.

37. In my opinion, both of these features hold a distinct advantage over the presentation of G. von Rad.

38. Cf., e.g., L. Köhler, *ThR* NF 7, 1935, 272f.

39. In this regard, see below, chap. 3, n. 219.

40. See above, sec. 2.d.

41. L. Köhler, ET *Old Testament Theology* (London and Philadelphia, 1957). Also cf. Köhler's remarks in *ThR* NF 7, 1935, 255f.; and 8, 1936, 55f., 247f.

42. L. Köhler, *ThR* NF 7, 1935, 272, 276. Cf. the foreword to his *Theologie* (4th ed.), v–vi.

43. H. H. Rowley's structure is similar, although it is more detailed and thus somewhat closer to the Old Testament materials themselves: revelation and the means of revelation, God, humanity, individual and community, ethics, death and afterlife, the day of Yahweh (eschatology). See H. H. Rowley, *Faith* (London, 1956, and later editions).

44. By way of contrast, see J. L. McKenzie, *A Theology of the Old Testament* (Garden City, N.Y., 1974), whose discussion of Israel's experience of God begins with the cult.

45. It is little wonder that the *Theology of the Old Testament* by P. Heinisch (1940), coming from a Roman Catholic perspective, gave a stronger role to dogmatic theology. E.g., here one finds the following main sections: the nature of God, the characteristics of God, preparation for the secret of the trinity (angel, wisdom, word, and name of God), creation, salvation, and the messiah. Another Roman Catholic description is the work by P. van Imschoot (*Théologie de l'Ancien Testament*, vol. 1, Paris, 1954; vol. 2: *Humanity*, 1956). Volume 1 (*God*) appeared in English in 1965 (New York). A third volume (judgment and salvation, and eschatology) was planned but did not appear. It is clear that dogmatics also determined the structure (God, God and the world, revelation, etc.). For additional Catholic works, see J. Scharbert, "Die biblische Theologie," 7f.

46. Weiser, *Die theologische Aufgabe der alttestamentlichen Wissenschaft* (BZAW 66; 1936, 207–224 (= *Glaube und Geschichte im Alten Testament*, 1961, 182f.).

47. See above, sec. 2.a.

48. E. Jacob, *Théologie de l'Ancien Testament* (Neuchâtel and Paris, 1955). The second revised and supplemented edition appeared in 1968. In the foreword to this new edition, E. Jacob describes his position within the debate about Old Testament theology carried on since the appearance of the first edition. He supplements his views on pp. 22–26 by making his own determination as to the place of a theology of the Old Testament within both the other branches

of Old Testament criticism and the other disciplines of theology. He argues that an Old Testament theology should be both systematic and historical.

49. An English translation of E. Jacob's first French edition appeared in 1958: *Theology of the Old Testament* (London and New York). J. Barr has offered his criticism of what he considers to be too much emphasis by E. Jacob on the etymology and derivation of the roots of Hebrew words ("Review of E. Jacob, *Theology of the Old Testament*," *JSS* 5, 1960, 168).

50. The works that appeared in the English-American regions during this pause received attention for the most part at a much later time. See, e.g., M. Burrows, *An Outline of Biblical Theology* (Philadelphia, 1946); and O. J. Baab, *The Theology of the Old Testament* (New York, 1949). For a discussion of both of these works, see J. H. Hayes and F. C. Prussner, *Old Testament Theology*, 192–198. See also H. Graf Reventlow, *Problems of Old Testament Theology*, who provides additional scholarly literature.

51. English translations of the second (1954) and the third (1966) Dutch editions of Th. C. Vriezen's *Theology* appeared in 1958 and 1970 respectively (see *An Outline of Old Testament Theology* [Newton Centre, Mass.: Charles T. Branford Co., 1970]). In contrast to von Rad (see below), the third edition, faced with confirming the unity of the Old Testament, intentionally set forth a synopsis of the Old Testament witnesses.

52. See n. 24 above. See Jepsen, p. 19.

53. Thus W. Zimmerli, *TRE* 6, 442 (in borrowing from G. A. F. Knight).

54. G. von Rad, "Grundprobleme einer biblischen Theologie des Alten Testaments," *ThLZ* 68, 1943, 225–234; and idem, "Kritische Vorarbeiten zu einer Theologie des Alten Testaments," in L. Hennig, ed., *Theologie und Liturgie* (1952), 9–34. Von Rad expanded these critical reflections on method in his "Offene Fragen im Umkreis einer Theologie des Alten Testaments," *ThLZ* 88, 1963, 401–416 (= TB 48, 1973, 289f.); and in his "Antwort auf Conzelmanns Fragen," *EvTh* 24, 1964, 388–394.

55. Cf. once more D. G. Spriggs, *Two Old Testament Theologies*. In addition, see H. Graf Reventlow, *Problems of Old Testament Theology*, 59–65; J. H. Hayes and F. C. Prussner, *Old Testament Theology*, 23ff.; and R. Smend, *Deutsche Alttestamentler*, 226f. See n. 2 above for von Rad.

56. For a discussion, see H. Graf Reventlow, *Problems of Old Testament Theology*, 62, 110–111.

57. Cf. the similar views of G. E. Wright, *God Who Acts: Biblical Theology as Recital* (SBT 8; London, 1952; Naperville, Ill., 1958), and elsewhere. For a discussion of Wright's Old Testament theology, see J. H. Hayes and F. C. Prussner, *Old Testament Theology*, 224f.

58. For a discussion, see the preliminary, methodological reflections at the beginning of part 2 in vol. 1 and the foreword to vol. 2, where von Rad (*Old Testament Theology*) debates his critics.

59. Particularly in G. von Rad, *Wisdom in Israel* (Nashville, 1972), 337f.

60. For a discussion of the problem of salvation history, see H. Graf Reventlow, *Problems of Old Testament Theology*, 87–110.

61. For the proposals that von Rad has offered for addressing these problems, see H. D. Preuss, *Das Alte Testament in christlicher Predigt* (1984); and M. Oeming, *Gesamtbiblische Theologien der Gegenwart* (2d ed., 1987).

62. Zimmerli wrote a friendly review that sought to continue the discussion. This review is recommended reading before as well as after working through von Rad's theology (*VT* 13, 1963, 100–111). F. Baumgärtel wrote a less friendly, even scathing critique (*ThLZ* 86, 1961, 801–816, 895–908).

63. Cf., e.g., F. Hesse, "Kerygma oder geschichtliche Wirklichkeit?" *ZThK* 57, 1960, 17–26; V. Maag, "Historische oder ausserhistorische Begründung alttestamentlicher Theologie?" *SThU* 29, 1959, 6–18; and the discussions by H. Graf Reventlow, *Problems of Old Testament Theology*, 77 (and the literature he cites).

64. In regard to this, see also M. Honecker, "Zum Verständnis der Geschichte in Gerhard von Rads Theologie des Alten Testaments," *EvTh* 23, 1963, 143–168.

65. One should not overlook the fact that the relationship between faith (*kerygma*) and history as well as the juxtaposition of the individual *kerygmata* (proclamations) in von Rad's theology has a certain propinquity to the New Testament theology of Rudolf Bultmann (1948–1953).

66. Cf. C. A. Keller (*ThZ* 14, 1958, 308), cited by W. H. Schmidt, *VuF* 17, 1972, 13 n. 27.

67. Cf. concerning this issue, e.g., John Bright, *The Authority of the Old Testament* (Nashville and New York, 1967); and G. E. Wright, *The Old Testament and Theology* (New York, 1969).
68. G. von Rad, *ThLZ* 88, 1963, esp. 405, n. 3a: "What does Old Testament theology have to do at all with this almost univocally expressed question about "unity" or a "center?"
69. The Old Testament "has no focal-point such as is found in the New" (G. von Rad, *Theology*, 2:362). Cf., however, 2:427: "A theology of the Old Testament will therefore have to do further work upon the question of what is the typical element in Jahwism."
70. Here many things call to mind Herder or even Gunkel.
71. See above, sec. 2.d.
72. Cf. in this regard also J. Strange, "Heilsgeschichte und Geschichte: Ein Aspekt der biblischen Theologie," *SJOT* 2, 1989, 100–113 (+ 136–139); and N. P. Lemche, "Geschichte und Heilsgeschichte: Mehrere Aspekte der biblischen Theologien," *SJOT* 2, 1989, 114–135.
73. See A. Jepsen, n. 24 above, and nn. 60–66 above. In addition, see (only a selection!) H. Graf Reventlow, "Grundfragen alttestamentlicher Theologie im Lichte der neueren deutschen Forschung," *ThZ* 17, 1961, 81–98; Chr. Barth, "Grundprobleme einer Theologie des Alten Testaments," *EvTh* 23, 1963, 342–372; R. C. Dentan, *Preface to Old Testament Theology* (2d ed.; New York, 1963); H.-J. Stroebe, "Überlegungen zur Theologie des Alten Testaments," in H. Graf Reventlow, ed., *Gottes Wort und Gottes Land, FS H.-W. Hertzberg* (1965), 200–220; idem, "Geschichte, Schicksal, Schuld und Glaube," *BBB* 72 (1989), 268f.; G. Fohrer, "Der Mittelpunkt einer Theologie des Alten Testaments," *ThZ* 24, 1968, 161–172; S. Wagner, "Zur Frage nach dem Gegenstand einer Theologie des Alten Testaments," in D. Rossler, ed., *Fides et communicatio*, ES M. Doerne (1970), 391–411; E. Jacob, *Grundfragen;* R. Smend, *Die Mitte des Alten Testaments* ThSt 101; 1970; idem, "Die Mitte des Alten Testaments," *Gesammelte Studien* 1 (1986), 40f.; E. Würthwein, "Zur Theologie des Alten Testaments," *ThR* NF 36, 1971, 185–208; W. Zimmerli, "Alttestamentliche Traditionsgeschichte und Theologie," in H. W. Wolff, ed., *Probleme biblischer Theologie: FS G. von Rad* (1971), 632–647; W. H. Schmidt, "'Theologie des Alten Testaments vor und nach G. von Rad," *VuF* 17, 1972, 1–25; G. F. Hasel, *Old Testament Theology: Basic Issues in the Current Debate* (Grand Rapids, 1972); idem, "Methodology as a Major Problem in the Current Crisis of Old Testament Theology," *BTB* 2, 1972, 177–198; W. Zimmerli, "Erwägungen zur Gestalt einer alttestamentlichen Theologie," *ThLZ* 98, 1973, cols. 81–98; G. F. Hasel, "The Problem of the Center in the Old Testament Debate," *ZAW* 86, 1974, 65–82; E. Osswald, "Theologie des Alten Testaments—Eine bleibende Aufgabe alttestamentlicher Wissenschaft," *ThLZ* 99, 1974, cols. 641–658; C. Westermann, "Zu zwei Theologien des Alten Testaments," *EvTh* 34, 1974, 96–112; W. Zimmerli, "Zum Problem der 'Mitte des Alten Testaments,'" *EvTh* 35, 1975, 97–118; J. Gamberoni, "Theologie des Alten Testaments," *ThG* 66, 1976, 332–342; E. Otto, "Erwägungen zu den Prolegomena einer Theologie des Alten Testaments," *Kairos* NF 19, 1977, 53–72; M. E. Tate, "Old Testament Theology: The Current Situation," *RExp* 74, 1977, 279–300; H. Graf Reventlow, "Basic Problems in Old Testament Theology," *JSOT* 11, 1979, 2–22; R. Martin-Achard, "A propos de la théologie de l'Ancien Testament," *ThZ* 35, 1979, 63–71; A. H. J. Gunneweg, "'Theologie' des Alten Testaments oder 'Biblische Theologie'?" in A. H. J. Gunneweg and O. Kaiser, eds., *Textgemäss: Aufsätze und Beiträge zur Hermeneutik des Alten Testaments, FS E. Würthwein* (1979), 39–46; *Sola Scriptura*, 1983, 227f.; R. Rendtorff, "I principali problemi di una teologia dell' Antico Testamento," *Protest.* 35, 1980, 193–206; G. F. Hasel, "A Decade of Old Testament Theology: Retrospect and Prospect," *ZAW* 93, 1981, 165–183; H. Graf Reventlow, *Problems of Old Testament Theology* (1985); J. A. Soggin, "Den gammaltestamentigla teologin efter G. von Rad," *SEÅ* 47, 1982, 7–20; idem, "Teologia dell' Antico Testamento oggi," *Protest.* 39, 1984, 125–137; idem, *Horizons in Biblical Theology* 6 (1984); P. Höffken, "Anmerkungen zum Thema Biblische Theologie," in M. Oeming and A. Graupner, eds., *Altes Testament und christlicher Verkündigung, FS A. H. J. Gunneweg* (1987), 13–29; H. Graf Reventlow, "Zur Theologie des Alten Testaments," *ThR* NF 52, 1987, 13–29; G. F. Hasel, "Old Testament Theology from 1978–1987," *AUSS* 26, 1988, 133–157; and J. Høgenhaven, *Problems and Prospects of Old Testament Theology* (Sheffield, 1988). Additional literature is mentioned in J. H. Hayes and F. C. Prussner, *Old Testament Theology*, 219f.

74. Brief descriptions of the world of Old Testament faith that investigate Old Testament ideas, without, however, wishing to set forth a "theology of the Old Testament," include E. Jones, *The Greatest Old Testament Words* (London, 1964); and N. H. Snaith, *The Distinctive Ideas of the Old Testament* (New York, 1964).

75. Cf. similarly, A. Deissler, *Grundbotschaft;* and W. H. Schmidt (see below, p. 23).

76. See also the brief sketch by W. Zimmerli in *TRE* 6, 445–454. For a discussion of Zimmerli, see R. Smend, *Deutsche Alttestamentler,* 276f.

77. See the discussion below in sec. 4.

78. There was a kind of "canonization" of Mesopotamian literature developed in the so-called Cassite period. However, this contrasted with the biblical process of canonization in regard to reasons, character, and purpose (see H. Klengel, ed., *Kulturgeschichte des alten Vorderasien,* 1989, 315, 317).

79. In regard to these questions, see several contributions in M. Klopfenstein et al., eds., *Mitte der Schrift? Ein jüdisch-christliches Gespräch* (1987). Also see R. Rendtorff, "Zur Bedeutung des Kanons für eine Theologie des Alten Testaments," in H.-G. Geyer et al., eds., *"Wenn nicht jetzt, wann dann?"* FS H.-J. Kraus (1983), 3–11; and M. Heymel, "Warum gehört die hebräische Bibel in den christlichen Kanon?" *BThZ* 7, 1990, 2–20. For overestimating the importance of the "final form" of Old Testament texts, the critical remarks of H.-J. Hermisson, in E. Blum et al., eds., *Die hebräische Bibel und ihre zweifache Nachgeschichte,* FS R. Rendtorff (1990), should be taken to heart.

80. At this point, it certainly should not be overlooked that the arrangement of the "Christian" Old Testament, as over against the Hebrew Tanak, has not been structured by the Christian church but rather fully (not just in essence) derives from the LXX of (Hellenistic) Judaism. In respect to this, further critical inquiries should be directed to the remarks by E. Brocke, "Von den 'Schriften' zum 'Alten Testament'—und zurück?" in E. Blum et al., eds., *Die hebräische Bibel,* FS R. Rendtorff (1990), 589; see below, p. 22.

81. B. S. Childs, *Introduction to the Old Testament as Scripture* (London and Philadelphia, 1979).

82. Cf. J. A. Emerton, *VT* 36, 1986, 376–378; and G. F. Hasel, *AUSS* 26, 1988, 154. For this matter, see also J. H. Hayes and F. C. Prussner, *Old Testament Theology,* 268–273; and J. Høgenhaven, *Problems and Prospects of Old Testament Theology,* 68f., 83f. A very critical assessment of Childs, which does not, however, go into his Old Testament theology, is found in M. Oeming, *Gesamtbiblische Theologien der Gegenwart* (2d ed., 1987), 186–209.

83. B. S. Childs has summarized briefly his understanding of this issue in his presentation, "Die Bedeutung des Jüdischen Kanons in der alttestamentlichen Theologie," in M. Klopfenstein et al., eds., *Mitte der Schrift?* 269–281. Cf. e.g., his statement on p. 280: "The purpose of an Old Testament theology is to reflect only on this part of the Christian canon, but to do so by regarding it as Christian scripture." Critical of this position is W. E. Lemke, "Is Old Testament Theology an Essentially Christian Theological Discipline?" *HorBiblTheol* 11, 1989, 59–71. Lemke (p. 67) gives the following description of "Old Testament Theology" which necessarily (and rightly so) opposes the corresponding thesis of Childs: "Old Testament Theology is an exegetical and theological discipline which seeks to describe in a coherent and comprehensive manner the Old Testament understanding of God in relationship to humanity and the world." The issue of determining the relationship of the Old Testament to the New Testament is not, in and of itself, necessary to carry out the enterprise of Old Testament theology. Jews also should be able to partake in their own respective tasks.

84. Cf. above, p. 11. See also R. E. Clements and W. C. Kaiser, Jr.

85. This work of E. A. Martens appeared in England under the title *Plot and Purpose in the Old Testament* (Leicester, 1981).

86. Also for these reasons, the work of Martens is to be regarded as significantly different from the more fundamentalist presentation of W. C. Kaiser, Jr. (*Toward an Old Testament Theology,* 5th ed.; Grand Rapids, 1981) which seeks to handle everything under the leading idea of promise.

87. J. Vermeylen (*Le Dieu de la promesse et le Dieu de l'alliance,* Paris, 1986) similarly combines a description of Old Testament Israel's faith in its complexity with a historical delineation (preexile, exile and Persian period, postexile, and Hellenistic period). He also seeks to

discover the possible unanimity or common understandings in the Old Testament. The volume is enriched by discussions of literary sources, witnesses, and redactions as well as theological questions, making it actually a combination of an Old Testament introduction and a history of Israelite-Jewish faith that probes the dominant, theological questions and problems of each particular epoch. This combination is the central problem of the book, but it also, at the same time, provides it its coherence.

88. Cf. the remarks about B. S. Childs earlier in sec. 2.f.

89. Going beyond this position, H. Seebass (Der Gott der ganzen Bibel, 1982, 219 n. 5) has reasoned that an Old Testament theology representing a Christian, theological faculty can scarcely be something other than a biblical theology that includes both Testaments. This is the case, argues Seebass, if Old Testament theology does not wish to be what is in actuality a history of religion. Unfortunately, his own outline of a comprehensive biblical theology demonstrates that, at least for the present time, it is impractical for many reasons to attempt to carry out this program. Nevertheless, one should constructively consider certain points at their appropriate place.

90. The traditiohistorical studies of H. Gese have indeed resulted in important investigations of individual Old Testament traditions and themes (cf., above all, Zur biblischen Theologie, 1977; 3d ed., 1989; and Vom Sinai zum Zion, 1974; 3d ed., 1990). However, his work has not been shaped into a comprehensive description of an Old Testament theology. For a discussion of his work, see, e.g., the first and second volumes of Biblisch-Theologische Studien (1977 and 1978); as well as M. Oeming, Gesamtbiblische Theologien der Gegenwart (2d ed., 1987). Also see J. H. Hayes and F. C. Prussner, Old Testament Theology, 260–264. Some critical questions about the traditiohistorical approach are found in H. D. Preuss, Das Alte Testament in christlicher Predigt (1984), 32, 68f.

91. R. Rendtorff, "Theologie des Alten Testaments—Überlegungen zu einem Neuansatz," NGTT 30, 1989, 132–142.

92. See above, pp. 6f. and 14f.

93. A. H. J. Gunneweg correctly places in question and criticizes such a position. See his Understanding the Old Testament (OTL; London and Philadelphia, 1978), 78.

94. For a different view, see the previous work of F. Baumgärtel, "Erwägungen zur Darstellung der Theologie des Alten Testaments," ThLZ 76, 1951, cols. 257–272. For more contemporary scholars who represent a different view from mine on this issue, see G. F. Hasel (Old Testament Theology) and E. Otto ("Erwägungen zu den Prolegomena einer Theologie des Alten Testaments"). According to Otto, Old Testament theology endeavors to proceed from modern questions concerning the contribution of the Old Testament to the contemporary and salutary form of existence.

95. See W. H. Schmidt, VuF 17, 1972, 22.

96. See the discussion under sec. 4 below.

97. W. Zimmerli, Theology, 12.

98. For comparisons to the ancient Near East, see, above all, the following most important collections of texts: AOT (2d ed.); ANET (3d ed.); RGT (2d ed.); and TUAT. For a general orientation, the following serves well: H. W. Haussig, ed., Wörterbuch der Mythologie, vol. 1: Götter und Mythen im Vorderen Orient (1965; 2d ed., 1985; cited as WdM). See also H. Klengel, ed., Kulturgeschichte des alten Vorderasien (1989). For the entire problem, see C. Westermann, "Sinn und Grenze religionsgeschichtlicher Parallelen," ThLZ 90, 1965, cols. 489–496 (printed also in TB 55, 1974, 84f.). Works that provide an entree into and survey of this field include the following. FOR ANCIENT EGYPT: A. Erman, Die Religion der Ägypter (1934; and more recent printings); S. Morenz, Ägyptische Religion (1960); J. Assmann, Ägypten: Theologie und Frömmigkeit einer frühen Hochkultur (1984); H. Brunner, Grundzüge der altägyptischen Religion (1983; 3d ed., 1989). Also see the following articles: "Ägyptische Religion" (J. Bergman) and Ägypten II: Ägypten und Israel" (R. J. Williams) in TRE 1, 465–492, 492–505 (also see accompanying literature); and M. Görg, "Ägypten," NBL I, cols. 36–49. FOR MESOPOTAMIA: H. W. F. Saggs, Mesopotamien (1966); Th. Jacobsen, The Treasures of Darkness (New Haven and London, 1976); K. Bergerhoff, Mesopotamien und das Volk Gottes (1983); J. Bottéro, Mésopotamie: L'écriture, la raison et les dieux (Paris, 1987); and J. Bot-

téro and S. N. Kramer, *Lorsque les dieux faisaient l'homme: Mythologie mésopotamienne* (Paris, 1989). Also see the articles "Assyrien und Israel" (W. G. Lambert) and "Babylonien und Israel" (W. G. Lambert) in *TRE* 4, 265–277, and *TRE* 5, 67–79 (see accompanying literature); see also *TRE* 5, 79–89, for Babylonian and Assyrian religion (W. von Soden); and W. Röllig and M. Görg, "Babylonien," *NBL* I, cols. 227–233. FOR THE HITTITES: O. R. Gurney, *Die Hethiter* (1969); and E. and H. Klengel, *Die Hethiter* (1970). Also see the article "Hethitische Religion" in *TRE* 15, 290–297 (J. Ebach). FOR SYRIA, CANAAN, and UGARIT: H. Gese, M. Höfner, and K. Rudolph, *Die Religionen Altsyriens, Altarabiens und der Mandäer* (1970) (includes the contribution by H. Gese); D. Kinet, *Ugarit: Geschichte und Kultur einer Stadt in der Umwelt des Alten Testaments* (SBS 104; 1981) and O. Loretz, *Ugarit und die Bibel* (1990). See also the article "Kanaan" in *TRE* 17, 539–556 (F. Stolz), and the accompanying literature. FOR PERSIA: G. Widengren, *Die Religionen Irans* (1965).

99. H. Wildberger, *EvTh* 19, 1959, 77.
100. Ibid, 78.
101. Cf. W. H. Schmidt, *VuF* 17, 1972, 9.
102. W. Zimmerli, *VT* 13, 1963, 105. Cf. S. Wagner, in D. Rossler et al., eds., *Fides et communicatio*, FS M. Doerne, 409.
103. See, above all, G. von Rad, *ThLZ* 88, 1963, col. 405; and idem, *Theology,* 2:362. Nevertheless, even von Rad inquires after representations of the faith "typical of Yahwism" (*Theology,* 2:428; cf. *ThLZ* 88, 1963, col. 406).
104. In this regard, cf. the works by R. Smend ("Die Mitte des Alten Testaments"); G. F. Hasel (*Old Testament Theology*); J. Høgenhaven (*Problems and Prospects of Old Testament Theology*); J. H. Hayes and F. C. Prussner, *Old Testament Theology,* 257–260; and H. Graf Reventlow, *Problems of Old Testament Theology,* 125–133.
105. In this regard, see R. Smend, "Die Mitte des Alten Testaments," *Gesammelte Studien* 1 (1986), 57ff.
106. D. H. Odendall wishes to renew this attempt ("Covenant—the Centre of the Old Testament?" *NGTT* 30, 1989, 143–151).
107. Accordingly, see S. Terrien, *The Elusive Presence: Toward a New Biblical Theology* (San Francisco, 1978).
108. Cf. also in regard to this W. S. Prinsloo, *The Theology of the Book of Joel* (BZAW 163; 1985), 1f.
109. See, e.g., K. Barth, *KD* I/1, 334ff.
110. See, e.g., W. Zimmerli, *Theologie* (6th ed.), 123. Cf. Eng. ed., *Theology,* 141.
111. This is formulated in a similar way by K. Schwarzwäller, *Das Alte Testament in Christus* (Th St 84; 1966), 55: Salvation history is the "history of God's self-disclosure."
112. One rejoices in the fact that one now has Jewish conversation partners who have entered the discussion about the "center of the Old Testament." Cf. the collection of essays, M. Klopfenstein et al., eds., *Mitte der Schrift? Ein jüdisch-christliches Gespräch* (1987); and E. Brocke, "Von den 'Schriften' zum 'Alten Testament'—und zurück?" in E. Blum et al., eds., *Die hebräische Bibel,* FS R. Rendtorff (1990), 581–594. It is Brocke's opinion that the search for a center of the Old Testament may not be an exegetical or a methodological problem but rather a "Christian-existential" one (p. 584). This opinion, however, has already been brought into question by the Jewish contributions in the above-mentioned collection. E.g., the Jewish interest in determining a center is clear from the emphasis given to the Torah as the most important corpus of texts within the Tanak. This view derives from the value and placement of the Torah within the Tanak as a whole.
113. C. Westermann, *Elements of Old Testament Theology,* 9.
114. R. Smend, "Die Bundesformel," 23 (= *Gesammelte Studien* 1, 1986, 55).
115. See, above all, S. Herrmann, "Die konstruktive Restauration: Das Deuteronomium als Mitte biblischer Theologie," in H. W. Wolff, ed., *Probleme biblischer Theologie,* FS G. von Rad (1971), 155–170. Cf. also A. Deissler, *Grundbotschaft,* 91f.
116. See p. 15 and n. 73 above.
117. Cf. the discussion below in chap. 3.5.

118. W. H. Schmidt, *VuF* 17, 1972, 12 (n. 25).
119. W. H. Schmidt, *Das erste Gebot* (ThEx 165; 1969); and idem, *Alttestamentlicher Glaube in seiner Geschichte* (6th ed.); etc.
120. "This expression received classic formulation especially in Judaism" (see in this regard the critical survey of R. Smend, "Die Mitte des Alten Testaments," *Gesammelte Studien* 1 (1986), 63ff.).
121. W. Dietrich, "Der rote Faden im Alten Testament," *EvTh* 49, 1989, 232–250.
122. The same may be said for the effort by H. Spieckermann to point to the characteristics of God mentioned in the formula in Exod. 34:6, including its prehistory and dissemination throughout the Hebrew Bible, as the center for Old Testament theology ("Barmherzig und gnädig ist der Herr . . . ," *ZAW* 102, 1990, 1–18). One especially needs to explain how it was, e.g., that Israel came to know that Yahweh is "compassionate."
123. Cf. J. W. Rogerson, "What Does It Mean to Be Human?" (n. 3 above).
124. Ibid., 298.
125. M. Oeming (*Gesamtbiblische Theologien der Gegenwart,* 2d ed., 1987, 139f.) has discussed the degree to which von Rad's understanding of history was influenced by the circle of W. Pannenberg (*Revelation as History,* trans. D. Granskou; New York, 1968).
126. In agreement with R. Martin-Achard ("A propos de la théologie de l'Ancien Testament").
127. In this regard, see R. Rendtorff, "Geschichte und Überlieferung," in R. Rendtorff and K. Koch, eds., *Studien zur Theologie der alttestamentlichen Überlieferungen,* FS G. von Rad (1961), 81–94 (= TB 57, 1975, 25ff.).
128. So H.-J. Stoebe, "Überlegungen zur Theologie des Alten Testament," 203.
129. Cf. the similar view of E. Jacob, *Grundfragen,* 41.
130. Cf. G. von Rad, *Theology,* 2:425: "Ancient Israel found something of importance for herself expressed in [the election]."
131. Thus A. Soete, *Ethos der Rettung—Ethos der Gerechtigkeit* (1987), 41.
132. Cf. H.-J. Hermisson, "Zur Erwählung Israels," in H. Schroer, ed., *In Memoriam Gerhard Krause* (1984), 37–66. He says on p. 37: "The theme of the "election of Israel" belongs to the central expressions of Old Testament theology. One could even see in this theme the (or, more precisely, a) center of the Old Testament." However, he then remarks on p. 39: "It is already a rule of good taste that one should not seek to comprehend the entire Old Testament under it" (i.e., election). As everyone would agree, one cannot debate what may be a matter of "taste."
133. R. Smend, "Die Mitte des Alten Testaments," 55 (= *Gesammelte Studien* 1, 1986, 81).
134. For an analysis of this question, although with different emphases, see R. Smend, "Theologie im Alten Testament," in E. Jungel et al., eds., *Verifikationen,* FS G. Ebeling (1982), 11–26 (= "Die Mitte des Alten Testaments" *Gesammelte Studien* 1, 1986, 104ff.).
135. In this regard, see J. Blenkinsopp, "Old Testament Theology and the Jewish-Christian Connection," *JSOT* 28, 1984, 3–15; cf. also W. Dietrich, *EvTh* 49, 1989, 249.
136. Cf. B. S. Childs, *Theology,* 8f.
137. For a different understanding, see, above all, A. H. J. Gunneweg ("'Theologie' des Alten Testaments oder 'Biblische Theologie'?"); cf., however, in addition, M. E. Tate ("Old Testament Theology: The Current Situation").
138. Cf. also H. Strauss, "Theologie des Alten Testaments als Bestandteil einer biblischen Theologie," *BN* 24, 1984, 125–137.
139. Cf. the similar views of H. Wildberger, "Auf dem Wege zu einer biblischen Theologie," *EvTh* 19, 1959, 70–90.
140. Cf. also G. von Rad, TB 8 (3d ed., 1965), 136: "The Yahwistic faith of the Old Testament is election faith, i.e., primarily salvation faith."
141. "The open-ended character of introductory questions swings the door wide open to a radical restructuring of Old Testament theology" (B. Seidel, WZ Halle 38/1989, [1], 81).
142. E.g., Deuteronomistic influence on Isaiah 6 or Isaiah 1–32.
143. K. Koch, *Die Profeten,* vol. 1 (2d ed., 1987), 120. Cf. ET, *The Prophets,* vol. 1: *The Assyrian Period,* trans. Margaret Kohl (Philadelphia, 1983).
144. Cf. the important statement of S. Herrmann, "Die Abwertung des Alten Testaments als Geschichtsquelle: Bemerkungen zu einem geistesgeschichtlichen Problem," appearing in *Sola Scriptura,* Kongressband Theologenkongress Dresden, 1990.

Chapter 2. The Old Testament's Statements about Election

1. The literature includes: K. Galling, *Die Erwählungstraditionen Israels* (BZAW 48; 1928); M. Buber, "Die Erwählung Israels" (1938), in Buber's *Werke*, vol. 2 (Schriften zur Bibel; 1964), 1037–1051; Th. C. Vriezen, *Die Erwählung Israels nach dem Alten Testament* (AThANT 24; 1953); K. Koch, "Zur Geschichte der Erwählungsvorstellung in Israel," *ZAW* 67, 1955, 205–226; H. Wildberger, *Jahwes Eigentumsvolk* (AThANT 37; 1960); H. H. Rowley, *The Biblical Doctrine of Election* (1950; 2d ed., London, 1964); H.-J. Zobel, "Ursprung und Verwurzelung des Erwählungsglaubens Israels," *ThLZ* 93, 1968, cols. 1–12; H. Wildberger, "Die Neuinterpretation des Erwählungsglaubens Israels in der Krise der Exilszeit," in H.-J. Stoebe et al., eds., *Wort, Gebot, Glaube,* FS W. Eichrodt (1970), 307–324 (= TB 66, 1979, 192ff.); idem, "בחר *bḥr* erwählen," *THAT* 1, cols. 275–300; H. Seebass, "בחר *bḥr*," *ThWAT* 1, cols. 592–608; idem, "Erwählung. I: Altes Testament," *TRE* 10, 1982, 182–189 (literature); H.-J. Hermisson, "Zur Erwählung Israels." FS G. Krause, 1982, 37–66; and G. Braulik, "Erwählung (Altes Testament)," *NBL* I, cols. 582f. Cf. also L. Köhler, *Theologie* (4th ed.), 65–67; E. Jacob, *Théologie,* 163ff.; R. E. Clements, *Theology,* 87ff.; W. Zimmerli, *Theology,* 43–48; and W. H. Schmidt, *Alttestamentlicher Glaube* (6th ed.), 134ff.
2. See above, p. 24.
3. Cf. in this regard J. Scharbert, " 'Erwählung' im Alten Testament im Licht von Gen 12, 1–3," in *Dynamik im Wort,* FS KBW (1983), 13–33.
4. Cf. *THAT* 1 and *ThWAT* 1 (see n. 1 above).
5. *AHw* 1, col. 407.
6. Cf. K. Koch, *EKL* (1st ed.), vol. 3, col. 268.
7. So, e.g., G. von Rad, *Theology,* 1:178.
8. Cf. in this regard H. H. Rowley, *The Biblical Doctrine of Election,* 95ff.
9. Cf. Vol. II, 10.1.
10. The Priestly document later on places its emphasis on Noah's piety (Gen. 6:9 and 7:1b).
11. Cf. Vol. II, 14.6.
12. Cf. O. Bächli, "Die Erwählung des Geringen im Alten Testament," *ThZ* 22, 1966, 385–395.
13. Cf. the evidence in *THAT* 1, col. 281; and *ThWAT* 1, col. 593.
14. Cf. T. Veijola, *Verheissung in der Krise* (Helsinki, 1982).
15. Cf. W. Eichrodt (*Theology,* 1:53) for Israel's self-awareness of election, grounded already in the destiny of the ancestors. Cf. also B. S. Childs, *Theology,* 93ff.
16. According to Isa. 19:25, also a later addition, Yahweh even calls Egypt "my people." Amos 9:14 is also a later addition.
17. Cf. Vol. II, chap. 6.
18. "What was this but an act of election" (G. von Rad, *Theology,* 1:7; cf. 1:166).
19. Cf. more about this below, chap. 3.5.
20. Cf. Th. C. Vriezen, *Erwählung.*
21. This "knowing" clearly means here "to elect"; cf. 2 Sam. 7:20; Jer. 1:5; and Exod. 33:17b.
22. H. Seebass (*ThWAT* 4, col. 593) states: "Moreover, this certainly expresses a simple understanding of election that, for instance, also occurs in Gen. 24:7 (Abraham); Josh. 24:3 (your father); 1 Kings 11:32 (Jeroboam I); Jer. 43:10 (Nebuchadrezzar at the conquest of Egypt); Hag. 2:23 (Zerubbabel); 2 Sam. 7:8; 2 Chron. 17:7; Ps. 78:79 (David); and Num. 3:12, 41, 45; 8:16, 18 (Levites)."
23. "Holy" is used to refer only to persons, not to things, in the Old Testament.
24. In the last passage, the ל = *l* points to affiliation (cf. *GK,* no. 129).
25. Cf. the discussion of this text below, chap. 3.5.a.
26. H. Seebass, *ThWAT* 1, col. 603.
27. See Vol. II, chap. 8.
28. See Vol. II, 10.1.
29. In this regard, see H. D. Preuss, *Deuteronomium* (EdF 164; 1982), 182ff.; and R. Rendtorff, "Die Erwählung Israels als Thema der deuteronomischen Theologie," in J. Jeremias and L. Perlitt, eds., *Die Botschaft und die Boten,* FS H. W. Wolff (1981).
30. "There is certainly no conscious recognition that this is a new theological insight now to be proclaimed; rather, it points to a previous understanding of the relationship between Yahweh and Israel" (H.-J. Hermisson, "Zur Erwählung Israels," 43).

31. Th. C. Vriezen, *Die Erwählung Israels,* 51; and H. Wildberger, *THAT* 1, col. 285.

32. H.-J. Hermisson, "Zur Erwählung Israels," 47: ("and that can only mean to come back to an exclusive relationship with Yahweh and away from the nations").

33. Both R. Rendtorff ("Die Erwählung Israels als Thema der deuteronomischen Theologie," 77f.) and H.-J. Hermisson ("Zur Erwählung Israels," 43) refer to Deut. 32:8f. (LXX) in order to point to this possible prehistory. Rendtorff also refers to Psalm 82.

34. Cf. Vol. II, chap. 8. For this formula, see H. Seebass, *ThWAT* 1, cols. 599f., and *TRE* 10, 183f. H. Spieckermann appears to want to derive the thoughts about election entirely from the "sphere of temple theology" (*Heilsgegenwart,* FRLANT 148, 1989, 148f.).

35. Th. C. Vriezen, *Die Erwählung Israels,* 47.

36. H. Wildberger, *THAT* 1, cols. 288f. For Deuteronomy as the "center" of the Old Testament, see the preceding discussion.

37. Deut. 4:37; 7:13; and 23:6; cf. Isa. 43:4 and 48:14.

38. H.-J. Hermisson, "Zur Erwählung Israels," 57.

39. See Vol. II, chap. 15.

40. See Vol. II, 15.7.

41. Cf. H. Wildberger, "Neuinterpretation."

42. See Vol. II, 14.6.

43. See below, chap. 3.8.

44. See G. Braulik, "Das Deuteronomium und die Geburt des Monotheismus," in his *Studien zur Theologie des Deuteronomiums* (SBAB 2; 1988), 257–300.

45. "The Chronicler uses the verb בחר = *bāḥar* without literary precedent eleven times: but the objects of this divine election are the king, the place for the cult and the tribe of Levi. The term was never employed in this way in earlier times. However, to the Chronicler these specific acts of election were more important than the one act of the election of Israel" (G. von Rad, *Theology,* 1:352–353; cf. 1 Chron. 15:2; 28:4; 2 Chron. 7:12, 16; 12:13; 29:11; and 33:7). However, could one say that, for the Chronicler, the "election of Israel" was a presupposed topos, a current conception that he now wanted to make more specific?

46. For the postexilic period, see esp. H. Wildberger, *THAT* 1, cols. 293–297.

47. See below, chap. 3.1, 2.

48. See Vol. II, chap. 6.

49. See below, chap. 3.3.b. and pp. 143f.

50. See below, chap. 3.9.a.

51. "Instead of a theogony or 'kratogony' to speak of the origin of the forms and concentrations of power, there appears an *ethnogony* under the defining feature of divine election" (K. Koch, "Qädäm: Heilsgeschichte als mythische Urzeit im Alten [und Neuen] Testament," in J. Rohls and G. Wenz, eds., *Vernunft des Glaubens: Wissenschaftliche Theologie und kirchliche Lehre,* FS W. Pannenberg (1988), 253–288; citation from 285).

52. See below, chap. 3.2.

53. See now K.-F. Pohlmann, *Die Ferne Gottes—Studien zum Jeremiabuch* (BZAW 179; 1989), 113f.

54. K. Galling, *Erwählungstraditionen,* 93 (with reference to J. Hempel).

55. Cf. Vol. II, chap. 14.

56. Cf. the grounds in Ps. 89:34f.; Isa. 14:24; and 45:5–7, although these do not make direct reference to "election."

57. According to G. von Rad (*Theology,* 2:424), the relationship between history that is believed and history that is "real" hinges on this question.

58. For the question of a "covenant," see below, chap. 3, n. 219.

Chapter 3. The Election and Obligation of the People

1. In agreement with R. Smend, "Der Auszug aus Ägypten: Bekenntnis und Geschichte," in *Zur ältesten Geschichte Israels* (*Gesammelte Studien* 2; 1987), 27–44. For the question about a pre-Israelite Yahwism and a YHWH before the exodus, which is possibly reflected even in some Old Testament texts, see the "new paradigm" by J. C. de Moor, *The Rise of Yahwism*

(BETL 91; 1990), 221 and passim. This study is somewhat fanciful and offers some trouble-some suggestions concerning dates. Also see below, the so-called Kenite hypothesis (chap. 4.1.a.).

2. See K. Galling, *Die Erwählungstraditionen Israels* (BZAW 48; 1928), 5–26; H. Lubsczyk, *Der Auszug Israels aus Ägypten* (1963); G. Fohrer, *Überlieferung und Geschichte des Exo-dus* (BZAW 91; 1964); A. F. Lenssen, *Der Auszug aus Ägypten im Zeugnis der Bibel* (1966); G. J. Botterweck, "Israels Errettung im Wunder am Meer," *BuL* 8 (1967), 8–33; E. W. Nichol-son, *Exodus and Sinai in History and Tradition* (Oxford, 1973); P. Weimar, *Untersuchungen zur priesterschriftlichen Exodusgeschichte* (1973); W. Gross, "Die Herausführungsformel," *ZAW* 86, 1974, 425–453; P. Weimar and E. Zenger, *Exodus: Geschichten und Geschichte der Befreiung Israels* (SBS 75; 1975); S. I. L. Norin, *Er spaltete das Meer: Die Auszugsüber-lieferung in Psalmen und Kult des alten Israel* (CB OT 9; Lund, 1977); M. A. Klopfenstein, "Auszug, Wüste, Gottesberg," in B. Rothenberg, ed., *Sinai* (1979), 17–31; J. L. Ska, *Le pas-sage de la mer* (AnBib 109; Rome, 1986); R. Smend, "Der Auszug aus Ägypten," 27–44; the thematic volume *Exodus, ein Paradigma mit bleibender Wirkung, Conc* (D), 23, 1987, vol. 1; and M. Görg, "Exodus," *NBL* I, cols. 631–636. Also see E. Jenni, "יצא *ys'* hinausgehen," *THAT* 1, cols. 755–761; G. Wehmeier, "עלה *'lh* hinaufgehen," *THAT* 2, cols. 272–290; H. D. Preuss, "יצא *yāṣā'*," *ThWAT* 3, cols. 795–822; and H. F. Fuhs, "עלה *'ālāh*," *ThWAT* 6, cols. 84–105. Cf. also H. H. Rowley, *Faith*, 40ff.; G. von Rad, *Theology*, 1:175–179; W. Zimmerli, *Theology*, 21–27, 43–48; and W. H. Schmidt, *Alttestamentlicher Glaube* (6th ed.), 36ff.

3. Exod. 13:22 (20f. = redactional?); 14:5, (6?), (7?), 9aα, 10bα, (11–12?), 13, 14, 19β, 20, 21 aβ, 24*, 25(b), 27aβb, 30, (31?a?). For a German translation of this reconstructed text, see R. Smend, "Der Auszug aus Ägypten," 38f. I continue to think that the best case can be made for placing the Yahwist within the time of the Davidic and Solomonic empire (i.e., ca. 950 B.C.E.). For this dating, I follow the arguments by L. Schmidt (*EvTh* 37, 1977, 230–247); W. H. Schmidt (*BZ* NF 25, 1981, 82–102); and H. Seebass (*TRE* 16, 441–451). Also see the more detailed work of K. Berge, *Die Zeit des Jahwisten* (BZAW 186; 1990).

4. It must be stressed that there is not another setting in the history of Israel that is appropriate for this song. The terse language and the fact that neither the place nor the time needs to be mentioned suggest that the song belongs to this literary and historical context. For a different view, see P. Weimar and E. Zenger, *Exodus*, 71ff. They argue that the song originates in Jerusalem during the early period of David's rule.

5. "All true, living confession, however, occurs in *one* sentence" (*Praise and Lament in the Psalms*, trans. Keith R. Crim and Richard N. Soulen [Atlanta, 1981], 107).

6. The Song of Moses (Exod. 15:1–18) is a later text that develops more fully the brief song in Exod. 15:21. This later text already has in view the journey from Egypt to Zion (v. 17).

7. The historical questions associated with the exodus are described and discussed in detail in P. Weimar and E. Zenger, *Exodus*, 100–138.

8. Exod. (13:20?); 14:1, 2*, 3, 4, 8*, 9a b, 10abβ, 15–18, 21b, 22–23, 26, 27aα, 28–29. R. Smend provides a German translation of this reconstructed text ("Der Auszug aus Ägypten," 39f.). A third possible source, in addition to J and P, that mentions a "flight" may be found in Exod. (13:17–19?); 14:5a (6??), 19a, 25a. These verses are occasionally attributed to the E frag-ments. In addition, the texts that speak about the "fear of God" are often attributed to a par-ticular source (Exod. 14:24ab, 25a, 27b, 28b).

9. For the background and problems of the numerical data (600,000 men without wives and chil-dren, etc.), cf. G. Beer, HAT I/3, 68f.

10. *TUAT* I/6, 544ff.

11. Cf. below, sec. 7.

12. For more precise details, see the descriptions in the various "histories of Israel" (H. Donner, A. H. J. Gunneweg, S. Herrmann).

13. Cf. below, sec. 5.a.

14. "The so-called historical texts of the Bible are not actually historical texts. The Yahweh faith exercised much more in these texts a surprising freedom. This faith gave individual historical acts now and again their deepest meaning for a particular situation by attributing them to Yah-weh." Thus, P. Weimar and E. Zenger, *Exodus*, 95.

15. See the forced interpretation by I. Willi-Plein (*Das Buch vom Auszug*, vol. 2: *Moses*, 1988,

90): "The water driven by the wind could not flow over the high west bank and therefore was diverted along both sides, moving to the north and the south."

16. Cf. below, pp. 44, 210f., 217f.
17. Cf. F. Kohata, *Die Endredaktion (R^P) der Meerwundererzählung* (AJBI 14; 1988), 10–37.
18. Cf. F. A. Spina, "Israelites as *gērîm,* 'Sojourners,' in Social and Historical Context," in C. L. Meyers and M. O'Connor, eds., FS D. N. Freedman (Winona Lake, Ind., 1983), 321–335.
19. This occurs thirteen times in the Old Testament, often in Deuteronomistic texts (e.g., Deut. 5:6; 6:12; 7:8; 8:14; 13:6, 11; Jer. 34:13). Cf. *ThWAT* 3, cols. 805, 814 (with secondary literature).
20. Cf. Vol. II, 15.3.
21. Cf. Vol. II, 13.4.
22. Cf. H. D. Preuss, *Deuterojesaja: Eine Einführung in seine Botschaft* (1976), 42–45; K. Kiesow, *Exodustexte im Jesajabuch* (OBO 24; 1979); H. Simian-Yofre, "Esodo in Deutero-isaias," *Bibl* 61, 1980, 530–553; E. Zenger, "Der Gott des Exodus in der Botschaft der Propheten—am Beispiel des Jesajabuches," *Conc* (D) 23, 1987, 15–22; and H. M. Barstad, *A Way in the Wilderness* (JSS Mon. 12; Manchester, 1989).
23. Cf. below, chap. 4.6.d.
24. Exod. 3:20; Judg. 6:13; Neh. 9:17; Pss. 78:11f.; and 106:7, 21f. Then Deut. 4:34; 6:22; 7:19; 26:8; and 29:2 (מוֹפֵת [*môphēt,* "wonder"] and אוֹת [*'ôt,* "sign"]; cf. the articles in *THAT* and *ThWAT*).
25. Exod. 34:10; Jer. 21:2; Micah 7:15; Pss. 9:2; 26:7; 40:6; 71:17; 72:18; 86:10; 96:3; 105:2, 5; 107; 111:4ff.; 136:4; and 145:5. The understanding is characteristically different in the Book of Job: Job 9:10; cf. 5:8f.; and 37:5, 14, 16.
26. D. Conrad, *ThWAT* 6, col. 578. See there the article "פלא *pl'* " and the literature on the theme "Wunder im Alten Testament."
27. Cf. Vol. II, 15.3. For the exodus in the ancient legal texts, see also n. 56 below (and the literature listed).
28. Cf. H. D. Preuss, *Deuteronomium* (EdF 164; 1982), 187f.
29. F. Crüsemann, "Der Exodus als Heiligung," in E. Blum et al., eds., *Die hebräische Bibel,* FS R. Rendtorff (1990), 117–129. What follows is related to this essay.
30. See J. A. Soggin, "Kultätiologische Sagen und Katechese im Hexateuch," *VT* 10, 1960, 341–347 (= *O. T. and Oriental Studies,* Rome, 1975, 72ff.); N. Lohfink, *Das Hauptgebot* (AnBibl 20; 1963), 113ff.; and J. Loza, "Les catéchèses étiologiques dans l'Ancien Testament," *RB* 78, 1971, 481–500.
31. Exod. 10:2; 12:27; 13:8; Deut. 4:9ff.; 6:7–20; 11:19ff.; 32:7; and Josh. 4:6, 21.
32. Thus, e.g., according to J. Scharbert, "Das 'Schilfmeerwunder' in den Texten des Alten Testaments," in M. Carrez et al., eds., *De la Torah au Messie,* FS H. Cazelles (AOAT 212; 1981), 395–417.
33. Cf. Pss. 18:15f.; 66:5ff.; 68:7ff.; 74:12f.; 77: (6ff.?), 16ff.; 78:12f., 43ff.; 80:6ff.; 81:11; 89:11; 103:7; 105:23, 37f., 43; 106:9f., 21; 114; 135:8f.; 136:10ff.; cf. Exod. 15:4ff.; Isa. 63:12f.; Jer. 32:20f.; Nahum 1:4; Hab. 3:8; Neh. 9:9–11, 18; and Dan. 9:15. See J. Kühlewein, *Geschichte in den Psalmen* (1973); and E. Haglund, *Historical Motifs in the Psalms* (CB OT 23; Malmö, 1984). Further, see S. I. L. Norin, *Er spaltete das Meer.*
34. For Isa. 63:7–64:11, see I. Fischer, *Wo ist Jahwe? Das Volksklagelied Jes 63,7–64,11 als Ausdruck des Ringens um eine gebrochene Beziehung* (SBB 19; 1989).
35. For more on Psalm 114, see below, sec. 2.
36. S. I. L. Norin, *Er spaltete das Meer,* 171ff.
37. Cf., e.g., Exod. 3:8, 17 (J); Jer. 2:6; Hos. 2:17; Amos 9:7; Ps. 81:11; and Josh. 24:17 (predeuteronomistic). Amos 3:1 is redactional, while Amos 2:10 is Deuteronomistic.
38. Nehemiah 9 is here, however, dependent on Exod. 32:4, 8; and 1 Kings 12:28.
39. Exodus 3:11 indicates that in earlier texts Moses also can be the subject of the verb for "leading out" (cf. Exod. 32:1, 7, 23; 33:1). However, these latter texts make it clear that it is Moses, not Yahweh, who "led out" Israel.
40. This usage is entirely missing, e.g., in First Isaiah, Hosea, Amos, Micah, Nahum, Habakkuk, and Zephaniah. For more exact information, see the articles in *THAT* and *ThWAT* mentioned in n. 2 above.

41. H. F. Fuhs, *ThWAT* 6, col. 97.
42. For the following, cf. the literature listed in n. 2 above, and especially the works by H. Lubsczyk and A. F. Lenssen. Further, see S. Herrmann's article, "Exodusmotiv. I: Altes Testament," *TRE* 10, 732–737 (and the literature).
43. Exod. 13:9; 16:1; 18:1; 20:2; 29:46 (P); 32:4, 8, 11; Lev. 11:45; 19:36; 22:33; 25:38; 26:13, 45; Num. 15:41; 23:22; 24:8; Deut. 4:20; 5:6; 6:12, 21; 7:8; 8:14; 29:24 (and many other places in Deuteronomy); Josh. 24:6, 17; Judg. 2:12; 6:8; 1 Sam. 8:8; 10:18; 12:6, 8; 1 Kings 8:16, 21, 51, 53; 9:9; 12:28; 2 Kings 17:7, 36; Jer. 2:6; 16:14; 32:20f.; Dan. 9:15; Amos 2:10; Neh. 9:18; etc. Cf. Ps. 81:11. Therefore, predominantly either in passages influenced by Deuteronomistic language and thought or in later texts.
44. Judg. 19:30; 1 Sam. 8:8; 2 Sam. 7:6 ("since the time when I . . . "); cf. Deut. 9:7; 1 Kings 6:1; 2 Kings 21:15; and Jer. 7:25. Cf. the remarks about P above, pp. 42f.
45. Cf. once more the corresponding articles in *THAT* and *ThWAT*.
46. K. Elliger, BK XI/1, 151.
47. Deut. 7:8; 9:26; 13:6; 15:15; 21:8; 24:18 (nowhere else in the Hexateuch!); 2 Sam. 7:23; Jer. 15:21; 31:11(?).
48. Deut. 7:8; and 9:26. For the other cases (not combined with פדה = *pādâ*, "redeem"), cf. H. D. Preuss, *Deuteronomium* (EdF 164; 1982), 187.
49. Deut. 6:12; 7:6ff.; 8:14 (and often in Deuteronomy); Hos. 2:10, 22; 11:3; 12:10; 13:4; Micah 6:6–8; 7:8–20; Amos 3:1f.; Pss. 105:37–41; 114:1–8; and 136:10–16.
50. Hos. 11:1ff.; 13:4; Exod. 20:2f. (= parallel); Deut. 6:14; 7:4; 13:6, 11; and often (also in the Deuteronomistic literature).
51. Cf. the preamble of the Decalogue; Amos 3:1f.; Hos. 12:7, 9, 15; and Micah 6:4f. Cf. also 1 Kings 8:9; 2 Kings 21:8; Ezek. 20:10f.; Pss. 81:6; and 105:43–45.
52. Hos. 12:10; Amos 2:10; Deut. 6:10–12, 15; and 8:6–10. Cf. already Exod. 3:8; 34:10 (J); and Exod. 13:17 (E?).
53. Amos 3:1f.; and Micah 6:3f. Cf. the "murmuring stories" in Exodus and Numbers, and, in addition, 1 Sam. 8:7ff.; and 10:17f. Also cf. 1 Sam. 15:1ff.; 2 Sam. 7:5f.; and 1 Kings 12:28.
54. Amos 2:6–10; 3:1f.; Hos. 2:4ff.; 7:15f.; 11:1ff.; 12:10; 13:1ff.; Micah 6:5; Jer. 2:4ff.; and 11:1ff.
55. Hos. 2:16; 11:5; 12:10, 13f.; Amos 9:7, 9f.; and Micah 6:13ff.
56. Lev. 19:33f., 35f.; 25:35ff.; Deut. 6:12, 21, 23; 7:8, 19; 8:6–16, 17b; 10:19; 13:6, 11; 15:15; 16:1, 3, 6; 23:5, 8; 24:18, 22; 25:17; 26:8; Hos. 2:10, 13; 11:5; 12:10f., 12; 13:4a, 11; Amos 2:8; 3:1, 12, 14; 9:1, 7, 8; Micah 6:6f., 13ff.; Jer. 7:21ff.; and often. Cf. also Exod. 22:20; and 23:9, 15. See J. Pons, "La référence au séjour en Egypte et à la sortie d'Egypte dans les Codes de Loi de l'Ancien Testament," *ETR* 63, 1988, 169–182.
57. Cf. Vol. II, 13.4.
58. It is once again striking that none of these references is found in First Isaiah.
59. Cf. Ezek. 20:13ff., 34ff.; also Jer. 2:4ff.
60. Thus with H. Spieckermann, *Heilsgegenwart* (FRLANT 148; 1989), 150f., who on pp. 150–157 offers an engaging interpretation of Psalm 114.
61. The citations are from H. Spieckermann, *Heilsgegenwart,* 151, 155, 157.
62. Cf. above, p. 44.
63. Cf. *TRE* 14, 713–718 (literature).
64. For the angel, tent, and countenance, cf. below, chap. 5.3 and chap. 4.4.b, c.
65. For the scholarly discussion (with literature), cf. H. D. Preuss, *Deuteronomium,* 144–147; S. Kreuzer, *Die Frühgeschichte Israels in Bekenntnis und Verkündigung des Alten Testaments* (BZAW 178; 1989); and D. R. Daniels, VT Suppl 41, 1990, 231–242.
66. For the function of the exodus tradition in the Psalms, see above, p. 45.
67. Cf. J. Kegler, "Das Zurücktreten der Exodustradition in den Chronikbüchern," in R. Albertz et al., eds., *Schöpfung und Befreiung,* FS C. Westermann (1989), 54–66.
68. Compare 2 Chron. 3:2 with 1 Kings 6:1; Solomon's prayer in 2 Chronicles 6:24–29 drops 1 Kings 8:51–53, which refers to the exodus; 2 Kings 21:10–16 is absent in 2 Chron. 33:10–17, as are 1 Kings 12:28 and 2 Kings 21:15. 2 Kings 17:7, 36 is missing in Chronicles, which is probably due to the precursor's reference to the Northern Kingdom.
69. J. Kegler, "Das Zurücktreten der Exodustradition in den Chronikbüchern," 64.

70. Cf. the survey provided above in chap. 2, and, in addition, Vol. II, chaps. 7 and 8.
71. Cf. W. Zimmerli, *Theologie* (6th ed.), 19.
72. Following the translation by G. Braulik (German Ecumenical Version). E. Brunner-Traut
    (*Frühformen des Erkennens*, 1990) points out that in ancient Egyptian society the individual
    was the constitutive entity, not the larger family or the tribe (pp. 82f.). "The individual was
    not a member of a communal whole" (p. 84).
73. See L. Rost, "Die Bezeichnungen für Land und Volk im Alten Testament," in *Das kleine
    Credo* (1965), 76–101; H. W. Wolff, "Volksgemeinde und Glaubensgemeinde im Alten
    Bund," *EvTh* 9, 1949/1950, 65–82; H. W. Hertzberg, *Werdende Kirche im Alten Testament*
    (ThEx NF 20; 1950); F. Maass, "Wandlungen der Gemeindeauffassung in Israel und Juda,"
    ThViat 2, 1950, 16–32; W. Eichrodt, *Israel in der Weissagung des Alten Testament* (1951);
    H.- J. Kraus, *Das Volk Gottes im Alten Testament* (1958); O. Bächli, *Israel und die Völker*
    (AThANT 41; 1962) [concerning Deuteronomy]; N. A. Dahl, *Das Volk Gottes* (2d ed., 1963);
    C. Westermann, "God and His People: The Church in the Old Testament," *Interp* 17, 1963,
    259–270; N. Lohfink, "Beobachtungen zur Geschichte des Ausdrucks יהוה עם," in H. W.
    Wolff, ed., *Probleme biblischer Theologie*, FS G. von Rad (1971), 275–305; idem, "Unsere
    grossen Wörter" (1977), 111–126 ("Gottesvolk"); G. Chr. Macholz, "Das Verständnis des
    Gottesvolkes im Alten Testament," in W. Eckert et al., eds., *Jüdisches Volk—Gelobtes Land*
    (1971), 169–187; N. Füglistre, "Strukturen der alttestamentlichen Ekklesiologie," *Mysterium
    Salutis* IV/1, 1972, 23–99; J. J. Stamm, "Wandlungen in der Gestalt der Gemeinde nach dem
    Alten Testament," *EMM* 117, 1973, 31–39; idem, *Judentum und Kirche: Volk Gottes* (Theol-
    ogische Berichte, vol. 3, 1974); H.-J. Zobel, "Das Selbstverständnis Israels nach dem Alten
    Testament," *ZAW* 85, 1973, 281–294; J. Schreiner, ed., *Unterwegs zur Kirche: Alttesta-
    mentliche Konzeptionen* (1987); and J. Høgenhaven, *Gott und Volk bei Jesaja: Eine Unter-
    suchung zur biblischen Theologie* (1988). In addition, see A. R. Hulst, "גּוֹי/עַם *'am/gôy* Volk,"
    THAT 2, cols. 290–325; R. E. Clements, "גּוֹי *gôy*," *ThWAT* 1, cols. 965–973; and E. Lipiński,
    "עַם *'am*," *ThWAT* 6, cols. 177–194; cf. also R. E. Clements, *Theology*, 79ff. See J. Golding-
    gay's diachronic study of the Old Testament's different presentations of the people of God,
    from a migrating clan, to a theocratic people, to a state, to a remnant, to a community of hope
    (*Theological Diversity and the Authority of the Old Testament*, Grand Rapids, 1987, 59ff.).
74. It is, nevertheless, striking that the combination "YHWH, the God of Israel" occurs for the
    first time in Exod. 5:1 (then again in Exod. 24:10) and not at all in Genesis or in Exodus 1–4.
75. Cf. Vol. II, chaps. 10 and 14.
76. See Exod. 1:6f. Whether the ancestor was given the name "Israel" is debated. The thesis that
    it was is especially represented by H. Seebass, *Der Erzvater Israel und die Einführung der
    Jahweverehrung in Kanaan* (BZAW 98; 1966).
77. The possibility of Israel's being only a small group at the time of its origins could also explain
    why there are scarcely any archaeological traces of this group migrating into Canaan. There
    is very little archaeological evidence for an Israelite "conquest." See in regard to this I. Finkel-
    stein, *The Archaeology of the Israelite Settlement* (Jerusalem and Leiden, 1988); V. Fritz,
    "Conquest or Settlement? The Early Iron Age in Palestine," *BA* 50/2, 1987, 84–100; and M.
    Weinfeld, "Historical Facts behind the Israelite Settlement Pattern," *VT* 38, 1988, 324–332.
78. L. Rost, "Die Bezeichnungen für Land und Volk im Alten Testament," 89.
79. See the data provided in *ThWAT* 6, col. 185.
80. אלהים(ה) עם (*'am [hā]'ĕlōhîm*, "people of God") occurs only in Judg. 20:2 and 2 Sam. 14:13;
    otherwise always יהוה עם (*'am yahweh*, "people of YHWH"). Cf. N. Lohfink, in H. W. Wolff,
    ed., *Probleme biblischer Theologie*, FS G. von Rad (1971), 276. See in this essay's notes the
    complete listing of the 359 occurrences.
81. Cf. the expression כְמוֹשׁ עם (*'am kĕmôš* = "people of Chemosh") in Num. 21:29. J. C. de Moor
    discusses whether one finds the "people of YHWH" already in the Egyptian texts that men-
    tion the Shashu bedouin (see below, chap. 4.1.a.).
82. For the evidence found in the contexts of intercessory prayer (outside the Psalter), see N.
    Lohfink, in H. W. Wolff, ed., *Probleme biblischer Theologie*, 291, n. 59.
83. 1 Kings 8:16, 30, 33, 34, 36 (2), 38, 41, 43, 44, 50, 51, 52, 56, 59, and 66.
84. "More than two-thirds of all instances of יהוה עם = *'am yahweh* ("people of YHWH") occur

in Yahweh speeches, speeches in the name of Yahweh, or prayers addressed to Yahweh. The expression belongs mainly to the context of dialogue between Yahweh and Israel, and less so to the situation of speaking about Israel" (N. Lohfink, in H. W. Wolff, ed., *Probleme biblischer Theologie*, 280).

85. For these prayers, cf. H. D. Preuss, *Deuteronomium* (EdF 164; 1982), 24, 82, 103, 141, 146f., and 184f.
86. See the data in N. Lohfink, in H. W. Wolff, ed., *Probleme biblischer Theologie*, 283f., n. 36.
87. E. Lipiński, *ThWAT* 6, col. 187.
88. Cf. below, sec. 5.c. In speaking of the origin of the covenant formula, R. Smend has pointed out that it derives from the expression יהוה עם = *'am yahweh* ("people of YHWH"; *Die Bundesformel* ThSt 68; 1963 [= "Die Mitte des Alten Testaments," *Gesammelte Studien*, I, 1986, 11ff.]. Also see N. Lohfink, in H. W. Wolff, ed., *Probleme biblischer Theologie*, 296ff.).
89. N. Lohfink, ibid., 302.
90. The LXX translates עם (*'am*) with λαός (*laos*), and גוי (*gôy*) with ἔθνος (*ethnos*).
91. See *ThWAT* 1, cols. 970f.
92. According to A. Cody, "When Is the Chosen People Called a Gôy?" *VT* 14, 1964, 1–6, this is especially the case when Israel is placed over against the nations (cf., e.g., Gen. 12:2; 18:18; and Deut. 9:14), or something is stressed that the other nations also have.
93. In this connection the reference is not insignificant, for "people" is not a term that is used in the ancient Near Eastern cultures surrounding Israel at that time. "The conception of people and a theology of history are entirely foreign to the ancient Near East" (W. von Soden, *TRE* 5, 82; and idem, *Denken und Begriffsbildung im Alten Orient*, 1974, 35f.). See *ThWAT* 6, col. 189.
94. Deut. 4:20; 9:26, 29; 1 Kings 8:51, 53; Isa. 47:6; 63:17; Joel 2:17; 4:2; Micah 7:14, 18; Pss. 28:9; 74:2; 78:62, 71; 94:5, 14; and 106:5, 40. Cf. also Exod. 34:9. Earlier evidence is probably found in Deut. 32:8f. For a later discussion, see below, sec. 9.c.
95. A. R. Hulst, *THAT* 2, col. 314.
96. The Holiness Code does not specifically call Israel a "holy *people*" but rather addresses them as "holy ones" (cf., e.g., Lev. 19:2; 20:26). For this, cf. H. F. Fuhs, "Heiliges Volk Gottes," in J. Schreiner, ed., *Unterwegs zur Kirche* (see above, n. 73), 143–167.
97. Cf. above, pp. 45f.
98. See G. Gerleman, "ישראל *yiśrā'ēl Israel*," *THAT* 1, cols. 782–785; H.-J. Zobel, "ישראל *yiśrā'ēl*," *ThWAT* 3, cols. 986–1012 (see the literature); R. Albertz, "Israel. I: Altes Testament," *TRE* 16, 368–379 (cf. the literature); and O. Margalith, "On the Origin and Antiquity of the Name 'Israel,' " *ZAW* 102, 1990, 225–237.
99. Cf. the mention of an "Israel" on the stele of Pharaoh Merneptah; cf. above, pp. 41f.
100. Cf. above, sec. 3.d. and p. 75.
101. E.g., in Ugarit and Ebla; cf. *THAT* 1, col. 782; *ThWAT* 3, col. 988; and *TRE* 16, 369.
102. Cf. H.-J. Zobel, *ThWAT* 3, cols. 988ff.; and R. Albertz, *TRE* 16, 369f.
103. For the problem of the "unifying bond" of this association of tribes ("amphictyony"?), see below, sec. 3.e.
104. R. Albertz, *TRE* 16, 370.
105. H.-J. Zobel, *ThWAT* 3, col. 998.
106. For the linguistic usage of the prophets, cf. L. Rost, *Israel bei den Propheten* (BWANT 71; 1937) and H.-J. Zobel, *ThWAT* 3, cols. 992f., 1006ff.; see also the following note.
107. For the use of "Israel" in Isaiah, cf. also J. Høgenhaven, *Gott und Volk bei Jesaja*, 5ff. (also see on pp. 20ff. "Israel" in Hosea, Amos, and Micah).
108. For the "ecclesiology" of Deuteronomy and the Deuteronomistic History, cf. F.- L. Hossfeld, "Volk Gottes als 'Versammlung,' " in J. Schreiner, ed., *Unterwegs zur Kirche*, 123–142 (esp. 128ff.).
109. For the very differentiated usages of ישראל = *yiśrā'ēl* ("Israel"), יהודה = *yĕhûdâ* ("Judah"), גולה = *gôlâ* ("exiles"), and עם (*'am*, "people") in the books of Ezra, Nehemiah (and Chronicles), see, above all, H. C. M. Vogt, *Studie zur nachexilischen Gemeinde in Esra und Nehemia* (1966).
110. Cf. the informative survey by H.-J. Zobel, *ThWAT* 3, cols. 1003–1011.
111. Cf. Vol. II, 12.3.

286

Notes to Chapter 3

112. R. Albertz, *TRE* 16, 371.
113. Cf. below, pp. 83f. and 89; and Vol. II, chap. 12.
114. W. Eichrodt, *Israel in der Weissagung des Alten Testaments* (1951), 21.
115. Cf. the significance of the genealogies in the Old Testament and the study of these by M. Oeming, *Das wahre Israel* (BWANT 128; 1990), 9f.
116. See L. Rost, *Die Vorstufen von Kirche und Synagoge im Alten Testament* (BWANT 76; 1938), although see also W. Schrage, *ZThK* 60, 1963, 178–202; H.-P. Müller, "קהל *qāhāl* Versammlung," *THAT* 2, cols. 609–619; J. Milgrom, H. Ringgren, and H.-J. Fabry, "עדה *'edāh*," *ThWAT* 5, cols. 1079–1093; F.-L. Hossfeld, E.-M. Kindl, and H.-J. Fabry, "קהל *qāhāl*," *ThWAT* 6, cols. 1204–1222; and F.-L. Hossfeld, "Volk Gottes als 'Versammlung,' " 108.
117. For the law of the community in Deut. 23:2–9, cf. H. D. Preuss, *Deuteronomium* (EdF 164; 1982), 142f. (literature); also see *THAT* 2, col. 615, and *ThWAT* 6, cols. 1211f.
118. For the occurrences in Chronicles, cf. F.-L. Hossfeld, *ThWAT* 6, cols. 1215ff.
119. F.-L. Hossfeld, *ThWAT* 6, col. 1214. For קהל (*qāhāl*) and עדה (*'ēdâ*) in P, cf. also K. Elliger, HAT I/4, 1966, 70 (along with footnotes 20f.).
120. F.-L. Hossfeld, *ThWAT* 6, col. 1215.
121. See below, chap. 5.3.
122. For עדה = *'ēdâ* ("congregation"), cf. also Num. 32:2, 12, 13; Josh. 18:1; 20:6, 9; and 22:12, 16ff., 20, 30.
123. "The preexilic period knows of a nation but not a 'church.' In the prophetic period the idea of a 'church' begins to take shape and to detach itself from that of a nation. In the post-prophetic period, the idea of a 'church' not only appears alongside that of a nation but also comes to receive greater prominence" (O. Eissfeldt, "Volk und 'Kirche' im Alten Testament," in his *Geschichtliches und Übergeschichtliches im Alten Testament,* 1947, 10; see pp. 9–23 for the entire essay).
124. Cf. below, sec. 5.b.
125. J. Hausmann, *Israels Rest* (BWANT 124; 1987), 123–125.
126. Cf. Vol. II, 14.8.
127. Pss. 9:10, 19; 10:8, 14, 18; 12:6; 14:6; 22:25; 35:10; 37:14; 40:18; 49:3; 69:34; 70:6; 74:21; 86:1; 107:41; 109:22, 31; 140:13; and Ps. 35:20. For the "poor" in the Psalms, see H.-J. Kraus, BK XV/1, 108–111.
128. For the night visions in Zechariah, cf. H.-G. Schöttler, *Gott inmitten seines Volkes: Die Neuordnung des Gottesvolkes nach Sach 1–6* (TThSt 43; 1987).
129. According to F. Maass, "neglecting circumcision (Gen. 17:14), profaning the Sabbath (Num. 15:32–36), blaspheming God (Lev. 24:10–16), sacrificing at unholy places (Lev. 17:9), failing to observe the Passover festival (Num. 9:13) and the fasts of propitiation (Lev. 23:29), the consumption of blood (Lev. 7:27), etc., are to be punished by death in accordance with the law." The community "exists by reason of its faithfulness to the law" (*ThViat* 2, 1950, 28).
130. Cf. L. Köhler, *Theologie* (4th ed.), 48: "The nation is neither a census of its citizens nor the mathematical calculation of its size. Rather, the nation is represented by any number of citizens." Cf. H. W. Wolff, *EvTh* 9, 1949/1950, 73f.
131. Cf. Vol. II, chap. 15.
132. M. Noth, *Das System der zwölf Stämme Israels* (BWANT IV/1; 1930, reprinted 1966). For additional scholarly literature, see O Bächli, *Amphiktyonie im Alten Testament,* (1977). Cf. the continuing discussions that are both critical and supportive of this thesis: M. Metzger, "Probleme der Frühgeschichte Israels," *VuF* 22, 1977, 30–43, with accompanying literature; R. Smend, "Zur Frage der altisraelitischen Amphiktyonie," *EvTh* 31, 1971, 623–630 (= "Zur ältesten Geschichte Israels," *Gesammelte Studien* 2, 1987, 210ff.); A. H. J. Gunneweg, *Geschichte Israels* (6th ed., 1989), 45–54; and W. H. Schmidt, *Alttestamentlicher Glaube* (6th ed.), 124ff. An instructive survey of the more recent scholarship concerning these issues is provided by J. D. Martin, "Israel as a Tribal Society," in R. E. Clements, ed., *The World of Ancient Israel* (Cambridge, 1989), 95–117.
133. So G. Fohrer in his comprehensive critique of the hypothesis of an amphictyony: "Altes Testament—'Amphiktyonie' und 'Bund'?" *ThLZ* 91, 1966, cols. 801–816, 893–904 (= BZAW 115; 1969, 84ff., esp. 90f.). Cf. also his study in *ZAW* 100, Supplement, 1988, 244–248.

134. The question as to whether there was the same kind of "amphictyony" elsewhere in the ancient Near East is discussed by O. Bächli, *Amphiktyonie im Alten Testament,* 33–41.
135. As a consequence of what R. Smend calls the "ubiquity of the amphictyony" (*EvTh* 31, 1971, 628), additional hypotheses have sought to find their footing on this foundational hypothesis. We shall not go into a discussion of these since they are even more uncertain than the basic hypothesis itself. These additional hypotheses, among others, include: amphictyonic officials, amyphictyonic proclamations of law, YHWH war as a cultic act of the amphictyony, amphictyonic festivals, etc.
136. Cf. below, chap. 5.2.
137. Judges 20:27b is generally regarded as an addition. However, cf. below, chap. 5, n. 23.
138. G. Fohrer, BZAW 115, 98.
139. Thus H.-J. Zobel, *Stammespruch und Geschichte* (BZAW 95; 1965), 84f.
140. Cf. F. Maass, *ThViat* 2, 1950, 18: "This continuing encounter with Yahweh, that did not necessarily occur within the cult but could also occur outside of it, delayed the disintegration of the nation."
141. Thus with O. Eissfeldt, "Der geschichtliche Hintergrund der Erzählung von Gibeas Schandtat," in A. Weiser, ed., *Festschrift Georg Beer* (1935), 19–40 (= *KS* 2, 1963, 64ff.); and K.-D. Schunck, *Benjamin* (BZAW 86; 1963), 57ff.
142. G. Fohrer, BZAW 115, 100ff.
143. Ibid., 102.
144. So with S. Herrmann, *A History of Israel in Old Testament Times,* rev. ed., trans. John Bowden (London and Philadelphia, 1981).
145. For the problem of the secular tribe of Levi, cf. Vol. II, 9.3.
146. Cf. H.-J. Zobel, "Zusammenschlüsse von Stämmen in der vorstaatlichen Zeit Israels," *Theologische Versuche* XIV, 1985, 29–37. He tries to demonstrate the existence of a large number of groupings of Israelite tribes in the period prior to state formation. However, he also argues that one finds in the term "Israel" something approaching a totality of tribes prior to state formation who were developing a collective awareness of unity. "Israel" certainly emphasizes this union of tribes in the premonarchial period, although, as Judges 5 demonstrates, still in a not fully developed form (p. 34).
147. Cf. above, sec. 3.b.
148. Cf. above, secs. 3.a and 9.a; in addition, cf. the various presentations of the history of ancient Israel (H. Donner; A. H. J. Gunneweg; and S. Herrmann [see above, n. 144]).
149. Cf. A. H. J. Gunneweg, *Geschichte Israels* (6th ed., 1989), 34–44.
150. Cf. the survey in the thematic collection "Anfänge Israels," in the journal *Bibel und Kirche* (1983, no. 2). See the contributions by N. Lohfink, H. Engel, and H.-W. Jüngling (with literature). Cf. also R. Albertz, "Israel. I: Altes Testament" *TRE* 16, 368–379, esp. 374f.; and the collection of texts, *Ethnologische Texte zum Alten Testament,* vol. 1 (1989).
151. Did this provide the so-called "minor judges" their function (Judg. 3:31; 10:1–5; 12:8–15)?
152. H.-J. Zobel, "Das Selbstverständnis Israels nach dem Alten Testament," *ZAW* 85, 1973, 281–294. Zobel (p. 281) writes that, in spite of the significance that the event of the exodus and the exodus tradition assumed in Israel, it is rather amazing "that no one has undertaken to use them as the basis to elucidate what is distinctive to Israel." Cf., however, H. D. Preuss, *Jahweglaube und Zukunftserwartung* (BWANT 87; 1968), chap. 1, and the present outline of a "theology of the Old Testament."
153. See H. D. Preuss, " . . . ich will mit dir sein!" *ZAW* 80, 1968, 139–173; and *ThWAT* 1, cols. 485–500. Also R. Winling, *RScRel* 51, 1977, 89–139; and M. Görg, *ThG* 70, 1980, 214–240. Cf. also Vol. II, 6.5.
154. See below, chap. 4.3.
155. For אֵל (*'ēl*) in this context, see *ThWAT* 3, cols. 817f. with literature. Here, a non-Israelite speaks. For the Balaam speeches, see H.-J. Zobel, in E. Blum et al., eds., *Die hebräische Bibel,* FS R. Rendtorff (1990), 141–154.
156. Although it is not sustained throughout, see the Old Testament's differentiation between the two (below, chap. 4.4.g).
157. H.-J. Zobel, *ZAW* 85, 1973, 286. Concerning this point, see also H. W. Wolff's essay "Gottesglaube und Selbstverständnis Altisraels," in his volume *Wegweisung* (1965), 54–77.

158. G. von Rad, *ThLZ* 88, 1963, col. 405; and idem, *Theology*, 1:119.
159. Cf. above, chap. 2.3.
160. See H. W. Robinson, "The Hebrew Conception of Corporate Personality," (BZAW 66; 1936), 49–62; W. Eichrodt, *Krisis der Gemeinschaft in Israel* (1953); J. Scharbert, *Solidarität in Segen und Fluch im Alten Testament und in seiner Umwelt* (BBB 14; 1958); L. Wächter, *Gemeinschaft und Einzelner im Judentum* (1959; 1961); J. de Fraine, *Adam und seine Nachkommen* (1962); and H. W. Wolff, *Anthropologie des Alten Testaments* (1973) 309–320. See also W. Eichrodt, *Theology*, 2:231–267; L. Köhler, *Theologie* (4th ed.), 149–154; Th. C. Vriezen, *Theologie*, 181–188; and H. H. Rowley, *Faith*, 99ff.
161. Cf. Vol. II, 15.7.
162. The expression "corporate personality" is often used to capture this understanding. Cf. H. W. Robinson and especially the detailed discussion of J. de Fraine (see n. 160 above).
163. See H. Seidel, *Das Erlebnis der Einsamkeit im Alten Testament* (1969).
164. Cf. Vol. II, 12. 3.
165. "My God" occurs some 130 times in the Old Testament. See, e.g., Pss. 3:8; 5:3; 18:3; 22:2, 11; 25:2; 31:15; 63:2; 68:25; 84:4; 89:27; 91:2; 102:25; 118:28; and 140:7. Also see Exod. 15:2; Isa. 40:27; Jer. 31:18; etc. For a discussion, see O. Eissfeldt, " 'Mein Gott' im Alten Testament," *ZAW* 61, 1945–1948, 3–16 (= *KS* 3, 1966, 35ff.). Cf. also R. Albertz, *Persönliche Frömmigkeit und offizielle Religion* (1978); and H. Vorländer, *Mein Gott* (AOAT 23; 1975). The two last-named authors certainly stress too much the distinction between personal piety and official religion. While Albertz makes the necessary acknowledgment of the "pluralism of religious interiority," the distinction between personal piety and official religion derives, not so much from the Old Testament, but more from being imposed upon it from the outside. See, e.g., Deuteronomy's or Hosea's polemics against the piety of the people.
166. Cf. J. Scharbert, "Unsere Sünden und die Sünden unserer Väter," *BZ*, NF 2, 1958, 14–26; and idem, *Solidarität in Segen und Fluch im Alten Testament*.
167. F. Baumgärtel judges things differently, *Die Eigenart der alttestamentlichen Frömmigkeit* (1932). Cf., however, H. van Oyen, *Ethik des Alten Testaments* (1967), 159: "Individualism is a product of the enlightenment and liberalism and could not at all come into consideration in the ancient world."
168. So R. Knierim, *Die Hauptbegriffe für Sünde im Alten Testament* (1965), passim; and others.
169. It should remain here an open question as to whether this feeling of solidarity could or ought to be regarded as a nomadic legacy.
170. J. Hempel, *Das Ethos des Alten Testaments* (BZAW 67; 2d ed., 1964), 34. Also see his discussion of "collectivism and individualism" on pp. 32–67 and 93.
171. K. Elliger, "Das Gesetz Leviticus 18" (*ZAW* 67, 1955, 1–25 = TB 32, 1966, 232ff.), has shown that Leviticus 18 has in view an Israelite extended family where, in the normal situation, four generations lived together.
172. For the function of genealogies in the Old Testament, see n. 115 above.
173. Cf. Vol. II, 11.1.d.
174. In response to David's intercession, YHWH "repented" of the evil that he had intended yet to do (2 Sam. 24:16ff.).
175. Cf. Vol. II, 6.5.
176. Cf. Vol. II, 11.7.d.
177. Cf. J. Scharbert, *Solidarität in Segen und Fluch*, 113ff.; and J. Hempel, *Das Ethos des Alten Testaments*, 46ff.
178. According to H. Ringgren (*ThWAT* 1, col. 14): "This contradiction actually is never resolved in the Old Testament." See the entire article on אָב (*'āb*) in cols. 1–19.
179. Cf. Vol. II, 7.7 and 15.7. For this matter, also see M. Saebø, "Vom Individuellen zum Kollektiven," in R. Albertz et al., eds., *Schöpfung und Befreiung*, FS C. Westermann (1989), 116–125.
180. W. Eichrodt, *Theology*, 2:265.
181. For a discussion of this tradition and its various problems, see W. H. Schmidt, *Exodus, Sinai und Mose* (EdF 191; 1983), 71–90; idem, *Alttestamentlicher Glaube* (6th ed.), 46ff.; P. Maiberger, "סִינַי *sinay*," *ThWAT* 5, cols. 819–838; and J. van Seters, "Comparing Scripture with Scripture: Some Observations on the Sinai Pericope of Exodus 19–24," in G. M. Tucker

et al., eds., *Canon, Theology, and Old Testament Interpretation,* FS B. S. Childs (Philadelphia, 1988), 111–130. Cf. also G. von Rad, *Theology,* 1:187–279; B. S. Childs, *Theology,* 53ff.; W. Zimmerli, *Theology,* 48–58; and S. Terrien, *The Elusive Presence* (New York, 1978), 106ff. In addition to these literary-critical and redactional evaluations, see T. B. Dozeman, *God on the Mountain* (SBL MS 37; Atlanta, 1989).

182. See H. Utzschneider, *Das Heiligtum und das Gesetz* (OBO 77; 1988).

183. For this, see below, sec. 8.a.

184. "To be elected implies special responsibility. It does not merely mean to be loved" (Th. C. Vriezen, *Theology,* 167). Cf. H. H. Rowley, *The Biblical Doctrine of Election* (2d ed., 1964), 43, 45.

185. See, above all, E. Zenger, *Die Sinaitheophanie* (1971; idem, *Israel am Sinai* (1982) (this includes a discussion of Rᴾ as the editor of the entire unit of Exod. 19:25–20:21); and L. Perlitt, *Bundestheologie im Alten Testament* (WMANT 36; 1969), 232ff.

186. See J. Halbe, *Das Privilegrecht Jahwes Ex 34,10–26* (FRLANT 114; 1975).

187. Concerning these units, see also Chr. Hinz, "Feuer und Wolke im Exodus," *EvTh* 27, 1967, 76–109 (esp. 91ff., which culminates, to be sure, in a critical conversation with J. Moltmann).

188. What follows continues the insights of Zenger (cf. n. 185 above).

189. Cf. the "broken covenant": Lev. 26:15; Num. 15:31; Deut. 17:2; 31:16, 20; Josh. 7:11, 15; 23:16; Judg. 2:20; 2 Kings 18:12; Isa. 24:5; Jer. 11:10; 34:18; Hos. 6:7; and 8:1. Also cf. Deut. 29:24; 1 Kings 11:10; 2 Kings 17:15; Jer. 22:9; and Ps. 78:10, 37.

190. W. Zimmerli, TB 19, 215f.; see L. Perlitt, *Bundestheologie,* 233.

191. For the theology of the *kābôd* ("glory"), see below, chap. 4.4.d. P. Weimar offers detailed analysis of the Priestly Sinai texts and their relationship to Genesis 1 and Genesis 6–9* (P) in his essay "Sinai und Schöpfung," *RB* 95, 1988, 337–385.

192. A cipher for the exile?

193. U. Struppe, *Die Herrlichkeit Jahwes in der Priesterschrift* (ÖBS 9; 1988), 27.

194. Cf. M. Noth, *Das zweite Buch Mose (Exodus)* (ATD 5) for this passage.

195. Cf. further Vol. II, chap. 13.

196. For this, see also H.-J. Zobel, "Der frühe Jahwe-Glaube in der Spannung von Wüste und Kulturland," *ZAW* 101, 1989, 342–365. Zobel (pp. 346f.) indicates that the ancient descriptions of the theophany of YHWH are formed independently of any Canaanite model. "The reason for this is probably that the appearance of God in the Old Testament always accompanies the process of divine revelation. Accordingly, this special character of Israelite Yahwistic faith as a revealed religion is there from the start. This characteristic feature is underscored by the Sinai theophany standing at the beginning. Sinai may be described as the birth of the relationship not only of Yahweh with Israel but also of Israel with Yahweh."

197. Above all, see L. Perlitt, *Bundestheologie,* 167–181.

198. With L. Perlitt, *Bundestheologie,* 178.

199. For the "ascending" of YHWH (the mountain is thus not his dwelling place!), see Gen. 11:5, 7; 18:21; Exod. 3:8; and Num. 11:17. Cf. below, chap. 5.1.

200. L. Perlitt, *Bundestheologie,* 235.

201. Cf. Gen. 31:22; 34:25; 40:19f.; Josh. 1:11; 3:2; and Hos. 6:2. E. Zenger sees the third day as "a turning point in the chain of events" (*Israel am Sinai,* 1982, 181).

202. Exodus 19:9b, possibly a later interpretation, classifies the theophany as an "answer." According to P. Welten ("Gott Israels—Gott vom Sinai," *BThZ* 1, 1984, 225–239, esp. 233f.), this interpretation of the theophany of Sinai, introduced in Exod. 19:19b, is significant for understanding the personality and exclusivity of YHWH.

203. E. Zenger makes the improbable argument that Exod. 33:18, 21a, 22; and 34:6–8, 29–31* should be attached here (*Sinaitheophanie,* 101).

204. E. Zenger, *Sinaitheophanie,* 158.

205. An overview of scholarly opinion is found in E. Zenger, *Sinaitheophanie,* 13ff.; and W. H. Schmidt, EdF 191, 71–90.

206. For this, see H. D. Preuss, *Deuteronomium* (EdF 164; 1982), 145–147, 236f. (and literature). G. von Rad (*Theology,* 1:121–125) classifies this as an ancient text and as the kernel of the Hexateuch.

207. For this, cf. below, sec. 7.
208. YHWH's "word of promise (Exodus 3f.; 6), act of deliverance (Exodus 14f.), and help of those in distress (Exodus 15–17) precede the giving of the law (Exodus 20ff.); the legislation and orders for life do not need to create the community, for these are its inevitable consequences" (W. H. Schmidt, *Alttestamentlicher Glaube,* 6th ed., 46).
209. Following S. Mowinckel (*Le décalogue,* Paris, 1927), above all, G. von Rad, "Das formgeschichtliche Problem des Hexateuch (1938)," TB 8 (3d ed., 1965), 9–86 (esp. 20ff.).
210. So esp. W. Beyerlin, *Herkunft und Geschichte der ältesten Sinaitraditionen* (1961); cf., however, also M. Weinfeld, *ThWAT* 1, cols. 794ff.
211. Cf. W. H. Schmidt, *Exodus, Sinai und Mose,* 106–109 (and literature). This thesis was important for O. Procksch, *Theologie,* 94ff.
212. Cf. again W. H. Schmidt, *Exodus, Sinai und Mose,* 79–82 (and literature); and P. Maiberger, "סיני *sinay,*" *ThWAT* 5, cols. 819–838 (according to him, Sinai was certainly located in the vicinity of Kadesh).
213. Cf. S. Herrmann, "Sinai," *BHHW* 3, cols. 1801f., and the map found in cols. 1803f.
214. See there the (deliberate?) association of סיני = *sinay* ("Sinai") and סנה *sĕneh* ("thornbush"). Cf. P. Maiberger, "Dornbusch," *NBL* I, cols. 440f.
215. See W. H. Schmidt, *Exodus, Sinai und Mose,* 44; BK II/1, 145; and L. E. Axelsson, *The Lord Rose Up from Seir* (CB OT 25; Stockholm (Lund?), 1987). For different emphases, see J. C. de Moor, *The Rise of Yahwism* (BETL 91; 1990), 111f. See below, pp. 143f.
216. For this, see W. H. Schmidt, *Exodus, Sinai und Moses,* 110–130 (and literature), and below, pp. 143f.
217. Exod. 2:18; 3:1; 4:18; 18:1ff.; Num. 10:29; and Judg. 4:11.
218. For this, see L. Perlitt, "Sinai und Horeb," in H. Donner et al., eds., *Beiträge zur alttestamentlichen Theologie,* FS W. Zimmerli (1977), 302–322; cf. also P. Maiberger, *ThWAT* 5, cols. 830ff. For a different view, see Chr. Levin, "Der Dekalog am Sinai, *VT* 35, 1985, 190f.
219. For this, see above all: D. J. McCarthy, *Old Testament Covenant: A Survey of Current Opinions* (Growing Points in Theology; Oxford, 1972); idem, *Der Gottesbund im Alten Testament* (SBS 13; 1966); L. Perlitt, *Bundestheologie im Alten Testament* (WMANT 36; 1969), 156ff.; N. Lohfink, SBAB 8 (1990), 325ff.; E. Kutsch, *Verheissung und Gesetz* (BZAW 131; 1973), 75ff.; idem, "ברית *bĕrît* Verpflichtung," *THAT* 1, cols. 339–352 (cf. *TRE* 7, 397–403); and M. Weinfeld, "ברית," *ThWAT* 1, cols. 781–808. Also see: W. Zimmerli, "Erwägungen zum 'Bund': Die Aussagen über die Jahwe-ברית in Ex 19–34," in H. J. Stoebe et al., eds., *Wort, Gebot, Glaube: Beitrage zur Theologie des Alten Testaments,* FS W. Eichrodt (AThANT 59; 1970), 171–190; W. Eichrodt, "Darf man heute noch von einem Gottesbund mit Israel reden?" *ThZ* 30, 1974, 193–206; L. Wächter, "Die Übertragung der Beritvorstellung auf Jahwe," *ThLZ* 99, 1974, cols. 801–816; J. Scharbert, " 'Bĕrît' im Pentateuch," in M. Carrez et al., eds., *De la Torah au Messie,* FS H. Cazelles (1981), 163–170; E. W. Nicholson, *God and His People* (Oxford, 1986), esp. 121ff., which point to the individual key texts (most are similar to L. Perlitt); idem, "Covenant in a Century of Study since Wellhausen," *OTS* 24, 1986, 54–69; R. A. Oden, Jr., "The Place of Covenant in the Religion of Israel," in P. D. Miller, Jr., et al., eds., *Ancient Israelite Religion,* FS F. M. Cross (Philadelphia, 1987), 429–447; N. Lohfink, "Bund," *NBL* I, cols. 344–348; and R. Davidson, "Covenant Theology in Ancient Israel," in R. E. Clements, ed., *The World of Ancient Israel* (Cambridge, 1989), 323–347. For another perspective, see Chr. Levin, *Die Verheissung des neuen Bundes* (FRLANT 137; 1985). Cf. further: W. Eichrodt, *Theology,* 1:36–45; L. Köhler (4th ed.), 43ff.; G. von Rad, *Theology,* 1:129–135; and W. H. Schmidt, *Alttestamentlicher Glaube* (6th ed.), 129ff.
220. For Exodus 34 and the Yahwistic interpretation of the Sinai covenant, cf. also J. Scharbert, "Jahwe im frühisraelitischen Recht," in E. Haag, ed., *Gott, der einzige* (1985), 160–183, esp. 163ff.
221. Cf. Mark 14:24 and Matt. 26:28.
222. For Exod. 24:1–11, see also F.-L. Hossfeld, *Der Dekalog* (OBO 45; 1982), 190–204; and W. H. Schmidt, "Wort und Ritus," *PTh* 74, 1985, 68–83 (esp. 72ff.). Cf. also A. Deissler, *Grundbotschaft,* 87ff.
223. The greatest difficulty confronting E. Kutsch's interpretation is his view that the two "parts"

of the blood refer to distinctively different things: sacrifice, on the one hand, and duty on the other (*Verheissung und Gesetz,* 82ff.; cf. his article "Das sogenannte 'Bundesblut' in Ex xxiv 8 und Sach IX 11," *VT* 23, 1973, 25–30).

224. Chr. Levin, "Der Dekalog am Sinai," *VT* 35, 1985, 165–191 (esp. 177, although with a different view of the Sinai tradition's incorporation of the Decalogue).

225. For the covenant (*běrît*) of the ancestors, cf. Vol. II, 6.6. For the Davidic covenant (*běrît*), see Vol. II, 7.2.

226. For this, see E. Kutsch, *THAT* 1, col. 340. For a critical response to these etymological derivations along with some important reflections on the statements about covenant in the Old Testament, see J. Barr, "Some Semantic Notes on the Covenant," in H. Donner et al., eds., *Beiträge zur alttestamentlichen Theologie,* FS W. Zimmerli (1977), 23–38.

227. Cf. *AHw* 1, cols. 129f.

228. Cf., however, also (with E. Kutsch) the Akkadian word *barû: AHw* 1, col. 109.

229. M. Görg, in H.-J. Fabry, ed., *Bausteine biblischer Theologie,* FS G. J. Botterweck (BBB 50; 1977), 25–36.

230. J. Wellhausen, *Prolegomena to the History of Ancient Israel* (Cleveland and New York, 1957), 417–419; idem, *Israelitische und jüdische Geschichte* (9th ed., 1958), 15ff.

231. J. Wellhausen, in R. Smend, ed., *Grundrisse zum Alten Testament* (TB 27; 1965), 73f.

232. R. Kraetzschmar, *Die Bundesvorstellung im Alten Testament* (1896). Also see, in addition, the older work of P. Karge, *Geschichte des Bundesgedankens im Alten Testament* (1910).

233. J. Pedersen, *Der Eid bei den Semiten* (1914).

234. W. Eichrodt, *Theology,* 1:36–45 (see above, chapter 1: "Setting the Stage," and pp. 8ff.). Cf., e.g., W. Eichrodt, *Theology* (5th ed.), 1:9ff.

235. L. Köhler, *Theologie* (4th ed., 1966), 43–59.

236. J. Begrich, "Berit," *ZAW* 60, 1944, 1–11 (= TB 21, 55ff.).

237. Ibid., 7ff. (= TB 21, 61ff.).

238. Ibid., 7 (= TB 21, 62).

239. Ibid.

240. We shall examine the Old Testament views of law below in sec. 6.

241. Thus H. W. Wolff, "Jahwe als Bundesvermittler," *VT* 6, 1956, 316–320 (= TB 22, 2d ed., 1973, 387ff.); and M. Noth, *Gesammelte Studien zum Alten Testament,* vol. 1, 3d. ed. (TB 6; 1966), 142–154.

242. J. Hempel, *RGG,* 3d ed., vol. 1, col. 1514.

243. For this, see A. Jepsen, "Berith: Ein Beitrag zur Theologie der Exilszeit," in his *Der Herr ist Gott* (1978), 196–210.

244. For this, see J. Scharbert, *ThWAT* 1, cols. 282f.; and M. Weinfeld, *ThWAT* 1, col. 785.

245. Sefire I A: *KAI,* no. 222, l. 40 (*ANET,* 3d ed., 660a; *TUAT* I/2, 181f.). Mari: ARM II, 37 (*ANET,* 3d ed., 482b).

246. See also Deut. 7:9; 12; 8:18; 1 Kings 8:23; Neh. 1:5; and 9:32.

247. For E. Kutsch and L. Perlitt, see the citations in n. 219 above.

248. For this, see above, p. 69.

249. For this, cf. H. D. Preuss, *Deuteronomium* (EdF 164; 1982), 158f.

250. Cf. for this also H. Cazelles, "Les structures successives de la 'berît' dans l'Ancien Testament," in R. Martin-Achard, ed., *Permanence de l'Ancien Testament: Recherches d'exégèse et de théologie* (Cahiers de la Revue de théologie et de philosophie, 11; 1984), 33–46.

251. Cf., e.g., Deut. 4:13, 23; 5:2f.; 9:9, 11, 15; 10:8; 17:2; 28:69; 29:8, 11, 13, 20, 24f.; 31:9, 16, 20, 25f.; 1 Kings 11:11; 19:10, 14; 2 Kings 17:15; 23:2f.; etc.

252. Cf. the later texts Pss. 25:10, 14; 44:18; 50:16; 78:10, 37; 103:18; Zech. 9:11; and Dan. 9:27.

253. Cf. above, pp. 65f.

254. Cf. also Vol. II, chap. 6.

255. For a different view, see A. Jepsen, "Berith," 200.

256. For this, cf. the evidence in n. 189 above.

257. Cf. already J. Wellhausen, *Israelitische und jüdische Geschichte* (9th ed., 1958), 14ff.

258. For this, cf. above, sec. 3.e.

259. M. Weinfeld argued it was unknown outside Israel (*ThWAT* 1, col. 807). Cf., however, N. Lohfink's indication of a possible Assyrian example of a contract between king, people, and

deity (Esarhaddon with the nation and the god Assur) in "Gott im Buch Deuteronomium," in J. Coppens, ed., *La notion biblique de Dieu* (BETL 41; Louvain, 1976), 101–126, esp. 115, n. 52; cf. also H. D. Preuss, *Deuteronomium,* 68. For the term *adê,* see now K. Watanabe, *Die adê-Vereidigung anlässlich der Thronfolgeregelung Äsarhaddons* (1987), 6–26; for the text, see 181f. He sees the term recited within the context of making a "political or public oath."

260. I accept the argument that Joshua 24 is not completely Deuteronomistic (so L. Perlitt, *Bundestheologie,* 239ff., n. 219), but rather has an older (probably JE) text at its kernel. For this, see also now J. C. de Moor, *The Rise of Yahwism* (BETL 91; Louvain, 1990), 177ff.

261. This means they cannot have the highly placed theological position that H. Gese has attributed to them (*Vom Sinai zum Zion* [3d ed., 1990], 21, 34–36).

262. L. Perlitt, *Bundestheologie,* 129ff.

263. For the "covenant of David," cf. Vol. II, 7.2.

264. Cf. Mal. 2:10, 14; and Prov. 2:17.

265. For Ezekiel 16 (vv. 1–43), cf. Th. Krüger, *Geschichtskonzepte im Ezechielbuch* (BZAW 180; 1989), 139ff.; for vv. 44ff., see pp. 325ff.

266. For this, cf. Vol. II, 11.10.

267. Cf. above, pp. 74f.

268. Cf. R. Rendtorff, " 'Covenant' as a Structuring Concept in Genesis and Exodus," *JBL* 108, 1989, 385–393.

269. For this, cf. above all R. Smend, *Die Bundesformel* (ThST 68; 1963) = *Die Mitte des Alten Testaments* (1986), 11ff. His argument that the entire formula derived from the time of Josiah does not appear to me to be demonstrable. Cf. further N. Lohfink, *ZKTh* 91, 1969, 517–553 (= SBAB 8, 1990, 211ff.); H. H. Schmid, in D. Luhrmann and G. Strecker, eds., *Kirche,* FS G. Bornkamm (1980), 1–25; and also W. H. Schmidt, BK II/1, 285f. Cf. also N. Lohfink, *ThPh* 65, 1990, 172–183 concerning Ps. 100:3.

270. Jer. 24:7; 30:22; 31:1, 33; 32:38; Ezek. 11:20; 14:11; 36:28; 37:23, 27; cf. 34:24; Zech. 8:8. These texts chronologically may be grouped around the Babylonian exile. For the "Exile," see B. J. Diebner, *NBL* I, cols. 625–631.

271. Exod. 6:7; Lev. 26:12; Deut. 29:12; 2 Sam. 7:24; cf. Jer. 7:23; 11:4. In Deut. 26:17f. the formula is used in both ways.

272. These three texts are situated in Shechem.

273. R. Smend, *Die Bundesformel,* 16 = *Die Mitte des Alten Testaments,* 24. For עם יהוה ('*am yahweh,* "people of YHWH"), see above, sec. 4.a.

274. Cf. below, sec. 10.f.

275. Cf. above, p. 42.

276. According to B. Stade (*Biblische Theologie des Alten Testaments,* vol. 1, 1905, 46), "Yahweh, Israel's God," was the "fundamental idea" of the religion of Israel.

277. See the book cited in n. 182 above.

278. For this, see Chr. Dohmen, "Was stand auf den Tafeln von Sinai und was auf denen vom Horeb?" in F.-L. Hossfeld, ed., *Vom Sinai zum Horeb* (1989), 9–50 (cf. his article in *ThWAT* 5, col. 830).

279. Cf. above, p. 70.

280. Cf. below, chap. 4.4.b.

281. For this, see J. Hahn, *Das goldene Kalb* (1981); also see the commentaries and Chr. Dohmen, *ThWAT* 5, col. 830.

282. For this, see Chr. Dohmen, *Das Bilderverbot* (BBB 62; 2d ed., 1987); S. Schroer, *In Israel gab es Bilder* (OBO 74; 1987), 81–104; and H. Utzschneider, *Hosea, Prophet vor dem Ende* (OBO 31; 1980), 88–104.

283. Compare Exod. 32:30f. to the "great sin" in 2 Kings 17:21.

284. E. Zenger, *Israel am Sinai* (1982), 186. For an illustration of this "natural inclination," one can refer to the bronze bull statuettes which point to a premonarchial, Israelite, agricultural clan sanctuary in the hills of Samaria. For this, see R. Wenning and E. Zenger, "Ein bäuerliches Baal-Heiligtum im samarischen Gebirge aus der Zeit der Anfänge Israels: Erwägungen zu dem von A. Mazar zwischen Dotan und Tirze entdeckten 'Bull Site,'" *ZDPV* 102, 1986, 75–86. Cf. further the find of the "calves" in Ashkelon.

285. See Chr. Dohmen, *Das Bilderverbot;* and below, sec. 8.c. Dohmen (pp. 66–132) sees in Exodus 32 a differently demarcated basic stratum and several redactions (i.e., a basic narrative with additions; the kernel is only in vv. 1–20). In regard to the text, cf. P. Weimar, *BN* 38/39, 1987, 117–160, including literature listed.

286. Cf. also W. Zimmerli, *Theology,* 73–74.

287. Cf. E. Aurelius, *Der Fürbitter Israels* (CB OT 27; Stockholm, 1988).

288. Cf. the accounts given in the various histories of ancient Israel.

289. However, cf. Exod. 2:14; 4:1; 5:15ff.; 6:9; and 14:11ff.

290. For this, see R. Knierim, "לין *lûn* rebellieren," *THAT* 1, cols. 870–872, esp. cols. 871f. He states: "The term *lûn* is at the center of Old Testament theology, for it discloses a form of sin where God's people as a whole reject both the history of liberation that has been divinely wrought and therefore its own salvific future. This sin occurs during the menacing time in between (i.e., the wilderness period), the time between liberation (the exodus) and fulfillment (the conquest), and results from blindness and impatience that lead to the misunderstanding of God. With the exception of Josh. 9:18 and perhaps Ps. 59:16, the verb לין appears in the Old Testament only in the 'murmuring stories.' " See also K.-D. Schunck, "לין *lûn*," *ThWAT* 4, cols. 527–530.

291. Cf. below, sec. 9.a.

292. For Numbers 16–17, cf. F. Ahuis, *Autorität im Umbruch* (1983).

293. For these texts, see, above all, V. Fritz, *Israel in der Wüste* (1970); G. W. Coats, *Rebellion in the Wilderness* (Nashville and New York, 1968); G. I. Davies, *The Way of the Wilderness* (Cambridge, 1979); R. A. Adamiak, *Justice and History in the Old Testament* (Cleveland, 1982); and A. Schart, *Mose und Israel im Konflikt* (OBO 98; 1990). Cf. also G. von Rad, *Theology,* 1:293ff.; and W. Zimmerli, *Theology,* 175–177.

294. However, it has been debated as to whether a segment of the Elohist source, itself fragmentary, may be included. V. Fritz (*Israel in der Wüste*) thinks that he can point to a group of narrative texts that derive from the sphere of the southern tribes and that predate the Yahwist. The Yahwist, thinks Fritz, certainly reshapes these texts thematically. Fritz and Adamiak (*Justice and History in the Old Testament*) also find in the Yahwist's description a warning directed against the monarchy. This warning, they think, originates in the time when the possession of the land appears to be safe.

295. Cf. also Vol. II, 11.9.

296. Exod. 16:35; Num. 14:33f.; 32:13; Deut. 2:7; 8:2, 4; 29:4; Josh. 5:6; Amos 2:10; 5:25; Ps. 95:10; and Neh. 9:21.

297. For this, cf. Th. B. Dozeman, "Horeb/Sinai and the Rise of the Law in the Wilderness Tradition," in D. J. Lull, ed., SBL Sem. Pap., 28 (Atlanta, 1989), 282–290; and M. A. Sweeney, "The Wilderness Traditions of the Pentateuch: A Reassessment of Their Function and Intent in Relation to Exodus 32–34," in D. J. Lull, ed., SBL Sem. Pap., 28 (Atlanta, 1989), 291–299.

298. For this, see A. Alt, *Die Ursprünge des israelitischen Rechts* (1934) (= *KS* 1, 1953, 278ff.); M. Noth, *Die Gesetze im Pentateuch* (1940) (= TB 6, 3d ed., 1966, 9ff.); E. Würthwein, "Der Sinn des Gesetzes im Alten Testament," *ZThK* 55, 1958, 255–270 (= *Wort und Existenz,* 1970, 39ff.); F. Horst, *Gottes Recht* (TB 12; 1961); R. Kilian, "Apodiktisches und kasuistisches Recht," *BZ* NF 7, 1963, 185–202; E. Gerstenberger, *Wesen und Herkunft des 'apodiktischen Rechts'* (WMANT 20; 1965); G. Fohrer, "Das sogenannte apodiktisch formulierte Recht und der Dekalog," *KuD* 11, 1965, 49–74 (= BZAW 115, 1969, 120ff.); W. Richter, *Recht und Ethos* (StANT 15; 1966); A. Jepsen, "Israel und das Gesetz," *ThLZ* 93, 1968, cols. 85–94 (= *Der Herr ist Gott,* 1978, 155ff.); W. Zimmerli, "Das Gesetz im Alten Testament," in his *Gottes Offenbarung* (TB 19; 2d ed., 1969), 249–276; H. Schulz, *Das Todesrecht im Alten Testament* (BZAW 114; 1969); R. Brunner, ed., *Gesetz und Gnade im Alten Testament und im jüdischen Denken* (1969); G. Liedke, *Gestalt und Bezeichnung alttestamentlichen Rechtssätze* (WMANT 39; 1971); V. Wagner, *Rechtssätze in gebundener Sprache und Rechtssatzreihen im israelitischen Recht* (BZAW 127; 1972); H. Rücker, *Die Begründungen der Weisungen Jahwes im Pentateuch* (1973); J. Halbe, *Das Privilegrecht Jahwes Ex 34, 10–26* (FRLANT 114; 1975); H. Gese, "Das Gesetz," in his *Zur biblischen Theologie* (3d ed., 1989), 55–84; W. Schottroff, "Zum alttestamentlichen Recht," *VuF* 22, 1977, 3–29 (also literature); R. Smend and U. Luz, *Gesetz* (1981); H. D. Preuss, *Deuteronomium* (EdF 164;

1982) (and literature); G. Braulik, "Gesetz als Evangelium: Rechtfertigung und Begnadigung nach der deuteronomischen Tora," *ZThK* 79, 1982, 127–160 (= SBAB 2, 1988, 123ff.); H.-J. Boecker, *Recht und Gesetz im Alten Testament und im altes Orient* (2d ed., 1984); D. Patrick, *Old Testament Law* (Atlanta, 1985); K. Koch, "Gesetz I: Altes Testament," *TRE* 13, 40–52 (also the literature); R. Martin-Achard, *La loi, don de Dieu* (Aubonne, 1987); E. Otto, *Wandel der Rechtsbegründungen in der Gesellschaftsgeschichte des antiken Israel: Eine Rechtsgeschichte des 'Bundesbuches' Ex XX 22–XXIII 13* (1988); idem, *"Gesetz" als Thema Biblischer Theologie* (JBTh 4; 1989); and idem, *Thinking Biblical Law* (*Semeia* 45), 1989. Cf. also W. Eichrodt, *Theology,* 1:70–97; L. Köhler, *Theologie* (4th ed., 92–96), 190–199; G. von Rad, *Theology,* 1:190–203; W. Zimmerli, *Theology,* 112; C. Westermann, *Theologie,* 154ff.; R. E. Clements, *Theology,* 104ff.; B. S. Childs, *Theology,* 51ff.; and W. H. Schmidt, *Alttestamentlicher Glaube* (6th ed.), 343–346.

299. For Old Testament justice as civil justice with stipulations for punishments, as a justice of "leniency," and so on, see H. Seebass, *Der Gott der ganzen Bibel* (1982), 102–113.

300. Section 8 of this chapter will go further into the Decalogue, especially the first and second commandments.

301. For this, cf. also P. Weimar, "Bundesbuch," *NBL* I, cols. 348–356 (and literature).

302. Cf. *ANET* (3d ed.), 159ff., 523ff.; *TUAT* I/1, 1982; I/3, 1983; *Orientalisches Recht* (HdO supplementary vol. 3), 1964; and W. Fikentscher et al., eds., *Entstehung und Wandel rechtlicher Traditionen* (1980) (see the essays by J. Krecher on Sumerian law and W. Helck on ancient Egyptian law). For ancient Near Eastern law, cf. the overview by W. Schottroff, "Zum alttestamentlichen Recht," 10ff.; and K. Koch, *TRE* 13, 40–42.

303. Cf., e.g., the comparative study of law by E. Otto, *Rechtsgeschichte der Redaktionen im Kodex Ešnunna und im "Bundesbuch"* (OBO 85; 1989).

304. A. Jepsen, *Untersuchungen zum Bundesbuch* (BWANT 41; 1927).

305. See the reference in n. 298 above.

306. For this, see A. Alt, *KS* 1, 285ff.

307. A. Alt considered the occasional presence of the direct address in the Covenant Code to be a secondary interpolation, an insertion of a stylistic feature belonging to other genres (*KS* 1, 287).

308. Thus, e.g., R. Hentschke, "Erwägungen zur israelitischen Rechtsgeschichte," *ThViat* 10, 1965/1966, 108–133.

309. For the interpretation of the contents, cf. H.-J. Boecker, *Recht und Gesetz,* 135ff.

310. For this, see L. Köhler, "Die hebräische Rechtsgemeinde," in his *Der hebräische Mensch* (1953), 143ff.; and H. Niehr, *Rechtsprechung in Israel* (SBS 130; 1987), who also takes a look at the Near Eastern context of ancient Israel.

311. E.g., even the Code of Hammurabi sets forth a better position for women than Old Testament law.

312. Cf. for this Vol. II, 15.3.

313. For punishments in ancient Near Eastern law, cf. H.-J. Boecker, *Recht und Gesetz,* 31f.; then also W. Eichrodt, *Theology,* 1:78–79. For the death penalty in ancient Near Eastern law, cf. R. Haase, *Einführung in das Studium keilschriftlicher Rechtsquellen* (1965), passim; and V. Korošec, "Die Todesstrafe in der Entwicklung des hethitischen Rechts," in B. Alster, ed., *Death in Mesopotamia* (Copenhagen, 1980), 199–212 (with literature for the larger ancient Near East).

314. As the specified texts indicate, we know relatively little about these minor judges. Thus they have been considered as holders of a variety of offices who carried out different functions. M. Noth considered them to be the spokespersons, not of casuistic but of apodictic law, while H.-J. Kraus viewed them as mediators of the covenant within cultic festivals. M. Metzger combined both of these views. W. Richter saw these minor judges as representatives of an order of civil jurisprudence during the time of the transition from a tribal constitution to a city constitution. And there are many other views. For an orientation to this discussion, see H. N. Rösel, "Die 'Richter Israels,' " *BZ* NF 25, 1981, 180–203; and Chr. Schäfer-Lichtenberger, *Stadt und Eidgenossenschaft im Alten Testament* (BZAW 156; 1983), 344ff. (he sees them in the framework of a "segmentary society").

315. H.-J. Boecker, *Recht und Gesetz,* 131.

316. For this, see H. W. Gilmer, *The If-You Form in Israelite Law* (Missoula, Mont., 1975).

317. Cf. H.-J. Boecker, *Recht und Gesetz,* 133.
318. A. Alt, *KS* 1, 291.
319. See, e.g., E. Otto, *Wandel der Rechtsbegründungen in der Gesellschaftsgeschichte des antiken Israel* (1988); and Vol. II, 12.3.
320. A. Alt, *KS* 1, 302ff.
321. Thus in Alt's translation (*KS* 1, 318).
322. A. Alt, *KS* 1, 323.
323. See above, pp. 71f.
324. G. von Rad ("The Form-Critical Problem of the Hexateuch," in G. von Rad, *The Problem of the Hexateuch and Other Essays,* trans. E. W. T. Dicken [New York, 1966], 1–78) points out in this connection that S. Mowinckel (*Le décalogue,* Paris, 1927) already saw in the narratives about the events of Sinai the account of Israel's New Year's festival that may have been rendered in the language of literary myth.
325. Cf. above, sec. 5.a.
326. Cf. to this H. D. Preuss, *Deuteronomium* (EdF 164; 1982), 45ff.
327. Cf. above, sec. 3.e, for a discussion of the so-called amphictyony.
328. In a similar way, A. Klostermann had already maintained that the laws were shaped by the oral proclamation in the cult. This was true, above all, for Deuteronomy, which is so strongly permeated by the style of preaching (*Der Pentateuch,* 1893; *Der Pentateuch,* Neue Folge, 1907).
329. M. Noth, *Gesetze im Pentateuch,* 49 (see TB 6, 81).
330. Cf. also G. von Rad, *Theology,* 1:203, although with attentuated emphases.
331. Cf., e.g., W. Zimmerli, TB 19, 256ff.
332. See G. von Rad, *Studies in Deuteronomy,* trans. D. M. G. Stalker (SBT 9; London, 1953). His Deuteronomy commentary appeared later (ATD 8; 1964, etc.). See also his *Theology,* 1:219–231.
333. G. von Rad, *Theology,* 1:192.
334. Ibid., 1:194.
335. Ibid., 1:194; cf. 2:393.
336. Ibid., 1:196.
337. Ibid., 1:196.
338. Ibid., 2:393 (cf. 388–391).
339. Ibid., 2:395. Cf. 2:269: In Ezekiel "Jahweh's commandments have turned into a law that judges and destroys."
340. Ibid., 2:397.
341. Ibid., 2:393.
342. In 1951 H.-J. Kraus, in commenting on M. Noth's understanding of the law, noted concerning the historical-theological continuities of the law: "The theological significance of the work of Noth must finally be recognized in particular by the systematic theologian. We are in a period when the discussion about the problem of 'Gospel and Law' is directed to the critical results of exegetical methodology."
343. Cf., e.g., the collection of essays, *Gesetz und Gnade,* ed. R. Brunner (1969).
344. Cf. also J. Belzer, "Apodiktik/apodiktisch," *NBL* I, cols. 122–124.
345. For this, see G. Heinemann, "Untersuchungen zum apodiktischen Recht," diss. (Hamburg, 1958).
346. Thus R. Hentschke, *ThViat* 10, 1965/1966, 114ff.
347. For these, cf. the account of S. Herrmann, *A History of Israel in Old Testament Times,* rev. ed., trans. J. Bowden (Philadelphia, 1981), 60, n. 30. Cf. also *LÄ* I, cols. 67–69. Egyptian parallels are also given in R. Kilian, "Apodiktisches und kasuistisches Recht." Cf. also the literature listed in n. 302 above.
348. In this regard, J. Halbe (" 'Altorientalisches Weltordnungsdenken' und alttestamentliche Theologie," *ZThK* 76, 1979, 381–418) is correct in his critical debate with the various works of H. H. Schmid.
349. Cf. H. Schulz, *Das Todesrecht im Alten Testament;* and R. Knierim, *Semeia* 45, 1989, 9–14.
350. For this, see W. Schottroff, *Der altisraelitische Fluchspruch* (WMANT 30; 1969).
351. For this, see, above all, H.-W. Jüngling, *ThPh* 59, 1984, 1–38; F. Crüsemann, " 'Auge um

Auge . . . ' (Ex 21, 24f): Zum sozialgeschichtlichen Sinn des Taliongesetzes im Bundesbuch," *EvTh* 47, 1987, 411–426; and C. Locher, *Die Ehre einer Frau in Israel* (OBO 70; 1986), 315ff.

352. V. Wagner (*Rechtssätze in gebundener Sprache und Rechtssatzreihen im israelitischen Recht*), has received more recognition in criticizing Alt's theses about apodictic law and in pointing to a "pedagogic" shaping of legal statements, than he has from his own thesis of a literary form of legal statements with a common deep structure in ancient Near Eastern and Old Testament law.

353. A. Alt, *KS* 1, 303–305.

354. G. Fohrer, *Das sogenannte apodiktisch formulierte Recht und der Dekalog;* and E. Gerstenberger, *Wesen und Herkunft des "apodiktischen Rechts."*

355. K. Elliger, "Das Gesetz Leviticus 18," *ZAW* 67, 1955, 1–25 = TB 32, 1966, 232ff. Also see his HAT I/4, 1966, 229ff.

356. Therefore S. Herrmann speaks of "normative" law rather than apodictic law. He certainly sees from the beginning of apodictic formulations on a process that is esp. typical for Israel ("Das 'apodiktische Recht': Erwägungen zur Klärung dieses Begriffs," *MIO* 15, 1969, 249, 249–261 [= TB 75, 1986, 89ff.]).

357. For a more precise form-critical investigation of the individual forms, see G. Liedke, *Gestalt und Bezeichnung alttestamentlicher Rechtssätze.*

358. For the sapiential admonition, see W. Richter, *Recht und Ethos.*

359. In the sphere of casuistic law, more of Alt's views have held up, including that of a common ancient Near Eastern life setting in secular jurisprudence.

360. Cf. the analogous distinction between "aspective" and "perspective" law in E. Brunner-Traut, *Frühformen des Erkennens* (1990), 96: "Aspective law formulates the individual case in a concrete and graphic fashion, while perspective law subsumes abstract, general, common, analogous cases within a single rule."

361. E. Otto, "Kultus und Ethos in Jerusalemer Theologie: Ein Beitrag zur theologischen Begründung der Ethik im Alten Testament," *ZAW* 98, 1986, 162. He further argues (pp. 161ff.): "The form-critical differentiation between casuistic and apodictic law does not point to a difference in origin between a genuine Israelite law of God and a non-Israelite secular law. Rather, the differentiation is due to functional differences of the law within Israelite society. Apodictic law has its roots in the family. There it establishes the boundary for the legal administration of the death penalty and ensures the fundamental norms of the common life and the survival of the family through the death sanction. Distinguished from this, not by its origin but according to its function, is casuistic law which, originally stemming out of a family-structured society, did not, to begin with, establish sanctions as did apodictic law. Rather, casuistic law seeks to work out settlements between the families of a transfamilial, legal community of the clan and then later of the local legal community. In the course of the history of Israelite jurisprudence, apodictic law moved from the family and into the transfamilial legal institution of justice administered at the gate, while casuistic law increasingly took over the function of establishing sanctions. Apodictic and casuistic law did not originally require as an inner- or extra-tribal law religious or even cultic legitimation. The foundation of the law was obtained rather from the function of securing the survival of the family through the protection of norms important for survival and through the regulation of conflict in the transfamilial legal community. The law sought to limit the violence between families of a tribe or local legal community that would threaten survival. However, the sacral norms of divine law are originally strictly differentiated from the above. The oldest collection of sacral law that has been preserved is found in Exod. 34:12–26* (par. Exod. 23:15–19*). This collection contains norms for the order of the cult that are considered to be the will of God. However, they do not transmit an ethical impulse for everyday life in Israelite society."

362. For this, see J. Halbe, *Das Privilegrecht Jahwes Ex 34, 10–26* (FRLANT 114; 1975); also J. Scharbert, "Jahwe im frühisraelitischen Recht," in E. Haag, ed., *Gott, der einzige* (1985), 160–183. In a fashion analogous to Otto (*ZAW*, 98, 1986, 161ff.; see n. 361 above), Scharbert (p. 171) states: "This Yahweh federation, that is, this 'Israel,' needs no personal and punitive law, because its regulation is entrusted to the tribal heads, the 'elders,' who

represent the primary groups, that is, the associations of the clans. However, the groups who wish to belong to Israel needed a sacral law that unites them. Through the acknowledgment of this law, these groups were bound to Yahweh." Thus Yahweh's privileges are mentioned as well as those of Israel.

363. With the exception of Exod. 21:6, which has האלהים (hā'ĕlōhîm, "the God")? Cf. J. Scharbert, "Jahwe im frühisraelitischen Recht," 179.
364. Cf. H. Rücker, Die Begründungen der Weisungen Jahwes im Pentateuch.
365. W. Zimmerli, Das Gesetz und die Propheten (1963), 68–81.
366. Ibid., 77.
367. Cf. M. Klopfenstein, "Das Gesetz bei den Propheten," in M. Klopfenstein et al., eds., Mitte der Schrift? (1987), 283–297; and G. M. Tucker, "The Law in the Eighth-Century Prophets," in G. M. Tucker et al., eds., Canon, Theology, and Old Testament Interpretation, FS B. S. Childs (Philadelphia, 1988), 201–216.
368. W. Zimmerli, Das Gesetz und die Propheten, 78.
369. Ibid., 81–93.
370. G. von Rad, Theology, 1:196.
371. See above, sec. 6.c.
372. "Blessing" and "curse" were not original components of the conclusion of the Book of the Covenant. On the one hand, Exodus 23:20–33 is not uniform and was added later. On the other hand, the content of this section has different emphases. For this, see J. Halbe, Das Privilegrecht Jahwes, 483ff. As for the punishment of God and the punishment of human beings according to the law in Exodus 21–22, see A. Schenker, Versöhnung und Widerstand (SBS 139; 1990).
373. For this, see H.-J. Fabry, "Noch ein Dekalog! Die Thora des lebendigen Gottes in ihrer Wirkungsgeschichte," in M. Bohnke and H. Heinz, eds., Im Gespräch mit dem dreieinen Gott: Elemente einer trinitarischen Theologie, FS W. Breuning (1985), 75–96.
374. For the curse, see, in addition to the work of W. Schottroff mentioned in n. 350 above, V. Wagner (see n. 298 above), 32ff. For the effect of the curse, cf. also H. Hempel, "Die israelitischen Anschauungen von Segen und Fluch im Lichte altorientalischer Parallelen," in idem, Apoxysmata (BZAW 81; 1961), 1–29.
375. V. Wagner, Rechtssätze in gebundener Sprache und Rechtssatzreihen im israelitischen Recht, 38.
376. W. Zimmerli, Das Gesetz und die Propheten, 86f.
377. Ibid., p. 91.
378. Ibid., p. 93.
379. For this, see A. K. Fenz, Auf Jahwes Stimme hören (1964). Cf. Vol. II, 11.8.a.
380. Cf. for this, above all: H. Gese, Das Gesetz, 55–84, esp. 75ff.; and P. Stuhlmacher, "Das Gesetz als Thema biblischer Theologie," in idem, Versöhnung, Gesetz und Gerechtigkeit (1981), 136–165.
381. Thus H. Gese, Zur biblischen Theologie (3d ed., 1989), 59.
382. For this, see M. Köckert, "Leben in Gottes Gegenwart: Zum Verständnis des Gesetzes in der priesterschriftlichen Literatur," JBTh 4 (1989), 29–61.
383. Cf. Vol. II, chap. 13.
384. The most important published texts and the literature that pertains to them are noted in H. D. Preuss, Deuteronomium (EdF 164; 1982), 217–219. One should add to these, above all, TUAT I/2, 1983; and S. Parpola and K. Watanabe, eds., Neo-Assyrian Treaties and Loyalty Oaths (Helsinki, 1988).
385. Thus W. Zimmerli, TB 19 (2d ed.), 268.
386. For this, see K. Baltzer, Das Bundesformular (WMANT 4; 2d ed., 1964), 97f.: "It continues to be astonishing that Israel recognized and experienced its relationship to God in such a straightforward way. This (covenant) form is closely connected with both Israel's history and its law. In this way Israel is set apart from what was characteristic of other religions in its environment. The other ancient Near Eastern gods were described primarily by reference to the seasons of nature and cultic mythology. By contrast Israel acknowledged that Yahweh had revealed himself in history. Israel knew that Yahweh was a just God and not a capricious one."
387. W. Zimmerli, TB 19 (2d ed.), 271.

388. Ibid., 276. Cf. A. Jepsen, *Der Herr ist Gott* (1978), 161f.
389. Cf. esp. for this G. Braulik, *Gesetz als Evangelium;* and M. Köckert, "Das nahe Wort," *ThPh* 60, 1985, 496–519.
390. See W. Zimmerli, BK XIII/1, 449f.; and H. Gese, in H. Donner et al., eds., *Beiträge zur alttestamentlichen Theologie, FS* W. Zimmerli (1977), 140–151, for the statement in Ezek. 20:25, so unusual for the Old Testament ("Moreover, I gave them statutes that were not good and ordinances by which they could not have life") and problems associated with it (either a fundamental statement of a unique kind or related to the subsequently mentioned sacrifice of the firstborn [Exod. 22:28]; the verse nevertheless is still rather enigmatic, theologically speaking, in its judgment of divine commandments).
391. For Deut. 9:1–6, see esp. G. Braulik, "Die Entstehung der Rechtfertigungslehre in den Bearbeitungsschichten des Buches Deuteronomium," *ThPh* 64, 1989, 321–333; esp. 328ff.
392. For this, cf. B. S. Childs, *Theology,* 84ff. Also see Vol. II, chap. 13, concerning the Old Testament cultus.
393. Cf. the commentaries for Ezra 7 and Nehemiah 8.
394. For this, see H.-J. Kraus, "Freude an Gottes Gesetz," *EvTh* 10, 1951/1952, 337–351.
395. For this, see Vol. II, 9.3 and 13.3.
396. This recognition does not come first from more recent scholarship. One could have read such a view already in A. Bertholet (*Biblische Theologie des Alten Testaments,* vol. 2, 1911, 1).
397. For this process and its possible (also political and social) background, see F. Crüsemann, "Der Pentateuch als Tora," *EvTh* 49, 1989, 250–267 (literature). For the assessment of the Torah in the postexilic and early Jewish period, see also J. Maier, *Zwischen den Testamenten* (NEB AT, Supplement, vol. 3, 1990), 212ff.
398. For a more precise study, see U. Kellermann, "Anmerkungen um Verständnis der Tora in den chronistischen Schriften," *BN* 42, 1988, 49–92.
399. U. Kellermann, *BN* 42, 1988, 51 (on pp. 51ff. and esp. the tables on pp. 67–70 for the passages from Chronicles, Ezra, and Nehemiah). "The cult is endangered in every period, and its technical operation and its material maintenance must be secured."
400. U. Kellermann, *BN* 42, 91.
401. For this, cf. H. D. Preuss, *Deuteronomium* (EdF 164; 1982), 84–90 (and the literature cited), and H. von Lips, *Weisheitliche Traditionen im Neuen Testament* (WMANT 64; 1990), 51–62 (literature).
402. For scholarly literature, see R. Smend, *Das Mosesbild von H. Ewald bis M. Noth* (1959); E. Osswald, *Das Bild des Mose in der kritischen alttestamentlichen Wissenschaft seit J. Well-hausen* (1962); K. Koch, "Der Tod des Religionsstifters," *KuD* 8, 1962, 100–123 (= K. Koch, *Studien zur alttestamentlichen und altorientalischen Religionsgeschichte* (1988), 32ff. with supplements); F. Baumgärtel, "Der Tod des Religionsstifters," *KuD* 9, 1963, 223–233; S. Herrmann, "Mose," *EvTh* 28, 1968, 301–328 (TB 75, 1986, 47ff.); H. Schmid, *Die Gestalt des Mose* (EdF 237; 1986) which lists additional literature; G. W. Coats, *Moses: Heroic Man, Man of God* (JSOT Suppl 57; 1988); and E. Aurelius, *Der Fürbitter Israels* (CB OT 27; 1988). See also B. S. Childs, *Theology,* 108ff.
403. M. Noth, *A History of Pentateuchal Traditions,* trans. B. W. Anderson (Englewood Cliffs, N.J., 1972), 156–175; and G. von Rad, *Theology,* 1:289–296. For a complete survey of scholarship, see H. Schmid, *Die Gestalt des Mose.*
404. I do not wish to enter into the discussion about whether Moses is to be identified with the Egyptian Bay/Beya. For this, see E. Knauf, *Midian* (1988), 135ff.; and J. C. de Moor, *The Rise of Yahwism* (BETL 91; 1990), 136ff. In addition, there should be no question as to whether YHWH (and, along with him, Yahwism) precedes Moses (cf. below, chap. 4.2 and following). However, the important question is whether this plays a decisive, theologically influential role for the Old Testament or even within it.
405. John Bright, *Early Israel in Recent History Writing* (SBT 19; 1956), 53.
406. For the pictures of Moses in the sources of the Pentateuch, cf. G. von Rad, *Theology,* 1:289–296. For different emphases, see G. W. Coats; cf. also W. Zimmerli, *Theology,* 81–83; and W. Eichrodt, *Theology,* 1:289–296. For Exodus 3–4, cf. also G. Fischer, *Jahwe unser Gott* (OBO 91; 1989).
407. For these texts, see, above all, E. Aurelius, *Der Fürbitter Israels.*

408. For the picture of Moses in P, see F. Kohata, *Jahwist und Priesterschrift in Exodus in 3–14* (BZAW 166; 1986), 77–80.
409. "He became what he was, not through study or learning but through the enlightenment of direct, divine assurance" (H. Schultz, *Alttestamentliche Theologie,* 5th ed., 1896, 89).
410. Cf. p. 42 and pp. 76f.
411. Cf. above, p. 69 and below, pp. 143f. for this area (Sinai, Horeb, mountain of God) and also for the connections with the so-called Midianite hypothesis.
412. Is it an accident that the name YHWH is missing in Exodus 1 and 2?
413. These kinds of death sentences are certainly always ventured until someone regularly appears who resurrects once again those who are said to be dead.
414. K. Koch, *KuD* 8, 1962, 107.
415. Ibid., 113f.
416. Ibid., 114.
417. Ibid., 117 (as a question). Similar to K. Koch is R. Rendtorff, "Die Entstehung der israelitischen Religion als religionsgeschichtliches und theologisches Problem," *ThLZ* 88, 1963, cols. 735–746 (= TB 57, 1975, 119ff.); cf. also pp. 152f. ("Mose als Religionsstifter?").
418. F. Baumgärtel, *KuD* 9, 1963, 223ff.
419. Ibid., 229.
420. Ibid., 233 (= N. Söderblom, *Das Werden des Gottesglaubens,* 1916, 310).
421. "Yahweh and Israel are placed together in an indissoluble relationship" (O. Procksch, *Theologie,* 69).
422. Cf. below, chap. 5.2.
423. See J. J. Stamm, *Der Dekalog im Lichte der neueren Forschung* (2d ed., 1962) (cf. *ThR* 27, 1961, 189ff., 281ff.); J. Schreiner, *Die zehn Gebote im Leben des Gottesvolkes* (1966); H. Schüngel-Straumann, *Der Dekalog—Gottes Gebote?* (SBS 67; 2d ed., 1980); L. Perlitt, "Dekalog. I: Altes Testament," *TRE* 8, 408–413 (see literature); F.-L. Hossfeld, *Der Dekalog* (OBO 45; 1982); F. Crüsemann, *Bewahrung der Freiheit: Das Thema des Dekalogs in sozialgeschichtlicher Perspektive* (1983); J. Vincent, "Neuere Aspekte der Dekalogforschung," *BN* 32, 1986, 83–104; F.-L. Hossfeld, "Zum synoptischen Vergleich der Dekalogfassungen: Eine Fortführung des begonnenen Gesprächs," in F.-L. Hossfeld, ed., *Vom Sinai zum Horeb* (1989), 73–117 (see literature); N. Lohfink, "Kennt das Alten Testament einen Unterschied von 'Gebot' und 'Gesetz'? Zur bibeltheologischen Einstufung des Dekalogs," *JBTh* 4 (1989), 63–89; and E. Otto, "Alte und neue Perspektiven in der Dekalogforschung," *EvErz* 42, 1990, 125–133. Also see B. S. Childs, *Theology,* 63ff.
424. For the different numeration and wording of the text in the Christian church as well as for the interpretation of the Decalogue in the New Testament and in catechisms, see B. Reicke, *Die zehn Worte in Geschichte und Gegenwart* (1973).
425. For a more exact discussion, see the works of F.-L. Hossfeld, *Der Dekalog;* and A. Jepsen, "Beiträge zur Auslegung und Geschichte des Dekalogs," *ZAW* 79, 1967, 277–304 (= A. Jepsen, *Der Herr ist Gott,* 1978, 76ff.).
426. Thus F. Horst, *RGG* (3d ed.), II, col. 70. For this papyrus, see E. Würthwein, *Der Text des Alten Testaments* (4th ed., 1973), 37 and 130f.; and A. Jepsen, "Beiträge zur Auslegung und Geschichte des Dekalogs," 76–78.
427. Cf. p. 77.
428. Cf. N. Lohfink, "Zur Dekalogfassung von Dt 5," *BZ* NF 9, 1965, 17–32 (= Lohfink, SBAB 8, 1990, 193ff.).
429. The work of R. Kittel is often mentioned as an example of such a reconstruction in which one modifies the commandments into prohibitions and reduces the longer commandments and prohibitions to conform with the short wording of an "original" or "basic" form (A. Jepsen). See R. Kittel, *Geschichte Israels,* vol. 1 (4th ed., 1921), 582. See also the criticism raised by L. Perlitt, *TRE* 8, 411.
430. See W. H. Schmidt, "Überlieferungsgeschichtliche Erwägungen zur Komposition des Dekalogs," VT Suppl 22, 1972, 201–220.
431. F.-L. Hossfeld, "Dekalog," *NBL* I, cols. 400–405 (together with K. Berger for the New Testament); see esp. p. 402.
432. Cf. also A. Jepsen, "Beiträge zur Auslegung und Geschichte des Dekalogs," 78ff.

433. Thus, e.g., M. Buber, P. Volz, W. Eichrodt, and H. H. Rowley.
434. Cf. Vol. II, 13.5.
435. See n. 423 above.
436. See N. Lohfink, "Das deuteronomische Gesetz in der Endgestalt—Entwurf einer Gesellschaft ohne marginale Gruppen," *BN* 51, 1990, 25–40.
437. Thus, e.g., with F.-L. Hossfeld and L. Perlitt (see n. 423 above).
438. So with A. Jepsen.
439. Cf. below, sec. b, and chap. 4.7.c.
440. Cf. above, p. 62.
441. See below, secs. 10.b and 10.c, for the first and second commandments.
442. Cf. above, pp. 141f. and 151f.
443. For more detail, see R. Albertz, "Hintergrund und Bedeutung des Elterngebots im Dekalog," *ZAW* 90, 1978, 348–374.
444. For the place of the wife in marriage and regulations concerning marriage, see, above all: F. Crüsemann, "'. . . er aber soll dein Herr sein' (Gen 3,16): Die Frau in der patriarchalischen Welt des Alten Testaments," in F. Crüsemann and H. Thyen, *Als Mann und Frau geschaffen* (1978), 13–106; there 25ff., 42ff.; E. Otto, "Zur Stellung der Frau in den ältesten Rechtstexten des Alten Testaments," *ZEE* 26, 1982, 279–305; K. Engelken, *Frauen im Alten Israel* (BWANT 130; 1990); and E. Gerstenberger, "Ehebruch," *NBL* I, cols. 479–481. Cf. Vol. II, 11.1.e.
445. Thus A. Alt, "Das Verbot des Diebstahls im Dekalog," *KS* 1 (1953), 333–340.
446. Cf. Vol. II, 12.4.
447. Cf. F.-L. Hossfeld, *Vom Sinai zum Horeb,* 113ff.
448. Cf. F. Crüsemann, *Bewahrung der Freiheit,* 8ff.
449. In addition to the literature mentioned in n. 423 above, cf. R. Knierim, "Das erste Gebot," *ZAW* 77, 1965, 20–39; W. H. Schmidt, *Das erste Gebot* (ThEx 165; 1969); cf. W. H. Schmidt, *Alttestamentlicher Glaube* (6th ed.), 82–91; M. Saebø, "Kein anderer Name," *KuD* 22, 1976, 181–190; N. Lohfink, "Gott. Polytheistisches und monotheistisches Sprechen von Gott im Alten Testament," in N. Lohfink, ed., *Unsere grossen Wörter* (1977), 127–144; O. Keel, ed., *Monotheismus im Alten Israel und seiner Umwelt* (1980); B. Lang, ed., *Der einzige Gott* (1981); E. Haag, ed., *Gott, der einzige* (1985); M. Hutter, "Das Werden des Monotheismus im alten Israel," in N. Brox et al., eds., *Anfänge der Theologie,* FS J. Bauer (1987), 25–39; J. Tigay, *You Shall Have No Other Gods* (Atlanta, 1986) (see below, n. 542); idem, *Der eine Gott der beiden Testament* (JBTh 2; 1987); and M. Görg, "Monotheismus in Israel—Rückschau zur Genese," *RHS* 32, 1989, 277–285. Cf. also G. von Rad, *Theology,* 1:203–212, 216ff.; and W. Zimmerli, *Theology,* 115–120.
450. Cf. below, chap. 4.7.c. "Zeal and holiness are in fact only differently shaded expressions of one and the same characteristic of Jahweh" (G. von Rad, *Theology,* 1:205).
451. Cf. *ThWAT* 1, col. 568.
452. Cf. also Vol. II, chap. 15 ("Israel and the Nations").
453. Cf. below, under sec. 8.c.
454. The movement under Pharaoh Akhenaton pushing for the exclusive worship of the sun god Aton was atypical for Egypt and also could not be carried out. In addition, this religion was bound up with the mediating role of the king, making it improbable that there was any influence on the faith of Israel. See below, sec. 8.c.
455. Deut. 4:28; 5:7; 6:14; 7:4, 16, 25; 8:19; 11:16, 28; 12:2, 3, 30, 31; 13:3, 7, 8, 14; 28:64; and 32:17; etc. Then see, e.g., Judg. 2:17; 2 Kings 17:35, 37f.; etc. For this subject, see J. P. Floss, *Jahwe dienen—Göttern dienen* (BBB 45; 1975).
456. W. H. Schmidt, *Alttestamentlicher Glaube* (6th ed.), 86.
457. N. Lohfink, *Unsere grossen Wörter* (1977), 142.
458. This is true in spite of or even on account of the argumentation of F. W. Golka, "Schwierigkeiten bei der Datierung des Fremd götterverbotes," *VT* 28, 1978, 352–354. Cf. for this topic W. H. Schmidt, *Das erste Gebot,* 12ff.
459. Cf. H. Gross, "Gotteserfahrung im Alten Testament," in A. Paus, ed., *Suche nach Sinn—Suche nach Gott* (1978), 139–175.
460. F. Crüsemann, *Bewahrung der Freiheit,* 45.

461. See Vol. II, chaps. 6–8.
462. Cf., e.g., the corresponding sections in O. Loretz, *Ugarit und die Bibel* (1990). For Baal: *WdM* 1, 253–274; for El: *WdM* 1, 279–283.
463. F. Crüsemann, *Bewahrung der Freiheit,* 46.
464. Cf. below, chap. 5.5. For the role of Satan in these matters, cf. below, chap. 5.6.
465. Cf. F. Lindström, *God and the Origin of Evil* (CB OT 21; Lund, 1983).
466. Since there was no desire later on to continue the severity of this statement, "the Satan" was inserted at this place (1 Chron. 21:1). Cf. below, chap. 5.6.
467. For the problem of obstinacy, cf. F. Hesse, *Das Verstockungsproblem im Alten Testament* (BZAW 74; 1955). For the obstinacy of pharaoh, cf. now F. Kohata, *Jahwist und Priesterschrift in Exodus 3–14* (BZAW 166; 1989), 216ff. (etc.). For Isa. 6:9, cf. the numerous pieces of literature mentioned in the commentaries, and R. Kilian, *Jesaja 1–39* (EdF 200; 1983), 112ff., (literature). Also see G. von Rad, *Theology,* 2:214–216.
468. For this, see, above all: K.-H. Bernhardt, *Gott und Bild* (1956); W. Zimmerli, "Das zweite Gebot," in his *Gottes Offenbarung* (TB 19; 2d ed., 1969), 234–248; idem, "Das Bilderverbot in der Geschichte des alten Israel," in K.-H. Bernhardt, ed., *Schalom: Studien zu Glaube und Geschichte Israels,* FS A. Jepsen (1971), 86–96 (= TB 51, 247ff.); G. von Rad, "Aspekte alttestamentlichen Weltverständnisses," *EvTh* 24, 1964, 57–73 (= TB 8, 3d ed., 311ff.); W. H. Schmidt, "Ausprägungen des Bilderverbots? Zur Sichtbarkeit und Vorstellbarkeit Gottes im Alten Testament," in H. Balz and S. Schulz, eds., *Das Wort und die Wörter,* FS G. Friedrich (1973) (cf. his *Alttestamentlicher Glaube,* 6th ed., 91ff.); Chr. Link, "Das Bilderverbot als Kriterium theologischen Redens von Gott," *ZThK* 74, 1977, 58–85; Chr. Dohmen, *Das Bilderverbot* (BBB 62; 2d ed., 1987); cf. *NBL* I, cols. 296–298; R. S. Hendel, "The Social Origins of the Aniconic Tradition in Early Israel," *CBQ* 50, 1988, 365–382; and F.-L. Hossfeld, "Du sollst dir kein Bild machen!" *TThZ* 98, 1989, 81–94. Cf. also G. von Rad, *Theology,* 1:212–219.
469. For the different designations for idols (esp. פֶסֶל = *pesel* as a molded work and מַסֵכָה = *massēkâ* as a molded work with valuable decoration), cf. Chr. Dohmen, *Das Bilderverbot,* 41ff.
470. For this topic and the examples given, see the corresponding article in *ThWAT* and H. D. Preuss, *Verspottung fremder Religionen im Alten Testament* (BWANT 92; 1971).
471. Cf. below, chap. 4.7.e.
472. W. Zimmerli, TB 19 (2d ed.), 246.
473. F.-L. Hossfeld, *TThZ* 98, 1989, 93.
474. Cf., e.g., J. Renger, "Kultbild," *RLA* VI, 307–314; D. Wildung, "Götterbild(er)," *LÄ* II, cols. 671–674. Cf. also O. Keel, *Die Welt der altorientalischen Bildsymbolik und das Alte Testament* (2d ed., 1977), 210–220; T. Jacobsen, "The Graven Image," P. D. Miller, Jr., et al., eds., *Ancient Israelite Religion,* FS F. M. Cross (Philadelphia, 1987), 15–32; and J. Assmann, "Die Macht der Bilder: Rahmenbedingungen ikonischen Handelns im Alten Ägypten," *Visible Religion* (Leiden), 7, 1990, 1–20.
475. In the Egyptian "Monument of Memphite Theology," *AOT* (2d ed.), 6; *ANET* (2d and 3d eds.), 5.
476. Cf. H. D. Preuss, *Verspottung fremder Religionen im Alten Testament,* passim.
477. Hos. 3:4; 4:11–19; 8:4–6; 9:10; 10:1–6; 13:1–3, 14; and 14:2–9.
478. Isa. 40:19f.; 41:6f., 21–29; 42:17; 43:8–13; 44:9–20; 45:14–17; 45:18–25; 46:1–7; 47:12–15; and 48: 3–5.
479. Cf. Vol. II, 11.3 and 4.
480. *Enuma eliš,* Tablet VI: *AOT* (2d ed.), 122; *ANET* (2d and 3d eds.), 68; *RGT* (2d ed.), 110.
481. For these questions, see E. Zenger, " ' Hört, auf dass ihr lebt' (Jes 55,3)," in J. Schreiner, ed., *Freude am Gottesdienst: Aspekte ursprunglicher Liturgie,* FS J. G. Plöger (1983), 133–144. The citation is found on p. 135.
482. See O. Keel, *Jahwe-Visionen und Siegelkunst* (SBS 84/85; 1977), 37–45. What Keel (p. 37, n. 50) writes that is critical for the "great theological summons" reflects the Old Testament's own continuing polemic against idols that intentionally opposes this identification of idol and deity.
483. R. S. Hendel ("The Social Origins of the Aniconic Tradition in Early Israel") sees rather the condemnation of the monarchy as the origin of the imageless worship of God in Israel. He likewise combines this with "socio-cultural" arguments, although of another kind.

484. Chr. Dohmen, *NBL* I, col. 296; J. C. de Moor wishes, among other things, to derive the prohibition against images once more from Moses (*The Rise of Yahwism;* BETL 91, Louvain, 1990, 170).
485. V. Fritz, *Tempel und Zelt* (WMANT 47; 1977), 167. Cf. also F.-L. Hossfeld, *TThZ* 98, 1989, 86.
486. For this, see below, chap. 5.2.
487. Above all, see K.-H. Bernhardt, *Gott und Bild.*
488. Cf. F.-L. Hossfeld, *TThZ* 98, 1989, 89 (literature). For Exodus 32, see above, pp. 77f; For the "sin of Jeroboam," see above, p. 77 and below, p. 216.
489. For the plural, see below, pp. 113f.
490. Cf. also G. Glaser, "Schauen ohne Bild: Zur alttestamentlichen Gotteserfahrung," *GuL* 55, 1982, 92–105.
491. Gen. 31:19, 30ff.; Judg. 6:25ff.; 17:4f (here one is able to see how such an image appeared and what its components were); 18:14ff., 24; 1 Sam. 19:13 (here the idol dressed up by Michal can serve as a substitute for David!); etc.
492. For this area as a whole, see S. Schroer, *In Israel gab es Bilder* (OBO 74; 1987). See esp. pp. 301ff. for the Old Testament semantic field. For a succinct overview of the seals and the finds of archaeology that pertain to the investigation of Israelite religion, see the essays by N. Avigad (pp. 195–208), W. G. Dever (pp. 209–247), and J. S. Holladay, Jr. (pp. 249–299), in P. D. Miller, Jr., et al., eds., *Ancient Israelite Religion,* FS F. M. Cross (Philadelphia, 1987).
493. For this and a look at the images of female gods, see esp. S. Schroer (*In Israel gab es Bilder*).
494. According to 1 Kings 18:21, the people did not answer Elijah's question posing an alternative between YHWH and Baal. This alternative was simply not understood.
495. According to O. Loretz (*Ugarit und die Bibel,* 1990, 210–215), the throne cart of YHWH in the Jerusalem temple possibly carried a cult figure. Psalm 17:15, according to Loretz, offers the evidence for this.
496. Cf. V. Fritz, *Tempel und Zelt,* 41ff., 48ff.
497. Cf. A. Reichert, "Massebe," *BRL* (2d ed.), 206–209.
498. Cf. K. Galling, "Aschera," *BRL* (2d ed.), 12f.
499. Cf. O. Loretz, *Ugarit und die Bibel,* 1990, 83–88. See the additional literature mentioned there and the references. Cf. further, S. M. Olyan, *Asherah and the Cult of Yahweh in Israel* (SBL MS 34; Atlanta, 1988). An etymological explanation of the name is attempted by B. Margalit, "The Meaning and Significance of Asherah," *VT* 40, 1990, 264–297.
500. These texts are now in *TUAT* II/4, 1988, 556–558, 561–564. For the texts (with literature), cf. O. Loretz, *Ugarit und die Bibel,* 71f.; K. A. D. Smelik, *Historische Dokumente aus dem alten Israel* (1987), 137–145, 161; P. K. McCarter, Jr., "Aspects of the Religion of the Israelite Monarchy: Biblical and Epigraphic Data," in P. D. Miller, Jr., et al., eds., *Ancient Israelite Religion,* FS F. M. Cross (Philadelphia, 1987), 137–155; and E. S. Gerstenberger, *Jahwe—ein patriarchaler Gott?* (1988), 46ff. S. Mittmann (*ZDPV* 97, 1981, 139–152) is certainly skeptical about the reading "Asherah." Cf. also the translations in *TUAT* II/4, 557f., 563f., and the other reading by W. H. Shea, "The Khirbet El-Qom Tomb Inscription Again," *VT* 40, 1990, 110–116.
501. For this problem, U. Winter, *Frau und Göttin* (OBO 53; 1983); and R. Laut, *Weibliche Züge im Gottesbild israelitisch-jüdischer Religiosität* (1983).
502. "On the other side, the radical faith in one deity possibly was much more suited for establishing the foundation for the equality of all people and the egalitarianism of the sexes" (E. S. Gerstenberger, *Jahwe—ein patriarchaler Gott?* 50). For the problem of "YHWH as a male deity," cf. below, chap. 4.7.f.
503. Cf. many of the citations found in n. 449 above, esp. the collections edited by E. Haag (for this, see B. Lang, *ThQ* 166, 1986, 135–142), O. Keel (for this, see B. Lang, *ThQ* 163, 1983, 54–58), and B. Lang. Also cf. the contribution by N. Lohfink and the work by J. H. Tigay (cf. n. 542 below). Further, see L. Ruppert, "Jahwe und die Götter," *TThZ* 84, 1975, 1–13; C. Thoma and M. Wyschogrod, eds., *Das Reden vom einen Gott bei Juden und Christen* (1984); F.-L. Hossfeld, "Einheit und Einzigkeit Gottes im frühen Jahwismus," in M. Bohnke and H. Heinz, eds., *Im Gespräch mit dem dreieinen Gott: Elemente einer trinitarischen The-*

ologie, FS W. Breuning (1985), 57–74; B. Lang, "Zur Entstehung des biblischen Monotheismus," *ThQ* 166, 1986, 135–142; M. Hutter, "Das Werden des Monotheismus im alten Israel," in J. Brox et al., eds., *Anfänge der Theologie,* FS J. B. Bauer (1987), 25–39; D. L. Petersen, "Israel and Monotheism: The Unfinished Agenda," in G. M. Tucker et al., eds., *Canon, Theology, and Old Testament Interpretation,* FS B. S. Childs (Philadelphia, 1988), 92–107; M. Görg, "Monotheismus in Israel," *RHS* 32, 1989, 277–285; W. H. Schmidt, "'Jahwe und . . .' Anmerkungen zur sogenannten Monotheismus-Debatte," in E. Blum et al., eds., *Die Hebräische Bibel und ihre zweifache Nachgeschichte,* FS R. Rendtorff (1990), 435–447; and J. C. de Moor, *The Rise of Yahwism* (BETL 91; Louvain, 1990). Cf. also H. Graf Reventlow, *ThR* 52, 1987, 264–267; B. Lang, "Vor einer Wende im Verständnis des israelitischen Gottesglaubens?" in his *Wie wird man Prophet in Israel?* (1980), 149–161; Th. C. Vriezen, *Theology,* 23–25; and P. van Imschoot, *Theology of the Old Testament,* vol. 1 (1965), 30ff.
504. For the history of scholarship and the state of the discussion, cf. the contribution by N. Lohfink in E. Haag, ed., *Gott, der einzige* (1985), 9–25. In addition, see D. L. Petersen, "Israel and Monotheism."
505. Cf. W. von Soden, *Einführung in die Altorientalistik* (1985), 144.
506. For the same "monotheistic" tendencies in Mesopotamia, cf. B. Hartmann, "Monotheismus in Mesopotamien?" in O. Keel, ed., *Monotheismus im Alten Israel and seiner Umwelt,* 49–81. For Akhenaton's "monotheism," cf. E. Hornung's essay in Keel, ibid., 83–97. Cf. also N. Lohfink, *Unsere grossen Wörter,* 131ff. J. C. de Moor, *The Rise of Yahwism,* 42–100, shows that on occasion Israel's environment came to experience a "crisis of polytheism."
507. In my judgment, the burial of gods (Gen. 35:1–4) does not have this meaning. This thesis is esp. represented by B. Lang (*Der einzige Gott,* 66–68), although the texts cited by him from the Old Testament do not provide the desired support. 1 Sam. 7:2–14 is redacted by the Deuteronomistic scribes; Jer. 44:18 does not refer only to the siege of Jerusalem in 587/586.
508. Cf. again the examples in S. Schroer, *In Israel gab es Bilder;* and U. Winter, *Frau und Götter.*
509. Cf. n. 284 above. For El as a steer, cf. *RGT* (2d ed.), 218f., 220, 223.
510. Whether at times there have been revolutions (so O. Keel and F. Stolz in the collection of essays edited by O. Keel, *Monotheismus im Alten Israel und seiner Umwelt*) appears to me to be neither provable nor probable.
511. Cf. in what follows the different contributions in E. Haag, ed., *Gott, der einzige* (1985). Cf. also the outline of early Israelite religion attempted by D. N. Freedman (" 'Who Is like Thee among the Gods?' The Religion of Early Israel," in P. D. Miller, Jr., et al., eds., *Ancient Israelite Religion,* FS F. M. Cross [Philadelphia, 1987], 315–335) and the contribution by T. N. D. Mettinger, "The Elusive Essence: YHWH, El and Baal and the Distinctiveness of Israelite Faith," in E. Blum et al., eds., *Die Hebräische Bibel und ihre zweifache Nachgeschichte,* FS R. Rendtorff (1990), 393–417.
512. Cf. Vol. II, 6. 3.
513. Cf. H.-P. Müller, "Gott und die Götter in den Anfängen der biblischen Religion: Zur Vorgeschichte des Monotheismus," in O. Keel, ed., *Monotheismus im Alten Israel und seiner Umwelt,* 99–142. See pp. 114ff. F. Stolz makes a different assessment in the same volume (pp. 155ff.).
514. Cf. also P. Welten, "Gott Israels—Gott vom Sinai," *BThZ* 1, 1984, 225–239.
515. "The later monotheism in Israel is the spiritual extension of the original knowledge of God" (Th. C. Vriezen, *Theology,* 23).
516. B. Lang (*Wie wird man Prophet in Israel?* 1980, 157) thinks, however, that all efforts to find a monolatrous program in the nomadic religion of the patriarchs or in the work of Moses continues to be an "exegetical romanticism about the wilderness." So what! The issue does not involve a "program." What would he say to J. C. de Moor (*The Rise of Yahwism*) who expresses a different perspective when he traces the influence of monolatry back even earlier to the Egyptian worship of Amun-Re?
517. Cf., e.g., below, chap. 4.6.b.
518. Cf. also below, chap. 4.4.f.

519. J. Scharbert, "Jahwe im frühisraelitischen Recht," in E. Haag, ed., *Gott, der einzige* (1985), 160–183.
520. See also above, 3.3.e. For the "Canaanites," see also n. 668 below.
521. Regarding these matters in the Yahwist, see E. Zenger, "Das jahwistische Werk—ein Wegbereiter des jahwistischen Monotheismus?" in E. Haag, ed., *Gott, der einzige*, 26–53; and F.-L. Hossfeld, "Einheit und Einigkeit Gottes im frühen Jahwismus," in M. Bohnke und H. Heinz, eds., *Im Gespräch mit dem dreieinen Gott: Elemente einer trinitarischen Theologie*, FS W. Breuning (1985), 60–68. For the dating of the Yahwist, see above, n. 3.
522. E. Zenger, "Das jahwistische Werk—ein Wegbereiter des jahwistischen Monotheismus?" 50–51.
523. Cf. G. Hentschel, "Elija und der Kult des Baal," in E. Haag, ed., *Gott, der einzige*, 54–90; and P. Weimar, "Elija," *NBL* I, cols. 516–520.
524. Thus with G. Hentschel, "Elija und der Kult des Baal," 60f.
525. According to G. Hentschel, "Elija und der Kult des Baal," 84 (cf. pp. 88ff.), Elijah demanded already in the earliest form of the narrative (vv. 21, 30, 40) "compliance with the first commandment."
526. For Baal as a weather god and dispenser of rain, cf. O. Loretz, *Ugarit und die Bibel* (1990), 73–78. See there the additional literature and the references to the Ugaritic texts. Cf. also for Baal, *WdM* 1, 253–274.
527. For the divine judgment on Carmel in the narrative's final form, cf. also H. D. Preuss, *Verspottung fremder Religionen im Alten Testament* (BWANT 92; 1971), 80–100.
528. G. Hentschel, "Elija und der Kult des Baal," 86.
529. For this, see H.-W. Jüngling, "Der Heilige Israels: Der erste Jesaja um Thema 'Gott,' " in E. Haag, ed., *Gott, der einzige*, 91–114.
530. Cf. below, chap. 4.7.b.
531. Isa. 1:4; 5:19, 24; 10:20; 12:6; 17:7; 29:19; 30:11, 12, 15; 31:1; cf. "the Holy One of Jacob" in 29:23 and in 10:17 "his = Israel's Holy One." H.-W. Jüngling ("Der Heilige Israels: Der erste Jesaja um Thema 'Gott,' " 99ff.) classifies as Isaianic 1:4; 5:19–24; 30:11 (12, 15); and 31:1 in addition to 6:3.
532. Cf. below, 4.3, 3.4.d. and 3.7.b.
533. Cf., for this, Vol. II, 15.2.
534. For this, see, above all, H. Vorländer, *Mein Gott* (AOAT 23; 1975); R. Albertz, *Persönliche Frömmigkeit und offizielle Religion* (1978); and M. Rose, *Der Ausschliesslichkeitsanspruch Jahwes: Deuteronomische Schultheologie und die Volksfrömmigkeit in der späten Königszeit* (BWANT 106; 1975).
535. For this, see P. Höffken, "Eine Bemerkung zum religionsgeschichtlichen Hintergrund von Dtn 6,4," *BZ* NF 28, 1984, 88–93.
536. Cf. Gen. 12:6f.; 28:16ff.; Judges 6; 1 Sam. 7:16; 9:12; 14:35; 2 Sam. 15:7; 1 Kings 3:22ff.; 15:14; 18:30; 19:14; etc.
537. Cf. n. 500 above.
538. Cf. G. Braulik, "Das Deuteronomium und die Geburt des Monotheismus," in E. Haag, ed., *Gott, der einzige*, 115–159.
539. Cf. A. Deissler, *Grundbotschaft*, 25. For the translation of Deut. 6:4, cf. also R. W. Moberly, VT Suppl 41, 1990, 209–215.
540. See, however, B. Lang, *Der einzige Gott*, 74ff., for the interests of the "YHWH alone movement."
541. Thus also B. Lang, *Der einzige Gott*, 53–57.
542. See J. Tigay, *You Shall Have No Other Gods*. Cf. in addition his "Israelite Religion: The Onomastic and Epigraphic Evidence," in P. D. Miller, Jr., et al., eds., *Ancient Israelite Religion*, FS F. M. Cross (Philadelphia, 1987), 157–194; and (with reservations) J. D. Fowler, *Theophoric Names in Ancient Hebrew* (JSOT Suppl 49; Sheffield, 1988).
543. Now it is a curious argument to oppose this position by saying that there was no evidence for this in the official religion (thus H. Niehr in his review of Tigay's book: *BZ* NF 33, 1989, 298f.), since previously the opposite has often been maintained, i.e. the official religion may have been "Yahwistic," while personal piety may have been "polytheistic." Cf. thus, e.g., M. Rose or B. Lang.

544. Cf. J. C. de Moor, *The Rise of Yahwism,* pp. 10–41.
545. Cf. H.-D. Hoffmann, *Reform und Reformen* (AThANT 66; 1980). Cf. also H. Donner, *Geschichte des Volkes Israel und seiner Nachbarn in Grundzügen,* vol. 2 (1986), 331f., who makes critical remarks concerning the reform of Hezekiah.
546. Cf. above, sec. 8.c.
547. For these problems and others, see E. S. Gerstenberger, *Jahwe—ein patriarchaler Gott?* (1988); see pp. 38–50, "Jahwe und seine Aschera."
548. See also H. Vorländer, "Der Monotheismus Israels als Antwort auf die Krise des Exils," in B. Lange, ed., *Der einzige Gott,* 84–113 (134–139, 145–148: notes and literature).
549. See H. Wildberger, "Der Monotheismus Deuterojesajas," in H. Donner et al., eds., *Beiträge zur alttestamentlichen Theologie,* FS W. Zimmerli (1977), 506–530.
550. Cf. C. J. Labuschagne, *The Incomparability of Yahweh in the Old Testament* (Leiden, 1966).
551. Cf. *ThWAT* 2, cols. 272f.
552. Isa. 41:1–5, 21–29; 43:8–13; 44:6–8; and 45:18–25.
553. G. Braulik, "Das Deuteronomium und die Geburt des Monotheismus," in E. Haag, ed., *Gott, der einzige,* 151: "Theologically, Deutero-Isaiah thus begins where Deuteronomy in chap. 4 has arrived with its teaching about God." See also his (pp. 154ff.) interpretation of God in the Song of Moses (Deuteronomy 32).
554. The data in the fifth century B.C.E. texts of the Jewish colony of Elephantine, located on the Nile (see *AOT,* 2d ed., 450–454; *ANET,* 2d and 3d eds., 491ff.), significantly deviate from this picture. These texts indicate that not only YHWH but also other gods were worshiped. Cf., e.g., H. Donner, *Geschichte Israels,* vol. 2 (1986), 382f.; and F. Stolz, in Keel, ed., *Monotheismus im Alten Israel und seiner Umwelt,* 166, 172.
555. For "the traces of the history of Yahweh faith in the Psalms," cf. G. Schmuttermayr, "Vom Gott unter Göttern um einzigen Gott," in FS H. Gross (1986), 349–374.
556. Thus H. Vorländer, "Der Monotheismus Israels als Antwort auf die Krise des Exils," 106: "The Israelites were stimulated and supported in the shaping of their monotheistic faith by the Persians." Cf. also B. Lang, *ThQ* 166, 1986, 139.
557. See below, sec. 10.a.
558. Cf. N. Lohfink, *BiKi* 38, 1983, 58: "Above all . . . the binding together of the segmentary form of society with the exclusive worship of Yahweh is without an analogy." For the "Canaanites," see n. 668 below.
559. J. Schreiner has produced an instructive outline of this development, "Ein Volk durch den einen Gott," in J. Schreiner and K. Wittstadt, eds., *Communio sanctorum: Einheit der Christen, Einheit der Kirche,* FS P.-W. Scheele (1988), 15–33.
560. So with M. Rose, *Der Ausschliesslichkeitsanspruch Jahwes,* 144f.
561. See Vol. II, chap. 15.
562. For this, see H. Wildberger, "Israel und sein Land," *EvTh* 16, 1956, 404–422; W. Eckert, N. P. Levinson, and M. Stöhr, eds., *Jüdisches Volk—gelobtes Land* (1970); P. Diepold, *Israels Land* (BWANT 95; 1972); E. Cortese, *La terra di Canaan nella storia sacerdotale del Pentateuco* (Brescia, 1972); Th. F. Kane, *God Who Gives* (Pamplona, 1973); W. D. Davies, *The Gospel and the Land* (Berkeley, 1974); R. Rendtorff, *Israel und sein Land* (ThEx 188; 1975); F.-W. Marquardt, *Die Juden und ihr Land* (1975); W. Brueggemann, *The Land* (Philadelphia, 1977); A. Ohler, *Israel, Volk und Land* (1979); A. G. Auld, *Joshua, Moses and the Land* (Edinburgh, 1980); G. Strecker, ed., *Das Land Israel in biblischer Zeit* (1983); and E. W. Davies, "Land: Its Rights and Privileges," in R. E. Clements, ed., *The World of Ancient Israel* (Cambridge, 1989), 349–369. See also W. Zimmerli, *Theology,* 64–69.
563. Cf. R. E. Clements, *Theology,* 92f.
564. Cf. the Meša inscription concerning Gad (*KAI,* no. 181,1. 10; *RGT* (2d ed.), 256; *TUAT* I/6, 648).
565. This would not be surprising, if it is true, e.g., that the "Moses group" immigrating into the land may have been relatively small, as most have assumed.
566. For this, see J. G. Plöger, "אֲדָמָה," *ThWAT* 1, cols. 95–105; J. Bergmann and M. Ottoson, "אֶרֶץ," *ThWAT* 1, cols. 418–436; H. H. Schmid, "אֲדָמָה *'ădāmâ* Erdboden," *THAT* 1, cols. 57–60; and "אֶרֶץ *'ereṣ* Erde, Land," *THAT* 1, cols. 228–236. Further, L. Rost, "Die Bezeichnungen für Land und Volk im Alten Testament," in L. Rost, *Das kleine Credo* (1965), 76–101.
567. L. Rost, "Die Bezeichnungen für Land und Volk im Alten Testament," 78.

568. Ezekiel often uses the expression of אדמת ישראל = *'admat yiśrā'ēl* ("land of Israel").
569. H.-J. Zobel, *Stammesspruch und Geschichte* (BZAW 95; 1965).
570. For the historical as well as sociological problems of the conquest, cf. the descriptions in the histories of Israel by H. Donner and A. H. J. Gunneweg. Also see W. Thiel, *Die soziale Entwicklung Israels in vorstaatlicher Zeit* (2d ed., 1985), 88ff; and V. Fritz, "Conquest or Settlement?" *BA* 50, 1987 (no. 2), 84–100; I. Finkelstein, *The Archaeology of the Israelite Settlement* (Jerusalem, 1988); and H. Weippert, *Palästina in vorhellenistischer Zeit* (1988). See further, M. Weinfeld, "Historical Facts behind the Israelite Settlement Pattern," *VT* 38, 1988, 324–332; and E. Otto, *ThRev* 85, 1989, cols. 3–10.
571. For this, see R. Kilian, "Die Priesterschrift: Hoffnung auf Heimkehr," in J. Schreiner, ed., *Wort und Botschaft* (1967), 226–243.
572. Thus, in regard to the various verses, see N. Lohfink, *Die Priesterschrift und die Geschichte*, VT Suppl 29, 1978, 189–225 (= *Studien zum Pentateuch*, SBAB 4, 1988, 213–253); see 222f., n. 29. For Joshua 13–21, see E. Cortese, *Josua 13–21* (OBO 94; 1990).
573. For the patriarchal narratives, see Vol. II, chap. 6. Also see there the "fathers" in the Deuteronomic and Deuteronomistic literature.
574. Cf. J. Ha, *Genesis 15* (BZAW 181; 1989). For a different evaluation, see H. Mölle, *Genesis 15*, 1988 (vol. 62).
575. For its "theology of the Land," cf. P. Diepold, *Israels Land, 562*; M. Weinfeld, *Deuteronomy and the Deuteronomic School* (Oxford, 1972), 313ff.; H. D. Preuss, *Deuteronomium* (EdF 164; 1982), 191–194 (including literature); and L. Perlitt, in G. Strecker, ed., *Das Land Israel in biblischer Zeit*, 46–58.
576. For the statements about the fruitfulness of the land, cf. Chr. Gottfriedsen, *Die Fruchtbarkeit von Israels Land* (1985).
577. W. H. Schmidt, BK II/1, 164f. (literature); D. E. Skweres, *Die Rückverweise im Buch Deuteronomium* (AnBib 79; 1979), 157–165.
578. Usually with ארץ = *'ereṣ*, only Deut. 31:20 has אדמה = *'ădāmâ*. According to W. H. Schmidt, BK II/1, 138f., Exod. 3:8, 17 is suspected of being a Deuteronomistic addition.
579. S. Schwertner seeks to make an extensive differentiation, "Das verheissene Land," diss. (Heidelberg, 1967) (cf. *ThLZ* 93, 1968, cols. 787–790) (different waves of immigration; the peaceful as compared to a more militant conquest; possession of the land contrasted with room to live; the ancestors who were more nomadic, while the Moses group by contrast came from sedentary forms of existence; etc.).
580. "The heavens will rain oil, the brooks will flow with honey" is the wording, e.g., in an Ugaritic Baal text (*KTU* 1.6 III 6–7; cf. *KTU* 1.3 II 38–41; cf. O. Loretz, *Ugarit und die Bibel* [1990], 16 and 74). These are not exactly parallel in wording, since oil, honey, and dew (however, not milk) are mentioned.
581. Cf. the description of the land in the narrative of Sinuhe: *TGI* (2d ed.), 4, ll. 80ff.
582. Cf. *ThWAT* 1, col. 546 and K.-D. Schunck, "לין *lûn*," *ThWAT* 4, cols. 527–530. Cf. above, sec. 5.e.
583. For this semantic field, cf. Deut. 1:7f., 20f., 22, 31, 37–39; 4:1, 5, 21, 38; 6:10f., 18f., 23; 7:1f.; 8:1, 7–10; 12:1; 19:2, 14; etc.; cf. Exod. 6:8; Num. 15:18; Jer. 2:7; 23:23, and *ThWAT* 1, cols. 544–547, as well as on ירש *yrš* in *THAT* 1 and *ThWAT* 3; and N. Lohfink, "Kerygmata des deuteronomistischen Geschichtswerks," in J. Jeremias and L. Perlitt, eds., *Die Botschaft und die Boten*, FS H. W. Wolff (1981), 87–100, and *BZ* NF 27, 1983, 124–133. N. Lohfink thinks that there may have been a preexilic Deuteronomistic narrative of the conquest of the land, a narrative whose basic component presently extends from Deuteronomy 1 to Joshua 22.
584. Cf. Josh. 1:13, 15; 21:43ff.; 22:4; 23:1; 1 Kings 5:18; 8:56; also 1 Chron. 22:9; 23:25; 2 Chron. 6:41; 14:5; and Heb. 3:4ff. See *ThWAT* 5, cols. 304ff.
585. This contrasts esp. with Ezekiel, probably because of the situation of the exile.
586. Hos. 8:1; 9:15: house of YHWH = the land?
587. See A. Madl, *ThWAT* 6, cols. 893–898.
588. Deut. 4:26–28, 29–31; 11:17; 28:21, 51, 63; 29:21–27; Josh. 23:13, 15; 1 Kings 8:46ff.; 9:3–9; 13:34; 14:15f.; 2 Kings 17:7ff.; 18:11f.; 23:25–27; 25:21; etc.; cf. Lev. 26:20, 32f., 34f.
589. We shall not discuss at this point the fact that there were only elements of Israel that must go into exile. For the theme of the "land" in the setting of the exile, cf. D. L. Smith, *The Religion of the Landless* (Bloomington, Ind., 1989).

590. Deut. 4:1, 5; 5:16, 31; 6:1, 10; 7:1f., 11; 8:1, 9ff.; 11:22, 29, 31f.; 12:1, 19; 15:4f., 7; 17:14; 18:9; 19:1, 8f., 14; 25:15; 26:1; 27:3; 28:21, 63; 30:16; 30:16; 31:20f.; Josh. 23:15f.; 2 Kings 17:23; Amos 5:27; 7:17; and Jer. 7:5–7.

591. Deut. 21:23; 24:4; 1 Kings 14:16; 15:26, 30, 34; 16:20; 22:53; 2 Kings 3:3; 10:29; etc.; cf. Lev. 18:25, 27f.; Num. 35:31; Jer. 2:7; and 3:2.

592. Deut. 4:1; 6:17; 8:1; 11:8, 22–25; 12:1, 28; 16:20; 18:9; 19:8–10; 21:1; 23:21; 27:3; Josh. 13:1, 6; 23:5ff.; and Judg. 2:21ff.: mostly the Deuteronomic, legal stratum.

593. Cf. *ThWAT* 5, cols. 304f., and above, pp. 119f. G. von Rad makes a plea for a Deuteronomic theme: "Es ist noch eine Ruhe vorhanden dem Volke Gottes," TB 8 (3d ed., 1965), 101–108.

594. Cf. Ruth 4:9; and R. de Vaux, *Das Alte Testament und seine Lebensordnungen* I (2d ed., 1964), 268. According to G. Wanke ("Jeremias Ackerkauf—Heil im Gericht?" in V. Fritz et al., eds., *Prophet und Prophetenbuch*, FS O. Kaiser, 1989, 265–276), Jeremiah 32 does not contain a promise of salvation, but rather a recognition of judgment. Wanke finds the following relationship between symbolic act and symbolic event: "Even as the farm bought by the prophet continues to be withheld from cultivation through the safekeeping of the deed of purchase in a sealed clay container for a long period of time, so the land in the future will continue to be withheld from cultivation by its owner" (p. 271). Even if one agrees with Wanke's view of v. 15 (a secondary explanation), nothing in the text suggests the connection between the safekeeping of the deed of purchase and the nonusage of the farm.

595. Gen. 17:8; 28:3f.; 36:7; 37:1; 47:9 (2); Exod. 6:4: all P; outside P, only Ezek. 20:38.

596. Amos 9:13–15; Hos. 2:20, 24f.; Joel 2:18–27; 4:18; Isa. 30:18–26; 60:15ff.; Jer. 31:12–14; Ezek. 36:9ff., 29ff.; and Zech. 8:11f.

597. W. Zimmerli, *Gottes Offenbarung* (TB 19; 2d ed., 1969), 197.

598. See H. D. Preuss, *Deuterojesaja: Eine Einführung in seine Botschaft* (1976), 45f. In Deutero-Isaiah, the discussion of the land is limited just to this destruction; Isa. 49:8 is an addition.

599. For a more precise presentation, see H. Simian, *Die theologische Nachgeschichte der Prophetie Ezechiels*, 1974 (vol. 14).

600. For the terminology, cf. Num. 33:50–34:15 (supplement to P). Cf. n. 572 above for Joshua 13–21 (what is probably the exilic, postexilic "program" of the Priestly document).

601. Cf. above, p. 121, and n. 587.

602. See R. Hanhart, "Das Land in der spätnachexilischen Prophetie," in G. Strecker, ed., *Das Land Israel*, 126–140 (also see there the relation of the land of Israel to the entire earth in these texts, something not discussed here).

603. Or does this mean only Jerusalem, i.e., the temple?

604. See H.-J. Hermisson, *Sprache und Ritus im altisraelitischen Kult* (WMANT 19; 1965), 107ff. Critical for "Levitical piety" and "Levitical songs," which are readily mentioned in these contexts is the work of M. Tsevat, *ThWAT* 2, col. 1018, who rightly refers to ancient Near Eastern personal names.

605. Cf. also G. von Rad, *Verheissenes Land und Jahwes Land im Hexateuch* (TB 8; 3d ed., 1965), 87–100; esp. 88f.

606. See E. Lipiński, "נחל *naḥal*," *ThWAT* 5, cols. 342–360.

607. Exod. 15:17 has here a special place both in its naming of the temple mountain as YHWH's נחלה = *naḥălâ* ("inheritance") and in its context ("the Song of Moses").

608. Cf. above, sec. 3.b.

609. See W. Dommershausen, "גורל," *ThWAT* 1, cols. 991–998.

610. In Num. 26:55f.; 33:54; 34:13; 36:2f.; Josh. 13:6; 14:1f.; 15:1; 16:1; 17:1, 14, 17; and often in Joshua 18–20. A. G. Auld (*Joshua, Moses and the Land*) assumes the possible existence of an older (Deuteronomistic Historian) foundation text behind the report concerning the division of the land in Joshua 13ff. He argues that rather often an original *gĕbûl* is replaced by *gôrāl* in the present text. E. Cortese (*Josua 13–21: Ein priesterschriftlicher Abschnitt im deuteronomistischen Geschichtswerk;* OBO 94, 1990) sees P at work here.

611. The allocation of these chapters to the Priestly source (even if later texts have augmented this section and it now exists in a post-Priestly redactional form) appears to me to be made probable by the study of E. Cortese (*Josua 13–21*).

612. G. Dalman (*AuS* II, 42) thinks he is able to speak more precisely about this (cf. *ThWAT* 1, col. 994).

613. Thus with F. Horst, *Gottes Recht* (TB 12; 1961), 208.

614. The Levites did not participate in the possession of land (Num. 18:20; Deut. 10:9; 12:12; 14:27, 29; 18:1; Josh. 14:4; and 18:7). Rather, they were the נחלה = *naḥălâ* of YHWH. See Vol. II, 9.4.

615. See M. Tsevat, "חלק *ḥālaq* II," *ThWAT* 2, cols. 1015–1020.

616. See H.-J. Fabry, "חבל *ḥbl* I," *ThWAT* 2, cols. 699–706 (esp. 705).

617. See N. Lohfink, *Die Landverheissung als Eid* (SBS 8; 1967), 65ff.; P. Diepold, *Israels Land* (1972), 29ff., 56ff.; and A. Ohler, *Israel, Volk und Land* (1979), 24ff.

618. Deut. 1:7, 35, 37; 2:29; 3:25; 4:21f.; 9:1; 11:31; 12:10; 30:18; 34:3; Josh. 22:19; Ezek. 47:13ff.; and Num. 20:12; differently Deut. 4:45–49.

619. See W. Bolle, "Das israelitische Bodenrecht," diss. (Berlin, 1939); F. Horst, "Das Eigentum nach dem Alten Testament," *Gottes Recht* (TB 12; 1961), 203–221; R. de Vaux, *Das Alte Testament und seine Lebensordnungen* I (2d ed., 1964)," 264ff.; U. Küppel, *Das israelitische Bodenrecht im Hexateuch*, diss. (Fribourg/Schweiz, 1971); J. Ebach, "Sozialethische Erwägungen zum alttestamentlichen Bodenrecht," *BN* 1, 1976, 31–46; H.-J. Boecker, *Recht und Gesetz im Alten Testament und im Alten Orient* (2d ed., 1984), 77–81; and J. Ebach, "Bodenrecht," *NBL* I, cols. 313f. For the ancient Near East, cf. *Orientalisches Recht*, (HdO supplementary vol. 3), 1964; K. Baltzer, "Naboths Weinberg (1. Könige 21): Der Konflikt zwischen israelitischem und kanaanäischem Bodenrecht," *WuD* NF 8 (1965), 82ff.; see *RLA* and *LÄ* for the words Ackerbau, Besitz , Eigentum, Grossgrundbesitz, Landschenkung, Landwirtschaft, etc.; H. Klengel, ed., *Kulturgeschichte des alten Vorderasien* (1989) (see there the terms *Eigentum, Kauf, Pacht*). Cf. also S. Schwertner diss., "Das verheissene Land," 165–168.

620. This was a tenet "which one could call the Magna Carta of the Old Testament law of the land" (H.-J. Boecker, *Recht und Gesetz im Alten Testament und im Alten Orient, 77*).

621. For the stipulations concerning impoverished Israelites becoming slaves (Lev. 25: 39ff.), cf. F. Crüsemann, "Der Exodus als Heiligung," in E. Blum et al., eds., *Die Hebräische Bibel und ihre zweifache Nachgeschichte, FS R.* Rendtorff (1990), 117–129, esp. 124f.

622. Is it an accident that 587 minus 538 equals 49 years?

623. See A. Meinhold, "Jubeljahr. I: Altes Testament," *TRE* 17, 280f. (see the literature).

624. Thus, A. Meinhold, *TRE* 17, 281.

625. Thus following K. Baltzer, "Naboths Weinberg (1. Könige 21)," 73–88. More skeptical is R. Bohlen, *Der Fall Naboth* (TThSt 35; 1978).

626. Cf. W. Thiel, "Die Anfänge von Landwirtschaft und Bodenrecht in der Frühzeit Altisraels," AOF 7 (1980), 127–141.

627. The texts in *TUAT* I/3, 210ff.; additional examples come from Alalakh. For these, see W. Thiel, *Die soziale Entwicklung Israels in vorstaatlicher Zeit*, 52ff. (also see pp. 93ff. for the Israelite law concerning land).

628. Cf. Vol. II, 15.3.

629. Cf. above, sec. 9.c.

630. For them, see Vol. II, 9.3.

631. So in the Meša inscription: *KAI*, no. 181, l. 10. Cf. n. 564 above.

632. Cf. L. Perlitt, in G. Strecker, ed., *Das Land Israel*, 47, concerning the Deuteronomic and Deuteronomistic statements of the land: "According to Israel's own reflection or description, the history of Yahweh began with Israel outside the land and without the land: in revelation and salvation, in guidance and accompaniment. Conversely, Israel was then over a thousand years without a land, Israel the subject of the love of God. However, one must still go a step farther: for the Yahweh from Sinai, Canaan was also a strange land. Therefore he must now conquer it for himself and his own."

633. Cf. M. Weippert, "Fragen des israelitischen Geschichtsbewusstseins," *VT* 23, 1973, 415–442. Cf. n. 589 above.

634. For the further effects of this idea, see M. Buber, *Israel und Palästina* (1950).

635. Cf. also P. Weimar, "Die Jahwekriegserzählungen in Exodus 14, Josua 10, Richter 4 und 1 Samuel 7," *Bibl* 57, 1976, 38–73. According to Weimar, these narratives belong to the context of the dispute with the institution of kingship. Furthermore, he thinks that there was already an older description of the miracle at the sea in Exodus 14 that preceded the Yahwist.

636. Cf. above, p. 42.

637. Cf. M. J. Benedict, *The God of the Old Testament in Relation to War* (New York, 1927;

reprinted, 1972); H. Fredriksson, *Jahwe als Krieger* (Lund, 1945); G. von Rad, *Holy War in Ancient Israel* (Grand Rapids, 1991); R. Smend, *Jahwekrieg und Stämmebund* (FRLANT 84; 2d ed., 1966) (= "Zur ältesten Geschichte Israels," *Gesammelte Studien*, vol. 2, 1987, 116ff.); F. Stolz, *Jahwes und Israels Kriege* (AThANT 60; 1972); M. Weippert, "'Heiliger Krieg' in Israel und Assyrien," *ZAW* 84, 1972, 460–493; P. D. Miller, Jr., *The Divine Warrior in Early Israel* (Cambridge, Mass., 1973; 2d ed., 1975); A. Malamat, *Early Israelite Warfare and the Conquest of Canaan* (Oxford, 1978); P. C. Craigie, *The Problem of War in the Old Testament* (Grand Rapids, 1978); J. Ebach, *Das Erbe der Gewalt* (1980); M. C. Lind, *Yahweh Is a Warrior* (Scottdale, Ont., 1980); N. Lohfink, ed., *Gewalt und Gewaltlosigkeit im Alten Testament* (1983), esp. his essay "Die Schichten des Pentateuch und der Krieg," 51–110; H. D. Preuss, "מלחמה *milḥāmāh*," *ThWAT* 4, cols. 914–926 (literature); F. Stolz, ed., *Religion zu Krieg und Frieden* (1986), including the essay by H. H. Schmid, "Heiliger Krieg und Gottesfrieden im Alten Testament," 49–65; N. Lohfink, "Der gewalttätige Gott des Alten Testament und die Suche nach einer gewaltfreien Gesellschaft," JBTh 2 (1987), 106–136; S.-M. Kang, *Divine War in the Old Testament and in the Ancient Near East* (BZAW 177; 1989); N. Lohfink, "Der 'heilige Krieg' und der 'Bann' in der Bibel," *IKZ* 18, 1989, 104–112; G. H. Jones, "The Concept of Holy War," in R. E. Clements, ed., *The World of Ancient Israel* (Cambridge, 1989), 299–321; A. van der Lingen, *Les guerres de Yahvé* (LeDiv 139; Paris, 1990); and J. A. Soggin, "Krieg. II: Altes Testament," *TRE* 20, 19–25 (literature). Cf. also J. Hempel, *Gott und Mensch im Alten Testament* (BWANT 38; 2d ed., 1936), 33–44; L. Köhler, *Theologie* (4th ed.), 7f.; G. E. Wright, *The Old Testament and Theology* (New York, Evanston, London, 1969), 121ff.; W. Zimmerli, *Theology*, 59–64; E. A. Martens, *God's Design* (Grand Rapids, 1981), 41ff.; and W. H. Schmidt, *Alttestamentlicher Glaube* (6th ed.), 118ff.

638. H. Fredriksson, *Jahwe als Krieger*, 107.

639. Ibid., 112. Fredriksson evaluates the role of the conception of YHWH as warrior to be only positive for the general image of God. The conception of Yahweh as warrior "(a) has given the image of Yahweh the character of a living, active deity; (b) has prepared the way for monotheism; and (c) has caused to stand out strongly certain essential characteristics of Yahweh" as, e.g., YHWH's power, strength, and holiness.

640. Cf. below, chap. 4.6.d.

641. *AOT* (2d ed.), 108–129; *RGT* (2d ed.), 106–110; *ANET* (3d ed.), 60–72, 501–503.

642. Thus, e.g., in Num. 31:28, 49; Deut. 2:14, 16; Josh. 5:4, 6; 6:3; 17:1; Judg. 20:17; 1 Sam. 16:18; 17:33; 2 Sam. 17:8; Isa. 41:12; Jer. 6:23; 38:4; 39:4; 41:3; 48:14; 49:26; 50:30, 42; 51:32; 52:7, 25; Ezek. 27:10, 27; Joel 2:7; 1 Chron. 28:3; etc. From time to time, the expression גבור חיל = *gibbôr ḥayyil* (occasionally plural, "mighty warrior") (1 Chron. 12:9; 2 Chron. 17:13) is also used for YHWH (see below).

643. Cf. Isa. 51:9f.; Pss. 68:22, 31; 74:13f.; 77:17, 20; 89:11; 104:6–9; Job 9:13; and 26:11–13.

644. Cf. below, chap. 4.6.d.

645. "Yahweh usually does not have weapons in these descriptions. In the hymns where creation is described with motifs from the battle with chaos, weapons are entirely absent" (H. Fredriksson, *Jahwe als Krieger*, 78). For YHWH's weaponry (bow, arrow, sword, spear, shield, staff, etc.), cf. ibid., 94–101.

646. Cf., e.g., Isa. 17:12–14; 27:1; Ezek. 29:3–5; 32:2–4; Nahum 1:4; and Hab. 3:6–15.

647. Cf. F. Stolz, *Struckturen und Figuren im Kult von Jerusalem* (BZAW 118; 1970), 72–101. This volume also contains translations of texts.

648. Thus, in the epilogue to the Code of Hammurabi: *TUAT* I/1, 79. For this goddess, cf. *WdM* 1, 81–89; for her warlike character, see p. 85, e.g., "Ishtar of Arbela was the Assyrian goddess of war purely and simply." Cf. also J. Bottéro and S. N. Kramer, *Lorsque les dieux faisaient l'homme* (Paris, 1989), 203–337.

649. "In the Ugaritic texts 'Anat appeared as both fighter and lover. Her power to wage battle was celebrated in great detail" (O. Loretz, *Ugarit und die Bibel*, 1990, 79). On pp. 79f. there is an example of a text and (pp. 81ff.) the indication that wild battle scenes of Anat could live on in biblical texts that tell of YHWH's wrath, as, for example, Isa. 63:1–6 (see below). Cf. also *WdM*1, 235–241;; and *RGT*, 2d ed., 214f.

650. Pss. 7:7; 10:12; 35:23; 44:24, 27; 59:5f.; and 74:22.

651. Cf. below, chap. 5.2.

652. Cf. pp. 144ff. and F. Fredriksson, *Jahwe als Krieger,* 50–55.
653. Cf. *ThWAT* 4, cols. 916–917.
654. Cf. n. 649 above, and the text cited there.
655. Cf. *ThWAT* 1, cols. 912f.
656. N. Lohfink (*JBTh* 2, 126, n. 33; [see n. 637 above]) denies (also on the basis of apologetic reasons owing to his justifiable love for a powerless society) that Exodus 14 was a war narrative, a view, however, that does not itself do justice to the text. S.-M. Kang, *Divine War in the Old Testament and in the Ancient Near East,* 114–125, who finds here only a late theological understanding of this event, is also wrong.
657. Deut. 25:17–19; 1 Sam. 15:2f. Cf. Gen. 14:7; Num. 13:29; 14:25, 43, 45; 24:20; Judg. 3:13; 6:3, 33; 7:12; 10:12; 12:15; 1 Sam. 14:48; 15:5–7, 15, 18; 27:8; 30:1; 2 Sam. 1:1, 8; and 1 Chron. 4:43; 18:11.
658. Thus F. Stolz, *Jahwes und Israels Kriege,* 99. For נֵס (=*nēs*), cf. also H.-J. Fabry, *ThWAT* 5, cols. 468–473, esp. 471f.; and C. Houtman, *OSt* 25, 1989, 110–120.
659. For this phenomenon in the history of religions and the phenomenology of religion, see C. Cople, "Zur Bezeichnung und Bezeugung des 'Heiligen Krieges,' " *BThZ* 1, 1984, 45–57, 189–214; for the Old Testament, see pp. 199–202.
660. For these texts and this period (conquest and securing of the land), cf. also E. S. Gerstenberger, *Jahwe—ein patriarchaler Gott?* (1988), 50–66 ("Jahwe der Stammeskrieger"). There, e.g., he writes on p. 65: "Tribal religions are generally led by males. The ideas of god correspond to the functions of war and defense that are observed in the tribe. However, the female element is also directly integrated." S.-M. Kang (*Divine War in the Old Testament and in the Ancient Near East,* see p. 145) contests the notion that in the "canonical" tradition of the Old Testament the "historical" battles that occurred mainly in the time of David are described as YHWH wars. Rather, YHWH war occurs much more in a regular way in later (mostly Deuteronomistic) theological interpretation.
661. Cf. below, chap. 4.4.f.
662. E. S. Gerstenberger, *Jahwe—ein patriarchaler Gott?* 56.
663. Cf. I. L. Seeligmann, "Menschliches Heldentum und göttliche Hilfe," *ThZ* 19, 1963, 385–411; and L. Schmidt, *Menschlicher Erfolg und Jahwes Initiative* (WMANT 38; 1970).
664. Cf. W. Zimmerli, *Theologie* (6th ed.), 52. See also the English edition (*Theology,* 62).
665. See N. Lohfink, "Die Schichten des Pentateuch und der Krieg," 75ff.
666. Cf. Exod. 6:26; and Num. 1:3, 52; 2:3. Then Pss. 44:10; and 60:12 = 108:12.
667. Cf. above, sec. 3.a.
668. Cf. *ThWAT* 4, col. 916.
669. "Frequently encountered as a military technical term" (H. Fredriksson, *Jahwe als Krieger,* 10): Deut. 20:1; 21:10; Judg. 20:28; 1 Sam. 8:20; Amos 5:3; Job 39:21; with YHWH as subject: Judg. 5:4; Isa. 42:13; Hab. 3:13; Zech. 14:3.
670. Cf. above, sec. 1. For יָצָא/יֹצִיא (*yāṣā'/yôṣî'* "go out, bring out"), cf. *ThWAT* 3, cols. 795–822.
671. Cf. above, p. 42, and see J.-L. Ska, "La sortie d'Egypte (Ex 7–14) dans le récit sacerdotal (Pᵍ) et la tradition prophétique," *Bibl* 60, 1979, 191–215.
672. See P. Welten, *Geschichte und Geschichtsdarstellung in den Chronikbüchern* (WMANT 42; 1973), 79ff., 115ff. S. J. de Vries, *1 and 2 Chronicles* (FOTL 11; 1989); see there the regulations under "Battle Story," "Battle Report," and "Quasi-Holy War Story." N. Lohfink ("Die Schichten des Pentateuch und der Krieg," 51f.) points out in connection with a work by S. Japhet that the Books of Chronicles appear to know nothing of a mighty invasion of the land by the people of Israel.
673. Cf. Vol. II, 7.5.
674. Cf. Vol. II, 9.2.
675. P. Welten, *Geschichte und Geschichtsdarstellung in den Chronikbücher,* 170f.
676. The German translation is provided by P. Welten, *Geschichte und Geschichtsdarstellung in den Chronikbücher,* 140.
677. "Highly imaginative imitation of Israel's primitive holy-war narrative" (S. J. de Vries, *1 and 2 Chronicles,* 434; see 2 Chron. 13:3–21; 14:8–14; 20:1–30; and 25:5–13).
678. Thus, G. von Rad, *Holy War in Ancient Israel,* 40; see the description that follows on pp. 40ff.
679. Cf. below, under d.

680. J. Wellhausen, *Israelitische und jüdische Geschichte* (3d ed.), 26 (= 9th ed., 1958, 24).
681. G. von Rad, *Holy War in Ancient Israel,* 93.
682. See ibid., 115–127.
683. R. Smend, *Jahwekrieg und Stämmebund,* 637.
684. "It is not that the cultic element had been entirely absent in YHWH war in the ancient period. This absence would not be expected at the beginning, because there already is a religious process at work in the name itself. And cultic forms are almost always a factor in one way or another" (R. Smend, *Jahwekrieg und Stämmebund,* 27). For a critique of the interpretation of YHWH war as a cultic institution, see also G. Fohrer, *History of Israelite Religion,* trans. D. E. Green (Nashville, 1972), 87–94.
685. R. Smend, *Jahwekrieg und Stämmebund,* 30. Perhaps it was (also) the experience of the powerfulness of YHWH in war and their own strength under this deity that led the tribes to form early Israel.
686. F. Stolz, *Jahwes und Israels Kriege.*
687. M. Weippert, "'Heiliger Krieg' in Israel und Assyrien."
688. For the theory and practice of war among the neighbors of Israel, see the literature listed in *ThWAT* 4, cols. 914f., 917, and, above all, the description in part 1 (pp. 11–110) of the work by S.-M. Kang, *Divine War in the Old Testament and in the Ancient Near East* (Berlin, 1989).
689. How the "conquest" (= settlement) of Israel or of its various parts is actually carried out (infiltration model; invasion model; revolution model; a longer period of symbiosis; different forms and incursions; etc.) will not be discussed at this point. Cf. n. 570 above. For the view that the conquest was chiefly a military action and for an analysis of the "tactics" used during this invasion, cf., e.g., A. Malamat, *Early Israelite Warfare and the Conquest of Canaan.*
690. Oddly enough, P. D. Miller investigates Exodus 15 with his mythical-historical schematic, but not Exod. 13:17–14:31 (*The Divine Warrior in Early Israel*).
691. That the Old Testament narratives of YHWH war and the ban cause problems for contemporary readers (and among them not only those who have been influenced by the New Testament) and Christians has led many Old Testament scholars to engage in apologetic, hermeneutical, and historical reflections on this issue. Cf. M. J. Benedict, *The God of the Old Testament in Relation to War;* P. C. Craigie, *The Problem of War in the Old Testament;* and J. Ebach, *Das Erbe der Gewalt.* Further, see H. D. Preuss, "Alttestamentliche Aspekte zu Macht und Gewalt," in *Macht und Gewalt* (vol. 14), 1978, 113–134.
692. M. C. Lind, *Yahweh Is a Warrior.*
693. For M. Rose, the "demilitarization of war" present there is a result of secondary redaction (*BZ* NF 20, 1976, 197–211). However, cf. for all of this N. Lohfink, "Die Schichten des Pentateuch und der Krieg," in N. Lohfink, ed., *Gewalt und Gewaltlosigkeit im Alten Testament,* 61–64.
694. Conquest: from the judges to David; "a theology of defeat" (Num. 14:39–45; Deuteronomy 32; and Psalm 78); kings and prophets; and Deuteronomic and Deuteronomistic writings. Oddly enough, the Books of Chronicles are missing.
695. S.-M. Kang, *Divine War in the Old Testament and in the Ancient Near East.*
696. For this, see N. Lohfink, "חרם *ḥāram*," *ThWAT* 3, cols. 192–213 (literature); idem, "Bann," *NBL* I, cols. 237f.; idem, "Der 'heilige Krieg' und der 'Bann' in der Bibel," *IKZ* 18, 1989, 104–112; and P. Welten, "Bann I: Altes Testament," *TRE* 5, 159–161.
697. "The words with the root *ḥrm* I are especially situated in the semantic field of war and destruction": N. Lohfink, *ThWAT* 3, col. 195. The term often occurs with נכה = *nākâ,* "slay."
698. However, apostate individuals according to Deut. 13:2–12 are subject to the death penalty. The distinction between the ban and the death penalty probably consists of the fact that in the former the possessions (and the family) are also exterminated. "This punishment is toned down in the postexilic period (cf. Ezra 10:8; Lev. 27:29)" (Lohfink, *NBL* I, col. 237).
699. Cf. also H. D. Preuss, *Deuteronomium* (EdF 164; 1982), 32, 81f., 101, 134, 140, 189; and N. Lohfink, *ThWAT* 3, col. 212.
700. Laws pertaining to war are found in Deut. 20:1–20; 21:10–14; and 23:10–15 (cf. 25:17–19). Addresses pertaining to war occur in Deut. 1:2f., 29–33; 2:24f., 31; 3:12f., 28; 7:17–24; 9:1–6; 11:22–25; and 31:1–6, 7f., 23. For the warlike spirit of Deuteronomy and its back-

ground, cf. H. D. Preuss, *Deuteronomium,* 188f. Cf. N. Lohfink, *ThWAT* 3, cols. 209ff.; and
idem, "Die Schichten des Pentateuch und der Krieg," *Gewalt und Gewaltlosigkeit im Alten Testament,* 65ff.

701. N. Lohfink (*NBL* I, col. 238) sees here a literary resistance against the Assyrian "empire propaganda, which consciously displays military terror." YHWH was capable of great actions of annihilation for the benefit of Israel.
702. Isa. 34:2, 5; Jer. 50:21, 26; 51:3; 2 Chron. 20:33; and Dan. 11:44.
703. N. Lohfink, *NBL* I, col. 237.
704. Cf. e.g., N. Lohfink, *ThWAT* 3, cols. 205f.
705. *KAI,* no. 181, ll. 16f.; *RGT* (2d ed.), 256; and *TUAT* I/6, 649.
706. Cf. the commentaries and the dealing with "Saul's rejection" mentioned in Vol. II, 7.2.
707. Cf. J. A. Soggin, "Der prophetische Gedanke über den heiligen Krieg als Gericht gegen Israel," *VT* 10, 1960, 79–83 (= *Old Testament and Oriental Studies,* Rome, 1975, 67ff.); and D. L. Christensen, *Transformations of the War Oracle in Old Testament Prophecy* (Missoula, Mont., 1975).
708. See R. Bach, *Die Aufforderungen zur Flucht und zum Kampf im alttestamentlichen Prophetenspruch* (WMANT 9; 1962).
709. Isa. 3:25; 13:4; 21:15; 22:2; 30:32; 42:25; Jer. 4:19; 6:4, 23; 18:21; 21:4f.; 28:8; 46:3; 49:2, 14; Ezek. 27:27; 39:20; Hos. 10:9, 14; Joel 2:5; Amos 1:14; Obadiah 1; and Zech. 14:2.
710. Cf. Vol. II, 14.12.
711. Thus often N. Lohfink, e.g., *IKZ* 18, 1989, 105.
712. Cf. Vol. II, 14.12; and 15.4.
713. Cf. 1 Kings 20:18; Micah 3:5; Zech. 9:10; Ps. 120:7; Qoh. 3:8; then also Deut. 20:10–12; Josh. 11:19; 2 Sam. 8:10; 11:7; 1 Kings 2:5; Isa. 27:4f.; and 1 Chron. 18:10.
714. See H. H. Schmid, "Frieden. II: Altes Testament," *TRE* 11, 605–610 (literature).
715. See R. Bach, ". . . , der Bogen zerbricht, Spiesse zerschlägt und Wagen mit Feuer verbrennt," in H. W. Wolff, ed., *Probleme biblischer Theologie,* FS G. von Rad (1971), 13–26. Cf. also Hos. 1:5; 2:20; Jer. 49:35; Micah 5:9f.; and Zech. 9:10.
716. Vol. II, 15.4.
717. Thus N. Lohfink, "Der gewalttätige Gott des Alten Testaments und die Suche nach einer gewaltfreien Gesellschaft," JBTh 2 (1987), 119f.
718. Isa. 26:3, 12; 32:14ff.; 60 (cf., however, also v. 12); 65:17ff.; Ezek. 34:25ff.; and 37:26ff.
719. With N. Lohfink, *IKZ* 18, 1989, 106f.
720. Thus N. Lohfink, "Der gewalttätige Gott des Alten Testaments und die Suche nach einer gewaltfreien Gesellschaft," 133.
721. N. Lohfink, *IKZ* 18, 1989, 108. What Lohfink further says then about power and powerlessness reaches (both significantly and legitimately) beyond the Old Testament.
722. N. Lohfink, "Der gewalttätige Gott des Alten Testaments und die Suche nach einer gewaltfreien Gesellschaft," 106–136, esp., e.g., 107, 121, 133f., etc. He certainly draws throughout on R. Girard's view of power and freedom from power.

Chapter 4. The God Who Elects

1. Intense theological discussions about YHWH, his manner of behaving, and the possibility and impossibility of his compassion within perhaps a more theoretical teaching about God are found, according to L. Schmidt (*"De Deo,"* BZAW 143, 1976), in Job 1; Gen. 18:22ff.; and the Book of Jonah, assuming that his literary and redactional theses concerning these texts are correct.
2. For the "Kenite/Midianite hypothesis," cf. above, pp. 40, 60f., 69, 98. For Exod. 6:1–8, cf. also E. A. Martens, *God's Design* (Grand Rapids, 1981), 12ff.
3. Cf. Vol. II, 6.3–5.
4. Cf. יהוה בשם קרא = *qārā' bĕšem yhwh* ("call on the name of Yahweh") in Gen. 12:8; 13:4; 21:33; 1 Kings 18:24; etc.
5. *AOT* (2d ed.), 261: in a Babylonian prayer. This form of address is not identical with the "prayer to an *unknown* God," to whom one calls because one does not know which god one has sinned against. Cf. *RGT* (2d ed.), 133.

6. *AOT* (2d ed.), 128f.

7. See O. Grether, *Name und Wort Gottes im Alten Testament* (BZAW 64; 1934); J. Mehlmann, *Der Name Gottes im Alten Testament* (Rome, 1956); R. Mayer, "Der Gottesname Jahwe im Lichte der neuesten Forschung," *BZ* NF 2, 1958, 26–53; S. Herrmann, "Der alttestamentliche Gottesname," *EvTh* 26, 1966, 281–293 (= TB 75, 1986, 76ff.); J. Kinyongo, *Origine et signification du nom divin Yahvé à la lumière de récents travaux et de traditions sémitico-bibliques* (BBB 35; 1970); E. Jenni, "יהוה Jhwh Jahwe," *THAT* 1, cols. 701–707; G. H. Parke-Taylor, יהוה–*Yahweh: The Divine Name in the Bible* (Waterloo, Ont., 1975); H. von Stietencron, ed., *Der Name Gottes* (1975) (see in this volume H. Gese, "Der Name Gottes im Alten Testament," 75–89); and M. Rose, *Jahwe* (ThSt 122; 1978); cf. his essay in *TRE* 16, 438–441; D. N. Freedman, P. O'Connor, "יהוה JHWH," *ThWAT* 3, cols. 533–554; and H. D. Preuss, "Jahwe," *EKL* (3d ed.), vol. 2, cols. 789–791 (literature). J. C. de Moor presents an unusual explanation of the name YHWH in connection with his far-reaching theses about pre-Israelite YHWH religion (*The Rise of Yahwism,* BETL 91, Louvain, 1990, 234ff.). See also W. Eichrodt, *Theologie,* 1:116ff.; G. von Rad, *Theologie* 1:193ff.; P. van Imschoot, *Theology of the Old Testament* (1965), 1:1:7ff.; A. Deissler, *Die Grundbotschaft des Alten Testaments* (1972), 48ff.; W. Zimmerli, *Theologie* (6th ed., 1989), 12ff.; W. H. Schmidt, BK II/1, 169–180 (literature); idem, *Alttestamentlicher Glaube,* 63ff.

8. The material is found in R. Kittel, *RE* (3d ed.), vol. 8, 529ff.; cf. O. Eissfeldt, *RGG* (3d ed.), vol. 3, cols. 515f.; and *ThWAT* 3, col. 542.

9. Cf. E. Jenni, *THAT* 1, col. 31.

10. Due in part to the plea of H. Ewald (1803–1875)? According to a student anecdote, he is supposed to have begun his lectures in Göttingen with the "authentic professorial prayer": "Great Yahweh, who Gesenius in Halle still continues to call Jehovah, stand by us!" Thus, according to O. Eissfeldt, *Adonis und Adonaj* (1970), 8.

11. In Qoheleth and Esther, God is spoken of only in a veiled manner: "help from another quarter" (Esth. 4:14).

12. In Canticles, the interpretation or rather the reading of שלהבתיה = *šalhebetyâ* in 8:6 is debated. Is it a compound word with the short form of the divine name יה = *yâ* ("flame of Yah" as a superlative construct), or is it a so-called intensive suffix? Cf. the commentaries.

13. יהוה = *yahweh* in Job 12:9 is probably a scribal mistake.

14. For the personal names, see *ThWAT* 3, cols. 539–541.

15. The literary analysis of the composition of the text leads, in my opinion, invariably to a Yahwistic (Exod. 3:1abα, 2–4a, 5–7, 8*, 16–17*) and an Elohistic (Exod. 3:1bβ, 4b, 6, 9–15*) narrative strain. Verse 15 may be a later continuation. Cf. for this, W. H. Schmidt, BK II/1, 107ff.; for a different assessment, see M. Saebø, "Offenbarung oder Verhüllung?" in J. Jeremias and L. Perlitt, eds., *Die Botschaft und die Boten,* FS H. W. Wolff (1981), 45–48. For the Elohist, see P. Weimar, *NBL* I, cols. 527–532.

16. In opposition to L. Köhler, the name is hardly to be regarded as a normal substantive with a י = *y* prefix. Cf. E. Jenni, *THAT* 1, cols. 702f.

17. M. Rose (*Jahwe*) regards the short form as the original form of the name and thinks that the long form may have been introduced for the first time under Josiah. This thesis breaks apart because of what are clear, older, extra-biblical occurrences of the long form. These include the Meša inscription (*TUAT* I/6, 649) and the texts from Kuntillet 'Ajrud and Khirbet el-Qom (*TUAT* II/4, 557, 563f.). See n. 25 below and see above, pp. 111,115.

18. This is why other explanations and etymological derivations are excluded: "the one who causes to fall," "the one who casts lightning," "the one who blows," not to mention others. Cf. *ThWAT* 3, col. 549. Also cf. O. Procksch, *Theologie,* 439: "The more complicated one imagines the derivation to be, the more improbable it is." J. C. de Moor (*The Rise of Yahwism,* BETL 91, 223ff.) sees in YHWH a tribal ancestor deity, who had nothing to do with the exodus, as Psalm 68; Habakkuk 3; Deuteronomy 32 and 33; and Judges 5 demonstrate in their earliest strata. The name of this deity may have been אל = *'ēl*, El, which was later connected or even identified with יהוה = *yahweh*. As יהוה-אל = *yahweh-'ēl*, the resulting meaning would be "May El be present or active (e.g., as a helper)."

19. For this, cf. the interpretation of Philo (*Vita Mosis* I 74f.), cited in H. Gese, *Der Name Gottes im Alten Testament,* p. 76.

20. In spite of the objection, which is not convincing, by R. Bartelmus (*HYH: Bedeutung und Funktion eines hebräischen "Allerweltswortes,"* ATSAT 17, 1982.

21. Cf. W. von Soden, "Jahwe 'Er ist, Er erweist sich,'" *WO* 3/3, 1966, 177–187 (= *Bibel und Alter Orient,* BZAW 162, 1985, 78ff.).

22. Cf. M. Saebø, "Offenbarung oder Verhüllung?" in J. Jeremias and L. Perlitt, eds., *Die Botschaft und die Boten,* FS H. W. Wolff (1981), 43–55. He assumes (pp. 52f.) that the name of YHWH originated through the reduplication of the short form יה = *yâ.* This view that requires him to adopt changes is improbable.

23. This is true, e.g., also in terms of the statement that human beings are made in the "image" of God in Gen. 1:26ff. (cf. Vol. II, 11.3).

24. O. Grether, *Name und Wort Gottes im Alten Testament,* 8.

25. Cf. above, pp. 111, 114. See then *KAI,* nos. 192–197; Y. Aharoni, *Arad Inscriptions* (Jerusalem, 1981), 2:18, 21; 3:16, 40; 4:21; 5:21; 9:18. See n. 17 above, for further references. Cf. also *ThWAT* 3, cols. 536–538, for the extra-biblical evidence. The seal of "*miqnyaw,* servant of YHWH" (8th cent.?) was published by F. M. Cross in L. Gorelick and E. Williams-Forte, eds., *Ancient Seals and the Bible* (Malibu, Calif., 1984), 55–63. Cf. also N. Avigad, "The Contribution of Hebrew Seals to an Understanding of Israelite Religion and Society," in P. D. Miller, Jr., et al., eds., *Ancient Israelite Religion,* FS F. M. Cross (Philadelphia, 1987), 195–208. Cf. also *BRev* 5, 1989, 31.

26. Cf. n. 17 above.

27. Cf. *WdM* 1, 291f.; O. Loretz, *Ugarit und die Bibel* (1990), 88. For a different view, see J. C. de Moor, *The Rise of Yahwism,* 113ff. (YW = Yammu?!). S. Dalley, "Yahweh in Hamath in the 8th Century BC: Cuneiform Material and Historical Deductions" (*VT* 40, 1990, 21–32), seeks to demonstrate an Akkadian equivalent *IA(u)* for the short form *YH(w).*

28. See H.-P. Müller, "Gab es in Ebla einen Gottesnamen Ja?" *ZA* 70, 1980, 70–92. For the Akkadian *yaḥwi,* "[the deity] has brought [a child] to life" (or may do this), cf. H. B. Huffmon in G. E. Wright, ed., *The Bible and the Ancient Near East,* FS W. F. Albright (Baltimore and London, 1971), 283–289. Also see *ThWAT* 3, cols. 543f.

29. Since B. Stade, *Geschichte des Volkes Israels,* vol. 1 (1887), 130ff., see esp. E. Kautzsch, *Biblische Theologie des Alten Testaments* (1911), 47ff.; L. Köhler, *Theologie* (4th ed.), 27f.; G. von Rad, *Theology,* 1:8–10; W. H. Schmidt, *Alttestamentlicher Glaube* (6th ed.), 71ff. Critical of this hypothesis are, e.g., O. Procksch, *Theologie,* 74ff., 81; and also, although for different reasons, J. C. de Moor, *The Rise of Yahwism,* 223.

30. Since this was scandalous later on for P, it probably transferred Moses' encounter with God to Egypt (Exod. 6:2ff.).

31. Cf. above, pp. 41f., 55f., 58f., 78, 102f., 106, 112f.

32. Cf. S. Herrmann, "Der alttestamentliche Gottesname," 78, 82ff. (= TB 75, 1986, 76ff.); and R. Giveon, *Les Bédouins Shosou des documents égyptiens* (Leiden, 1971). Cf. above, p. 69.

33. S. Herrmann has demonstrated that the Tetragrammaton יהוה = *yahweh* (YHWH), and not only the short forms יהו = *yāhû* or יה = *yâ,* conforms to the Egyptian sequence of consonants *YH3* (*Der alttestamentliche Gottesname,* 286ff. = TB 75, 1986, 81ff.). For a different explanation, see J. C. de Moor, *The Rise of Yahwism,* 111.

34. Cf. above, chap. 3.8, chap. 3.10, and chap. 3.8.d, "The Formation of Monotheism." What J. C. de Moor (*The Rise of Yahwism,* 113f.) believes he is able to conclude appears to me to be nothing more than a heavily hypothetical construction.

35. See A. S. van der Woude, "צבא *ṣābā'* Heer," *THAT* 2, cols. 498–507 (esp. col. 499 and the combinations appearing in H.-J. Zobel, *ThWAT* 6, col. 879); also see *THAT* 2, cols. 960f, for the expression יהוה צבאות שמו = *yahweh ṣĕbā'ôt šĕmô* ("YHWH Sebaoth is his name"). Also see T. D. Mettinger, *The Dethronement of Sabaoth* (CB OT 18; Lund, 1982, p. 12) for a table of precise percentages for the occurrence of this expression throughout the Old Testament. Also see H.-J. Zobel, "צבאות *ṣĕbā'ôt,*" *ThWAT* 6, cols. 876–892 (literature). Cf. also L. Köhler, *Theologie* (4th ed.), 31ff.; and above, chap. 3, n. 652.

36. H.-J. Zobel, *ThWAT* 6, col. 892.

37. The expression יהוה צבאות שמו = *yahweh ṣĕbā'ôt šĕmô* ("YHWH Sebaoth is his name") is found in the "participial hymn" (A. S. van der Woude, *THAT* 2, col. 960) in Isa. 47:4; 48:2; 51:15; 54:5; Jer. 10:16; 31:35; 32:18; 46:18; 48:15; 50:34; and 51:19, 57; the expanded form that adds אלהי = *'ĕlōhēy* ("God") occurs in Amos 4:13; 5:27. This expression does not occur in any

early text. Through these concluding remarks, the worshiping, postexilic community emphasizes the power of YHWH who is praised. The reference to the (earthly) hosts is no longer recognizable.

38. See C. T. Begg, "The Absence of YHWH *ṣĕbā'ôt* in Isaiah 56–66," *BN* 44, 1988, 7–14.
39. 1 Kings 18:15; 19:10, 15; 2 Kings 3:14. Cf. the prophetic message formula כה אמר יהוה צבאוֹת = *kōh 'āmar yahweh ṣĕbā'ôt* ("thus says YHWH Sebaoth") in 1 Sam. 15:2; 2 Sam. 7:8 (= 1 Chron. 17:7) and then many times in Isaiah, Jeremiah, Zechariah, Haggai, and elsewhere.
40. Cf. the overview of the explanations in H.-J. Zobel, *ThWAT* 6, cols. 880f.
41. Cf. below, chap. 5.2.
42. However, not all of the time! In Isaiah, one has κύριοΩ Σαβαώθ = *kyrios Sabaōth,* while in other scriptures one has κύριο των δυνάμεων = *kyrios tōn dynameōn.* This points to different translators; however, perhaps also to a different understanding of the expression. Cf. H.-J. Zobel, *ThWAT* 6, cols. 878f. See E. Tov, in M. Klopfenstein et al., eds., *Mitte der Schrift?* (1987), 241f., 251.
43. A. S. van der Woude, *THAT* 2, col. 505. Cf. H.-J. Zobel, *ThWAT* 6, col. 885: One can decide on the relationship of צבאוֹת = *ṣĕbā'ôt* and ark "in such a way that the element of YHWH war belongs also to the royal majesty of YHWH and other features. But the term *ṣĕbā'ôt* and the ark do not give definition to the element of the enthroned king."
44. Cf. below, sec. 3.
45. Cf. the use in the laments: Pss. 59:6; 69:7; and 80:5, 8, 15, 20. See also 2 Sam. 7:26 = 1 Chron. 17:24 in the prayer of David. For the numerous occurrences in Isaiah 1–39, cf. H.-J. Zobel, *ThWAT* 6, cols. 889–891.
46. Cf. n. 37 above.
47. See n. 35 above.
48. See W. H. Schmidt, "אלהים *'aelōhīm* Gott," *THAT* 1, cols. 153–167; H. Ringgren, "אלהים," *ThWAT* 1, cols. 285–305; and H. Vorländer, "Elohim," *NBL* I, cols. 526f. Cf. also O. Loretz (et al.), *UF* 7 (1975), 552f.
49. For both of these, see below under b and c.
50. Cf. the examples in *ThWAT* 1, col. 291.
51. Cf. W. Eichrodt: This is a plural "serving to expand and reinforce the concept in question, and to elevate the person designated by it to the status of a general representative of his class" (*Theology,* 1:185).
52. Cf. Th. C. Vriezen, *Theology,* 196.
53. W. H. Schmidt, *THAT* 1, col. 154.
54. Cf. the lists in H. Ringgren, *ThWAT* 1, cols. 294f.; and W. H. Schmidt, *THAT* 1, cols. 163f.
55. For this, see above, chap. 3.5.c.
56. See *THAT* 1, cols. 161f. For the expression, "God of Abraham/Isaac/Jacob," "God of my/your father," and others, cf. Vol. II, 6.3 + 4; *ThWAT* 1, cols. 298f.; and *THAT* 1, cols. 157ff.
57. See the literature cited in n. 87 below.
58. Cf. *ThWAT* 1, cols. 219f.; H. D. Preuss, *Deuteronomium* (EdF 164; 1982), 180f. (literature); A. Alghisi, "L'espressione 'Altri Dèi' nella fraseologia deuteronomistica (Deut.–2 Reg.; Jer.)," *RivBibl* 33, 1985, 135–163 and pp. 105f., 111f. above. For the occurrences of אלהים אחרים = *'ĕlōhîm 'ăḥērîm* ("other gods") in the Book of Jeremiah and otherwise, see, above all, H. Weippert, *Die Prosareden des Jeremiabuches* (BZAW 132; 1973), 215–227.
59. Cf. above, pp. 105f., 111f.
60. Cf. the material in H. Ringgren, *ThWAT* 1, cols. 302–304.
61. *ThWAT* 1, col. 290.
62. Cf. *ThWAT* 1, col. 301; and *THAT* 1, col. 157.
63. Cf. above, p. 140.
64. Cf. H. D. Preuss, *Einführung in die alttestamentliche Weisheitsliteratur* (1987), 127ff.; D. Michel, *Qohelet* (EdF 258; 1988), 95ff.; and idem, *Untersuchungen zur Eigenart des Buches Qohelet* (BZAW 183; 1989), 274ff.
65. אלהים = *'ĕlōhîm* ("God") occurs 229 times , but יהוה = *yahweh* ("YHWH") only 44 times. In the rest of the Psalter as a whole, אלהים = *'ĕlōhîm* ("God") occurs only 29 times, while יהוה = *yahweh* (YHWH) occurs 642 times.
66. Cf. above, chap. 3.8.d.
67. Cf. W. H. Schmidt, "אל *'el* Gott," *THAT* 1, cols. 142–149; F. M. Cross, "אל," *ThWAT* 1, cols.

259–279; D. O. Edzard, "Il," *RLA* V, 46–48; and E. Otto, *NBL* I, cols. 507f. See also *WdM* 1, 279–283; and W. Eichrodt, *Theology,* 1:178–185.

68. Cf. M. H. Pope, *El in the Ugaritic Texts* (VT Suppl 2; Leiden, 1955); and O. Loretz, *Ugarit und die Bibel* (1990), 66–73, 153–156.

69. Cf. W. Schmidt, "Jerusalemer El-Traditionen bei Jesaja," *ZRGG* 16, 1964, 302–313; and E. Otto, "El and Jhwh in Jerusalem," *VT* 30, 1980, 316–329.

70. For the latter, cf. below, pp. 256f.

71. For the absence in Chronicles: J. P. Weinberg, "Gott im Weltbild des Chronisten: Die vom Chronisten verschwiegenen Gottesnamen," *ZAW* 100, Supplement, 1988, 170–189.

72. Exod. 15:11; Pss. 29:1; 89:7; Dan. 11:36. Or is there here (at least on occasion) an אל with an enclitic *m?* Cf. *ThWAT* 1, cols. 272f.

73. Cf. above, sec. 2.a.

74. Cf. Vol. II, 6.3.

75. For the problem of עליון (אל) = ('*ēl*) '*elyôn* that occurs also in Ugarit and Sefire (*KAI*, 222A, 11) as a divine epithet, cf. G. Wehmeier, *THAT* 2, cols. 282–287; and esp. H.-J. Zobel, "עליון '*eljôn*," *ThWAT* 6, cols. 131–151 (literature). For Gen. 14:18ff., cf. H.-J. Zobel, "Der frühe Jahwe-Glaube in der Spannung von Wüste und Kulturland," *ZAW* 101, 1989, 360–363.

76. Cf. *THAT* 1, cols. 143–145; *ThWAT* 1, col. 274.

77. For the problem of the translation (e.g., "God Olam" or "God of Eternity" or "the eternal [ancient] God"), etc., cf. *ThWAT* 1, cols. 273f.

78. Cf. Vol. II, 6.3 and 4.

79. Cf. *ThWAT* 1, cols. 274f.; M. Weippert, "שדי *Šaddaj* (Gottesname)," *THAT* 2, cols. 873–881; and, above all, K. Koch, "*Šaddaj,*" *VT* 26, 299–332 (= *Studien zur alttestamentliche und altorientalische Religionsgeschichte,* 1988, 118f.).

80. M. Weippert, *THAT* 2, col. 881.

81. K. Koch, "*Šaddaj,*" 329 (= *Studien zur alttestamentliche und altorientalische Religionsgeschichte,* 148).

82. For the German translation (with literature), see *TUAT* II/1, 1986, 138–148.

83. Cf. K. Koch, *Studien zur alttestamentliche und altorientalische Religionsgeschichte* (1988), 27ff.; and M. Delcor, "Des inscriptions de Deir 'Alla aux traditions bibliques, à propos des *šdyn,* des *šedim* et de *šadday,*" in FS J. Scharbert, 1989, 33–40.

84. Cf. H.-J. Zobel, "Bileam-Lieder und Bileam-Erzählung," in E. Blum et al., eds., *Die hebräische Bibel und ihre zweifache Nachgeschichte,* FS R. Rendtorff (1990), 141–154.

85. For the use of the appellations of God in the Book of Job, see below, pp. 186f., and n. 88.

86. W. H. Schmidt, *THAT* 1, col. 148.

87. Cf. O. Eissfeldt, " 'Mein Gott' im Alten Testament," *ZAW* 61, 1945–1948, 3–16 (= *KS* 3, 1966, 35ff.).

88. Overall, the Book of Job shows some peculiarities in its use of the appellations of God and of the name of YHWH. YHWH occurs only in the narrative frame of the book (Job 1 and 2 and 42:7ff.), and then in the speeches of God in Job 38:1–42:6 where it is stressed that they are the answer of YHWH; however, the occurrence of this name in 12:9 is a scribal mistake. By comparison, אל = '*ēl* ("God") occurs 55 times, אלהים = '*ĕlōhîm* ("God") 4 times, and שדי = *šadday* ("mountains"?) 31 times in Job.

89. Cf. below, sec. 4.e.

90. Cf. H. D. Preuss, *Deuteronomium* (EdF 164; 1982), 16–18 (literature).

91. Occurrences, below, sec. 4.e. (thus not in the Deuteronomistic History?).

92. Occurrences, below, sec. 4.e.

93. Cf. Vol. II, 8.1.

94. Cf. T. D. Mettinger, *The Dethronement of Sabaoth* (CB OT 18; Lund, 1982). Differently, H. Seebass, *TRE* 10, 184; and H. Weippert, *BZ* NF, 1980, 76–94. Cf. also B. Janowski, JBTh 2 (1987), 173–180. See there additional literature.

95. G. von Rad, *Theology,* 1:184–185.

96. See W. Zimmerli, *Erkenntnis Gottes nach dem Buche Ezechiel* (AThANT 27; 1954) (= TB 19, 2d ed., 41ff.).

97. Cf. above, pp. 145f., and below, chap. 5.4.

98. Above all, see S. Mowinckel, *Psalmenstudien II. Das Thronbesteigungsfest Jahwäs und der Ursprung der Eschatologie* (Christiania (Oslo), 1922; reprint, Amsterdam, 1961); A. von

Gall, ΒΑΣΙΛΕΙΑ ΤΟΥ ΘΕΟΥ (1926); O. Eissfeldt, "Jahwe als König," *ZAW* 46, 1928, 81–105 (= *KS* 2, 1962, 172ff.); H.-J. Kraus, *Die Königsherrschaft Gottes im Alten Testament* (BHTh 13; 1951); A. Alt, "Gedanken über das Königtum Jahwes," *KS* 1, 1953, 345–357; H. Schmid, "Jahwe und die Kulttraditionen von Jerusalem," *ZAW* 67, 1955, 168–197; M. Buber, *Königtum Gottes* (3d ed., 1956); J. Gray, "The Hebrew Conception of the Kingship of God: Its Origin and Development," *VT* 6, 1956, 268–285; D. Michel, "Studien zu den sogenannten Thronbesteigungspsalmen," *VT* 6, 1956, 40–68; L. Rost, "Königsherrschaft Jahwes in vorköniglicher Zeit?" *ThLZ* 85, 1960, cols. 721–724; V. Maag, "Malkût JHWH," VT Suppl 7, 1960, 129–163 (= *Kultur, Kulturkontakt und Religion*, 1980, 145ff.); J. Gray, "The Kingship of God in the Prophets and Psalms," *VT* 11, 1961, 1–29; J. Schreiner, *Sion-Jerusalem, Jahwes Königssitz* (StANT 7; 1963); J. D. Watts, "Yahweh Mālak Psalms," *ThZ* 21, 1965, 341–348; W. H. Schmidt, *Königtum Gottes in Ugarit und Israel* (BZAW 80; 2d ed., 1966); E. Lipiński, *La royauté de Yahwé dans la poésie et le culte de l'Ancien Israel* (Brussels, 1965); M. Treves, "The Reign of God in the Old Testament," *VT* 19, 1969, 230–243; J. A. Soggin, "מלך *maelaek* König," *THAT* 1, cols. 908–920; L. Ruppert, "Jahwe—der Herr und König," in K. Hemmerle, ed., *Die Botschaft von Gott* (1974), 112–127; J. H. Ulrichsen, "JHWH *mālāk:* Einige sprachliche Beobachtungen," *VT* 27, 1977, 361–374; J. Coppens, "La royauté de Yahwé dans le Psautier," *EThL* 53, 1977, 297–362; and 54, 1978, 1–59; F. Stolz, "Erfahrungsdimensionen im Reden von der Herrschaft Gottes," *WuD* NF 15, 1979, 9–32; J. Gray, *The Biblical Doctrine of the Reign of God* (Edinburgh, 1979); W. Dietrich, "Gott als König," *ZThK* 77, 1980, 251–268; P. Welten, "Königsherrschaft Jahwes und Thronbesteigung," *VT* 32, 1982, 297–310; H. Ringgren, K. Seybold, and H.-J. Fabry, "מלך *melek* u. Deriv.," *ThWAT* 4, cols. 926–957; E. Zenger, "Herrschaft Gottes/Reich Gottes. II: Altes Testament," *TRE* 15, 176–189; J. Jeremias, *Das Königtum Gottes in den Psalmen* (FRLANT 141; 1987); N. Lohfink, "Der Begriff des Gottesreichs vom Alten Testament her gesehen," in J. Schreiner, ed., *Unterwegs zur Kirche* (1987), 33–86; E. Otto, "Mythos und Geschichte im Alten Testament: Zur Diskussion einer neuen Arbeit von Jörg Jeremias," *BN* 42, 1988, 93–102; O. Loretz, *Ugarit-Texte und Thronbesteigungspsalmen* (UBL 7; 1988); B. Janowski, "Das Königtum Gottes in den Psalmen," *ZThK* 86, 1989, 389–454; L. Schmidt, "Königtum. II: Alten Testament," *TRE* 19, 327–333 (esp. 330–332); M. Z. Brettler, *God Is King* (JSOT Suppl 76; Sheffield, 1989); R. Scoralick, *Trishagion und Gottesherrschaft: Psalm 99 als Neuinterpretation von Tora und Propheten* (SBS 138; 1989). Cf. also W. Eichrodt, *Theology,* 1:194–200; A. Deissler, *Grundbotschaft,* 109ff.; W. H. Schmidt, *Alttestamentlicher Glaube* (6th ed.), 170–178. For the history of interpretation of the individual texts as well as of the common theme, see esp. O. Loretz, UBL 7. Whether and to what extent the predicate of king for YHWH is only metaphor (thus M. Z. Brettler) depends upon how little or how much stock one places in the term "metaphor." The YHWH enthronement psalms show in an exemplary and most clear fashion that not everything is said when the royal predicate is set forth as an isolated metaphor. Rather, the predicate is always enriched and made concrete with other statements (see below).

99. Exod. 15:18; 1 Sam. 8:7; Isa. 24:23; 52:7; Ezek. 20:33; Micah 4:7; Pss. 47:9; 93:1; 96:10 (= 1 Chron. 16:31); 97:1; 99:1; and 146:10.

100. Num. 23:21; Deut. 33:5; 1 Sam. 12:12; Isa. 6:5; 33:22; 41:21; 43:15; 44:6; Jer. 8:19; 10:7, 10; 46:18; 48:15; 51:57; Micah 2:13; Zeph. 3:15 (cf. LXX); Zech. 14:9, 16, 17; Mal. 1:14; Pss. 5:3; 10:16; 24:7, 8, 9, 10; 29:10; 44:5; 47:3, 7, 8; 48:3; 68:25; 74:12; 84:4; 95:3; 98:6; 99:4; 145:1; 149:2; and Dan. 4:34.

101. N. Lohfink ("Der Begriff des Gottesreichs vom Alten Testament her gesehen," 38, n. 10) refers, however, to the narrative frame of the Book of Job with its scene in the heavenly court. Even so, it is clear that this scene of the royal court was given no impressive significance in the later Book of Job. Neither this scene nor the Satan occurs again in Job 3–42.

102. Especially clear in Exod. 15:18; Isa. 6:5; 24:23; 52:7; Jer. 8:19; Micah 4:7; Pss. 24:7–10; 48:3; and 146:10; and the YHWH enthronement psalms.

103. Cf. Vol. II, chap. 7.

104. O. Loretz disputes the thesis that the enthronement psalms have their own literary form (UBL 7, 435ff.).

105. מלכות = *malkût* ("dominion"): Pss. 103:19 and 145:11f.; מלוכה = *mĕlûkâ* ("kingship"):

Obadiah 21 and Ps. 22:29; ממלכה = *mamlākâ* ("sovereignty"): 1 Chron. 29:11; ממשלה = *memšālâ* ("rule"): Pss. 103:22; 114:2 and 145:13; in Dan. 3:33; 4:31; 6:27 and 7:27, Aram. (מלכו[ת](א) = *malkû([t]ā'*) ("royalty") in combination with שלטן = *šālĕtān* ("dominion").

106. Gen. 48:15; 49:24; Ezekiel 34; Pss. 23:1; 80:2. Cf. Ps. 28:9; Isa. 40:11; and often. See J. A. Soggin, "רעה *r'h* weiden," *THAT* 2, cols. 791–794 (literature).

107. 1 Kings 22:19; Isa. 6:1; 66:1; Jer. 3:17; 17:12; Ezek. 1:26; Pss. 9:5, 8; 11:4; 29:10; 33:14; 47:9; 89:15; 93:2; 103:19; and 2 Chron. 18:18.

108. See M. Görg, "שׁב *jāšab*," *ThWAT* 3, cols. 1012–1032.

109. J. C. de Moor (*The Rise of Yahwism*, 118ff. and often) finds a reference to YHWH as the king of Bashan (vv. 23 and 25) in the older parts of Psalm 68 (= 2–25; v. 36 may be an addition from the time of Solomon), dating from the time around 1220 B.C.E. Are we witnessing here the contrasting of the often popular late dating in contemporary scholarship with an early dating?

110. Cf. M. Metzger, *UF* 2, 1970, 150. Cf. also below, sec. 4.e., and above, pp. 146 + 151f.

111. Cf. below, chap. 5.1.

112. For the special problem of Ps. 29:10a (YHWH's enthronement over the "flood"), cf. B. Janowski, "Das Königtum Gottes in den Psalmen," 421; M. Görg, *ThWAT* 3, col. 1031; and O. Loretz, UBL 7, 171–178.

113. 1 Sam. 4:4; 2 Sam. 6:2; 2 Kings 19:15; 1 Chron. 13:6; Isa. 37:16; Pss. 80:2; and 99:1 (here כרובים = *kĕrûbîm* does not have the definite article).

114. J. C. de Moor assesses the matter differently (*The Rise of Yahweh*, 101ff.), on the basis in part at least of risky hypotheses and theses.

115. Thus according to N. Lohfink, "Der Begriff des Gottesreichs vom Alten Testament her gesehen," 35ff. The citation is found on p. 40. Cf. E. Zenger, *TRE* 15, 176.

116. O. Loretz assumes on the basis of this section of text from the preexilic festival of enthronement that originally there was a statue of YHWH on a throne or a throne cart, or an empty throne symbolizing the presence of YHWH (UBL 7, 249–274). Cf. above, pp. 110f.

117. For Psalm 29, cf. moreover the detailed examination by O. Loretz, UBL 7, 76–248, with the division into two parts and late dating.

118. Cf. below, chap. 5.2.

119. For this problem, see M. Görg, *ThWAT* 3, cols. 1028f. O. Keel makes the attempt to reconstruct this through drawings and illustrations (*Jahwe-Visionen und Siegelkunst*, SBS 84/85, 1977, 26). Cf. the discussion of the cherubim below, chap. 5.4.

120. Cf. B. Janowski, "Das Königtum Gottes in den Psalmen," 429f. For this title, see R. Scoralick, *Trishagion und Gottesherrschaft*, 29ff. (see n. 98 above).

121. Cf. Vol. II, 8.2, and for this subject, see F. Crüsemann, *Der Widerstand gegen das Königtum* (WMANT 49; 1978), 42ff.

122. Cf. K. Seybold, *ThWAT* 4, col. 949.

123. Originated in connection with the building of the temple? Thus, E. Zenger, "Herrschaft Gottes/Reich Gottes," 177.

124. Cf. W. H. Schmidt, *Königtum Gottes in Ugarit und Israel;* O. Loretz, *Ugarit-Texte und Thronbesteigungspsalmen;* and idem, *Ugarit und die Bibel* (1990), 96–109, for a more detailed study with additional texts. In Egypt, Amun-Re above all had the title "king of the gods" (cf. *WdM* 1, 331–333), while in Mesopotamia, e.g., it was Anu (*RGT,* 2d ed., 142). Additional references in *RGT* (2d ed.), 176f., 220, 226, 235.

125. According to K. Baltzer (*Die Biographie der Propheten,* 1975; see the index), the prophets might have been seen as the "viziers" of YHWH who set forth the kingship of God. J. Gray (*The Biblical Doctrine of the Reign of God*) shapes too broadly the theme of the "sovereignty of God" that, for him, takes in the remnant, the servant of God, the messiah, and many other topics. Similarly, this is true of J. F. Walvoord.

126. For Psalm 96, cf. also O. Loretz, UBL 7, 317–331.

127. Cf. below, pp. 173f.

128. Cf., e.g., *KTU* 1.3 III, 29–31, or *KTU* 1.6 I, 56–62.

129. For the enduring kingship of El and the periodic regaining of kingship by Baal as seen in the Ugaritic texts, cf. O. Loretz (*Ugarit-Texte und Thronbesteigungspsalmen;* and idem, *Ugarit und die Bibel*).

130. O. Eissfeldt has not given full credit either to the influence of ancient Near Eastern figures of speech or to the recognition that there is hardly a realistic striving of Israel for sovereignty

over the world! ("Jahwes Königsprädizierung als Verklärung national-politischer Ansprüche Israels," in FS J. Ziegler, vol. 1, 1972, 51–55 = *KS* 5, 1973, 216–221).

131. W. H. Schmidt, *Alttestamentlicher Glaube* (6th ed.), 173.
132. "The *mlk*-idea stands under a polemical-apologetic portent": K. Seybold, *ThWAT* 4, col. 950. It "may have originated then with the building of the Jerusalem temple: it is not genuinely Yahwistic, but rather is mediated through a Canaanite-Jebusite source" (E. Zenger, *TRE* 15, 178).
133. Cf., however, above, p. 153.
134. See H. Spieckermann, *Heilsgegenwart* (FRLANT 148; 1989), 165–179.
135. For Deutero-Isaiah, cf. N. Lohfink, "Der Begriff des Gottesreichs vom Alten Testament her gesehen," 66–71.
136. Cf. Vol. II, 7.7.
137. Cf. above, chap. 3.2.
138. For the role of the nations in Deutero-Isaiah, cf. Vol. II, 15.6 and 7.
139. *Enuma eliš* IV 28 (*AOT,* 2d ed., 117; *ANET,* 3d ed., p. 66). For the Akkadian divine epithet *šarru* (king, lord, owner), cf. K. L. Tallquist, *Akkadische Götterepitheta* (Helsinki, 1938; reprint, Hildesheim, 1974), 232–237. See there pp. 366f. for "Marduk as Lord, 'Shepherd,' Ruler, and King."
140. For the second-mentioned text, cf. pp. 66f.; for Exod. 15:18, cf. also n. 145 below.
141. Thus T. Veijola, *Das Königtum in der Beurteilung der deuteronomistischen Historiographie* (Helsinki, 1977) (see the index).
142. For these, also H.-J. Kraus, *Theologie der Psalmen* (BK XV/3; 1979), 105–113; compare to him, however, P. Welten, "Königsherrschaft Jahwes und Thronbesteigung."
143. That in the postexilic period the Psalter became the "court hymnal of King Yahweh" (thus N. Lohfink, "Der Begriff des Gottesreichs vom Alten Testament her gesehen," 73) is indeed an attractive proposition but hardly verifiable exegetically.
144. It appears doubtful to me that we know as much about a preexilic Israelite enthronement festival with a throne cart and cult image of YHWH as O. Loretz thinks we do (UBL 7, passim; above all, pp. 411ff.).
145. The syntax of subject + verb = inversion, placing emphasis on the subject: Pss. 93:1; 96:10 (1 Chron. 16:31); 97:1; 99:1 (cf. the corresponding *yiqtol*-subject in Ps. 146:10) and 1 Kings 1:18 the "Adonijah *mālak.*" For this form, cf. the discussion by R. Scoralick, *Trishagion und Gottesherrschaft,* 22ff.; and O. Loretz, *Ugarit-Texte und Thronbesteigungspsalmen,* 413ff. (the formula is often secondary). In Exod. 15:18, the singular occurs: subject + *yiqtol!* Cf. H. Spieckermann, *Heilsgegenwart* (1989), 110 (with a reference to the parallels in *KTU* 1.2 IV, 32: "Baal is king/let Baal be king"): "Yahweh's kingship is understood rather clearly in the song of the Sea of Reeds to be a result of his victory over a mythical, dangerous, enemy. Since the preformative conjugation has been chosen for the royal predication, as was the case in the assimilated Canaanite tradition, the ingressive and durative aspects are also stressed. Contrary to its custom and enticed by the possibility of the combination of the act of the exodus and Canaanite mythology, Israel has here clearly dared to imagine the inception of Yahweh's kingship (as a result of a theomachy)."
146. For the order of qatal + subject, see Ps. 47:9. Cf. Isa. 24:23; 52:7.
147. The word order here, however, is *qatal* (verb) + subject!
148. For the thesis of the intermittent loss of royal sovereignty (concerning Marduk but not Baal!) and, linked with that, the rejection of its application to YHWH, cf. P. Welten, "Königsherrschaft Jahwes und Thronbesteigung"; and B. Janowski, "Das Königtum Gottes in den Psalmen," *ZThK* 86, 1989, 425ff. For the Babylonian New Year's festival (ritual), cf. now *TUAT* II/2, 1987, 212ff.
149. B. Janowski, *ZThK* 86, 1989, 433.
150. For Psalm 93, cf. H. Spieckermann, *Heilsgegenwart,* 180–186.
151. J. Jeremias (*Das Königtum Gottes in den Psalmen*) seeks to set forth a more differentiated chronology: Psalm 47: preexilic; Psalm 93: early or middle monarchy; Psalms 95 and 99: within the orbit of Deuteronomic and Deuteronomistic theology; Psalms 96 and 98: within the orbit of Deutero-Isaiah's theology; and Psalm 97: the Hellenistic period. For the late postexilic dating of Psalm 99, cf. also R. Scoralick (*Trishagion und Gottesherrschaft*). The final form of Psalm 47 is hardly preexilic.

152. Thus with E. Otto, *BN* 42, 1988, 98f.; and B. Janowski, *ZThK* 86, 1989, 406.
153. O. Eissfeldt, *KS* 1, 190.
154. B. Janowski, *ZThK* 86, 1989, 445.
155. Cf. below, chap. 5.1.
156. "The study of temple theology, from Israel to the Canaanites, reveals that the temple has its origins in the heavens. The heavens are not the object of divine creativity but rather the dramatic stage for the display of divine power and splendor" (H. Spieckermann, *Heilsgegenwart*, FRLANT 148, 1989, 167).
157. For comparison, the following is helpful. When the Hittites added to their goddess Wurunšemu the title "queen," they designated her as queen of the land of the Hatti, as queen of heaven and earth, as the caretaker of royal sovereignty, and as the mistress of divine justice. Cf. H. Klengel, ed., *Kulturgeschichte des alten Vorderasien* (1989), 243, 247.
158. For the role of the (ה)קדצ = *sdq(h)* of YHWH ("righteousness of YHWH") in the YHWH enthronement psalms, cf. below, p. 175.
159. See B. Janowski, *ZThK* 86, 1989, 408ff.
160. Thus E. Otto (*BN* 42, 1988, 100) and B. Janowski (*ZThK* 86, 1989, 417f.).
161. "Are the Psalms acquainted with *theologia gloriae*? Clearly yes, in the form of *Soli Deo gloria*" (Spieckermann, *Heilsgegenwart*, 225).
162. Cf. Micah 2:13; 4:7; Zeph. 3:15; Jer. 3:17; 10:7, 10; 17:12; 51:57; and Mal. 1:14.
163. The sentence "Temple theology is mainly not eschatologically oriented" (H. Spieckermann, *Heilsgegenwart*, 222) does not correspond with the facts of the case (e.g., see the YHWH enthronement psalms).
164. Cf. H. Merklein, *Jesu Botschaft von der Gottesherrschaft* (SBS 111; 1983), 37, 39.
165. Thus W. Dietrich, "Gott als König," 252 (cf. p. 268).
166. Cf. Vol. II, 14.11 and 12.
167. For some aspects of the relationships between divine sovereignty and world power in the period of Persian hegemony, cf. J. Maier, *Zwischen den Testamenten* (NEB AT, Supplement, vol. 3, 1990), 56. The Persian empire was powerful and fragile at the same time. "This evident contradiction between demonstrative, celebrated power on the one hand and the experience of peril on the other confirmed the monotheistic claim, so impressively formulated during the exile by Deutero-Isaiah, for the God of Israel in regard to the difficult question of power. . . . The experience of fragility attributed to this world power made relative all earthly power, and confirmed the ancient liturgical confession of the royal sovereignty of YHWH." Also the postexilic imaginings of the divine court with angels, etc., are occasioned by Persian prototypes of the king's court and royal audience (cf. ibid., pp. 194, 197). Cf. below, chap. 5.4.
168. YHWH both gives and also takes away the royal power of earthly foreign rulers: Dan. 2:37; 3:32; 4:14, 21, 28f., 32; 5:18–28; and 6:26–28.
169. Cf. Vol. II, 7.6 and 7.
170. Differently, however, N. Lohfink ("Der Begriff des Gottesreichs vom Alten Testament her gesehen," 37): "For the Old Testament as a whole, as we hold it today in our hands, the statement 'Let Yahweh be King' is formative. Cf. B. Janowski's statement that extends the theme to both Testaments: 'Let God be/become King' is of central significance" (B. Janowski, "Das Königtum Gottes in den Psalmen," 391).
171. That the royal sovereignty of God was also not a main theme in early Judaism is demonstrated by O. Camponovo, *Königtum, Königsherrschaft und Reich Gottes in den frühjüdischen Schriften* (OBO 58; 1984). The preaching of the βασιλεία by Jesus actually appears to have been a new emphasis.
172. W. H. Schmidt, *Alttestamentlicher Glaube* (6th ed.), 121.
173. Cf. R. Albertz and C. Westermann, "חור *rûah* Geist," *THAT* 2, cols. 726–753 (there cols. 742f.) [literature]; J. Scharbert, "Der 'Geist' und die Schriftpropheten," in R. Mosis and L. Ruppert, eds., *Der Weg zum Menschen*, FS A. Deissler (1989), 82–97; and M. Dreytza, *Der theologische Gebrauch von RUAH im Alten Testament* (1990). Cf. also L. Köhler, *Theologie* (4th ed.), 96–105; W. Eichrodt, *Theology*, 2:46–68, 131–134; and W. H. Schmidt, *Alttestamentlicher Glaube* (6th ed.), 121ff. (cf. also his essay in *TRE* 12, 170–173; literature).
174. Cf. also the Akkadian *šāru(m)* (*AHw* 3, 1192f.).
175. Cf. *THAT* 2, cols. 742f.
176. The double portion mentioned in 2 Kgs. 2:9 is the portion of the firstborn; cf. Deut. 21:17.

177. Cf. Vol. II, 10.3 and 4. Micah 3:8 is regarded mainly as an addition. Cf. J. Scharbert, "Der 'Geist' und die Schriftpropheten."
178. For רוח = *rûaḥ* ("spirit") in Ezekiel, see W. Zimmerli, BK XIII/2, 1262–1265.
179. Ezek. 3:12, 14; 8:3; 11:1, 24; 37:1; 43:5; Isa. 40:13; 61:1; 63:14; Zech. 7:12; 2 Chron. 15:1; 20:14; 24:20; and Neh. 9:30.
180. Do we have here the assignment of prophecy to the Torah? Thus A. H. J. Gunneweg, "Das Gesetz und die Propheten," *ZAW* 102, 1990, 169–180.
181. Cf. in addition Isa. 29:10; Hos. 4:12; 5:4; and Zech. 13:2 about negative forms and activities of spirits.
182. For the "spirit" as a part of Old Testament anthropology, see Vol. II, 11.2. Cf. similarly for Egypt: *RGT* (2d ed.), 59. רוח אלהים = *rûaḥ 'ĕlōhîm* in Gen. 1:2 is probably to be understood and thus translated as a superlative use of אלהים = *'ĕlōhîm*: "the divine (great) storm" that refers to the description of chaos before (!) creation (cf. the commentaries and monographs on Genesis 1 and above, sec. 2.a.)
183. Cf. H. Gross, "Der Mensch als neues Geschöpf," in R. Mosis and L. Ruppert, eds., *Der Weg zum Menschen*, FS A. Deissler (1989), 98–109.
184. Compare to David above. K.-D. Schunck made the judgment therefore that the spirit of God was always a continuing gift ("Wesen und Wirklichkeit des Geistes nach der Überlieferung des Alten Testaments," in his *Altes Testament und Heiliges Land*, 1989, 137–151, esp. 146).
185. L. Köhler, *Theologie* (4th ed.), 99.
186. Cf. H. D. Preuss, *Verspottung fremder Religionen im Alten Testament* (BWANT 92; 1971), 171, 206, 240, and often.
187. H. H. Schmid makes some good observations and has some interesting ideas about this pattern ("Ekstatische und charismatische Geistwirkungen im Alten Testament," in C. Heitmann and H. Mühlen, eds., *Erfahrung und Theologie des Heiligen Geistes*, 1974, 83–100).
188. G. Pfeifer, *Ursprung und Wesen der Hypostasenvorstellungen im Judentum* (1967), 15.
189. See H. Simian-Yofre, "פנים *pānîm*," *ThWAT* 6, cols. 629–659 (literature; from this, see esp. F. Nötscher, "*Das Angesicht Gottes schauen" nach biblischer und babylonischer Auffassung*, 1924 [repr. 1969]; and J. Reindl, *Das Angesicht Gottes im Sprachgebrauch des Alten Testaments*, 1970); A. S. van der Woude, "פנים *pānîm* Angesicht," *THAT* 2, cols. 432–460. For "see," cf. H. F. Fuhs, *ThWAT* 7, cols. 251f.
190. For the surrounding cultures, cf. *ThWAT* 6, cols. 648f., and *THAT* 2, col. 454. For the goddess Tinnit/Tanit as *pny baal* on a Phoenician votive tablet from Carthage, cf. H. Gese, *Die Religionen Altsyriens* (1970), 206f.; and *WdM* 1, 311f.
191. Cf. Vol. II, 13.3.
192. Cf. the numerous psalm texts.
193. For the problematic חלה (את) פנים = *ḥillâ ('et) pānîm* ("to appease/to induce to show favor"), see *ThWAT* 6, cols. 641f.; *THAT* 2, cols. 456f.
194. Cf. below, sec. 4.d, e.
195. For the expression לפני יהוה = *lipnê yahweh* ("before YHWH"), cf. *ThWAT* 6, cols. 652–655.
196. See S. Wagner, "סתר *sātar* u. Deriv.," *ThWAT* 5, cols. 967–977; L. Perlitt, "Die Verborgenheit Gottes," in H. W. Wolff, ed., *Probleme biblischer Theologie*, FS G. von Rad (1971), 367–382; S. E. Balentine, *The Hidden God: The Hiding of the Face of God in the Old Testament* (Oxford, 1983); and R. Texier, "Le Dieu caché de Pascal et du Second Isaïe," *NRTh* 111, 1989, 3–23.
197. L. Perlitt ("Die Verborgenheit Gottes," 373) points correctly to the assumed association of Psalm 104 with the great hymn to the sun by Akhenaton who says in this regard: "When you rise they live, when you set, then they die" (*AOT*, 2d ed., 18; cf. also J. Assmann, *Ägyptische Hymnen und Gebete* (1975), 221; something of a divergent translation is provided in *RGT*, 2d ed., 46). For the concealment of a deity in the faith of the countries surrounding Israel, see S. E. Balentine, *The Hidden God*, 24ff., and, e.g., *RGT* (2d ed.), 62: "beautiful face" = merciful (in reference to an Egyptian deity).
198. Deut. 31:17f.; 32:20; Isa. 8:17; 54:8; 57:17; 59:2; 64:6; Jer. 33:5; Ezek. 39:23f., 29; Pss. 10:11; 13:2; 22:25; 27:9; 30:8; 44:25; 69:18; 88:15; 102:3; 104:29; and 143:7. Cf. also Ezek. 7:22; 2 Chron. 30:9 with different verbs. For the semantic field, cf. S. E. Balentine, *The Hidden God*, 1ff., 115ff.
199. "The individual who prays in Israel shares with the one who prays in Mesopotamia the ex-

perience of the silence of God. . . . However, it is only in Israel that this experience produced the precise notion of the 'hiddeness' of God. This common oriental phenomenon of the silence of God experienced individually or cultically, however, becomes an exception when the idea is applied to YHWH's acts in history. This experience of the hiddeness of Yahweh is the intrinsically agonizing, defining characteristic of Israel" (L. Perlitt, "Die Verborgenheit Gottes," 367 and 373). Cf. also *RGT* (2d ed.), 182 (the Hittite deity Telepinu "disappeared").

200. L. Perlitt, "Die Verborgenheit Gottes," 382.

201. For the complex passage of Exod. 33:18–23, cf. J. Reindl, *Das Angesicht Gottes im Sprachgebrauch des Alten Testament,* 55ff.; then also see above, pp. 77f., and below, p. 169f., concerning "majesty." Cf. also *ThWAT* 6, cols. 636f. For this subject, see also L. Köhler, *Theologie* (4th ed.), 110f.

202. Cf. below, sec. 4.c.

203. H. Simian-Yofre, *ThWAT* 6, col. 649.

204. Ibid., col. 650. Cf. A. S. van der Woude, *THAT* 2, col. 442.

205. Formed from the root לאך = *lā'ak* (also attested in Ugaritic). Cf. D. N. Freedman, B. E. Willoughby, and (H.-J. Fabry), "מלאך *mal'āk* Bote," *ThWAT* 4, cols. 887–904 (there 896–903) (literature); R. Ficker, "מלאך *mal'āk* Bote," *THAT* 1, cols. 900–908 (see there 904–908); H. Seebass, "Engel: II. *Altes Testament," TRE* 9, 583–586 (literature); J. A. Akao, "Yahweh and Mal'ak in the Early Traditions of Israel," *IrBibStud* 12, 1990, 72–85 (esp. for Exodus 3); and H. Röttger, *NBL* I, cols. 539–541. And cf. also P. Heinisch, *Theologie des Alten Testaments* (1940), 75ff.

206. Cf. below in chap. 5.4.

207. In Zech. 12:8, the reference to the angel of YHWH is probably a gloss.

208. For the different forms of angels in the Book of Daniel, cf. K. Koch (and others), *Das Buch Daniel* (EdF 144; 1980), 205ff. (literature).

209. Thus, especially according to G. von Rad, *Theology,* 1:285–289, "Jahweh's aid to Israel personalized" (p. 286). Cf. also W. Eichrodt, *Theology,* 2:23–29.

210. O. Procksch, *Theologie,* 51: "The God of revelation in the hidden God."

211. Cf. above, sec. 4.b.

212. "The actualization of the presence of the unseen God" (L. Köhler, *Theologie* 4th ed., 109; "agent of his support": *ThWAT* 4, col. 897).

213. For Satan, cf. below, chap. 5.6.

214. Cf. *THAT* 1, col. 907, and *ThWAT* 4, col. 901. In addition, see A. S. van der Woude, *NedThT* 18, 1963/1964, 4ff. Only the messenger of God in contrast to the customary messenger; not a special angel, but simply "the angel of YHWH"; hypothesis of revelation; theory of representation; theory of identity; theory of hypostasis; logos theory.

215. See C. Westermann, "כבד *kbd* schwer sein," *THAT* 1, cols. 794–812 (there 802ff.); M. Weinfeld, "כבוד *kābôd," ThWAT* 4, cols. 23–40 (literature); T. N. D. Mettinger, *The Dethronement of Sabaoth* (CB OT 18; Lund, 1982), 80–115.

216. References are found in M. Weinfeld, "כבוד *kābôd," ThWAT* 4, cols. 30ff.

217. For the theology of the temple, see Vol. II, chap. 8.

218. Cf. below, sec. 7.b. According to R. Rendtorff (*KuD* Beiheft 1, 5th ed., 1982, 31) the "glory of Yahweh is that dimension of the activity of Yahweh recognizable to human beings, in which he reveals himself in his power."

219. H. Spieckermann, *Heilsgegenwart* (FRLANT 148; 1989), 223 (cf. pp. 220–225).

220. Cf. W. Schmidt, "Jerusalem El-Traditionen bei Jesaja," *ZRGG* 16, 1964, 302–313 (esp. pp. 308f.; here certainly without the corresponding substantive, but indeed with the verb *kbd*).

221. Cf. below, chap. 5.2.

222. Cf. M. Noth, BK IX/1, for this text.

223. See C. Westermann, "Die Herrlichkeit Gottes in der Priesterschrift," in H. J. Stoebe et al., eds., *Wort, Gebot, Glaube: Beiträge zur Theologie des Alten Testaments,* FS W. Eichrodt (1970), 227–249 (cf. his article in *THAT* 1, cols. 808–810); and U. Struppe, *Die Herrlichkeit Jahwes in der Priesterschrift* (ÖBS 9; 1988).

224. Cf. above, chap. 3.5.a. This text is in its structure fundamental for the other P passages (cf. C. Westermann, "Die Herrlichkeit Gottes in der Priesterschrift," 243f.).

225. See D. N. Freedman, B. E. Willoughby, and (H.-J. Fabry), "עָנָן *'ānān*," *ThWAT* 6, cols. 270–275.
226. Cf. below, chap. 5.3. Therefore, also in P and Ezekiel with the verb שׁכן = *šākan* ("settle down/dwell") but not however ישׁב = *yāšab* ("sit/inhabit").
227. The *kābôd* had a "three-dimensional, clearly circumscribed size, descended now and then from heaven, and was the means by which Yahweh himself was present" (R. Rendtorff, *KuD* Beiheft 1, 5th ed., 1982, 29).
228. Thirteen times in the Priestly texts.
229. Cf. U. Struppe, *Die Herrlichkeit Jahwes in der Priesterschrift*, 59.
230. For these 'murmuring' narratives, cf. above, chap. 3.5.e.
231. See B. Janowski, " 'Ich will in eurer Mitte wohnen,' " *JBTh* 2 (1987), 165–193.
232. A so-called hymn of self-praise by YHWH (praise of himself by himself), a literary form also evidenced in Israel's cultural environment (e.g., *TUAT* II/5, 646–649), although there with another function, is found within the Old Testament only in Deutero-Isaiah and in the God speeches of the Book of Job. Cf. H. D. Preuss, *Deuterojesaja: Eine Einführung in seine Botschaft* (1976), 21 and 89 (literature); and his essay in H. Donner et al., eds, *Beiträge zur alttestamentlichen Theologie, FS* W. Zimmerli (1977), 339–342. Also see below, sec. 6.b.
233. Cf. above, chap. 3.5.d.
234. Cf. M. Noth, ATD 5, 212; and C. Westermann, *THAT* 1, col. 808.
235. Cf. above, sec. 4.b.
236. Cf. there the semantic field.
237. Cf. below, chap. 5.2, and above, sec. 4.d.
238. See A. S. van der Woude, "שֵׁם *šēm* Name," *THAT* 2, cols. 935–963 (there 953ff. with literature): "A specific Deuteronomy theology of the Name does not . . . exist" (col. 955). Thus also H. Weippert, *BZ* NF 24, 1980, 76–94; B. Janowski, *JBTh* 2, 1987, 173–186; H. Seebass, *TRE* 10, 184f.; and E. Würthwein, ATD 11/1, 102f. The frequent reference to R. de Vaux (in F. Maass, ed., *Das Ferne und nahe Wort, FS* L. Rost; BZAW 105, 1967, 220f.) is certainly no longer convincing. Cf. M. Rose, *Der Ausschliesslichkeitsanspruch Jahwes* (BWANT 106; 1975), 82ff. Then see H. D. Preuss, *Deuteronomium* (EdF 164; 1982), 13, 16–18, 90 (also the additional literature); N. Lohfink, "Zur deuteronomischen Zentralisationsformel," *Bibl* 65, 1984, 297–329; and T. N. D. Mettinger, *The Dethronement of Sabaoth* (CB OT; Lund, 1982), 38–79.
239. Cf. for Ugarit: *KTU* 1.2:7f.; 1.16:VI:56. For this, see H. D. Preuss, *Deuteronomium*, 17.
240. M. Weinfeld, *ThWAT* 4, col. 38: " . . . more abstract . . . "; similarly also T. N. D. Mettinger, *The Dethronement of Sabaoth.*
241. B. Janowski, *JBTh* 2 (1987), 174.
242. Thus more frequently in exilic and postexilic texts; see B. Janowski, *JBTh* 2 (1987), 177, n. 52. Cf. below, chap. 5.1.
243. Thus B. Janowski, *JBTh* 2 (1987), 178 (with H. Weippert).
244. Therefore, in his treatment of YHWH as a national deity, B. Stade formulated the superscription of his section 35 to read: "Yahweh defender of law and morality, though he is not just" (*Biblische Theologie des Alten Testaments*, I, 1905, 88).
245. See F. Crüsemann, "Jahwes Gerechtigkeit (*ṣedāqā*/*ṣädäq*) im Alten Testament," *EvTh* 36, 1976, 427–450 (his reference list on p. 432, nn. 27 and 28, is to be supplemented); and J. Krašovec, *La justice (ṢDQ) de Dieu dans la Bible hébraïque et l'interprétation juive et chrétienne* (OBO 76; 1988). Cf. also P. Stuhlmacher, *Gerechtigkeit Gottes bei Paulus* (FRLANT 87; 1965), 113–145; K. Koch, "צדק *ṣdq* gemeinschaftstreu/heilvoll sein," *THAT* 2, cols. 507–530; B. Johnson, "צדק *ṣadaq* u. Deriv.," *ThWAT* 6, cols. 898–924; and J. Scharbert, "Gerechtigkeit: I. Altes Testament," *TRE* 12, 404–411 (particularly pp. 408–410; the forensic character is certainly overemphasized here). Cf. also L. Köhler, *Theologie* (4th ed.), 16f.; and G. von Rad, *Theology*, 1:370–383. For the history of criticism, see esp. J. Krašovec, *La justice (ṢDQ) de Dieu*, 11ff.
246. See below, sec. 4.h. However, cf. also P. Heinisch, *Theologie des Alten Testaments* (1940), 57ff. According to Heinisch, YHWH is just, because he rewards the good and punishes the wicked (p. 58).
247. Cf. above, chap. 3.10.

248. Thus K. Koch, "*Ṣdq* im Alten Testament," diss. (Heidelberg, 1953), 63. Cf. A. Dünner, *Die Gerechtigkeit nach dem Alten Testament* (1963), 94.

249. For the difference between these two terms, see D. Michel, "Begriffsuntersuchung über ṣaedaeq-sedaqa and 'aemet-'aemuna," Habilitationsschrift (Heidelberg, 1964) (צדק = *ṣedeq* points to the general bearing of YHWH, צדקה = *ṣĕdāqâ* refers to a concrete display of salvation, i.e., an act of salvation).

250. In Amos 5:24, righteousness more probably has to do with the performance of righteousness by human beings (cf. 5:7; 6:12).

251. See H. Brunner, "Gerechtigkeit als Fundament des Thrones," *VT* 8, 1958, 426–428 (= Brunner, *Das hörende Herz;* OBO, 1988, 393ff.). Cf. to Ma'at: *WdM* 1, 373f.

252. Cf. Vol. II, 8.1 + 2.

253. For this, see A. Rosenberg, "The God *Ṣedeq*," *HUCA* 36, 1965, 161–177; H. H. Schmid, *Gerechtigkeit als Weltordnung* (BHTh 40; 1968), 75–77 with sources and literature; see pp. 78ff. also for the taking over of Canaanite concepts. Also see F. Crüsemann, "Jahwes Gerechtigkeit (*ṣedāqā/ṣādāq*) im Alten Testament," 439; F. Stolz, *Strukturen und Figuren im Kult von Jerusalem* (BZAW 118; 1970), 216, 218f.; see 181ff. also for the deity Salem; and K. Koch, *THAT* 2, col. 509.

254. Cf. the references in Rosenberg, *HUCA* 36, 163f. Also see F. Grödahl, *Die Personennamen der Texte aus Ugarit* (Rome, 1967) (see the index, p. 412); and B. Johnson and H. Ringgren, *ThWAT* 6, cols. 902f.

255. See R. Grieshammer, "*Maat* und *Ṣedeq*," in *Göttinger Miszellen* 55, 1982, 35–42; cf. B. Johnson, *ThWAT* 6, cols. 900–902 for the religiohistorical material.

256. For the connection between the sanctuary of Zion and the sun deity, cf. also J. Morgenstern, "The Gates of Righteousness," *HUCA* 6, 1929, 1–37; and B. Janowski, *Rettungsgewissheit und Epiphanie des Heils* (WMANT 59; 1989).

257. Cf. further Vol. II, chap. 8.

258. For these, see above, sec. 3.

259. Thus with K. Koch in his dissertation, "*Ṣdq* im Alten Testament" (Heidelberg, 1953). Cf. his *THAT* 2, passim. In regard to the cultic theophany, more skepticism is appropriate than one finds presented in Koch (cf. Vol. II, 13.4).

260. See H. H. Schmid, *Šalôm "Frieden" im Alten Orient und im Alten Testament* (SBS 51; 1971); and O. H. Steck, *Friedensvorstellungen im alten Jerusalem* (ThSt 111; 1972).

261. Cf. W. Zimmerli, "Abraham und Melchisedek," in F. Maass, ed., *Das Ferne und Nahe Wort,* FS L. Rost (BZAW 105; 1967), 255–264.

262. Pss. 4:2; 5:9; 7:9, 18; 9:9; 17:1; 22:32; (24:5); 31:2; 35:24, 28; 36:7, 11; 40:11; 48:11; 50:6; 51:16; 65:6; 69:28; 71:2, 15, 16, 19, 24; 72:1; 88:13; 89:17; 96:13; 97:2, 6; 98:2, 9; 99:4; 103:6, 17; 111:3; 116:5; 119:40, 106, 123, 138, 142, 160, 164; 143:1, 11; and 145:7. Psalm 31:2 was certainly significant also for Luther; cf. his 1. Psalm lecture 1513/14, etc. For this, see E. Mühlhaupt, ed., *D. Martin Luthers Psalmen = Auslegung,* vol. 2 (1962), 30–35.

263. For the semantic field, cf. esp. J. Krašovec, *La justice (ṢDQ) de Dieu,* passim.

264. Cf. F. Crüsemann, "Jahwes Gerechtigkeit (*ṣedāqâ/ṣādāq*) im Alten Testament," 438.

265. Pss. 4:2; 5:9; 9:5; 31:2; 35:24; 71:1f.; 119:40; 143:1f., 11.

266. Pss. 7:18; 22:32; 35:28; 40:10f.; 50:6; 51:16; 71:24; 88:12f.; 89:17; 97:6; and 145:7 (–9).

267. Pss. 9:9; 35:24; 50:6; 96:13; and 98:2f., 9.

268. Pss. 11:7; 33:5; 37:28; 99:4; and 103:6. The context of 99:4 is especially important.

269. Pss. 96:13f.; 97:6, 8; 98:1–3, 9; and 99:4.

270. H. van Oyen, *Ethik des Alten Testaments* (1967), 52, speaks of a "righteousness that is beneficial and exclusive."

271. Cf. C. F. Whitley, "Deutero-Isaiah's Interpretation of *sedeq*," *VT* 22, 1972, 469–475; J. J. Scullion, "*Ṣedeq-Ṣedaqah* in Isaiah cc. 40–66," *UF* 3, 1971, 335–348; F. V. Reiterer, *Gerechtigkeit als Heil* (1976); H. D. Preuss, *Deuterojesaja: Eine Einführung in seine Botschaft* (1976), 83–87; and F. Crüsemann, "Jahwes Gerechtigkeit (*ṣedāqā/ṣādāq*) im Alten Testament," 443ff.

272. For these, see Vol. II, 15.7.

273. Thus K. Koch, "*Ṣdq* im Alten Testament," diss. (Heidelberg, 1953), 15, 37ff., 66 (esp. 39): "within my *ṣdq*" (cf. 41:2; 45:13).

274. Cf., e.g., C. Westermann, ATD 19, for this text.
275. Cf. C. Westermann, ATD 19, 132f.; and H. D. Preuss, *Deuterojesaja*, 21. Against this position, see F. Crüsemann, *Studien zur Formgeschichte von Hymnus und Danklied in Israel* (WMANT 32; 1969), 45f., n. 2.
276. Isa. 41:2, 26; and 45:19, 21, 23, 24f. In 41:26, צדיק *ṣaddîq* signifies simply, "that is correct."
277. The "righteousness of YHWH" and the "word" are connected in Isa. 41:26 and 45:19, 23 (24f.); cf. 63:1.
278. Isa. 56:1; 58:8; 59:16f.; 62:1f.; and 63:1. For this text, see esp. O. H. Steck, "Tritojesaja im Jesajabuch," in J. Vermeylen, ed., *The Book of Isaiah* (Louvain, 1989), 361, 406.
279. This combination, consequently, cannot be explained as a result of redaction as R. Rendtorff has attempted to do (*Das Alte Testament: Eine Einführung*, 1983, 211f.).
280. For the "remnant" (Ezra 9:15), cf. Vol. II, 14.8.
281. M.-L. Henry, *Glaubenskrise und Glaubensbewährung in den Dichtungen der Jesajaapokalypse* (BWANT 86; 1967), 93.
282. This finding comes up short in H. Graf Reventlow, *Rechtfertigung im Horizont des Alten Testaments* (1971), 112–115.
283. P. Stuhlmacher, "Zum Thema: Biblische Theologie des N.T.," in K. Haacker et al., eds., *Biblische Theologie heute* (BThSt 1; 1977), 25–60 (repeatedly, e.g., p. 44 and esp. p. 57).
284. See J. Hempel, "Die israelitischen Anschauungen von Segen und Fluch im Lichte altorientalischer Parallelen," in J. Hempel, *Apoxysmata* (BZAW 81; 1961), 30–113; S. Mowinckel, *Psalmenstudien V. Segen und Fluch in Israels Kult und Psalmendichtung* (1924, and reprint); F. Horst, "Segen und Segenshandlungen in der Bibel," *EvTh* 7, 1947/1948, 23–37 (= TB 12, 1961, 188ff.); J. Scharbert, *Solidarität in Segen und Fluch im Alten Testament und in seiner Umwelt* (BBB 14; 1958); C. Westermann, *Der Segen in der Bibel und im Handeln der Kirche* (1968); G. Wehmeier, *Der Segen im Alten Testament* (1970); J. Scharbert, "ברכה/ברך," *ThWAT* 1, cols. 808–841 (literature); C. A. Keller and G. Wehmeier, "ברך *brk* pi. segnen," *THAT* 1, cols. 353–376; C. W. Mitchell, *The Meaning of BRK "To Bless" in the Old Testament* (Atlanta, 1987); and Chr. Gottfriedsen, "Beobachtungen zum alttestamentlichen Segensverständnis," *BZ* NF 34, 1990, 1–15. In Wehmeier and the articles in *THAT* and *ThWAT*, there are also distinctions between the noun and the verb, subjects and objects, and kinds of sentences and textual groups. More precise is H.-P. Müller, "Segen im Alten Testament: Theologische Implikationen eines halb vergessenen Themas," *ZThK* 87, 1990, 1–32; see pp. 3–19 for the literary and grammatical form of blessing.
285. Thus with G. Wehmeier, *Der Segen im Alten Testament*, 67f., who notes that the term occurs 398 times, 71 of which are the noun.
286. Thus with F. Horst, TB 12, 188.
287. According to Chr. Gottfriedsen ("Beobachtungen zum alttestamentlichen Segensverständnis"), YHWH is the subject of the blessing since the Yahwist.
288. G. Wehmeier, *Der Segen im Alten Testament*, 66.
289. Ibid., 227.
290. Above all, see J. Hempel, "Die israelitischen Anschauungen von Segen und Fluch im Lichte altorientalischer Parallelen."
291. C. Westermann attempts to recognize a history of blessing in the Old Testament (*Der Segen in der Bibel*, 43–61), as does G. Wehmeier, *Der Segen im Alten Testament*. Chr. Gottfriedsen assumes there are two sources of the Old Testament understanding of blessing, namely, the nomadic tribe and the civilized land ("Beobachtungen zum alttestamentlichen Segensverständnis").
292. See G. Wehmeier, *Der Segen im Alten Testament*, 119ff., 160ff.: 38 times in the Hebrew Old Testament, and twice in Aramaic (Dan. 2:19; 4:31), e.g., Pss. 18:47; 34:2; 41:14; 66:8, 20; 68:20; and 145:2; however, also Gen. 9:26; 24:27, 38; Josh. 22:33; 1 Sam. 25:32; 2 Chron. 20:26; etc.; in Isa. 66:3 the reference is to an idol.
293. Differently, I. Willi-Plein, "Genesis 27 als Rebekkageschichte," *ThZ* 45, 1989, 315–334; there pp. 320ff.
294. Cf. J. Scharbert, *ThWAT* 1, cols. 814ff., and the analogous curses in Deut. 28:16–19 to the blessing and curse formulae. Cf. also G. Wehmeier, *Der Segen im Alten Testament*, 119f.
295. Only here the qal occurs as a passive participle.

296. Chr. Gottfriedsen ("Beobachtungen zum alttestamentlichen Segensverständnis") has argued that the original blessing formula had the objective of establishing community with the one addressed. However, he is able to prove only by various reductionisms that the abbreviated blessing formula אתה ברוך = *bārûk 'attâ* ("blessed are you"), without anything in addition, may have stood at the beginning of the history of the blessing.
297. J. Scharbert, "ברך / ברכה," *ThWAT* 1, col. 819.
298. Cf. G. Wehmeier, *Der Segen im Alten Testament.*
299. See, however, C. Westermann, *Der Segen in der Bibel und im Handeln der Kirche.* Cf. his *Elements of Old Testament Theology:* "The Saving God and History" (35–84); "The Blessing God and Creation" (85–117). Cf. also G. Wehmeier, *Der Segen im Alten Testament,* 228, etc. Critical of this is F. J. Helfmeyer, "Segen und Erwählung," *BZ* NF 18, 1974, 208–223.
300. Thus D. Vetter, *Jahwes Mitsein ein Ausdruck des Segens* (1971). For this formula, cf. also, e.g., H. D. Preuss, " . . . ich will mit dir sein!" *ZAW* 80, 1968, 139–173 (cf. *ThWAT* 1, cols. 485–500); R. Winling, *RScRel* 51, 1977, 89–139; and M. Görg, *ThG* 70, 1980, 214–240.
301. F. Horst, TB 12, 199.
302. See H.-P. Müller, *Ursprünge und Strukturen alttestamentlicher Eschatologie* (BZAW 109; 1969), 144ff.
303. See J. Scharbert, *Solidarität in Segen und Fluch im Alten Testament und in seiner Umwelt,* 141ff.
304. Cf. H. D. Preuss, *Deuteronomium,* 171 (and literature).
305. See K. Seybold, *Der aaronitische Segen* (1977). For this text and for the small silver plate discovered in 1986 with an inscription reminiscent of Num. 6:24–26, although not with the identical text, cf. M. C. A. Koppel, "The Poetic Structure of the Priestly Blessing," *JSOT* 45, 1989, 3–13.
306. For the "indicative, jussive, ambiguity" in blessing sayings, cf. H.-P. Müller, "Segen im Alten Testament: Theologische Implikationen eines halb vergessenen Themas," *ZThK* 87, 1990, 4–11.
307. Cf. K. Berge, *Die Zeit des Jahwisten* (BZAW 186; 1990), 273–310.
308. Thus in Gen. 12:3; then further 18:18 and 28:14; cf. also Exod. 12:32: request for blessing by the pharaoh. Cf. also Vol. II, 6.5.
309. See W. Schottroff, *Der altisraelitische Fluchspruch* (WMANT 30; 1969) (see also pp. 163ff. for the blessing formula); H. C. Brichto, *The Problem of "Curse" in the Hebrew Bible* (Philadelphia, 1963); and J. Scharbert, "ארר," *ThWAT* 1, cols. 437–481 (literature).
310. H.-P. Müller, *Ursprünge und Strukturen alttestamentlicher Eschatologie,* 165.
311. Cf., e.g., the "curse of Agade," which the god Enlil imposes because of a crime of King Naramsin and which is actualized by the invasion of the Guteans. Cf. the text in J. S. Cooper, *The Curse of Agade* (Baltimore and London, 1983), and the interpretations of the text by, e.g., J. Krecher and H.-P. Müller, "Vergangenheitsinteresse in Mesopotamien und Israel," *Saec.* 26, 1975, 13–44 (pp. 23f.). In contradistinction to this text, which cannot be verified as likely "historical," Deuteronomy 28 reflects an authentic, exilic experience. For the powerfully effective curse in ancient Near Eastern contract texts, cf. *RGT* (2d ed.), 153f.; and *TUAT* I/2, 1983, 143, 151, 157, 159, 169ff.
312. For this formula, cf. below, sec. 7.d.
313. C. Westermann, *Das Alte Testament und Jesus Christus* (1968), 46–48; and idem, *Der Segen in der Bibel und im Handeln der Kirche,* 40–42; cf. also G. Wehmeier, *THAT* 1, col. 371f.; and his *Der Segen im Alten Testament,* 224f.
314. Prov. 10:6f.; 11:11, 26; cf. also 3:33; 5:18; 20:21; 22:9; 27:14; 28:20; and 30:11.
315. Cf. below, sec. h.
316. Cf. H. D. Preuss, *Einführung in die alttestamentliche Weisheitsliteratur,* 179ff.
317. C. Westermann, *Elements of Old Testament Theology,* 98–101.
318. Cf. below, sec. 6.d.
319. See H.-P. Müller, *Ursprünge und Strukturen alttestamentlicher Eschatologie* (BZAW 109; 1969), 148ff.; see pp. 129–171 for the "aspect of finality" associated with blessing.
320. G. Wehmeier, *Der Segen im Alten Testament,* 230.
321. H.-P. Müller, "Segen im Alten Testament: Theologische Implikationen eines halb vergessenen Themas," *ZThK* 87, 1990, 3; cf., however, also pp. 20 and 26ff.
322. See the collection, K. Koch, ed., *Um das Prinzip der Vergeltung in Religion und Recht des*

Alten Testaments (WdF 125; 1972). Also see G. von Rad, *Wisdom in Israel,* 124–137; and *Theology,* 1:391–401, 418–441.

323. So according to K. H. Fahlgren, *Ṣĕdāḳā nahestehende und entgegengesetzte Begriffe im Alten Testament* (Uppsala, 1932).

324. Thus K. Koch. Cf. also G. von Rad, *Theology,* 1:264–268.

325. Thus according to K. Koch, WdF 125, 132.

326. Thus, e.g., K. Koch, "Alttestamentliche Ganzheitsdenken und Sündenbegriff," *ThG* 23, 1980, 20–28.

327. In Lev. 20:9, 11, 12, 13, 16, 27 (P); cf. also Josh. 2:19; 1 Kings 2:37; Ezek. 18:13; and 33:4, 5.

328. G. Gerleman, *THAT* 1, col. 449.

329. H. Graf Reventlow, "Sein Blut komme über sein Haupt," *VT* 10, 1960, 311–327; and K. Koch, "Der Spruch 'Sein Blut bleibe auf seinem Haupt' und die Israelitische Auffassung vom vergossenen Blut," *VT* 12, 1962, 396–416; both articles are also found in WdF 125, 412ff. and 432ff.

330. Cf. also Vol. II, 11.9.b.

331. In this connection, K. Koch (WdF 125, 442ff.) introduces in great detail the Israelite view of (spilt) blood. Also cf. A. Christ, Blutvergiessen im Alten Testament (diss., Basel, 1971), 1977.

332. Cf. the important article by K. Koch, "Gibt es ein Vergeltungsdogma im Alten Testament?" *ZThK* 52, 1955, 1–42 (= WdF 125, 130ff.). Also G. von Rad, *Wisdom in Israel,* 24–137; *Theology,* 1:264–268, 391–401, 418–441; and H. D. Preuss, *Einführung in die alttestamentliche Weisheitsliteratur,* 39f., 51–54 (literature).

333. See H. H. Schmid, *Gerechtigkeit als Weltordnung,* (BHTh 40; 1968); G. von Rad, *Wisdom in Israel,* 77–78; and H. Gese, *Lehre und Wirklichkeit in der alten Weisheit* (1958) (he investigates also the question about the origin of this thought).

334. Prov. 11:20; 13:25; 15:6; 17:13; 18:10, 11, 16; 19:4, 5, 7, 23; 20:13, 17; 21:18, 20f.; 22:8f.; 28:10, 18; and 29:6, 23, 25. Cf. also the images from nature in 22:8 and 25:23.

335. Thus K. Koch, WdF 125, 134.

336. Additional examples are found in Prov. 10:3; 15:25; 22:22f.; and 23:10f.

337. For the possible restrictions, see below, p. 186.

338. These observations are critical of the thesis of C.-A. Keller ("Zum sogenannten Vergeltungsglauben im Proverbienbuch," in H. Donner et al., eds., *Beiträge zur alttestamentlichen Theologie,* FS W. Zimmerli [1977], 223–238), according to which the successful life is due only to the correct handling of social rules.

339. Cf. H. Gese (*Lehre und Wirklichkeit in der alten Weisheit*). Further, cf. H. D. Preuss, "Das Gottesbild der älteren Weisheit Israels," *VT* Suppl 23, 1972, 117–145 (literature); and *Einführung in die alttestamentliche Weisheitsliteratur,* 52 + 204, n. 64.

340. Or do we already have here an "initial formulation of the problematic nature of the connection between deed and consequence in view of the contradictory experience of everyday life"? Thus E. Otto, "Die 'synthetische Lebensauffassung' in der frühköniglichen Novellistik Israels," *ZThK* 74, 1977, 393, n. 71.

341. For the "fear of YHWH," see Vol. II, 11.8.b.

342. Cf. H. D. Preuss, *Einführung in die alttestamentliche Weisheitsliteratur,* 53; and VT Suppl 23, 1972, 126–128.

343. See K. Koch, WdF 125, 168ff.; G. von Rad, *Theology,* 1:453–459; *Wisdom in Israel,* 203–226; H. D. Preuss, *Einführung in die alttestamentliche Weisheitsliteratur,* 69ff. For similar texts in Israel's environment, cf. *TUAT* III/1, 1990, 102ff., 110ff.

344. Job 4:7–11; 5:1–7; 8:20; 11:20; 15:17–35; 18:5–21; and 20:23–29; cf. the fourth friend, Elihu, in Job 34:10–12 and 36:5–7, 12–15. For Job 4:7–11, cf. in particular F. Horst, WdF 125, 207ff.: the discussion here is not only about a sphere of activity that effectuates fortune but also about the "breath of God," i.e., God's personal intervention.

345. Job 6:9–10, 12; 9:22–24; 10:15f.; 16:9–17; 19:6f.; 27:2, 5f., 7–23; chaps. 23 and 31.

346. Cf. D. Michel, *Untersuchungen zur Eigenart des Buches Qohelet* (BZAW 183; 1989).

347. Cf. still Qoh. 5:9ff.; 6:7ff.; 7:15; 8:10–14; and 9:1–3, 11.

348. See the more complete discussion in H. D. Preuss, *Einführung in die alttestamentliche Weisheitsliteratur,* passim (above all, pp. 172ff.).

349. See M. Saebø, "Chronistische Theologie/Chronistisches Geschichtswerk," *TRE* 8, 74–87 (literature).

350. See esp. G. von Rad, *Das Geschichtsbild des chronistischen Werkes* (BWAT IV/3; 1930), above all, pp. 10ff.
351. 1 Chron. 10:13f.; 28:2f.; 2 Chron. 15:2f.; 16:12; 24:14ff.; 25:14, 20; 26:16–21a; 33:1–20; and 35:20–25.
352. Cf. above, sec. 4.2.a.
353. Cf. W. Roth, "Deuteronomistisches Geschichtswerk/Deuteronomistische Schule," *TRE* 8, 543–552 (literature). Also see the survey of works on the Deuteronomistic history by H. Weippert (*ThR* 50, 1985, 213–249); and H. D. Preuss (appears also in ThR). See further G. von Rad, *Theology*, 1:327–347; and H. D. Preuss, *Deuteronomium*, 20–26. Cf. further below, p. 216.
354. Cf. also Vol. II, 7.1.
355. Therein "each generation" "experienced the whole Jahweh" (G. von Rad, *Theology*, 1:332).
356. Cf. M. Brettler, "Ideology, History and Theology in 2 Kings XVII 7–23," *VT* 39, 1989, 268–282.
357. Cf. H. W. Wolff, "Das Kerygma des deuteronomistischen Geschichtswerks," *ZAW* 73, 1961, 171–186 (= TB 22, 1964, 308ff.).
358. Cf. Vol. II, 6.5, and above, chap. 3.9.a.
359. E. Zenger, *BZ* NF 12, 1968, 16–30.
360. Cf. H. D. Preuss, *Einführung in die alttestamentliche Weisheitsliteratur*, 161 (literature, pp. 217f., n. 280).
361. E. Otto, "Die 'synthetische Lebensauffassung' in der frühköniglichen Novellistik Israels," *ZThK* 74, 1977, 371–400. However, according to Otto, the Succession Narrative already begins with 2 Samuel 7.
362. Moreover, the motif of YHWH's providence is for E. Otto ("Die 'synthetische Lebensauffassung' in der frühköniglichen Novellistik Israels," 385, n. 54) "in origin independent . . . of the synthetic interpretation of life."
363. Ibid., 387.
364. Ibid., 387ff.
365. H. D. Preuss, *Einführung in die alttestamentliche Weisheitsliteratur*, 154–159 (literature). Cf. p. 245.
366. For the extent of the association between deed and consequence over a period of time, see also Th. Krüger, *Geschichtskonzepte im Ezechielbuch* (BZAW 180; 1989), 90f. On pp. 86–96 is found a good, critical view of the theses of K. Koch and the scholarly debate.
367. E. Otto, "Die 'synthetische Lebensauffassung' in der frühköniglichen Novellistik Israels," 395. Also pp. 395–399 for what follows.
368. Ibid., 397; cf. 399.
369. For the numerous references in the psalms, cf. K. Koch, WdF 125, 148ff. (Ps. 18:26f. is esp. characteristic). Cf. also K. Seybold, *TRE* 12, 463f.
370. K. Koch, WdF 125, 141ff.
371. For the location and use of the expression "his blood guilt turns back upon him," cf. the cultic, legal texts Lev. 20:9, 11–13, 16, 27; and Ezek. 18:13. Cf. also for this topic the contributions of H. Graf Reventlow and K. Koch in WdF 125, 412ff. and 432ff. See above, sec. 4.h.
372. Cf. H. W. Wolff, BK XIV/1, 2d ed., XVII–XXIII; and J. Jeremias, "Hosea/Hoseabuch," *TRE* 15, 586–598 (literature) for the proclamation of Hosea as a whole.
373. Cf. the more complete description of them in Vol. II, chap. 10.
374. H. H. Schmid, "Amos. Zur Frage nach der 'geistigen Heimat' des Propheten," *WuD* 10, 1969, 85–103, = *Altorientalische Welt in der alttestamentlichen Theologie* (1974), 121ff. Schmid is of the opinion that Amos argues out of a common, human knowledge. This thesis already fails at 3:2.
375. Cf. Vol. II, chap. 14.
376. K. Koch, WdF 125, 156ff.
377. E.g., Prov. 10:24; 11:2, 27; 18:3, 6; Judg. 9:23f.; Ps. 37:15; etc. In addition, see H. D. Preuss, *ThWAT* 1, cols. 542–544.
378. See Vol. II, 11.8.e, 9.b.
379. See K. Koch, WdF 125, 161f. (see pp. 160ff. with additional lexicographical examples of terms with "double meanings").
380. H. H. Schmid, *Gerechtigkeit als Weltordnung* (BHTh 40; 1968); idem, *Altorientalische Welt*

in der alttestamentlichen Theologie (1974); and idem, "Unterwegs zu einer neuen biblischen Theologie?" in K. Haacker et al., *Biblische Theologie heute* (BThSt 1; 1977), 75–95.
381. U. Luck, *Welterfahrung und Glaube als Grundproblem biblischer Theologie* (ThEx 191; 1976); idem, "Inwiefern ist die Botschaft von Jesus Christus 'Evangelium'?" *ZThK* 77, 1980, 24–41; and idem, "Der Weg zu einer biblischen Theologie des Neuen Testaments," *DPfrB* 88 (No. 9/10), 343–346.
382. Cf. H. H. Schmid, *Wesen und Geschichte der Weisheit* (BZAW 101; 1966); G. von Rad, *Wisdom in Israel* (1972); H. D. Preuss, *Einführung in die alttestamentliche Weisheitsliteratur* (1987).
383. J. Scharbert, "Das Verbum *PQD* in der Theologie des Alten Testaments," *BZ* NF 4, 1960, 209–226 (= WdF 125, 278ff.).
384. Ibid., 283.
385. Ibid., 125, 141ff.
386. Ibid., 298.
387. J. Scharbert, "*ŠLM* im Alten Testament," in H. Gross and F. Mussner, eds., *Lex tua veritas,* FS H. Junker (1961), 209–229 (= WdF 125, 300ff.).
388. Thus J. Scharbert, WdF 125, 308f.; references on pp. 306f., nn. 45ff.
389. Ibid., 312ff.
390. Ibid., 315ff.
391. Ibid., 125, 322.
392. Ibid., 324.
393. Cf. above, pp. 179f.
394. J.Scharbert also refers to these, WdF 125.
395. R. L. Hubbard, "Is the 'Tatsphäre' always a sphere?" *JETS* 25, 1982 (No. 3), 257–262.
396. Ibid., 259.
397. J. Halbe, "'Altorientalisches Weltordnungsdenken' und alttestamentliche Theologie," *ZThK* 76, 1979, 381–418.
398. For the problem of biblical theology according to J. Halbe, see " 'Altorientalisches Weltordnungsdenken,' " 415ff.
399. Ibid., 383f.
400. Ibid., 385ff. Similarly also K. Koch, "צדק *ṣdq* gemeinschaftstreu/heilvoll sein," *THAT* 2, cols. 507–530 (esp. 509f. and 516f.).
401. J. Halbe, "'Altorientalisches Weltordnungsdenken,' " 387f.; cf. 413.
402. Ibid., 385.
403. Ibid., 395ff.
404. Author's addition.
405. J. Halbe, " 'Altorientalisches Weltordnungsdenken,' " 399.
406. Ibid., 400.
407. Ibid., 401.
408. Ibid., 403.
409. Cf. above, pp. 94f.
410. J. Halbe, " 'Altorientalisches Weltordnungsdenken,' " 414.
411. See also O. Kaiser, *Ideologie und Glaube: Eine Gefährdung christlichen Glaubens am alttestamentlichen Beispiel aufgezeigt* (1984).
412. Cf. R. Knierim, "World Order," *Horizons in Biblical Theology,* 3, 1981, 63–123 (see pp. 63–101 for "world order").
413. J. Krecher and H.-P. Müller, *Saec.* 26, 1975, 42.
414. Cf. above, sec. 4.f.
415. Cf. G. von Rad, *Wisdom in Israel* (1972), 144–176; H. D. Preuss, *Einführung in die alttestamentliche Weisheitsliteratur* (esp. pp. 60–67). Further, see W. Eichrodt, *Theologie,* 2:83–89; G. von Rad, *Theology,* 1:447–449.
416. Cf. also Exod. 28:3; 2 Sam. 14:2, 17–20; 1 Kings 3:9, 12, 28; Isa. 28:23ff.; 31:2; Jer. 10:12; 51:15; Job 4:12–16; and 11:6.
417. Continuing with these questions: O. Keel, *Die Weisheit spielt vor Gott,* 1974; and H.-J. Hermisson, "Observations on the Creation Theology in Wisdom," in J. G. Gammie et al., eds., *Israelite Wisdom,* FS S. Terrien (1978), 43–57.

418. Cf. above, p. 163.
419. Cf. H. D. Preuss, *Einführung in die alttestamentliche Weisheitsliteratur,* 85–87 (literature).
420. Ibid., 137–151 (with literature); and M. Küchler, *Frühjüdische Weisheitstraditionen* (OBO 26; 1979).
421. See B. Janowski, " 'Ich will in eurer Mitte wohnen,' " *JBTh* 2 (1987), 165–193 (see p. 191 with literature).
422. See O. Grether, *Name und Wort Gottes im Alten Testament* (BZAW 64; 1934); L. Dürr, *Die Wertung des göttlichen Wortes im Alten Testament und im antiken Orient* (1938); G. Gerleman, "רבד *dābār* Wort," *THAT* 1, cols. 433–443; W. H. Schmidt et al., "רבד *dābar*," *ThWAT* 2, cols. 89–133 (literature); cf. W. H. Schmidt, *Alttestamentlicher Glaube* (6th ed.), 296–300. Cf. also W. Eichrodt, *Theologie,* 2:71–80; O. Procksch, *Theologie,* 468–475; and C. Westermann, *Elements of Old Testament Theology,* 15–27.
423. Cf. above, sec. 4.g.
424. Cf. W. H. Schmidt, *ThWAT* 2, cols. 101f.
425. Cf. the analogy of the "problem of the translation" of John 1:1 ("In the beginning was the Word") in Goethe's *Faust* I (study scene; Faust with the poodle).
426. It begins with "When the heavens above (still) were not named, the earth below was (still) not named . . . " (*AOT,* 2d ed., 109; *RGT,* 2d ed., 108). For the importance of the (divine) word in Mesopotamia, cf. H. Lutzmann, *ThWAT* 2, cols. 98–101. Also according to the Egyptian viewpoint, Re created the gods through the naming of his bodily members, i.e., through their names (E. Hornung, *Das Totenbuch der Ägypter,* 1979, 60 = Saying 17.3). For Re, cf. *WdM* 1, 389–393.
427. Num. 15:31; Deut. 5:5 (pl.); 2 Sam. 12:9 (?); 1 Chron. 15:15; 2 Chron. 30:12; 34:21; and 35:6.
428. Cf. Vol. II, 9.4.
429. Exod. 4:28; 24:3, 4; Num. 11:24; Josh. 3:9; 1 Sam. 8:10; 15:1; Jer. 36:4, 6, 8, 11; 37:2; 43:1; Ezek. 11:25; Amos 8:11; 2 Chron. 11:4; and 29:15.
430. The prophetic word is meant in Jer. 36:4, 6, 8, 11; 37:2; 43:1; Ezek. 11:25; and 2 Chron. 11:4.
431. For example, this was different in Egypt, where the human word of wisdom that was beautiful speech and spoke "of God" was also named the "word of God." Cf. P. Kaplony, "Der Schreiber, das Gotteswort und die Papyruspflanze," *ZÄS* 110, 1983, 143–173. Proverbs 30:5 is (also terminologically) the major exception.
432. See above, sec. 4.d.
433. Thus with L. Köhler, *Theologie* (4th ed.), 91.
434. Cf. more exactly Vol. II, 10.4.
435. Cf., e.g., Isa. 8:5; Hos. 1:2; Amos 3:8; and Zech. 1:9. Then cf. Isa. 1:10, 20; 16:13; Jer. 1:7; 20:8f.; 23:28; 27:13; Amos 3:13; 4:1; etc.
436. Cf., e.g., Jacob in Bethel (Gen. 28:12); the Joseph Story (Genesis 40–41); and the prophets (Num. 12:6–8; Daniel 2; 4). The Hittites also were aware of the juxtaposition of dream and oracle, but probably not the creatively active and prophetic word of God. Cf. M. Hutter, "Bemerkungen über das 'Wort Gottes' bei den Hethitern," *BN* 28, 1985, 17–26.
437. For these formulae of the word event as well as the use of רבד = *dibbēr* in the prophets, cf. Vol. II, 10.4, and L. Rost, *Studien zum Alten Testament* (BWANT 101; 1974), 9ff., 39ff.
438. For the connection of Deut. 8:3b and Isa. 55:3, cf. L. Perlitt, "Wovon der Mensch lebt," in J. Jeremias and L. Perlitt, eds., *Die Botschaft und die Boten,* FS H. W. Wolff (1981), 424f. For Isa. 55:3: E. Zenger, " 'Hört, auf dass ihr lebt' (Jes 55:3): Alttestamentliche Hinweise zu einer Theologie des Gotteswortes," in J. Schreiner, ed., *Freude am Gottesdienst: Aspekte ursprunglicher Liturgie,* FS J. G. Plöger (1983), 133–144.
439. The Mari letters prior to the formation of Israel (eighteenth–seventeenth centuries B.C.E.) attest to a god's speaking through human "prophets." The prophetic words at Mari are, in addition, related more to incidental, single occurrences, and not to the interpretation of larger historical contexts and events of history. For this topic, cf. among others F. Ellermeier, *Prophetie in Mari und Israel* (1968) (for this, see J. G. Heintz, *Bibl* 52, 1971, 543–555); E. Noort, *Untersuchungen zum Gottesbescheid in Mari* (AOAT 202; 1977); and A. Schmitt, *Prophetischer Gottesbescheid in Mari und Israel* (BWANT 114; 1982). Cf. further Vol. II, 10.2.
440. Cf. Vol. II, 10.7 for the problem of "false prophets."
441. See below, sec. 5.e.

442. Cf. below, sec. 5.c.
443. Cf. in Vol. II, 10.6 and 14.7.
444. 118 times with אל היה *hāyâ 'ēl* ("was to") as predicate; cf. *THAT* 1, col. 439. For this, see W.
     Zimmerli, BK XIII/1, 89; and W. H. Schmidt, *ThWAT* 2, cols. 120f.
445. See E. Zenger, " 'Hört, auf dass ihr lebt' (Jes 55,3)," 137.
446. W. H. Schmidt, *ThWAT* 2, col. 126.
447. In the form of "inspiration"? Cf. R. Rendtorff, *EvTh* 22, 1962, 626 (= TB 57, 65).
448. Ibid., 65f. (= 626f.).
449. Deut. 12:28; 15:15; 24:18, 22; 28:14; 30:14–17, 19; 27:3, 8, 26; 28:58; 29:28; 31:12, 24; and
     32:46. In the Deuteronomistic History, e.g., see Josh. 8:34; and 2 Kings 23;24. Cf. G. Braulik,
     "Ausdrücke für 'Gesetz' im Buch Deuteronomium," *Bibl* 51, 1970, 39–66 (= SBAB 2, 1988,
     11ff.; see there [21; cf. Bibl 51, 49; see also W. H. Schmidt, *ThWAT* 2, cols. 124f.]) as a sum-
     mary: "the *dĕbārîm* in 4:10, 13, 36; 5:5, 22; 9:10; and 10:2, 4 refer to the Decalogue. *Dābār*
     in 15:15 and 24:18, 22 and *dĕbārîm* in 12:28 mean the concrete, preceding, individual stipu-
     lations. *Dābār* in 4:2; 13:1; and 30:14 and *dĕbārîm* in 1:18; 6:6; and 11:18 refer to the entire
     Mosaic "Law," namely, the paraenetic section and the contiguous, individual command-
     ments. In 28:14 *dĕbārîm* designates this 'Law' probably along with the Decalogue."
450. 1 Kings 15:29; 16:12; 22:38; 2 Kings 10:17; 24:2; cf. 2 Sam. 24:19; 1 Kings 12:15; 14:18;
     16:34; 17:16; 2 Kings 1:17; 2:22; 4:44; 9:36; etc. A particular Deuteronomistic redaction,
     the Deuteronomistic Priestly source, is often seen here. Cf. W. Dietrich, *Prophetie und
     Geschichte* (FRLNT 108; 1972). Above all, see p. 88.
451. Through Hebrew מלא *millē'* ("fulfilled") or הקים = *hēqîm* ("established"): 1 Kings 1:14; 2:27;
     1 Kings 2:4; 6:12; 8:20; and 12:15; cf. Deut. 9:5; 1 Sam. 1:23; 2 Sam. 7:25. Then see Josh.
     21:45; 23:15; 1 Sam. 3:19 (cf. Isa. 55:11!). For the references outside the Deuteronomistic
     History, cf. W. H. Schmidt, *ThWAT* 2, cols. 122f.
452. According to the Babylonian epic of creation, Marduk creates and makes to vanish by means
     of his word (*Enuma eliš* IV 19–26: *AOT*, 2d ed., 117; *ANET*, 3d ed., 66). For Egypt, see
     n. 453 following.
453. In addition to the monotheistic stretto that is self-evident for the Old Testament, the most im-
     portant distinction between the "active word of the one God of creation" in Genesis 1 and
     thus Israel and the creative word of the Egyptian God Ptah in the so-called "monument of
     the Memphite Theology" resides in this manner of historical continuation (*TUAT* I/6, 585ff.;
     RGT, 2d ed., 31f.; *ANET*, 3d ed., 4–6). For Ptah: *WdM* 1, 387–389. For this history of reli-
     gions inquiry, cf. K. Koch, "Wort und Einheit des Schöpfergottes in Memphis und
     Jerusalem," *ZThK* 62, 1965, 251–293 (= *Studien zur alttestamentlichen und altorientalis-
     chen Religionsgeschichte*, 1988, 61ff. with addenda and corrections). Cf. the evaluation of
     the word in Egypt: J. Landee, "Das Schöpfungswort im alten Ägypten," in FS H. E. Obbink
     (Utrecht, 1964), 33–66; and J. Bergmann, *ThWAT* 2, cols. 92–98. For creation through a
     word of God, see also *RGT* (2d ed.), 32, 52; cf. 129f.
454. Cf. F. Kohata, *Jahwist und Priesterschrift in Exodus 3–14* (BZAW 166; 1986), 226f.,
     310–315. For the relationships between the Priestly story of creation and the later P de-
     scription of the Sinai event (Exod. 24:15b–18a) as well as the construction of the tent of
     meeting (Exod. 39:43; 40:17), cf. also P. Weimar, "Sinai und Schöpfung," *RB* 95, 1988,
     337–385, esp. 358ff.
455. Cf. H. D. Preuss, *Verspottung fremder Religionen im Alten Testament* (BWANT 92; 1971),
     192–237.
456. For this question, see above pp. 163 and 194f.
457. Cf. W. H. Schmidt, *ThWAT* 2, cols. 128–133 ("Ansätze zur Hypostasierung").
458. See W. Eichrodt, "Offenbarung und Geschichte im Alten Testament," *ThZ* 4, 1948, 321–331;
     H. Haag, " 'Offenbaren' in der hebräischen Bibel," *ThZ* 16, 1960, 251–258; R. Rendtorff,
     "Die Offenbarungsvorstellungen im Alten Israel," in W. Pannenberg, ed., *Offenbarung als
     Geschichte* (1961; 5th ed., 1982; KuD Beiheft 1), 21–41 (= TB 57, 1975, 39ff.); H. Schus-
     ter, *Offenbarung Gottes im Alten Testament* (1962); W. Zimmerli, " 'Offenbarung' im Alten
     Testament," *EvTh* 22, 1962, 15–31; R. Schnackenburg, "Zum Offenbarungsgedanken in der
     Bibel," *BZ* NF 7, 1963, 2–22; F. Schnutenhaus, "Das Kommen und Erscheinen Gottes im Al-
     ten Testament," *ZAW* 76, 1964, 1–22; F. Dumermuth, "Biblische Offenbarungsphänomene,"

ThZ 21, 1965, 1–21; F. Baumgärtel, "Das Offenbarungszeugnis des Alten Testament im Lichte der religionsgeschichtlich-vergleichenden Forschung," *ZThK* 64, 1967, 393–422; A. Deissler, "Gottes Selbstoffenbarungen im Alten Testament," in *Mysterium Salutis,* vol. 2 (1967), 226–271; W. Zimmerli, *Gottes Offenbarung* (TB 19; 2d ed., 1969); R. Knierim, "Offenbarung im Alten Testament," in H. W. Wolff, ed., *Probleme biblischer Theologie,* FS G. von Rad (1971), 206–235; M. Saebø, "Offenbarung in der Geschichte und als Geschichte," *StTh* (Oslo) 35, 1981, 55–71; and J. J. Petuchowski and W. Strolz, eds., *Offenbarung im jüdischen und christlichen Glaubensverständnis* (1981). Cf. also E. Sellin, *Theologie des Alten Testaments* (2d ed., 1936), 45–57; L. Köhler, *Theologie* (4th ed., 83ff.); E. Jacob, *Grundfragen,* 25ff.; G. Fohrer, *Grundstrukturen,* 33ff.; C. Westermann, *Elements of Old Testament Theology,* 25–27; W. H. Schmidt, *Alttestamentlicher Glaube* (6th ed.), 100–105. G. von Rad's theology lacks a corresponding thematic discussion, although he often speaks about "revelation." Cf. an example of this in his *Theology,* 2:357–387.

459. Moreover, it is valid to say that revelation "is no objective, comprehensible phenomenon but rather a personal experience that befalls human beings" (G. Fohrer, *Grundstrukturen,* 38).
460. Cf. above, chap. 3.5.e.
461. Cf. above the appropriate subdivisions in chap. 4. For the priestly casting of lots, cf. Vol. II, 9.4.
462. Cf. M. Ottoson et al., "חלם *ḥālam,*" *ThWAT* 2, cols. 986–998 (literature).
463. For the following esp. R. Rendtorff, "Die Offenbarungsvorstellungen im Alten Israel"; also H. Haag and the appropriate articles in *THAT* and *ThWAT.*
464. H.-J. Zobel, *ThWAT* 1, col. 1029.
465. "The general oriental character of Old Testament language not only shows that Israel, at least in this respect, had no special conception of revelation. It also makes it necessary to ask if the experience of 'revelation' for Israel could not be seen essentially in ontological, cosmological, and empirical categories. Or theologically stated: one asks whether divine revelation does not also essentially involve the experience of God within the horizon of human experience and knowledge. This would explain then why a special 'revelation,' thus for instance one of Yahweh, requires from the outset a common language with which to communicate it" (R. Knierim, in H. W. Wolff, ed., *Probleme biblischer Theologie,* FS G. von Rad, 1971, 214f.).
466. R. Rendtorff, "Die Offenbarungsvorstellungen im Alten Israel," treats this term only in a footnote (p. 23, n. 11).
467. This also can refer to one person doing this to another: 1 Sam. 20:2, 12f.; 22:8, 17; and Ruth 4:4.
468. H.-J. Zobel, *ThWAT* 1, col. 1026: "Revelation seizes the entire person and is most closely entwined with history."
469. W. Zimmerli, *EvTh* 22, 1962, 16.
470. R. Knierim, in H. W. Wolff, ed., *Probleme biblischer Theologie,* FS G. von Rad (1971), 211. The words in parentheses are added by the author.
471. R. Rendtorff, "Die Offenbarungsvorstellungen im Alten Israel," 23. For the verb, cf. also F. Schnutenhaus, "Das Kommen und Erscheinen Gottes im Alten Testament," 10f.; and H. F. Fuhs, "ראה *ra'ah,*" *ThWAT* 7, cols. 225–266 ("Complementary term to גלה"; "God steps out of the concealment of his divine nature and is revealed in and through every possible form of human experience of reality. *rā'â* designates, then, the process of revelation itself" (ibid., 250).
472. For the difference between ראה = *rā'â* ("see") and ידע = *yāda'* ("know"), cf. the thoughts of R. Knierim that are worth consideration, in H. W. Wolff, ed., *Probleme biblischer Theologie,* FS G. von Rad (1971), 219f.
473. Ibid., 217.
474. D. Vetter, *THAT* 2, col. 700. See also above, sec. 4.d.
475. Cf. also Exod. 6:1; 14:31; 16:32; 34:10; Josh. 23:3; 24:7; Judg. 2:7; and Ps. 66:5.
476. R. Rendtorff, "Die Offenbarungsvorstellungen im Alten Israel," 26.
477. Cf. above, chap. 3.1, 2.
478. Cf. *ThWAT* 1, 562–568 (literature).
479. For the few corresponding texts that speak of a "going forth" of YHWH (יצא = *yāṣā'*) as a theophanic or epiphanic event, see *ThWAT* 3, cols. 803f.; and F. Schnutenhaus, "Das Kommen und Erscheinen Gottes im Alten Testament," 2–5.

480. Cf. above, pp. 64f., 66f., 175.
481. For the "coming from the south," see the (differing) results from L. E. Axelsson, *The Lord Rose Up from Seir* (Lund, 1987); and J. C. de Moor, *The Rise of Yahwism* (BETL 91; Louvain, 1990).
482. For these texts, cf. *ThWAT* 1, cols. 559–562.
483. F. Schnutenhaus, "Das Kommen und Erscheinen Gottes im Alten Testament," 17; cf. *ThWAT* 1, cols. 567f.
484. See R. Schlichting, *LÄ* IV, cols. 555–559 (literature); J. Bergmann, *ThWAT* 3, cols. 485f.; and G. J. Botterweck, *ThWAT* 3, cols. 487–491.
485. Cf. to the following, above all, W. Zimmerli, "Ich bin Jahwe," and "Das Wort des göttlichen Selbsterweises (Erweiswort), eine prophetische Gattung," in *Gottes Offenbarung* (TB 19; 2d, 1969), 11–40, 120–132. Cf. Zimmerli, *Theology*, 17–27. Then see R. Rendtorff, "Die Offenbarungsvorstellungen," 32ff.
486. The reference is found in the so-called Elohistic Psalter, so that יהוה = *yahweh* should replace the present אלהים = *'ĕlōhîm* ("God").
487. W. Zimmerli, TB 19 (2d ed.), 14.
488. See Th. Krüger, *Geschichtskonzepte im Ezechielbuch* (BZAW 180; 1989), 199ff.
489. W. Zimmerli, TB 19 (2d ed.), 20.
490. In the discussion between W. Zimmerli and R. Rendtorff, the question is, "Where is Yahweh 'seen' or 'known'?" "There are four alternatives: (a) in his addresses promising action; (b) in the acts following a promise; (c) only in his acts; or (d) in the traditiohistorical unity of both addresses and acts. Both scholars agree that possibility (c) is to be excluded. In determining the relationship between promise and action, Zimmerli leans toward alternative (a), while Rendtorff prefers to stress alternative (b) and especially alternative (d)" (R. Knierim, in H. W. Wolff, ed., *Probleme biblischer Theologie*, FS G. von Rad, 1971, 218).
491. Cf. F. Kohata, *Jahwist und Priesterschrift in Exodus 3–14* (BZAW 166; 1986), 173ff.; and W. Zimmerli, TB 19 (2d ed.), 61ff.
492. W. Zimmerli, TB 19 (2d ed.), 24.
493. Gen. 15:7; 26:24; 28:13; 31:11ff.; and 46:3; cf. Exod. 3:6; and Josh. 5:14.
494. Cf. H. D. Preuss, *Deuterojesaja: Eine Einführung in seine Botschaft* (1976), 89 (literature). Cf. pp. 193, 263, 277.
495. For the normal way of knowing God (esp. through a process of experience, even through a concrete sensory perception: Ezek. 20:42; Josh. 3:10), cf. I. L. Seeligmann, "Erkenntnis Gottes und historisches Bewusstsein im alten Israel," in H. Donner et al., eds., *Beiträge zur alttestamentlichen Theologie*, FS W. Zimmerli (1977), 414–445.
496. See W. Zimmerli, *Erkenntnis Gottes nach dem Buche Ezechiel* (AThANT 27; 1954) (= TB 19, 2d ed., 1969, 41ff.); further, R. Rendtorff, "Die Offenbarungsvorstellungen," 35ff.
497. That the Old Testament references in 1 Kings 20:13, 28 are the kernel of a prophetic tradition of the form of this prophetic saying, as Zimmerli assumes (TB 19, 2d ed., 54ff.), is today no longer widely accepted, since these texts are no longer assigned to such an early date. And I. L. Seeligmann asks with justification whether the derivation of the formula from the legal or prophetic demonstration of proof is correct or whether one should not instead think of entirely concrete experiences that allowed one to arrive at a knowledge of God, for instance, as a consequence of seeing or hearing (in H. Donner et al., eds., *Beiträge zur alttestamentlichen Theologie*, FS W. Zimmerli (1977), p. 239). He points, e.g., to Gen. 8:11; Exod. 3:7; Josh. 3:10; 24:7; Judg. 2:7; 17:13; 1 Sam. 20:33; Isa. 5:19; Ezek. 20:42; and Job 13:1f.
498. Zimmerli's register of textual references is found in TB 19 (2d ed.), 43, nn. 5–11; 44, n. 12.
499. Ibid., 49.
500. For the false priority of "being" over "event" in theology, cf. C. Westermann, "Das Alte Testament und die Theologie," in his *Erträge der Forschung am Alten Testament* (TB 73; 1984), 9–26.
501. For Exod. 6:1–8, cf. also: E. A. Martens, *God's Design* (Grand Rapids, 1982), 12ff.
502. For כבוד יהוה = *kābôd yahweh* (YHWH) as the sign and means of revelation according to the witness of the Priestly document, cf. above, sec. 4.d. and n. 474.
503. Cf. also above, pp. 204f.
504. W. Zimmerli, TB 19 (2d ed.), 65.

505. Cf. S. Talmon's essay in J. J. Petuchowski and W. Strolz, eds., *Offenbarung im jüdischen und christlichen Glaubensverständnis*, 32: "Revelation does not answer the questions concerning the identity of the deity who is made known but rather is the manifestation of his deeds in the past and in the present. And these acts have a determinative value for the future."

506. For this topic, cf. the overview by P. Eicher, *Offenbarung: Prinzip neuzeitlicher Theologie* (1977).

507. Thus W. Pannenberg in *Offenbarung als Geschichte*, 9f.

508. H. Haag (" 'Offenbaren' in der hebräischen Bibel," 256ff.) points correctly to the significance of "telling" (נגד = *nāgad*, hiphil) for the Old Testament revelatory event.

509. In opposition to R. Rendtorff (*EvTh* 22, 1962, 638 = TB 57, 77) it should be said that for the Old Testament history possessed a certain ambiguity. The preexilic prophets of judgment (esp. Jeremiah) have necessarily experienced this ambiguity, because *their* interpretation of history could also be contested and thus might not evoke faith in those to whom they spoke.

510. In regard to this point, P. Althaus ("Offenbarung als Geschichte und Glaube," *ThLZ* 87, 1962, cols. 321–330) has already cast a critical light on the problematic concept set forth by W. Pannenberg ("The revelation of history is open to anyone who has eyes to see").

511. Thus W. Eichrodt, *ThZ* 4, 1948, 324.

512. Zimmerli's antipathy toward "interpretation" (e.g., *EvTh* 22, 1962, 24; present in the citation of Rendtorff) cannot be accepted.

513. Nevertheless, one can indeed surmise what "the God who is proclaiming himself as the subject in his name" should be (thus W. Zimmerli, TB 19, 2d ed., 126), or what it means when it is said "in this event Yahweh himself has declared himself for the faith of Israel" (*Theology*, 25). However, these statements are prone to misunderstanding and are unclear. Zimmerli is criticized by Rendtorff for giving "remarkably little value to the name of Yahweh" (*EvTh* 22, 1962, 22). He thinks Zimmerli views revelation as a fixed positivistic hypostatization.

514. For the phenomena of revelation mentioned in this connection (smoke, fire, cloud, sound, etc.), cf. above, pp. 66f.; and F. Dumermuth, "Biblische Offenbarungsphänomene." For the Sinai theophany as "revelation," cf. also H.-J. Zobel, "Der frühe Jahwe-Glaube in der Spannung von Wüste und Kulturland," *ZAW* 101, 1989, 346f.

515. "We are not able honestly and simply to say: God has revealed himself in the exodus of Israel out of Egypt, but we can only say: Israel has experienced this event as the fundamental act of salvation in which God has revealed himself as the one who is" (Rendtorff, in *Offenbarung im jüdischen und christlichen Glaubensverständnis*, 47f.)

516. Cf. below, sec. 6.

517. I cannot find in the text of Qoh. 3:11ff. any discussion about transcending the fear of God through the speech of God as "revelation" and that this revelation may occur in earthly joy (against N. Lohfink, *BiKi* 45, 1990, No. 1, 31f.; cf. pp. 35f. regarding "natural revelation" in Qoheleth).

518. Cf., e.g., M. Saebø, "Offenbarung in der Geschichte und als Geschichte," 67. According to him, concentrated, condensed history as well as "natural revelation" is found in the experiential sayings of wisdom. I would ask what the books of Job and Qoheleth would think about that.

519. This is true in spite of the criticism of J. Barr, "Revelation through History in the Old Testament and in Modern Theology," *Interp* 17, 1963, 193–205.

520. See (in addition to much in n. 458 above that could be mentioned again): G. von Rad, "Theologische Geschichtsschreibung im Alten Testament," *ThZ* 4, 1948, 161–174 (= *Gottes Wirken in Israel*, 1974, 175ff.); H. Gese, "Geschichtliches Denken im Alten Orient und im Alten Testament," *ZThK* 55, 1958, 127–145 (= *Vom Sinai zum Zion*, 3d ed., 1990, 81ff.); H. W. Wolff, "Das Geschichtsverständnis der alttestamentlichen Prophetie," *EvTh* 20, 1960, 218–235 (= TB 22, 2d ed., 1973, 289ff.); R. Rendtorff, "Geschichte und Wort im Alten Testament," *EvTh* 22, 1962, 621–649 (= TB 57, 1975, 60ff.); I. Seeligmann, "Hebräische Erzählung und biblische Geschichtsschreibung," *ThZ* 18, 1962, 305–325; idem, "Menschliches Heldentum und göttliche Hilfe," *ThZ* 19, 1963, 385–411; J. Hempel, *Geschichten und Geschichte im Alten Testament bis zur persischen Zeit* (1964); G. von Rad, "Der Anfang der Geschichtsschreibung im alten Israel," in his *Gesammelte Studien zum Alten Testament* (TB 8), 3d ed., 1965, 148–188; B. Albrektson, *History and the Gods* (CB OT 1; Lund, 1967); idem, *Theologie als Geschichte*, (Neuland in der Theologie, vol. 3; 1967); R. Smend, *Elemente*

alttestamentlicher Geschichtsdenkens (ThSt 95; 1968) (= "Die Mitte des Alten Testaments," *Gesammelte Studien* I, 1986, 160ff.); C. Westermann, "Zum Geschichtsverständnis des Alten Testaments," in H. W. Wolff, ed., *Probleme biblischer Theologie, FS* G. von Rad (1971), 611–619; M. Weippert, "Fragen des israelitischen Geschichtsbewusstseins," *VT* 23, 415–442 (literature); J. Krecher and H.-P. Müller, "Vergangenheitsinteresse in Mesopotamien und Israel," *Saec.* 26, 1975, 13–44; G. von Rad, "Das Wort Gottes und die Geschichte im Alten Testament," in his *Gottes Wirken in Israel* (1974), 191–212; D. Grimm, "Geschichtliche Erinnerungen im Glauben Israels," *ThZ* 32, 1976, 257–268; G. Wallis, "Die geschichtliche Erfahrung und das Bekenntnis zum Jahwe im Alten Testament," *ThLZ* 101, 1976, cols. 801–816; J. Kegler, *Politisches Geschehen und historisches Verstehen* (1977), 414–445; S. Herrmann, *Zeit und Geschichte*, 1977; I.L. Seeligmann, "Erkenntnis Gottes und historisches Bewusstein," in FS W. Zimmerli, 1977, 414–445; Chr. D. Müller, *Die Erfahrung der Wirklichkeit* (1978); P. Gibert, *La Bible à la naissance de l'histoire* (Paris, 1979); J. Jeremias, "Gott und Geschichte im Alten Testament," *EvTh* 40, 1980, 381–396; J. van Seters, "Histories and Historians of the Ancient Near East: The Israelites," *Or* 50, 1981, 137–185; R. Schmitt, *Abschied von der Heilsgeschichte?* (1982); J. van Seters, ed., *In Search of History* (New Haven and London, 1983); K. Koch, "Geschichte/Geschichtsschreibung/ Geschichtsphilosophie. II: Altes Testament," *TRE* 12, 569–586 (literature); and J. N. Carreira, "Formen des Geschichtsdenkens in altorientalischer und alttestamentlicher Geschichtsschreibung," *BZ* NF 31, 1987, 36–57. Cf. also L. Köhler, *Theologie* (4th ed.), 77–80; E. Jacob, *Théologie*, 148ff.; J. L. McKenzie, *A Theology of the Old Testament* (1974), 131ff.; C. Westermann, *Elements of Old Testament Theology*, 217–221; H. Graf Reventlow, *Problems of Old Testament Theology*, 71–87; and W. H. Schmidt, *Alttestamentlicher Glaube* (6th ed.), 100ff.

521. See J. Kegler, *Politisches Geschehen*, 7ff.
522. For the debate concerning the different depictions of history (those of the Old Testament and those of contemporary scholarship), cf. G. von Rad, *Theology*, 2:v–viii. M. Deming sharpens the question in his investigation of fact and fiction ("Bedeutung und Funktionen von 'Fiktionen' in der alttestamentlichen Geschichtsschreibung," *EvTh* 44, 1984, 254–266). Concerning "fiction," he writes (see p. 262): " . . . a kind of description of history which indeed narrates what is historically unfounded, but is nevertheless related to history in that it seeks to uncover a truth in the past that will not emerge in mere description." Cf. also above, chap. 1.
523. See R. Rendtorff, "Geschichte und Überlieferung," in R. Rendtorff and K. Koch, eds., *Studien zur Theologie der alttestamentlichen Überlieferungen, FS* G. von Rad (1961), 81–94 (= TB 57, 1975, 25ff.).
524. K. Koch, *TRE* 12, 572; E. Jacob (*Theologie*, 149) cites H. W. Robinson: "History might be called the sacrament of the religion of Israel."
525. Cf. V. Fritz, "Weltalter und Lebenszeit. Mythische Elemente in der Geschichtsschreibung Israels und bei Hesiod," *ZThK* 87, 1990, 145–162.
526. J. Krecher and H.-P. Müller, "Vergangenheitsinteresse in Mesopotamien und Israel," 32f.
527. For the writing of history in the ancient Near East and the understanding of history emerging from this historiography, see the examples of texts in *TUAT* I/4–6. In addition to the works mentioned in n. 520 above, which include H. Gese, B. Albrektson, J. Krecher and H.-P. Müller, J. N. Carreira, and J. van Seters, and the work by H. Cancik mentioned in n. 547 below; cf., e.g., also: H.-G. Güterbock, "Die historische Tradition und ihre literarische Gestaltung bei Babyloniern und Hethitern bis 1200," *ZA* 42, 1934, 1–91; 44, 1938, 45–145; A. Kammenhuber, "Die hethitische Geschichtsschreibung," *Saec.* 9, 1958, 136–155; E. Otto, "Geschichtsbild und Geschichtsschreibung in Ägypten," *WO* 3/3, 1966, 161–176; idem, *Geschichte als Fest* (1966); H. Cancik, *Mythische und historische Wahrheit* (SBS 48; 1970); H. H. Schmid, "Das alttestamentliche Verständnis von Geschichte in seinem Verhältnis zum gemeinorientalischen Denken," *WuD* NF 13, 1975, 9–21; J. von Beckerath, "Geschichtsüberlieferung im Alten Ägypten," *Saec.* 29, 1978, 11–17; A. K. Grayson, "Assyria and Babylonia," *Or* 49, 1980, 140–194; H. A. Hoffner, "Histories and Historians of the Ancient Near East: The Hittites," *Or* 49, 1980, 283–332; H. Tadmor and M. Weinfeld, eds., *History, Historiography and Interpretation: Studies in Biblical and Cuneiform Literatures* (Jerusalem and Leiden, 1983); E. Brunner-Traut, *Frühformen des Erkennens: Am Beispiel Altägyptens*

(1990) (98ff.); and M. Cwik-Rosenbach, "Zeitverständnis und Geschichtsschreibung in Mesopotamien, *ZRGG* 42, 1990, 1–20. See also the brief remarks by K. Koch, *TRE* 12, 570ff.

528. Cf. the examples in *TUAT* II/4.

529. *TUAT* II/4, 555f.

530. Cf. M. Oeming, *Das wahre Israel* (BWANT; 1990).

531. Cf. the literature cited in n. 527 above and n. 547 below.

532. In the Babylonian "Weidner Chronicle" (by A. K. Grayson, *Assyrian and Babylonian Chronicles,* Locust Valley, N.Y., 1975, no. 19), the destiny of kings is described in terms clearly very close to the Deuteronomistic History. This destiny of kings is dependent upon their behavior toward the temple of Marduk, the Esagila, in Babylon. Cf. also E. Osswald, "Altorientalische Parallelen zur deuteronomistischen Geschichtsbetrachtung," *MIO* 15, 1969, 286–296.

533. Cf. H. Cancik, *Mythische und historische Wahrheit,* 9f., 90ff.

534. In addition, this literature has no term for "mistake" (intellectual as well as historical). See W. von Soden, *WO* 4, 1967, 38–47 (= BZAW 162, 1985, 99ff.), and his *Sprache, Denken, und Begriffsbildung im Alten Orient* (1974), 39.

535. B. Albrektson, *History and the Gods;* and idem, *Theologie als Geschichte.*

536. Cf. L. Cagni, *The Poem of Erra* (Malibu, 1977); for the Tukulti-Ninurta Epic, cf. the particulars in Krecher, *Saec.* 26, 1975, 26. Cf. for both texts H. Klengel, ed., *Kulturgeschichte des alten Vorderasien* (1989), 302f., 395; and for the Erra Epic, see J. Bottéro and S. N. Kramer, *Lorsque les dieux faisaient l'homme* (Paris, 1989), 680–727. For the prayers concerning pestilence, cf. *RGT* (2d ed.), 191–196 ("the sins of the father come upon the son": 195; cf. Jer. 31:29; Exod. 18:2). The lament over Ur: *TUAT* II/5, 700–707; and P. Michalowski, *The Lamentation over the Destruction of Sumer and Ur* (Winona Lake, Ind., 1989).

537. דברים = *děbārîm* is perhaps appropriately rendered "order of events."

538. Cf. Vol. II, 7.8.

539. H. D. Wendland, *Geschichtsanschauung und Geschichtsbewusstsein im Neuen Testament* (1938), 15.

540. See W. Werner, *Studien zur alttestamentlichen Vorstellung vom Plan Jahwes* (BZAW 173; 1988). However, he maintains that all texts from Isaiah and most from Deutero-Isaiah are late.

541. See n. 520 above.

542. For such etiologies, cf., e.g., Gen. 19:26 (Lot's wife as a pillar of salt); 19:36f. (origins of the Moabites and the Ammonites); Genesis 27 (the relationship of Israel and Edom); Josh. 4:20ff. (twelve stones in Gilgal); 6:25 (the Canaanite clan in Jericho); and 8:28 (Ai as a heap of debris). See B. O. Long, *The Problem of Etiological Narrative in the Old Testament* (BZAW 108; 1968); B. Diebner and H. Schult, *Ätiologische Texte im Alten Testament* DBAT, no. 5, 1974; 6, 1974, 6–30; 7, 1974, 2–17; 10, 1975, 2–9; and F. W. Golka, "The Aetiologies in the Old Testament," *VT* 26, 410–428; 27, 1977, 36–47.

543. Cf. the "historicizing" of the agrarian festivals. See Vol. II, 13.4.

544. Thus with J. Hempel, *Geschichte und Geschichten im Alten Testament,* 60ff.

545. Cf. Vol. II, 14.2 + 3.

546. "For the people of the Old Testament history is the intellectual expression of faith" (I. L. Seeligmann, *ThZ* 19, 1963, 385).

547. Cf., e.g., I. L. Seeligmann, *Hebräische Erzählung und biblische Geschichtsschreibung;* J. Hempel, *Geschichten und Geschichte im Alten Testament,* 152ff.; and H. Cancik, *Grundzüge der hethitischen und alttestamentlichen Geschichtsschreibung* (1976).

548. R. Smend, *Elemente alttestamentlichen Geschichtsdenkens,* 5.

549. Ibid., 37.

550. G. Mensching, *Vergleichende Religionswissenschaft* (2d ed., 1949), 66; cf. M. Noth, *Gesammelte Studien* 1 (TB 6; 3d ed., 1966), 245.

551. Cf. for this contrast, K. Löwith, *Weltgeschichte und Heilsgeschehen* (1953), 168ff.

552. Cf. for these questions, M. Saebø, "Offenbarung in der Geschichte und als Geschichte."

553. The following is certainly true: "In the period and intellectual sphere in which the Succession Narrative originated, a 'purely profane' historiography would be an impossibility" (C. Westermann, in H. W. Wolff, ed., *Probleme biblischer Theologie,* FS G. von Rad, 1971, 613).

554. For this, see H. Schnabl, *Die Thronfolgeerzählung Davids* (1988) (see there the older literature). Schnabl includes also 2 Sam. 21:1–14 (without v. 7 and places it before 2 Samuel 9). Cf. above, pp. 189f., 210f.

555. C. Westermann, in H. W. Wolff, ed., *Probleme biblischer Theologie*, FS G. von Rad (1971), 614, wants to add to these "theological" passages others in 2 Samuel (6:12–17; 7: however, these probably do not belong to the Succession Narrative); 8:6, 14b; 10:12b; 12:1–13; 14:11, 17; 15:7f., 25f., 31; 16:8, 10, 23; 18:28; 20:19; and 21:2, 14.

556. Thus, e.g., by E. Würthwein, *Die Erzählung von der Thronfolge Davids—theologische oder politische Geschichtsschreibung?* (ThSt 115; 1974); cf. also H. Schnabl, *Die Thronfolgeerzählung Davids.*

557. For this, see L. Schmidt, "Josephnovelle," *TRE* 17, 225–258 (literature); and also W. Dietrich, *Die Josepherzählung als Novelle und Geschichtsschreibung* (BThSt 14; 1989). Cf. above, chap. 2.8 and chap. 4.4.h.

558. "Behind these subtle markings of character the hand of God is apparent; he is the one who is capable of forming and leading human beings in order that they become just in their dealings" (W. Dietrich, *Die Josepherzählung als Novelle und Geschichtsschreibung*, 58).

559. For this two-fold casuality of human and divine action in history, cf. I. L. Seeligmann, "Menschliches Heldentum und göttliche Hilfe"; and also L. Schmidt, *Menschlicher Erfolg und Jahwes Initiative* (WMANT 38; 1970).

560. Also see P. F. Ellis's *The Yahwist* (Notre Dame, Ind., 1968).

561. For him, see H. Seebass, "Jahwist," *TRE* 16, 441–451 (literature). In addition, see S. Tengström, "Die Auffassung von der Geschichte im jahwistischen Werk und im Alten Testament," in *Gott und Geschichte* (Wissenschaftliche Beiträge der Ernst-Moritz-Arndt-Universität Greifswald; 1988), 21–46; and K. Berge, *Die Zeit des Jahwisten* (BZAW 186; 1990).

562. In the historiography of Israel, primeval history has to do with "ethnogony instead of theogony": K. Koch, *TRE* 12, 572. For the foundational and fundamental, primeval period in myth and in history, see Koch, "Qädäm: Heilsgeschichte als mythische Urzeit im Alten (und Neuen) Testament," in J. Rohls and G. Wenz, eds., *Vernunft des Glaubens: Wissenschaftliche Theologie und kirchliche Lehre*, FS W. Pannenberg (1988), 253–288.

563. The significance of the land as the central commodity of salvation and Israel's awareness that it did not occupy the land beginning with the primeval period both have significance for the development of the Israelite consciousness of history overall. M. Weippert ("Fragen des israelitischen Geschichtsbewusstseins," 428) has emphasized that history is best described as a "great etiology of . . . the possession of the civilized land" as well as the (Deuteronomistic) loss of the land.

564. Is it the Yahwist who inserts the list of unconquered areas in Judg. 1:27ff.? This is possible, since these areas were incorporated into the empire of David and Solomon (2 Sam. 24:5–7; 1 Kings 4:7–19), i.e., "when Israel grew strong" (Judg. 1:28). The Yahwist is likely to be assigned to the period of the empire. Cf. now K. Berge, "Die Zeit des Jahwist"; and also M. Noth, *The History of Israel* (2d ed.: New York, 1960), 216–224.

565. Cf. more precisely in Vol. II, chap. 10, as well as W. Zimmerli, "Wahrheit und Geschichte in der alttestamentlichen Schriftprophetie," *VT* Suppl 29, 1978, 1–15.

566. Cf. H. W. Wolff, "Geschichtsverständnis der alttestamentlichen Prophetie"; S. Herrmann, *Zeit und Geschichte* (1977), 53ff.; R. Schmitt, *Abschied von der Heilsgeschichte?*, 63–89; and G. von Rad, *Theology*, 2:176–187.

567. Also J. Jeremias (*EvTh* 40, 1980, 393) speaks of the "prophetic interpretation of history."

568. Cf. Vol. II, 10.4.

569. H. W. Wolff, *EvTh* 20, 1960, 222 (= TB 22, 293).

570. Isa. 41:17–20; 43:16–21; 48:20f.; 49:7a, 9–13; and 52:7–10, 11f.

571. "In prophecy the universal, historical interest awakened, because it recognized the coming of the God of Israel as the unique Lord of all reality": H. W. Wolff, *EvTh* 20, 1960, 229 (= TB 22, 301). Cf. also S. Herrmann, *Zeit und Geschichte* (1977), 62ff.

572. Cf. Th. Krüger, *Geschichtskonzepte im Ezechielbuch* (BZAW 180; 1989).

573. S. Herrmann, *Zeit und Geschichte* (1977), 54.

574. For this, cf. n. 353 above. Cf. also (with emphases other than the ones represented here): L. Eslinger, *Into the Hands of the Living God* (JSOT Suppl 84; 1989); and M. A. O'Brien, *The Deuteronomistic History Hypothesis: A Reassessment* (OBO 92; 1989).

575. Cf. above, sec. 4.e.

576. For the Deuteronomistic historiography (including the Deuteronomistic Priestly redaction) in the Books of Samuel, cf. also R. Bickert, "Die Geschichte und das Handeln Jahwes: Zur Eigenart einer deuteronomistischen Offenbarungsauffassung in den Samuelbüchern," in A. H. J. Gunneweg and O. Kaiser, eds., *Textgemäss: und Beiträge zur Hermeneutik des Alten Testaments*, FS E. Würthwein (1979), 9–27. For the assessment of the monarchy, cf. also Vol. II, chap. 7.

577. For P's narrative style, cf. S. E. McEvenue, *The Narrative Style of the Priestly Writer* (An Bibl 50; Rome, 1971).

578. For this, see, above all: K. Elliger, "Sinn und Ursprung der priesterlichen Geschichtserzählung," *ZThK* 49, 1952, 121–143 (= TB 32, 1966, 174ff.); N. Lohfink, "Die Priesterschrift und die Geschichte," *VT* Suppl 29, 1978, 189–225 (= *SBAT* 4, 1988, 213ff.); and P. Weimar, "Sinai und Schöpfung," *RB* 95, 1988, 337–385. Cf. also above, p. 199, and the subject index.

579. See below, pp. 232f.

580. *AOT* (2d ed.), 120f.; *ANET* (2d and 3d eds.), 67f.; *RGT* (2d ed.), 109. For the primeval flood in Mesopotamian texts, cf. *RGT* (2d ed.), 115–122; and J. Bottéro and S. N. Kramer, *Lorsque les dieux faisaient l'homme* (Paris, 1989), 564–601.

581. Cf. below, pp. 235f. For Mesopotamian theogonies, see J. Bottéro and S. N. Kramer, *Lorsque les dieux faisaient l'homme*, 471–478.

582. "The divine speech is the descriptive means to combine historical experience with the question of meaning" (S. Herrmann, *Zeit und Geschichte*, 1977, 44).

583. E. Cortese has recently shown that these chapters are to be assigned to P (*Josua 13–21: Ein priesterschriftlicher Abschnitt im deuteronomistischen Geschichtswerk* [OBO 94; 1990]). For the land in P, cf. also above, pp. 119f., 121f., 122f.

584. Creation to Abram: אלהים = 'ĕlōhîm; Abraham to Moses: שדי אל = 'ēl šadday; from Moses on: יהוה = yahweh.

585. Cf. above, sec. 4.d.

586. Cf. below, chap. 5.3.

587. Cf. above, p. 188, and there n. 349.

588. See *TRE* 8, 77f.

589. Cf. M. Oeming, *Das wahre Israel* (BWANT 128; 1990).

590. Cf. above, p. 159.

591. Cf. Vol. II, 9.3.

592. Cf. (besides G. Wallis, "Die geschichtliche Erfahrung und das Bekenntnis zu Jahwe im Alten Testament") also S. Kreuzer, *Die Frühgeschichte Israels in Bekenntnis und Verkündigung des Alten Testament* (BZAW 178; 1989).

593. M. Honecker, *EvTh* 23, 1963, 167.

594. Cf. S. Herrmann, *Zeit und Geschichte* (1977), 122.

595. Cf. Th. Boman, *Das hebräische Denken im Vergleich mit dem griechischen* (1952; 5th ed., 1968); W. Eichrodt, "Heilserfahrung und Zeitverständnis im Alten Testament," *ThZ* 12, 1956, 103–125; J. Muilenburg, "The Biblical View of Time," *HThR* 54, 1961, 225–252; B. S. Childs, *Myth and Reality in the Old Testament* (2d ed.; London, 1962) (73ff.); M. Sekine, "Erwägungen zur hebräischen Zeitauffassung," *VT* Suppl 9, 1963, 66–82; P. Neuenzeit, " 'Als die Fülle der Zeit gekommen war . . . ' (Gal 4:4): Gedanken zum biblischen Zeitverständnis," *BiLe* 4, 1963, 223–239; S. G. F. Brandon, *History, Time and Deity* (New York and Manchester, 1965); J. Barr, *Biblical Words for Time* (2d ed., London, 1969); J. R. Wilch, *Time and Event* (Leiden, 1969); H. W. Wolff, *Anthropologie des Alten Testaments*, (1973) (127–140); S. J. de Vries, *Yesterday, Today and Tomorrow* (Grand Rapids, 1975); A. Petitjean, "Les conceptions vétérotestamentaires du temps," *RHPhR* 56, 1976, 383–400; S. Herrmann, *Zeit und Geschichte* (1977) (85ff., 96ff.); N. Wyatt, "The Old Testament Historiography of the Exilic Period," *STh* 33, 1979, 45–67 (esp. 53ff.); S. D. Vries, "Das Verständnis der Zeit in der Bibel," *Conc* (D) 17, 1981, 96–109; R. Schmitt, *Abschied von der Heilsgeschichte?* (1982) (esp. 101ff.); idem, *Die Zeit* (Schriften der Carl-Friedrich-von-Siemens-Stiftung, vol. 6; 1983); A. Lacocque, "La conception hébraïque du temps," in *Bulletin du Centre Protestant d'Etudes et de Documentation*, 36, 1984, 47–58; K. Koch, "Qädäm: Heilsgeschichte als mythische Urzeit im Alten (und Neuen) Testament," in J. Rohls and G. Wenz,

eds., *Vernunft des Glaubens: Wissenschaftliche Theologie und kirchliche Lehre*, FS W. Pannenberg (1988), 253–288. Cf. also G. von Rad, *Theology*, 2:99–125.

596. For this, see the literature in n. 625 below.

597. For each of the Hebrew terms, cf. the articles in *THAT* and *ThWAT* as well as J. Barr, *Biblical Words for Time*. In addition, see J. Wilch, *Time and Event*, for עת = '*ēt;* S. J. de Vries, *Yesterday, Today, and Tomorrow*, for יום = *yôm;* and K. Koch, *Qädäm*, for קדם = *qedem.*

598. Cf. Vol. II, 14.9.

599. Exod. 10:13; 12:17; Num. 9:15; 11:32; Deut. 4:10; 9:24; Josh. 10:12; Judg. 19:30; 1 Sam. 8:8; 2 Sam. 7:6; Isa. 11:16; Jer. 7:22; 11:4, 7; 31:32; 34:13; Ezek. 16:4f.; Hos. 2:17; and Ps. 78:42.

600. L. Köhler, *Theologie* (4th ed.), 75.

601. This was similar in Egyptian; cf. H. Brunner, "Zum Zeitbegriff der Ägypter," *StGen* 8, 1955, 589 (= *Das hörende Herz* [OBO 80; 1988], 336).

602. A study that provides a comprehensive consideration of these distinctions in the Old Testament and that examines the significance of the afformative and preformative conjugation in the Hebrew verbal system for the Old Testament understanding of time unfortunately doe not exist. An initial effort has been presented by W. Zimmerli ("Die Weisung des Alten Testaments zum Geschäft der Sprache," *Gottes Offenbarung*, TB 19, 2d ed., 1969, 277–299, esp. 287f.). Zimmerli's effort has been continued by Th. Krüger, *Geschichtskonzepte im Ezechielbuch* (BZAW 180; 1989), 19–38 (literature). For ancient Semitic languages, cf. M. Cwik-Rosenbach ("Zeitverständnis und Geschichtsschreibung in Mesopotamien," 3–5).

603. Th. Krüger, *Geschichtskonzepte im Ezechielbuch*, 20 + 22.

604. More precisely in ibid.

605. In addition to Qoheleth, Sirach also has reflected over time; cf., e.g., Sir. 18:26 and 39:16–21, 33f.

606. S. de Vries, "Das Verständnis der Zeit in der Bibel," 97 (see also *Yesterday, Today, and Tomorrow*): What counts in wisdom literature is "not so much the isolated case or the single occurrence but rather what may be cataloged and made ascertainable in an abstract way."

607. By contrast, cf. Egypt: "The first birth of time occurred in the mythical past": L. Kaksy, *LÄ* VI, col. 1361.

608. Cf. Vol. II, 13.5.

609. Cf. above, p. 141f.

610. H. W. Wolff points to the significance of the temporal key word טרם = *ṭerem* ("not yet, before") in the Yahwist (*Anthropologie*, 130).

611. G. von Rad, ATD 2, commenting on this passage.

612. Exod. 16:35; Num. 14:33f.; 32:13; 33:38; Deut. 1:3; 2:7; 8:2, 4; 29:4; and Josh. 5:6. Dependent upon these: Amos 2:10; 5:25 (Deuteronomistic); Neh. 9:21; and Ps. 95:10.

613. For this, see K. Galling, "Das Rätsel der Zeit im Urteil Kohelets," *ZThK* 58, 1961, 1–15; G. von Rad, *Wisdom in Israel*, 138–143; N. Lohfink, "Gegenwart und Ewigkeit; Die Zeit im Buch Kohelet," *GuL* 60, 1987, 2–12; M. Laumann, "Qoheleth and Time," *BiTod* 27, 1989, 305–310; and D. Michel, *Untersuchungen zur Eigenart des Buches Qohelet* (BZAW 183; 1989); see there the index for the word "time" ("Zeit").

614. According to N. Lohfink (*GuL* 60, 1987, 7), this is a cry of joy, "because behind the passing moment shines eternal duration."

615. Or is Qoheleth citing here a view belonging to someone else?

616. "What makes human beings actually become human, namely, the question concerning meaning that goes beyond the present moment, is at the same time that for which they suffer" (D. Michel, *BiKi* 45, 1990, 23; there 22f. for Qoh. 3:11). I do not recognize in Qoheleth, by contrast, one who was "full of hunger for eternity," nor do I find in this book a positive "reference to eternity" (differently, N. Lohfink, *GuL* 60, 1987, 3 + 9). While Lohfink argues that Qoh. 3:11ff. deals with the amount of time given to humanity [49], he also has contended that for Qoheleth "we cannot ourselves determine the content of time" [5], for "in the background of reality, it is another who has time in his hand" [6]).

617. Cf. P. Höffken, "Des Menschen Zeit—Hiobs Zeit," in W. C.-W. Clasen and G. Lehnert-Rodiek, eds., *Zeit(t)räume* (1986), 121–133.

618. Cf. Vol. II, 13.4. "For "liturgical time," see A. Lacocque, "Le conception hébraïque du temps," in R. Martin-Achard, ed., *Permanence de l'Ancien Testament: Recherches d'exégèse et de théologie* (Cahiers de la Revue de théologie et de philosophie, 11; 1984), 48ff.; cf. also G. von Rad, *Theology*, 2:102–105. For von Rad, cf. in this case F. Mildenberger, *Gottes Tat im Wort* (1964), 32ff.

619. Here only more recent literature for this topic is to be pointed out, which therefore closes the door to earlier scholarship: G. Larsson, *The Secret System* (Leiden, 1973); idem, "The Chronology of the Pentateuch: A Comparison of the MT and LXX," *JBL* 102, 1983, 401–409; and J. Hughes, *Secrets of the Times* (JSOT Suppl 66; 1990). Cf. also A. Jepsen, "Zeitrechnung," *BHHW* 3, cols. 2211–2214.

620. Cf. the articles "Kalendar" and "Chronologie" in *LÄ* III and I respectively.

621. Cf. Mishnah b. Pes. X. 5 [= 116b] (with reference to Exod. 13:8 and Deut. 6:23): "In each generation each individual is to be regarded by us as though he himself may have been brought forth from Egypt."

622. G. von Rad, *Theology*, 2:106; i.e., as the narrators saw it.

623. Following a suggestion by N. Wyatt (*StTh* 33, 1979, 55).

624. Above all, see K. Koch, "Spätisraelitisches Geschichtsdenken am Beispiel des Buches Daniel," *HZ* 193, 1961, 1–32; K. Koch, et al., *Das Buch Daniel* (EdF 144; 1980).

625. See H. Brunner, "Zum Zeitbegriff der Ägypter," *StGen* 8, 1955, 584–590 (= *Das hörende Herz* [OBO 80; 1988], 327ff.); S. G. F. Brandon, *History, Time and Deity*; S. Morenz, *Untersuchungen zur Rolle des Schicksals im ägyptischen Religion* (1960); E. Otto, "Zeitvorstellungen und Zeitrechnung im Alten Orient," *StGen* 19, 1966, 743–751; W. von Soden, *Sprache, Denken und Begriffsbildung im Alten Orient* (1974); J. Assmann, *Zeit und Ewigkeit im alten Ägypten* (1975); idem, "Das Doppelgesicht der Zeit im altägyptischen Denken," in *Die Zeit*, 189–223; L. Kákosy, "Zeit," *LÄ* VI, cols. 1361–1371; and M. Cwik-Rosenbach, "Zeitverständnis und Geschichtsschreibung in Mesopotamien," *ZRGG* 42, 1990, 1–20.

626. Cf. the article "Kalendar" in *RLA* and *LÄ*.

627. Cf. W. von Soden, *Sprache, Denken und Begriffsbildung im Alten Orient*, 37.

628. S. Morenz shows that the "point in time" or "date" of the creation of the world in Egypt was thought about differently than in the Old Testament (*Ägyptische Religion*, 1960, 167–191).

629. Prologue of the Codex of Hammurabi, *TUAT* I/1, 40.

630. Cited by S. Morenz, *Ägyptische Religion* (1960), 80. On pp. 80ff., there are numerous references to "my, your, his, their time" in Egyptian.

631. Cf. J. Assmann, *Zeit und Ewigkeit im Alten Ägypten*, 41ff.; and idem, "Das Doppelgesicht der Zeit im altägyptischen Denken," 198ff. Further, see E. Brunner-Traut, *Frühformen des Erkennens* (1990), 101f., 156. He notes the contrast with the Israelite understanding of time that is properly viewed in connection with the Israelite form of historiography (pp. 108f.).

632. J. Assman, "Das Doppelgesicht der Zeit im altägyptischen Denken," 201.

633. J. Jeremias, *EvTh* 40, 1980, 381.

634. Cf. above, chap. 3.6, and Vol. II, 13.4, 9, as well as 6.d below.

635. See G. von Rad, "Das theologische Problem des alttestamentlichen Schöpfungsglaubens," in *BZAW* 66 (1936), 138–147 (= *Gesammelte Studien* 1 [TB 8], 3d ed., 1965, 136ff.); R. Rendtorff, "Die theologische Stellung des Schöpfungsglauben bei Deuterojesaja," *ZThK* 51, 1954, 3–13 (= TB 57, 1975, 209ff.); G. von Rad, "Aspekte alttestamentlichen Weltverständnisses," *EvTh* 24, 1964, 57–73 (= TB 8, 3d ed., 1965, 311ff.); C. Westermann, "Das Reden von Schöpfer und Schöpfung im Alten Testament," in F. Maass, ed., *Das Ferne und nahe Wort*, FS L. Rost (BZAW 105; 1967), 238–244; idem, "Neuere Arbeiten zur Schöpfung," *VuF* 14, 1969 (H. 1), 11–28; L. I. J. Stadelmann, *The Hebrew Conception of the World* (AnBib 39; Rome, 1970); W. Zimmerli, *Die Weltlichkeit des Alten Testaments* (1971); H. H. Schmid, "Schöpfung, Gerechtigkeit und Heil," *ZThK* 70, 1973, 1–19 (= *Altorientalische Welt in der alttestamentlichen Theologie*, 1974, 9ff.); C. Westermann, *Genesis 1–11* (1974) (BK I/1); R. Albertz, *Weltschöpfung und Menschenschöpfung* (1974); L. Vosberg, *Studien zum Reden vom Schöpfer in den Psalmen* (BEvTh 69; 1975); F. de Liagre-Böhl and H. A. Brongers, "Weltschöpfungsgedanken in Alt-Israel," *Persica* 7, 1975–1978, 69–136; R. Lux, "Schöpfungstheologie im Alten Testament," *ZdZ* 31, 1977, 416–431; O. H. Streck, "Zwanzig Thesen als alttestamentlicher Beitrag zum Thema: 'Die jüdische-christliche Lehre von der Schöpfung in Beziehung zu Wissenschaft und Technik,'" *KuD* 23, 1977, 277–299; idem, *Welt und Umwelt* (1978); A. Anger-

storfer, *Der Schöpfergott des Alten Testaments* (1979); R. Martin-Achard, *Et Dieu crée le ciel et la terre* . . . (Geneva, 1979); S. Wagner, " 'Schöpfung' im Buche Hiob," *ZdZ* 34, 1980, No. 3, 93–96; H. D. Preuss, "Biblisch-theologische Erwägungen eines Alttestamentlers zum Problemkreis Ökologie," *ThZ* 39, 1983, 68–101; E. Zenger, *Gottes Bogen in den Wolken* (SBS 112; 1983); E. Otto, "Schöpfung als Kategorie der Vermittlung von Gott und Welt in Biblischer Theologie," in H.-G. Geyer et al., *"Wenn nicht jetzt, wann dann?"* FS H.-J. Kraus (1983), 53–68; P. Doll, *Menschenschöpfung und Weltschöpfung in der alttestamentlichen Weisheit* (SBS 117; 1985); K. Eberlein, *Gott der Schöpfer—Israels Gott* (1986); H. D. Preuss, *Einführung in die alttestamentliche Weisheitsliteratur* (1987) (there 177ff.); and *La création dans l'Orient ancien* (LeDiv 127; Paris, 1987); R. Rendtorff, " 'Wo warst du, als ich die Erde gründete?' Schöpfung und Heilsgeschichte," in *Freiden in der Schöpfung* (ed. G. Rau et al.), 1987, 35–37; H. Spieckermann, *Heilsgegenwart* (FRLANT 148; 1989); M. Schubert, *Schöpfungstheologie bei Kohelet* (1989); and in the thematic issue, "Frieden, Gerechtigkeit, Schöpfung," *BiKi* 44, 1989, no. 4. Cf. also W. Eichrodt, *Theology,* 2:93–117; Th. C. Vriezen, *Theology,* 343–347; E. Jacob, *Théologie,* 110–121; G. Fohrer, *Grundstrukturen,* 149ff.; G. von Rad, *Theology,* 1:136–139; H. Graf Reventlow, *Problems of Old Testament Theology,* 134–154; C. Westermann, *Elements of Old Testament Theology,* 85–117; W. Zimmerli, *Theology,* 32–43; W. H. Schmidt, *Alttestamentlicher Glaube* (6th ed.), 197ff.; J. Goldingay, *Theological Diversity and the Authority of the Old Testament* (Grand Rapids, 1987), 200ff.

636. See H. Gese, "Die Frage des Weltbildes," in his *Zur biblischen Theologie* (3d ed., 1989), 202–222; Cf. also W. Eichrodt, *Theology,* 2:89–92; L. Köhler, *Theology* (4th ed.), 140ff.; and, e.g., *RGT* (2d ed.), 100f., 108f.

637. For the Book of Job's statements about God, the world, and humanity, cf. also A. Bertholet, *Biblische Theologie des Alten Testaments,* vol. 2 (1911), 121–135.

638. For the problematic מבול = *mabbûl* ("flood") in Ps. 29:10, cf. D. T. Tsumura, *UF* 20, 1988, 351–355 and B. Janowski, *ZThK* 86, 1989, 421. Cf. n. 112 above.

639. Cf. the references in the dictionaries.

640. The ancient Near Eastern comparative material is found in "La création dans l'Orient ancien," in M. Eliade, ed., *Quellen des alten Orients I: Die Schöpfungsmythen* (1964). For Mesopotamia, see J. Bottéro and S. N. Kramer, *Lorsque les dieux faisaient l'homme* (Paris, 1989), above all, 478–679, and pp. 526–564 for the Atra-ḥasis epic. For this epic, see also W. G. Lambert and A. R. Millard, *Atraḥasis,* (Oxford, 1969); and W. von Soden, *ZA* 68, 1978, 50–94. Cf. also the selection of texts in *RGT* (2d ed.) and along with this *WdM* 1, 121–124, 183, 309f., 405.

641. For the exegetical-hermeneutical positions concerning the Old Testament activity of creation and its special activity for Israel, cf. K. Eberlein, *Gott der Schöpfer—Israels Gott,* 24ff.

642. Cf. O. Loretz, *Ugarit und die Bibel* (1990), 167–172, who provides a detailed comparison with *KTU* 1.3 III 20–31 and attempts to reconstruct an early form of Psalm 19A.

643. Since in the Ugaritic text mentioned in the previous footnote the message going out about cosmic things is understandable only to the gods, one should not too quickly remove Ps. 19:4 as a later addition.

644. H. Spieckermann's effort to demonstrate the original unity of Psalm 19 as a whole has not been convincing (*Heilsgegenwart,* FRLANT 148, 1989, 60–72).

645. For this psalm see, among others, O. H. Steck, "Der Wein unter den Schöpfungsgaben," *TThZ* 87, 1978, 173–191; E. von Nordheim, "Der grosse Hymnus des Echnaton und Psalm 104," in FS E. Link (1978), 51–74; and H. Spieckermann, *Heilsgegenwart* (FRLANT 148; 1989), 21ff.

646. *AOT* (2d ed.), 15–18; *ANET* (3d ed.), 369–371; *RGT* (2d ed.), 43–46.

647. Cf. H. D. Preuss, *Verspottung fremder Religionen im Alten Testament* (BWANT 92; 1971), 108–110.

648. Thus K. Seybold, *ThZ* 40, 1984, 1–11.

649. Cf. the nightly worship services in Isa. 30:29; Ps. 134:1; and 1 Chron. 9:33.

650. Thus with J. Hempel, *FF* 35, 1961, 119–123; cf. also H. D. Preuss, *Verspottung fremder Religionen im Alten Testament,* 106. Another meaning, although also under the superscription "The Royal Human Being," is given by H. Spieckermann, *Heilsgewissheit,* 227ff. In speaking about this, Spieckermann says that, in contrast to Genesis 1, Psalm 8 points more clearly to humanity's position of dominion than to "the office of king" (235; cf. 238).

651. Cf. H. Spieckermann, *Heilsgegenwart,* 73ff.: "Of the maintenance of creation."

652. Prov. 14:31; 16:4; 17:5; 19:17; 21:13; cf. 16:19; 22:2; and 29:13.
653. Cf. n. 417 above, and the essay by H.-J. Hermisson mentioned there ("Observations on the Creation Theology in Wisdom").
654. For the statements about creation in the Book of Job, cf. S. Wagner, "'Schöpfung' im Buche Hiob"; J. Lévêque, in *La création dans l'Orient ancien*, 261ff.; and H. D. Preuss, *Einführung in die alttestamentliche Weisheitsliteratur* (1987), 90ff.
655. Isa. 41:4b; 42:8; 43:10b–13; 44:24b, 25–27; 45:6b, 7, 12, 18b, 21b; 46:9b, 10; 48:12b, 13; 50:2b, 3; and 51:12, 15, 16. Cf. pp. 168f., 205f.
656. H.-P Müller, "Altes und Neues zum Buche Hiob," *EvTh* 37, 1977, 297.
657. Cf. H. Rowold, *The Theology of Creation in the Yahweh Speeches of the Book of Job* (Ann Arbor: University Microfilms, 1977).
658. Cf. above, sec. 4.i, for this, and Prov. 8:22ff.
659. Cf. M. Schubert, *Schöpfungstheologie bei Kohelet*, 259.
660. Qoh. 1:13; 2:26; 3:10, 11; 5:17, 18; 6:2; 8:15; 9:9; 12:7; cf. 3:13.
661. For עוֹלָם = *'ôlām* in Qoh. 3:11, see above, pp. 222f., and M. Schubert, *Schöpfungstheologie bei Kohelet*, 139ff.
662. The verbs used for the creative works of YHWH/God in the Old Testament are עשׂה (*'āśâ*, "make"), ברא (*bārā'*, "create"), יצר (*yāṣar*, "form"), יסד (*yāsad*, "establish"), קנה (*qānâ*, "create"), and כון (*kûn*, "found"). פעל = *pā'al* ("make") occurs only in Isa. 41:4; Prov. 16:4; and Job 36:3. Cf. also נטה = *nāṭâ* ("stretch out") in Isa. 40:22; 42:5; and Ps. 104:2; and רקע = *rāqa'* ("spread out") in Isa. 42:5; 44:24; and Ps. 136:6. For יצר = *yāṣar* ("form"), cf. also Jer. 18:1–12. As a noun, see מעשׂה = *ma'aśe* ("work"). For all of these and for their use in Israel's cultural environment (e.g., for the conception of pottery-shaped forms = יצר = *yāṣar*, "to form"), see the appropriate articles in *THAT* and *ThWAT*.
663. M. Schubert, *Schöpfungstheologie bei Qoheleth*, 117ff.
664. Qoh. 2:24–26; 3:12, 22; 5:17–19; 7:13f.; 8:15; 9:7–9; 11:7–10; 12:1; cf. 9:10.
665. For the sapiential discussions of creation, see also H. D. Preuss, "Aus der Arbeit der Projektgruppe 'Biblische Theologie' der Wissenschaftlichen Gesellschaft für Theologie," *ThZ* 39, 1983, 82ff. (literature).
666. See O. Loretz, *Ugarit und die Bibel* (1990), 66ff., 156ff. For the verb קנה = *qānâ* ("create") in Gen. 14:19, 22, cf. E. Lipiński, *ThWAT* 7, cols. 67f., which certainly is to be translated "owner."
667. Cf. above, pp. 143f., etc.
668. Cf. Vol. II, 13.4. K. Engelken has attempted to show that "Canaan/Canaanites" refer to a territorial region. He argues that while these terms did not designate an ethnic group, they were a social expression ("city dweller, "merchant"). See *BN* 52, 1990, 47–63.
669. Still later, Jer. 27:5ff. moves outside of Israel to associate these lines with Nebuchadrezzar through whom YHWH acts in history.
670. Cf. in more detail W. Eichrodt, *Theology*, 2:167–185; and P. van Imschoot, *Theology of the Old Testament*, vol. 1 (1965), 98ff. Cf. also above, sec. 5.f, for the time of "time." For the Atra-ḫasis epic, see n. 640 above.
671. Cf. for the creative activity of maintenance also Gen. 26:12; 27:27f.; 49:25; Jer. 8:7; 10:13; 33:25; Isa. 40:26; Hos. 2:10ff.; Pss. 65:7–14; 107:35ff.; 147:8f.; 148:6; Job 9:7ff.; 34:13–15; and 38:25f.
672. For the statements about creation in the Book of Jeremiah, one may refer to the delightful little study by H. Weippert: *Schöpfer des Himmels und der Erde* (SBS 102; 1981).
673. For this, see A. Angerstorfer, *Der Schöpfergott des Alten Testaments*.
674. Ibid., 225.
675. Cf. Vol. II, 11.3.
676. For this so-called *dominium terrae* and the verbs רדה = *rādâ* ("rule over") and כבשׁ = *kābaš* ("subdue"), cf. N. Lohfink, *Unsere grossen Wörter* (1977), 165ff.; and K. Koch, "Gestaltet die Erde, doch heget das Leben!" in H.-G. Geyer et al., eds., *"Wenn nicht jetzt, wann dann?"* F.S. H.-J. Kraus (1983), 23–36; Cf., however, the note following.
677. Thus, e.g., according to P. Heinisch, *Theologie des Alten Testament* (1940), 118, who argues this is still so. Thus the Old Testament could not state that in addition to the creation of humanity by God (or in Israel's environment by gods) there was another act of creation that

had brought forth the king in this primeval time, a view probably represented, however, in a recently discovered Babylonian text. For this, see W. R. Mayer, "Ein Mythos von der Erschaffung des Menschen und des König," *Or* 56, 1987, 55–68. For an attempted interpretation of this text (esp. in its relationship to Old Testament ideas), see H.-P. Müller, "Eine neue babylonische Menschenschöpfungserzählung im Licht keilschriftlicher und biblischer Parallelen—Zur Wirklichkeitsauffassung im Mythos," *Or* 58, 1989, 61–85. For a skeptical view of the interpretation of Lohfink and Koch, see J. Scharbert, in W. Baier et al., eds., *Weisheit Gottes, Weisheit der Welt,* vol. 1 (1987), FS J. Cardinal Ratzinger, 241–258. Cf. Vol. II, 11.3.

678. For the absence of blessing for the land animals in Genesis 1, cf. the commentaries. This text probably sought to avoid a "conflict" or possible "conflict" between humanity and animals.

679. Cf. below, chap. 5.3.

680. Cf. N. Lohfink, *Unsere grossen Wörter,* 160; and esp. P. Weimar, "Sinai und Schöpfung," *RB* 95, 1988, 337–385.

681. For the statements about creation in Deutero-Isaiah, cf. R. Rendtorff, "Die theologische Stellung des Schöpfungsglaubens bei Deuterojesaja"; E. Haag, "Gott als Schöpfer und Erlöser in der Prophetie des Deuterojesaja," *TThZ* 85, 1976, 193–213; H. D. Preuss, *Deuterojesaja: Eine Einführung in seine Botschaft* (1976), 58–61 (literature); W. Kirchschläger, "Die Schöpfungstheologie des Deuterojesaja," *BiLe* 49, 1976, 407–422; A. Angerstorfer, *Der Schöpfergott des Alten Testaments,* 119ff.; J. Vermeylen, in *La création dans l'Orient ancien,* 183ff.; and K. Eberlein, *Gott der Schöpfer—Israels Gott,* 73ff.

682. Isa. 40:22; 42:5; 44:24, 27; 45:18; 48:13; 50:2; and 51:9, 10, 13, 15.

683. K. Eberlein, *Gott der Schöpfer—Israels Gott,* 93.

684. Cf. also Isa. 41:17–20; 43:16–21; 44:2; 45:11–13; 50:2; and 54:4–6.

685. G. von Rad, *Theology,* 2:240–242.

686. Isa. 41:20; 42:16, 25; 43:10, 19; 48:6, 7, 8; 49:23; and 52:6. Cf. K. Eberlein, *Gott der Schöpfer—Israels Gott,* 174ff.

687. Cf. A. Angerstorfer, *Der Schöpfergott des Alten Testament,* 154–156.

688. Cf. L. Vosberg, *Studien zum Reden vom Schöpfer in den Psalmen;* and K. Eberlein, *Gott der Schöpfer—Israels Gott,* 190ff., 246ff.

689. If the so-called doxologies of judgment in the Book of Amos (Amos 4:13; 5:8f.; 9:5f.; also 8:8?) originated during the context of the exile, the previous argumentation would be expanded by these texts. They speak without exception both hymnically and doxologically of YHWH as the creator, all stand directly after pronouncements of judgment, and all could consequently have the function of (exilic) doxologies of judgment. With these doxologies of judgment, justice is given through the community which speaks here these proclamations of judgment.

690. Cf. L. Köhler, *Theologie* (4th ed.), 71: "The history of creation in the Old Testament does not answer the question: How did the world come about? with the response: God has created it. Rather, the Old Testament answers the question: Where does the history of the people of God have its meaning? with the response: God has provided the meaning of the history of the people of God through creation" (ibid).

691. For these mythological elements in the Old Testament, there is an extensive body of literature of which here only a selection follows: H. Gunkel, *Schöpfung und Chaos in Urzeit und Endzeit* (2d ed.), 1921; O. Kaiser, *Die mythische Bedeutung des Meeres in Ägypten, Ugarit und Israel* (BZAW 78; 2d ed., 1962); A. Ohler, *Mythologische Elemente im Alten Testament* (1969); H.-P. Müller, *Mythos, Tradition, Revolution* (1973); M. K. Wakeman, *God's Battle with the Monster* (Leiden, 1973); O. Keel, *Jahwes Entgegnung an Ijob* (FRLANT 121; 1978); B. Otzen, H. Gottlieb, and K. Jeppesen, *Myths in the Old Testament* (London, 1980); C. Petersen, *Mythos im Alten Testament* (BZAW 157; 1982); J. Ebach, *Leviathan und Behemoth* (1984); U. Steffen, *Drachenkampf* (1984); C. Kloos, *Yhwh's Combat with the Sea* (Amsterdam and Leiden, 1986); and H. H. Schmid, ed., *Mythos und Rationalität* (1988). Cf. also C. Westermann, BK I/1, 39–46; and W. H. Schmidt, *Alttestamentlicher Glaube* (6th ed.), 194ff.

692. The following terms are used for the dragon/chaos monster: תְּהוֹם = *tĕhôm* ("deep"): only Hab. 3:8 and Prov. 8:24, 28; רַהַב = *rahab* ("Rahab"): Isa. 51:9; Ps. 89:11; Job 9:13; 26:12; cf. Pss. 74:12–17 and 18:15ff.; לִוְיָתָן = *liwyātān* ("Leviathan"): Isa. 27:1; Pss. 74:14; 104:23;

344 Notes to Chapter 4

Job 3:8; 40:25; cf. Ps. 89:10–15 and Hab. 3:8–15. בהמות = běhēmôt ("Behemoth"): Job 40:15 (24); תנין = tannîn ("Tannin"): Isa. 27:1; 51:9; Jer. 51:34; Ezek. 29:3; 32:2; Ps. 74:13; and Job 7:12; נחש = nāhāš ("serpent"): Amos 9:3; Isa. 27:1; and Job 26:13; ים = yām ("Yam"); Isa. 51:9f.; Ps. 74:13f.; Job 3:8 (amended); 7:12; and 26:12; and בטן = beṭen ("belly"): Jonah 2:3. The sea dragon in the Old Testament at times is no longer the waters of chaos but rather an animal found therein: Isa. 27:1. Cf. further the images of a threat of flood = threat of chaos = assault of nations, often in statements of trust in the psalms or in looking back at the earlier salvific acts of God: Psalms 46; 48; and 148:7–11; cf. 24:2; 29:3; 33:6f.; 36:7; 65:8; 77:20; and 104:5–9; then cf. Isa. 51:9f.; Jer. 5:22; Job 9:5–13; 26:5ff.; and 38:6, 8–11; cf. Prov. 3:20; 8:29; and 30:4. For this topic, see Th. Römer, "La rédecouverte d'un mythe dans l'Ancien Testament: La création comme combat," ETR 64, 1989, 561–573.

693. AOT (2d ed.), 117ff.; ANET (2d and 3d eds.), 66f.; and RGT (2d ed.), 108f. For this text and additional Mesopotamian theogonies and cosmogonies, cf. now esp. J. Bottéro and S. N. Kramer, Lorsque les dieux faisaient l'homme (Paris, 1989), 470ff., 526ff., 602ff.

694. KTU 1.1–6. For this, see D. Kinet, Ugarit (SBS 104; 1981), 65ff.; O. Loretz, Ugarit und die Bibel (1990), 73ff., 108ff., 156ff. For לויתן = liwyātān in Ugaritic texts (there ltn), cf. O. Loretz, Ugarit und die Bibel, 92f. For Yam: WdM 1, 289–291; for Mot: ibid., 300–302; cf. also RGT (2d ed.), 216f.; 222–224, 231–238 and for the Hittite weather god Telepinu: RGT (2d ed.), 182.

695. An actual myth of creation to this point has not been discovered in the Ugaritic texts. Nevertheless, one can still conclude that El was a creator deity and that Baal was the one who maintained creation. Cf. J.-L. Cunchillos, in La création dans l'Orient Ancien, 79ff.; and O. Loretz, Ugarit und die Bibel, 153ff., 156ff.

696. "God conducts a continuing battle to defend his work" (L. Köhler, Theologie, 4th ed., 74); cf. Isa. 17:12–14; Jer. 5:22; Hab. 3:10; Nahum 1:4; Pss. 74:13; 89:10f.; 104:7; Job 26:12; and 38:8–11.

697. L. Köhler, Theologie (4th ed.), 72.

698. Cf. for these texts the interpretations of H. Weippert (Schöpfer des Himmels und der Erde).

699. For these, compare Amos 9:11–15; Hos. 2:20–25; Isa. 11:1–9, 10ff.; Jer. 31:31–40; 32: 36–41; and 33:10–13; then, above all, see Isa. 65:17–25; 66:22; Ezek. 47:1–12; and Joel 4:18.

700. Cf. above, pp. 220, 227f., 231f. for the maintenance of creation.

701. O. H. Steck, "Alttestamentliche Impulse für eine Theologie der Natur," ThZ 34, 1978, 206f.

702. For a discussion of this demarcation (against, e.g., C. Westermann, R. Albertz, or G. Liedke), see H. D. Preuss, "Biblisch-Theologische Erwägungen eines Alttestamentlers zum Problemkreis Ökologie." ThZ 39, 1983, 89f.; cf. K. Eberlein, Gott der Schöpfer—Israels Gott, 17ff., 42ff.

703. This pointed statement formulated in 1936 by G. von Rad (TB 8, 3d ed., 136) is as true in its core meaning today as it was then.

704. Thus in reference to H. W. Robinson; cited by Th. C. Vriezen, Theology, 188.

705. Cf. the different verbs in n. 662 above. Also through the word, through battle.

706. Cf. above, sec. 4.f.

707. H. H. Schmid, "Schöpfung, Gerechtigkeit und Heil" (= Altorientalische Welt in der alttestamentlichen Theologie). For his theological formulation, cf. K. Eberlein, Gott der Schöpfer—Israels Gott, 54ff.

708. H. Gross ("Die Schöpfung als Bund," in W. Baier et al., eds., Weisheit Gottes, Weisheit der Welt, vol. 1, 1987, FS J. Cardinal Ratzinger, 127–136) wishes therefore to connect creation and covenant from Genesis 9 forward and even to regard this as a possible center of the Old Testament.

709. The traditiohistorical separation of the creation of the world from the creation of humanity (see R. Albertz, Weltschöpfung und Menschenschöpfung) no longer plays a significant role in the statements about creation in the most important writings of the Old Testament (cf. the Yahwist, Priestly source, and Deutero-Isaiah).

710. Cf. above, sec. 3.

711. Differently R. Knierim, in H. W. Wolff, ed., Probleme biblischer Theologie, FS G. von Rad (1971), 229. He lists Gen. 8:22; 27:28; 49:24–26; Deut. 7:13; Pss. 18:8–16; 29; 104:10ff., 24, 28–30; 107:25–29; Isa. 45:12; and Amos 4:13. He says: "All of this and much more

makes evident to the worshiper of Yahweh that he is the God of the world. Yahweh faith has grasped the revelation of God in nature not only through 'historicizing' but also through the recognition that Yahweh is revealed in nature itself." Here a somewhat more equivocal concept of revelation is used. Are "manifestations" (so Knierim) to be equated with revelation? That the YHWH worshiper finds YHWH active in many ways is one thing. That YHWH reveals himself in these various activities is another matter. Whence, then, does the worshiper of YHWH know something of God?

712. Cf. A. Eitz, "Studien zum Verhältnis von Priesterschrift und Deuterojesaja," diss. (Heidelberg, 1969), 61. For "land," cf. above, pp. 117ff.

713. Cf. E. Otto, "Schöpfung als Kategorie der Vermittlung von Gott und Welt in Biblischer Theologie in der alttestamentlichen Weisheit," p. 66: "Israel speaks of creation in the thorough examination of the painful experience of empirical, historical reality. . . . When YHWH is brought to expression in language as the creator, it is in reaction to empirical experiences of suffering. He is called upon, for he is the principal one who transcends this world when it is endangered by chaos."

714. Cf. also E. Sellin, *Theologie,* 15–38; and W. Eichrodt, *Theology,* 1:206–227 (sec. 6).

715. Cf. above, pp. 140f.

716. For YHWH's "justice," see above, sec. 4.f.

717. *AOT* (2d ed.), 109; *ANET* (2d and 3d eds.), 60f.; *RGT* (2d ed.), 32, 108. For Egypt: E. Hornung, *Der Eine und die Vielen* (1971), 134ff.; also S. Morenz, *Ägyptische Religion* (1960), 170ff., 183. For Mesopotamia, cf. n. 581 above.

718. Cf. over against this, e.g., the description of the gods during and after the primeval flood in the Epic of Gilgamesh, Tablet XI, 113ff. These gods are frightened, crouch down like dogs, cry and weep, swarm like flies over the sacrifices, and so forth (*AOT,* 2d ed., 178f.; *ANET,* 2d and 3d eds., 94f.); see also the beginning of the Epic of Atra-hasis (see pp. 226f. and *ZA* 68, 1978, 55): "When the gods like men . . . " For the senescence, e.g., of Re, see *RGT* (2d ed.), 36.

719. Exod. 15:11; 34:10; Deut. 10:14; Isa. 2:11; 37:16; 55:8f.; 57:15; Jer. 10:6; Micah 4:13; Pss. 92:6; 93:1; 95:4f.; 99:2; 113:4; 145:3; 147:5; etc.

720. Cf. above, chap. 3.8.c.

721. Cf. only *KTU* 1.11:1–3.

722. Cf. above, p. 150, and Vol. II, 6.4.

723. Cf. the following: H.-P. Müller, "קדשׁ *qdš* heilig," *THAT* 2, cols. 589–609; W. Kornfeld and H. Ringgren, "קדשׁ *qdš* u. Deriv.," *ThWAT* 6, cols. 1179–1204; D. Kellermann, "Heiligkeit. II: Altes Testament," *TRE* 14, 697–703; and J. G. Gammie, *Holiness in Israel* (Minneapolis, 1989). Cf. also L. Ruppert, "Jahwe—der lebendige und heilige Gott," in K. Hemmerle, ed., *Die Botschaft von Gott* (1974), 128–141; W. Eichrodt, *Theology,* 1:270–282; L. Köhler, *Theologie* (4th ed.), 34ff.; Th. C. Vriezen, *Theology,* 149–152; and W. H. Schmidt, *Alttestamentlicher Glaube* (6th ed.), 178ff.

724. Exod. 3:5; 15:13; cf. 19:23; 28:43; Josh. 5:15; Isa. 11:9; 27:13; 48:2; 52:1; Ps. 2:6; and Neh. 11:1.

725. Isa. 6:3 with its relationship to the Zion tradition suggests that the predicate "holy" was used also for gods in Israel's environment. Relevant passages are mentioned in *THAT* 2, col. 598; and, e.g., *RGT* (2d ed.), 59. See W. H. Schmidt, "Wo hat die Aussage: Jahwe 'der Heilige' ihren Ursprung?" *ZAW* 74, 1962, 62–66. In addition, the consciousness of something "holy" is probably a religious, phenomenological, anthropological, and fundamental constant.

726. This does not occur at all in Genesis, and thus not in the ancestral traditions! However, it occurs esp. often in Isaiah (Isa. 1:4; 5:19, 24; 10:17; 29:23; 30:11f., 15; and 31:1) and then in Deutero-Isaiah and Trito-Isaiah (Isa. 41:14, 16; 43:3, 14f.; 47:4; cf. 40:25; 41:20; 45:11; and 60:14).

727. Cf. above, chap. 3.3.a.

728. Cf. W. Zimmerli, " 'Heiligkeit' nach dem sogenannten Heiligkeitsgesetz," *VT* 30, 1980, 493–512; F. Crüsemann, "Der Exodus als Heiligung," in E. Blum et al., eds., *Die Hebräische Bibel und ihre zweifache Nachgeschichte,* FS R. Rendtorff, 1990, 117–129; and cf. above, p. 45.

729. According to Hanna Wolff, however (*Neuer Wein—Alte Schläuche,* 1981), the statement of

the holiness of God participates in the corruption of the image of God in the Old Testament, so that one entrusts again this book to the Jews and should no longer acknowledge it to be Holy Scripture that is the foundation of the faith for Christians.

730. Cf. also M. du Buit, "La sainteté du peuple dans l'Ancien Testament," *VS* 683 (vol. 143), 1989, 25–37.

731. J. Maier, *Zwischen den Testamenten* (NEB AT, Supplement, vol. 3, 1990), 220.

732. Thus also in Israel's environment: cf., e.g., *KAI*, 37A, 7; 69, 12; 74, 9; 76B, 2f.

733. The Old Testament wisdom literature uses the predicate "holy" for YHWH or God only in Prov. 9:10 and 30:3, each time in a somewhat altered form (plural), and in Job 6:10. The construct, "the Holy One of Israel," does not occur in the wisdom literature.

734. Exod. 20:5f.; 34:14; Num. 25:11–13; Deut. 4:23f.; 5:9f.; 6:15; 29:19; 32:16, 21; Josh. 24:19; 1 Kings 14:22; 2 Kings 19:31 (= Isa. 37:32); Isa. 9:6; 26:11; 42:13; 59:17; 63:15; Ezek. 5:13; 8:3, 5; 16:38–42; 23:25; 35:11; 36:5f.; 38:19; 39:25; Joel 2:18; Nahum 1:2; Zeph. 1:18; 3:8; Zech. 1:14f. 8:2; Pss. 78:58; 79:5; also Cant. 8:6? See B. Renaud, *Je suis un Dieu jaloux* (Paris, 1963); G. Sauer, "קִנְאָה *qin'ā* Eifer," *THAT* 2, cols. 647–650; W. Berg, "Die Eifersuch Gottes . . . ," *BZ* NF 23, 1979, 197–211 (literature); and E. Reuter, "קנא *qn'*," *ThWAT* 7, cols. 51–62. Cf. also Th. C. Vriezen, *Theology*, 153–154; and W. H. Schmidt, *Alttestamentlicher Glaube* (6th ed.), 87f.

735. Cf. to this above, chap. 3.8.d.

736. For this, see J. Scharbert, "Formgeschichte und Exegese von Ex 34:6f und seiner Parallelen," *Bibl* 38, 1957, 130–150; R. C. Dentan, "The Literary Affinities of Exodus XXXIV 6f," *VT* 13, 1963, 34–51; H. Spieckermann,"Barmherzig und gnädig ist der Herr . . . ," *ZAW* 102, 1990, 1–18. Cf. also *TRE* 5, 223.

737. While the hymn of self-praise in the Old Testament is found only in Deutero-Isaiah and in Job 38f., it is frequent in Israel's environment (Mesopotamia). Cf. H. D. Preuss, *Deuterojesaja* (1976), 89 with literature. Cf. above, pp. 168f., 205f., 229.

738. This translation is based on M. Noth's German translation of this passage (ATD 5).

739. Additional texts, which allude to the formula or parts of it, are found in H. Spieckermann, "Barmherzig und gnädig ist der Herr . . . , " *ZAW* 102, 1990, 1f., n. 4.

740. See H.-J. Stoebe, "רחם *rhm* pi. sich erbarmen," *THAT* 2, cols. 761–768; and H. D. Preuss, "Barmherzigkeit. I: Altes Testament," *TRE* 5, 215–224 (literature).

741. Exod. 33:19; Deut. 13:18; 30:3; 1 Kings 8:50; 2 Kings 13:23; Isa. 14:1; 55:7; Jer. 12:15; 33:26; 42:12; Zech. 10:6; etc.; then 2 Chron. 5:13; 7:3, 6; 20:21; Ezra 3:11; Neh. 9:17, 19, 27, 31; 13:22; and Pss. 23:6; 25:6f.; 40:12; 51:3; 69:17; 77:10; 103:4; 106:46; 119:77, 156; 145:9; cf. Dan. 9:9, 18; and Hab. 3:2.

742. See H.-J. Stoebe, "חנן *hnn* gnädig sein," *THAT* 1, cols. 587–597; and D. N. Freedman and J. Lundbom, "חנן u. Deriv.," *ThWAT* 3, cols. 23–40.

743. The one possible exception is Ps. 112:4.

744. Cf. J. Schreiner, "Unter Gottes Treue," in R. Mosis and L. Ruppert, eds., *Der Weg zum Menschen*, FS A. Deissler (1989), 62–81.

745. See K. Koch, "denn seine Güte währet ewiglich," *EvTh* 21, 1961, 531–544.

746. For חסד = *hesed* and אמת = *'ěmet*, cf. also the corresponding article in *THAT* and *ThWAT*. Also see E. Kellenberger, *hǎsǎd wǎ'aemǎt als Ausdruck einer Glaubenserfahrung* (AThANT 69; 1982); and S. Romerowski, "Que signifie le mot *hesed?*" *VT* 40, 1990, 89–103.

747. Cf. also Vol. II, 11.10.

748. See H.-J. Kraus, "Der lebendige Gott," *EvTh* 27, 1967, 169–200 (= *Biblisch-theologische Aufsätze*, 1972, 1ff.); H.-J. Zobel, "Der kanaanäische Hintergrund der Vorstellung vom lebendigen Gott: Jahwes Verhältnis zu El und zu Baal," *WZ* Greifswald 24, 1975, 187–194; and S. Kreuzer, *Der lebendige Gott*, 1983 (BWANT 116); cf. also E. Jacob, *Théologie*, 28–32; and W. H. Schmidt, *Alttestamentlicher Glaube* (6th ed.), 183–190.

749. Cf. to the deceased Baal: *KTU* 1.5; VI, 9f., 23f. For the "resurrection" of Baal, see n. 751 below.

750. Also on two (or three) ostraca from Lachish (No. 3 and No. 6; also 12, 3?) , *TUAT* I/6, 521, 624; *KAI* I, 35f., H.-J. Kraus calls it a "word of consecration" (= *Biblisch-theologische Aufsätze*, 10). For this above all, see S. Kreuzer, *Der lebendige Gott*, 30–145.

751. *KTU* 1, 6. III, 2–4, 20f. Cf. W. Schmidt, "Baals Tod und Auferstehung," *ZRGG* 15, 1963, 1–13.
752. *KTU* 1, 4; IV, 4–6. Cf. *RGT* (2d ed.), 65, for the Egyptian king as the "living god."
753. Cf. the comments by H.-J. Zobel, "Der kanaanäische Hintergrund der Vorstellung vom lebendigen Gott," 189f.
754. Cf. J. Hempel, "Jahwegleichnisse der israelitischen Propheten," *ZAW* 42, 1924, 74–104 (= *Apoxysmata* [BZAW 81; 1961], 1ff.); idem, "Die Grenzen des Anthropomorphismus Jahwes im Alten Testament," *ZAW* 57, 1939, 75–85; E. L. Cherbonnier, "The Logic of Biblical Anthropomorphism," *HThR* 55, 1962, 187–206; H. Gollwitzer, *Die Existenz Gottes im Bekenntnis des Glaubens* (1963), 113f. (literature); J. Lindblom, "Die Vorstellung vom Sprechen Jahwes zu den Menschen im Alten Testament," *ZAW* 75, 1963, 263–288; H. Kuitert, *Gott in Menschengestalt* (1967); U. Mauser, *Gottesbild und Menschwerdung* (1971); J. Jeremias, *Die Reue Gottes* (BSt 65; 1975); Ch. Abramowitz, "In the Language of Man," *Dor le Dor* 9, 1981, 139–143; E. Jüngel, "Anthropomorphismus als Grundproblem neuzeitlicher Hermeneutik," in E. Jüngel et al., eds., *Verifikationen,* FS G. Ebeling (1982), 499–521; Th. H. McAlpine, *Sleep, Divine and Human, in the Old Testament,* 1987 (JSOT Suppl. 38); A. Schenker,"Anthropomorphismus," *NBL* I, cols. 109–111; cf. also L. Köhler, *Theologie* (4th ed.), 4ff.; P. Heinisch, *Theologie des Alten Testaments* (1940), 32f.; Th. C. Vriezen, *Theology,* 171–174; 144ff.; and E. Jacob, *Grundfragen,* 18ff.
755. Cf. W. Eichrodt, *Theology,* 1:210–214.
756. Cf. above, sec. 7.c.
757. Gen. 3:8; 8:21; 32:31; Num. 11:1, 18; 14:28; 1 Sam. 5:11; 13:14; 26:19; 2 Kings 19:16; Isa. 7:13, 18; 43:3f.; 52:10; Jer. 9:11; Nahum 1:3; Pss. 2:4; 8:4; 33:13; and 37:13.
758. Gen. 6:5f.; 9:5; Exod. 32:35; Deut. 12:31; 32:35; Isa. 61:8; 62:5; Jer. 9:23; Hos. 11:8; Zeph. 3:17; and Jonah 3:10.
759. Thus P. Heinisch (*Theologie des Alten Testaments,* 1940, 29f.) encounters problems in attempting to prove from the Old Testament his statement about "God as a perfect, pure spirit."
760. Thus esp. in Hosea: God as husband (Hos. 2:4ff.; cf. Ezek. 16:8f.), father (Hos. 11:1ff.; cf. Exod. 4:22; Isa. 63:16; 64:7), bird catcher (Hos. 7:12), lion (Hos. 5:14; 13:7; cf. Amos 3:8), leopard (Hos. 13:7), mother bear (Hos. 13:8; cf. Lam. 3:10), and pus and caries (Hos. 5:12).
761. For anthropomorphisms in the religions of Israel's cultural environment, cf. *RLA* I, cols. 113f. (E. Ebeling) and *LÄ* I, cols. 311–318 (E. Otto). Cf. also O. Keel, *Die Welt der altorientalischen Bildsymbolik* (2d ed.), 1977, 157ff.
762. "The anthropomorphisms are evidence of the inadequacy of human speech about God, but they also bear witness to the living relation to Him that compels the faithful to speak of Him" (Th. C. Vriezen, *Theology,* 173).
763. From the abundant literature on this theme (in the Old Testament sphere), one may mention: U. Winter, *Frau und Göttin* (OBO 53; 1983); R. Laut, *Weibliche Züge im Gottesbild israelitisch-jüdischer Religiosität* (1983); F. J. Stendebach, "Vater und Mutter: Aspekte der Gottesvorstellung im alten Israel und ihre anthropologische wie soziologische Relevanz," in FS KBW (1983), 147–162; E. S. Gerstenberger, *Jahwe—ein patriarchaler Gott?* (1988); and O. Keel, "Jahwe in der Rolle der Muttergottheit," *Or* 53, 1989, 89–92. Cf. also B. S. Childs, *Theology,* 39f.
764. Cf. "Astarte, *the* god of the Sidonians" (1 Kings 11:5). Cf. above, sec. 2.a. For the problem of Asherah beside YHWH in recent texts, see above, pp. 110f.
765. Cf. above, chap. 3.8.c.
766. Cf. above, chap. 3.10.a.
767. According to O. Keel ("Jahwe in der Rolle der Muttergottheit"), YHWH assumes the role of Ishtar during the ending of the flood (Gen. 8:20–22). See the Epic of Gilgamesh, Tablet XI, 116ff, 164ff. This means the mother, who will not see destroyed what she has brought forth with pain and effort. Cf. *AOT* (2d ed.), 178f.; *ANET* (2d and 3d eds.), 94f.; *RGT* (2d ed.), 121f. (lines 164ff. are not translated). F. J. Stendebach ("Vater und Mutter," 153ff.) refers to deities who are bisexual or who are both father and mother in Israel's environment. He offers religiophenomenological, religiosociological, and religiopsychological reflections on these questions (with bibliography).
768. Cf. J. Jeremias, *Die Reue Gottes.*

769. C. K. H. Miskotte, *Wenn die Götter schweigen* (1963), 139.
770. Cf. the following selection from the abundance of literature: V. Maag, "Gottesverständnis des Alten Testaments," *NedThT* 21, 1966/67, 162–207 (= *Kultur, Kulturkontakt und Religion*, 1980, 256ff.); K. Hemmerle, ed., *Die Botschaft von Gott* (1974) (contains three contributions by L. Ruppert on YHWH); J. Coppens, ed., *La notion biblique de Dieu* (BETL 41; Louvain, 1976); W. Eichrodt, *Gott im Alten Testament* (1977); E. Zenger, "Wie spricht das Alte Testament von Gott?" in *Möglichkeiten des Redens über Gott* (1978), 57–79; H. Gross, "Gotteserfahrung im Alten Testament," in A. Paus, ed., *Suche nach Sinn—Suche nach Gott* (1978), 139–175; W. H. Schmidt, "Gott. II: Altes Testament," *TRE* 13, 608–626 (literature); D. Patrick, *The Rendering of God in the Old Testament* (Philadelphia, 1981); N. Lohfink (et al.), *"Ich will euer Gott werden": Beispiele biblischen Redens von Gott* (SBS 100; 1981); H. Seebass, *Der Gott der ganzen Bibel* (1982), 35ff.; and H. D. Preuss, "Gotteslehre. 4. Altes Testament," *EKL* (3d ed.), vol. 2 (1988), cols. 296–300 (literature). Cf. also the comments above (pp. 140 + 147) on אלהים = *'ĕlōhîm* and יהוה = *yahweh* as well as the literature cited on pp. 104f., 107f., and 111 for the first and second commandments and for the question about Old Testament monotheism.
771. Cf. above, pp. 148, 151, 184ff.
772. The argument that Qoheleth, e.g., held strongly to the first commandment (so W. H. Schmidt, *Alttestamentlicher Glaube*, 6th ed., 309) does not appear to me really to hit the mark.
773. Cf., e.g., B. R. Forster, "Wisdom and the Gods in Ancient Mesopotamia," *Or* 43, 1974, 344–354; W. Barta, "Der anonyme Gott der Lebenslehren," *ZÄS* 103, 1976, 79–88; and B. Couroyer, "Le 'Dieu des Sages' en Egypte," *RB* 94, 1987, 574–603; 95, 1988, 70–91, 195–210.

Chapter 5. The World of God and the World Distant from God

1. See M. Metzger, "Himmlische und irdische Wohnstatt Jahwes," *UF* 2, 1970, 139–158; and B. Janowski, " 'Ich will in eurer Mitte wohnen': Struktur und Genese der exilischen Schekina-Theologie," *JBTh* 2 (1987), 165–193.
2. Cf. above, pp. 68f., and also H.-J. Zobel, "Der frühe Jahwe-Glaube in der Spannung von Wüste und Kulturland," *ZAW* 101, 1989, 344.
3. ירד = *yarad* ("descend"): Exod. 19:11, 18, 20; 34:5; cf. Gen. 11:5, 7; 18:21; Exod. 3:8; 33:9; Num. 11:17, 25; 12:5; Neh. 9:13; and Micah 1:3.
4. For the problem of מבול = *mabbûl* ("flood") in Ps. 29:10, cf. above, chap. 4, n. 638.
5. Exod. 15:17; 1 Kings 8:13, 39, 43, 49 (= 2 Chron. 6:2, 30, 33, 39); Isa. 4:5; 18:4; Pss. 33:14; and 104:5.
6. For the cherubim, see below, sec. 4.
7. B. Janowski, "Das Königtum Gottes in den Psalmen," *ZThK* 86, 1989, 389–454 (esp. 415).
8. Cf. H. Seebass, *TRE* 10, 14; N. Lohfink, "Zur deuteronomischen Zentralisationsformel," *Bibl* 65, 1984, 297–329.
9. Cf. H. D. Preuss, *Deuteronomium* (EdF 164; 1982), 13, 16–18, 90; and B. Janowski, JBTh 2 (1987), 173–180. For this point, cf. above, chap. 4.4.e, and Vol. II, 8.2.
10. Both statements are incorporated into Deut. 12:5. Then with לשכן = *lĕšakkēn* ("to dwell") in Deut. 12:11; 4:23; 16:2, 6, 11; 26:2—thus not in the Deuteronomistic History! With לשום = *lāśûm* ("to place") in Deut. 12:21; 14:24; then in the Deuteronomistic texts 1 Kings 8:29f., 44f.; 9:3; 11:36; 14:21; 2 Kings 21:4, 7; and 23:27.
11. *KTU* 1. 2:7f.; 1.16: VI:56; cf. *KAI*, 14, l. 18 (*'Ešmun 'azar* inscription).
12. See T. N. D. Mettinger, *The Dethronement of Sabaoth* (CB OT 18; Lund, 1982).
13. See above, chap. 4.1.b.
14. Thus, e.g., in B. Stade, *Biblische Theologie des Alten Testaments* (1905), 103f.: From Ezekiel on, Yahweh now is the one who "has taken up residence" in heaven (see p. 291). Different, e.g., is the view of G. von Rad, *Theology*, 2:346: "It is unsatisfactory to explain this variety of ideas simply as the result of the devious history of the cult. The odd flexibility of these ideas and the open way in which they are mentioned must themselves have been in line with

the insight which Israel had into Jahweh's nearness and presence, and with her lack of need to reduce them to a fixed dogmatic standard and harmonise them." Cf. also L. Köhler, *Theologie* (4th ed.), 60.

15. Cf. also Jer. 3:17; 17:12—YHWH's throne in Jerusalem. Pss. 93:2; 103:19—in heaven.

16. M. Metzger, *UF* 2, 145.

17. "The (destroyed) sanctuary is in the first case a place of prayer where the name of Yahweh is present; Yahweh himself, however, is not bound to the temple, but rather he is 'enthroned/dwells' (יָשַׁב = *yāšab*) in heaven and hears there the prayers of his 'servant' Solomon and his people Israel": B. Janowski, *JBTh* 2 (1987), 177 (see pp. 175ff. also for the stratification of 1 Kings 8:14–66). Cf. above, pp. 170f.

18. See above, chap. 4.4.d.

19. See B. Janowski, *JBTh* 2 (1987), 181; also see pp. 184ff., for P (Exod. 29:45f., and often).

20. Cf. B. Janowski, *JBTh* 2 (1987), 187. See esp. p. 181, n. 75 for the "sojourning (YHWH) in the midst of Israel" as an expression of election theology.

21. R. Schmitt, *Zelt und Lade als Thema alttestamentlicher Wissenschaft* (1972); H.- J. Zobel, "אֲרוֹן," *ThWAT* 1, cols. 391–404. Cf. also G. von Rad, *Theology*, 1:234–241, for the tent and the ark.

22. For this, see also H. Spieckermann, *Heilsgegenwart* (FRLANT 148; 1989), 88–96; and B. Janowski, "Das Königtum Gottes in den Psalmen," *ZThK* 86, 1989, 389–454 (there pp. 428–446).

23. Judg. 20:27f. is often regarded as a gloss. Cf., however, H.-J. Zobel, "אֲרוֹן," col. 399: "That the note . . . is editorially secondary says nothing about its historical value."

24. R. Schmitt, *Zelt und Lade als Thema alttestamentlicher Wissenschaft*, 173.

25. H.-J. Zobel, "אֲרוֹן," col. 402: the portable sanctuary of the house of Joseph.

26. Comparative material is found in H.-J. Zobel, "אֲרוֹן," cols. 396f.

27. Cf. R. de Vaux, *Das Alte Testament und seine Lebensordnungen* II (2d. ed., 1966), 120.

28. For this combining, cf. J. Jeremias in H. W. Wolff, ed., *Probleme biblischer Theologie*, FS G. von Rad (1971), 183–198. Critical of this is H. Spieckermann, *Heilsgegenwart*, 196, n.22. Cf. also above, chap. 4.1.b.

29. See L. Perlitt, *Bundestheologie im Alten Testament* (WMANT 36; 1969), 40–42.

30. Cf. above, pp. 77 + 101f.

31. See H.-J. Zobel, "אֲרוֹן," 400f.

32. See likewise below, sec. 3.

33. For the possible connection between the tent and the ark, see H.-J. Zobel, "אֲרוֹן," cols. 395f.; there also is a reference to G. von Rad's increasingly significant differentiation between the different "theologies" of the tent and ark (ark = idea of dwelling and throne; tent = idea of encounter).

34. For כפרת = *kappōret* as the covering of the ark according to P, see Vol. II, 11.10 and 13.4.

35. For this, see p. 257f. For the relationship of the ark and the cherubim, cf. E. Würthwein, ATD 11/1, 1977, 89ff.

36. Cf. T. N. D. Mettinger, *The Dethronement of Sabaoth* (CB OT 18; Lund, 1982), 19–37.

37. See H. Spieckermann, *ZThK* 86, 1989, 94f.

38. See B. Janowski, "Das Königtum Gottes in den Psalmen," 428–446.

39. R. Schmitt, *Zelt und Lade als Thema alttestamentlicher Wissenschaft* (1972); K. Koch, " אֹהֶל," *ThWAT* 1, cols. 128–141; and C. R. Koester, *The Dwelling of God* (CBQ MS 22; Washington, D.C., 1989).

40. Cf. also V. Fritz, *Tempel und Zelt* (WMANT 47; 1977), 100ff., 112ff.

41. Thus according to K. Koch,"אֹהֶל," col. 134.

42. J. Wellhausen, *Prolegomena to the History of Ancient Israel* (Cleveland and New York, 1957), 37.

43. Cf. M. Görg, *Das Zelt der Begegnung* (BBB 27; 1967).

44. For this passage, see also B. Janowski, *JBTh* 2 (1987), 184f., 190.

45. Cf. above, sec. 2.

46. Other designations in P, which are probably to be assigned to different redactional strata, are מִשְׁכָּן = *miškān* ("tabernacle"); מקדש = *miqdāš* ("sanctuary"); המקדש = *hammiqdāš* ("the sanc-

tuary"); and אהל = *'ōhel* ("tent"). For these, see R. Schmitt, *Zelt und Lade als Thema alttestamentlicher Wissenschaft*, 219ff.

47. Cf. P. Weimar, "Sinai und Schöpfung," *RB* 95, 1988, 337–385. Cf. above, pp. 65f. + 167f.
48. See R. Schmitt, *Zelt und Lade als Thema alttestamentlicher Wissenschaft*, 228ff.
49. K. Koch, *ThWAT* 1, col. 140.
50. See R. Schmitt, *Zelt und Lade als Thema alttestamentlicher Wissenschaft*, 180ff. For a different view, see A. H. J. Gunneweg, "Das Gesetz und die Propheten," *ZAW* 102, 1990, 169–180 (post-Priestly texts that refer to Moses, i.e., to the Torah, give precedence to the Torah as the *medium revelationis* over the temple and sacrificial cult).
51. Sometimes also with (the secondary addition?) "the meeting."
52. For the discussion of this verse, the thesis of a gap prior to v. 7, and the unclear reference of לו = *lô*, cf. M. Görg, *Das Zelt der Begegnung*, 151ff.; and R. Schmitt, *Zelt und Lade als Thema alttestamentlicher Wissenschaft*, 198f., 276f. Whether these are texts from E or are additions to J is debated.
53. Cf. for ירד = *yārad* ("descend") also Gen. 11:5, 7; Exod. 19:11, 18, 20; and 34:5; all J. Cf. above, sec. 1.
54. Has Joshua here supplanted other priests? Are these texts additions that wished to bring Joshua closer to Moses?
55. K. Koch, *ThWAT* 1, col. 136 (cf. Exod. 18:7?).
56. Cf. above, sec. 2.
57. The theses of M. Görg about this (*Das Zelt der Begegnung*, 97, 121ff., 134ff.) are already problematic because of the unfounded conjecture of making Gihon into Gibeon in 1 Kings 1:38 (in spite of 1 Chron. 21:29). Cf. the criticism by R. Schmitt, *Zelt und Lade als Thema alttestamentlicher Wissenschaft*, 195f. For this subject, cf. also V. Fritz, *Tempel und Zelt* (WMANT 47; 1977), 94f.
58. Over against G. von Rad, "Zelt und Lade," TB 8 (3d. ed., 1965), 109–129. For a critical discussion of the research on this topic, cf. R. Schmitt, *Zelt und Lade als Thema alttestamentlicher Wissenschaft*, 256ff.
59. Thus also W. Eichrodt, *Theology*, 1:109–112; and R. de Vaux, *Ancient Israel: Its Life and Institutions* (New York, 1961), 294–302.
60. K. Koch, *ThWAT* 1, col. 138.
61. H. Schultz, *Alttestamentlicher Theologie* (5th ed., 1896), 470–492; M. Görg, "Keruben in Jerusalem," *BN* 4, 1977, 13–24; idem, "Die Funktion der Serafen bei Jesaja," *BN* 5, 1978, 28–39; D. N. Freedman and P. O'Connor, "כרוב, *kĕrûb*," *ThWAT* 4, cols. 322–334; E. T. Mullen, *The Assembly of the Gods: The Divine Council in Canaanite and Early Hebrew Literature* (HSM 24; Chico, Calif., 1980); S. Schroer, *In Israel gab es Bilder* (OBO 74; 1987); P. D. Miller, Jr., "Cosmology and World Order in the Old Testament: The Divine Council as Cosmic-Political Symbol," *HorBiblTheol* 9/2, 1987, 53–78; V. Hirth, "Die Keruben—Vorstellung und Wirklichkeit zur Zeit des Alten Testaments," *Theologische Versuche*, 17, 1989, 15–22; idem, *Gottes Boten im Alten Testament* (1975); C. Westermann, *Gottes Engel brauchen keine Flügel* (1957); and M. Welker, "Über Gottes Engel," *JBTh* 2 (1987), 194–209. Cf. also W. Eichrodt, *Theology*, 2:194–205.
62. So with Th. C. Vriezen, *Theology*, 179–180.
63. H.-P. Müller refers to a similar expression ("Let us create a figure of clay") from the mouth of the goddess Belet-ili in a 1987 published, New Babylonian narrative of the creation of humanity (*Or* 58, 1989, 63f.). No female beings also belong to the court of YHWH, since, according to Gen. 1:27, the human beings created by "us" and "after our image" include both man and woman?
64. Cf. especially *KTU* 1.2:I:13ff.; also *RGT* (2d ed.), 34.240. For this subject, see H. Gese, in H. Gese, M. Höfner, and K. Rudolph, *Die Religionen Altsyriens, Altarabiens und der Mandäer* (1970), 100f.; and O. Loretz, *Ugarit und die Bibel* (1990), 56ff.
65. For a more detailed discussion, see W. Eichrodt, *Theology*, 2:202–205; O. Keel, *Jahwe-Visionen und Siegelkunst* (SBS 84/85; 1977), 15ff., 152ff., etc. and S. Schroer, *In Israel gab es Bilder* (OBO 74; 1987), 121ff.
66. For this, see above, sec. 2.

67. For the later development of this connection, see Exod. 25:18–22; cf. 26:1, 31; 36:8, 35; 37:7–9.
68. See B. Janowski, "Das Königtum Gottes in den Psalmen," *ZThK* 86, 1989, 389–454 (see there esp. 428ff. and literature).
69. Cf. O. Keel, *Jawe-Visionen und Siegelkunst;* and T. N. D. Mettinger, *The Dethronement of Sabaoth* (CB OT 18; Lund, 1982), 19ff.
70. Cf. N. Lohfink, "Der Begriff des Gottesreichs vom Alten Testament her gesehen," in J. Schreiner, ed., *Unterwegs zur Kirche* (1987), 33–86, esp. 47: "The ark as a throne (pedestal) of YHWH and the conception of Yahweh as the one enthroned upon the cherubim could both be already premonarchial (brought together at Shiloh) before being included later in the ideology of kingship."
71. V. Hirth, *Theologische Versuche,* 17, 18.
72. Cf. above, sec. 1.
73. M. Görg (*BN* 5, 29f.) derives the term from a Middle Egyptian root: *sfr/srf* "griffin."
74. Cf. also the Ugaritic "Baal, the rider of the clouds" (*KTU* 1.2:II:7 etc.) and Pss. 18:11; 68:5. See *RGT* (2d ed.), 215–218, 228, 232.
75. It is not always easy to limit clearly the "angel of YHWH" to a single form. For this, see above, chap. 4.4.c. For the problematic nature of this figure, see V. Hirth, *Gottes Boten im Alten Testament* (1975). Cf. also, P. van Imschoot, *Theology of the Old Testament,* vol. 1 (1965), 107ff.; and H. Röttger, *NBL* I, cols. 537f.
76. The gods of Ugarit, Mesopotamia, and Egypt also dealt with each other and with human beings through "messengers." Cf. H. Gese, M. Höfner, and K. Rudolph, *Die Religionen Altsyriens, Altarabiens und der Mandäer* (1970). See in this volume, H. Gese, 170f., 198. Also see O. Loretz, *Ugarit und die Bibel* (1990), 89; and E. Otto, *LÄ* I, col. 846f. In Mesopotamia it was especially the so-called *lamassu* who assumed the functions of messengers and protection and then operated as forces of "good." Cf. *RLA* VI, pp. 446–455 and *WdM* 1, 46, s.v. "Botengötter."
77. Gen. 6:1–4; Exod. 15:11; Zech. 14:5; Pss. 29:1; 78:25; 82:6; 89:6–8; Job 1:6; 2:1; 5:1; 15:15; Dan. 4:14; 8:13; etc. Cf. above, p. 130.
78. Cf. the "corrupter" in Exod. 12:23; the angel of pestilence in 2 Sam. 24:16; 2 Kings 19:35; and 1 Chron. 21:15.
79. "Far from clashing with monotheism, this conception lays the greatest stress on the majesty of Yahweh" (Th. C. Vriezen, *Theology,* 180).
80. See K. E. Grönger, *TRE* 9, 586–596.
81. Cf. also J. Maier, *Zwischen den Testamenten* (NEB AT, Supplement, vol. 3, 1990), 34, 108f., 203.
82. Cf. W. Eichrodt, *Theology,* 2:223–228; G. Wanke, "Dämonen. II: Alten Testament," *TRE* 8, 275–277; and M. Görg, "Dämonen," *NBL* I, cols. 375–377 (Altes Testament); also see E. S. Gerstenberger and W. Schrage, *Suffering* (Nashville, 1988), who offer, in my opinion, an important evaluation.
83. Cf. B. Meissner, *Babylonien und Assyrien,* vol. 2 (1925) (see the index); H. W. F. Saggs, *Mesopotamien* (1966), 449ff.; H. Gese, M. Höfner, and K. Rudolph, *Die Religionen Altsyriens, Altarabiens und der Mandäer,* 171; O. Loretz, *Ugarit und die Bibel,* 90; and *WdM* 1, 46–49, 274–276.
84. Thus L. Köhler, *Theologie* (4th ed.), 148.
85. Thus H. Haag, *Teufelsglaube* (1974), 166.
86. Thus also in Mesopotamia. Cf. to this: H. Wildberger, BK X/3, 1347–1349. For the names, see also H. Donner, *ZThK* 87, 1990, 291f.
87. For Azazel: Vol. II, 13.4.
88. Cf. Exod. 28:33–35; Lev. 19:27f.; Deut. 14:1; Ezek. 27:31; Amos 8:10; etc. For similar practices in Ugarit, cf. O. Loretz, *Ugarit und die Bibel,* 109–115. Also see Vol. II, 11.1d, 6.
89. See more exactly N. Lohfink, "Ich bin Jahwe, dein Arzt," in "*Ich will euer Gott werden*" (SBS 100, 1981), 11ff.
90. For Satan, see below, sec. 6.
91. L. Köhler, *Theologie* (4th ed.), 148.
92. Cf. R. Schärf, "Die Gestalt des Satans im Alten Testament," in C. G. Jung, *Symbolik des Geistes* (1953), 151ff.; H. Haag, *Teufelsglaube* (1974); P. L. Day, *An Adversary in Heaven*

(HSM 43; Atlanta, 1988). For the Satan (with further evaluation): also see H. D. Preuss, *Einführung in die alttestamentliche Weisheitsliteratur* (1987), 104–107 + 210.

93. Cf. the overview of scholarship in G. Fohrer, *Studien zum Buche Hiob* (BZAW 159; 2d ed., 1983), 43, n. 14.

94. Thus, L. Köhler, *Theologie* (4th. ed.), 167.

95. Cf. to the heavenly prosecutor the heavenly defender (Job 33:23ff.)

96. Cf. to these literary and redactional questions concerning the Book of Job the overview by H. D. Preuss, *Einführung in die alttestamentliche Weisheitsliteratur* (1987), 72ff.

97. See H. Haag, *Teufelsglaube*, 192ff.; and J. Maier, *Zwischen den Testamenten* (NEB AT, Supplement vol. 3, 1990), 34, 211f.

98. Deut. 32:39; 1 Sam. 2:6f.; 2 Kings 6:33; Isa. 45:7; Amos 3:6; Qoh. 7:13f.; Job 1:21; and 2:10. Is Isa. 45:7 already directed against Persian dualism? Cf. p. 107.

99. For the Old Testament view of suffering, see Vol. II, 11.6.

100. See V. Maag, "Tod und Jenseits nach dem Alten Testament," *SThU* 34, 1964, 17–37 (= *Kultur, Kulturkontakt und Religion*, 1980, 181ff.); and Th. Podella, "Grundzüge alttestamentlicher Jenseitsvorstellungen," *BN* 43, 1988, 70–89. See also W. Eichrodt, *Theology*, 2:210–223.

101. Thus 66 times in the Old Testament. For the debated etymology of the word, see G. Gerleman, *THAT* 2, cols. 837f.; and Th. Podella, *BN* 43, 1988, 75f. Sometimes Sheol is called simply "the land," or "the earth": Exod. 15:12; Num. 16:30, 32; 1 Sam. 28:13; etc. For its names and appellations, see N. J. Tromp, *Primitive Conceptions of Death and the Nether World in the Old Testament* (BibOr 21; Rome, 1969), 21ff.

102. For the death, dying, and resurrection of human beings according to the Old Testament, see Vol. II, 11.1.d, 7.b, d.

103. Cf. L. Köhler, *Theologie* (4th ed.), 142. He regards Sheol as "the precursor of hell and the parallel of hades."

104. Cf. Chr. Hardmeier, " 'Denn im Tod ist kein Gedenken an dich...' (Psalm 6,6): Der Tod des Menschen—Gottes Tod?" *EvTh* 48, 1988, 292–311.

105. Cf. in addition Isa. 7:11; Hos. 13:14; and Prov. 15:11.

106. Cf. the "arms" and "throat" of Sheol: Hab. 2:5 and elsewhere.

107. For the dimunition of life as the power of death, cf. Vol. II, 11.1.d, 7.b. Cf. also *RGT* (2d ed.), 50, 60.

108. Jer. 2:6; 13:16; Pss. 44:20; 107:10, 14; Job 3:5; 10:21f.; 16:16; 38:17; etc.

109. Cf. above, sec. 1 of this chapter. For the conception of the world, cf. above, chap. 4.6.a.

110. Gen. 37:35; 44:29, 31; Num. 16:31–33; Deut. 32:22; Isa. 5:14; 14:9; 38:10; Ezek. 31:15ff.; Amos 9:2; Jonah 2:7f.; Pss. 9:14; 16:10; 30:4; 63:10; 88:4–7; 89:49; 95:4; 107:10–16; Prov. 1:12; 7:27; 9:18; Job 7:9f.; 10:21; 16:22; 17:13f., 16; 21:13; 26:6; 38:16f.; and Qoh. 9:5, 10.

111. V. Maag, *SThU* 34, 1964, 23: a "cabinet of wax figures" (cf. Job 3:13ff.). Hebrew רפאים = *rĕpā'îm* ("shades"): Isa. 14:9; 26:14, 19; Ps. 88:11; Job 26:5 (of רפא = *rāpā'* "to be languid"). For the figures thus named in the Ugaritic texts: D. Kinet, *Ugarit* (SBS 104; 1981), 90ff.; and O. Loretz, *Ugarit und die Bibel* (1990), 128–134, 208 (literature). Cf. also Th. Podella, *BN* 43, 1988, 85ff.; and *WdM* 1, 304f.

112. Isa. 8:19 and 29:4.

113. 2 Sam. 12:23; Pss. 78:39; 94:17; 115:17; Job 3:11ff.; 7:9f.; 10:21; and 14:12–14.

114. Not to be confused with "souls," "shadows" may even not be described.

115. L. Köhler, *Theologie* (4th ed.), 143.

116. Thus with V. Maag, *SThU* 34, 1964, 20.

117. For this, see M. Hutter, *Altorientalische Vorstellungen von der Unterwelt* (OBO 63; 1985); and *WdM* 1, 130–132.

118. *AOT* (2d ed.), 183–186; *ANET* (2d and 3d eds.), 97–99, 507. See further A. Schott and W. von Soden, *Das Gilgamesch-Epos* (1958, 1963), 100–106. Cf. also "Inanna's Descent into the Underworld," *ANET* (2d and 3d eds.), 52–57, 106–109; and J. Bottéro and S. Kramer, *Lorsque les dieux faisaient l'homme*, 318–330.

119. Thus with V. Maag, *SThU* 34, 1964, 20.

120. Cf., e.g., contemporary statements about grandmother or another relative in the grave, in the cemetery, in heaven, etc.

121. See, e.g., H. Gese, M. Höfner, and K. Rudolph, *Die Religionen Altsyriens, Altarabiens und der Mandäer*, 119ff., 135ff., etc.; *WdM* 1, 253ff., 300ff.; D. Kinet, *Ugarit*, 65ff., 90ff.; and O. Loretz, *Ugarit und die Bibel*, 73–75, 89. Cf. *RGT* (2d ed.), 231–238.

122. For these mourning customs and the problem of the worship of the dead, cf. J. Nelis, "Toten-verehrung," *BL* (2d ed.), cols. 1774–1777; O. Loretz, *Ugarit und die Bibel*, 109–115; Th. J. Lewis, *Cults of the Dead in Ancient Israel and Ugarit* (HSM 39; Atlanta, 1989); and Vol. II, 11.1.d + 7.b.

123. For this, see Vol. II, 11.1–4.

124. Cf. V. Maag, *SThU* 34, 1964, 18–20.

125. O. Loretz (*Ugarit und die Bibel*, 88f., 125–143, 183, 218) is too confident in his judgment that the "fathers" (Abraham, etc.) were originally deified and worshiped as ancestors and then later in the postexilic period were transformed into prominent "ancestors."

SELECT INDEX OF BIBLICAL CITATIONS

(Old Testament books are listed in the order of the Hebrew Bible.)

INDEX OF SUBJECTS

372

Index of Subjects

Swear (Oath; also YHWH's) 243
Symbolic Actions 215

Tabernacle. *See* Tent (of Meeting)
Tablets of the Ten Commandments
  (Decalogue) 74, 77, 101, 254, 292
Talion Formula 83, 88
Tanit/Tinnit 321
Telipinu 322, 344
Temple (Jerusalem) 33, 49, 110, 1256,
  153f., 158, 167–176, 212, 237, 240,
  247, 251–254, 256f.
Tent (of Meeting) 100, 168f. 218,
  233, 254–256
Theogony 112, 215, 217, 231, 239,
  280
Theophany 64f., 66f., 129, 175, 187,
  202–204, 251, 334
Throne (of YHWH) 153, 173, 226,
  251–252, 253f., 257
Tiamat 217, 235
Time (Understanding of) 209,
  219–226
Torah 18, 227, 277
Tribal Sayings 61f., 118, 182
Trito-Isaiah 25, 178, 240
Tukulti-Ninurta Epic 212

Ugarit/Ugaritic Texts 111, 126, 142,
  148f., 155f., 187, 236, 239, 245, 251,
  256, 258, 262, 301, 306, 309, 323,
  324, 341, 342, 344, 346, 351, 352
Universalism 38
Ur 212
Uraeus Serpent 257
Utu 174

Vetitive 89

War (of YHWH) 40–42, 104, 120,
  128–138, 145, 181, 244, 246
Weidner Chronicle 336

Whole (Thinking about) 62, 184
Wife (of YHWH) 82, 104, 111, 116,
  239, 245
Wilderness (Wandering) 46, 79–80,
  120, 237, 256
Wisdom (of YHWH) 95, 194f., 227f.,
  230
Wisdom Lists 228, 233
Wisdom Literature 3, 7, 25, 35, 48,
  51, 55, 57, 95, 122f., 128, 153, 163,
  183, 185–188, 191f., 195, 204, 208,
  220, 228–230, 241, 248f., 263, 330,
  346
Wisdom of Solomon 187, 195, 200,
  227, 261
Wonder (Miracle) 44
Word (of YHWH) 195–200, 212, 219,
  235, 244
Work 231
"World Order" 88, 179, 191f., 237
Worldview 226, 251, 352

Yahwist 25, 32, 38, 41–43, 56, 65, 66,
  84, 112, 128, 139, 142, 154, 182,
  198, 213, 214, 222, 231, 238, 255,
  293, 313
Yam 236
YHWH (Name of) 112, 139–144,
  151
YHWH Enthronement Hymns
  152–159
YHWH War. *See* War (of YHWH)

Zeal (of YHWH) 73, 91, 103, 105,
  151, 41, 244
Zechariah (Book of) 35, 57, 122,
  138f., 168, 258, 260
Zerubbabel 29
Zion 33, 35, 122, 146, 173–178, 247,
  251. *See also* Jerusalem
Zion Torah 92f.
Zion Tradition 146f., 153, 155, 240